THE
CHICAGO
SCHOOLS

THE
CHICAGO
SCHOOLS

A Social and Political History

MARY J. HERRICK

with a Foreword by ROBERT J. HAVIGHURST
and an Introduction by MORRIS JANOWITZ

SAGE PUBLICATIONS

Beverly Hills / London

To my father, and to all those others,

many unrecognized and unknown,

who gave the best they knew

to the children of Chicago

Acknowledgments

Since early historical data on Chicago is relatively scarce, perhaps because of the great fire, the generous help of Archie Motley, librarian of the Chicago Historical Society, has been especially valuable. The collection of historical data of the Chicago Teachers Union on Margaret Haley and on early teacher organization was similarly useful. The Citizens Schools Committee and the Chicago Principals Club also allowed use of their early files. Librarians in eight major libraries in the Chicago area were generous with time; those in the Education library of the University of Chicago showed special interest.

Mrs. John L. Hancock permitted use of the unpublished autobiography of her father, the first examiner, and Dr. Helen Newman and Edward E. Keener lent clippings and correspondence. The staff of the University of Chicago research project on School and Society in Chicago, particularly Robert J. Havighurst, Robert L. McCaul, and Mrs. Elizabeth Murray, was helpful in many ways. Mrs. Marion Westover prepared the final text with meticulous care.

A considerable number of informed and responsible persons within and without the school system took time to read and make suggestions on sections in which they had particular insight, to assure accuracy and objectivity.

The faith of Morris Janowitz, Arthur Hillman, Earl Johnson, and Senator Paul Douglas that such a study would contribute to a better understanding on the part of present and prospective teachers, Board members, and general public as to how Chicago schools came to be as they are is in large part responsible for the completion of this book.

Mary Herrick

FOREWORD

The current wave of interest in urban education has brought a large volume of research and a great deal of scientific competence to bear on problems of education in big cities. Most of this has been done with the conceptual tools of the sociologist, though some attention has been given to this topic by political scientists and economists.

Thus the research literature on urban education has reached an impressive size, mainly since 1960. Every student of contemporary educational problems has become fairly familiar with the problem and its various suggested solutions.

However, there has been almost no treatment of urban education from the point of view of the historian. All we have in most books or research monographs is a brief and almost stereotype introduction on the "historical background."

Therefore this book by Mary Herrick is a useful one. It views the public schools of a great city vertically through the time dimension, rather than horizontally through the social space dimension. Especially detailed in its presentation of events during the present century, it shows the connections between past and present in such a way that the reader gets a superior understanding of the present.

Every big city is at the same time unique and similar to other big cities. It is to be hoped that we will eventually be able to read accurate histories of the school systems in several of the larger American cities.

The present book has also the quality of "immediacy" due to the fact that Mary Herrick has spent her career in the Chicago school system, and that her father was a Chicago school principal. Her immediate perceptions are part of the book, as well as her thorough collection and analysis of School Board minutes, newspaper reports, published statements and unpublished minutes of the proceedings of various community organizations.

Thus the book is a unique product, one of what we may hope will become a series of socio-historical studies of education in our big cities.

Robert J. Havighurst

INTRODUCTION

By 1970, dissatisfaction with the quality and effectiveness of public school education, especially in the "inner city," had reached unprecedented levels. The decade of the 1960's has seen experimentation in the form of demonstration projects in education, federal aid to low income schools, widespread efforts at preschool education and integration by means of busing. It was a period of marked increase in unionization by teachers and a gradual increase in per pupil expenditure.

But the results have hardly been impressive and the demands for basic changes in the school system persist and grow in intensity. One cannot escape the question: are the problems of public education in the United States now so deep and so fundamental that the nation is truly facing a unique crisis? Is the crisis actually raising the specter of a collapse and a fundamental transformation of the system of public education?

There are many who believe that such is the case. A new system and a new approach are required. Somehow parents must gain more power and influence over the professional administrator and the unionized teacher. One approach is the demand for comprehensive community control. Another is the idea of a voucher system in which the government would give hard cash to each parent who would then purchase on the free market the kind of education he believes appropriate for his children. These solutions—realistic or utopian—are beyond the drawing board stage; they are actually being tested in one form or another. Should they succeed, they would transform the public school system as we now know it.

But I do not believe that either of these experiments—as they are conceived by their advocates—will succeed. Comprehensive community control has already revealed inherent difficulties. Both of these innovations will make some progress and will make a positive contribution toward improving the quality of public education, but I do not believe that the public education system will be dismembered or transformed suddenly and drastically by any specific approach. Change will continue to be incremental. In part, I believe this to be the case because there is no viable alternative.

In part, this is so because the crisis in public education is not without historical counterparts. Mary Herrick's detailed and vivid history of the Chicago Public school system and the Board of Education of the city of Chicago presents a valuable perspective from which to evaluate the current crisis. We have sufficient theories about the origins, nature and scope of current dilemmas in public education, but we are short on adequate and accurate documentation of the historical facts in depth. Therefore, her social history of public education in the city of the "steelmakers and hog butchers" of America is a relevant and timely contribution.

Of course, no satisfaction or respite can be derived from a knowledge of past difficulties. In fact, I do believe that the scope of the crisis of the contemporary period emerges as greater and more extensive in numbers and magnitude, but not as fundamentally unique. The potential resources that might be mobilized are correspondingly greater.

There is no need to conclude that history merely repeats itself when one has finished reading this exciting account. But it is important to be informed that, already by 1890, outside experts including university professors, were preparing school surveys which were only partially implemented. By 1920, the movement toward school efficiency was well launched in order to overcome administrative difficulties, but had limited impact because of the narrow definitions of performance that were employed. Already by the 1930's, the public school system of Chicago (as elsewhere in the country) was faced with a financial crisis which has never been adequately solved. It is true that in previous periods the school system showed greater flexibility in dealing with foreign immigrants than with the sons and daughters of the Black population. To teach a foreign language in the school system as a device to help the transition of immigrant families tragically seemed more natural than to make the necessary cultural adjustments to serve the needs of the Black community.

In this sense the current issues in public education are unique; can the schools deal successfully with the demands and aspirations of the Black community? The crisis is a long standing one to the extent that the public schools have traditionally failed to deal successfully with lower income groups. But it is a new crisis because it involves the pressing realities of Black and white.

It is abundantly clear that there will be no single solution as new forms of education evolve both within and outside the public school system. Mary Herrick's social history helps to identify which efforts are new and which are adaptations of the old. Her story underlines the fact that, in the past, the main thrust of reform and change was through local and community efforts. Only very recently does it become clear to Chicago and to other major urban centers that national solutions are required. Her book helps make it clear that in the 1970's progress in public education requires articulating the Chicago public schools into a national system of finance, training and standards of performance. It will require a reasonable, effective and humane system of public inspection. But none of these national developments will hinder local initiative. To the contrary, only when we have a truly national system of public education can there be effective decentralization and community participation.

Morris Janowitz

University of Chicago

CONTENTS

APPENDIXES

The Author

Mary Herrick, A.B., Northwestern University, M.A., University of Chicago, has been (with time off for graduate work in sociology and political science) a most unusual teacher from 1916—when she obtained her first teaching post (at the magnificent salary of $75 per month!) until her retirement in 1961. For over twenty-five years, Miss Herrick taught at DuSable High School in Chicago. During most of that period she also supervised student teachers for the University of Chicago's Graduate Department of Education.

Miss Herrick's role in the teachers' union movement has also been an active one—commencing with her membership in the Federation of Women High School Teachers (1923-1937), which she served as president from 1933-1936. She was Chairman of the Joint Board of Teachers Unions which became the basis of the Chicago Teachers Union (founded in 1937)—a union in which she has been an active member to the present day. Miss Herrick also served as the American Federation Teachers' research director from 1956 to 1958, and as a vice-president of the AFT from 1935-1940 and 1958-1962.

In addition to the labor movement, Miss Herrick has also been active in many civic and community enterprises—including Settlement House work, the League of Women Voters, the Chicago Urban League, VISTA, and the Citizens Schools Committee of Chicago.

In recognition of her contributions as teacher and humanitarian, she has been the recipient of awards from: the University of Chicago's Alumni Association (for Civic Service), Frontiers of America (Black business and professional men), the DuSable Alumni Association (which gave a $1,000 Scholarship Fund in her honor), Phi Delta Kappa (the Black Teachers Sorority), the Chicago Commission on Human Relations, and the Mayor's Commission on Senior Citizens.

She served on the Illinois State Commission on Human Relations and was invited to the White House Conferences on Children and Youth in 1950 and 1960, and to the President's Conference on Education in 1965. Between 1928 and 1955 she participated actively in changes to the curriculum on social science in the Chicago Public Schools. She is the author of papers and pamphlets published by the Chicago School System, the Chicago Teachers Union, the

American Federation of Teachers, the Citizens Schools Committee, by journals specializing in matters relating both to teaching and delinquency, and coauthor of the text, *Government in Action.*

Most recently, Miss Herrick has done research for the Havighurst-McCaul Project on Society and Education in Chicago and for a section of the Douglas Report on Urban Problems.

Part I

PUBLIC EDUCATION

IN EARLY CHICAGO

Chapter 1

THE SCHOOLS OF FRONTIER CHICAGO

The late afternoon October sun was still bright as two men closed the door of the log cabin where they had worked all day, and stopped a moment to look around them. To the south and west stretched miles of dusty, open prairie and reedy marshland. To the east, beyond a narrow swamp and a strip of yellow sand, lay the long blue horizon of a great and empty sea. To the north, a row of rude buildings straggled along the muddy bank of a stream, not really wide enough to be called a river. This was the Chicago of 1833. It took six weeks for new settlers to reach there from the eastern seaboard by river, canal, lakes, and muddy roads, and ten days for the weekly mail to come by pony from Detroit.

But 1833 had been a busy year in the little settlement and rapid changes were visibly taking place. In March there had been only twenty houses, but during the summer 160 structures of one kind or another were hastily put together, some as shelter for those who stayed, some to accommodate—with lodging and supplies—the settlers passing through with destinations farther west. On the recommendation of a young West Point engineer named Jefferson Davis, the sand bar which blocked the mouth of the river had been cut and a few small ships had already entered it. There was excited talk about digging a canal to connect the little river in Chicago with a creek not far west which drained into the Mississippi. On August 10, twenty-eight voters of the settlement had approved the incorporation of Chicago as a town. On September 26th, a council of Indian chiefs camping near the town had agreed to move their people not only away from the Chicago area but, by 1835, entirely across the Mississippi. It had been promised that they should be paid yearly in goods. Only a year before, over panic at the Blackhawk War, the whole population of the settlement crowded within the wooden walls of the fort built in 1816. It was encouraging to feel the danger of Indian attack was now gone.

21

The Sale of School Land

Early in October, 1833, a petition signed by 95 voters presented to the new town government asked that the square mile of land which Richard Hamilton and young John Bates—who had just received his state auctioneer's license—had just spent four days selling be put on the market immediately. Hamilton was an "old" settler of two years' standing.[1] * Born in Kentucky, he had studied law in Louisville, and in 1827 been admitted to the bar in Illinois. He had come to the tiny lake settlement after the legislature had appointed him Probate Judge, Clerk of the Circuit Court, Recorder of Deeds, and Notary Public for Cook County when that area was separated from Peoria in 1831. The Cook County officials had added to his titles by making him County Commissioner of School Lands, responsible for school property in each township of the county.

Hamilton was disturbed by the demand that the land be sold so soon. There had only been twelve families with children in 1830, fewer than thirty children in the settlement in 1832, and not many more a year later. Two of every three adults were men out to make their fortunes in the wilderness as fast as they could—and without too many questions as to "how." Hamilton expressed some doubts as to whether those who had scrawled their names on the petition were as much concerned about schools (for other people's children) as about getting land cheap for speculation. His doubts were indignantly seconded by the town druggist, Philo Carpenter, who publicly challenged some of the names as fraudulent, since their owners could not legally be voters. The state law required six month's residence and ownership of property or previous payment of at least $3.00 in taxes before a man could vote.[2] But the new town government nevertheless accepted the petition, and as the state law required the land to be sold as soon as three-fourths of the white voters of the township so asked, Richard Hamilton reluctantly arranged the sale.

The square mile under question did indeed look like a good prospect for speculation. Its northern edge was only a quarter mile from the southern-most houses of the town and the eastern side only a short distance from the lake The surveyors who laid out the townships by order of Congress had even given names to some of their lines as streets. The school land ran south down an imaginary line named State Street, and west along an imaginary Madison for a mile. In the four days of the auction, all but four of these theoretical city blocks had been sold. Hamilton himself had reserved these four, including the one likely to be most valuable—where "State Street" met "Madison."

A total of $38,619.74 was realized by the sale, most of it in promises to pay.[3] The state law allowed purchasers of school lands three years to complete payment of the auction price if they paid their ten percent interest in advance. All the prospective buyer really needed, in fact, was a little faith in the future. The average price of a forty-foot lot on "State Street" was $20, for which a man need only put down $2.00 in interest.[4] In a few months he

*Notes and References begin on p. 409.

might be able to sell his claim for $20 or more in cash, and buy new land on the same kind of gambling margin. The average return on an acre of this land was $67. Since literally millions of the acres granted to the states by Congress for schools had already been sold at a dollar an acre or less, it was clear that Hamilton and Bates had not acted in collusion with land speculators. But within two years, land almost immediately adjacent—advertised as being along the much-talked-of canal route—was selling at five times this price, even though the crowd at the sale laughed when Hamilton, who was also in charge of the canal land sale, claimed that there would be 50,000 people in Chicago some day.

The land sold in October was the gift of the federal government. When the disputed claims over western lands of the seaboard states had been settled by establishing the Northwest Territory as part of the public domain of the United States, Congress had stipulated in the Ordinance of 1785 that in each of the six-mile "Congressional Townships" the surveyors must mark off one square mile to be set aside for a school. On the charts, Section 16 was to be so marked. The unbelievable waste of this gigantic gift to twenty-nine states is one of the starkest tragedies in the history of the United States.[5] As early as 1831 more than one-fourth of the 985,141 acres given to Illinois in Section 16 squares had already been sold, much of it at less than $1.25 an acre. Unscrupulous pioneers had already cut the valuable wood off much of the Section 16 timberland, sometimes without authorization, and occasionally abandoning their claim after the trees were cut. The Illinois school code bounty of $8.00, still offered to any citizen who will bring suit against those who cut and remove logs from school land, is a dim echo of this once common practice.[6]

At least Chicago's Section 16 had been kept intact and now yielded a hypothetical school fund of $38,618.74 paying interest. Moreover four of the blocks were not sold in 1833. Two of these lay along the river, between streets now called Polk and Harrison. Another was at the northwest corner of the section at Madison and Halsted, and the last was the northeast corner where "State" met "Madison." These four scraps brought no revenue for ten years. In 1843 the State and Madison block was divided into 16 lots, rented on a seven-year lease for "no less than $30" a year, and the others were let for "agricultural purposes."

The First Schools in Chicago

There had been little schooling for the children of the settlement before the sale of the land. In 1832 Richard Hamilton had donated a twelve-foot-square log stable north of the river. Here a young Easterner named John Watkins taught reading to four white and eight Indian children as they sat on old boxes. There were also twenty children in a school at the little Presbyterian church and a handful of boys at the Baptist church. According to state law, income from school lands was to be divided among the schools of the township according to the number of children enrolled and according to some accounting of the number of days attended. This kind of numerical record entitled the teacher to a share in the public money if "orphans and indigent scholars" were admitted. Teachers did not have to admit "pauper" children who were "bound out" if those responsible for them promised they would be taught to read and write.

The first money from the Chicago school fund was paid in 1834 to Miss Eliza Chappell, who kept the school in the Presbyterian church. A year later the other two schools also shared in the public funds. There was no other source of income for these schools but $2.00 per quarter paid by parents.[7] Not only the salaries of the teachers, but rent of space, heating, and books and equipment, if any, must come from the interest on the fund. Women teachers were paid $200 a year and men $500. Each teacher was a law unto himself, left to his own devices to keep order and dispense knowledge.

In the last half of the year 1837, five schools, which now held 325 children in a town of four thousand people, were closed. The nationwide depression had punctured the land speculation bubble and the interest income from the fund dried up. A young teacher who had come from Alton to teach in Chicago wrote home that "The great school fund, for which Chicago has been so celebrated, is all loaned out, and can not now command enough interest to support even one district school."[8]

But 1837 had brought to the Chicago schools changes other than those caused by the depression. In that year the town got a new city charter from the legislature as recognition of its growth from 360 to 4,000 people. An alderman was to be elected to a city council by each of six wards, and a mayor by the city to preside over the council. The new charter gave the council some authority and responsibility for schools to the extent that the County Commissioner of School Lands, now called the School Agent, must make a report to the council every six months on the exact state of the school fund and the income from the unsold school land, if any. More important still was the formal organization of the schools under the direction of seven unsalaried school inspectors, to be appointed by the council. These inspectors were to examine applicants for teaching on their fitness, select books for the schools, provide enough buildings for them, and visit them regularly. The division among the schools of the money from the school fund income was also their responsibility.[9]

The new law also provided that each separate school district elect three trustees, who would actually hire teachers for their schools and were responsible for seeing that "all white children in the district could attend." Seventy-seven persons were listed as Negro in Chicago in 1837, but there is no record of the number of Negro children or whether they attended. The trustees could also levy a local school tax in their districts up to one-half of one percent of the value of the property in the district, to be used for any necessary expenses except teachers' salaries, which were to be provided from the school fund income. Since there was no punishment for not paying the school tax, no one really paid it. In 1836 one district had borrowed $200 from the school land fund to provide a district school house; when it had not been paid back by 1840, the city council took action against the trustees—who begged for delay, so that knowledge of the emergency might "make possible the collection of some taxes."

The city government steadily extended its control over the schools. In 1839 the legislature amended the new city charter not only to give the city council, instead of the county, full control of school lands and funds, but also the right to appoint the local district trustees as well as the seven inspectors. The council furthermore had the right to choose text books and prescribe the course of study. This right they did not use, and in 1841 turned all such matters over to the inspectors. But the right to control all school contracts, now becoming big enough to be politically useful, the council kept tight hold of.[10]

Depression and Boom

The city council had more pressing problems after 1837 than worrying about primers. The growing town had accumulated a per capita debt of $2.85 and was brought up short in the depression, unable to pay its debts. All city employees and other creditors were paid in "scrip" at 40 percent discount. One teacher could not even get $4.00 a week for board and room. The years between 1837 and 1841 were bleak, as "the mudhole in the prairie" which had been growing at such a tremendous rate suddenly stood still. Land speculators left for greener fields. The seven little churches were almost empty. The slaughter houses poured only a trickle of filth into the river, and no one objected to cows on the wooden sidewalks. Only the noisy grogshops kept up their business. When the state government went bankrupt in 1841, and could pay only twenty cents on the dollar on its outstanding bonds, there were bankruptcies throughout the state, including Chicago.[11]

The "internal improvements" program went dead. The work on the long planned Illinois and Michigan Canal, the planking and replanking of muddy roads, and the building of bridges all stopped. The Irish laborers who had come to work on these projects at $16 a month were idle. Penniless refugees from the 1840 potato famine, they were not held in high regard by the native population who considered them "clannish roisterers" and distrusted their religion. The Germans and Scandinavians were more readily accepted. In 1843, 2,256 out of the 6,082 people in Chicago were foreign-born. Some 13 percent of the townspeople were Irish, another 13 percent were German or Norwegian, and 11 percent were from other parts of Europe or from Canada. The foreign groups were becoming politically powerful, the Irish then among the Whigs and the Germans among the Democrats.

In the discouraging confusion of unemployment and depression, little attention was paid to the schools. When there had been only $3,062 in sight to operate them for 325 children in 1837, they had been closed. In 1841, however, when there was only $3,007.36 for the same number of children, they remained open, by the simple device used for the first—but unfortunately not for the last—time, of giving more children to each teacher and having fewer teachers to pay. The general public was worried about things more immediate and practical than what children did in school.

The depression did not last. In 1842 everything began to flourish again. The speculation in land, the canal trade, grain production, and the new railroads all returned in a rush. Only 212 bushels of grain had been shipped out in 1841, but ships a year later were loaded with 586,907 bushels. The muddy roads were replanked and, in 1846, 70,000 creaking wagon loads trundled into the city over them. In 1848, with fanfare and jubilation, the completion of the canal was celebrated and sixteen boats went through on its first day. The canal cut off two weeks in shipping sugar from New Orleans to Buffalo. Orders began to come in to Cyrus McCormick's new reaper factory.

Ever since 1836 there had been talk of railroads. In November, 1848, the first ten miles on the line to Galena were finished, and a load of wheat was hauled on it from Des Plaines to a wharf on the river. In 1850, for $45,000, the city council sold the Illinois Central Railroad the site of the second Fort Dearborn, long abandoned, along the river east of Michigan Avenue. The state gave the road a two-hundred-foot strip on either side of its right of way and a considerable amount of other land as well. In 1852 the city presented the whole lake front to the Illinois Central if it would build a breakwater to keep the waves from eating the shore along Michigan Avenue. The state received 7 percent of the gross earnings of the railroad, but all the town got was the breakwater. By 1854 six railroads were pulling loads into Chicago over 2,933 miles of track.

Real estate values in Chicago shot up dramatically. The school land lot on the corner of State and Madison, once listed at $20, was worth $17,500 in 1851 and $40,000 in 1855. The taxable real estate which had been valued at $238,842 in 1837 was worth $4,995,466 ten years later, even before the canal and the railroads were in operation. The town of 1840 with 4,470 people and 1842 with 6,593, in 1850 soared to 29,963, and to 38,733 and 60,662 two and three years later. And at mid-century more than half its people were foreign-born.[12]

Enrolment and Income

The tremendous explosion of population, production, and wealth had little influence on the schools except to intensify their problems. Between 1837 and 1847 the population had increased four and one-half times, but school expenditures had risen only three times. The new wealth had no influence on the fixed amount of the school fund, nor even on the rents set for seven years in 1843 on the unsold land. A new state law increased the contribution from the state a little, but not enough to pay the costs of educating the additional children. In 1843 eight teachers were hired to teach the 818 "scholars" who enrolled—more than one hundred pupils for each.

By 1845 the paper value of the school land fund was $46,848, but $16,300 had been lost by unwise investments. That same year the town donated some tax money, and the average class for the 18 teachers was only 72 children. Even with these huge teaching loads, only between nine and ten percent of the population between the ages of five and twenty-one were even enrolled, and of those enrolled, no more than two-thirds were present at any one time. However, Chicago was doing better by its children than many other cities of this period: in 1845, Indianapolis had only three percent of its children of school age in public school, and Detroit only one percent.[13]

After 1847, there was a little more money available for schools in the city. In 1847 the total income had been $10,000, a third of which was spent on instruction. Of this total, $4,000 came from the school land fund, which had been increased by a gift from the state of some of the "canal lands" which had not been sold in 1834, and $6,000 from the increased state funds and from local taxes. In 1848 the school fund got another gift. The town finally was awarded the rents on wharves along the river, whose users had refused to pay the amounts set by the city council. The claim for unpaid rents was $60,000, and the council voted to give anything over $30,000 to the school fund. Therefore in 1848 the schools had $21,757 to spend. Two years later the federal government gave to fifteen of the new states in the Mississippi Valley millions of acres of the swamp lands within their borders which the federal land offices had not sold. Illinois put the proceeds of the sale of its share into its state school fund.[14]

Even with more aid from the state and some help from the city council, however, the financial situation of the schools failed to improve, since the number of children enrolled increased at least as fast as the income. In 1850 there were 21 teachers for 1,919 children enrolled, and in 1853, in a city now of 60,000 population, 34 teachers struggled to teach 3,086 children. As the population grew less transient, the ratio of children to adults increased. In 1837 only a third had been under twenty-one years of age. By 1850, 45 percent were of school age.[15] Moreover, by 1850 with more than half the population foreign-born, some of the children did not speak English, and many parents as well lacked understanding of the traditions of their new country. Many of the children of these newcomers had never been in school at all.

Housing and Teaching in Frontier Schools

Teaching in Chicago schools between 1834 and 1854 was no bed of roses, either for teachers or "scholars." As the teachers were to keep order and dispense knowledge, the difficulty of achieving the first objective increased so rapidly that the second became almost submerged. The average number of children per teacher ranged between 80 and 100 for most of the first twenty years—an impossible task for a constantly changing succession of untrained teachers. Nor was it their fault that they were not trained. Only two private academies undertook to train teachers in 1833 and they were both in Massachusetts. The head of one of these, S. R. Hall, wrote a little book called *Lectures on School Keeping* which was distributed by New York State to its teachers, but the teachers in Illinois had no help from any source. There was no publicly supported training for the state of Illinois until 1852 nor for teachers in Chicago until 1856.

The most successful teachers were Easterners who had attended the private academies. But these, if young men, seldom remained in such a financially unrewarding occupation and quickly left for business or a professional career. If they were young women, like Eliza Chappell, they quickly married.[16] As the number of children in the rapidly growing town increased, the fixed amount of income from the school fund actually decreased, as interest payments on loans became delinquent in successive periods of economic depression. The number of children confronting each teacher therefore increased. Some teachers became bitter tyrants in sheer self-defense. In 1836 one teacher was beaten up by the older boys in his school, and his successor was praised for keeping a stout inch-thick stick in his desk ready for use. Others by genuine good nature and a reputation for fairness won the respect of their pupils and survived. One such was A. D. Sturtevant who, with two assistants, somehow managed the 543 children who crowded the school—called "Miltimore's Folly"—during its first year. He remained as a teacher for sixteen years. But many teachers never finished the year they started and few returned for a second.

One "scholar" of this period claimed that if children "ever advanced beyond the point where they were left by their early teachers, it was in spite of their elementary instruction and not because of it."[17] He himself attended a school which met in the abandoned barracks of old Fort Dearborn, and details with glee how he pulled the bricks out of the fireplace and brought down the chimney—bricks, soot, and all—on his teacher and schoolmates. Putting a shotgun shell in the wood for the stove was also a frequent way of interrupting boredom. His father sent him to a private school in 1845.

From the beginning of the Chicago school system there were never enough seats for the children who came, and there were many who never came at all. Only a few of the children were housed in the old barracks. The schools quickly grew too large for the small churches, and rooms and buildings were rented wherever they could be located. One Sarah Kellogg was employed to teach in 1837 at $10 a week but could not "keep school" because no space could be found.

The only building owned by any of the school districts was a frame house at Madison and Dearborn, built on school land. All the buildings were bare, had little light or ventilation, and uneven stove heat in cold Chicago winters. All the spaces used were without ornament or equipment for school purposes, and none had enough seats on days when attendance was high.

There was no real change in the situation until 1845, when the house at Madison and Dearborn was sold for $45.00 and the inspectors got the city to agree to build a school across Madison Street on a piece of "canal land" which had been given to the school fund. The new brick building was three stories high and very plain inside and out. It cost $7,500 and was nicknamed "Miltimore's Folly," after the inspector who had been most insistent on its construction. The mayor, Augustus Garrett, who had opposed the new building, commented acidly that its plainness was the best thing about it, as "It could easily be converted into a factory or an insane asylum for those responsible for its erection."[18] The mayor's fears that it would not be filled were unfounded. It housed 543 children from two adjacent school districts as soon as it opened, and the next year 843 children appeared from one district alone. By 1854 the seven buildings used for schools were so overcrowded that one thousand children who came to enroll were turned away.

The early classroom procedures in these first schools were described by one of the "scholars."

> "We mumbled the Lord's Prayer with careless lips, read a chapter of the Bible in mock unison and then read at the top of our voices as rapidly as possible every word in 40 pages of coarse print in Kirkhams' Grammar. Those who got through first won the coveted award of being able to do what they pleased till the drones were through."[19]

This could not have been a very enlightening experience, particularly for those who were still struggling with the alphabet. Mastery of a text book, almost any text book, was the goal. In the earliest schools, a child brought to class any book he could find. In 1840 the inspectors made a list of books they recommended, but they had no money to buy them, nor any power to compel parents to do so. Poor children who could not afford them, did without, if they came to school. Much of a teacher's time was spent listening to children recite from the books by memory, in concert or singly. Reading was taught by memorizing the alphabet, and then spelling words without attention to meaning. A teacher spent much of his time in mending quill pens and setting copy for those who were learning to write. As the numbers of children grew, by sheer necessity teachers used the Lancastrian method of having older children drill the younger ones. In no other way could three teachers in "Miltimore's Folly" have "taught" 543 children.

The 1840 book list approved by the inspectors included a primer, three grades of readers, an arithmetic, a speller, a grammar, and Peter Parley's First, Second, and Third Books of History. The readers contained stories and some pictures of good children who obeyed their parents, loved to go to school, and gave money to poor children. They also contained speeches and poems to be learned for recitation on "Declamation Days." Peter Parley's history had a very conservative outlook on most subjects. The Second Book, for instance, describes Louis XVI as an "amiable and benevolent prince, tortured by ferocious persecutors." Slavery in this country was taken for granted as being better than living in Africa, although the slave trade was described as "horrid." The three books are a chatty summary of the current prejudices of the day generously sprinkled with dates and long lists of places and distances to be memorized. The accompanying geographical coverage described Africa as a peninsula, largely desert, where the Negroes were gay but cruel to their enemies. Some of the arithmetic was more relevant. There were problems to work like the following:

> If there are 11 seats and 7 pupils on each seat, how many scholars are there?
> If lots are bought for $10 and sold at a 20% profit, what is the price?
> If a man can lay 9 rods of plank road in a day, how much can he lay in a week?

But the "scholars" not only had to memorize the multiplication tables, they had to learn the Greek and Latin names of numbers, English money and measurements, weights and measures from the Bible, and "up to sextillions by the French and English methods."

The total curriculum was narrow, no matter how many years were spent in school. In 1840 the inspectors counted 64 children studying geography and history, 29 grammar, and 57 arithmetic.[20] Since there were 317 enrolled, presumably more than half were still struggling with the alphabet and learning to read.

Control by Inspectors and City Council

Some glaring deficiencies in instruction and school financing did not go without notice. As early as 1838 a special committee of citizens made an extensive report to the city council, commenting on the fact that most of the children actually attended school for only about one-fourth of each term and lamenting that "Compulsory education is opposed by the prejudice which regards it as interference with family rights and duties, and yet it seems almost a necessity."[21] The committee felt that the irregularity of attendance was due in part to the condition of the places where children were expected to learn.

The troubled school inspectors were concerned with other phases of their responsibility than merely the inadequate housing and attendance. The 1838 report of the "special committee" indicated the basic problem:

> "It is well known that from the period of the first settlement of this place, the cause of education has received very little attention. This important interest which lies at the foundation of our social and political institutions has hitherto been left like an exotic, to struggle for a precarious existence under the blighting chill of apathy and neglect."

The committee went on to point out the lack of uniformity among the district schools in text books or methods of instruction. They wanted boys and girls separated on the New England pattern. Vacancies in teaching positions should be filled immediately. A general city school tax should be levied and collected. There is no indication that the inspectors resented these criticisms; but they lacked the means to correct them, either through current resources, legal authority, or support of the political and economic leaders of the city. Those who shrewdly and carefully planned the economic miracles which were transforming Chicago from frontier settlement into a bustling center of commerce and trade showed little concern about the schools. Exceptions were Richard Hamilton, William B. Ogden and John Wentworth.

The inspectors did try to improve matters. In 1840 they had made a list of text books; in 1841 they recommended creation of a high school to take older children out of the crowded, ungraded rooms—but nothing came of it. Their one recommendation that was really carried out in all the schools was the continuation of Bible reading every day at the opening exercises. In 1846 they set the school year as four quarters of 12 weeks each, with one week free between quarters. For this service they were paying some men teachers $800 a year and a few women as much as $500 by 1850. At the same time the city council took the matter of training teachers into its own hands, and ruled that all teachers in Chicago should meet weekly with the inspectors as a teachers' institute. No questions were raised as to the qualifications of the inspectors to give such instruction; after all, the council had appointed them.

In 1849, from the superior level they felt their schools had attained, the inspectors had looked back on previous accomplishments with scorn. The 1849 report states that the schools had been a complete failure until 1840, and that even in that year they were unsatisfactory:

> "A few miserably clad children, unwashed and uncombed, were huddled into small, unclean and unventilated apartments, seated upon uncomfortable benches, taught by listless and indifferent tutors, who began their vocations with dread, and completed their unpleasant duties with pleasure." [22]

They continue with the rosy contrast presented by their 1849 schools,

> "Now the school reports of the township show the names of 2,000 pupils, two-thirds of whom are in daily attendance in spacious, ventilated, well regulated rooms, where they are taught by those whose duty is their pleasure. The scholars are neat in person and orderly in behavior."

A little more soap and water may have been used than in 1833 and 1840, but the report sounds more like a campaign speech for the next appointment for inspector than a summary of the facts. Their official records for the year showed 1,794 children taught by 18 teachers, while more than half the enrolled children in town were actually going to private schools.

Differences of opinion had begun to arise between inspectors and among parents as to what the schools should include in their teaching. In 1841 a teacher of music had been hired at $16 a month, and the children liked to sing. But in 1842 some parents suggested this was an unnecessary extravagance and the teacher was dismissed, to the expressed disappointment of the children. In 1846 the children themselves took up a collection to pay for a music teacher, and one was employed the next year. A century of argument in Chicago on "fads and frills" in education had begun.

Some of the best ideas advanced by the inspectors simply could not be put into effect in 1840 or 1849—or at any other time—in ungraded rooms of from 70 to 100 children of all ages from five to twenty-one, at all levels of achievement, taught by teachers with no training for even less difficult tasks. Even when 800 children were housed in one building, the rooms remained ungraded, and coordination between classes, as well as among the separate districts, did not exist. The "principal" in the larger buildings had his hands full just trying to keep order in the halls, on the stairways, and outside the doors. Individual records, either of attendance or achievement, were not kept; only tallies of the total numbers present—required to get local and state money. It was little wonder that comparatively few children came to school under the circumstances.

Private Schools

In 1850 there were 13,500 children of school age in Chicago, only 1,919 of whom were enrolled in the district schools. There were more children in private and parochial schools than in the public schools, and thousands were in no school at all. Since there was no public education beyond the ungraded elementary schools, all secondary education was under private auspices. In 1837 the state law authorizing Chicago's charter as a city had specifically stated that a high school for the city was legal, and three years later the inspectors urged that one be set up in order to relieve the crowded elementary rooms. But there never was enough money to proceed, and any "scholar" who had ambition to go further had to pay for his education. There were several Catholic secondary schools. In 1844 a school for boys on Madison near Michigan was chartered as "the University of St. Mary's of the Lake." Two years later St. Xavier's Academy for girls and St. Ignatius College for boys were added. Non-sectarian secondary schools included a "Normal School," which did not train teachers, and a Female Academy which did. More than 200 private schools opened their doors to Chicago children between 1850 and 1870. Parents who could afford it did not send their children to the noisy, crowded, disorganized district schools, and instead paid tuition, which averaged $5 for one course (with more for "extras"), in the private schools.

There were, fortunately, forces in Chicago and in the state at work to get public support for more effective schools. Many of the settlers were quite indifferent to education, and quite as willing to make a fat profit from speculation in school lands as were some of their sons and grandsons a generation later from child labor. There were always some, nevertheless, who saw in the new nation not just an escape from the rigid class lines of European society nor merely an opportunity to amass wealth by exploiting the untapped resources of what was to them an empty continent. To these earnest idealists, free public education was the avenue of opportunity for all, the fulfillment of a great human dream. All over the country a few such devoted souls attempted to translate the dream into reality.

In colonial Massachusetts, the colony had required, in laws adopted 1642 and 1647, simple schools set up in each settlement. While Virginia was still claiming distant Illinois as part of her territory in 1778, Thomas Jefferson had tried to get his state to organize and support a system of free schools, but the House of Burgesses had failed to do so. The Ordinance of 1787 nevertheless proclaimed that "Religion, morality and knowledge being necessary to good government, schools and the means of education shall be forever encouraged."

Not only Jefferson, but Washington, Madison, Franklin, Adams, and others whose leadership created the new United States, had stressed the necessity for free, publicly supported education if the new nation was to fulfill its destiny. The general concepts of the need for an educated citizenry to manage self-government, the responsibility of government for seeing that such education was provided, the tradition of the separation of public education from any established state churches, and the right of individuals to achieve status and power regardless of lineage were passively accepted; but few spent thought and energy putting them into effect or in pointing out inconsistencies in current practice. Such men as Horace Mann, however, whose energetic leadership had helped create the climate out of which the State Board of Education had developed in Massachusetts (of which he became head in 1837), had made himself heard—even on the frontier, and had given impetus to the drive for free schools there.

As early as 1820, thirteen of the twenty-three states in the Union had made some kind of statutory provision for free public education, although many of the laws were ineffective because the school taxes mentioned in them were not compulsory. In 1825 the General Assembly of the new state of Illinois had passed such a law. It required that a "common school or schools" be organized in every county. To help pay the cost of these schools, the state government was to set aside two dollars of every hundred received by the state treasurer for a state school fund. A majority of the voters in each school district could authorize a property tax on all property in the local district, besides. There was such an uproar about the local school tax that it was made voluntary in 1827 by requiring that no one could be taxed for schools unless he gave his personal consent to do so in writing. At the next session of the legislature, the whole law of 1825 was repealed.

State Aid to Local Schools

Illinois did have some money to put into a state school fund, however, even if the 1825 law was premature. Not only had the federal government given each local township a section of land for a local school, it had given the state 5 percent of the proceeds of the sales of land within the state by the federal land offices. Two-fifths of this gift was to be used for roads, and three-fifths for schools, one-sixth of the school share being reserved for "seminaries and colleges." As early as 1822 the income for schools from this source was $5,955 in one year. Of course, only the interest was to go to schools. Then in 1836, after the closing of the National Bank, the "surplus revenue" of the federal government was distributed to the states. Illinois' share amounted to $478,000, which the legislature assigned to the state school fund. At the end of the year (1836), the Illinois state school fund had reached the imposing total of $948,955 on paper—but only on paper. All of the principal had been spent in a reckless and frequently futile program of "internal improvements," but the state obligated itself to pay 6 percent interest on the nonexistent fund each biennium to help the public schools.[23] This $114,000 interest is clearly recognizable in the current budgets of the state today. The $57,000 a year thus apportioned at first brought only a very small amount to the little settlement at Chicago, as only one-fifth of the people of the state lived in its whole northern half.

The failure of the 1825 law to produce any effective results did not daunt the earnest minority. In 1834 they assembled in a "state convention" in Vandalia, then the state capital, to coordinate their efforts. People came from all over the state. Concerned citizens in Chicago met in the Presbyterian church to choose three delegates to go to Vandalia. Abraham Lincoln represented Sangamon County. Stephen A. Douglas acted as secretary to the convention. Its report was circulated throughout the state urging the adoption of a system

> "which would carry to every man's door the means of educating his children as the offspring of freemen should be taught, [and asking the question] shall it be said that Illinois is too poor to educate her sons and daughters? To hesitate upon this subject is to charge the people with a want of spirit and an ignorance of the character of the age in which they live."[24]

Ten years later a similar group met in Peoria to urge a compulsory school tax in every district, and that the secretary of state of Illinois serve as an ex-officio state superintendent of schools. The second "state convention" on schools, held by interested citizens in Peoria in 1844, had urged that provision be made for teachers' institutes; in 1846, meeting in Chicago, the same group invited the handful of local teachers to the affair—thereby raising their morale and arousing more interest in schools among the general public. In 1845 the three men teachers in Chicago had helped to organize a state society of teachers. Women were not supposed to speak at such meetings, as Susan B. Anthony pointed out indignantly to a similar group in New York State in 1848.

In 1847 an inquiry from the state could locate only 21 countries in which any local school tax was levied. A state law that year had allowed a local compulsory tax for schools if approved by two-thirds of the voters in a district. Proponents of the law vigorously attacked large property owners, accusing them of unwillingness to help other people's children. In that year, also, William B. Ogden, early mayor and shrewd Chicago businessman, as chief officer of the Northwest Educational Society, presided over a meeting of school supporters from several states. The meeting stressed the need for better teaching and pointed out the wisdom of hiring women, as they could be obtained more cheaply than men. In January, 1849, on the first day of the sixteenth session of the General Assembly of Illinois, a great public meeting of school enthusiasts from all parts of the state met in the hall of the State House of Representatives, declaring that the "property owners of the state must be taxed to educate the children of the state." When the separate office of State Superintendent of Public Instruction was created in 1854, Ninian Edwards, the first incumbent, urged a school property tax which would give "every child in the state the right to be educated and to all an equal right." In 1855 the legislature finally did provide a two-mill state school tax, authorize collectible local school taxes, and required that a free school be open in each school district for at least six months of the year.

A Town With Many Problems

In 1854 the public schools of Chicago had been open for twenty years. Their development had lagged far behind that of the town of which they were a part, and in some ways behind those of comparable communities, in most of which the number of children per teacher was considerably lower. But the city itself had grave problems, which, like those of the schools, were intensified by the speed of its growth. Cholera killed 5 percent of the population in 1854. The new waterworks completed that year to replace the rotten wooden water pipes let dead fish through. Those who could afford it bought water at 10 cents a barrel. Smallpox epidemics occurred every year, and tuberculosis and infant diseases took a heavy toll. One in every sixty inhabitants died of "consumption" in 1853. The streets were just two feet above the level of the river and in rainy weather were impassable even for empty wagons.

But to the enthusiastic promoters of the city's future, the progress of the seventeen-year-old town was plainly visible. There were 159 miles of wooden and brick sidewalks, 27 miles of streets where the mud was covered with loose wooden planks, four miles of wharves along the river and its branches, ten bridges, a gas works, street lamps (turned off at midnight) and a new waterworks. As the business streets expanded, the little frame houses were rolled away to the west and south as more and larger stores and factories went up in their places. Subdividers began selling the swamplands to the west. The council approved the first city plan, aimed to pull the city out of the mud. The shallow Chicago river was to be dredged so that boats of deep draft could pass through and the dirt puled on the streets till they had been raised twelve feet. Houses were to be jacked up to that level.

The schools had always been an afterthought for most Chicagoans in midst of the moneymaking bustle. But even the schools had new plans after twenty years. In 1853 the city council had authorized the employment of a superintendent of schools who would serve as a kind of secretary to the school inspectors and "bring order and unity" into the school districts. In 1854 the inspectors agreed on an appointment and Chicago's first superintendent of schools began a monumental task.

Chapter 2

FRONTIER SCHOOLS BECOME A TOWN SYSTEM

In September, 1854, the public schools of Chicago began the long, slow—still unfinished—process of transforming great huddles of children into a skilled professional enterprise with definite goals and rational means of attaining them. Often the work was directed by people with no real sense of their own purposes or of the needs of the children before them. The new superintendent, John Dore, had no authority whatsoever over his 34 teachers and 3,000 children other than that granted him by the seven school inspectors. The ungraded schools in each district were completely independent of each other in methods, books, and procedures, except in the requirement for counting their children. These schools differed from isolated, primitive, rural schools only in the huge numbers of children each teacher struggled with. There were "principals" in buildings of several rooms, like Miltimore's Folly, but they were kept busy moving children in and out, and had no time for supervision, even had they known how to help teachers with their impossible task. In employing a superintendent, the city council and inspectors apparently wanted someone to do for all the schools what the principals tried to do within one building—"introduce order and unity." Superintendents were a new and untried device in 1854; the advanced Boston school system had not employed one until 1850.

Superintendents and Their Untrained Teachers

Superintendent Dore had come to Chicago from the well-organized Boylston Street school in Boston. The anarchy he found in the Chicago schools was even worse than he anticipated when he accepted the position. No one really knew what school any given child belonged in, or what progress he might have made.

37

There were no records for an individual child, either of his attendance or of his work. In spite of the text lists, so patiently made by the inspectors, there was practically no uniformity in books being used.

In the two years' time of his service, Superintendent Dore managed to get every child's name recorded somewhere, and a daily record kept at least of his attendance. He himself gave a general examination to every child in the schools, so that it might be possible for a teacher to classify the "scholars" according to their level of progress, even in the ungraded rooms. He explained that this examination was too great a labor to expect of the school inspectors. The new superintendent was surprised that the children knew as much as they did, and admitted that the unsupervised schools had done better than could have been expected of them, except in grammar. He insisted on uniformity in the books used. He urged strongly that the inspectors provide a high school, which he felt would serve many purposes. It would reduce the number of older children in the ungraded rooms. It could provide training for future teachers. And it would follow the trend in other cities which Chicago was boastful about emulating in other ways—an argument always useful in Chicago.

The first report of the new superintendent in 1855 had several suggestions for the improvement of the schools. One was that the city council must pay for the sweeping and washing of school rooms and the making of fires (all duties heretofore performed by pupils). He suggested that the council plant some trees around the bare school buildings. Dore commented on the "migratory character" of pupils and the limited extent of their training, caused in part by parents keeping children out of school for "frivolous reasons." He added that if it is now the acknowledged duty of the public to provide schools for the education of its children, the responsibility assumed by the public implies a like duty on the part of parents to see that their children attend. He commented that "A truant law in some cities of the Eastern states has had a wonderful effect." Boston had had such a law since 1850.

Then Superintendent Dore lamented the lack of training of his teachers:

> "It has long been conceded that to become proficient in any art or profession, an apprenticeship is necessary, but by some unaccountable oversight, the art of teaching has been considered an exception, or rather has received no consideration at all. School agents or trustees have not exercised the same judgment in the employment of teachers that they exercise in their own private affairs."[1]

Disturbed at the low regard in which the public schools were held, he continued,

> "Shall there be an inferior class of schools which the more fortunate will not patronize because they can afford to pay high tuition, and which the less fortunate but proud spirited will not patronize because they are the schools of the common people? Or shall it be a

class of schools so elevated as to be worthy of the patronage of the whole community?"

In his second report Dore had sharp criticisms to make of the methods of instruction in use. Too much time was spent on memorizing unimportant details. Pupils were being required to commit an entire grammar text to memory before they received any instruction in the application of its principles. Grammar could be learned at ten, he said, and is now being postponed till children reach thirteen or fourteen years of age. Reading is out loud, rather than individual. In order to improve the attitudes of parents, he urged that they visit the schools and show a lively interest in what the teachers are trying to do. Many parents had come during the year as a result of his invitations.

Superintendent Dore had the support of the inspectors in the limited efforts he made, but the actual control of the schools remained completely in the hands of the inspectors and of the city council, who by a two-thirds vote could remove the superintendent from office at any time. Each inspector was responsible for certain schools, where he appointed and dismissed teachers without even thinking of consulting the superintendent.[2] After two years of service. John Dore resigned, went into business, became an affluent "first citizen," was elected to the State Senate and for a year served as president of the fifteen-man Board of Education which in 1857 replaced in name and number the seven inspectors.

Superintendent Dore's successor, William Harvey Wells, was one of the most effective administrators in the early history of public education. He left his mark not only on the city and its schools, but on growing school systems throughout the Middle West. He was able to transcend to some degree, by positive and sometimes dramatic leadership, the welter of checks and balances of the economic and political forces which actually controlled the schools.

Wells had been born on a farm in Connecticut, forty-four years before coming to Chicago, and had managed to get an education only by great personal effort. When he was seventeen he got one year's schooling at a private academy near his home; he taught in a district school for a year, and then became an assistant at the academy. At twenty-two, he spent eight months at Andover Teachers' Seminary, which, in 1823, S. R. Hall had made the first teacher training institution in the country, and where he later spent eleven years as a teacher himself. In 1845 Dartmouth College gave him an honorary Master of Arts degree. In 1846 he published a new kind of grammar, where examples of good usage were taken from the great literature he wanted his students to read. As the principal of an academy in Massachusetts, he had become the first editor (1848) of a publication called the "Massachusetts Teacher," and served as president of the newly organized Essex County Teachers Association and then of the Massachusetts State Teachers Association. In 1854 he was asked to head the Westfield State Normal School, one of the new Massachusetts normal schools. Just before he accepted the superintendency in Chicago in 1856, he was one of the initiators of the American Normal School Association. Few people of his generation had as intimate knowledge of the rising standards of education, and of the successful efforts being made to meet them.

William Harvey Wells not only knew *about* teaching; he was a teacher himself who spared no efforts in his own performance. In his country school he had heard about cloth maps and bought some, out of his meager salary of $10.00 a month. (When other teachers came from distances to see them, the school board finally paid for them.) He heard about blackboards and made one, and his mother came to help him paint it. Though he had difficulty with his eyes all his life, he was so eager to learn that he persuaded others to read to him when his eyes tired. Many of his students have recorded their appreciation of his enthusiastic interest, not only in what he was teaching them, but in them as people, and of his ability to generate student enthusiasm for what teacher and pupil were doing together. One remembered the clear, eager ring in his voice. A pupil in the academy he directed wrote, after forty years:

> "He made his scholars feel life to be a cheery business. I have never seen a man who combined the organizing ability, administrative faculty and the personal influence for character with such earnest and philosophical method. He imparted a desire to master and made students sanguine of success."[3]

Not only could William Wells teach, he knew how to help others learn how—a gift invaluable to the schools of Chicago in 1856. He did his best to help the teachers of Chicago understand that as teachers they were not simply imparting instruction to passive little "objects." They were to arouse the interest of their pupils and to direct their energy. He explained that "mental discipline," the catchword of the day, could not be accomplished by rote memorization, but required consciously directed effort on the part of the learners. He stressed the need of children for sympathy and understanding, and told his teachers in his Saturday morning training classes that a kind word to a desponding pupil might accomplish more than any reprimand and that punishment not aimed to help a child develop self-discipline was worse than useless.

Wells was particularly concerned that the Chicago schools were so far behind the procession of other cities in primary education, since primary education over the country had improved more in the last eight years than in the previous fifty. He insisted that the salaries of primary teachers be raised to those of teachers in the upper grades, as had already been done in St. Louis. He told the primary teachers that their work was the foundation for all other education, and reminded them that a large part of the children never went farther than the primary years.

Wells did his best to reduce the size of primary classes. In his 1859 report he said, "It is humilitating to admit that there are so many as 150 scholars in one primary room, with four or five little children on a seat built for two." He wanted each child to have a seat by himself, and suggested it did little good to scold children so crowded together for whispering to each other. In 1859 the average primary class in Chicago was 81. He managed to reduce it to 77 by 1860, and pointed out in his report that the average in St. Louis was 60, in New York, 50, and in Cincinnati, 45. In some Chicago schools 200 small children with more than one teacher were all meeting in one room. He was concerned that in most primary schools even the youngest children were supposed to sit quietly during the day without relaxation or movement, and sometimes without anything to do. They must have recreation and action, Wells said, even though it was just marking on paper. Reading must never be taught without teaching the meaning of the words covered and care must be used in pronunciation, particularly for the children of the foreign-born.

He felt it would be a good idea to admit four-year-olds, as was done in Boston, if there were money enough for buildings and teachers. Since there was not, he urged that the entrance age be raised from five years to six, so that those who were allowed to come should have a better chance to learn. He wrote to forty cities for their practice on age of admission and reported that seven large cities were already excluding five-year-olds. This change was made in 1865, after he was no longer superintendent.

A Graded System and a High School

William Harvey Wells was also deeply concerned with the other end of his academic spectrum, the new high school. It opened in 1856 with 169 boys and girls and grew to 324 in his eight years of service. High schools were new everywhere. Philadelphia had opened one in 1838 and New York City in 1849. In 1848 Philadelphia had introduced a normal training course for teachers, and Superintendent Wells similarly included a two-year course for teachers in Chicago's high school in its first year. Since he himself had been the principal of two academies of recognized standing in the East, he knew what he wanted in the new Chicago institution—and the normal training was one of his first goals. Within two years the new high school was sending back into the Chicago schools a few teachers with at least some training for their work. A few made an immediate difference, since in 1860 there were only 123 teachers altogether to teach 14,000 children.

Not everyone could attend the new high school; but anyone twelve years old or older was permitted to take the written examination which would admit him. To prevent "outside influence," applicants were known only by number on the examination paper. Then a public examination for honors was given—an exciting occasion, held in a large hall, with parents and general public invited. One newspaper referred to the high school examinations as local "Olympic Games." The honors awarded were highly regarded and motivated younger "scholars" to greater effort.

A student who enrolled in the new high school had his choice of three courses. He could take a strictly classical course with Latin and Greek the major subjects. This would fit him for college. He could enroll in the English course which replaced all the required classics but Latin with some reading in English literature, and included an appalling list of sixteen other subjects such as navigation, surveying, astronomy, mineralogy, logic, "intellectual and moral science," political economy, and the Constitution of the United States. Finally, he might enter the two-year normal course if he were sixteen years of age; in this, he learned no foreign languages but added United States and "general" history, "mental philosophy," and theory of teaching.[4]

Superintendent Wells specified in theory of teaching not only the procedures of instruction in a graded school system but his new ideas on "oral instruction" in primary and grammar grades. By this method, teachers were to interest children by telling them facts about the world around them, as well as teaching reading and arithmetic tables. The practice was justified in current pedagogy as helping children "to cultivate observation and secure accurate use of language." Helping children to understand their own environment was not yet orthodox, but it was particularly useful as the science taught in academies and high schools was still "facts," without laboratories, and the practical suggestions made in the course of study were useful to the teacher.

Superintendent Wells' best known professional accomplishment was the grading of the entire school population and the preparation of a complete graded curriculum. Within five years after his appointment, he accomplished the major miracle of dividing 14,199 children into 10 grades plus the high school grades. The 123 teachers were reassigned to teaching these separate grades using the detailed, monumental course of study worked out by the superintendent for each grade. The tenth grade was for five-year-olds. There were four other primary grades and five grammar grades. That such a revolution in procedure—and in the long established daily activities of teachers—was accomplished so quickly and so thoroughly was a tribute to the superintendent's administrative ability and to his skill with people, both teachers and Board members. The minimum standards he set apparently did not seem unreasonable to most of his teachers. They were to post a regular schedule with specific times assigned for the important subjects such as reading, spelling, and arithmetic. Children in the same grade should be grouped for efficient instruction, although it was admitted that this "could scarcely be done if the teacher had more than fifty scholars." The reading lesson was not to be left until the children knew the meaning of every word. A fifteen-minute grammar lesson on one day should be reviewed the next.

Superintendent Wells' book, *A Graded Course of Instruction with Instructions to Teachers,* published first in 1862, and reissued in two later editions (with slightly different titles), gave detailed instructions on material to be covered in each grade. The five-year-olds in the tenth grade should learn colors, shapes, and the alphabet. Children in the next grade, six-year-olds, should learn to tell time, count to 100, know some addition tables forward and backward, and read simple words. After five years of school, the "scholars" should know multiplication and division tables, Roman numerals to one thousand, and have finished "half a second reader." By the end of the next year they should be able to spell the Books of the Bible, know about solids such as cubes and parallelopipeds. In the next year, the teacher was cautioned not to have the children memorize the number of square miles in each state, but to take 100 words from newspapers for spelling lessons. In what is now seventh grade, the children should be one-third through a fourth reader, and in grammar, "to the verb." They should have heard of the hanging gardens of Babylon, the Pyramids, the Trojan War, Julius Caesar, the Crusades, Columbus, and George Washington.

Thousands of copies of Superintendent Wells' book were sold over a period of years in its three editions, and its contents adopted as official curriculum all over the Northwest states.[5] Advertisements in the 1866 edition are illuminating. Teachers were urged to buy *A Young Citizen's Catechism*, Fowle's *Bible Reader* (price $1.00), or Cheever's *Life in the Sandwich Isles*, an account of "Degradation and barbarism enlightened by civilization and Christianity."

School Housing for Children and Adults

Perhaps Superintendent Wells' pedagogy may seem passé today, but his hard-headed hammering on the need for seats for school children is unfortunately not unfamiliar a hundred years later. When Superintendent Dore arrived in 1854 the seven school buildings in Chicago had been so overcrowded that a thousand children were turned away. In Wells' first report (1856) he grieved that he could not accommodate 3,000. Eight years later, when he left, 5,000 children were turned away for lack of space. In his 1859 report Wells stated that Chicago now has "the smallest amount of room and the smallest number of teachers in proportion to the number of pupils of any city in the Union, simply because the population of our city has increased faster than any other."[6] He urged the city council to issue bonds to build school buildings.

Wells' plan for new buildings was a kind of small educational park where a grammar school was the center of a cluster of nearby smaller primary schools for not more than 600 pupils. When constructed, however, the buildings were not very good, hastily erected without real planning for light and air. When finished, they were still bare and barren of most kinds of school equipment. The Brown School, built in 1857—and used for one hundred years thereafter—was the first to substitute crude steam heat for stoves.

Getting a school building erected was a slow process, even though the actual construction might be a hasty, sloppy job. Delays were caused by the division of authority between the Board of Education and the city council. The Board was supposed to choose the sites, but the council actually bought them with school money. Not for more than 50 years would the Board of Education have the right of eminent domain. Board members, impatient at long delays in the purchase of sites recommended, charged angrily that aldermen were in collusion with owners of the sites and were profiteering in the sale of land. The council on its part took pains to forbid teachers and other employees to·have "any pecuniary interest in articles purchased or work done" in the schools; Board members and superintendent were threatened with dismissal by the council if they took rewards from book concerns or were involved in the sale of texts. There is evidence of such implication for at least some of the charges and inferences on both sides.

In spite of the lag in the construction of buildings, the school enrollment rose from 6,826 in 1855, to 14,199 in 1860, and to 29,080 in 1865. There were twice as many teachers in 1855 as in 1850–42 instead of 21–but there were four times as many children, 6,826 instead of 1,919, with each teacher supposed to be in charge of 160. Even so, these 6,826 were only 21 percent of the Chicago school-age population from 5 to 21, some of whom actually came and were turned away. In 1860 there were 123 teachers for 14,199 children, 115 per teacher, on the average. In 1865 the year after Wells left, there were twice as many teachers, 240, but also twice as many children, 29,080.[7] In spite of vigorous effort, Wells had been able to exercise little effect on school housing and overcrowded class rooms.

Besides the monumental work of grading the school system and inaugurating the high school, Superintendent Wells also incorporated some new services into the structure and curriculum during his term. In 1857 a teacher had volunteered to teach immigrants who wanted to learn English, and children, willing to come after working all day, if the Board of Education would allow the use of a room at night. After seven years of such volunteer service, Wells got the approval of the Board for pay for night-school teachers, and in 1864 five evening schools admitted 3,800 students. Similar schools were being opened in Cincinnati, St. Louis, and New York. Evening high-school classes were added in 1868. Another basic addition to the school system was the introduction of physical training. Luther Haven, president of the Board of Education in 1858, grew increasingly concerned at the "crooked" spines, pale faces, and generally poor physical condition of the children he saw in his school visits. In 1861 gymnastics (without equipment) was introduced into the new graded curriculum. The boys in the high school built a gym for the school at the cost of $100. President Haven wanted playgrounds outside the schools, but the city council could see no sense in such extravagant waste of money for expensive land–just for a place for children to play.

Superintendent William Harvey Wells

In 1864 after eight years of energetic, effective effort, William Wells resigned. In eight years' time he had channeled the Chicago schools in directions they followed for decades. He had turned the tide of public opinion toward some concern, rather than scorn, for the public schools. Although less than half of all the children who went to any school attended the public schools in 1850, by 1860 the reverse was true. In spite of his lack of authority, and in spite of the political exploitation of jobs and contracts—increasing as the number of projects and the amount of school expenditures rose—he had made a school system. He lamented the danger of the "fetid tide of official corruption," which threatened the future of the country, but he was more successful in facing it than many of those who succeeded him. The 1857 amendment to the city charter which had changed the seven inspectors into a fifteen-man "Board of Education" had also wiped out the remnants of the old district system, with their separate trustees.[8] The new centralization had been useful in helping the superintendent structure his graded system, although it left him with fifteen people to deal with instead of only seven.

Many of the concerns he expressed are still problems more than one hundred years later. On grading children's work, he felt that "Records of scholarship that are kept in schools are almost always based on attainment, which too often fails entirely of being a record of intellectual progress." The Saturday morning Teachers' Meeting, which the council had ordered the school inspectors to hold for all teachers (instead of teaching on Saturday), Wells reduced to one Saturday a month, and actually gave the teachers something worth coming for. He wanted the principals to have more time to help the teachers. He hoped for further decrease in corporal punishment. He believed in freedom of speech as a citizen and felt free to disagree with some of the war-time policies of the government. He refused to allow military training in the high school during the war. Wells did not want to put muskets in the hands of boys.

But most of all, Wells was deeply concerned because so many children were not in school at all. In his 1856 report he had said that between 3,000 and 5,000 children in Chicago had never been in school a day in their lives. In his 1857 report a modern chart of the attendance curve shows only a slight diminution in truancy and absentees. He urged support for evening schools. He took pride in the record that only 28 percent of those who entered high school in Chicago failed to graduate, while more than half of those who entered the Philadelphia high school dropped out. He was disappointed because Chicago was the only large city which had absolutely no provision for books for poor children, and did not even require vaccination to protect the children's health. He did not consider his work done, by any means. But his eyesight was becoming much worse and he was far from well.

A school is a relationship among human beings, not a place, a group of objects, nor a list of subjects. The greatest single contribution of William Wells to Chicago was his kindling of faith within his teachers that their work was of the first importance, that it was appreciated, and that it was worthy of their best efforts. They felt that he understood their problems and was concerned about them as people. When his resignation was announced the teachers themselves held a meeting in his honor at the high school. The Chicago Tribune of January 6,

1864, describes the superintendent's last speech to his staff. He told them of his own bitter experiences as a nineteen-year-old novice in an isolated country school, of the weeks he spent struggling between his own inexperience and ignorance of how children act, and his anxious desire to have them learn. "Night after night, after the children left, I would sit and weep in mortification and discouragement. I lost so much weight that the buttons on my only coat became too loose." Then he went on:

> "I have never known a more competent, laborious and successful body of teachers than that which I meet today. You are also appreciated by the Board of Education and they intend to give you substantial evidence of this. My health demands that I leave, and I am going to the Mediterranean for six months. May every blessing attend you in your continued efforts to elevate and improve the public schools, and may a generation of children be made wiser and better by your self sacrificing labors." [9]

To this the teachers responded by a resolution read by George Howland, principal of the high school, "that his uniform kindness and encouragement have contributed very greatly to the pleasure as well as the success of the teachers in the public schools, . . . have won for him an affectionate regard, and that his devotion and zeal in the duties of his office furnish an example worthy of imitation by all." Mr. Howland then presented the retiring superintendent with a gold watch worth $400—no small gift from less than 260 teachers with salaries ranging from $250 to $1000 a year—"as a visible token of the esteem and kind regard they wish to express."

William Wells continued his service to the schools for many years after his resignation and entry into the insurance business. He was immediately appointed a member of the Board of Education by the city council and served as its president between 1872 and 1874. He then refused reappointment because it took too large a share of his time. He was one of the first members of an Illinois State Board of Education which helped establish the Illinois State Normal School in 1872. But Wells did not limit his public leadership to formal education. He helped to establish a public library after the great fire, and served as director of the Library Board until his death. He was instrumental in the founding of the Chicago Astronomical Society and the Chicago Academy of Science, and took part in the Chicago Historical Society. His own interest in the dramatic story of Chicago led him to write a history of the early schools as a part of his 1857 report.

When William Wells died in 1885, more than twenty years after he left the school system, every newspaper in Chicago commented on the contributions he had made to the life of the city. The Herald wrote, "The city loses an earnest advocate of the cause of popular education." The Advance Intelligencer paid this tribute: "Few men had as broad and warm sympathy for their fellows. It would be hard to name a philanthropic project which did not commend his cooperation." The Public Library Board attended the funeral in a body, as did the Board of Education, which adopted the following resolution:

"His connection with the school system marked an era in its history. Under Mr. Wells, what was crude and provisional was brought to thorough organization and efficiency. It is not too much to say that his work was the foundation of whatever is best and most permanent in our present educational system."

More significant, however, than public tributes by official bodies, was a letter to Mrs. Wells, signed by thirty-three of forty-seven teachers who had known him in 1854, telling her how "Well we remember when he first came, his kindly greetings, his warm friendship, his words of cheer and his intense zeal and enthusiasm."[10]

Clearly, the personality, the skill, and the breadth of leadership of the superintendent of schools was from this time on to be a significant factor in the shaping of the city's schools.

Income and Salaries

The failure of Superintendent Wells to solve the school housing problem in spite of very real effort was due in part to the inelasticity of the sources of school income and in part to the lack of school interest on the part of many of the city's "movers and shakers." Though the actual value of the unsold school lands skyrocketed as the population mounted, its income did not rise in proportion to its value. The four blocks of the original section which had not been sold in 1835 were now worth $860,000, and the land which had been disposed of for $38,000 was now worth, on a conservative estimate at least thirty million dollars. The Board of Education had talked of selling the remaining lots in the center of the city but the School Land Agent pled publicly in 1855 to have the lands kept for the future. Said he, "If the real estate yet belonging to the school fund, though but a fragment of what it once was, shall be judiciously managed and kept, the next generation may be in possession of a revenue adequate for the support of the grandest system of public schools of any city in the world!"[11]

The valuable land was not bringing in any such tremendous income at the time, partly because the leasing of it had been a political perquisite, used to create partisan support rather than to obtain revenue for the schools. When block 87 along the river was leased in 1858, the rent had been set for $800. The president of the Board of Education called attention to the fact that the lessee of a privately owned block adjacent to it and worth no more, was paying $5,667 in rent. In 1865 the Board of Education was allowed by the council to appoint the school land agent. But the council kept its fingers, some of which had a reputation of being "sticky," on the school property. It appointed appraisers for the lands in 1870, but when their report set the current value of the school land at $2,616,424, the council did the lessees the favor of reducing the appraised value to $1,852,424. The loss of 6 percent interest to the schools on the politically inspired reduction was $46,000 a year. This obvious manipulation of the school lands for personal and partisan profit became a hot political issue. In 1862 "Long John" Wentworth, several times a school board member, one-time mayor, and now Union Republican congressman, attacked "the bankers" as robbers of the school fund.[12] At the height of Civil War bitterness, in 1864, the Republicans accused the Democrats in the council of using reductions in the value of the lands to help the Democratic Chicago Times, which was accused of being secessionist.

In any case, there were grave suspicions and open charges that mismanagement of the school fund and lands was one reason for the dire financial straits of the schools. The enrollment and total costs of the schools were increasing so fast, however, that even the best management of this one resource would not have produced enough to make even meager ends meet. In 1855 the total expenditures had been $16,546; in 1860, $69,630; in 1865, $176,000; and by 1870, $527,444. The gap between the income from the interest on the school fund and the rent from the lands had been filled to some degree in 1857 by a 2 mill tax for schools on the property of the city (raised to three mills in 1865[13]), and by a share of a state property tax for schools authorized by the legislature in 1855. The state tax was a 2 mill levy on all property in the state and was distributed after 1854 by a full-time State Superintendent of Public Instruction, elected by the people of the state for four years on the "off" years to bypass the "heated political passions" of presidential elections.

In 1867 the legislature allowed the city council to increase the property tax for schools to 5 mills in case there had been a deficit the year before. Any bonds for school buildings had to be authorized by the council, but the interest and principal had to be repaid from school money. The state school tax was divided among the counties in proportion to the number of white children. "Persons of color" could get school money individually in proportion to the taxes they paid and educate their children as best they could. (This last clause was ignored in Chicago, but not in most of Illinois.)[14] The president of the Chicago Board of Education complained that the 1861 state allocation of $18,817.69 to Chicago was unfair and urged that there be a more equitable division of state funds. In 1871, when the Chicago school enrollment had almost tripled, only $35,000 was allotted from the state school fund, not even twice the allocation of ten years before.

The stringency in the financial resources of Chicago schools not only slowed down the construction of desperately needed buildings, it kept teachers' salaries down to a level below those paid to other city employees, and below that of teachers in some other cities. The change in proportion of women to men teachers from five to one in 1854 to sixteen to one in 1871 was both a result and a continuing cause of the low salary scale. The change had been greatest during the Civil War, but the lack of money for men's higher salaries after the war kept their number low. Men high-school teachers in the 50's and early 60's received $1,000 a year, four times the $250 paid some women teachers in the primary and grammar grades Men in the lower grades received twice as much as women. Women high-school teachers also received half the salary of their male colleagues. The Chicago Inter Ocean for October 3, 1863, noted an increase in salaries for elementary teachers, "Lady teachers remain at $300 for three and one-half years, and then may get $400." By 1868 the superintendent was being paid $4,500, the one high-school principal $2,500, a male elementary principal $2,200, and a woman principal $1,200. In 1856 a Chicago policeman had been paid $800 a year and a woman teacher $250, neither with any specific qualifications required.

Salaries for teachers did not improve even if the opportunities for being trained as a teacher did. In 1865 the normal division of the high school offered a half a year of experience in teaching under guidance in a practice school. A twenty-year-old girl named Ella Flagg was put in charge, and she arranged to have students work in rooms in a school in a very poor neighborhood. Ella Flagg had attended the Brown School at the age of thirteen when her family moved to Chicago, and had taught arithmetic there as a child monitor under the old Lancastrian system. After she took the two-year normal course, she returned to the Brown School as its assistant principal, at eighteen. Like Wells, she tried to interest her student teachers in the children as well as in the rigid methods of instruction they were taught to apply. In 1866 the program for teaching under guidance was reduced from a half year to two weeks by the Board of Education. In 1871 Ella Flagg asked to be transferred to high-school teaching, since she was no longer willing to try to make teachers out of children just two years out of elementary school, particularly when it was impossible to weed out the hopelessly incompetent (sponsored by Board members and other politically powerful persons).[15] In that year the normal division was separated from the high school and located in six rooms of a building standing on the present site of the Chicago State College (for many years after 1897 called the Chicago Normal School). Superintendent Wells' successor asked the Board to lengthen the normal training by at least another half year to "give the young ladies more culture," but the Board discouraged both lengthening the term and raising standards of admission for the normal school.[16]

In 1873 the second director of "practice" education resigned, following the announcement by the Board of Education that incompetent students could be dismissed only by Board action, and that the teachers in the normal school could not prevent the graduation of anyone approved by the Board. In 1877 the Board closed the normal school entirely, claiming there were more applicants to fill the vacancies of a staff of 700 than there were vacancies. Opponents of the closing alleged that the Board's motive was to do away with the training requirement for prospective teachers and to restore to itself the unquestioned control of all appointments on a personal or political basis.[17] One hundred seventy-nine teachers had profited from the training given by young Ella Flagg in her four years of effort. But in 1870 less than half the women teachers in the Chicago schools had graduated from the four-year high school, or the two-year normal division, and the majority had attended only elementary school.[18]

Exploitation by Local Politicians

The temper of the times accepted use of public office for private profit and personal power as a matter of course, and there were few open protests against it. Some school board members expressed surprised irritation at any criticism of the manipulation of school lands and contracts, or of appointments and promotions. As in other cities of the United States in that day, government employees were expected to show their "loyalty" and gratitude not by doing their work well, but by helping those who provided their jobs to remain in power. Teachers, who constituted approximately half the city employees, were included in this system as a matter of course. Those who failed to show the required "loyalty" could expect to be dismissed without further ado. Some of the Board members could easily rationalize the use of their position for personal profit or for the advantage of the political party: "After all," said they, "it's always been done this way! Why do you think people accept these unpaid jobs?"

The schools had made great progress in organization, in the morale of teachers, in the improvement of teaching methods, and in the respect of the general public since 1854. They had increased in enrollment from 3,500 pupils, with 47 teachers, to more than 21,000 with 223 teachers in 1864, and then to 40,000 and 570 teachers by 1871.[19] But in spite of the efforts of Alderman Richard Hamilton, Congressman John Wentworth, and ex-Superintendent Wells, the public schools of Chicago were not considered of great importance by the decision-makers of the city, public or private.

Chapter 3

THE TOWN BECOMES AN INDUSTRIAL CITY

The failure of succeeding Boards of Education to put into effect the hope of Superintendent Wells that they would reward their teachers more generously, and the opposition of many members toward any effort to improve the training of teachers, must have been particularly discouraging to the next superintendent, Josiah Pickard. As state superintendent of education in Wisconsin, his finest achievement had been the creation of a state normal school. In Chicago he had to watch a small experiment in teacher training be whittled away until nothing at all remained. By 1875 sixteen cities in the United States had set up some kind of training system to provide teachers. Chicago was the only one of the sixteen which failed to continue its teacher training program.

That Superintendent Pickard had less effect on Chicago schools than his predecessor was probably not entirely his fault. The dramatic events in the city's history during his thirteen years in office eclipsed the slow development of a school system which had never seemed too important to most of its citizens in any case. His term began in the heat of the Civil War, followed by a disastrous depression. The city was just emerging from the depression when the great conflagration of 1871 destroyed a large share of the city including a third of the school buildings. An even deeper and longer depression fell on the city, as it began to recover from the fire, in which the rumblings of bitter labor conflict could be heard in what had become a great industrial city.

Pickard's efforts, however, were not entirely without result. He gave complete support to the idea of evening schools, and not only persuaded the Board to pay teachers for them, but asked for a part-time day school for working children (which he did not get). Only Cincinnati, Boston, and New York had preceded Chicago in establishing evening schools. In 1874 high-school classes were offered in the evening schools. He managed to get the Board of Education to request the

State Agricultural College (now the University of Illinois) to place a polytechnic institute in Chicago.[1] When this plan failed, the city council was asked for funds for such a school. All these plans came to nought in his term of office, but they indicated a considerable understanding of what the public schools should be offering to children and to the city. He was successful in getting three special rooms for truants in which "sloyd" or manual training in woodwork was taught, and in encouraging the council to require small pox vaccination for all children in the schools in 1867. In 1869 a graded course in music was added to the curriculum and in 1876, under his leadership, the Board took over the room for deaf mutes which, like the evening school, had begun in a school building at private expense.[2]

In his annual report to the Board in 1865, Pickard proposed "truant police," pointing out that ten percent of the children enrolled one month were absent the next. Boston had used truant officers since 1850, and added to its force in 1862. The Annual Report of the Board of Education for that year underlined the serious problem of child labor. "Many a child," it said, "has been sacrificed mentally and morally as well as physically to the pecuniary interest of the parent."[3] In 1873 the superintendent stated that corporal punishment had been abandoned "by request." In his 1876 report Superintendent Pickard made the eminently sensible comment that "the common practice of suspension of wilful non-attendants was only a 'reward for truancy.' "

Effect on Schools of the Civil War

Each of the major historical events of Superintendent Pickard's administration left its mark on the Chicago school system. During the war the proportion of women teachers to men rose to sixteen to one—six times the national average of the time, according to the census of 1870. Since the pay levels for women were roughly half that of men, any subsequent increase in the number of men required either more money or some increase in the already unbearable class load. Since no more money was available, the proportion of women increased rather than decreased. In 1885 there were twenty-three women to one man in Chicago schools. Only in Philadelphia was the ratio higher, twenty-five to one. In New York it was six to one and in Cincinnati, four to one.[4] A woman elementary teacher was paid on approximately the same level as a seamstress. Salaries were not raised during the war, although prices of clothing, fuel, and food doubled by 1862.

A more dramatic result of the war came in 1863. Tension was high in Chicago between the Lincoln Unionist Republicans and the Democrats, particularly the Irish, who were at the bottom of the economic pile in Chicago and felt threatened by the possible economic competition of Negroes. They rioted against a few Negro dock workers who had "taken the jobs of their brothers." The most serious effect of these wartime tensions on the schools was the passage by the city council of the so-called Black School Law of 1863.

The Underground Railroad had operated openly during the war and the number of Negroes in Chicago had noticeably increased. Under pressure from the Irish and other groups, in 1863, the city council adopted an ordinance requiring that all Negro children go to segregated Negro schools.[5] The parents of Negro children in the already established schools refused to obey the ordinance and continued to send their children to the schools in which they were already enrolled. Then the school board ruled that a child with only one-eighth Negro blood might attend the regular schools. Finally the pressure of delegations of Negro citizens on the mayor and on the Board of Education brought about the repeal of the measure in 1865. A separate evening school for Negroes, however, was maintained between 1863 and 1870.

The Negro citizens in Chicago actually suffered less discrimination in education than those in the rest of the state.[6] The Chicago school system had not excluded Negro children, although it had never received state funds for them. Some Chicago Negroes had prospered and were recognized as important leaders in the life of the city—James Jones for one. Many Chicago churches before the Civil War had earnestly protested the evils of slavery, the Fugitive Slave Law, and the Kansas-Nebraska Bill, but statements of protest did not indicate opposition to segregation, containing opinions that "the two races could never live on terms of civil or social equality,"[7] and that it would be a good idea to send the Negroes back to Africa. There were separate sections for Negroes in theaters in Chicago, and unions did not admit them. But they had gone to school with all the other children, and continued to do so.

When the soldiers came home at the end of the war and government war expenditures ceased, there was a period of great unemployment. One-half the "mechanics" in Chicago were idle as late as 1869. Unskilled labor was a drug on the market, and actual hunger and suffering were widespread. But both the population and the number of children coming to school continued to increase without proportional increase in school income or school seats. At the end of the war the schools were $30,000 in debt. The city council finally authorized bonds up to $1,200,000 for more buildings, and some ten were built, amid cries of extravagance and criticisms of the council. The additional capacity, however, still did not decrease the lag in seating. The income from the school fund and the rents did not change, and the additional sum for each child from the state was less than a dollar each. The total expenditure for 29,080 children in 1865 was $176,966 or $8.60 per capita, and in 1870 for 38,934 children, $415,810 or $11 per capita. The only gain in school income was from an increase in the local property tax from 2 mills to 5 mills to meet the deficit of 1865. It was continued at 5 mills thereafter, and in 1879 was divided, with 2 mills being spent on salaries and 3 mills on buildings.[8]

Effects on Schools of the Great Fire

The city and its schools had not recovered from the effects of the war and the depression when the greatest single calamity in its history fell upon it. In two days in October, 1871, the whole heart of the city burned itself out. In a city of 300,000 people, the homes of 98,000 were lost and at least 35,000 left completely without food or shelter. Two hundred million dollars worth of property was destroyed, including fifteen school buildings—a third of all the school housing. The schools still standing were for some time used to shelter the homeless. The high-school building housed the courts for a year, and classes were not reopened until 1874. The burned school buildings were not replaced for three years, and no new ones were built. All city, county, and school records went up in smoke, including the records of titles to school lands and funds. In the confusion, fraudulent titles to some of the school lands in outlying townships were accepted and recorded, and as much as $200,000 worth permanently lost. Neither the city nor the state collected property taxes in Chicago for a year, interest was not paid on loans made from the school funds, and rents were not collected on the land. The lessees wanted rents reduced because of the fire and finally the city agreed that the rents due and not paid on school lands should be cut forty percent.[9] One positive benefit of the fire was the final enforcement of an 1867 law requiring safe exits for school buildings.

In the race for rebuilding the city after the fire the schools lost out. Priorities were given to other services. In 1872 the city council authorized $4,581,000 to rebuild the water system, $2,637,000 for new sewers; it built a new city hall, a bridewell, dug two tunnels under the river, and finally borrowed $1,171,500 for construction and operation of schools. The city had many more sources of income than had the schools, which had to rely on the local property tax, from which it now derived $765,968 of the $827,502 spent in 1875 on 49,121 children. The city could and did levy heavy special assessments for paving, sidewalks, lights, and sewers, and could require licenses for increasing numbers of business activities. For the sewers and water pipes, the city estimated what it needed and set about to find the money. To the schools, the city council said, "You have only so much money; fit what you do, to what you have." In 1875 one-fifth of all the children attended school only a half day, and in 1880 the per capita expenditure, which had risen to $13.49 in 1875, fell back again to the 1870 level of $11.70. There were 10,000 more children, but only $30,000 more dollars. The prolonged depression of 1873-1879 reached its height in 1877, and all the evening schools closed for lack of funds. The situation was made worse in 1878 by the defalcation of the city treasurer with a large amount of public money. The mayor cut 20 percent from all appropriations including schools. Teachers were paid in scrip (promises to pay later) with an 18 percent average loss.[10]

The decade following the fire was a difficult period for the schools in many ways. The new state constitution of 1870 had proclaimed that "The General

Assembly shall provide a thorough and efficient system" of free schools for all the children of the state, but it had not furnished the means to do so. It abolished all special legislation for cities, but it did not abolish classifying them. Therefore when it passed a new school law in 1872 referring "only to cities over 100,000," it applied only to Chicago. The new law limited the control of Chicago schools to some extent, and increased state control, but not state support.

The city council no longer had the power to dismiss the superintendent. The Board of Education employed him now, and could dismiss him at the end of one year of service. The fifteen members of the Board were to be appointed by the mayor for three years, five each year, and must be "affirmed" by the city council. The council retained its control over school sites and bonds for schools. The city treasurer still kept all school funds, which could be withdrawn on Board order only if countersigned by the mayor and city clerk. The Board might levy taxes, employ teachers, rent buildings, fix salary schedules, select text books, lay off school districts for administrative purposes, and "maintain discipline and examine and expel scholars." It was to choose its own president from among its members, employ a secretary, keep records and present an annual report. The Board not only appointed the superintendent, it appointed his supervisory staff—with or without his recommendation. The schools were actually governed, and teachers appointed or dismissed, by committees of the Board, which meant that most of the decisions on matters under their jurisdiction were made without reference to the whole Board. The number of committees grew to 79 by 1885. The superintendent had general management of instruction and supervision of the teaching staff. There were 476 teachers in 1872, 696 in 1870, 895 in 1880 and 1,296 in 1885. The 1872 law forbade giving public funds to sectarian schools, and threatened, with a fine of $500 and twelve-months' imprisonment, any teacher who profited by the purchase of books, apparatus, or furniture.[11]

Responsibility Diffused and Achievement Low

The lot of the Chicago school superintendent was not a happy one. He had no clear authority in any situation. If he attempted changes, he collided with vested interests within the schools, within the Board, and outside the system. He had no control over the appointment or dismissal of teachers and principals and could only use persuasion in his supervision of them. If he did not like the assistants the Board chose for him, he could not change them. If he did like them, they might be dismissed anyway. After Superintendent Pickard had served twelve years, the Board demoted his two assistant superintendents without his approval and installed in their place a young man from Detroit named Duane Doty. Pickard felt he was being pushed out for Doty, and resigned, going to the University of Iowa (of which he later became president). Apparently his suspicion was justified, because in two weeks Doty was made superintendent.

The story of the Doty appointment had a lurid sequel. One of the demoted assistants wrote an anonymous letter to the Board denouncing a woman who, he claimed, was responsible for the political manipulation which brought Doty to Chicago to displace him.[12] The woman's husband heard the letter read at the board meeting, went to the aggrieved man's home and shot him. The assailant was acquitted of murder on a plea of self-defense.[13] This inauspicious introduction to his office did not help Superintendent Doty establish rapport with his teachers, although his major contribution in his three years of service was a sensible simplification of the records teachers were required to keep. The Board dismissed him in 1880 and he went off to the company town of Pullman, to the south of Chicago, to serve as agent for Mr. Pullman's Palace Car Works.

The next superintendent had remained in the school system a long time. George Howland had begun his career in 1858 as a teacher in the new high school, becoming its principal in 1860. As superintendent from 1880 to 1891, he met his growing group of teachers once a year. He gave examinations to qualify them and recommended those who passed to the Board of Education for appointment. He suggested to the successful applicants that they get letters from their ward committeemen. It was well known that Mr. Howland's recommendation went "a long way" with ward committeemen. The Board, however, accepted or ignored his recommendations as it pleased, and was free to appoint applicants he did not recommend.

In 1880 Superintendent Howland published a book called *Practical Hints for Teachers in the Public Schools*. He urged principals to remember that teachers with sixty restless children needed help, particularly new ones. Teachers entered the profession too young to have read very much or done careful study in any area, and for many teaching was just a makeshift to tide a young person over until he could find something better. Primary teachers particularly needed help. Of the 90,000 children in Chicago schools, 28,000 were in first grade, 16,000 in second, and only 9,000 in fourth.

He offered some suggestions on discipline. Making children "mind" was no end in itself. Too much time was put into worrying about whispering and tardiness, and not enough in making classes interesting to children. Keeping them after school solved no problems. "Obedience must be immediate and absolute," said Howland, might be true perhaps for soldiers, but not for children. He asked that parents not be told to beat a recalcitrant child.

George Howland had definite criticisms of current teaching methods. "Memory heaps up rubbish as well as treasures," said he, and classed memorizing definitions without any use of them as rubbish. In recitations, children should not merely repeat something from a book, get a mark, and sit down—while the other children paid no attention until their names were called from a shuffled file of cards. Students should not merely be corrected, they should be encouraged to express themselves and debate among each other. Education must not be merely a "desultory haphazard learning of unconnected facts."

An 1874 study issued by the Bureau of Education and signed by 26 college presidents, 14 state superintendents of education, and 25 local superintendents, also criticized the military precision required of children in the schools of that decade, and the overemphasis on conformity in punctuality, attendance and silence. They showed concern that the ratio of school population to the entire population of American cities ranged only from 5 to 16 percent. In Chicago 12 percent of the population were enrolled, but average attendance was only 9 percent. Only 28 percent of those between five and twenty-one years were in the Chicago public schools and only 14 percent came regularly.[14]

One citizens organization in Chicago during this period made a study of what it saw as the vital educational questions of the day. The Committee on Education of the Citizens Association in 1881 recommended that there be compulsory education for 60 days a year for the 25,000 children of Chicago who had never been in any school—*if* and when seats could be provided for them. They felt that the high school derogated manual labor, when in fact the city needed laborers and skilled tradesmen, and urged that courses in sewing and blacksmithing be offered. They wanted physiology taught to prevent drunkenness. They held up to ridicule the method of treating children like identical "India rubber bags" to "receive mental nutriment in equal quantities at fixed times."[15]

During Superintendent Howland's term of office, public discussion grew over the kind of people who were being appointed to the Board of Education, and sharp talk about the mayor's paying off his political debts by appointing people to whom he was obligated and who would be sure to award contracts to the "right people." In 1885 Victor Lawson of the Chicago Daily News openly attacked the basis of appointment of the members of the Board of Education.[16] In the same year the Chicago Woman's Club urged the appointment of Mrs. Ellen Mitchell, a member of the club, as a member of the Board of Education. After a three-year campaign of committees to the mayor and pressure from the husbands of club members, Mrs. Mitchell was appointed. In 1890 a second woman, Miss Mary E. Burt, was appointed by Mayor Dewitt Cregier.

Question as to the quality of school board members was growing in other cities also. A report from the Office of Education in 1885 stresses this general concern:

"Men chosen to serve on the city school boards ought to be foremost citizens in respect to intelligence, integrity of character, public spirit, sound judgment and social standing. In practice, it has been found extremely difficult to reach ths standard. The school boards are probably few and far between among whose members there are not some persons unqualified for a trust of such importance. This office is not infrequently used by young politicians and old politicians of inferior order as a stepping stone to coveted political places. . . . It is too often traded off by politicians for assistance in running the political machine to incompetent persons. . . . Everywhere there are unscrupulous politicians who do not hesitate to use every opportunity to sacrifice the interest of the schools to their purposes. . . . Without doubt this is the supreme educational problem."[17]

The building shortage did not lessen. The bonds issued by the council after the Civil War had built ten buildings in four years, but the new space had not even kept up with increasing enrolments, and basements and other unsuitable space had to be rented. By 1882, 12,919 children were on a half-day schedule. In 1876 only 9 percent of the floor space had any kind of artificial lighting, and in 1881 steam heat was still a novelty. By 1886, after the passage of the first compulsory education law by the legislature, there were only one-third enough seats if all the children were present who were required to attend by law. The city council passed an ordinance requiring that "reasonable care" must be exercised in ventilating, cleaning, and constructing buildings. The ordinance on cleanliness provided no extra funds for such purpose, but it did replace a previous ordinance passed by the city council in 1867 ordering school buildings to be cleaned by prisoners from the House of Correction.[18] The school buildings put up in this period had 63 seats in a class room. By 1890 the newest buildings had only 54 seats.

According to the Bureau of Education, in 1885 the average city school class size was between 60 and 70. New York had a maximum of 75 allowed in a primary room, and 60 in a grammar grade. Some enthusiastic reformers insisted on 30; but the Bureau of Education stated that "Enough teachers for 30 would involve an expenditure beyond the means available in this present society." It would be an improvement, said they, if the class size could be reduced to 55. But Chicago was not the only city with massive school housing problems in the 1880's. In 1881 New York City schools turned away 9,189 children for lack of seats and the president of the Board of Education claimed there were at least 20,000 children out of school for lack of room. The superintendent of San Francisco schools in 1883 said he had some class rooms with 80 children standing around the walls.[19]

Three significant trends in public education in Chicago emerged during the twenty years after the Civil War. One dealt with the idea that books were not the only thing with which schools should be concerned, and that "mental discipline" was not their major goal. A second trend in Chicago was response to the demands of ethnic groups for change in the curriculum. The third, which was nationwide, was the rising demand for child labor laws and compulsory education.

Demands for Vocational Education and Ethnic Control

The change in educational theory took the form of emphasis on manual training, and the beginnings of vocational education. Industry was changing.

Manual labor was less useful as more skills were being required in industrial production; only the public schools could provide them on a large scale. In Europe, particularly in the German states, schools had been providing such training for some time. At the Paris Exposition of 1867 an exhibition of manual training and technical education in European schools had attracted world-wide attention and had impressed visitors from the United States. But the teaching of manual skills in America was a departure from accepted educational theory, and Superintendent Howland, for one, had little enthusiasm for it. Feeling that a high school should be a "poor man's college" and not a place for "practical education," Howland grieved at the dropping of Greek from the high school curriculum. Others in the system urged its use, however, and business and industrial leaders even gave private financial support to experiments in "practical education."

In 1876 Superintendent Pickard's truant boys at work on "sloyd," the Swedish term for woodworking, coincided with experiments in Boston and other city schools in the early '80's. In 1885 the Chicago Woman's Club, alert to new trends in education, urged further experiment with manual training programs in Chicago schools. The next year, one year's work in manual training and woodworking was offered at the North Division High School and extended to two years in 1887. Business and industrial leaders, increasingly impressed with the value of such training and impatient with the slow progress in public schools, set up an experimental school of their own. A board, including such business giants as Marshall Field, Richard Crane, and John Crerar, hired as the school's director Henry Belfield, who as principal had introduced the manual training course at North Division. Tuition of up to $100 a year was paid by enough students to operate the school.[20]

In 1890 the Board of Education opened a fourth secondary school, called the English and Manual Training High School, which offered a three-year course much like that of the private school after which it was modeled. In 1891 Richard Crane paid for equipment and a teacher's salary to provide manual training in one elementary school, and the Chicago Herald did the same for the Jones School. By 1896 twelve elementary schools had rooms equipped with manual training tools. Pressure from outside the schools for vocational education continued and culminated, in the first decade of the twentieth century, with a controversial plan copied after the German system.

The second element of change in the schools of the 1880's was pressure from the immigrant population. Chicago was a city of European immigrants. By 1850, 52 percent of the population had been born outside the United States. In 1857, 3,400 had arrived in one day on the Michigan Central Railroad. The total proportion of foreign-born declined a little after 1850, but the number of their children, many of them still speaking languages other than English at home, steadily increased. In 1870, 48.35 percent were foreign-born, and in 1880, 40.7 percent. Poles and Polish Jews had begun to come in the 1870's, Russian Jews and Czechs in the 1880's and Italians in the 1890's. The census of 1890 showed

40.9 percent of the city's population foreign-born, and 37 percent the children of foreign-born parents.[21]

The earliest, largest, and most vocal ethnic groups were the Irish and the Germans, each of whom constituted approximately one-fifth of the people of the city. The Irish, Roman Catholics and now Democrats in politics, had come to escape the desperate years of potato famine in Ireland. They had little or no education or technical skills and were poor when they arrived. They tended to be hostile to other groups which threatened their economic status, including the Negroes and the Poles. The mayor of Chicago in 1855 had accused them of being "a hopelessly criminal race, with no respect for law and order." But their "clannishness" stood them in good stead in politics and they quickly developed leaders and found jobs in the growing local government. Many of their children went to parochial schools, and many of their daughters became teachers in public elementary schools.

The Germans came to Chicago in a steady stream after 1848. Many of them had some education or skill, and were able to attain middle-class status more quickly than the Irish. They were both Catholic and Protestant, but more of them Lutheran than Catholic. While some sent their children to Catholic or Lutheran schools, a much larger percentage of Germans sent their children to the public schools than was the case with the Irish. In 1870 all public notices were published in German as well as in English.

Almost all the ethnic groups had their own organizations, religious or social (or both), and expressed publicly their continued interest in their native lands, such as the demonstration celebrating Bismarck's victory over the French in 1871. A Slavic Union, a Scandinavian Union, several Polish and Czech societies and numerous German Turnvereins kept the old cultures alive in the new country. The German Protestants, with the Scandinavians, were the largest group of Lutherans in any city in the United States. Only New York City, with a much larger population, had more Jews and Catholics than Chicago with its five synagogues and twenty-five parishes. The "Know Nothing" native Americans and other such groups as the "American League" were hostile toward all the immigrants. The religious antagonisms of Europe intensified those already existing in America, and both religious and ethnic prejudices played a significant part in Chicago's political and educational life.

The political leadership of the city depended on the support of ethnic groups. One of the hot political controversies to develop early along ethnic lines concerned the sale of liquor. Almost all the immigrant groups openly resented the efforts of the W.C.T.U. and others to control or forbid their use of liquor. In 1855 when the mayor tried to enforce an ordinance barring the selling of liquor "on the premises," forbidding sales to minors under 18, and raising the license fee of saloons to $300, the governor had to call out the National Guard to quell the "Lager Beer" riots. In 1865 seven million gallons of beer were brewed in Chicago, and the per capita consumption was thirty-nine gallons a year. Joseph Medill was the last "dry mayor" in Chicago. He was roundly defeated in 1873 by the People's Party, organized around the liquor issue, and his Sunday closing law promptly repealed. The fact that the supporters of the Sunday closing law were also ardent supporters of civil service reform as well as expansion of public education did not help gain support for the cause of schools among many ethnic groups. Carter Harrison I, mayor of Chicago five times (beginning the first of his terms in 1879), was a Yale graduate and from an old native family, but he could speak German to his Democratic followers—and according to his son (also with a long career as mayor), "sing a German ditty." Harrison was under attack consistently by Protestant clergy for the support given him by the "great unwashed." But naturalized voters outnumbered the native-born in 20 of the city's 34 wards, and continued to elect him as mayor.

The Germans were the group most concerned about the public schools. The Irish united with them, however, in demanding that the reading of the Bible in class be stopped. In 1869 the president of the Board of Education, himself foreign-born, had recommended the elimination of Bible reading, since Lutherans and Catholics did not approve of it, to make the public schools scrupulously non-sectarian. Protestant revival meetings vigorously supported reading the Bible in school. For five years the issue was debated, with public meetings and petitions   arguing both sides. In 1874 the Board finally ordered Bible readings eliminated from the curriculum and from opening exercises of the public schools as well.[22]

The Germans wanted not only negative but positive changes in the schools. They gave warm support to the introduction of physical training and to the extension of music and drawing. But most of all, they wanted their children growing up knowing how to speak the German language. They did not approve of the practice, however, common in some of the parochial schools in solidly foreign neighborhoods, of having *all* instruction in a language other than English. In some Polish parochial schools this was the practice even after World War I. The Germans wanted their children to know English, but they did not want them to lose the German language and the traditions of German culture.

In 1865 German organizations demanded that German be offered in the public schools for those who wanted to learn it. This request was publicly opposed by Scandinavian and other ethnic organizations, but a German program was nevertheless introduced in the six upper grades of one elementary school. A year later the Board provided that German might be taught in one school per area if 150 parents asked for it. By 1870 eight German teachers were instructing 2,597 pupils in the Chicago schools, and, by 1892, 242 teachers of German had 34,547 pupils in the language—about one-fourth of all the children enrolled.[23] The issue of teaching German became a state-wide controversy after two state superintendents of public instruction in 1873 and 1887 urged that all elementary instruction be in English only, in both public and parochial schools. Both were defeated, the large German group in the East St. Louis area adding to the opposition from Chicago. German continued in the upper grades in Chicago until World War I, when it was completely dropped in the era when the Bismarck Hotel was rechristened "The Mark Twain."

A much more basic educational problem for many years received little attention. Many of the children of immigrants never came to school at all. In 1871 only 16 percent of the children enrolled in the Chicago public schools had foreign-born parents, although almost half of the population was foreign-born. Many of the immigrants remained desperately poor. The crowded slums of Chicago's West Side housed a population of 162,000 in the 1880's, second only to those of New York. In 1882 half the children born in these slums died before they were five years old, at a rate three times that of the rest of the city. By 1853 the County Poor House was overflowing, but until 1870 it still took in the insane and some dependent children. In 1858 the Home for the Friendless was overcrowded as soon as it opened. Boys arrested for drunkenness, with no one to pay their fines, were thrown into the County Jail or Bridewell with hardened criminals. Fines on prostitutes maintained the House of Good Shepherd and the Erring Woman's Refuge for Reform. In 1888 the Board of Education was urged to furnish a teacher for the children in the Waif's Mission. It did so after three years. It was also asked to provide a teacher for children in the Bridewell. It did that six years after the request was made.

Child Labor in Chicago

Many of the children not in school were working in factories or dingy home sweatshops, or on the streets as newsboys or bootblacks. Even if they had established homes, the wages for unskilled labor after the Civil War were not sufficient to feed a family on current prices, and a woman might earn only $1.25 a week for domestic service. There was no security in any kind of unskilled work during the disastrous depressions in the '60's, '70's, and '80's. Laws making education compulsory, discussed earnestly since the Civil War, were frequently drafted without any recognition of the facts either of dire poverty or of child labor.

Some laws were passed, however, to enforce compulsory education and to reduce child labor. In 1877 the legislature had attempted to regulate child labor by an act which made it unlawful for anyone having custody of a child under fourteen years of age to allow him to engage in occupations "injurious to health, or dangerous to life and limb." There was no procedure for enforcement included in the law. In the same year, another law had been adopted to prohibit the employment of boys under twelve in Illinois coal mines, and also of women and girls. In 1879 the age limit was raised in mines to fourteen years for illiterate boys and in 1883 for all boys. A study by the Illinois Bureau of Labor Statistics in 1880 found 5,673 children in Chicago working ten to fifteen hours a day pulling basting threads in garment sweatshops in slum tenements for fifty cents a week. The Bureau in 1882 estimated that 5 percent of all the children in the state between eight and fifteen years of age had not attended school at all, that at least one-third of these were working, and that the rest were neglected and on their way to becoming delinquents.

In 1883 the General Assembly adopted the first compulsory education law in Illinois. All children between eight and fourteen were required to attend school for at least twelve weeks in any one year, unless excused by the Board of Education "for good cause"—which included not having a school within two miles of their homes. If a parent or guardian failed to obey this law, nevertheless, he might be fined from $5 to $20 by a justice of the peace; if school directors failed to enforce it, they might be fined $10 if a taxpayer took the trouble to sue them. This law was not enforced anywhere in the state. In 1888 the State Superintendent of Public Instruction, in his annual report for 1888-1889, gave an estimate of 135,329 children under fifteen in Illinois who were not in school, most of whom had never gone to school. The 1885 school census in Chicago had reported 169,384 persons between six and twenty-one in Chicago, of whom 79,276 were enrolled in public schools.

Five years after the passage of the 1883 compulsory education law, a member of the Chicago Board of Education moved that the Board appoint a committee to devise ways of enforcing it. The Chicago Woman's Club had urged some action and had sent the Board the following petition:

> "Whereas the appalling increase of crime among youth, the large number of vagrant children, and the employment of child labor in the City of Chicago is fraught with danger to the commonwealth,
> Therefore, we, the Chicago Woman's Club, respectfully ask your honorable body immediately to take the necessary measures to ensure the enforcement of the Illinois Statute of 1883, providing for compulsory education." [24]

Not all the voices raised on the matter of compulsory education were affirmative, however. The Chicago Times of March 30, 1884, claimed in an editorial that child labor and compulsory education laws would close down manufacturing plants and make children idle and vicious. In the same period, the Chicago Inter Ocean declared, "Compulsory ecucation is preposterous. Education is not necessary for everyone."[25]

The committee appointed by the Board of Education made its report. It was a very limp document, pointing out that there simply was not room in the present schools for more children than those already attending. "If there were enough school houses, it would not be found a hard task to get children to attend," said the report optimistically, but concluded that very little could be accomplished to compel school attendance in Chicago "without greater facilities than are now at the command of the Board." In order to show that the Board's heart was in the right place, however, the committee recommended several actions for the Board to take, "to show the people that the spirit of the law is cordially recognized by the Board." The Board should publicize the law and its intention to enforce it "where practicable." Free text books should be provided for "indigent" children; provision should be made for educating "pauper" children. A department of compulsory education should be established by the Board.[26]

As a result of this report three truant officers were appointed, one for each section of the city, and a public meeting called in the name of the Board of Education, to which the Chicago Woman's Club and "other bodies interested in the enforcement of the compulsory education law" were invited. The mayor offered to "direct the entire police force to aid in enforcement" of the law. On January 19, 1889, a much larger public meeting was held by the civic agencies concerned about compulsory education. The next week, the Board increased the number of truant officers from three to seven, "three of whom shall be ladies," and added a clerk to record complaints from principals and the police. Superintendent Howland pointed out the clear connection between compulsory education and child labor, and stated that as a result of the agitation on both problems, a number of employers were now refusing to employ boys under fourteen without a permit from the Board of Education.

In 1889 the General Assembly amended the 1883 law by raising the time a child must attend school in one year from 12 to 16 weeks, 8 weeks of which must be consecutive. Boards of Education were required to appoint at least one truant officer. Children might attend private schools only if the "common branches" were taught in English. The Chicago Board of Education made some real effort to enforce the 1889 law. It appointed twelve truant officers instead of seven. Fifty-five thousand circulars were printed in seven languages, German, Italian, Bohemian, Swedish, Polish, Yiddish, and Norwegian, and sent home to parents. The Board asked 171 private and parochial schools for the names of their pupils within the age limits of the new law, but only 32 responded. To discourage child labor, the Board sent a circular to 2,591 proprietors of shops, stores, and factories, asking for the names of children in their employ, and urging them not to hire children between seven and fourteen. Only 300 answers were received on this mailing, but one firm alone sent the names of 175 children under fourteen.[27] No one did anything about the children in the street trades.

This energetic campaign did result in increased enrolment, but it also brought increased problems, the result of decades of neglect. The teachers had known all along that children were not little automatons arranged in neat and orderly rows, obedient to every wish of authority; but some of the earnest advocates of compulsory education felt that a "child" was a helpless, gentle creature who would welcome the guidance of the school. When the truant officers began herding children in from the highways and byways of the city streets, many of them turned out to be neither helpless nor gentle. Superintendent Howland reported that 3,528 enrolled were "subject for reform schools." The Committee on Compulsory Education of the Board reported to that body that large numbers of incorrigibles in the schools, "when brought to school by the attendance agent, cause sufficient disturbance to have their absence heartily desired by the teacher and the principal." The committee recommended placement in a separate room or building under a different system of discipline.

It added that many of the children brought in from the streets were physically filthy, "not fitted for the ordinary class room." Moreover, they soon dropped out of class or were suspended for misconduct. There was discussion of the need for a parental school where such children could be sent, but nothing was done about it.[28]

In 1888 the truant officers of the Board investigated the cases of 17,500 children, and placed 9,799 of them in parochial, evening, or day schools. They found that some of the working children were not in extreme poverty, although some were. A committee of the Chicago Woman's Club founded the School Children's Aid Society to provide clothes for needy children. The County Board was asked to appropriate funds to clothe and feed poor children whose parents and guardians could not support them, so that "they might attend school and be saved from the pernicious effects of bad company and often very evil associates." But even in 1890-1891, the Board of Education issued 820 work permits to children under fourteen, "whose necessities had compelled them to seek employment."

The effort to enforce compulsory education was strengthened very little, in 1891, by the passage of the first general state child labor law. This law forbade the employment of any child under thirteen without a certificate; but a Board of Education might issue such a certificate provided the labor of the child was needed for the support of any aged or infirm relative and provided the child had attended school for at least eight weeks in the current year. No proof of age need be required by employers and no means were provided for enforcing the law. The city council adopted an ordinance requiring work permits for children under fourteen. The Board of Education detailed one of its truant officers to visit factories and notify employers of the provisions of the city ordinance. One person in a vast, industrial city of now more than a million could scarcely cover the ground. In 1892 the Chicago Board of Education approved the report of a citizens' committee recommending two significant changes in state and local laws on school attendance. First, all children under thirteen should attend all the time, not just sixteen weeks a year. Second, there should be enforceable penalties for adults who wilfully deprived children of an education. The truant officers had reported countless instances of such abuse but they had no weapons to deal with those who openly refused to comply with the law. This report also called attention again to the provisions for "the care, maintenance and education of neglected and wayward children" who were demoralizing classrooms. Provision for their "bodily care, and proper preparation for contact with others in a schoolroom" was urgently needed, according to the report. It quoted statistics from the County Jail and the Bridewell as to the large number of children annually placed under arrest, for whom neither the school nor any other institution had shown any concern before they became the enemies of society.

Since 1889, the staff at Hull House, the new settlement on Halsted Street headed by Jane Addams, had been among the strong voices speaking in behalf of the children of the streets. One of its residents, Mrs. Florence Kelley, urged that the state authorize an investigation of the sweatshop system in the garment industry in which many small children were employed. The tracing of a small-pox epidemic to such a tenement workshop focused attention on the practice. Governor Peter Altgeld appointed Mrs. Kelley director of such an inquiry, and as a result of her work and that of Miss Addams, who obtained the backing of the labor organizations in the state, a new child labor law went into effect in 1893.

The new law did not include many items its sponsors had wanted, but it did have some means of implementation. It still required only sixteen weeks' school attendance in one year, but there were to be twelve weeks of consecutive attendance instead of eight. It authorized, but no longer required, Boards of Education to employ a truant officer. But it flatly forbade employment of children under fourteen in factories and workshops. Children under sixteen must furnish affidavits giving their age. Every employer must post on his wall a list with the names, ages, and addresses of all children under sixteen in his employ. The law provided for the appointment of a chief factory inspector and twelve deputies, and Governor Altgeld appointed Mrs. Kelley as chief inspector for the state. Disappointed that the law did not include children in stores and in the street trades, Mrs. Kelley in her first report, in 1894, stated that there were still thousands of children between seven and fourteen not in school, and that the street-trades children roamed the city, lawless and irresponsible. She felt that there was little gained by taking children out of factories if they did not go to school. She was disturbed by the number of working children over fourteen who could not even write their own names.

Mrs. Kelley was appalled at the attitude of some of the people in the schools. Principals expelled children at the age of eleven because they were incorrigible and sent them to Mrs. Kelley with a written request that they be given work permits. She felt that these were the children most in need of help from the school and that the factory certainly would not improve their incorrigibility. She was highly critical of the failure of the Board of Education to see that the under-age children discovered by her inspectors actually went to school.[29]

The report of the Board Committee on Compulsory Education in 1894 to the Board was an even more defeatist document than the prevous one of 1888. It based its recommendations on a report from a committee of citizens to the effect that

> "Careful research into the history of pauperism and criminality
> seems to show that the child's bent is fixed before his seventh year.
> If childhood is neglected, the child will mature lawless and
> uncontrolled and the final end will be the jail or the poorhouse...."

The Board washed its hands of children over seven who would not behave, asked that the Department of Compulsory Education be abolished, and, in its place, kindergartens be maintained.[30] It did not seem to occur to them (as it has not occurred to others seventy-five years later) that the skill of a teacher lies not in his ability to impart information to those who want to learn, but in his skill in getting those who have not cared to learn, to want to do so. The truant officers were kept, however, and the slow effort to provide a "thorough and efficient education" for all children continued.

Conflict Over an Emerging Labor Movement

Child labor was only one facet of the economic situation in the city which caused conflict during the three decades after the Civil War. The increasing tension between an emerging labor movement and a powerful group of employers openly hostile to organized labor conditioned attitudes on educational policy long after most of the actual violence had subsided. The great fire may have hastened the conflict by widening the gap between the "haves" and the "have-nots." It was no longer so easy to enter the city with bare hands, take up land, start a business and become wealthy. It did happen, but to fewer and fewer people. The affluent got credit quickly after the fire and grew richer; the disadvantaged found themselves more handicapped than before. Chicago was rebuilt after the fire with tremendous speed. Credit became available immediately and within one year forty million dollars of new buildings sprang up, many of stone construction. A week after the fire contracts were let for a new Palmer House, a new Field and Leiter store, and a new Illinois Central Railroad station. The debris picked up in the wake of the fire was dumped into the lake to extend the city's shore line. The non-existent public library was "replaced" by a gift of 7,000 volumes collected in Great Britain with Queen Victoria's blessing by Thomas Hughes, author and member of Parliament. Two months after the fire, 5,000 little cottages were built on the west side to replace the 10-by-25-foot cabins in which whole families (and their animals) had lived before the fire. The grain elevators were rebuilt and with the stockyards (which had prospered during the war and were not damaged by the fire), did a profitable business even during the nationwide 1873 depression. After all, if the unemployed in the eastern cities had any money at all, they were spending it on something to eat.

After the fire Chicago no longer looked like a frontier town. But its "movers and shakers" lost none of their frequently ruthless drive toward wealth and power. The new Palmer House with silver dollars in its barber shop floor was a symbol of determination that Chicago should be the first, the biggest, and perhaps the showiest in modern living. Chicago now packed more meat than Cincinnati and surpassed St. Louis as a center of trade. George M. Pullman, whose first job in Chicago had been to jack up the old Tremont House hotel to street level to escape the city's mud, was now sending "Pullman Palace" railroad cars around the country to demonstrate midwestern opulence.

Stores on State Street boomed. Field and Leiter sold ten millions worth of goods in a year. The balls in the big hotels during the winter displayed the luxurious living of the city. Organized sports flourished, too, White Stockings baseball players got large salaries of $2,500 apiece in 1872. With wealth the criterion of success, real estate values rose above pre-fire levels. In 1873 the city staged an Interstate Industrial Exposition as a jubilee celebration of the city's resurgence after the fire.

But wealth was only for the few. Wages had not kept up with the cost of living during the war, and the depression—a Pyrrhic aftermath of Appomattox—hit the poor people in Chicago hard. Thirty-four percent of the population were classed as unskilled labor, and were dismissed quickly when profits shrank. In 1879 food prices had almost doubled again, and one-half of the working men in the city did not earn enough to pay for rent and food for their families. Wives and children worked too. It was not merely that working people resented not sharing in the wealth flaunted in their faces; thousands of them were actually too hungry and destitute to care. Almost all were immigrants who had come to this country to escape just such grinding poverty and hopelessness, and they now saw little hope of security.

In addition to their bright hopes, however, the immigrants had brought with them some experience in European efforts to ameliorate economic hardship, and a general acquaintance with a whole range of European ideologies. The Irish and the Germans joined the labor unions and, together, exercised a majority in all the large unions except that of the seamen, who were Scandinavian, and the cigarmakers and printers, most of whom were native-born. The Irish brought with them a tradition of violence against injustice, and the Germans a knowledge of the philosophies of Marxists and anarchists. They did not intend to accept their fate passively.

The dissatisfied workers were not always agreed on what they were for, but they were quite clear on what they were against. They wanted no more ten-cent-a-day Chinese, like those who built the Union Pacific Railroad, brought in to compete with them. They wanted unpaid convict labor stopped. They wanted fake employment agencies, which took their money and failed to get them jobs, put out of business. They felt the city ought to do something to protect them against the widening gap between wages and rising prices of food. Toward this end a great crowd in 1873 stormed the city council to protest as man after man lost his job. They did not need the Citizens' Association report on tenements, in 1884, to tell them they were paying unfairly high rents; the report stated that some slum landlords collected as much as 40 percent of the total value of their property in rent in one year. But most of all, they wanted an eight-hour day. Only the small group of anarchists pooh-poohed that goal, claiming it was such a small gain that it was not worth the effort; but even they joined in the demand for it as a way of arousing opposition to the whole pattern of industrial society.

During the 1870's no single year passed without labor disturbances in Chicago. The nation-wide railroad strike in 1877 climaxed a long series of conflict, all the more violent in Chicago as the country's biggest railroad center. The Chicago Tribune headlines screamed "Red War" and "Social Convulsion." Militia had been called out in Baltimore and Pittsburgh; in Chicago a great mass meeting to support the strikers and attack the "railroad kings and capitalist press" was also ringed with National Guardsmen on the alert.[31]

The owners of industry were adamant against the eight-hour day. The Conservators League of America, a secret organization of business leaders, was organized to counteract such "labor troubles." The Illinois Manufacturers Association also began in 1884 as an instrument to oppose the eight-hour day. The legislature had long before sought to defend law and order by passing a statute in 1863 forbidding picketing or preventing any one from entering or working at a lawful business. Pinkerton private detectives defended plants with guns. With the business faction the press also opposed the eight-hour law—in no uncertain terms. In 1880 the Illinois State Register had called the eight-hour day a "movement too silly for lunatics," and stated that striking for it made no more sense than striking for pay without working at all. Both the Chicago Times and the Inter Ocean attacked the makers of the 1884 program of the newly formed State Federation of Labor as "employees who worked in gangs," who had the nerve to tell their employers what to do—when everyone knew that ten hours of work was necessary for the profitable use of expensive machinery. Some employers, furthermore, could not make any profits unless they employed children.[32]

The employers were clearly united, but the workers were not. Only a few older craft unions like the printers, brickmakers, and masons had almost 100 percent of the workers in their trades. The Knights of Labor had worked together with the Chicago Trade and Labor Assembly to seek state legislation. It was most powerful in the '70's, and admitted any man or woman who wished to join, whatever his occupation. In 1880 there were about 67,000 members of labor organizations of one kind or another among the half million people of the city. In 1884 members of all kinds of labor organizations in the state along with representatives of the Farmers' Grange, met in Chicago to unite on a program for action. An eight-hour day headed the list, and child labor and compulsory education laws followed. They wanted enforceable safety laws, payment for injuries at work, public inspection and regulation of factories, housing, and food, control or public ownership of railroads and waterways, and the recognition of the legal rights of unions.[33]

Two years later there were great strikes all over the country. The McCormick Works in Chicago closed in February because of a strike and reopened in March with non-union labor guarded by Pinkerton operatives and city police Sixty-two thousand workers in Chicago were threatening strikes. Marshall Field urged that the standing army be assigned to stop them. The Chicago Board of Trade asked Washington for 100,000 troops. The Citizens' Association raised $30,000 to pay a local militia to protect property rights.[34] The workers claimed that police and employers arrested them and held them indefinitely without charge, depriving them of their constitutional rights of freedom of speech and assembly by arrest without warrant or cause, and detention in jail without opportunity for habeas corpus or trial.

A mass meeting at a wide section of Randolph Street, called the Haymarket, was called on May 4 to demand that workers be given their civil rights. Mayor Harrison came to the meeting; after he left and the crowd was dispersing, a bomb was thrown at the massed policemen, shots were fired, and some policemen and workers were killed. Seven men were arrested for throwing the bomb, some of them known anarchists. Three of them were hanged, though a committee of responsible citizens pointed out to the court that there was no specific evidence against them. When Peter Altgeld ran for governor on a platform of an eight-hour day and Workmen's Compensation, he got the solid support of the working people of Chicago. Altgeld later opposed the use of federal troops to put down the Pullman strike of 1892 and pardoned three of the men accused in the Haymarket riot. Mayor Harrison said he did not think the men arrested were the ones who had committed the crime, and was reelected mayor in 1893 with the entire English press of the city against him.[35]

The scars left by decades of hatred, fear, and violence in bitter economic conflict were deep and lasting in Chicago. The distrust and hostility which caused them appeared over and over again in the next four decades, not only in the relations of workers and employers, but in significant disputes about the public schools.

Chapter 4

FRONTIER VILLAGE TO WORLD
METROPOLIS IN SIXTY YEARS

In sixty years the huddle of cabins in the mud had become a city of a million people drawn from far places, the second city of the nation and the fifth largest in the world. The swamps had been replaced by hundreds of miles of streets and two thousand acres of parks connected by wide boulevards. Five million dollars' worth of bonds were being sold to pay for a vast Exposition celebrating the discovery of the New World by Christopher Columbus, and the whole world had been invited to it. In ten years, between 1880 and 1890, the area of the city expanded from 35 square miles to 170, as suburb after suburb was annexed. In those annexations four whole townships and parts of four others had been taken into the city. These new areas had included thirty-three entire school districts and parts of eighteen others, with 30,000 pupils and 700 teachers. The Chicago school system inherited the remnants of Section 16 school lands in eight townships—as well as all the outstanding debts of the separate suburban school systems.[1]

By the end of the school year in June, 1890, there were 135,431 children enrolled and 3,001 teachers in the public schools of Chicago; $3,583,481 was spent on them in calendar year of 1890. The addition of the annexed schools had not been an unmixed financial blessing. In all of the schools in the outlying areas the financial year was coextensive with the school year. In Chicago it was not, and taxes were not levied either in the old districts or in Chicago to cover the expenses of the added schools for the last four months of the year. The average number of pupils for classes in the new large school system fell sharply after annexation, because the outlying towns lacked the huge enrolment with which the central city schools were burdened. The average was now down to 45, but the 63 seats in the old city classrooms were still full. The per capita cost rose to $26.54 with the lower class average.

Superintendent Howland resigned in 1891 after ten years in office and thirty-three years of service to the school system. He was replaced by Albert G. Lane. Elected as a Republican, Lane had served eight years as county superintendent of schools in Cook County. Although, like Ella Flagg Young, he had had only the two-year normal course in the old Chicago High school as formal education, Lane was generally recognized within the system as an effective administrator, and his election as president of the new National Education Association indicated similar recognition by his professional colleagues outside the city. He used what authority he had with tact, both with teachers and principals, and with the Board of Education. The Board frequently ignored his recommendations for appointments, but usually accepted the changes he proposed for the system.

Superintendent Lane welcomed the help of agencies outside the schools which showed interest in their progress. Under his direction manual training classes, after the pattern of the experimental room furnished by Richard Crane, were opened in ten more elementary schools as a regular part of the curriculum. The ten kindergartens which had been operated and financed since 1888 by the Froebel Association were finally incorporated into the system in 1892, and money for their operation was sanctioned by state law in 1895.[2] Night-school opportunities for immigrants and working youth were extended, and 14,530 students took advantage of them in 1893. The school for the Bridewell, which the Chicago Woman's Club had asked for in 1888, was finally provided and named the John Worthy School. Superintendent Lane urged also the provision of a residential parental school, and in 1899 the legislature approved an act to require that cities having a population of 100,000 or more "must establish one or more parental schools for the purpose of affording a place of confinement, discipline, instruction and maintenance for children of compulsory school age, who may be committed thereto" by the new Juvenile Court established at the same session.[3] In 1895 he supported the efforts of teachers to get a pension fund, eight years after such protection for old age had been provided for Chicago policemen and firemen.

Under Lane's direction, a general revision in the course of study throughout the system embodied many smaller changes sought by groups outside the schools. The Womens Christian Temperance Union had succeeded in getting the legislature to pass a law in 1889 requiring that school systems "instruct children in the evils of alcohol and narcotics." The Ladies Auxiliary of the Grand Army of the Republic wanted special exercises for Decoration Day. The Sons of the American Revolution gave a flag to each school and now flags and poles were furnished as well. The essay contest on patriotism sponsored by the Daily News was encouraged. The superintendent welcomed heartily the aid of the new Public School Art Society, sparked by Ellen Starr of Hull House, which provided pictures for the bare walls of school buildings, and of the School Children's Aid Society which furnished poor children with clothing so that they could come to class. In 1896 the Civic Federation sponsored the first "vacation school" in the

Medill School on the West Side. In 1897 the University of Chicago Settlement opened a second with funds from Mrs. Emmons Blaine. In that year the Chicago Woman's Club, with the cooperation of 43 suburban and city women's clubs, raised $9,600 to provide vacation schools for 2,000 children. Six thousand more asked to be admitted. Twenty percent of the children who were admitted were Italian, 18 percent Jewish, 18 percent German, 12 percent Irish and 1 percent Negro. Hull House and the Northwestern University Settlement also sponsored vacation schools. The cost for each child was about $3.00. Pressure for care for crippled children resulted in one class for them in 1899. School buildings were opened for free public lectures, sometimes illustrated, furnished by the Chicago Record Herald and by the faculty of the new University of Chicago.[4]

Changes in Curriculum and Training Teachers

Not all the pressures for change in the course of study were for positive additions. In 1893 a bitter war was waged over special subjects in the curriculum—which their enemies labeled "fads and frills." The inclusion of clay-modelling, drawing, music, physical culture, and German were all ridiculed by those who felt that too much money was being spent on the public schools, and that what money there was should be used to improve elementary education in what they considered the essentials, reading, writing and arithmetic. The issue was discussed in the press, in civic organizations, and in public meetings for five months. The growing Trades and Labor Assembly stoutly defended the special courses and said that if they were necessary for rich children in private schools, they were necessary for their children in public schools. The conflict was resolved for a while by a compromise. German would not be taught in the primary grades, only in the "grammar" grades; clay-modelling would be dropped except in kindergartens and for deaf mutes. There would be no drawing in first grade, and less in second and third, and there would be less singing in the first two grades. Physical education would be taught in the elementary schools by regular class teachers, not by specialists. Sewing would be dropped altogether. Supervisors in the special subjects would be added to the superintendent's staff to help the teachers with the subjects they had not been trained to teach.[5]

The newspapers mainly sided with the need for economy and deletion of all nonessentials. The Chicago Tribune was particularly hostile to the "fads and frills," and published no less than thirty editorials attacking them during the year 1893. On January 4, 1893, it urged cutting down the "mud pie making," foreign languages, singing, and drawing "to the lowest possible figures." When it was argued that narrowing the elementary school curriculum would not give equal opportunity to all children, the Tribune editorial on March 14, 1893, declared that such theories would compel "sending to college all the children of working men" who wanted to go. The Chronicle opposed physiology instruction as a fad and said the "less children and adults knew about their internal workings the better it was for their comfort and peace of mind." A little later when the Chicago Record Herald made a project of collecting funds for vacation schools, the Tribune protested that the Board of Education had no money for "alluring luxuries."[6] Since the attack on special subjects by the Tribune came just at the time when the newspaper was arranging a new lease on school land (under attack ever since as unfairly low), Tribune critics alleged that the demand for economy was its defense for losses in income for which the Tribune itself was responsible.

Superintendent Lane's most important contribution to the Chicago school system was a long step forward in the training of teachers, taken in 1896. There were 4,826 in the teaching force by 1895. The 300 high-school teachers almost all boasted college degrees, but few of the elementary teachers had more than a high-school education. Some old-timers, like Ella Flagg Young and Superintendent Lane himself, had attended only the original two-year normal course. After the early normal school had been closed in 1877 as an unnecessary expense, Chicago alone among the large cities had no provision for training teachers.

The procedure for becoming an elementary teacher had been very simple since 1877. A high-school graduate who could find a political sponsor was designated a cadet to learn from another (untrained) teacher, or, without any experience, was directly assigned as a substitute teacher. A very simple examination was given the applicants, but a letter from a ward committeeman was the only sure guarantee of appointment. In 1885, as he assigned to duty 70 cadets with no training of any kind, Superintendent Howland had mourned they would be helpless when confronted with 60 or 70 pupils, but he could do nothing about it. Superintendent Lane did something. In 1892 he opened an after-hours school course for cadets which they were required to attend for six months. He had planned to extend this extracurricular training from six months to a full year, but found a still better answer to the problem.

In the winter of 1895-1896 the Cook County Normal School offered to turn over its building and land on 68th Street to the city if the Board of Education would continue to use it as a normal school. After considerable discussion in the press and in Board meetings, the offer was accepted.[7] Colonel Francis W. Parker became head of the new normal school and brought with him a whole new range of ideas about children and pedagogy—and sharp criticism of the mechanical teaching methods characteristic of the normal schools of the day.[8] Some of Parker's ideas were not approved by all the members of the Board of Education. The mayor announced that he did not care, for example, for Parker's method of teaching reading. In 1899 Parker left the Normal School to head a new school for teachers at the University of Chicago; but he had already left a mark on the Chicago public schools.

Shortage of Seats for Children

Superintendent Lane's greatest disappointment lay in his failure to reduce the seating deficit. Twenty new buildings a year would have been necessary just to keep up with the added number of children, but not more than twelve were erected in any year. In 1893 14,086 children were still in half-day divisions, and in 1895, 13,507 in rented rooms in unsuitable buildings. In 1896 there were 295 school buildings, 296 rented rooms, and 213,825 children to squeeze into 202,231 seats. There *were* empty seats, but not near the children: the most crowded schools were still in the densely populated slums. In 1899 21,000 boys and girls still met in rented rooms or in half-day sessions. Delays by the city council in approving building sites, and unreasonably high prices for land bought (25 percent above a fair rate, according to the Record Herald of March 13, 1899), slowed down construction and reduced the number of schools which could be built with the money available. The number of high schools had been increased by the annexation of outlying districts—Lake View, Hyde Park, Jefferson, Bowen, Englewood, and Austin High Schools were in the areas added. In 1894 Marshall and Medill High Schools were built, and a new structure replaced the old Hyde Park building.

Graft in Land Leases and Property Taxes

The most dramatic conflict over schools in Superintendent Lane's administration had concerned matters completely outside his authority or control. It dealt—for almost a century to come—with the disposition of the increasingly valuable remaining school lands. The interest on the school fund, which consisted of the proceeds of the original sale plus a few later additions, once so all important, was now an almost negligible factor in school resources. In 1895 that income of $58,010 was a tiny part of the total expenditure of $6,334,328. But the rental from the scraps of Section 16 land which had not been sold in Chicago and the other eight townships, not wholly or partly within the city, was $247,482. A great many people thought it should have been much higher. Some of the land had been lost without payment of any kind, when forged titles were recorded after the fire.[9] In 1886 the Great Western Railroad had quietly bought up the leases on Blocks 87 and 88 along the river between Harrison and Polk, and then exercised the right of eminent domain given to railroads (but not to the Board of Education) to condemn this large and valuable area. The railroad paid $650,000—but on a fifty-year mortgage at only 5 percent—and proceeded to build a Grand Central Station on it the next year.[10] The only complete Section 16 land which came to the Chicago Board of Education through annexation was the Clearing Township section, now used as Midway Airport.

The school lands in the outlying townships had been badly managed. On land annexed in 1874 unpaid rentals amounted to $208,000. The council sold 271 acres of outlying school land at farm prices of $350 an acre in 1873. There had been a few accretions to the school lands, however, as land was forfeited instead of money in payment of loans from the school fund. A twenty-foot strip on the east side of State Street, under the Carson, Pirie Scott store, had been acquired in this way in 1862. During the '70's, after the fire and during the long depression, rentals were paid irregularly and the council reduced rents for some time by 40 percent. Bankruptcies had caused a loss of $43,000. When permanent stone structures began to replace the pre-fire wooden structures, lessees of the school land insisted on long-term leases. In 1872 the first ninety-nine-year lease was granted with a fixed rent, for the entire ninety-nine years, of 6 percent of twice its value in 1870.[11]

Most of the longer leases, however, had a clause allowing revaluation every five years, so that the income of the schools would increase as real-estate values rose. And real-estate values did rise. The most valuable land was the Madison and State Street block, already boasting the busiest corner in the world. On the corner of Madison and Dearborn was the building of the Chicago Tribune: in 1833 the property had been valued at $20. In 1855 the newspaper site had been valued at $15,000 and paid rent of $900; in 1880 it was valued at $194,400 with a rental of $9,664. The Chicago Daily News leased a lot on 175 West Madison Street. In 1855 it paid $482 a year on a lot valued at $8,040; in 1880 its value was $82,000 and the rent, $4,920.[12] Between 1880 and 1890 the population of the city more than doubled, rising from 503,298 to 1,205,660. The value of the land at the center of the city rose faster than the population.

When the appraiser made the five-year revaluation in 1885 a storm of protest issued from the lessees at the estimates set. The Tribune Building lot was valued at $444,000, not $194,000, with rent of $26,640, not $9,664. The Daily News property was listed at $140,000, not $82,000, and the rent set at $8,400, not $4,920. The total increase in all the estimates was a half million dollars, and the total value of all the land set at $8,976,746. The lessees challenged the appraisal in court, paying the rentals in escrow to the First National Bank (itself one of the lessees), until the Board and the twenty-two litigants arrived at an agreement. In 1888 the Board concurred that appraisals should be made at intervals of ten not five years, and that the leases, most of which would expire in 1930, should be extended to 1985. It was agreed that the appraisals be made by three "discreet persons," one of whom should be appointed by the Board of Education, one by a judge of the Circuit Court, and one by the judge of the Probate Court of Cook County.

The annexation of more than 100 square miles in 1889 and 1890, the prospect of the World's Fair, and an enormous increase of business volume in the city's central area raised the value of the land in huge jumps. Two tenants offered to increase their rentals immediately if they were given ninety-nine-year leases which guaranteed no further increases. One was John M. Smyth, whose furniture store was at Madison and Halsted. The other was the Chicago Daily News on West Madison. The Board accepted these offers, raised the rent on the

Symth land from $6,139 to $11,000 and on the Daily News from $8,400 to $14,400, with a promise of no change until 1985.[13] The Board claimed a financial victory, but comparison with rentals on adjacent land did not bear out the claim. Property similar to and close by the Daily News plot was rented in 1893 for $30,000 a year.

Appraisers were duly appointed to make revaluations for 1895 on all the other pieces of land. The involved lessees all sought to have leases without revaluation to 1985, also. Five such leases were granted to lessees in the State and Madison block, the best known of which was the Chicago Tribune, on the Madison and Dearborn corner. The Tribune owners agreed to pay $30,000 a year for ten years, and then to increase that amount by 5 percent, which would then be the rental from 1905 to 1985. Land directly across the street paid $60,000 a year on a ninety-nine-year lease. Another nearby building, occupying half the area of the Tribune lot, paid $27,000 on a ninety-nine-year lease.

The fact that the Tribune attorney was president of the Board of Education and a member of the Committee on School Fund Property lent substance to the firm belief, on the part of a considerable number of citizens, that the Chicago Tribune had deliberately cheated the school system with the connivance of Board members.[14] Governor Altgeld, addressing the State Senate on March 6, 1895, commented about the leases on school land obtained by the Tribune and the Daily News:

> "As these papers have much to say about patriotism and a higher citizenship, they should set a better example. Waving the flag with one hand, and plundering the public with the other, is a form of patriotism getting entirely too common, and is doing infinite harm to our country."[15]

However, it should be pointed out that the final rentals accepted quite willingly by the Tribune and other lessees were almost twice as high as those they had protested so violently in 1885. Argument over these leases justified the fears expressed by the president of the Board of Education in 1885 that pressure from powerful tenants of school lands might make the school lands a major issue in city politics.[16]

The school system needed all the money it could get from any source. The increased rentals, unfair though they might be, brought the receipts from that source up to $524,037, instead of the $247,482 collected in 1895. But the chief source of income now was the local property tax for schools, returns from which in 1896 were $5,145,161, 85 percent of the total. Approximately 5 percent of the year's income came from the state school fund, and the rest from rentals and interest on the original school fund. Including bonds issued for buildings, the per capita expenditure for 1895 was $26.12. But the high-school per capita cost was $58.68—and the enrolment now was almost 8,000, not the 300 of twenty years before, and rising at an accelerating pace. Neither the state nor the city showed any interest in increasing tax rates for education, and there was little hope for any immediate addition to school income after the rental of school lands had been fixed for the next 89 years. Decision on grants of state funds was in the hands of a rurally controlled legislature, jealous of the power of the expanding metropolis, reluctant to grant to it its fair share of representation, and critical of what "downstaters" considered the cultural aberrations of its alien population. The logrolling and even cruder pecuniary pressures put on members of the legislature by the city authorities were not used to increase funds or privileges for the schools. Other activities than schools were more useful politically, both to claim advances in services and to provide controllable jobs.

Chicago nevertheless did have tremendous problems it could not solve without legislative action. The sewerage problem had never been settled and became acute with recurring epidemics of typhoid fever, which brought the death rate from that cause in Chicago to the highest in the country. The hundred and more square miles of annexed territory needed paving, sidewalks, street lights, and sewers. The common assumption that any kind of public business naturally cost more than the same activity in well-managed private business was based on observable fact. Many owners of "well-managed" businesses were quite willing to cross public palms for favors which decreased their cost of profit-making, and increased the costs of municipal government. The financial problems of the city were indeed so great its leaders had little time for concern oer inadequate school income. The pupils did not vote. But the children still came in increasing numbers. Between 1885 and 1896 the enrolment increased from 79,276 to 213,825, and the number of teachers from 1,296 to 4,668. Child labor was becoming less profitable and the voices raised against it were being heard more clearly. Child labor and compulsory education laws were still weak and poorly enforced, but the temper of the times was changing. More and more children of the poorer immigrants were coming to class, bringing with them problems the school system was not prepared to face. There were as many attending parochial schools, however, as one fourth of the total public school enrolment.[17]

The city was not making use of some sources of income available to it. The public utility companies were making millions. Horse cars were replaced by trolleys, and steam engines scattered sparks from elevated structures which encircled the downtown area. Franchises were granted to utility companies with small compensation to the city but, it was rumored, large compensation to individual council members. Stocks were sold to the public for more than they were worth, in the case of street-car lines controlled by Charles Yerkes, for example, inflated with $5,000,000 of "water." The gas companies were given the use of the streets and forty-year franchises without any real regulation of prices to the consumer. When Yerkes finally departed, he left two monuments to the city—one, the University of Chicago Observatory on Lake Geneva, and the other, a tangled financial mess of local transportation facilities from which he had milked an enormous fortune for himself. The first street-car lines in 1870 had been granted the use of the streets in Chicago for 99 years by the state legislature, which was amenable to the same methods as those which worked so effectively on the city council. This franchise was revoked in 1874 and limited to twenty years, coming up again in 1894. In 1886 the street-car lines paid $30,533 to the city for the use of hundreds of miles of its streets. In 1888 all public utilities were to pay the city for the privilege of having a franchise and were to turn over 3 to 5 percent of their gross earnings to the city. A state law specified that public-utility franchises were personal property, liable to assessment and taxation at the same rate as real estate under the uniform property tax provision of the state constitution. So glaring and so impudent was the failure of the utilities to meet their legal liabilities to the public in these regards that in 1888 a drive for municipal ownership of public utilities began to gather momentum.

Efforts to Reform City Government

The World's Fair of 1893 dramatized the exciting and positive phases of the life of the city. But a year later a book written by William T. Stead, editor of the British Review of Reviews, focused on the seamy side. He named the book *If Christ Came to Chicago,* and it followed the tradition of the great revivals of Dwight L. Moody. Stead went through the city's slums and the "red light" districts. He saw the helplessness of the poor and the callous disregard of human needs by many of the powerful who had no compunctions about corrupting the city government for their own profit.

In 1894 the Civic Federation rebelled against local government conditions. It declared that the downtown streets were no better than pig wallows, and at the expense of its members hired seventy-five men to clean them up. Headed by a banker, Lyman Gage, and some other people of influence including Judges Murray Tuley and Edward Dunne, the Federation attacked the "gray wolves" in the council on their favors to the utilities and on their dishonest election conduct. They precipitated a grand jury investigation of elections with evidence they themselves collected, resulting in twenty-one convictions. They raided "gambling dens" operating illegally across the street from the City Hall—with open police protection.

In 1896, having developed the Municipal Voters League as an offshoot, they unearthed a $500,000 theft by the county board in contract kick-backs. They protested the political manipulation of the tax assessment process, by which the influential could escape and the poor and ignorant paid. The Hull House staff accused Alderman Johnny Powers of their Nineteenth Ward of buying votes by putting one out of every five voters in the ward on an occasional city payroll, whether he worked or not. In 1897 the Municipal Voters League managed to elect 20 of the 70 aldermen; even without a majority the new aldermen could stop some of the devious activities of the council. Of the council Judge Tuley said in 1896:

"No city council ever before known in Chicago has attained the degradation of the present one. For wilful disregard of duty, for unfaithfulness to trust, for open and barefaced corruption, it is unparalleled in the sublimity of its infamy." [18]

Status of Superintendent

This infamous council had been approving members of the Board of Education. The fate of Albert G. Lane as superintendent of schools illustrated how completely subservient they were to partisan politics. Both Mayor Harrisons, senior and junior, had grumbled at Lane's appointment and reappointments—because he had been a successful Republican politician and elected county superintendent on the Republican ticket. The second Carter Harrison made very clear that he was not interested in the less important jobs in the school system, but he did think the mayor had the right to choose the superintendent.[19] Moreover, objections had been raised by members of the Board of Education, including William Rainey Harper, president of the new University of Chicago (serving on the Board for one year), to Lane's lack of formal education. This was thereupon echoed by the mayor, who wanted "only the best for Chicago."

Superintendent Lane, accused of using his influence for the Republican party, was not reappointed in 1898. No evidence was adduced as to just how he had misused his office, unless it was wrong for a Republican to hold so important a post in a Democratic city. Lane's personal integrity was attested to by the fact that, over a long period of years, he had repaid every penny of the $33,000 county school money lost in a bank failure while he was county superintendent. He was not responsible for the loss, and had never been blamed for it, and was under no legal obligation to do anything about it. Such responsibility for public funds was a rare exception in Chicago of the 1890's—and for many years thereafter. Superintendent Lane was demoted to assistant superintendent and replaced by E. Benjamin Andrews.[20]

Andrews had the two qualifications the mayor wanted. He was an ardent Democrat and an articulate supporter of Bryan's free silver policy, to the dismay of some of the conservative trustees of Brown University, where he had been president. His former presidency of a distinguished Eastern university lent luster to the city, as well as rendering him safe from suspicions that he might get teachers to vote Republican. But the jungle of local politics in Chicago was no place for an academician who expected his ideas to be accepted with all due respect to his office and to his learning. There had never been any such built-in respect for a superintendent of schools in Chicago. The Board of Education resented his condescension to them, and for his part, he was appalled at their surprised opposition when he insisted on appointments and promotions and refused to accept their vetoes quietly as a proper superintendent should. He annoyed the Board extremely by sitting in the front row at its meetings and speaking without being spoken to.[21]

Moreover it was quite obvious to the teachers, harassed by huge class loads and low salaries, that he knew nothing about public education, and that some of his orders were utterly impossible to obey. Ella Flagg Young, now a district superintendent, resigned in protest against such arbitrary orders. The elementary teachers blamed his nomination on President Harper, who had made unflattering remarks about their lack of training.

Two months before his term was up in 1900, the Board handed Andrews his hat and a leave of absence for two months; whereupon he resigned and left to become chancellor at the University of Nebraska. The head of a midwest state university might have to deal with a rural state legislature, but he did not have the combination of Chicago city council, Chicago Board of Education, and a group of 4,000 teachers who were beginning to find their voices. Conflict between the current political order and the superintendent of schools was at that time resolved in San Francisco and Buffalo by the simple process of electing the superintendent on a partisan ticket.[22]

Superintendent Andrews' successor was Edwin J. Cooley, who vacated the principalship of the Lyons Township High School in LaGrange to head the Chicago Normal School after Colonel Parker. Superintendent Cooley knew his way around Chicago politics, and with wry humor and considerable skill he managed to curb some of the powers of the Board. The Board resented his obedience to a rule they themselves had nobly made, on the motion of member Chester Dawes that the superintendent should report all political efforts to influence his recommendations, when he read them a list of such efforts including the names of eight Board members.[23] His shrewd awareness of the actual sources of power gave him some weapons for dealing with them.

Changing Educational Philosophies

The 1890's introduced a new factor in the life of the city which began to have a significant impact on the school system. Established in 1892 under the energetic leadership of William Rainey Harper, with a large gift from John D. Rockefeller, the University of Chicago was becoming a positive force in many phases of Chicago life. John Dewey became the nationally known spokesman for a whole new outlook on education in general, and William Rainey Harper headed a commission which took a sharp look at the Chicago public schools and stated quite clearly what it did not like.

Changes in educational philosophy come slowly. In the 1890's there was first the clear emergence of a demand for professional training and professional status for teachers, and the conscious sharpening in every city of the long struggle— recognized so well by Superintendents Lane and Cooley—against a school system run as an adjunct to a local political organization. Now it was no longer publicly acceptable for teachers to be considered just one part of the untrained clerical employees of the city.

One of the agencies urging the professionalization of teaching was the National Education Association, then a small group directed for the most part by university presidents. During the decade of the 1890's this organization appointed two committees, one on secondary education, which came to be known as the Committee of Ten, and one on elementary education, known as the Committee of Fifteen. Neither proposed any radical changes in their reports, but each served as a catalyst in discussions of the many proposals being made. In the main they still held to the "mental discipline" theory, although their moderation provoked bitter attack from classicists like Chicago's Assistant Superintendent Nightingale, who cried, "We must stand in unbroken phalanx in maintaining the incomparable superiority of the thorough knowledge of the classics."

The N.E.A. high-school report did not visualize the possibility of universal secondary education, nor a national economy which would remove all under sixteen or eighteen from the labor force. It was mainly concerned with college entrance requirements, holding that

"Secondary education should prepare for the duties of life that small proportion of all the children in the country, small in number, but important to the welfare of the nation, who show themselves able to profit by an education prolonged to the eighteenth year, and whose parents are able to support them while they remain so long in school." [24]

In Chicago in 1894 there were 731 students in the last year in high school, out of a total enrolment of 185,000—less than four-tenths of 1 percent.

Both the N.E.A. and its committees steered clear of such mundane matters as political control of jobs and expenditures, although they complained loudly about the number of poor teachers. It was safer to acept the completely fallacious notion that "the school" was a proud and isolated institution, detached from the rough-and-tumble crudities of business and politics. Their reports, however, carried great weight and received respectful consideration in deliberations over the course of study in Chicago.

The pressures for change increased. Natural scientists wanted education to become a science, "based on scientific principles." Business and industrial leaders wanted workers who had enough general background to adapt quickly to new enterprises. Psychologists described individual differences. The budding sociologists discussed the influence of environment. John Dewey talked about "the whole child" and his need for concrete experience rather than abstractions. Jane Addams spoke eloquently for the youth on the city streets, and recognized the so-far-untouched problem of helping children of poor and alien backgrounds. And Jacob Riis in the 1890's declared to unheeding ears that the battle of the slums must be won in the schools. [25]

The Harper Report

The nationwide search for direction for public education was focused in Chicago through the report of a commission appointed by Mayor Harrison to study the entire school system. He appointed eleven men, including two members of the Board of Education and three city council members, and former Board member William Rainey Harper. Harper was chosen chairman of the commission and with his usual thoroughness and energy produced a 248-page report in a year's time. He invited as advisers the presidents of thirteen of the most prestigious universities in the country, from Harvard to Stanford, and the superintendents of schools of twelve of the largest cities. The report contained twenty specific recommendations, with reasons to substantiate them, and details for implementation, and supported by a wealth of footnotes. President Harper did not dodge the unpleasant realities, no matter how suavely he presented them. He sent questionnaires to principals, interviewed teachers, visited schools, and drew on his own shrewd observations as a member of the Board of Education.

None of the Harper recommendations which required legislation were put into effect for years, and some, such as the simple matter of a school principal being able to direct the engineer and janitors in his own school, are still not in effect seventy-two years later. But the reasons given for the recommendations mirror the actual workings of the 1898 Chicago school system.

Regarding the Board itself, the commission recommended that the mayor appoint only eleven Board members instead of the current twenty-one to which the Board had been enlarged (from its original fifteen) after the annexations. Their term should be four years instead of three. The Board should concern itself with legislating policy and leave the administration of schools to the superintendent and to a new official, to be called a business manager. The standing committees of the Board, which at one time had reached 79, should be reduced to three and not operate as independent agencies. The Board should have the right of eminent domain and be able to purchase sites completely independent of the city council; Board members should not represent a given section of the city. Two pages of quotations cite the evils of politically controlled Boards of Education, one to the effect that "The city councils of American cities are almost always composed of inferior men, with a large number, if not a majority of corrupt men."[26]

The superintendent of schools should have a term of six years, not one, the Harper Report continued. He should be removed during his term only for cause on written charges and by a two-thirds vote of the Board. He should have the right to appoint his own assistants. He should certificate all teachers, after an examination by a new Board of Examiners, and recommend all promotions or dismissals, which should stand as final unless a majority of the Board disapprove. He should be responsible for the choice of texts and for the course of study, which should not be determined by laymen. He should make clear the rights and responsibilities of principals, who should be able to control the engineers and janitors serving their buildings.

A business manager with a six-year contract should conduct all the business affairs of the schools, not the members of the Board of Education. He should appoint his own architect and other assistants under civil service rules, including janitors (under the current Board of Education rules the president of the Board signed all contracts).

Applicants for teaching positions must present a certificate of good physical condition from a physician and one of three kinds of proof of professional status—a certificate from the Chicago Normal School (then one year's training), a B.A. degree including nine months of study of teaching, or evidence of four years of successful teaching. An A.B. degree was required for high school, or three years of successful teaching in lieu of it, or six years of successful teaching plus "collegiate scholarship."

All candidates should be examined by a Board of Examiners. Teachers should be on probation for two years. Their salaries should recognize the grade of teaching, the length of service, and also success in teaching and advances in scholarship. More men teachers should be brought into the system even if it cost more money. Dismissal of a teacher should take place only on the recommendation of the superintendent after two changes in assignment have been permitted, unless a majority of the Board dissents.

In discussing the need for highly qualified teachers, the Harper Report stated:

> "In no city in the United States do more difficult conditions confront a school system. Not even in the lower wards of the borough of Manhattan, thickly populated by foreign-born residents, and in many instances by representatives of the lowest classes, is the problem of how to secure through the public school system that assimilation of heterogeneous elements which is the supreme need of our civilization, presented more definitely. In reviewing the school districts of Chicago, section after section is found where a large proportion of the school children comes from families to whom English is barely known and where under the best conditions the ideas and traditions of the home are utterly opposed to the requirements of American citizenship. The situation demands of Chicago teachers, broad culture and thorough professional training." [27]

In pointing out the reasons why not all teachers were of high caliber, the report stated plainly,

> "When teachers are appointed through personal or political influence, and when they are retained and even promoted for similar reasons, without any justification in their record as teachers, and

indeed against the unanimous opinion of those best qualified to judge, there is sure to be a large number of incompetents within the force."[28]

Admission to the Chicago Normal School should be by the Board of Examiners, and dismissal by the faculty of the school. The course should be extended from one year to two. There should be practice teaching under guidance, and graduates should be supervised by the Normal School faculty for a year after their assignment. There should probably be three normal schools, rather than only one. The Board of Education should encourage teachers' institutes and establish a library for the use of teachers.

The superintendent should review the course of study to reduce unnecessary repetition and to unify the work done within each grade, and between grades, particularly the elementary and the high schools. There should be a kindergarten in each school in the more thickly populated districts and eventually in every school.

The work of the high school should be better correlated not only with that of the elementary schools, but with that of the normal school. Enough teachers should be employed so that no class in a high school should be larger than 40 (data given on class loads cited a beginning Latin class of 70), and more men should be employed. A four-year commercial high school should be established in a central location, and two more manual training high schools opened, offering vocational skills for boys and "domestic economy" for girls. Teachers and principals should have more freedom in the choice of text books.

More detailed, systematic, and specific preparation for good citizenship is needed. To this end, the history of other forms of government and a thorough knowledge of our local, state, and national popular government are necessary, along with the duties as well as the rights of citizens. "The only intelligent, systematic and effective method of teaching patriotism," said the report, "is to make the school itself an ideal democracy where pupils learn to practice self government," an educational goal far different from that of "mental discipline."

The teaching of "special subjects," such as music, drawing, and physical culture should be encouraged and extended to seventh and eighth grades. "Vacation" schools should be open for children delinquent in school work or "unable to go out of the city." School yards should be open as playgrounds from 8 a.m. until sunset. There should be an ungraded room in each school for children who fall behind because of language or other difficulties. An ungraded room for truants should be considered. Steps must be taken toward a more adequate compulsory education law. The legislature should authorize the establishment of parental schools for "the forcible detention of persistently refractory pupils."

School accommodations must be increased. They can not be considered adequate until there is a "sitting" in a properly constructed and suitably situated building for every child of school age who is not in a private or parochial school. As soon as the finances of the Board allow, the number of pupils assigned each teacher engaged in actual instruction must be reduced.

"There are now 30,000 children in Chicago for whom fair provision is not made. Thirteen thousand are in rented buildings and 17,000 on half day sessions. . . . It is false economy that lessens the value of school instruction by 50 per cent in securing a saving of less than 20 per cent in school expenses. The public has not yet appreciated the full importance of this." [29]

There should be open competition in the presentation of plans for new school buildings. Play yards should be provided around every school. Bonds should be issued to obtain enough funds to replace all rented structures. The purposes for which a school building were to be used should be considered in its planning.

Four recommendations sound curiously modern for 1898. The first was support for John Dewey's ideas on teachers councils.

A Board of Education should provide for

"an establishment of school faculties and district councils and a general council, with proper representation to be chosen wholly or in part by the teachers themselves, and such faculties and councils should be given the right of direct recommendation to the Board on all matters concerned with the educational system of the city. It is a shameful fact that most teachers are afraid to speak boldly about abuses connected with the schools in which they are employed." [30]

Community Use of School Buildings

The second Harper Report recommendation urged use of school buildings for general community purposes. The opportunities offered in evening schools should be extended, including the present plan of free lectures. A special assistant principal should have charge of evening and vacation schools. The public school buildings are "notoriously underutilized." "They should become the center of the educational life of the community from infant to adult, in a sense far different from what has been true up to the present time."

The third recommendation urged decentralization and involvement of lay citizens from the community. The Board was asked to divide the city into special inspection districts to include not more than ten schools. Then the mayor should appoint six "resident commissioners" for terms of three years to visit the schools and report on discipline, sanitation, and the work of the schools to the Board. The "present tendency is to make the school system more and more a matter of expert control." This tendency should be modified by greater communication of the people with the system. "If the system of public instruction is not readily affected by public opinion, a feeling of dissatisfaction naturally arises." "The importance of the lay element in the educational system has strongly impressed itself on your commission." [31]

The fourth recommendation asked for periodic surveys. The Board should employ expert inspectors from time to time, to study the school system of the city and make reports and recommendations to the Board. "These inspectors should be recognized experts in educational affairs, and that they may be unbiased and untrammeled, they should be engaged from without the city."

The Harper Report recognized how deeply the school system was imbedded in the political and economic structure of the city; but it did not accept its exploitation as necessary. It supported firmly the demand for increased professional training, professional standards, and professional administration. The report outlined sharply the legitimate role of a Board of Education. And it was curiously modern in its emphasis on decentralized community "inspectors" and the need for "community schools." Its recommendations might have been ignored, but they could not be answered. Slowly, many of them actually went into effect. They are still worthy of thoughtful consideration by any student of the history of Chicago schools.

Contributions of the University of Chicago

The University of Chicago made two other important contributions to public education in Chicago besides the Harper Report, by the turn of the century. One was Hannah Belle Clark's 1897 doctoral dissertation, published as *The Public Schools of Chicago: A Sociological Study*, in the new Department of Sociology, the first of scores of such studies of Chicago school problems. That a study of schools could be a sociological work was in itself a novelty. The writer pointed out the double problem of the schools in

> "training children from homes of poverty and ignorance, if not of vice, to be honest, industrious and intelligent, and to adapt aliens to become active citizens in a country whose institutions, ideas and customs are in many cases radically different from those they learn from their fathers. The burden rests on the schools."

But, she went on,

> "You may search the records in vain to find any explicit reference to these conditions or to any need for special adaptation of the curriculum to foreign [born] clientage. They gain little or no insight into the workings of the society in which they live, the dependence

of every man on every other man, the relations of groups of men to
each other. They do not learn how Chicago is fed or clothed, and
not clearly how it is governed. . . . The significance of local political
divisions and activities, the resources and needs of the municipality,
such facts as these have at no time been included in the conception
of training for citizenship." [32]

Hannah Clark described numbers of children who left after third grade
without a glimmer of understanding of the world they lived in. Text books had
been meaningless to them. She said that the majority of all the children left by
sixth grade with merely a collection of unrelated—memorized—facts, and that
only 4 percent of those who stayed through eighth grade went on to high school.
Most of all, she lamented that, except for Superintendent Wells' great effort in
grading the schools, there had been no far-seeing leadership, no vision to work
toward in the Chicago public schools—only a following of the drift of the times
and changes in circumstances outside the schools themselves, and no appraisal of
changes once effected.

The second contribution of the University came through its influence on Ella
Flagg Young, and her communication of its finest contributions in the
philosophy of education to literally thousands of teachers in the system. The
bright young girl who had tried to teach normal school students how to interest
poor children in 1866 had married and become a widow. She served as
elementary teacher, high school teacher, normal school teacher, elementary
principal, and as a district superintendent, and had resigned from the system in
1899 in protest against the futility of the Andrews' regime. She had worked with
John Dewey in a seminar at the university since 1895, and the University of
Chicago invited her to be a member of its faculty when she left the system. She
remained at the university until 1904 and was granted a Ph.D. degree for her
work, *Isolation in the Schools.* Ella Flagg Young translated the heart of John
Dewey's ideas into a viable living philosophy which she herself exemplified and
which hundreds of teachers began to follow. When she left the university in
1904 she headed the normal school, and then as superintendent from 1909 to
1915, she became as significant a symbol of educational change as had William
Wells fifty years before, with whom she had begun her career.

Mrs. Young understood that what the teachers themselves did constituted the
reality of a school system, not what was written on paper as curriculum or
administrative order. In her thesis, "Isolation in the Schools," she made this
clear, pointing out that if the public school system was to

"meet the demands twentieth century civilization laid upon it, the
isolation of the great body of teachers from the administration of
the schools must be overcome. . . .
"The dangerous tendency is that the whole system will be looked at
as a great machine intended to take in children at one end, and

passing them along by means of one wheel or another, turn them out
at the other end, educated young citizens." [33]

Teachers were not to be operatives turning a crank on order. There must be
freedom for them as well as for administrators. Her efforts to develop teachers'
councils and her firm defense of the right of teachers to organize were evidence
to thousands of Chicago teachers of her sincerity. She really believed that
teachers, like children, must have a chance to learn for themselves—and
supported in their efforts to do so, whether she agreed with each action or not.

As the nineteenth century ended, the teachers set out to learn for themselves.
The next act in the drama of the Chicago public schools was theirs to play.

Part II

A PROFESSION

BEGINS TO TAKE SHAPE

Chapter 5

THE TEACHERS TAKE ARMS AGAINST A SEA OF TROUBLES

After 1898 a third force within the school system quickly aroused repercussions. No longer was there merely conflict between active superintendents and Boards of Education conditioned by relationships and ambitions quite apart from the purposes of the schools; from that time on, the teachers also had something to say. Right or wrong, wise or unwise, selfish or unselfish, they said what they had to say, so directly and forcefully that they could not be ignored, either by superintendents and Boards, or by the public at large. In fact, most of the dramatic movements in the school system for the next fifty years were the result of activities of a succession of teachers' organizations and of changes in alignments of the three forces—teachers, Board, and superintendent.

Neither Board or teachers had had any respect for Superintendent Andrews, to be sure, but for different reasons. With his usual cool appraisal of the forces he had to work with, Superintendent Cooley, Andrews' successor, made it very clear that he was an employee of the Board, and not a representative of the teachers. Mrs. Young, on the other hand, openly and staunchly defended the right of the teachers to organize—against the expressed desire of the Board to kill their organization. Not until 1947, after a series of major and minor wars, the Board, the superintendent, and the teachers (for a short while) would be at peace and working harmoniously together.

The failure of the powerful leaders of Chicago in politics and industry to give priority to the problems of the schools, the rapidity of the city's growth and population shifts, the ever-present lack of space for children, the huge class sizes, and the failure to adjust salaries—as the instruction required and as the cost of living rose steadily—were serious oversights. The general hand-to-mouth planning for schools, with whatever happened to be handy, had been going on for fifty years. The size and energy of teacher organizations in Chicago have been in direct proportion to the extent of their exasperation and frustration at the slow pace of change.

Early Teacher Organizations in Chicago

Three-quarters of a century later it seems strange that Chicago teachers did not organize to solve their problems sooner. Teachers had been told for years, however, that they were to be dedicated saints—above such things as low pay and political corruption. An early study of the Chicago Teachers Federation written in 1908, gave as the reason for "backwardness" in the organization, the "hearing of the greatness of their work as it was eulogized by press and pulpit."[1] The status given teachers in Europe may have influenced European immigrants to encourage their children to be teachers, even though that status in this country was much lower. When the Chicago Teachers Federation was organized in 1897 the comments of the press were illuminating. On November 14, 1898, the Chicago Times Herald rebuked the new organization, for the tactical blunder of asking for more pay, as showing "a spirit not creditable to a high standard of professional ethics." Again that year the paper declared that "A teacher was not worthy of her salary who did not earn more than she was paid. . .," a standard not applied to other activities in the city—then or at any other time. An editorial in the American Teacher and School Board Journal of June, 1899, advised the new Federation to "avoid the objectionable features of labor organizations" and to "seek to improve the work of the schools by improving the work done by its own members."

One reason for the lack of organization was the short stay of the average teacher in the school system—an average of only seven years. The short length of service indicated that very few teachers were held by the "missionary" theory; apparently most of them were the "maddened maidens meditating matrimony" of whom President Vincent of the University of Minnesota spoke with such despair twenty years later. In 1897, out of 4,800 teachers, 225 or 4 percent had taught twenty years or more and only a hardy 26, or .5 percent, including District Superintendent Ella Flagg Young, had survived more than thirty.[2]

The first organizations of teachers within the school system were of principals—the men principals in the George Howland Club who met on payday for a 35-cent lunch at the Palmer House, and the few women elementary principals in the Ella Flagg Young Club. Both groups had suggested to the Harper Commission in 1898 that there be a probationary period for teachers, and, the Young Club added, for principals also. The Howland Club wanted vacation schools, manual training, and classes of no more than 40. In October, 1899, members of both groups united to support a Chicago Principals' Club whose first act was to send a representative to Springfield to ask for more state school money to shore up its request for a 25 percent pay increase.

One suggestion on organizing teachers received considerable attention—the idea that teachers should elect councils to give them some voice in what happened to the schools—and to themselves. In 1898 Mrs. Young set up such a council in the area where she was district superintendent. The Harper Report in 1898, reflecting the thinking of John Dewey and Col. Francis Parker at the

University of Chicago, also recommended that the Board of Education establish councils in school faculties and in districts; it further urged a general council with representatives to be chosen wholly or in part by the teachers themselves, and that they be given "the right of direct recommendation to the Board on all matters connected with the educational system."[3] A voluntary council, in which superintendents and principals could out-vote teachers, was indeed arranged, but it was not accepted by the elementary teachers and had little influence.

The Harper Report commented that the "Development and recognition of organized and representative associations of teachers will focus the experience and thought of the five thousand Chicago teachers to the great advantage of the Chicago school system and will prove a wholesome stimulus to themselves."[4] Mrs. Young continued her interest in the council idea in her University of Chicago Ph.D. thesis, "Isolation in the Schools":

> "To secure freedom of thought for teachers, there must be organizations to consider questions of legislation. . . . The voice of authority not only must not dominate, but must not be heard in the councils. . . . There should be organized throughout the system councils whose membership in the aggregate should include every teacher and principal. The membership of each school council should be small enough to make the discussions deliberative, not sensational. Yet it should include the teaching corps of at least two different schools, so that the official character of principal and teacher meetings should be eliminated. . . . There should be second councils from the first, and a central council. . . ."[5]

The membership was not to be based on position in the schools. The superintendent, receiving recommendations, must still act in accordance with his judgment after referring his position to the councils. A 1903 statement from John Dewey furnished the philosophy of the council movement: "The remedy is not to have one expert dictating educational methods and subject matter to a body of passive, recipient teachers, but the adoption of intellectual initiative, discussion and decision throughout the entire school corps."[6]

In 1897, however, the council idea was still an idealistic theory, taken seriously by few.

Teachers in Chicago were deeply worried about much more practical problems. Most immediate was the imminent danger of collapse of the new teachers' pension law which had finally been passed in 1895. Pension laws were then a new experiment; only New York City had one for its teachers, set up in 1894, and there was not much experience on which to base them. Besides, there was considerable opposition to teachers having any pension, although Chicago police and firemen enjoyed them since 1890. In that year, on July 2, the Evening Post had reproached city officials for discriminating against teachers and asked, "Is it because a teacher has no saloon affiliations and can not give aid and comfort to the 'boys'?" On the other hand, when the law was passed in 1895, the Chicago Record complained that it would discourage thrift.

The actual trouble with the first Chicago teacher pension law was that it did not provide enough money to pay the pensions promised the contributors. Its sole source of income was the collection of a 1 percent salary contribution from everyone in the system, including non-teaching employees. No fixed amount had to be paid in before receiving a benefit. A teacher who had paid $8.00 was entitled to retire in 1896-97 (if she had taught twenty years) with a pension of $600 for the rest of her life. Teachers who had taught almost twenty years and left returned to the system to collect on such a bargain. Principals and high-school teachers, whose payments on a percentage basis were higher than those of elementary teachers because their salaries were higher, got proportionally no more in benefits. Since they stayed in service longer than the average elementary teacher, they saw their larger contributions disappearing rapidly— with nothing left for themselves. Men had to work twenty-five years to get the same pension as women who worked twenty. The sum of $25,194 collected in 1895-96 almost disappeared the first year.

The teachers' pension money was to be administered by the superintendent, one member of the Board of Education, and two teachers. The most constructive clause in the law guaranteed a teacher that she would not be dismissed until the end of the year in which she paid into the fund, rather than at any time the Board chose. It was clear by 1897, however, there would soon be nothing left in the fund for people still in the system, or for those who had retired, either.

The Chicago Teachers Federation

On March 16, 1897, a small group of teachers concerned with the disaster facing the pension fund met to discuss the problem at the Central Music Hall. That night they agreed to form an organization to "do something" about the pensions. By June, 1897, they had 300 members signed up. By December they had 2,567 paid-up members—more than half of all the teachers—and had obtained 3,567 signatures to a petition to the Board to "do something" about salaries. As the members poured in, they registered an accumulation of problems of which the pension was only one.

Most elementary teachers were getting the same salary in 1897 as that paid in 1877. The salary was $500 a year for beginners, who might after six years get $825. In 1895 the Board had seriously considered cutting the scale, in order to get money for buildings and contracts, for which the Board members showed more concern than for salaries. And the schools were still desperately overcrowded. The elementary teachers felt they were not treated like teachers, but like any city clerical employee. They knew very well that the high-school teachers "looked down" on them, and they promptly excluded principals and high-school teachers from their new organization. Early in 1898, when the salary petition had been unsuccessful, the new Chicago Teachers Federation told the Board of Education to close the schools if it did not have money to run them, and that bold pronouncement rang like a thunderclap throughout the school system.[7] A whole generation of timid inhibitions began to collapse. Teachers seized the intoxicating notion they could take arms against their "sea of troubles" and proceeded to do so with a vigor and daring which astonished and alarmed many observers, and sometimes, perhaps, themselves.

They hired a financial secretary and business manager—at a teacher's salary—for twelve months a year and proceeded to organize active committees on specific problem areas. These included press relations, pensions, rules of the Board of Education, councils, school finances, legislation, and educational matters. Under the vigorous leadership of Catherine Goggin, who left her classroom at the Jones School in 1898, and of Margaret Haley, who left the Hendricks School in 1900, they set to work with an enthusiasm few of them had ever felt before. By 1901 a printed weekly bulletin was going to all members. Ways and means committees began figuring out how to pay for all this on the small dues (a maximum of $5.00) possible on current salaries. Membership committees went to work in unorganized schools. A parliamentary law class was held before meetings. An "Educational Department" arranged for lectures on psychology and pedagogy by professors from the Normal School and the University of Chicago, and (up to 1904) for classes at the Art Institute. The widening possibilities of such an organization as the Chicago Teachers Federation gradually became evident to many hundreds of its members.

People thought of services the new Chicago Teachers Federation could render that had never occurred to them before. For instance, they set up a "Mortuary Department." Everyone who belonged paid in a half dollar to begin with. When a member died one-half of the total amount was given to the family of the deceased or paid for a funeral. Then everybody paid in another quarter so that the fund would never be empty. Even teachers who were not members of the Federation could belong to the "Mortuary Department."

Two important statements of policy and intent were made by the new organization. One, adopted at the first meeting in 1897, was a statement of purpose:

> "The object of this organization shall be to raise the standard of the teaching profession by securing for teachers conditions essential to the best professional service, and to this end, to obtain for them all the rights and benefits to which they are entitled, the consideration and study of such subjects as the Federation may deem necessary, the consideration and support of the pension law, and the study of parliamentary law."[8]

When Catherine Goggin was inaugurated as president of the Federation in June, 1899, her speech was significant enough to be printed in the current Chicago Teachers and School Board Journal. She began by explaining the difference between groups like the Kindergarten Primary Association and the Chicago Teachers Federation:

> "In these other organizations, these lines [purely professional] might be dwelt upon and developed. The Federation should have a broader outlook. It should consider all which properly comes within the scope of intelligent citizenship. Its endorsement should be a powerful aid, its disapproval equally mighty. It should so educate public sentiment that a newspaper which attempted to lower the teachers of the city in the estimation of the public should immediately feel the result of the attempt in its decreased circulation and depleted advertising columns. What a lever that quarter million souls is and how much greater might be their power united for the common good!"

The "broader outlook" took the Federation into the city council, the legislature, the courts, the political campaigns, the business organizations, the banks, the newspapers, and the women's clubs and suffrage association, to protect the economic and legal interests of teachers. It developed as a well organized and aggressively led group as any in the city, even among the professional political organizations.[9] One quaint contemporary comment was that "The clamor of the time is for action, and as an ideal course, located midway between the red handed hatchet of Carry Nation, and the ineffectiveness of stately resolutions, the one followed by the Federation is safely, sanely and powerfully inviting."[10] Before long, many of her opponents in Chicago would have preferred Carry Nation's futile histrionics to Margaret Haley's coolly calculated, successful tax suits. The history of the Chicago schools for the first quarter of the twentieth century is in large part the history of the Chicago Teachers Federation. It has left an indelible mark on Chicago schools.

The pension problem, however, got much worse before it got better. The fund simply could not pay the amounts promised to teachers under fifty years old who had paid their $8.00 for one year and then expected at least half pay for the rest of their lives. At the 1901 session of the legislature, the Federation tried to get half the receipts from streetcar licenses to bolster up the fund, but failed. But the high-school teachers, the principals, the non-teaching employees, and the teachers who did not want to stay in the system did manage, over the opposition of the federation, to get the 1 percent contribution made voluntary—whereupon 883 teachers resigned. The Federation opposed this bill and tried to get the governor to veto it, but failed. The pension benefits fell to one-third of the original promises and new teachers refused to pay in. In 1903 the non-teaching employess got a separate system from that of the teachers.

In 1907 the Federation urged new and more financially sound pension legislation. It became mandatory on all new teachers, but not on those already in service, and about one thousand teachers, out of a 6,400 total, still stayed out. Some of the original inequities had been removed. The contribution was no longer on a percentage basis, but a flat sum, the same for all, since the benefit was the same for all. Women now had to wait till they had completed twenty-five years of service, the same as men. The annual benefit was set at $400 with a teacher having to accumulate $450 (the contribution represented by 25 years of service) before becoming eligible. Each teacher paid $5 a year for the first five years of service, $10 for the second five years, $15 for the third five years, and $30 for the remainder of service. Disability payments were in proportion to amounts paid in. Teachers who left before completing twenty-five years might get half their contributions back. The pension fund rose from $41,886 in 1906 to $131,807 in 1907-08, and became a shaky but viable system.[11]

But there were two permanently significant things about the 1907 pension law. The first was that some public funds were added to the teachers' contributions. The total was not much—only the income from interest on school property tax money collected in one year, held to be spent the next. This interest was to go to the pension fund if it did not exceed 1 percent of the property tax collected. By 1915 this source began to evaporate as the money for the next year was borrowed against, and gradually disappeared entirely. But in 1911 the legislature did require that the Board of Education equal the teachers' contribution from its general fund; and in 1913 it was authorized to pay twice as much as the teachers deducted from their own pay.

The second change put the control of the pension board into the hands of the Chicago Teachers Federation where it remained until 1955—long after the Federation had ceased to be the dominant force among Chicago teachers. The board controlling the fund was changed from four members as in the 1895 law to nine members, three to be members of the Board of Education, and six to be teachers elected by the teaching force. As funds grew, attempts were made to oust the teachers from control. In 1913 the city council made an effort to put the pension fund under the Chairman of the Finance Committee of the council, Alderman Rothman—a movement thwarted by the Federation with the help of Alderman Charles E. Merriam, head of the Department of Political Science of the University of Chicago.

Federation Tax Suits

Pensions for teachers were new, and teachers had to learn the hard way how to make them work. But there was nothing new about paying salaries, and no increase in twenty years was the exception, not the rule, in city school systems. It was not difficult to see what to do—just pay more! The new Federation set out in its first year of existence to find out why they were not getting better salaries, and to get them. Within eight months after the first meeting, the Federation collected 3,567 signatures, from about 90 percent of the elementary teachers, to a petition for a salary increase. High-school teachers, principals, and other administrators, and some special teachers, such as those who taught German, had received increases of from 14 to 100 percent during the twenty-year period. A few elementary teachers had received as much as 6¼ percent more; but the great mass of primary and grammar grade teachers were getting not a cent more than in 1877. In 1898 the Board did act to extend the seven-year salary schedule to ten years, with an increment of $75 for the eighth year and $50 each for the ninth and tenth or eleventh, until a maximum of $1,000 was reached. However, this was only a paper victory. No teacher, no matter how long the service, ever got beyond the eighth year on this schedule and not for long.

The 1897 teachers' salary schedule was as follows:

	Primary Grades	Grammar Grades
First year	$500	$500
Second year	550	550
Third year	575	625
Fourth year	650	675
Fifth year	700	725
Sixth year	775	800
Seventh year	800	825 (max.)

The 1898 schedule was voted to add:

	Primary Grades	Grammar Grades
Eighth year	$875	$900
Ninth year	925	950
Tenth year	975	1,000
Eleventh year	1,000[12]	

The Board paid the $75 for the eighth step for four months only, between September, 1898, and January, 1899. Then it announced that there was no money to pay the $75 it had voted for the remaining six months of the school year, 1898-99. In January, 1900, the $50 increases were voted on the first seven steps, but not on the eighth. In 1901 the eighth step was paid. In 1902, all steps above the seventh were abolished and elementary teachers went back to the 1877 schedule unless they met Superintendent Cooley's new promotion requirements.

During the Christmas vacation of 1899 a committee of the Federation set out to find more money for salaries. Since at least 90 percent of the school income was derived from a tax on property within the city, levied by the City Council on each $100 of its "assessed valuation," it began on already known peculiarities of the assessment system. They checked the payment lists of large corporations in the city against the tax records and found that some of them, like Pullman, were paying no taxes at all. They hired an able attorney and decided to concentrate on the public utility corporations, whose city-granted franchises gave them practical monopolies in necessary services. All of these companies had fixed rates and were enjoying huge business. All of them paid some tax on their buildings and tangible properties, but none of them a tax on their valuable franchises. The Constitution of Illinois clearly required that the same tax be paid on the franchises as on the tangible property. There was even a special statute requiring that the property tax be paid on franchises. The corporations involved were the Union Traction Company, the City Railway Company, the Peoples Gas Light and Coke Company, the Chicago Edison Company, and the Chicago Telephone Company. The facts were clear. The statements made by these companies to their own stockholders set a value of approximately $200,000,000 on the untaxed franchises.

All this data was presented to the county tax assessors in 1900. They did nothing. Then the Federation sent Catherine Goggin and Margaret Haley to Springfield to present the facts to the State Board of Equalization. They did nothing. Then the Federation sued in the Circuit Court of Sangamon County for a mandamus to compel the State Board of Equalization to assess the franchises according to the law. Support from Mayor Harrison and the Board of Cook County Commissioners finally materialized. They got the mandamus; but the State Board of Equalization adjourned and announced that the court had no control over its decisions anyway. The utility corporations asked for and got an injunction from a Federal court to restrain the State Board from "assessing them twice," but the injunction was dissolved almost immediately. The Circuit Court in Springfield than gave the State Board three days to answer the mandamus or be in contempt of court. Before the three days expired, the State Board of Equalization met and adopted a new rule assessing the franchises at a nominal rate which had no relation to their actual value.

The Federation held the new rule to be a mere evasion of the law, and went to court again. On the complaint of Catherine Goggin, "taxpayer and president of the Chicago Teachers Federation," the Circuit Court in Springfield issued another mandamus to compel the State Board to obey the law. On an appeal to the State Supreme Court, a decision was rendered by that body on October 1, 1901, that the assessment on franchises of Chicago public utility corporations, made by the State Board of Equalization in 1900, was fraudulent—so low as to be no assessment at all—and ordered that these corporations be assessed according to the law. Finally the State Board complied with the law and set a new assessment.

The new assessment was so high that the taxes to be collected on it amounted to $2,300,000. Again the corporations went into the Federal Court complaining that railroads and other corporations were not assessed according to the law either, and that the rate set for them violated the uniformity clause of the state constitution. The Federal Court accepted the argument and reduced the assessments so leniently that the taxes to be collected would amount to only $600,000 instead of $2,300,000, and issued a permanent injunction against collection of the remaining $1,700,000.[13] Since the constitution required full valuation of all property to be taxed, as well as uniformity, the illegality of the general tax procedure in Illinois was clearly illustrated.

But $600,000 was a lot more than nothing. The Board of Education got $249,544.77 as its share, although the money was not turned over to the Board until July 9, 1902. When it came, the Board proceeded to appropriate it to pay coal bills, clean school houses, and "other purposes," and never even mentioned using it for salaries. The teachers had paid for lawyers and court fees out of special contributions as well as from dues to the organization, and were not about to be ignored. They were still on the 1897 schedule, because the eighth step had now been dropped by vote of the Board. However, the Board had voted the increase for 1898-99, but had not paid it for the last six months of the school year on the ground that there was no money. The Federation claimed that the new money should be used to pay this six months' salary. The Board refused to do so, and the Federation obtained an injunction against using $193,000 of the new money for anything but salaries appropriated legally by the Board for the year 1898-99. The case was assigned to Judge Edward F. Dunne in the Circuit Court, who ruled in favor of the Federation and got their sincere and lasting gratitude. He held that the Board could not abrogate its contract for the school year, when money was available, and that the teachers had an "equitable lien" on the money (as voted also by the City Council in 1900), fortified by the fact that the very fund under controversy was secured through the tax work of the teachers.[14] The teachers got their money, two years late. When Judge Dunne became mayor of Chicago in 1905 he appealed the decision on the permanent Federal injunction to the United States Supreme Court; with two judges dissenting, one of them Oliver Wendell Holmes, it failed to remove the injunction.

The details of this first major effort by the Federation are significant. They indicate not only the concerted determination of the teachers, but the complaisant attitude of the political authorities not only on tax assessment and collection but on law enforcement in general. The Federation members, however, saw that the machinery of government could be used by ordinary people for what they thought was just, if they were willing to stick it out. The taste of victory encouraged further effort; the Federation urged citizens to demand that aldermen insist on payment of franchise taxes *before* franchises were granted, and attempted or organize citizens by wards to put pressure on aldermen to this end. In January, 1902, they issued a circular threatening to close the schools if salaries were cut again (likely because the county assessors had reduced the assessed valuations in Cook County), and accusing the assessors of making the reductions in retaliation for the Federation victory. The assessors, the utilities, the aldermen, the State Board of Equalization, and the Board of

Education all resented the impertinent, unladylike independence of the Federation, and felt that the teachers were impinging upon their very valuable political prerogatives.

The Chicago Teachers Federation's next adventure in seeking more funds concerned the press. On the tax suits the newspapers had shown a wide variety of reactions. The first were almost unanimously disapproving, but success brought more respect. The Tribune for March 16, 1900, scolded the Federation, in trying to set the whole world straight, for treating the city like a small child. On December 7, 1900, it stated flatly that the problem of taxes was "outside the teachers' province," that their activities were regarded with silent or open disapproval, and that they were encouraging "political interference with the school system, a situation far worse than any defeat in the school system." The Chicago Chronicle on November 17, 1900, agreed that the "Tax cause was worthy," but "School ma'ams as lobbyists left an unfavorable impression"; "It was impertinent for public employees to lobby to get more pay for themselves." Apparently it was not impertinent for the corporations to use methods they saw fit, for decreased taxation and more profit for themselves. The Times-Herald, on January 27, 1900, charged that the teachers had been "thoughtless in characterizing the corporations as tax dodgers," and added on February 20, that "Teachers were assuming a responsibility beyond their legitimate sphere of action." But by October 10, 1900, the Daily News was supporting the Federation's tax suits and on March 18, 1901, urged them to persevere. The Chicago American on March 31, 1902, gave the Federation credit for the success of the suits, and the Record Herald on May 11, 1902, hoped quite respectfully that the Federation would continue its struggle to compel corporations to pay back taxes on capital stock.

Before beginning in its next drive to increase school income, the Federation used its strength to kill legislation which had been drafted as a result of recommendations of the Educational Commission appointed by Mayor Harrison in 1897. The Civic Federation introduced a bill to implement the recommendations in 1901 and 1903, providing for a nine-member appointed Board, a five-year term for the superintendent after a two-year probationary period, and for some control by the superintendent over a business manager. The Federation opposed the legislation, got the active opposition of the Chicago Federation of Labor against it, and was in considerable part responsible for killing the chances of its passage. The objections raised were that the centralization of power in one superintendent was dangerous.

The Federation's attitude may have been influenced by its bitter opposition at the time to Superintendent Cooley's secret marking plan and by his failure to ask for higher salaries, a resentment shared by the Principals' Club. He was accused of aligning himself against the teachers with the Union League Club, the Manufacturers' Association, and the Board of Education. The Federation had shown consistent suspicion of President Harper himself, because they believed the University of Chicago was working toward the exclusion from teaching of applicants who had not gone to the University. They felt his Report had derogated the Chicago teachers and minimized their contribution. They resented his disapproval of the ingrown character of the teaching force, and his sharp criticism of the lack of training of elementary teachers, most of whom, in 1898, had come in since 1877 without any training for teaching at all. Moreover, the Federation wanted an elected, not an appointed Board, and were supported in this goal by the Chicago Federation of Labor, which influenced a considerable number of votes in Springfield. The Board of Education introduced its own bill for a five-year term for superintendent in 1903, and the City Charter committee a similar measure in 1905, but none of these was enacted into law.

Investigation of School Land Leases

The search for more money continued. In the process the Federation took on the largest and most influential of all the Chicago papers as a permanent mortal enemy. It explored thoroughly the dark and sorry story of the school lands given to the city by the federal government for school purposes by the Ordinance of 1785. It found that the annual rent received from all the school lands in 1905 was only $500,000, estimated to be half what it should be at current land values. Since the land belonged to the Board of Education, no property tax was paid. But the Board was tax exempt, not the lessees, who should have paid the same rates on their long-term leases as private land owners. In his 1895 message to the legislature, Governor Altgeld had stated:

> "Years ago all school lands were leased by the Board of Education to various parties for a long term, but with the provision that there should be revaluation every five years, and that the rent would be six percent per annum on this revaluation. The purpose of this was to get the benefit of the advance in value as the city grew larger. Revaluations have been made from time to time, each much higher than the former, but the lessees, many of whom are prominent citizens, have been able to exert such an influence that the rent produced by this ground has always been far below that paid for ground belonging to private individuals in the same locality and no more desirable."

In 1895 a number of leases had been granted which removed the revaluation clause, providing for no real revaluation between 1915 and 1985.

Anyone seeking more money for Chicago schools could obviously not omit this source. The trouble was that the most flagrant offender was the Chicago Tribune itself. The Tribune held a ninety-nine-year lease running from 1886 to 1985 on the Madison and Dearborn lot on which it had built its headquarters. The president of the Board of Education in 1895 at the same time Chairman of the Committee on School Fund Property which had recommended the non-revaluation change, was also the Chicago Tribune attorney. In 1902 the Board of Education leased one floor in the Tribune Building for its officers and paid the Tribune $1,000 a year more than the Tribune was paying for the land. A member of the Board of Education in 1904 stated that the schools had already lost fifteen million dollars because of the leases. By 1905 the issue was at a boiling point, because there was a chance to change the lease. Besides, lessees who had not had the revaluation clause removed were suing in the courts to have it struck from their leases as well—litigation that was not settled until 1912.

The Federation began long before 1905 to raise the issue of school land leases, stating the case over and over in public meetings and in its publications, and intensifying its efforts during the 1905 discussions on lease changes. When Judge Edward Dunne became mayor in 1905 he appointed Jane Addams and other independents as Board of Education members. At their instigation the Board took a suit to court asking that the 1895 Tribune lease be declared illegal,[15] but the Circuit Court held the lease proper and binding. Their action against the Tribune was one of the reasons some of the Dunne Board members were accused of being "tools of the Federation." (One reason the Federation had given Judge Dunne enthusiastic support in his mayoralty campaign was that his opponent, Mayor Carter Harrison, supported the fixed evaluation leases.) When Miss Haley had no other issue at the moment, the school land leases were always at hand. The Chicago Federation of Labor likewise made the leases a continuing issue. But neither the News or any other paper mentioned them. Jane Addams once commented that "The press, with the opportunity of selecting its data, assumes the power, once exercised by the church, when it gave people only such knowledge as it deemed fit for them to have."[16] The Federation never got its revaluation and the leases still stand till 1985. But from then on, the Tribune seldom lost an opportunity of attacking the Federation on almost any ground, at any time.

The Federation did not spare the superintendent in its opposition to what it felt blocked the road to progress for teachers. It disagreed sharply on the steps he recommended be required for promotion on the salary scale. As early as 1884 a president of the Board of Education had lamented that teachers must inevitably be paid according to "position and length of service" because "in a large system it was practically impossible to pay according to the value of their work." This was probably especially true in a system where incompetents had obtained positions through political influence, and where their political support would make them more likely to get extra salary than competent teachers without such backing.

In 1901 Superintendent Edwin G. Cooley took a step toward rating teachers' competency. To avoid the problem of political influence, he made his ratings secret and thereby raised a storm of protest from all kinds of teachers. He recommended to the Board that the eighth step on the salary schedule, voted in 1898 but not really being used, be restored only to those who met certain qualifications. Applicants for the eighth step must take promotional examinations, the first of which would be given in 1902. (If teachers showed enough credits from a degree-giving institution or from the Normal School they might be excused from the promotional examination.) A grade of 80 percent was required for passing the examination. But in addition, the applicant must receive an 80 percent efficiency mark by her principal. These marks were recorded secretly, and no teacher was to know the result. If she took the examination and passed it, she would be notified as to whether she would be placed on the eighth step. If she were not notified, she would know she had less than an 80 percent secret marking. The principal would record his grades each year, but no teacher rated low was to be told what was wrong or how to improve. Superintendent Cooley said such discussion would only produce squabbling.

The Federation in 1901 opposed the whole scheme, and urged teachers not to take the promotional examinations, but to stick to length of service as basis for promotion to the eighth step. However, 900 teachers did prepare for the examination and were qualified. About one thousand teachers took a course at the Normal School evenings or summer in 1902-03.

The secrecy of the rating was the biggest point of controversy. The Chicago Federation of Labor urged Superintendent Cooley in 1903 to give each teacher a copy of her rating,[17] and in 1905 the new members of the Dunne Board gave the teachers the right to know their scores and arranged that teachers might go one afternoon a week for ten weeks to Normal extension classes every other year, without loss of pay.[18] Superintendent Cooley then dropped the promotional examination and required instead five courses of 36 hours each. Jane Addams was attacked by the Federation as a compromiser because she felt something must be done to help teachers improve. The Record Herald, May 21, 1906, suggested that the schedule be automatic for seven years, and if teachers had not reached a given standard by that time, dismiss them. Neither superintendent or Federation took up that suggestion. When Mayor Busse appointed a majority of the Board in 1907, the new members reverted to the original Cooley plan of secret markings and promotional examinations. A referendum taken by secret ballot in 1908 showed that 90 percent of the 3,000 teachers who chose to vote disliked the system. Mrs. Young finally did away with secrecy in 1909, during her term of office.

Affiliation of Teachers With Labor

Between 1897 and 1902 the Federation had found money for salary increases, protested the exploitation of school lands, objected to the secret scores and promotional pressures of Superintendent Cooley, and had won respect as a strong force from the political powers of Chicago. In 1902 the Federation took what was then a highly controversial step: it voted to affiliate with the Chicago Federation of Labor and applied for a "federal" charter from the American Federation of Labor. The Federation was the second group of teachers in the United States to take this action. Teachers in San Antonio, Texas, had preceded them by a few weeks. Nor were the members of the Federation entirely unanimous; some of the membership felt they were compromising their "genteel profession."

The arguments for the affiliation were many. Margaret Haley herself gave one reason:

> "The only people you can depend on to act permanently with you are those whose interest are identical with yours. We expect by affiliation with labor to arouse the workers and the whole people . . . to the dangers of confronting the public schools from the same interests and tendencies that are undermining the foundations of our democratic republic."[19]

Editorials in the Federation bulletins stated that the schools were powerless against organized wealth and that all public offices were under the control of those interests. School board members were not appointed for competence but because they were subservient to the mayor and to the vested interests. Affiliation with the Chicago Federation of Labor would mean the disappearance of special privilege. Teachers affiliated with labor would know better the home conditions of children, and parents would learn to appreciate the efforts of teachers.

An article in School and Society, October 16, 1915, claimed that Superintendent Cooley's pressures on the teachers may have helped precipitate the affiliation. Since he was not able to change the economic and political forces which hindered the progress of the schools, Cooley made no effort to reduce classes, increase salaries, or solve teachers' problems, but instead put pressure on teachers to resolve their own improvement of these situations and "really compelled them further to organize themselves and encourage the movement begun before his time to such a degree that one group of teachers allied themselves with the labor movement of Chicago." "If the Board had always been concerned only to serve the schools, teachers' organizations would never have become an issue."

Margaret Haley, a Dramatic Leader

One other element in the situation had a bearing on the affiliation—the vigorous, reforming spirit of Margaret Haley herself. That John Fitzpatrick's wife was a teacher, a Federationist, and a friend of Miss Haley's was not so significant. But that Miss Haley herself was an ardent exponent of the reforms in which John Fitzpatrick and other leaders of the Chicago Federation of Labor of that day were deeply involved, was significant. She was an official in the Municipal Ownership League working to get city ownership of the street-car lines. She believed in the Single Tax movement, and in the organization of citizens into independent political action. She was a leader in the Illinois woman suffrage movement, which labor was supporting. She campaigned at these efforts both before and after the labor affiliation of the Federation.

But Margaret Haley was not the stereotype of an earnest social reformer. She was a most attractive little woman who knew how to use her dainty femininity effectively. Her bright face, quick smile, clear blue eyes, and cheerful manner made her stand out in any crowd. She had rare gifts as a speaker and organizer. She planned the Federation meetings as carefully as if she were staging a play. There was always something new and exciting to report, dramatically presented. Her dicta were accepted by most of her followers as infallible. Her quick wit served her well in the council and the legislature, and in any kind of debate. She informed herself thoroughly on the issues in the controversies in which she engaged, and over and over proved that her adversaries did not know what they were talking about. Political leaders preferred not to have her as an opponent, and were loath to promise what might have brought them her support since they knew they would be expected to keep such promises.

William Hard, an editorial writer for the Tribune and a great admirer of Miss Haley's, in an American Magazine article for September, 1906, entitled "Chicago's Five Maiden Aunts," concluded that "Joining the Chicago Federation of Labor indicated unity between the fight of the teachers for a larger voice in the management of the school system and the fight of working men and women in general for a large voice in the management of the whole industrial system."

There was scandalized opposition to the affiliation in the Chicago press. Hard's newspaper, the Tribune, on January 24, 1902, exclaimed that it was not enough apparently for a teacher to teach. "She must also be a tradeunionist, a referendum enthusiast (for initiative, referendum and recall) a municipal ownership worker, and a politician generally. Discipline and efficiency in the schools will give way." The Daily News for November 12, 1902, stated flatly that labor affiliation for teachers was clearly untenable. The opposition of the metropolitan press continued as long as the affiliation continued. On January 27, 1905, the Chronicle held that a teacher must be neutral and that "Character and citizenship could not be taught by a teacher in a labor organization which taught hatred of other classes." In May of that year the same paper blamed the insubordination of children in school on labor union influence.

The Tribune, the News, and the Herald regularly capitalized on strikes, mentioning the Federation, although the Federation had said it did not intend to strike. On June 8, 1905, the Tribune accused the Federation of teaching "sedition, revolt against authority, disrespect for law, subversion of private and public rights" in answer to the Federation Bulletin of May 12 which said "Employers were responsible for the causes of strikes." On June 24, 1905, the Tribune urged the Board of Education to take strenuous action against the

Federation, assuring the Board that the "Mass of members would then desert the unholy alliance." (This was at the time when the Federation was urging the Board to revaluate the Tribune lease.) Not only the newspapers, but other publications took exception to the affiliation. The bulletin of the Merchants' Club in 1908 quoted Nicholas Murray Butler, President of Columbia University, against affiliation of police, firemen, and teachers with labor.

Not all the voices were negative, however. The Rockford Star on November 11, 1902, said great good would come from teachers' affiliation with labor. Jane Addams approved the union between teachers and labor as a step in the right direction. In Scribners, June, 1903, Graham Taylor said it was of immense value to the unions. In 1904 Margaret Haley was on the N.E.A. program to explain why teachers should organize locally, affiliate with labor, and "recognize that their struggle to maintain efficiency in the schools was the same great struggle which manual workers had been making for humanity to secure better living conditions for themselves and their children."[20] The Illinois State Federation of Labor endorsed heartily the right of the Federation to affiliate with labor, and denounced as un-American the attempts to intimidate the teachers.

Federation Activity in City Politics

The Federation not only affiliated with organized labor, it began a long career as an actively organized political force, working for or against the election of candidates for mayor and aldermen. The organization gave strong public support to Judge Edward F. Dunne for mayor when he was elected in 1905 and again in 1907 when he was defeated by William Busse. Dunne had not only decided the 1902 salary case in favor of the Federation, he supported municipal ownership of utilities, favored stronger pension and tenure protection for teachers, and wanted a revaluation of the 1895 school land leases. Women had been allowed to vote in the referendum on the city charter for Chicago in 1904, in which a large number of advisory opinion questions had been included, four of them dealing with schools. Four thousand two hundred nineteen teachers out of a possible 4,618 elementary teachers voted. The effective organization of the Federation drive in this referendum is registered in the vote on these school issues:

	Against	For
An elected Board of Education	243	3543
On permanent tenure for teachers	10	3948
On tax money for the pension fund	106	3728
On promotional examinations	316	3844

But they took an active part in the general city election as well, and were ready to work for their candidates in the 1905 mayoralty campaign. Miss Haley went from ward to ward denouncing the Harrison administration as the tool of the Yerkes traction ring and the protector or organized vice, and the impact of her campaigning was acknowledged by the professional politicians.

Judge Dunne was elected mayor in 1905. Miss Haley was among those he thanked publicly for support. He appointed to the Board of Education a number of distinguished people in his two-year term, among them Jane Addams, who was made chairman of the School Management Committee, Mrs. Emmons Blaine, Raymond Robins, Louis F. Post, John J. Sonsteby (later chief justice of the new Municipal Court), Dr. Cornelia De Bey, and Wiley Mills, who served as an alderman for many years. Although the new members were not a majority of the Board of twenty-one, they worked diligently and effected an unusual number of changes, most of which disappeared at the end of Mayor Dunne's term two years later. They eliminated the secrecy in ratings of teachers, substituted the opportunity for in-service training on school time for promotional examinations, and instituted a suit against the Tribune to require periodic evaluation of its lease. They withdrew a suit begun by a previous Board to appeal from Judge Dunne's salary decision in favor of the Federation.

Mrs. Blaine and Dr. De Bey presented a plan for an "official advisory committee of the teaching force of Chicago"—a council system which was to be independent of the Board of Education but have access to it.[21] But no definite action on the plan was taken by the Board before the 1907 mayoralty election and no council was ever established. The Federation, however, praised the action and felt that they had made some headway with the Board.

In 1905 Jane Addams found that

> "The teachers inside the system were unfortunately so restricted
> that they had no space in which to move about freely and the more
> adventurous among them fairly panted for air. ... The larger
> number of teachers in the Federation fretted individually and as an
> organization against the rigidity of administrative control, low salary
> rates from 'economy' boards, and their inability to say anything
> about curriculum."[22]

The other Board members accused the Dunne appointees of being too friendly with the Federation. However, Miss Addams felt that the Federation exaggerated some of its claims, that the charges of graft it brought against board members were true, but that the Federation sometimes mixed its theories with its facts—and she wanted only facts. In spite of her constructive efforts along the major directions in which it wished the schools to move, the Federation grew impatient with her objective outlook and methods, and finally accused her of having "sold out to the business men," and of having "had her opportunity and thrown it away."

The Dunne Board tried to improve the salary situation as well as the status of teachers, but did not succeed in that direction either. By 1905 Chicago had fallen far behind New York and Philadelphia in expenditures per child, and behind New York and Boston in teachers' salaries. The average salary of an elementary teacher in New York was $996 and in Chicago $717. The Dunne Board voted a $50 annual increase in 1907, but by April of that year, Dunne had been defeated in spite of the earnest efforts of Miss Haley and the Federation, and the new board members appointed by Mayor Busse cut back the $50 for 2,500 teachers the next year. The Dunne Board had prepared a plan for a ten-year schedule without promotional tests, but it never went into effect.

Most of the changes voted or proposed by the Dunne Board were lost in the political scuffle which arose as the new mayor pushed board members around in order to get immediate control of the Board. On May 20, 1907, Mayor Busse demanded resignations of twelve of the twenty-one Board members. When only three complied, the mayor arbitrarily removed seven from office, and five others resigned in protest. The members who were forced out took their protest to the Supreme Court of Illinois and were reinstated in January, 1908. The decision stated clearly that the mayor could not remove board members at will.[23] But the president of the Board had sent in his resignation as president to the mayor, pointing out that the schools had been an issue in the mayoralty election and that he wanted the new board to organize accordingly, and the reconstituted board, even with the members returned by court order, was no longer friendly to Federation policies for the schools.

There was no reason why the Busse-controlled Board should have looked with favor on the Federation. The Federation began to learn that the punishment of the "outs" negated the successes of the "ins" in the shifts of political quicksands, but it did not change its policies on active participation in city politics. A part of the punishment lay in the 1908 salary raises for office employees and other non-teaching employees of the Board, in which teamsters were raised from $960 to $1,020, but in which there were no increases for primary and grammar grade teachers. Instead of granting them salary raises in 1909, the President of the Board attacked the activities of the Federation as the "underground burrowings of conspiring rebels."[24] In January, 1909, principals received a salary increase and some high-school and special teachers, also.

The Federation took to the legislature and introduced a bill to require that seven-eighths of all the tax funds collected for educational purposes be used for salaries, alleging that the Board simply cut teachers' salaries whenever it had any other plans it wanted to carry out. This legislation did not pass, but a compromise measure did, in which repairs on buildings were to be charged to the building fund instead of the educational fund. Board member Sonsteby, a hold-over from the Dunne Board, represented the Federation in Springfield on the legislation and was paid $2,100 by them for expenses and services on the bill.[25] It was clear that the Federation was being punished for its independence and opposition to the "Establishment."

Chapter 6

THE BOARD ATTACK ON THE FEDERATION

The Federation probably did not do Edwin Cooley justice. He made an earnest effort to reduce child labor, working with Jane Addams and Mrs. Kelley in the Cook County Child Saving League, which cooperated with the legislative committee of the Chicago Federation of Labor in getting a new law passed in 1903. The law required that children who could not read and write at fourteen, must go to day or evening school until sixteen years of age, and be able to show the record of their attendance.[1] He appointed William J. Bogan to make a study of the new continuation schools in Eastern cities and in 1909 opened the first such school in Chicago. Thirteen years after Cooley resigned as superintendent he returned to the Chicago schools to continue to work at the development of continuation schools, as their director. He proposed that the Board take over the vacation schools, started by gifts and social agencies, praising their "free and interesting curriculum," and he managed to get seventeen such summer schools paid for by the Board in 1909. Twice the evening schools were closed for lack of funds, in 1901 and in 1905, and twice they were reopened. He saw that every new school had a playground, and tried to get more space around older ones. In 1907 he took over the city playgrounds adjacent to schools. Bath services in the crowded areas were increased. When the Daily News offered a course of free lecturers in 1907 they were accepted. New buildings included gymnasiums and had no more than 54 seats in a room, some only 48.

A two-pronged attack was made on the problem of insufficient seats. The Board adopted the policy in 1905 of putting up wooden "portable" school rooms adjacent to school buildings instead of using basements and other kinds of rented rooms, and a consistent attempt was made to obtain better use of the space available.[2] In 1905 11,000 children were on double shift, and few kindergartens in proper space. In 1909 the elementary children on half-day had been reduced to 3,200, but there were still 2,600 in rented rooms. In 1909 Superintendent Cooley listed the schools with empty space in the newspapers before the annual May 1 moving day, to encourage parents to move into those school districts, and then redistricted areas where there were empty seats left as residence areas became industrial. All schools were inspected for safety regularly after the Collinwood fire tragedy in 1907.

But the rapidly rising enrolment in the high schools, from 10,200 in 1900, 12,400 in 1905, to 17,800 in 1910, and the impact of more effective child-labor and compulsory-education law enforcement negated the gains in elementary school seats. In 1909 the eighteen high schools were becoming crowded, too.

Superintendent Cooley's calm, sardonic patience with his Boards of Education won him a few carefully unheralded victories. He was known to take out a proposal objected to at one meeting by the Chairman of the Committee on School Management, and quietly put it in the file of proposals for another meeting, and have it pass. But he knew better than to try the many things his record indicates he would have liked to accomplish.[3] The Federation was so concerned with the frustrations of teachers it gave little thought to those of a superintendent. When Edwin Cooley resigned in 1909 to go into the textbook business, Ella Flagg Young succeeded him. The Federation gave her its ardent support.

Superintendent Ella Flagg Young

Ella Flagg Young was an astonishing human being. Not more than five feet tall, she could scarcely control a situation by sheer overbearing size and impressive presence. A woman in a profession traditionally dominated by men, she quietly insisted on being considered on her merits, and so competently demonstrated them that critics had no choice but to recognize her achievements. In 1879 men applicants for the principalship were required to take an examination, but women were excused from it. Mrs. Young not only insisted on taking the examination, she passed at the head of the list and was assigned to one of the largest elementary schools instead of one of the very small primary schools given to women. A creative educational innovator to whom John Dewey paid high tribute as one whose experience and advice were invaluable to him, she knew how to state educational concepts simply so they would be easily understood by those with little academic training. Thus she disposed of the ancient shibboleth of "mental discipline" by remarking that no one would say it made no difference what a child ate, just so he had a good digestive system. She made clear to teachers that children really had learned nothing if what they were taught did not make sense to them in the light of their own experiences and interests. The mere external application of increasing numbers of separate courses was not education. Education must concern itself with the total experience and outlook of children, with the influence of their homes and communities as well as with formal education in school hours and in school buildings. Teachers and the schools must become parts of the communities they served.

Ella Flagg Young is the only recorded principal in Chicago schools who ever dismissed an incompetent school engineer, and was able to keep him dismissed. She won the respect of powerful political leaders, like the two Mayors Harrison, in whose home neighborhood lay her Skinner School, not by aiding their political careers, but by the recognized impact of her school on its community. When orders given her by her superiors seemed to her disastrous to children and the school system, she did not accept them with the usual helpless shrug; she resigned—and she resigned three times in her fifty three years in the Chicago Public Schools. She never lost her poise in dealing with those who opposed her. She simply acted, directly and consistently.

An idealist in a city where public affairs were generally considered outside the realm of personal ethics, she calmly and successfully withstood those who sought promotions for proteges, the book companies who pressed for contracts, business leaders who, she felt, wanted to use the schools for narrow ends, the conservatives in the schools who wanted to keep the status quo, and in a difficult period of confusion and transition, she managed to change the direction of a vast school system. As she looked at the forces arrayed against her hopes for the opportunities of children, she once said that the advance of public education, like

> "The emigrant's way over the Western desert, is marked
> By campfires long consumed and bones that bleach in the sunshine."

But she never lost her faith that a host of emigrants would follow and that schools would become increasingly useful to the kind of society she hoped for; and she herself never lessened her efforts toward an end she knew she would never see. When she left the superintendency, she was seventy years old. She put everything in her office in perfect order for her successor, quietly walked out and boarded a train for California—a gesture completely in keeping with the rest of her seventy years.

Mrs. Young's Educational Philosophy

Some of the Normal School faculty in 1905 had been hostile to Ella Flagg Young's talk of "the child" instead of methods, and her outspoken concern for children of the immigrants, of the tenements, and of the streets, who made up 67 percent of the pupils in Chicago's schools in 1909. She made more sense to teachers who flocked to her lectures and listened with understanding as she warned against motivating children by encouraging them to compete with each other, against using sarcasm—which was "worse than a whipping," and against punishing a whole group for the sins of a few. She told them that what was needed of children and teachers was cooperation, and that cooperation was not merely obedience, it was the conscious use of creative intelligence to reach a common, understood goal.

Mrs. Young maintained that the public schools were the most powerful agency to create "oneness" in our cosmopolitan society, so powerful that "sectional antagonism based on racial character" can be "unknown in our schools." In childhood, children could learn the unity of the human race, and she told them that "The Soul is not classified according to its world possessions, particular languages or the faith in which it is reared." The public schools must be for the poor and the rich, native and immigrant, all faiths and races, all meeting on a common ground.[4] Ella Flagg Young lived her own philosophy, and won the trust and faith of thousands of teachers. She gave them a belief to live by, a sense that the monotonous life in an isolated class room was a significant part of the great movement of human history—an ennobling adventure. But she agreed with the teachers that they should not be asked to undertake it for almost nothing, and gave practical evidence of her convictions on that score, as well. *Her* frustrations the Federation knew and understood.

The Chicago Teachers' Federation was quite conscious that Mrs. Young was trying to direct the school system to achieve the social end of greater opportunity not only for children but for the Federation too, in the face of the ever-increasing enrolment and ever-increasing gap between needs and resources. She did use every resource available. She welcomed the aid of the Chicago Woman's Club and sixty other groups in helping to keep the penny lunch program in operation in the low-income areas. By 1914 bath rooms with attendants existed in 77 schools in the crowded neighborhoods. More than half of the evening school enrolment of 38,000 were immigrants learning English and studying for naturalization papers. Mrs. Young served on the Child Labor Committee of the Illinois State Federation of Labor with Raymond Robins and Graham Taylor, and was deeply concerned that 30 percent of the children applying for age certificates for work were foreign born.[5] She limited the number of seats in an elementary classroom to 54, and persuaded the Board to limit the number to 40, which they voted to do "as soon as there was money." Her comment on this action was, "How long, O Lord, how long?"

The population of the city rose a half million between 1900 and 1910, from 1,600,000 to 2,185,000. There were not only more children, but a larger proportion of the total number of children were coming to school, and even more important, staying in class. Although a report made by the City Club Committee on Education in 1910 showed that only 67 percent of those who enrolled in first grade reached eighth grade, and only 6 percent of them graduated from high school, these figures indicated much greater holding power than comparable data ten years before. The high-school enrolment was now 25,000, and at a per capita level of $95 was costing more than $2,000,000 a year. One reason for the jump in high-school attendance was the opening of two-year commercial courses which offered immediate help in getting work. The seventh and eighth grades were also offering "pre-vocational courses" to keep children from leaving after sixth grade. Mrs. Young introduced sex education into the high schools and normal school, but the Board stopped it after protests from several groups.[6]

Elementary principals' salaries were increased in 1910, and Mrs. Young proposed a plan to pay a ten-year schedule for teachers, although there was insufficient money to put it into effect in 1910 and 1911. In 1912 the Board did vote increases for elementary and high-school teachers, but did not pay them for lack of funds. In the meantime, the cost of living was rising so fast that a $1,000 salary in May, 1913, could buy only what $693 would have bought in 1897. In February, 1914, after the high-school day had been lengthened by 20 percent, high-school salaries were increased by 10 percent and elementary salaries by 5 percent. When the Federation claimed credit for the increase, the Board issued a public statement that the Federation had nothing to do with it. Theoretically the elementary maximum had reached $1500 by 1914, but no teacher ever received that amount until 1918. The Board discussed closing the schools for two weeks at the end of the fiscal year in December, 1914, and suggested that the teachers should be willing to give up their pay raises. There was no sick leave at all for teachers until 1916, when the Board paid two-thirds of the $7 a day substitute's pay, instead of having the teacher pay it all. The instability of the salary policy of successive Boards of Education for twenty years was a bitter experience for the elementary teachers. The idea that they were deliberately discriminated against, and expected to take all the jolts, became fixed.

Cooley Plan and Labor Reaction

During Mrs. Young's superintendency, conflicting concepts in the purposes and methods of public education in the city burst into violent public debate. The dispute had begun as far back as the Harper Report of 1898 and exploded again in 1925, but its sharpest manifestation occurred in 1912 when the business organizations of the city proposed a dual system of schools. In the Harper Report, the German system of commercial training, separate from that of the "classical" schools, was suggested, and Edmund J. James had been quoted as praising the European system of one kind of school for those going into professions and another for those being trained in manual and other work skills.[7] In 1900 only one-sixth of all boys in Chicago between fourteen and eighteen were in school at all. By 1901 some business courses had been set up in the high schools, and in 1905 Superintendent Cooley suggested that the Jones School in the downtown area be used for a commercial high school, a project encouraged by resolution of the city council in 1909 (accomplished in 1938, and provided with a building in 1967). In 1910 some prevocational courses were prepared for children who would otherwise have stopped at sixth grade.

Both business and labor groups were anxious to have vocational training expanded. In October, 1908, representatives of the Chicago Federation of Labor appeared before the Board of Education offering to cooperate in the development of courses in industrial education.[8] In January, 1909, the Federation of Labor accepted an invitation from the Association of Commerce to appoint members of a joint committee to advise the Board on industrial education. In 1908, the Association had made a study of proposals for vocational education in the city and had published a pamphlet in 1909, "Industrial and Commercial Education in Relation to Conditions in the City of Chicago."

In 1911 the Commercial Club asked ex-Superintendent Cooley, working for a text book company for two years, to go to Europe to study vocational education there. When he returned he presented a plan which incorporated the European system of two kinds of non-interchangeable high schools, general and vocational. The Commercial Club, the Association of Commerce and the Civic Federation approved the plan and proceeded to have legislation drafted to put it into effect. The Illinois Manufacturers' Association and the Industrial Club supported the legislation when drafted. It provided for a dual system of schools beginning at seventh grade, one for general and "classical" education, and one for vocational. A special additional tax was to be levied to provide for the expensive equipment required for the vocational schools. These were to be taught by teachers from factories and other areas of vocational competence, and managed by special boards of "practical men and women." Attendance at the vocational schools was to be compulsory until eighteen, unless pupils were in some other school. The National Association of Manufacturers sponsored the idea in nation-wide campaigns and in 1913 published a report, "Industrial Education," in which the dual system in use in Wisconsin was given high praise. This report urged compulsory vocational education until age sixteen, and attendance at continuation schools thereafter. When opposition arose, the business organizations insisted that they knew the needs of industry and that these needs must determine the nature of vocational education and the methods by which such education should be implemented. They urged the passage of the Cooley Bill.

Not all the organizations which included business and professional leaders agreed, however. The City Club in 1912 had initiated a study of the problem financed by Mrs. Emmons Blaine, who had been a member of the Dunne Board of Education. Careful research by University of Chicago graduate students, under an advisory committee of which William J. Bogan, principal of Lane High School, was a member, came to a different conclusion. The City Club "Report on Vocational Training in Chicago and Other Cities," issued in 1912, stressed the obvious need for vocational courses for youth from twelve to sixteen years of age, and pointed out that of the fourteen-to-sixteen-year age group, more than half were out of school and idle. The club urged that the compulsory education age be raised to sixteen for all children, but strongly opposed a system of separate schools. They also prepared legislation and openly opposed the Cooley Bill.

Teachers at all levels were shocked by the Cooley Bill. The Federation and the Principals' Club sent representatives to Springfield to oppose the two-track system. Mrs. Young used all her influence against it, claiming it trained youth to accept lower-class status and blocked the social mobility which was the mark of American society. Other leaders in education and social thought were outspoken opponents of the proposal, including Dr. Charles H. Judd and Sophonisba Breckenridge of the University of Chicago, and John Dewey. The Illinois State Teachers Association opposed the bill in Springfield.

Chicago was a city where labor conflict had always been bitter. It was the center of open shop activities, and had developed large and effectively run local and state labor movements. The clash between business interests and labor organizations on the Cooley Bill was the climax of years of altercation in which each assumed the worst possible motives in the other group. The Chicago Federation of Labor accused business of trying to get cheap, submissive labor without the educational background American citizens should have, calling it the most direct of all the open-shop, anti-union drives ever made. The Illinois State Federation of Labor supported the City Club bill and marshaled votes against the Cooley Bill.[9] The Cooley measure was presented to the legislature three times, in 1913, 1915, and 1917, and failed each time. It became a sharp focus of class antagonism. Not only the labor leaders, but the educational opponents alleged that its sponsors wanted to train children for their convenience, not for the youths' own welfare. They claimed that the plan would assign the poor to dead-end schools with no chance for upward mobility. Its proponents never conceded that it had any undemocratic implications, and pointed to its use in Wisconsin.

By the time the bill failed for the third time in 1917, the Federal Vocational Act had been adopted, aid for vocational course equipment had been made available through matching federal aid to state and local funds, and vocational work in the high schools materially increased thereafter. Likewise in 1918-19 the continuation schools in Chicago became compulsory for one day a week for all employed non high school graduates who were under eighteen years, although there was no general agreement on arguments made by the Association of Commerce and the Commercial Club that continuation schools were needed to "minimize the increase of socialism" and to "combat unsound and dangerous economic and social doctrines."

The Board of Education as a government agency did not play a leading part in the dispute over the Cooley Bill. But it had worked closely with the Association of Commerce in a privately sponsored vocational-guidance project with children in schools, finally taken over by the school system in 1916. The Board also had allowed the Association to organize junior groups called Civic and Industrial Clubs in 1914, with programs directed by the Association. At least four members of the Board of Education were active in the Association.[10]

Certainly the open and effective opposition of the Chicago Teachers Federation and its allies in the labor movement to the Cooley legislation did not lessen the hostility with which the Board viewed the Federation and all its works.

Mrs. Young's greatest contribution to the Chicgo schools lay in her efforts to gave teachers pride in participation in and improvement of, the schools of which they were a part. There is no evidence that she supported—or that she approved—all of the Federation activities. But there is no doubt that she sought to establish a close and sympathetic relationship with the teaching staff and to impart a sense of involvement in school decisions. She was now able to bring to reality the kind of teachers' council she had begun talking about in 1899 and had proposed to the Dunne Board in 1907. The council was not recognized by the Board and met only on call of the superintendent, but it was heartily approved by the Federation. Its leaders and members felt that Mrs. Young was working with them toward a "strong, self-reliant and self-confident professional group of teachers," and felt that she agreed with their contention that "mere obedience to all knowing superiors" was not the chief requirement of a good teacher. Copies of her thesis, "Isolation in the Schools," were read by Federation members and became a source of justification and guidance for their leaders. A statement by John Dewey in the Elementary School Journal of December, 1903 (reprinted in a 1908 "Federation Report to Teachers") was apparently still true and was used in 1913 by the Federation:

> "If there is a single school system in the United States, where there is an official and constitutional provision for submitting questions of method of discipline and teaching and questions of curriculum, textbooks, etc., to the discussion and decision of those actually engaged in the work of teaching, that fact has escaped my notice."

Mrs. Young really tried it.

Just how far the members of the Federation understood Mrs. Young's far-seeing policies and her efforts to improve the quality of teaching is not easy to determine. But they gave her loyal support and warm personal admiration. They felt that she had recognized and suffered from the same selfish forces which they identified as the "enemy." She also recognized the validity of many of the Federation requests and recommended raises for the elementary teachers early in her administration (although the Board said it had no funds). She urged the Board to strengthen the pension fund, and it did vote $50,000 for this purpose in 1911. However, some high-school teachers and principals felt Mrs. Young was more concerned about the elementary teachers than about them.

When Mrs. Young resigned in 1913 in protest against lack of cooperation by a Board which clearly had no intention of reelecting her, the Federation urged her to stay. Mayor Harrison, who admired her and also wished her to remain, produced signed but undated resignations of the Board members he had appointed, and replaced them with appointees more friendly to Mrs. Young. She was then reelected and remained as superintendent until December, 1915.[11] When the Board and the Federation came into final overt, last-ditch conflict in 1915, Mrs. Young openly took the Federation's side during hearings of the Senate committee investigating the Federation. She also appeared publicly at a protest meeting held by the Chicago Federation of Labor. Whatever her private convictions on the training, efficiency, and actual performance of elementary teachers in Chicago, she did not think that enormous classes, low pay, and complete repression were the ways to improve them.

In the period of Mrs. Young's superintendency, the Chicago Teachers Federation meetings and bulletins ranged over a wide variety of subjects of general public interest as well as on specific school problems. Miss Haley was an active leader in the suffrage movement, and its activities were detailed for Federation members. Interest in municipal ownership continued unabated. The Seventeenth Amendment on direct election of Senators, in which William Lorimer's record played a part, got attention. Lorimer had been no friend of the Federation and his downfall and disgrace had proved the merit of their opposition. Discussions of the movement for initiative, referendum, and recall explained the importance of these legislative devices at length. The Federation supported processes of government which would "restore the government to the people." They continued their political action with open opposition to the election of William Hale Thompson in 1915 and thus concluded their seventeenth year in the free-swinging, all-inclusive direct style with which they had begun in 1898.

But in April, 1915, Carter Harrison II was defeated by William Hale Thompson. The Federation had opposed Harrison in 1905, and given measurable support to his opponent, Judge Edward Dunne. In 1915 it supported Harrison in the Democratic primary, because he had given his support to Mrs. Young. Harrison was defeated in the primary by Robert M. Sweitzer—many of whose campaign posters were in German. Harrison's ability to speak German and "sing a German ditty" were not enough to win him the important German vote.

There was nothing in Thompson's or Sweitzer's campaign oratory to encourage the Federation that either would do much to help the schools, although a group of principals gave a dinner for Thompson at the Union League Club. Ugly rumors were current that Thompson's major interest in the schools was to "get rid of the army of Catholic school teachers" and he accused Sweitzer of planning to fill the schools with adherents of the Pope. When Thompson was elected in April, his arrogance toward Mrs. Young aroused the anger of the Federation. The mayor disliked her statement that she had found two dead men and teachers long out of service on the payroll, and that she could obtain no explanation from Board members on the expenditure of $24,000 of payroll funds.[12] A tale is told that when Thompson was a seventh-grade boy at the Skinner School Mrs. Young sent him home for his parents; he never went back, never forgave her, and did not like her personally. In any case, he announced that he would have to approve the appointment of any principals in the schools.

The mayor became indignant when the Federation called his supporters on the Board "lunkheads," and demanded that he not reappoint a Board member named Rothman.[13] The Federation's position against Rothman was based on his effort to take over the teachers' pension funds when he was in the city council, an effort prevented by the Federation with the help of Alderman Charles E. Merriam, who gave public evidence that Rothman had failed to turn over any interest from the large police pension fund when it was under his direction. Other organizations also opposed Rothman's reappointment, but on August 31, 1915, the mayor reappointed him anyway. Mutterings of reprisals against the Federation were being heard at an accelerating rate.

Some unexpected voices were raised in defense of the Federation. On August 25, 1915, the Daily News in an editorial was still against teachers having a union, although it found the Federation was really needed, and that prior to its organization teachers had been "too often victims or beneficiaries of political influence. Give the teachers justice and they won't need a union." The wild talk about getting rid of teachers because of religion had been disturbing to many people. Even the Tribune, on August 14, 1915, praised the Federation for correction of tax abuses, admitting it gave protection to the "most important workers in the social organization."

Loeb Rule–Federation Outlawed

On September 1, 1915, Thompson's Board of Education met, and friction between it and the Federation exploded into open war to the finish. A new rule sponsored by Board member Jacob Loeb was added to the existing regulations. It forbade "Membership by teachers in organizations affiliated with a trade union, or a federation or association of trade unions, as well as teacher organizations which have officers, business agents or other representatives who are not members of the teaching force."[14] Not only the Federation, but the Principals Club and the Illinois State Teachers Association had paid employees, and there were also two small high-school organizations affiliated with the Chicago Federation of Labor. Loeb went out of his way to say publicly that he did not mean to include the Principals Club, ignored the affiliation of the high-school groups, and made it quite clear that the action was aimed at the Federation. Catherine Goggin and Margaret Haley were both paid a teacher's salary by the Federation. This action was not without precedent. The American Federationist for August, 1914, had attacked the Cleveland Board of Education for ruling that joining any part of the American Federation of Labor meant automatic resignation from the school system. There was considerable evidence that, in the Chicago case, the attack was supported by religious as well as labor prejudice.[15] In any case, the dogs of war were loose and running hard.

In nine days an overflow crowd filled the Auditorium Theater in a meeting of protest. Samuel Gompers himself came to speak. Louis Post, a member of the

Dunne Board, and now Assistant Secretary of Labor, came in a hurry from Washington. The newspapers carried first-page headlines on the speeches. "Halt Plot to Make Schools Serf Factories!" "Capitalism in Assault on Public Schools." Miss Haley urged that the people elect the Board of Education so that they might have something to say about their own schools. A Tribune poll taken on September 11 showed that non-Federation teachers were supporting the Federation. The Board refused to put into the record the protest of the high-school union groups.

On September 13, the Chicago Federation of Labor called a meeting of its members at the Auditorium to protest the rule–to which Mrs. Young came and received as hearty an ovation as did Margaret Haley herself. On September 15, the Board sent out blanks to teachers ordering them to sign pledges that they would not contribute to the suit the Federation had announced it would enter and reminding them that they were due for a $2.50 monthly raise. Months later the Federation quietly announced that the teachers had contributed $5,000 immediately. On September 18, the Daily News agreed that insubordinate teachers should be fired, but that the methods being used were "unfortunate." The Illinois Manufacturers Association sent a letter to the Board of Education approving the Loeb Rule. On September 21, Frank Walsh, chairman of the National Industrial Commission appointed by President Wilson came to Chicago to confer with Miss Haley and the officers of the Federation of Labor.

On September 23, the Federation asked for and obtained an injunction against the enforcement of the Loeb Rule. The court held that the rule was arbitrary and would make it impossible for any Chicago teacher to belong to the National Education Association, the Illinois State Teachers Association, the Chicago Men Teachers Union or the Federation of Women High School Teachers. On September 26, Mayor Thompson announced his support of the Loeb Rule, whether the court upheld it or not. Mrs. Ida Fursman, president of the Federation, called Thompson a traitor. Thompson retorted that the members of the Federation were "character assassins" and "lady sluggers"; they had bulldozed public officials long enough and it was "time for them to get to work on the 3 R's."[16]

On September 29, the Board narrowed its rule specifically to the Federation, claiming that the organization was "hostile to discipline, prejudicial to the efficiency of the teaching force, and detrimental to the welfare of the schools." On October 4, the city council met to consider school board appointments. The next morning the Tribune stated that Thompson had barred a crowd of 5,000 teachers, club women, and labor officials from the council meeting and the Herald added that city employees had filled all the seats long before the meeting began. Since no teacher could be dismissed until June by the terms of the 1895 pension law, without an individual trial, the Federation and the Board settled down to an armed truce till an active battle could take place at the end of the year.

The dispute drew nation-wide attention. The School and Society article (October 16, 1915), mentioned earlier, commented:

"Doubtless in its [the Federation's] fights against the encroach-
ments of interests, it has resorted to means not always desirable in
the teaching profession. . . . That teachers have affiliated with union
labor has nothing to do with the present questions, else other groups
of teachers and employees so affiliated would have come under the
rule. Affiliation with labor has brought a higher sense of civic
responsibility, as Mrs. Young pointed out to a state Senate
Committee. United efforts for the general welfare are so much
higher than one person grabbing for himself."

Federation Counterattack

While the Board action occupied the main ring of this circus, a fascinating
little side show was going on—a flank attack. On September 13, 1915, a
committee of five state senators appeared in Chicago to "investigate the conduct
of the Chicago schools." The chairman, Senator Perceval Baldwin, announced
that the committee would hold hearings for four months if necessary. The
committee made no effort to investigate the records or activities of the Board of
Education, but began promptly to summon the officers of the Federation. The
record of the actions of the state senate disclosed no authorization for such a
committee and it was admitted that no appropriation had been made for it,
although it was holding hearings in a luxurious suite in a downtown hotel. Miss
Haley charged that an illegal conspiracy was taking place and quoted two
members of the committee to the effect that a fake motion had been introduced
into the Senate record after the close of the legislative session. The official
printed record of the Laws of Illinois for 1915 shows no authorization for a
committee. Senator Canady, who had informed Miss Haley on September 1 that
something was wrong, said that he had sat in the front row all day June 19,
1915, and was positive no motion for a committee had been introduced or
approved. The record, which he said had been altered, indicated that Senator
Samuel Ettelson had made such a motion on June 19. But the record also
showed Senator Ettelson as absent from Springfield on that day.[17] Ettelson,
attorney for Samuel Insull, had since become Mayor Thompson's corporation
counsel.

Chairman Baldwin and his colleague, George F. Harding, expressed indignation at these accusations and announced they wished to employ an associate of
Jacob Loeb's brother at Sears and Roebuck, a bright young man named Julius
Rosenwald, to make the investigation. Strangely enough, however, no approach
seemed to have been made to Mr. Rosenwald, and the committee had already
hired (out of its non-existent funds) another young man named Meyer Stein.
Stein had sent a letter to committee members to assure them they would be
given their per diem pay and that the costs of the investigation would be taken
care of by unknown philanthropists. On September 17, the Herald stated that

five stenographers from Board of Education offices were being furnished to the committee at Board expense. On September 21, an anonymous circular attacking the Federation, purportedly published by the Chicago Parents' Federation, was distributed at the committee hearings. The circular stated that the Chicago Parents' Federation had been organized the week before and that it had 125,000 members (but no office, no address, nor any names.)[18]

On October 1, 1915, the Baldwin Committee folded up. It duly paid $360 rent to the LaSalle Hotel. Meyer Stein said he received $10 a day for ninety days, although Senator Canady inferred that he had been paid a lot more. In any case, he said, $2,358 had plainly been spent out of funds furnished by someone who wanted to slash the Teachers Federation and Mrs. Young in secret hearings, and he wanted to know where the money came from. At the beginning of the hearings, John Fitzpatrick and Victor Olander had sent all the details of the "fishy" committee hearings to the governor, who was now none other than the Federation's old friend, Edward F. Dunne. The Senate investigation was "postponed" and never heard from again. On October 9, the women suffrage group of which Miss Haley was an officer of the Illinois Political Equality League, demanded that the Senate investigate the matter of the forgery of the Senate records.

Knowledgeable newspaper reporters watched with delight the neatness and dispatch with which Margaret Haley stuck a pin in this paper bomb. They liked her anyway. She made exciting news, gave them reliable facts they could trust, and had spunk enough to say out loud some of the things about the city they would like to say and could not—and which their papers would not have printed had they written them. In a little paper called the Daybook, on September 24, 1915, Carl Sandburg (of the Daily News) wrote:

"Margaret Haley wins again! Often she loses. For fifteen years this one little woman has flung her clenched fists into the faces of contractors, school land lease holders, tax dodgers and their politicians, fixers, go-betweens and stool pigeons. . . . Over the years the Tribune, the News and the ramified gang of manipulators who hate Margaret Haley have not been able to smutch her once in the eyes of decent men and women of this town who do their own thinking. When Billy Hard quits the Tribune as an editorial writer, the first thing he is going to do is write the story of the work of Margaret Haley. He told how the teachers were driven, exploited, low-paid without even the right of petition. He rated her as a brilliant aggressive figure of heroic size. But he couldn't print it in the Tribune."

The Loeb Rule was stopped by injunction and the Senate investigation fizzled out, but the school land issue had raised its ugly head again in October of 1915. The Federation accused the Board of planning to sell some of the outlying school land, taken in when annexation had been made to the city. The defenders of the Federation said that the Loeb Rule, among other things, was intended to clear away the opposition to misuse of the lands. On October 13, the Board debated such sale.[19] One trustee said the land would be worth no more a hundred years from now and another claimed that because it paid no taxes it deterred the improvement of adjoining property—a non sequitur indeed. An editorial in the Herald for October 15, 1915, came close to an attack on the Tribune. It was headed "Look Out of the Window!" and went on "When any member of the School Board [which met in the Tribune Building at Madison and Dearborn] . . . is tempted to consider selling the landed estates of the schools, he should go to the front windows of the Board rooms, look south on Dearborn Street, and think how easy would be the financial going if even one-tenth of that landed estate had not been turned into cash fifty or sixty years ago." Loeb in testifying before the bogus Senate Committee, had been asked by Stein, the investigator with the mysterious philanthropic friends, whether the Federation's statements on school lands were not radical. He replied he didn't know the facts.[20]

In attacking the Board on its school land policy, Miss Haley mentioned the names of current Board members whose firms were defendants in a suit the Federation was bringing to compel taxation of capital stock of some twenty corporations which had been escaping taxation on a valuation of $250 millions a year. One such Board member was president of the so-called "Brick Trust" another, Alfred Urion, the attorney for Armour, was a defense attorney in the suit at the same time he was president of the Board of Education. She did not forget to pay tribute to Mr. Urion, too, as the author of legislation to take control of the pension fund away from the teachers. Mr. Rothman was the law partner of Roy O. West, president of the Board of Review, who would be compelled to assess the corporations if the suit were successful. A nephew of another Board member was the partner of Rothman and West. All had voted for the Loeb Rule. And for good measure she pointed out that the Board resented the part played by the Federation in the failure of the Cooley Bill and its impertinence in talking about municipal ownership of utilities and initiative and referendum.

In January, 1916, the Federation suffered a great loss. On January 4 returning to the hospital where she had been for two weeks, Catherine Goggin was struck by a truck on a dark street and killed. Her body lay in state in the City Council chamber, and on January 29 a notable list of speakers shared in a memorial service, including Mrs. William S. Hefferan, President of the Parent Teacher Association of the State, and William J. Bogan, principal of Lane High School. The newspaper accounts of the accident and ceremonies were uniformly respectful and the Herald, Post, and Journal paid warm tribute to her fairness her patient long years of hard work and the incongruity of her unselfish service and the bitter attacks then being made upon the Federation.

A forty-eight page issue of Margaret Haley's Bulletin on January 27, 1916, i filled with letters from schools, individuals, former Board members, women's clubs, labor organizations, the State Teachers Association, other teacher groups, the city council, and the Board of County Commissioners. Many distinguished people sent letters, including Mrs. Young, who had retired to California. She had known Catherine Goggin as a bright student in her practice school forty years before. She said "Her mind was of the legal type. Whenever the question of teachers' rights arose, she sought instinctively for the foundations on which those rights rested–foundations which had been recognized in the legally constituted courts and in the tribunals of social justice." Superintendent John D. Shoop sent a warm letter to the Federation.

Governor and Mrs. Dunne attended the ceremony in the city council chambers. The governor served as an honorary pallbearer with Judge William E. Dever, Peter Reinberg, President of the County Board, William J. Bogan, Louis Post, Frank P. Walsh, and the president of the Milwaukee Normal School, who was a past president of the N.E.A. Among the active pallbearers were Victor Olander, John Fitzpatrick, a vice president of the American Federation of Labor, and three members of the Chicago Men Teachers Union. The attendance at the ceremonies showed the depth and breadth of the roots of the Federation. The Board of Education had taken on a formidable task to uproot them.

The Federation went ahead with its union activities as if its right to do so had not been challenged. In April, 1916, the Chicago Teachers Federation joined with seven other teacher unions, including the two high-school groups in Chicago, to obtain a national charter from the American Federation of Labor. As the oldest and largest local, the Federation was Local Number One. The San Antonio local had now disappeared. Mrs. Ida Fursman president of the Federation, became a vice president of the new organization. Margaret Haley was asked to serve as organizer and trustee, and did go to Baltimore to help a struggling group of teachers. Just before the granting of a charter to New York Teachers she, with John Dewey, had addressed a meeting of a thousand teachers urging them to organize and affiliate with labor. The New York Times condemned the meeting and said if teachers "didn't like it, they should get out." The majority at the New York meeting, however, voted to organize and affiliate with labor and became Local Five of the American Federation of Teachers.[21] On April 27, 1916, Miss Haley spoke to the union local in Gary, where she opposed Superintendent Wirt, but did not attack the platoon plan.

New organization or not, it was clear that the conflict in Chicago between the Board and Federation was not ended. No teacher's contract extended farther than the end of one school year. In February, 1916, the Illinois State Teachers Association gave complete support to the Federation in its publication, the Illinois Teacher, pointing out that the Federation displayed an active interest "in every movement to advance education in the last 20 years." In its issue of October, 1915, the Association had quoted with disapproval a letter sent by the Illinois Manufacturers Association to the Board of Education and to Mayor Thompson, approving the Loeb Rule, "which would separate the schools from the Teachers' Federation because it was controlled by union labor."

The important women's organizations of the city held a mass meeting on the spoils system in March, 1916. Three recognized leaders discussed the current effort to coerce teachers—Mrs. Joseph K. Bowen of Hull House, Mary McDowell of the University of Chicago Settlement, and Harriet Vittum of the Northwestern University Settlement. On June 17, as the conflict over the status of the Federation approached a climax, another mass meeting of citizens was held in the auditorium. Mary McDowell presided; Jane Addams, Mrs. Willian Hefferan, and Alderman Charles E. Merriam spoke in behalf of the teachers' right to organize as they chose. A four-page statement signed by these persons along with Grace Abbott and Sophonisba Breckinridge of the University of Chicago School of Social Work, and John Fitzpatrick and Victor Olander of the labor movement, was distributed at this meeting. The Chicago high-school unions offered their complete support, financial as well as moral.

Teachers Dismissed Without Cause

In its own behalf, the Federation had sued and obtained a court ruling on May 1, 1916, to the effect that any rule basing employment of teachers on membership in societies or unions was null and void. Whatever happened would not be done on the basis of the Loeb Rule; but no individual teacher had any protection from Board action on June 27, when every teacher would be hired or dropped for the next year. At the Board meeting on that day, Board members were presented with two lists of teachers. One was the printed list of all teachers in service in June, 1916; the other was a typed list of 71 names which were to be voted on separately. Jacob Loeb had just been elected president of the Board. In response to a question from Board member Ralph Otis, as to the reason for the failure to rehire teachers, Loeb answered "You can not force me to give reasons for dismissal if I don't want to. I don't care to discuss each candidate." Five Board members left the room to try to prevent a quorum, but the vote on rehiring the blacklist proceeded anyway. Finally, sixty-eight teachers failed to be rehired, with no reasons given.[22] These included three district superintendents, four of the six elected teacher pension trustees, all of the officers of the Chicago Teachers Federation, and Federation delegates to the Chicago and Illinois State Federations of Labor. Every one of these teachers had superior, excellent, or good ratings or were Federation members who had been promoted to be principal or district superintendent. Twenty-one persons who were not members of the Federation were also on the list; all of these but two were rated inefficient. Loeb openly offered the district superintendencies to Board members for their friends.

With her customary crisp efficiency, Miss Haley took care of the immediate problem first. If four of the six teacher pension trustees were ineligible, the three Board of Education members of the pension board would constitute a majority of the remaining five. Since the current pension board filled any vacancies, the

Board of Education members could appoint teachers they could control. But the teachers who were dismissed were not legally separated from the system until July 1 and could function on the pension board until that time. The old pension board therefore met the evening of June 27, the four resigned as of July 1 and proceeded to elect four more good Federationists to replace those whose status was uncertain. That part of the Board's effort to minimize Federation influence was promptly thwarted.

The newspapers were not as vocal at the exhibition of the raw power of the Board in June as they had been in the previous September, when the Loeb Rule was passed. But the Herald denounced the firing of the 68 as the "greatest single blow at the integrity of popular education Chicago has seen in a generation. Competent teachers were dismissed without accusation, trial or conviction."

When the Federation (as usual) took this case to court, there was a ten-month wait for the disappointing decision, handed down in April, 1917, that

> "The Board has the absolute right to decline to employ or re-employ any applicant for any reason whatever or for no reason at all. The Board is responsible for its action only to the people of the city, from whom, through the mayor, the members have received their appointments. It is no infringement upon the constitutional rights of any one for the Board to decline to employ him as a teacher in the schools. The Board is not bound to give any reason for its action. Questions of policy are for the determination of the Board, and when they have once been determined by it, the courts will not inquire into their propriety."[23]

Miss Haley employed good lawyers who knew they had no specific law on their side, but they had presented arguments which might have justified court action. Six years later, with no legislative change in the specific areas concerned, the court not only *inquired* with a vengeance, but sent several Board members to jail. And even by April, 1917, a law regarding tenure of teachers was in process of being adopted—the unfavorable decision was already outdated.

Chapter 7

A TENURE LAW LEAVES MANY PROBLEMS UNSOLVED

Going back as far as the 1989 Harper Report, there had been discussions of tenure provisions and possible probation periods before tenure was establsihed. The Dawes rule, made by the Board itself in 1900, had required that changes in personnel must be recommended by the superintendent; but if the Board disregarded its own rule, even a direct and outspoken superintendent could do little about it. Superintendent Shoop was ignored completely by the Board in its actions on the sixty-eight. But so many people in the city were concerned it was now possible to get a tenure law of some kind when the legislature met in January, 1917. Not only were the labor forces in Springfield ready to act—with a considerable number of votes ready to be counted—the civic agencies like the women's clubs were behind such legislation and the people who had called the June 17 mass meeting, now organized into a group called the Public Education Association, were effective and outspoken. The directors included Mrs. William Hefferan, president of the Illinois Congress of Parents and Teachers, who had been a student at the normal school under Col. Parker, Mrs. Dunlap Smith, Carl Thompson of the Municipal Ownership League, Grace Abbott, George Mead, and Paul Harper of the University of Chicago. The president was Allen B. Pond of the City Club. In the next year this group issued four carefully reasoned and effective bulletins in behalf of new school legislation.

Teacher Tenure—The Otis Law

But there still were not enough votes to assure passage of any major new law in Springfield until two important additional sources of political power were added. Ralph Otis, a Board member who had voted for the Loeb Rule but not for firing the sixty-eight, put the able school board attorney, Angus Shannon, at work drafting an act which embodied many of the recommendations of the Harper Report of 1898. The Board as a whole did not sponsor the bill openly, at least at first, but Otis and some other individual Board members did. Not only did Angus Shannon work on it, but his frequent opponent, the able Federation attorney, Isaiah Greenacre, made some suggestions as did the officers of the Chicago Principals Club. Miss Haley was careful that the legislation was not identified as a Federation product for two reasons. One, that it was better if it were based on a principle, not as a defense of any one group; and two, that Speaker Shanahan of the House of Representatives had said if she had anything to do with the proposed legislation he'd be against it. But Victor Olander and the State Federation of Labor played an active part in its passage.

What Miss Haley did to help obtain tenure was more important than getting Federation credit for new legislation. Perhaps Speaker Shanahan did not like her, but a great many aldermen in the Chicago city council did. She had several times been able to get resolutions passed by the council when the current mayor did not approve. She managed now to get the council to direct its Committee on Schools, Fire, Police and Civil Service to recommend the preparation of new state legislation for the reorganization of the school system, an action which the City Council voted to approve December 7, 1916.[1] At public sessions of the committee held in October and November, a whole procession of education experts expressed in no uncertain terms their surprise at, and disapproval of, the doings of the Chicago Board. The content of the proposed legislation was not entirely the same as that worked out by Otis, but the ills it was to cure were the same, plainly set out for all to see. Miss Haley had the effective help of Alderman Charles E. Merriam, whose influence is indicated by the part played in the hearings by Charles H. Judd of the University of Chicago. Miss Haley did not like Dr. Judd.

Invited to appear were Superintendent William H. Maxwell of New York City, Superintendent Blewett of St. Louis, Superintendent Spaulding of Minneapolis, Superintendent Chadsey of Detroit, Leonard Ayres of the Russell Sage Foundation, who had been in charge of the schools of Puerto Rico, and Dr. Charles H. Judd. Superintendent Maxwell was ill, but sent a statement. The others appeared. Chadsey, Spaulding, and Ayres urged that the superintendent be in control of the entire system, with a definite term set by law, and that there be a small elected Board. Maxwell agreed that the Board should be elected and that teachers should have tenure after three years. Dr. Judd said ratings must be open to teachers and that indefinite tenure for teachers was necessary. Judd had just finished a survey of the Cleveland schools, and pointed out that there, as in Chicago, no clear distinction between authority of Board and superintendent existed. Spaulding objected to the power of the numerous standing committees of the Board and urged that teachers 'councils be set up. He was quoted in the Tribune of October 29, 1916, as testifying that he knew of no Board of Education that dictated to teachers as to what organizations they might belong.

The report included twelve criticisms of the Chicago Board of Education. It was too large. It attempted actual administration of the schools. The administration was divided among Board, superintendent, secretary, business manager, and separate Board committees which acted independently of the Board—actually ordering educational supplies without consulting anyone else. There was confusion between the authority of the Board and that of the city council. The Board was responsible to the mayor and not to the people. The annual election of the superintendent made it necessary for him to line up votes for reelection every year. The Board did not consult the educational staff in making decisions. The Board made a grave mistake in destroying continuity of teachers who were giving satisfactory service. Controlling the kinds of organizations to which teachers might belong was not a proper function of a Board of Education. Dismissal of teachers without charge or hearing was unanimously denounced. Machinery for recording the efficiency of teachers and of the school system was not being used.

To remedy these defects the report recommended legislation with the following provisions:

1. Election of a Board of Education of seven members for six-year terms, at a salary of $5,000 a year, on a non-partisan basis.
2. Power of eminent domain and control of choice of sites for school buildings in the hands of the Board, not the city council.
3. Appointment by the Board of an attorney, not under the superintendent.
4. Use by the Board of disinterested experts to report to the Board on the efficiency of the schools.
5. A four-year contract for a general superintendent of schools to organize and administer the entire system.
6. Right of dismissal of the superintendent after charges presented ninety days before decision, and answered by him.
7. Enactment of an administrative code to define functions of the superintendent and other educational employees.
8. Provision by ordinance for self-governing councils which might recommend directly to the superintendent.
9. Authorization of a standard salary schedule for all employees.
10. Tenure for teachers after a three-year probationary period.
11. Abolition of standing committees of the Board.
12. Biennial budgeting of school expenditures.
13. Increase in current resources through legislative action to permit use of modern educational methods, particularly for educational purposes.
14. Initiation by the superintendent only, of appointment and dismissal of teachers, subject to the approval of the Board.[2]

Miss Haley attended the sessions and reported them to the teachers. She is the only person recorded as asking questions at the hearings. These dealt with the method of electing councils in Minneapolis, specifically as to whether elementary teachers had their own council, whether a superintendent could stop calling the councils, whether the councils had a printed record in the records of the Board of Education, whether they met on school time, and whether the right of hearing before dismissal was a matter of law or of Board rule only.

Legislation embodying these specific proposals was drafted, introduced, and supported in the legislature by Alderman Robert Buck, chairman of the council committee which had made the study and the recommendations. Otis' proposal, drafted by the Board attorney, was also presented. Senator Baldwin, of investigating committee fame, presented a third. The Public Education Association printed a careful comparison of all three bills.[3] In the main, the Association supported the Otis proposal, but urged an examiners' commission, more power for the superintendent than the original bill included, and a clearer statement of what was meant by efficiency in teaching.

The Otis Bill allowed the Board to spend 75 percent of the anticipated real-estate taxes for a year before they were collected during the next year. The Buck Bill required setting up councils; the others did not. The Baldwin Bill allowed the Board to sell school lands without council approval and to borrow in anticipation of taxes not yet collected; it had no tenure for teachers or term for superintendent. The Buck Bill set up a non-partisan paid elected Board of seven, a superintendent with a four-year term in control of the entire system, but did not allow borrowing on future tax collections, which the Board was already beginning to do. It required that all Board meetings be public.

The Otis Bill passed. It provided for an eleven-member Board, appointed, not paid, with five-year terms. It gave the superintendent a four-year term, but no specific authority over the business manager or attorney, who reported directly to the Board. Teachers were given indefinite tenure after three years' probation with specific procedure for dismissal. The Board could borrow 75 percent of the taxes to be collected the following year. The law gave the Board the right of eminent domain. The superintendent, and two persons nominated by him to the Board, constituted a Board of Examiners. The city council was to levy taxes, "upon demand and under the direction of the Board," but would have no control over school lands or purchases of lands. A budget should be prepared and public hearings held upon it. Some specific powers were outlined for the Board and for the superintendent.

The Otis law had not been passed and signed by June 1917, but it was quite clear that some legislation giving teachers tenure would become a reality. The salaries of the ousted Federation members had been paid by members of the Federation and of the small high-school union locals, and the high-school groups had collected $200 to keep one of the dismissed district superintendents in Springfield working on legislation. On June 13, 1917, the Tribune carried a story that thirteen of the twenty-one Board members were now willing to take the Federationists back. When the time for reelection came, forty-nine were reinstated, including all those who had been dropped because of Federation membership.

By this time President Loeb and Mayor Thompson had sharply different attitudes toward World War I, which had broken out in April. Mayor Thompson announced that Chicago was the sixth German city of the world, that he hated the British and opposed the draft. Jacob Loeb, on the other hand, began looking for teachers who were pacifists and was horrified at the Tribune story that a spelling book used in the schools contained a eulogy of the Kaiser.[4] In any case Loeb began to go down paths divergent from those of the mayor and never really became a reliable ally of Thompson thereafter. Whether this break played a part in the rehiring of the Federationists is not clear.

Federation Loses Ground

Earlier in the spring of 1917 there were rumors that Loeb had proposed peace with Miss Haley if she would leave her labor affiliations. Miss Haley denied this categorically. But on May 21, 1917, the Federation did withdraw from the American Federation of Teachers, the Chicago Federation of Labor, the Illinois Federation of Labor, and the Women's Trade Union League. There is disagreement as to why. Miss Haley herself said that John Fitzpatrick advised her to disaffiliate.[5] Some say she did make a deal with Loeb to get the teachers back. Others say the Federation had lost members and spent so much money on suits and salaries for the suspended teachers, that it simply could not go on paying per capita to all the labor groups. It had lost half its membership in 1915 and 1916.[6] The executive secretary of the American Federation of Teachers, who was a member of the Chicago Men Teachers Union, stated that she left because she felt that winning local issues was more important than slowly building a national organization. When the Loeb Rule was finally deleted from the Rules of the Board of Education in 1924, the Federation made no move to resume its labor affiliations.

The last assumption seems borne out by the fact that the Federation also withdrew from the National Education Association a few months later. Several of its members, and particularly Miss Haley, had been active in the N.E.A. since 1901. In 1904 she had been the first woman to address the N.E.A. when she urged support for strong local organizations which could fight for tenure against low salaries and "factoryization of education" with the "same courage and persistence which labor unions have used."[7] In 1903 she had been largely responsible for a resolution, printed in a long report in 1905, which set in motion the study of teachers' salaries. She had helped in 1912 to engineer the nomination from the floor of Ella Flagg Young as president of the N.E.A. and had organized the campaign which elected her in opposition to the candidate presented by the official nominating committee. In that year, also, she presented a petition for a new department of the N.E.A. to be known as the Class Room Teachers Department, created in 1913. She supported for its president Florence Rood, who later became president of the St. Paul Teachers Union and, in 1932, of the American Federation of Teachers. In 1914 she had spoken at the N.E.A. convention on teacher councils.[8]

When Miss Haley withdrew in 1918 she gave as her reason the change in N.E.A. policy which turned over the choice of voting representatives from each state to the state associations in that state. The Federation had been active in the Illinois State Teachers Association, had worked to elect Ella Flagg Young its president in 1910, and had earnestly built up its membership in Chicago. But as the state association had begun to grow in power, the control of that power began to be concentrated in the hands of administrators rather than teachers. In 1916 the Federation had joined a loosely knit group of local organizations like their own, which assembled each year as the N.E.A. was meeting and was the backbone of the Class Room Teachers Department. It was called the League of Teacher Associations, and in this the Federation remained.

To this group of organizations Miss Haley sent a letter on May 27, 1918, to explain the reason for her withdrawal from the N.E.A. She quoted the recommendation, to be voted at the 1918 N.E.A. meeting, over control of the N.E.A. by a small group of delegates to be elected by the voting delegates of the component state associations. She cited the fact that while the Illinois State Teachers Association had 1,360 persons, mostly class room teachers, in attendance at its annual meeting in December, 1917, only 167 had been chosen voting delegates by the twelve divisions of the state. Of these 167, 42 were politically elected county superintendents, 53 were city superintendents, 36 were principals and only 14 were elementary teachers—although they made up the bulk of the members. These 167 were the only voting delegates from Illinois to the N.E.A., no matter who attended. When the N.E.A. based its membership on dues collected by state associations, its membership grew from 10,105 in 1918 to 52,850, but the voting delegates of the N.E.A. included very few class room teachers.[9]

Miss Haley had done as much as anyone to get some voice for class room teachers in the N.E.A. She was completely discouraged by the freezing of control in the hands of administrators and withdrew from the N.E.A. Her letter pointed out

> "It required years of struggle to get the N.E.A. to give any consideration whatever to the living and working conditions of the class room teachers and to recognize salaries, pensions and tenure as legitimate subjects for discussion. It actually took a revolution in 1903 to secure the appointment of a committee on Salary, Tenure and Pensions. For the first 50 years of the N.E.A., no class room teacher was ever elected to any office."

Apparently the leaders of the Federation felt the effort to function effectively in the American Federation of Teachers and in the National Education Association required more of them than they could now give. From 1916 to 1925 there were no issues of the Federation bulletin. Federation members took their turn as leaders in the League of Teacher Associations, and helped in the preparation of its strong report on teachers' councils in 1923.

But affiliated or not, Margaret Haley was still a part of the labor movement in Chicago, as the smaller high-school unions found out when they wanted one thing and she wanted another, even though they were paying per capita and she was not. Miss Haley was one of the moving spirits and skilled leaders in the new Chicago Farmer Labor Party, organized in 1918. She was on the executive committee which nominated John Fitzpatrick for mayor—and got for him 8 percent of the total vote cast, in 1919.[10] Her efforts in Fitzpatrick's behalf obviously did not raise her stock with William Hale Thompson, who won.

The Otis Law passed. The teachers had tenure. Jacob Loeb was a guest of the Federation at its annual luncheon in June, 1918, as a sign of peace. The Federation had won its fight for continued existence—and probably for continued labor affiliation, had it so chosen. Out of the struggle had come a tenure law for teachers, a weakening of direct and open control by the mayor and city council, and some strengthening of the power of the superintendent. In spite of the recommendation for direct election of the Board in the Buck Bill, the Federation had supported the Otis legislation, which did not give the superintendent control of the whole system. The Federation had opposed a recommendation to this end, when it was made in the Harper Report of 1898, because they feared an autocratic superintendent. The other teachers' groups in Chicago, the Illinois State Teachers Association, the Illinois Federation of Labor, and most of the civic groups in Chicago had also supported the new legislation, and had defended the right of teachers to organize as they chose.

It appeared that the schools of Chicago could now face an era of peace and concentrate on improving the services of the schools. Nothing could be farther from the truth. The new legislation sowed dragon's teeth, whose offspring, nurtured by William Hale Thompson, threw the schools into chaos for five years.

Competing Boards of Education

On June 18, 1917, Mayor Thompson appointed an entirely new Board of Education to comply with the Otis Law, which had reduced the membership of the Board from twenty-one to eleven, and had changed the length of their terms from four years to five. He reappointed only two of the previous Board members. One of these was Jacob Loeb. The council approved the eleven names; but after a vote to reconsider the approval was passed, no action was taken to vote upon approving them again, so that their status became uncertain. However, the eleven new members did take possession of the Board rooms, elected the business manager and attorney required by the Otis Law, and proceded to act as if they were the Board.

The old Board of twenty-one took the case to court and were reinstated as the legal Board on June 20, 1918, since the State Supreme Court held that the eleven had not been legally approved by the city council the second time. The twenty-one served as the Board until May 27, 1919, when Mayor Thompson appointed eleven more members. Jacob Loeb had been legally a member of the old Board and also on the original list of eleven; when the mayor made new appointments in 1919 he omitted Loeb, who then sued to keep his place. The court said he had been legally approved once for the new Board of eleven in 1917, and by suing he won his right on October 16, 1919, to continue as a Board member, even though not on the 1919 list of appointees. On October 20, 1919, the council approved the inclusion of Loeb on the Board, and there were for the first time since 1917, eleven whose legal membership on the Board was not questioned.[11] By 1919 Loeb had become the leader of the anti-Thompson faction on the old Board, and, from Thompson's point of view, had committed a grave crime in suing for reinstatement.

Superintendent John Shoop, who had been assistant superintendent to Mrs. Young, and succeeded her in office, was ill for most of his three years of service. He played practically no part in the duel between the Federation and the Board of Education or in the passage of the Otis Law. The Board ignored him in its action dismissing Federation leaders, and he offered no protest against this blatant infraction of the Board's own rule, adopted in 1900, that the superintendent should recommend changes in personnel.

Superintendent Shoop died in the fall of 1918 after the old Board of twenty-one had been returned to power in June. Loeb was responsible for the appointment of a committee of citizens to recommend a successor to Shoop, and for ignoring Thompson completely in the process of choosing the superintendent of schools. A committee of nine civic leaders recommended Charles E. Chadsey, Superintendent of Schools in Detroit, who had appeared at the City Council hearings in October of 1916. There he had spoken for a superintendent with power over the whole system, for civil service for all non-teaching employees, for an elected school board, and against a board as large as twenty-one (which was then also the number of Board members in Detroit). He had also spoken for tenure for teachers, and said that he would be willing to accept councils if his teachers to organize as they chose. The Board of twenty-one approved his employment as superintendent in March, 1919.

When Thompson ran for reelection in April, 1919, he promised to "kick Chadsey out."[12] When the third Thompson Board of eleven, which did not include Loeb, took over in May, 1919, it claimed the Otis Law was not in effect in March, 1919; it locked Chadsey out of his office and elected Peter Mortenson superintendent. Chadsey naturally said the law had been passed in 1917 and that of course he had a four-year term. In November, 1919, the Circuit court ruled that Chadsey was right and he was returned as superintendent. Then the Board on November 25 took away all the authority given to him by the Otis Law. Loeb, by this time reinstated, objected and defended Chadsey.

On November 26, 1919, Chadsey submitted a letter of resignation contending it was obvious that the Board would spare no effort to prevent his rendering any service to the schools of Chicago. He had taken his case to court to establish "as a matter of law that municipal political office holders have no right to interfere with the administration of the public school system." The courts levied fines and imposed jail sentences up to five days on the six members of the Board who had voted to render Chadsey's service futile, and on the Board attorney.[13] The Tribune commented that "The life and works of the school board proceed with the restraint of a Hottentot war dance." Mortenson was reappointed superintendent—but with a damaged reputation, as he was accused by the court of cooperating with the Board in the treatment accorded Chadsey.

The teacher organizations did nothing to help Chadsey. The Federation was suspicious of him because Loeb championed him so strongly. The Principals Club was annoyed at him because he refused to accept the traditional requirement of experience as an elementary school principal before appointment to a high-school principalship. The high-school teachers were snapped at by Chadsey when representatives of the voluntary high-school council urged him to do something about the choice of text books: he told them to be "responsible and study curriculum." By that time it was probably quite clear to him that he could do nothing to control Board manipulation of the choice of texts. Chadsey went off disgusted, to the calm and quiet of the office of Dean of the School of Education of the University of Illinois.

Creation of Teachers Councils

After four competing school boards and two in-and-out superintendents had run the Chicago schools for two and one-half years, there seemed to be an opportunity for peace. Superintendent Mortenson, under a cloud of criticism for his cooperation with the Thompson "Solid Six" in their persecution of Chadsey, at least tried to placate the teachers. The committee of high-school organizations which had been rebuffed by Chadsey on the text book problem came back to Mortenson with mounting problems in the too rapidly expanding high schools, and suggested that he reinstate and encourage the teachers' councils which had been practically inactive since Mrs. Young's day. The councils met only on call of the superintendent—and Shoop never called them. The high-school group had met on its own authority occasionally, but lacked status with any official body.

On March 12, 1919, the Board authorized the high-school teachers to form a council.[14] On August 31, 1921, Superintendent Mortenson recommended to the Board that councils for all teachers be set up on school time, as had the local councils in Mrs. Young's time, and that it be mandatory for the superintendent to call the councils at regular intervals. The Board approved the recommendations on September 15 and on October 11, and the Superintendent's *Bulletin* set up the framework of this new council system. The local school councils met every five weeks and elected their delegates to the thirty-nine group councils.

The central council was elected by the group councils and met with the superintendent every five weeks. The local and group councils met at 1:30 on Friday, on school time. The central council, though including five organization representatives without vote, was reorganized on a purely numerical and regional basis; but many other organization leaders were elected in their own schools as local school representatives.

The high-school teachers had plenty of problems. Enrolment in secondary schools had risen from 8,000 in 1898 and 12,700 in 1907, to 25,322 in 1915 and 31,500 by 1920. Since the per capita cost for high schools was more than twice that of elementary, pressure on the inelastic income of the schools was reaching a breaking point. In 1913 the Board of Education lengthened the high-school day to make it six clock hours, one hour longer than the elementary schools, and required that high-school teachers teach six classes instead of five, the norm for high schools all over the country. Since this arrangement saved salaries simply by not adding approximately one-fifth more teachers to the high-school teaching force, the high-school teachers were given a ten percent increase in pay (but a 20 percent increase in work). The teaching loads of high-school teachers in the early 1890's had been lower than those of elementary; but now there was little difference. In 1908 the new North Central Association of Schools and Colleges had refused approval to two of the Chicago high schools, on grounds of too large classes, inadequate space, and inefficient teaching. Just what changes were made to secure re-approval in 1910 are not recorded. In 1912 a group of men high-school teachers, and in 1914 a group of women, had followed the Federation example of affiliation with the American Federation of Labor and had enlisted the active support of the Chicago Federation of Labor in their efforts to improve conditions in the high schools. Members of both these small union groups belonged to and worked within the High School Teachers Club.

The High School Council held referenda on fourteen items between 1919 and 1922. Among these were record keeping, simplification of class books and report cards, counting of part-time teachers in making up class size averages, a five-hour, not a six-hour day, a maximum salary of $4,500 (for five hours), teacher participation in choosing a broader list of text books, freedom to choose books best suited to students, sabbatical leave, and more clerical help. Besides these referenda, resolutions on many other subjects were sent to the superintendent. Some of these dealt with the use of intelligence tests, vocational guidance, articulation of high and elementary schools, class size, control of pupils in lunch rooms, increasing use of portables, and "senseless questionnaires." [15]

The Elementary Council resolutions indicated their grief that money was not available to reduce the theoretical average elementary class load from 44 to 43, but rejoiced that more classes for non-English speaking pupils had been provided. Since children entered any time at age six, not just at the beginning of the semester, the councils urged a change in state law to allow them to enter before six, so that new pupils would not disrupt the large classes all year long. They reported "No progress on class interruptions," but enough history books for all children would soon be forthcoming. Electric lighting was promised for all schools as soon as possible.

The superintendent suggested to the Elementary Council that it approve of requiring two years of Normal training for all teachers entering the elementary schools; at present some were being admitted only on "outside experience." The elementary councils recommended that elementary teachers with degrees be allowed to teach in the high schools without examinations. In 1923 the councils asked that first-grade class size be kept down to 40, and that other elementary classes not go above an average of 44.6 More special rooms for sub-normal children were urged. They also asked for special Normal classes in the summer for experienced teachers, "as many of the teachers in the Chicago schools have not had the opportunity of receiving the training given by the Normal College."[16]

Several of the local council groups urged Mortenson to continue as superintendent when he had announced his resignation. On January 13, 1923, all group councils had taken action

> "to express their appreciation of the services rendered to the children of Chicago and to the cause of education by Superintendent Peter A. Mortenson, who, through the Class-Room Teachers Councils, is utilizing for the benefit of the school system, the collective experience of the classroom teachers, gained by daily personal contact with the children."

In March, 1923, the Federation protested against the Board threat to remove Mortenson.

Jail Sentences for Board Members

Superintendent Mortenson must have been particularly pleased by these warm words, because very few people beside the teachers had many encomiums for him. Reprimanded sharply and publicly by the court which sentenced the Board's "Solid Six" and their attorney, for playing along with them in the conspiracy against Chadsey, Mortenson was in no position to oppose the Thompson Board in its wild career of looting the schools between 1919 and 1923, although he did not use what little authority he had to stop them. An era of lawlessness ushered in by the beginning of prohibition in January, 1920, ended with Robert Crowe, Thompson's candidate for state's attorney, turning against Thompson. Crowe used the scandalous doings of the Thompson-controlled school Board, among other items, to attack him and his erstwhile supporter, Fred Lundin.[17]

There seemed to be little limit to what the Board tried to do, or little to what it actually accomplished for its own ends. It attempted to get additional authorization from the legislature to sell the remaining Loop and other school lands, and told the Federation and other groups to stop opposing the legislation or their salaries would be cut. All the teachers' groups opposed the legislation and were able to defeat it in the State Senate after it passed the House. Then the Board turned to the "honest graft" system of George Washington Plunkett of Tammany, tipping off their friends to proposed school sites so they could buy the land cheap and sell to the Board at high cost. The most flagrant example of this was the profit made on the Wendell Phillips High School land. In March, 1920, the superintendent asked for property at the rear of the Phillips building for athletics, as the school had no space around it. When the estate which owned the property was approached, it had already sold the land for $65,000. The Board bought it for $95,000 and allowed $100,000 in rents from the crowded buildings on the site to be collected by a third party, a buyer of the buildings only. School board members who apparently had been shut out of this arrangement brought it to the attention of State's Attorney Crowe.

There were other kinds of graft. Non-existent companies got huge contracts. School principals were directed by calls from Board members to order unwanted, unneeded equipment at quadrupled prices. Furniture was taken from schools to Board members' summer homes and replaced at such costs as $107 for one kitchen table. In 1921 the Board charged $8,714,065 to unitemized "incidentals." The politically oriented school engineers, to obtain salary raises, were accused of presenting $78,000 to Board members—supposedly in a silver tea pot.[18]

Civic Organizations Demand a Grand Jury Investigation

The Municipal Voters League, the Women's City Club, and other civic groups demanded a grand jury investigation and got it in May, 1922. Hearings continued through August. State's Attorney Crowe was harassed by lack of funds and considered asking for contributions to complete the investigation. The grand jury indicted a former Board president, a former vice president, the attorney (Mr. Bither had already served a jail sentence in the Chadsey case) and forty political favorites involved in illegal deals. Two school engineers were sent to jail for refusing to testify. The Federation protested their return to service in September, 1922, with full back pay.

Serious damage had been done to Mayor Thompson's status, even if the Board members had not been sentenced, as they were. Lundin deserted Thompson. Thompson's candidate for governor, Len Small, was compelled after a court trial to return $600,000 in interest on state funds. Newspapers denounced the waste and corruption of the Thompson regime, and repeated the charge that Thompson and Lundin had said to school trustees, "We're at the feed box now—and we're going to feed." Lundin was indicted for heading a group of twenty-three conspirators including some school board members who had robbed the school treasury of over a million dollars, and collected rake offs and campaign funds from contractors. Jacob Loeb testified against Lundin, giving details of Lundin's activities during the time of his own collaboration with the Thompson faction. Lundin was not convicted, but he left town. Thompson, left holding all the bags, announced he would not run for mayor in 1923 but would labor in obscurity for all the people.

Reform Board of Education

The Democratic candidate for mayor in 1923 was a judge with an impeccable reputation, William E. Dever. He had been induced by Graham Taylor of Chicago Commons to run for alderman in 1902. He knew the city and he knew the workings of the political system. But he found, as an alderman remarked forty years later, that "Chicago wasn't ready for reform." He tried to break up the syndicated bootlegging, knowing that ward committeemen and legislators were deep in it. Murders occurred in job lots, including that of an assistant state's attorney (of whose death Al Capone was accused, but not convicted). Dever urged municipal ownership of street cars, and lost the referendum. But he gave the school system four years of freedom from political interference, appointing seven competent, concerned citizens to the Board. The new Board made every effort to locate a new superintendent who would use this freedom to strengthen the educational authority of his office, to stop the waste of funds, and to improve educational standards.

William A. McAndrew was chosen for the superintendency. Mr. McAndrew was not new to the Chicago schools. In 1887 he had been one of the five teachers and later the principal at Hyde Park High School, where he had demonstrated his independence of political pressure by refusing to pass a politician's son, and in 1891 had been dismissed as a result. Rumor had it that the Board had been divided on his selection. Some members had preferred President William B. Owen of the Normal School, and some, William J. Bogan, principal of Lane High. But the teachers had approved of McAndrew's coming, the Elementary Teachers' Council giving him a warm welcome on March 22, 1924.[19] Miss Haley expressed her approval of his appointment. McAndrew had been assistant superintendent in the New York City schools and had experience in a big city system. Hope was expressed by many teachers and citizens that at last the schools were on their way to improving the education of children. In 1922 a new salary schedule went into effect, which gave a ten-step schedule for elementary teachers from $1,500 to $2,500 and for high-school teachers from $2,000 to $3,800, the most solid, permanent salary gains Chicago teachers had had in half a century. They did not know, of course, how permanent it was to be; it was not paid in full for twelve of the next twenty-one years. But in 1922 it was a hopeful sign of real concern for justice to the teachers.

McAndrew's Plans

The new superintendent entered upon his new responsibility with brisk efficiency on February 1, 1924. He made his goals plain early. He wanted greater efficiency in educational administration from top to bottom—and no nonsense about it. He made very clear that the present standards of achievement were not acceptable. To improve these standards he intended to have every teacher and every school meet certain fixed criteria, and set up a "line and staff" system of "close supervision" to see that they did. Teachers' meetings on school time (without their principals), telling the superintendent what to do, had no place in this scheme of things, nor did organizations not meeting on school time. Anyone foolish enough to use political influence would get nowhere.

> "Let's get a good junior high school system going, use the space in the overcrowded elementary schools effectively, get visiting teachers in the elementary schools, deans of boys and girls in the high schools, set up ways of measuring our successes in instruction, eliminate dead wood in the teaching staff, get teachers to school on time, get some buildings built, use the schools 12 months a year, tell the public what the schools need, and be on our way to having a good school system. . . ."

was in effect his program.[20] It seemed an eminently reasonable one to him, and he said so, without consulting his Board, the teachers' groups, or anyone else. After all, he was the one who knew what good schools were, and he was going to do his best to get them. Others had made a pretty bad mess of it already, and he was there to straighten things out for everybody.

McAndrew set about making changes immediately. A junior high-school system was to take care of seventh-, eighth-, and ninth-grade children, and new buildings for them would reduce the overcrowding in the other schools. Crowded elementary schools were to be organized on the "platoon system" (which had begun in Gary) so that children could be in school more hours in the day than double shifts allowed. School time must not be wasted on meetings of teachers, really of no value in improving the schools—which needed improvement so badly. But each of these three objectives was not to be accomplished by a simple order from the top. Each of them had deep roots in the long history of Chicago schools, and each had explosive possibilities. By June each of these issues had indeed exploded and the reverberations lasted not only as long as McAndrew, but for years thereafter.

Chapter 8

MODERNIZATION OF SCHOOLS
ORDERED BY SUPERINTENDENT

Junior high schools were not a new idea in Chicago, nor the United States. In 1918 four junior high or intermediate schools had been approved and set up in Chicago, and were in operation in 1924.[1] In December, 1923, before McAndrew was installed, the Chicago Board of Education had set up a committee of its own to study the possibility of using the junior high-school plan in Chicago. The committee recommended favorably upon its adoption on May 14, 1924. In 1913 William B. Owen, later president of the Chicago Normal College, had been chairman of an N.E.A. committee which heartily recommended the use of the junior high plan. In the 1916 survey of Cleveland schools made by Dr. Charles H. Judd of the University of Chicago the advantages of the junior high school system in Cleveland were stressed. The report pointed out that seventh- and eighth-grade pupils are physically and mentally different from those of lower grades, that the junior high school can offer a more stimulating course of study and experience, and it has a higher holding power at the eighth- and ninth-grade levels than the 8-4 system. Mrs. William H. Hefferan, the Board member with the most background on schools and a history of friendly attitude toward the teachers' organizations and councils, was enthusiastic about the junior highs.

Junior High Schools

Then why an explosion? It did not start with a big bang, but gathered force as discussion developed. Seven weeks after his arrival, Superintendent McAndrew met with the Elementary General Council. It reported to him that five of the group councils approved the introduction of junior high schools, six opposed, and twenty-eight asked for answers to the following questions:

1. What were the essential features of a junior high school system?
2. Will the junior high make a cleavage along class lines, becoming a substitute for senior high?
3. Can a junior high be incorporated in an elementary school?
4. Does it hold children in school and does it increase senior high failures?
5. What teachers will be eligible for appointment to junior high?

The superintendent stated that definite answers to these questions were not yet ready, but that the forthcoming report of the Board's committee would contain some of them. He explained that a junior high in general is not exclusively preparation for senior high, but is also for the child who must leave school after ninth grade. But it was not intended, he assured them, to cause class cleavage. Since elementary schools do not have enough children at the seventh- and eighth-grade levels to offer them a varied program, they would be better off in a school which could. He gave the members of the council a list of references on junior high schools for them to study, and added a characteristically acid touch in answer to the question on high-school failures. There were no data on the effect of junior high schools on senior high failures, but, said he, "High school teachers will knock the work of elementary teachers from any grade. Some of them now in Chicago say that the elementary teachers do not know their business." As for eligibility for junior high appointment, that would be determined in the future.

On April 9, the superintendent sent the secretary of the Elementary General Council a letter saying he saw no reason for holding their meetings on school time, and on April 22 he refused to call them at the usual time, as set down in the rules of the Board. The Board attorney ruled that he was obliged to call them, and he did so in May. When the elementary group councils then met in May, thirty-five of the thirty-nine councils presented resolutions urging that the "fullest publicity be given to all the essential features of the proposed Junior High School for Chicago, for public discussion of the same, to the end that parents and teachers may know what is proposed, and as far as possible, what results may be expected from the working out of this system." These resolutions were unanimously approved by the General Council and sent to the Board and to the superintendent, who still made no answer to the questions asked him in March.

On May 14 the Board referred these resolutions to the Committee on School Administration. The Board committee on that day published its report recommending the adoption of the junior high-school plan, and authorized the printing of 10,000 copies. Then, without further ado, the Board voted to install junior high schools throughout the system as soon as it could do so. The superintendent named five elementary schools to be remodeled immediately as junior high schools, appointed a district superintendent to administer them, and was authorized to provide for the transfer of their pupils. A motion made by Mr. James Mullenbach to postpone action on adoption of junior highs was lost.

McAndrew's obvious insistence on making changes quickly without bothering to answer questions raised by teachers (or anyone else) aroused resentment and suspicion. Rumors that he had been brought to Chicago to subdue teachers, and to support the domination of the schools by business interests, spread rapidly.[2] McAndrew's summary disposal of the whole council tradition antagonized most of the teaching force. His statements to the Councils in March on the provision for children who "must leave school at 9th grade" antagonized organized labor and reopened scars left by the fifteen-year-old bitter fight on the Cooley plan. The Tribune, the Association of Commerce, and business groups generally supported the junior high plan.

In June the Chicago Federation of Labor asked for a public hearing and one was held. After making an extensive study of junior high schools in other cities, Victor Olander suggested that the junior high-school plan be considered an experiment. He adduced evidence from Rochester, New York, where he alleged it had produced a definite class-conscious division based on "card catalogue intelligence tests" which clearly discriminated against lower-income working people.[3] Neither Board nor superintendent offered comment or assurances on this point at the hearing or at any time, and since the forces supporting the plan were those which had for years endorsed the Cooley plan, the labor groups from that time on opposed the plan as a deliberate effort to terminate children's educational opportunities and shunt them into lower paying jobs. The city council sent a communication to the Board from its June meeting listing complaints of parents from several wards that no announcement had been made as to where their children, displaced by the five new junior highs, would go. At a 46th ward meeting Miss Haley spoke against and the new junior high district superintendent, Joseph Gonnelly, for them. The alderman of the 46th ward, Oscar Nelson, who was also vice president of the Chicago Federation of Labor, urged the Board not to put the new system into effect until there had been much more discussion with the public. Superintendent McAndrew calmly ignored all of this activity and made no comments at all.

The teachers were concerned by the methods used to "put over" the junior high plan and by the possibility of its abuse. After all, they had opposed the Cooley plan for years. Victor Olander was invited by the teacher union groups to speak at a mass meeting which filled the Auditorium in October, 1924. He pointed out possible dangers which were clearly not imaginary, since the plan was openly advocated by powerful groups which had worked so long for the Cooley plan. McAndrew's unwillingness to discuss these issues intensified suspicions of his real intentions. The Federation of Women High School Teachers supported the junior high school on the basis of its own survey but had warned of possible misuse.[4] The Federation of Men Teachers followed Olander's original suggestion that the plan be considered an experiment and not adopted for the whole system at this time. But the Chicago Teachers Federation opposed the whole plan from beginning to end, and Miss Haley's flat and unyielding opposition to it—and to succeeding policies—became a major factor in McAndrew's career as superintendent in Chicago.

The Federation gave many reasons for its unqualified opposition. It objected to the failure of the superintendent to answer the questions sent him by the General Elementary Council. It objected to his scheduling an examination for junior high-school teachers in the summer of 1924 (without any authorization by the Board), calling it a threat to tenure. The certificate for elementary teachers included the right to teach in seventh and eighth grades. If a certificate was no longer good for all seventh and eighth grades, it could likewise be invalidated for any other grades merely by a superintendent's action, and the long and desperate struggle for tenure would be lost. No examination had been given to the elementary principals who had already been appointed to the five new junior highs. Most of the seventh- and eighth-grade teachers were the older teachers who had less formal training than the more recent graduates of the Normal School, and many of whom had been the backbone of the Federation. It was the younger teachers in the main who took the junior high school examination. The salaries for junior high teachers were not immediately announced; but since ninth-grade teachers got senior high salaries, it would be llkely to be higher than that paid elementary teachers. They actually did get 20 percent more than elementary teachers, had a 20 percent increase in school day, and a daily teaching load of from 300 to 500 children.

It was inevitable that the Federation would feel that the existence of a large body of junior high-school teachers, with a salary schedule and problems different from those of elementary teachers, clearly would threaten the dominant position of the Chicago Teachers Federation in the school system. In this they were correct. The younger teachers who took the junior high examination, and became enthusiastic about new approaches to teaching younger adolescents, resented the Federation's continued blanket opposition to the new system. Most of them joined one of the two high-school unions if they became members of an organization, and tended to oppose the Federation on all measures. The number of these teachers became sizable, even though only one-fifth of the seventh- and eighth-grade children were in junior high schools at the time they ceased operating in 1933.[5]

The Platoon System

The junior high schools did open in September, 1924, with the superintendent paying no attention to any opposition, mild or otherwise, from teachers or public. To his second proposal the teachers were united in their opposition; and no moderate voices were heard among them. When the junior highs had been promised, the Board committee in its report had been unanimously in favor. But on the "platoon system" for the elementary schools the Board committee was sharply divided, and presented a minority report strongly opposing the plan.

"Platoon schools" had been the invention of Superintendent William E. Wirt of Gary when he took over the schools in the new Indiana city built in 1907 by the United States Steel Corporation, on the empty sand at the foot of Lake Michigan. They were advocated as an economy measure by Superintendent Wirt, whose extreme right-wing connections had not enhanced his reputation, and by bitterly anti-union United States Steel, whose name was anathema to the entire labor movement. The plan, of course, proposed to use the school plant for a long day, with a half-day of class-room instruction and a half-day of supervised play and other non-academic activities, so that a building could accommodate larger numbers of children than could crowd into class rooms at any one time.[6]

Had the plan been proposed as a stop-gap while the Chicago school system increased the number of desperately needed school buildings, it might have met with a different reception. In fact, Mrs. Young *had* used it on this basis, without opposition of any kind. But it was not so presented, its proponents defending it instead as a desirable permanent improvement. In June, 1924, the Tribune, commending the idea as permanent policy, declared that the school must now take over "not only the scholastic training of the child, but the supervision of his play." The editorial deplored the fact that such assumption by the schools might even be "mildly socialistic," but even so, it was better than life in the "streets and alleys" and the "culturally impoverishment of the child in the great city. For such children, the family in many of its functions has already disappeared." Then it added that, besides offering guidance to children for a greater share of each day, the platoon plan would accommodate "more pupils per square yard, reduce overhead costs, require fewer buildings and less equipment and give more educational product for the taxpayers' money. Under the educational conditions of the modern city, the platoon plan is bound to come."

For several years the platoon plan had been the target of sharp criticism from national and local labor movements, as a way of short changing children and pleasing tax cutters. It had been tried in New York and Detroit against the active opposition of local labor bodies. As soon as it was suggested in Chicago the Chicago Federation of Labor circulated letters from a member of the Detroit Board of Education and from Detroit parents sharply opposing the idea, and pointed out that very little mention was made of the reasons given for its use in Gary, or in fact, little mention of its origin in Gary. They also used the report issued by a teachers' organization in Milwaukee, opposing the plan. The Federation of Labor argued that very small children would be pushed rapidly from place to place in a school building, would meet many teachers in one day, some of whom might deal with as many as 500 different pupils daily and that no one could say that this was educationally sound procedure. The Chicago Teachers Federation sent nine of its members to a number of cities where the platoon system had been tried; they returned with factual data to support the opposition. The thirty-nine area elementary councils voted unanimously against its use, and no teacher group in Chicago supported it.

When the Woman's City Club board took strong action supporting not only the junior high school but the platoon plan, without referring such action to its educational committee, the high-school teachers who belonged to the club resigned. They did so, not because the club disagreed with a minority of its members, but because its board obviously was not even willing to listen to any arguments against a decision they had already made without consulting the club's membership. It was the feeling of the resigning teachers that the husbands of some of the board members had determined the decision. This feeling was strengthened when Mrs. McAndrew was added to the board of the club. Public hearings on the platoon system were granted the labor representatives and the Chicago Teachers Federation on July 7, 1924, but the superintendent's only comment was that the plan was being used in sixty-six cities.[7]

Abolition of Teachers Councils

The opposition of the teachers' groups to McAndrew's program was definitely acerbated by his flippant destruction of the teachers' councils which had become the symbol to teachers of their important place in the system and in the teaching profession. They had been respected in principle–if not used in practice–for a quarter century. Only Mrs. Young and Superintendent Mortenson had ever really used them, and no great stir had been made when Superintendent Shoop had failed to call a meeting in his entire term of three years. But to be informed that a right which had been recognized for decades was forbidden, and to be told in a way that minimized the value to the school system of the contributions of the whole teaching force was a different matter.

McAndrew had called the councils as required by Board rules when he came and had met with the Elementary Teachers' General Council on March 22, 1924. The secretary of the group expressed the hope that relations between the delegate body and the superintendent might be pleasant and profitable to all concerned. Then she summarized the reports received from the thirty-nine group councils of elementary teachers. All had passed resolutions opposing the platoon system, most of them using the wording of a resolution adopted by the Chicago Division of the Illinois State Teachers' Association, to which high-school teachers also belonged. An eleven-point summary of the arguments against the plan as unsound educationally ended with a protest against any makeshift plan "except as an emergency measure to be abandoned as soon as adequate facilities permit." Then the five questions mentioned above on the junior high schools were presented to the superintendent, from twenty-eight of the group councils, six of whom had voted in favor of junior highs.

A discussion on decentralized control quoted a highly distinguished New York educator to the effect that

> "The management of any school system . . . would be much more intelligent if the intelligence of the whole body were used than if the school system were managed by the most intelligent person in this audience. For it stands to reason that the intelligence of the whole

teaching force must be immensely superior to that of any one person who is running it. . . ."

The highly distinguished educator was one William A. McAndrew. As he left the meeting the superintendent wished the delegates a pleasant vacation in case he did not see them again.[8] Since the Board rules called for a meeting in May *before* vacation, the remark indicated either that the council would not meet or that he would not be present if it did.

On April 9, McAndrew wrote the chairman of the General Elementary Council that he would notify the principals to hold a full school session on April 25, when the next local councils should meet, and objected to the exclusion of principals from the local meetings. On April 22, 1924, the superintendent's bulletin carried the statement that the councils would not be called "at this time," as it "does not appear to be a good time" to do so. On April 23, Mr. James Mullenbach, as a Board member, presented the Board with the specific By Laws of the Teachers Councils, approved as a whole September 1, 1922, which dealt with the mandatory calling of meetings by the superintendent. The date for local council meetings was April 25. They were not called. On May 6 the bulletin stated that no group council meetings would be held on school time. But on the same day the attorney of the Board notified the superintendent that the dates and manner of calling council meetings were set by the rules of the Board, and not by the superintendent. On May 7 the superintendent sent a communication to the Board to the effect that the councils met in

"accordance with rules and by-laws already adopted and approved by the superintendent of schools or amendments hereafter made and so approved. . . . I therefore make and approve the following amendments, viz., that no dismissals of pupils from their classes during regular school hours shall be made for the purpose of meetings of councils. I am filing with you . . . the rulings and regulations herein made."

On May 8 the superintendent notified principals that the president of the Board had informed him of an "hitherto unfiled and unrecorded document" on dismissal of children for council meetings, and "pending final decision, it would be well to follow this week last year's practice regarding council meetings." The group councils then met on the regular day, May 9, on school time. They reiterated their positions in opposition to the platoon plan and for delay in approving junior high schools, and their reports were presented to the Board on May 14, on which day the junior highs were approved by the Board. On May 15 the superintendent wrote the chairman of the General Council asking for postponement of its meeting as he was going to New York. It never was called and never met again.

On June 3, when a public hearing on the junior high schools was held in response to the request of the Chicago Federation of Labor, two members of the Elementary General Council and the chairman of the High School Council appeared to speak at 3 p.m., obviously on school time. Representatives of the Elementary General Council also appeared at a hearing of the Committee on School Administration on July 7, opposing platoon schools, which were approved by the Board on July 9. On September 8 all principals were notified that no classes should be dismissed for councils as the superintendent had amended the rules. The president of the High School Council pointed out that many high schools had a twelve-period day, and councils could not meet except on school time, a statement reiterated on July 17, 1925. On September 10 Mr. Coath moved that the Board allow high-school councils to meet on school time, but it was not approved. A minority of the Committee on School Administration moved that the superintendent's request to make councils permissive on his part be approved and the Board did approve it on September 24.

On February 11, 1925, Superintendent McAndrew presented his plan for Teachers Councils. On March 10 representatives of all the major teacher organizations and the Elementary and High School General Councils appeared before the Committee on School Administration unanimously opposing the plan. After their statements had been made, Mr. Mullenbach, who was the labor arbitrator in the men's clothing industry, made his own statement:

> "I do not know what kind of record this Board . . . will make, but I am certain in years to come, when the historians of educational development look back upon it that it will be of immense interest . . . to read of the tremendous reaction that took place in the school system of Chicago in 1924 and 1925 when the school councils that had been advocated by all the leading educators in this country for many years, were suddenly and ruthlessly withdrawn. . . . I feel ashamed as a citizen of Chicago, when I think of the teachers who teach the children of this city having less to say about the conditions and policies of our educational system than the humblest sewing girl working in the manufacture of men's clothing has to say about the conditions under which she works. . . . It looks to me like the degradation of a professional group that ought to be given a place of dignity in the community second to none. . . . I can not in all conscience accept the Superintendent's proposal."

Mr. Mullenbach and Mrs. Hefferan opposed the superintendent's plan for councils, but the School Administration Committee vote was a tie. Then two members of the committee presented a recommendation that McAndrew's plan be approved. A long history of the council movement in Chicago was presented by Mullenbach's subcommittee on Advisory Organization of the Teaching Force, on May 25, beginning with the Harper Report, quoting Ella Flagg Young and John Dewey, and stating the legal status of the Mortenson councils, and ending as with a quotation from the De Bey committee report of 1907:

"Even if it were true that all goodness and wisdom . . . dwell with the school authorities, the fact remains that in the end their decrees must be executed by the teachers. It is the teachers . . . that must be depended upon to give vitality to public school education.

"Teachers are neither soulless machines to be despotically manipulated by master hands, nor soldiers with no other function but unquestioning obedience, nor mechanical producers of the inanimate commodities of the factory, but are the personal guardians and guides of the children whom they teach. If they feel the weight of despotic hands, the less assertive will cringe in their official intercourse with superiors in authority, and be despotic in turn in their official intercourse with subordinates. Thus perpetuating itself, the despotic or degree promulgating policy must inevitably react upon the pupils, tending to turn some of them into little learning mediums, and others into little rebels, instead of making eager students of them all.

"In the opinion of your committee, the teaching force must be sympathetically considered and trusted. If they are to do the best for the children, the teachers must be consulted about educational policies, not now and then, or here and there, as real or apparent favorites of superiors in authority, but as a body of educators organically recognized by the Board and its employees. Their cordial acquiescence in the wisdom, justice and sincerity of the policies they are called upon to promote must be secured or their work will fall short of the highest possibilities. This acquiescence can not be secured either by preventing discussion or by ignoring recommendations. . . . The important thing is not that the recommendations of teachers be adopted regardless of merits, but that they be considered in good faith on their merits."[9]

The subcommittee recommended that the present "educational councils of the Chicago Public Schools be invited to submit a revised constitution for the purpose of placing the teaching body of the Chicago public school system into direct advisory relations with the Board."

This long document had been sent to the superintendent before the meeting. He answered it by a letter addressed to the employed secretary of the Board:

"This is to acknowledge your favor in transmitting the request of the Chairman of the School Administration Committee that I mull over the papers sent. Please advise the chairman that the matter is similar to the material . . . which was gone over on framing the document which the Committee on School Administration has.

Signed, William McAndrew"

On April 8, 1925, the Board approved McAndrew's plan for a council of organizations, in which the four principals and superintendent outvoted the three large groups of teachers and in which the small group of truant officers—for whom no educational requirements were set and who were chosen by the City Civil Service Commission—had the same votes as the Federation, with its thousands of teacher members. Meetings were to be held outside school time and principals were not to be excluded. It stated that bypassing principals and providing direct contact between teachers and superintendent was "repugnant to experience, discipline and efficiency." The record of the councils, said the superintendent, was "barren of educational results," unanimously contrary to the decisions of the Board of Education and was a "violent clamor" against giving more time to teaching.

The new plan set up a central council to furnish the superintendent with advice (when he asked for it) to be given by a representative from each of the twelve voluntary teacher organizations within the system, plus one elementary, and one high-school principal, one district, and one assistant superintendent. Since six of the large organizations representing teachers had appeared before the Board to oppose the plan before it was adopted, it clearly had little chance of success. In presenting it, the superintendent stated that, like all superintendents, he had been taking counsel with teachers all his school life, and that no formal machinery was necessary. Allegations that teachers were not free to discuss problems before principals were observed. "If anyone should be so inaccurate as to charge the Chicago teachers with faults, timidity would not be one of them," McAndrew replied. If Chicago has permitted a distortion to grow up of "the standard works on school management in which there is a direct line of control from Board through superintendents and principal down to teacher, a return to the generally approved system is desirable." The superintendent must organize, deputize and supervise. The schools need "close supervision."[10]

Tight Supervision and United Opposition

And "close supervision" he proceeded to give them. McAndrew marshalled ten district superintendents to support his stand on the councils. He required every teacher to check in on a sheet four times a day. He set up ratings for teachers and for schools, and demanded 100 percent performance in reading and arithmetic in every school, no matter what the background of the children, their need for extra kinds of help, or the size of classes in a school. He declared that the tests he had administered showed that the results of the instruction being given were "appalling and astounding."

McAndrew made no exceptions in his scathing criticism of the overcrowded schools and of all teachers. He assumed that slackness, indolence, and general inefficiency permeated the school system, and he managed to antagonize the most earnest and effective teachers even more than the least useful. In a standard school, said he, every child should reach 100 percent in reading, language, and "citizenship." Continued testing of results would make all teachers work hard enough for every child to accomplish such success. That a child attended sessions far larger than the average class size of 45, that he came from an illiterate home or one where English was not spoken, or that he was hungry or lived in a ward with the highest tuberculosis death rate in any city in the United States, made no difference.

The Superintendent claimed that in 1925 only 66 percent of the children could do simple sums in eighth grade, but in 1926, 292 schools showed every child 100 percent in arithmetic, and that while only 2 percent of all the children had excellent penmanship in March, 1924, 51 percent had in April, 1926—a state of affairs due, of course, to the force of the superintendent making the lazy teachers work. This was happening in the school system where Ella Flagg Young had said, long before, there was "No more unAmerican or dangerous solution of the difficulty involved in maintaining a high degree of efficiency in the teaching corps in a large school system . . . than that which is effected by what is termed 'close supervision.' "[11] The teachers knew only too well how these neat figures were prepared by principals and district superintendents who wanted promotions, while the real problems which hindered efficiency were not touched.

The school system and the city were again polarized as they had been by the Cooley plan and by the Loeb rule. The teachers' organizations which had welcomed the superintendent, and at least one of which had supported him on junior high schools, were now unanimously bitter in their reaction to his arrogant derogation of all Chicago teachers. McAndrew had even gone out of his way to criticize their clothes in an article in the Chicago Schools Journal for September, 1925, by saying that dowdy teachers were not as useful as well dressed ones. If instruction was not good, it was entirely the fault of teachers, and this "nonsense" about class size was an alibi; there was no relation between the size of classes and educational progress. A good teacher could handle 54 children as well as 42, said the superintendent when the Federation protested an increase in class size.[12] When the major teacher organizations were invited to the first meeting of his new council, the three high-school organizations refused to attend. Miss Haley came to represent the Federation but was not recognized, as she was not employed by the Board. But she suggested thereupon that the rules be changed so that the superintendent might choose the Federation's representative, so that they would "insure the Superintendent against the hazards of uncontrolled and uncontrollable utterances and opinions by guaranteeing at all times certainty of his ability to penalize for such utterances."[13]

The Federation of Women High School Teachers was the organization supporting the junior high schools, after a survey of its own. When it made a survey of the teaching load in the high schools—in many of which were twice as many children as seats—and sent it to the press and to the thirty civic groups with which it worked, its president, Beulah Berolzheimer, of Crane College, was called before the Board of Superintendents and told in no uncertain terms by the superintendent himself "that in public service, those who approached the public could look for dismissal." She duly reported to her group that "if members of our organization make public statements that do not correspond with the ideas of the superintendent, that the members might look for dismissal."[14]

In April, 1926, Miss Haley commented on the line and staff regime as one where the "Cabots speak only to the Lowells, and the Lowells speak only to God." The Men Teachers Federation urged that inefficiency be met by action, not by ratings—or by blanket denunciation, and that principals should work with teachers to improve instruction. The Joint Bulletin of the High School Federations in October, 1925, pointed out that while McAndrew had said $150,000 was being wasted on use of school time by the councils, he had added $10,000 a year for clerks to check the four daily signatures of each of the thousands of teachers on the time sheet. The publication charged that such a system was devised by industrial experts, it minimized each principal, and punished all teachers for the offenses of a few who could be dealt with more effectively as individuals by the principals. The system was based on the assumption that teachers had no professional responsibility; it claimed, and the organizations held, that education was not improved by mechanization in the guise of business efficiency.

McAndrew brushed aside all objections to any of the changes he had determined to make. He answered them categorically by saying that John Dill Robertson, when he retired as president of the Board of Education, had claimed that "unrest and antagonism in the minds of hundreds of Chicago's teachers [was] a matter of 30 years' standing." The Tribune of March 5, 1927, quoted McAndrew as telling a group of new principals "You have the hand of iron. Use it. If teachers or a wild bunch of citizens . . . try to run the schools, put a stop to it with the power you have."

In two and a half years' time, the gulf between the teachers of the city and the superintendent they had welcomed had become so deep and so wide that it could no longer be bridged. It was not that Miss Haley simply had her feelings hurt because McAndrew had paid no attention to her. It was not resentment by many teachers at the changes he proposed, with some of which they heartily agreed. But hard-working teachers in the system felt personally insulted by his blanket public tirades against the integrity, motives, and skill of the teaching force as a whole, and by his failure to give public recognition to, or help with, the problems with which they were struggling so desperately.

McAndrew on the other hand considered the teachers not only obstreperous but ungrateful. In his first year he had suggested a salary schedule which offered higher maxima than the 1922 scale, $3,250 instead of $2,500 for elementary teachers and $4,700 instead of $3,800 for high-school teachers. However, in order to get the money for higher salaries at the top, the 1922 schedule was actually reduced for teachers who had taught less than five years, by a total during those five years of almost $1,200 less than they were then receiving. All of the teacher groups opposed this specious kind of increase except the Men Teachers Federation, which asked the Chicago Federation of Labor to recommend better salaries, and was willing to try the new scale as a start. But Miss Haley came to the executive committee of the Federation of Labor (of which she was no longer a member), and prevented any such action on its part.

Since the total proposed schedule did not increase the total payroll, the teachers claimed it was offered in bad faith, particularly since neither Board nor superintendent showed any interest, for example, in the teachers' project to increase tax collections and get more *actual* money for the schools. The teacher organizations were already well aware that school finances were drifting into a very precarious state and were determined to do something about it, besides "platooning schools." The principals accepted the new schedule, as they got no cuts and a maximum of $5,500. The superintendent felt he had offered the teachers something much more important than councils, and that they were cutting off their own noses to spite their faces.

Superintendent Ignores Labor Leaders

The sharp and bitter differences which in two years had developed between the organizations of teachers and Superintendent McAndrew appeared also among the major social and economic forces in the city. These forces had been polarized for decades, and school issues had been among the most bitter causes of controversy among them. All of them had accepted the superintendent in the beginning of his term as a competent and intelligent person, able to pull the school system out of the morass of corruption and stagnation which the 1922 indictments had so plainly exposed. It is possible that a superintendent could have at least kept working good will with all groups, if he really tried. His program for efficiency pleased business. His plans for training citizenship for all children and for extension of adult education and community centers were in the direction sought by labor leaders in the city. But the superintendent congealed his own opposition. The spokesmen for organized labor had not opposed the junior high-school plan in the beginning. After all, it had been used in Chicago since 1918 and 2,000 children in overcrowded Chicago schools were already set up on the platoon plan in 1923–before McAndrew came–without protest either from teachers or labor leaders.

The high-handed manner in which McAndrew treated his employees, his open rudeness toward representatives of the labor movement, and his apparent warm alignment with anti-union, anti-school taxes, anti-teacher organization business forces lost him all support from the labor movement, which might have given him substantial help. In his treatment of employees, McAndrew followed the spirit if not the letter of the Loeb rule, that teachers should speak when spoken to, and that they were there to take orders from their betters. Not only the Federation, but the three high-school organizations, and the elementary group which had always opposed Miss Haley were united in resentment at the treatment accorded them, and all refused to cooperate with the superintendent's substitute for the councils. His open scorn of the right of organized employees to have any significant influence on decisions as to their work really antagonized organized labor, which would have objected whether teachers were affiliated with labor or not. The superintendent's bored, deliberate non-attention at the junior high-school hearings requested by Fitzpatrick and Olander—culminated with the distribution, as participants left, of mimeographed sheets prepared in advance as an answer[15]—in sharp contrast to his eager identification with the powerful, affluent elements in the city.

The conviction grew that McAndrew had indeed been brought to the city through the machinations of "big business" to squelch teachers, save taxes, cut expenses, and by use of "so-called" intelligence tests, reduce the opportunities open to children of laboring people. Certainly, the superintendent made no effort to create a better understanding of his point of view on these issues.

On the other hand, Superintendent McAndrew seemed to go out of his way to secure the approval and close cooperation of the leaders of business enterprise, in sharp contrast to his open distaste for labor and for political leaders. When a business leader spoke on "Chicago Schools for Chicago" at a luncheon meeting of the Association of Commerce, the superintendent used the material in his annual report and sent a printed copy of the speech to every school principal.[16] The speech stressed the need for sound civic training— "sound" according to the standards of the Association of Commerce, which had worked for the Cooley Bill, and, labor leaders alleged, for anti-union propaganda in the continuation schools. As one of his reasons for denouncing the quality of teaching in the schools, the superintendent quoted the complaints of business men.

The Association of Commerce hired a staff to supervise the activities it was permitted to sponsor in Chicago high schools: Civic and Industrial Clubs, and the "High School Presidents' Council of Chicago Public High School Organizations," which included student councils and many kinds of high-school clubs. In his 1924-25 report, the superintendent lauded the work of the Association of Commerce in the schools, and praised the contributions of the Union League Club, the Rotary Club, the Men and Women's City Clubs, and the Scouts. None of these agencies had offered any opposition to McAndrew's efforts to improve the schools. The Association of Commerce Magazine, Chicago Commerce, carried frequent articles on the schools, consistently praising the superintendent as a man of courage and foresight, a "citizen maker." He was quoted as saying "He was not going to tell business men what they should do for the schools, but proposed to ask the business men what the schools should do for them."[17]

In the 1924-25 annual report, McAndrew recorded that the Association of Commerce had been asked to send groups of ten volunteers, each to "look over" one school, and that principals had been told to cooperate with them. In discussing school problems McAndrew used phrases identified with industrial management, such as, "The purpose of a school system is not to please us who are in it, but as with all public service corporations, to satisfy the customers." Even in 1925, a considerable number of his audience lived in the suburbs, and many who lived in the city sent their children to private schools. The labor people, whose children did go to the public schools, asked who the "customers" really were. The annual report for 1926 described the "sampling day" when business leaders were invited to visit the schools. In making a speech to the Association of Commerce in that year, the superintendent quoted the opinions collected by the employer and his interests . . . neatness, tidiness, respect for authority." The firms quoted included anti-union corporations—and the very "public service corporations" against which the teacher organizations were at that moment preparing a suit because they cut down school income by failing to pay taxes on their capital stock. In 1927 the Union League Club organized a "Citizens Public Education Committee" of the "best elements" in the community. Invited were the Association of Commerce, the Real Estate Board, the Commercial Club, the Hamilton Club, the City Club, the Western Society of Engineers, the Chicago Woman's Club, and the League of Women Voters. Not invited was the Chicago Federation of Labor because "labor organizations would not be anxious to cooperate."[18] If McAndrew had tried to prove the rumors true that he had been brought to Chicago by conservative business men to serve their purposes, he could not have taken more direct steps to do so.

All this conflict was news, and the papers made the most of it. In his 1924-25 annual report the superintendent reprinted the headlines on his conflict with the teachers. In fine print they took two pages, listing objections from many sources. There were 35 headlines dealing with teacher criticisms of the superintendent and 18 on the superintendent's initiative in conflict with teachers, 10 on conflict between Board and superintendent and four on opposition by parents to proposed policies. Three dealt with actions taken by the city council criticizing the superintendent's actions. Sixteen were editorial defenses of the superintendent by newspapers. These were quoted in detail in the report.

The following give the general tenor of this support. The News said: "Public opinion should be stirred by the lone and fearless contest the Superintendent is making on behalf of the children in the schools"; The Herald Examiner, "Chicagoans generally have regarded these controversies as a 'Tempest in a Teapot' "; the Tribune, "The parents of Chicago and every citizen who has a regard for the city's youth ought to protest against this controversy. If they do not protest in such terms as will put the wrangling invaders where they belong, our school conditions will go from bad to worse and Chicago will not be able to get any competent, self-respecting educator to assume the impossible task of school direction." On December 31, 1925 the Tribune also praised McAndrew for being "refreshingly hard boiled and thick skinned."

In his report the superintendent added a page on the reduction of political influence on the schools, pointing out that there had been 520 attempts by Board members and others to influence him in 1924, but that in the current year this had occurred only five times. He added that it seemed to him "quite possible that the dissensions are exaggerated, and to a large degree, artificially manufactured," and that "It is regrettable that a desire to attract notice to stir up strife, should be responsible for the noisy lampoon repeated by the few in whose selfish interest it is manufactured and spread."[19] It was quite clear to William McAndrew that he had done exactly what a model superintendent was supposed to do and that those who disagreed with him were wrong on all counts.

But even as the papers defended and praised McAndrew, he was given warning by them which he did not take. On June 16, 1924, the Tribune published an editorial "Who Runs Our Schools?" It protested the

> "... preposterous manhandling to which the schools have been subject for years.... From the days of Cooley down to those of McAndrew, there has been one dog fight after another. No private business could survive such conditions.... But good or bad, the junior high plan is the responsibility of the school management, board and expert superintendent, and not of the politicians in the council, the Federation of Labor, or Miss Haley's organization.... The intervention of aldermen is an inexcusable invasion."

McAndrew ignored the aldermen's interest, a sign of general political concern.

In June, 1924, the Tribune published editorials explaining the value and advantages of the platoon plan and recognizing the sincerity of Olander's arguments against "educational snobbery" in the schools; the newspaper agreed with his resentment against it, but felt the junior high schools might serve to break down the bourgeois snippiness of the "white collar class" and that this was one of its advantages. The Tribune offered more intelligent, more respectful and more reasoned answers to the objections raised by labor than did the superintendent, who simply brushed them off.

On September 10 the Tribune warned him of the results of his unwillingness to compromise on lesser issues in order to achieve his major goals. McAndrew's

> "... platoon project and his junior high schools are two of the greatest educational advancements in Chicago in the last forty years. But if he were more of a business man in meetings and less of a school teacher, he would get along faster.... He should not jeopardize 'his big job' by his uncompromising attitude on teachers' councils.
>
> "The teachers' council controversy is after all small potatoes. It is concerned chiefly in forcing several thousand mature and women to toe the mark. Councils on school time may or may not be justified;

they are not in any case worth all the fighting. They are supported by a rule of the Board of Education which the superintendent seems to be ignoring. They are sanctioned legally by an opinion of the Board attorney. They are supported openly by four members of the Board and tacitly by others. . . . But in any case is the victory worth the fight? Will it not, if carried through, chiefly win the antagonism of thousands of teachers?

"A school system fighting its superintendent is a ruined school system. It is true that Margaret Haley, leader of the teachers, has been bellicose and unreasonable. It is true that much of the opposition of teachers and labor leaders has been motivated less by educational ideals than by a desire to obstruct Mr. McAndrew. But the need is to reduce friction, not to aggravate it. . . . Education in Chicago will not gain by antagonizing the bulk of the teaching force."

On October 3, 1924, the Tribune amplified this argument in an editorial titled "Is Teaching Labor or Professional Service?" It observed that the pay of teachers puts them in the ranks of labor, and that the low salaries will probably continue, pointing out that the only hope of maintaining the professional status of the teaching profession lay in the preservation of less tangible compensations such as personal dignity and "relative freedom from detailed supervision." If these rewards are not present, said the Tribune, the teachers will naturally ally themselves with labor. The development of "a defensive and antagonistic frame of mind toward the management will not help Chicago schools. Schools are not steel mills. Chicago's children can be rightly taught only by voluntary cooperation of all the force. A conquered teaching force will be worse than useless." Miss Haley herself could not have stated her point of view better! These, however, were the last good words for teachers from the Tribune for a long time.

But the superintendent did not modify his "school teacher" attitude of demanding from his employees total and abject obedience. He made no real answer to the objections to his program raised by labor. A group of thirty non-partisan civic agencies, including the P.T.A., urged him to call the councils.[20] And the political forces, aware that labor's voting power was far greater than that of the powerful business men, watched his career with growing attention. On May 6, 1925, Miss Haley spoke to the City Council Committee on Schools, Fire and Civil Service and the Council sent a resolution to the Board urging that meetings of the teachers' councils be called. It was already clear that the school conflict might become a major political issue.

Chapter 9

THE NON-TEACHER PAY ROLLS BECOME
THOMPSON PATRONAGE LISTS

Into the devil's caldron which was beginning to bubble, the superintendent, in October, 1925, had thrown in another ingredient. This time, he refused, temporarily, to obey the Board, which unanimously opposed his recommendation on an appointment. The issue centered on the employment of older teachers and getting rid of the "dead wood." In April, 1925, on the recommendation of the superintendent, the Board attorneys prepared a bill to retire all members of the teaching force over seventy with an annual payment beyond the pension, whose maximum was now $1,000.[1] The bill was presented in the legislature by a teacher legislator named Walter Miller, and passed the House. The Senate amended it, but the conference committee approved the original House form. This the Senate did pass on the last day of the session. The legislature then adjourned. The clerk of the House refused to send the bill to the governor for signature, because it had not been voted on in the House a second time, although there was no change whatsoever in the bill as it had been passed by the House. Since it did not go to the governor, it was not signed, and did not go into effect. The proposed law allowed for dismissal at age 75 in 1926, at age 74 in 1927 and by 1930 of all teachers who reached 70.

Setting Age Limits for Teachers

On October 14, 1925, McAndrew presented the name of William Campbell for reappointment as examiner. Mr. Campbell was now 73, and had been examiner since 1913. The Board unanimously refused to approve the reappointment and directed the superintendent to submit another name. Without waiting for further legislation, then, on the recommendation of the superintendent, the Board adopted a rule of its own on December 9, 1925, that no teacher over seventy, except the superintendent, should be employed in the schools. It then created a new category of teachers, called the "emeritus service"; these people were dropped from active service but were on call if needed, and were to be paid $1,500 a year.[2] On February 1, 1926, seventy teachers and principals were assigned to emeritus service, including Mr. Campbell. One was 83.

There was a stir over this action. The Federation took active exception to it. A considerable number of older principals were on the list. The Principals Club as an organization did nothing, although it was clear that any action taken by the Board could be changed by the Board and that the $1,500 payment could be stopped at any time. The Otis law was specific in reasons for dismissal, and age was not among them. Every teacher dismissed, according to the Otis law, was entitled to an individual trial. A number of those dismissed employed Governor Dunne's son to prepare a suit, and the Federation lawyer went over the brief. At the first hearing, the injunction asked for was denied, and the decision appealed to the Illinois Supreme Court.

In the meantime, after some prodding, the attorney general gave the Speaker of the House an opinion that the Miller Law had been passed legally, and it was finally sent to the governor on May 19, 1926, a year after its passage. He signed it, to go into effect July 1, 1926. In October, 1926, the State Supreme Court declared that the Board had no authority to pass its emeritus rule in December, 1925, and directed the Board to restore to service and pay all teachers retired under the Board's rule from February 1, 1926, to the end of the school year in June, 1926. Since the law as adopted set up a sliding scale for retiring from 75 years in 1926 to 70 in 1930, any one under 75 on the list was restored to active duty.[3] In 1927 the law was amended to pay teachers retiring at 65 $1,000 and a maximum of $1,500 for those retiring at 70, after 1930. This law was in effect until 1935.

The superintendent had lost face with the Board by agreeing to the retirement of teachers by a Board rule, and for trying to make an exception to his own recommendation in the case of the examiner. The Board paid almost a quarter million dollars in back salary to those who had been retired—for no services at all.

City Takes Over Non-Teaching Employees

McAndrew's next conflict with the Board dealt with the status of the clerks in the schools, who had been teachers since 1909. The background of the dispute as usual reached far back into the history of the school system and began, not with the clerks, but with the engineers and janitors who were not under the direction of the superintendent, but of the business manager, over whom the superintendent had no control. For years the engineers in each school had hired local people to sweep the schools. A woman hired to sweep was supposed to receive $25 a month for a floor in a large school; in actual fact many of them received less than $15 a month, and had to enlist the help of their children to do the work.[4] There was no check on the engineer's use of "contract" system funds. There had been long protest against this exploitation, beginning with the Harper Report in 1898, and from teachers, civic organizations, and Board members, there had also been objection to overtime payments to engineers, which raised the salaries of many of them above those of the principals in the same schools. In 1923 and in 1927 the Board had appointed committees of its members to report on maintenance of buildings in other school systems.

Change in the system was precipitated by a court case finally decided March 2, 1927, which had been brought by the Union of Stationary Firemen, who were the engineers' assistants, and who said the engineers did not respect their seniority rights. The Appellate Court held that the contract system was invalid and that janitors and firemen must be chosen by the City Civil Service Commission, all with civil service status and seniority rights. The decision cited an 1898 dictum of the Illinois Supreme Court, which held that employees of the Board of Education were under the jurisdiction of the City Civil Service Commissioners, except those exempted by the civil service act. Only those engaged in actual teaching were so exempt. The Board accepted the court decision, set a separate salary for janitors, and provided that thereafter they were to be appointed from civil service lists.[5] Since the local ward committeemen had worked with engineers to employ political favorites under the old system, there was a stir at first, quickly calmed by the speedy recognition that the system prevailing was to use temporary political appointees instead of persons who had passed any examination.

Now these matters were outside the superintendent's jurisdiction. He could not change the janitor system for better or for worse, any more than a principal had any authority over the engineer and janitors in his school. But the interpretation of the court ruling did not stop with engineers and janitors, or with the smaller groups of non-teaching employees, such as penny lunch workers, attendants in shower rooms and truant officers.

After the defeat of Mayor Dever in April, 1927, the Board attorney, prodded by a Board member who supported the resurgent Thompson, held that by the same reasoning as that used in the decision on janitors, the school clerks must also be under City Civil Service laws. Since 1909 the school clerks had been certified teachers assigned to clerical duties. On August 3, 1927 the Board adopted a resolution dismissing all 350 school clerks, ordering that their places be filled from civil service lists. McAndrew was up in arms. He helped the school clerks prepare a suit for an injunction against the action. Appearing as a witness, he stated that his name had been signed to papers filed by the attorney without his knowledge or approval, and that the injunction against the Board should be granted.[6]

Long before August, however, the devil's caldron had boiled over into the wildest mayoralty campaign the city had ever seen. The staid, judicial Mayor Dever had tried to enforce the prohibition law in a "wet" city, with disastrous political results to himself. The rising tide of syndicated gang control of bootlegging, which was buying off the agencies of justice, was not to be stemmed. Dever had lost control of his own political organization, many of his staff promised jobs by his opponent, former Mayor William Hale Thompson. Dever had never once interfered in the management of the schools and had angered Margaret Haley by refusing to do so in the dispute on councils. He had the detached, objective quality of a good judge, and his moderate statements as to what he had done and planned to do for the city were completely drowned out by the obstreperous, meaningless shouting of his opponent. His supporters called Thompson's backers "hoodlums." The "hoodlums" seized on the epithet, and used it to win support from the "ordinary people." Seizing the school issue as one of the areas in which existing conflict could be used to his advantage, Thompson announced he would fire McAndrew as he had fired Chadsey nine years before. Then he proceeded to use McAndrew as the whipping boy in a planned appeal to every kind of ethnic prejudice latent in the nationality groups in a city of recent immigrants.[7]

For his part, McAndrew seemed to go out of his way to help Thompson in his demagogic career. He emerged from his serene inner sanctum to take an active part in the campaign for Dever, a partisan act never performed by any superintendent of schools, before or after. He wrote and signed a letter urging votes for Dever—printed in the school print shops (non-union, of course)—sent by the Women's City Club to the principal of every school.[8] At a public dinner for Dever, given at the club, he appeared wearing a wide Dever paper streamer and a row of Dever buttons. Certainly he made no effort to keep his office above the storm.

William Hale Thompson's chief opponent in 1927 was not Dever. It was King George of England! No one ever quite knew which of the five King Georges, however, as Thompson talked in the present tense about the American Revolution as if it were George III he was going to "punch in the snoot." McAndrew for years afterward told that when someone asked Thompson which King George was the criminal, his response was, "Oh, are there two?" In any case, it was safe to attack the English in Chicago, as there were so few of them, particularly after praising the heroes of the Germans, the Poles, the Irish and the Italians—and George Washington, who somehow seemed to have shuffled off his shameful English antecedents. Though Thompson had been cooler than lukewarm about World War I in 1915, to please the thousands of Chicago Germans, he now became the chief spokesman of an ultra patriotic "America First" movement. "Big Bill the Builder" wanted the Volstead Act repealed, metering of city water stopped, no World Court, the University of Chicago kept from meddling with the schools, and the Superintendent of Schools and his unpatriotic text books kicked out. Of course, the whole campaign made no logical sense, but it generated a tremendous amount of impassioned oratory and inflated the egos of people who usually felt unimportant. Moreover, it covered up the contribution of a quarter million dollars from the bootlegging syndicate and the thorough job being done for Thompson by Al Capone and his organized gun-men.[9] The syndicate, incidentally, offered Dever $100,000 for his campaign fund, too—just in case.

This was not the Chicago of the thick rugs of the Union League Club, or the Chicago of the Association of Commerce or the Women's City Club. This was the Chicago of Yerkes and Lorimer, of Al Capone and gang murders, of bought votes, fixed taxes, and unreasoning, bitter, national, religious and racial prejudice. McAndrew had ignored all indications of its existence in his years as superintendent. There were some indications for him to see, had he chosen to do so. In 1926 Mayor Dever sent him a document prepared by a "Citizens' Committee on School Histories," of which a far right ex-Congressman named George Gorman was president. It denounced three American history texts in use in the schools as pro-British and set forth instances in which heroes of various other nationalities had been overlooked in these books. McAndrew paid no attention to such nonsense; but the Board, which had also received copies, appointed a Thompson Board member, who took them seriously, to confer with the board of superintendents.[10] In one of his off-hand remarks McAndrew one day criticized the old picture of three soldiers, called the "Spirit of '76," as not giving an accurate picture of what war really was like. At the next city council meeting, Bathhouse John Coughlin, alderman of the first Ward, made a ponderous denunciation of this traitorous remark—only to be answered angrily by Alderman William Meyering. Meyering had lost an arm in World War I, and in fact had been the first American soldier decorated for gallantry in action in the war, and *he* said he agreed with McAndrew.[11] Coughlin's resolution stopped right there.

The February, 1927, primary over, Thompson immediately began his attack in earnest on McAndrew. Miss Haley came out for Thompson. The Chicago Federation of Labor, whose vice president was now Alderman Oscar Nelson, a Thompson supporter, urged his election, as Thompson was not the representative of "big business." If the Federation wanted McAndrew out, out he should go.[12] Said Thompson, "I threw out Chadsey, who was imported here by the friends of British propaganda, and I'll throw out McAndrews." He accused the superintendent of conspiring with Merriam and Judd of the University of Chicago to "destroy the love of America in the hearts of children by encouraging teachers to attend special classes at 'Chicago University' at which a text was used which pictured George Washington as a rebel and a great disloyalist." Over and over he expounded his promises to repeal the Volstead Act, and the Chicago city water metering law, to kill the World Court, to kick out the unpatriotic text books, and to keep America first! He attacked the superintendent because nine new school buildings had been built so poorly that they were not safe for use.[13] That the contracts had been placed by the Board in his own previous regime was not mentioned. He declaimed that evil text books were being given children. But the president of the Dever Board, Charles Moderwell, couldn't be heard for the noise when he pointed out that they had been approved by Thompson's former Board of Education, and that the questionable history book by Muzzey was not even on the list. The Hearst papers supported Thompson and the America First campaign with enthusiasm.

Thompson won the election by a 51 percent majority. His opponents asserted that 100,000 or one-fifth of his votes were stolen. His plurality over his two opponents was 31,861. The Negro wards, then Republican, gave him 65,000 of his votes. But he won, took office in April, 1927, and proceeded to put some of his threats and promises into effect. By resignations and appointments he got a majority on the Board of Education. "Iron-Handed Jack" Coath was elected president. He had also been on the 1922 Thompson Board. Coath was an off-and-on supporter of Thompson, like Crowe and many other party notables whose rapid shifts from shocked denunciation to fulsome praise, or vice versa, were dizzying to watch. He was pleased that Thompson had picked him for Board president, and he proceeded to lay about him vigorously to carry out the Mayor's orders.

After the election the first shot at McAndrew was aimed by the city council. Alderman Wiley Mills, an ex-Dunne era Board member close to Miss Haley, sent a letter to McAndrew on May 16, asking him to explain a statement the Tribune had quoted him as making, before he came to Chicago, to the effect that he had been brought to Chicago to "loose the hold of the City Hall and certain outside agencies on the schools." Mills asked who had brought McAndrew here and what were these agencies. McAndrew's answer listed the names of the members of the Board of Education who had voted for his appointment. Then he summarized the entire statement from which the sentence had been lifted, saying that it had been made at a conference to which he was invited by the president of the Board, and that he had found that "city school systems which had ejected political influence from promotions, choice of sites and textbooks had improved their services." He added that his unsolicited election by the Board three weeks later had indicated to him that the Board "desired the schools to be managed according to the law here, and according to usage elsewhere." On May 19 the City Council Committee on Schools, Fire and Civil Service asked him to appear before them. The new Board of Education Committee on School Administration voted that he should obey the summons, but action on their recommendation was deferred for two weeks. In the meantime, McAndrew settled the matter himself. He wrote to the chairman of the council committee, "Your resolution suggests that you are proposing to try me before your committee. I don't see what, other than personal satisfaction to yourself, could come of it. Much as I love you, I'll have to deny myself that favor to you."[14]

Then on August 3, 1927, Todd, the attorney for the Board, ruled that teacher clerks must now be employed through the City Civil Service Commission, as were janitors. The superintendent had supported the clerks in their request for an injunction against he action of the Board.

Trial of McAndrew

On August 29 the attorney of the Board presented the charges of insubordination he had been ordered by the President of the Board to prepare against McAndrew, and by a vote of six to five the Board voted to suspend him pending trial.[15] The charges in August were based on his support of the school clerks. McAndrew employed as attorneys, Francis X. Busch, who had been Dever's respected corporation counsel, and Angus Shannon, the ex-school Board attorney who had drafted the Otis law. The charges were answered factually, and the suspicion that the action of the Board was merely a way to increase the number of patronage jobs was added forcefully. Apparently Todd, the current Board attorney, was not acceptable to Thompson, and Frank Righeimer, one of the mayor's proteges, was made prosecutor in the superintendent's trial. Righeimer had been appointed as County Judge for a short while to fill an unexpired term, but was defeated in 1922, and Thompson had gotten him appointed attorney to the Board of Education.[16]

In September the trial began. McAndrew read newspapers while it unfolded, and on November 20, he yawned, announced that he was leaving and would come back when and if the Board wished to dismiss the charges against him, as most of what was being said had nothing to do with them. Finally in March, 1928, the Board voted to dismiss him, two months after his four-term was over, with only Mrs. William Hefferan and James Mullenbach dissenting. McAndrew sued the Board for $6,000 in back salary and Thompson for $250,000 for libel, but withdrew the suits when a Circuit Court judge ruled that he had been unjustly dismissed, there being no basis for the charges either on grounds of insubordination or lack of patriotism.[17]

But for five months after McAndrew walked out of the trial the dreary repetition of ridiculous charges droned on. It got headlines all over the world. Some eighty teachers, principals, or other school officials who had objected to any of McAndrew's activities were summoned, or came voluntarily to testify against him, while "Iron-Handed Jack" Coath munched pretzels. Three pseudo-historians presented long tirades against the history books which were the ordinary ones in use all over the country. Trumped-up organizations with such names as the "Anti-British Citizens Committee on School Histories" made endless accusations. That mild social organization, the English Speaking Union, was accused of conspiring with the University of Chicago to bring McAndrew to Chicago to do its devilish work with evil books preaching that George Washington was a rebel—a statement, which, after all, did seem to be quite an obvious fact!

The mayor wrote a letter to the Board of Education which was read into the trial, ordering that specific Polish, German, and other ethnic heroes be "taught" in the schools.[18] Righeimer drew national attention by screaming at McAndrew, "And you left out of the schools the name of that great hero, Ethan Allen, who said he had only one life to give for his country!" Since that one noble sentiment was about all most Americans ever heard about Nathan Hale, even the audience at the trial laughed.[19] The announcement by Thompson's Public Library Board appointee, one Sport Hermann, that he was going to burn the pro-British books in a bonfire on the lakefront, further enlivened the dull proceedings. The book burning, of course, was a poignant idea for a city which never had a Public Library until the British author, Thomas Hughes, with Queen Victoria's blessing, collected and sent books after the fire of 1871 to replace the ones they thought must have been burned!

At the end, in March, 1928, only nine spectators were present to hear Righeimer's peroration, which summed up all the charges. "As early as 1916," he began, "the University of Chicago organized a Public Education Association, which found fault with Mayor Thompson's Board of Education, and tried to get the law amended to give the superintendent more power. Allen B. Pond, 'who belonged to this group fighting the Loeb rule,' was the organizer of the English Speaking Union." As a member of the "Pond organization," McAndrew was indifferent "to the effects on school children of un-American history books and other British propaganda; he treated the teaching force despotically; he imposed on the schools obsolete and unsound teaching methods by threats and intimidation" until citizens and teachers held meetings to protest. "But a leader was needed. They turned to William Hale Thompson for help. With characteristic courage and energy he espoused the cause of citizens, crying 'They shall not teach that George Washington was a rebel!' "[20] And then the farce was over.

Yet somehow the miracle of public education, in a vast system with a half million pupils, went on. Children learned, and most teachers did their best to teach. The vicious and absurd antics of the powers in office were taken in their stride by children and teachers. The editor of the Parker High School paper wrote an editorial on the McAndrew trial, ending,

"Rid our schools of that horrible British taint,
Make the history books tell things as they ain't!"[21]

The Board solemnly debated suspending him but reluctantly decided they had better not. Children make their own judgments, and the teachers were at least accomplishing some of the aims of public education in spite of the frustration and stupid nonsense.

Effects of Thompson's Regime

There were three aftermaths to the trial. The first was of no great importance to the school system. On October 11, 1929, George Gorman, the ex-Congressman who had sent the first statement attacking the history books to Mayor Dever, and who had appeared at length in the trial, wrote David Saville Muzzey, whose high-school history text had been attacked so viciously, that he had never read the book himself, and that the statements he had made—and sworn to—had been written by someone else; he had been misled and now found nothing in Muzzey's books to criticize. Board member Mullenbach read the letter into the Board record, and introduced a resolution that the Board of Education apologize to the people of the city for wasting their money on McAndrew's "so-called trial," to David Muzzey for the charges made by the Board against him, and to Charles E. Merriam and to Charles H. Judd for accusing them of conspiring against the children of Chicago. He also called to the attention of the State's Attorney of Cook County and of the Chicago Bar Association that Gorman, who was a member of the bar, had admitted that he knowingly testified falsely under oath. The resolution was sent to a committee, but never heard of again. Neither the lawyers nor the businessmen were anxious to take on the vindictive Thompson. Many of the "civic" groups opposed Thompson's ridiculous list of bond issues in 1928, totaling $78 millions, but the Association of Commerce did not take action even though the Civic Federation's analysis indicated financial trouble ahead, and the city's budget already showed a deficit.[22]

A Public Emergency Committee had been organized during the McAndrew trial to protest the whole outrageous procedure. In January, 1928, this committee stated that Board members were pledged to dismiss McAndrew before they were appointed by Thompson, that Coath, who had made the charges, was himself the judge who conducted the trial, that most of the hearings had nothing to do with the charges, and that the record showed that Coath himself had voted to approve every one of the books he now denounced. But the president of the University of Chicago, Max Mason, and of Northwestern University, Walter Dill Scott, were the moving spirits of this group, and Charles Merriam the chief spokesman, not the leaders of business and industry.

The second aftermath was the end of the fantastic drama of Thompson's own career, of which the McAndrew trial was one of the last major scenes. His tumultuous victory in 1927 went to his head. During the McAndrew trial, Thompson was off on a Presidential campaign junket, collecting ten-dollar memberships for his America First organization, a scroll from Huey Long inscribed to "one of the greatest living Americans," and a promise of support from William Randolph Hearst at San Simeon. But by the time of the April primary in 1928, the underworld support and control of the Thompson regime had become so evident that all his candidates went down to defeat. Crowe, who had been his nemesis in 1923, but was now his strongest partisan, was defeated for the Republican nomination for state's attorney by John Swanson. When Swanson's home and that of his sponsor, U.S. Senator Deneen, were bombed before the primary, Crowe had accused them of planting the bombs themselves.[23] There had been 107 gang murders the year after Thompson's election, and organized prostitution and bootlegging were flourishing. The amount of violence before and during the primary gave it the nickname of the "pineapple primary."

Thompson's candidate for governor, Len Small, already forced by the court to return $600,000 in interest on public money he had kept while State Treasurer, and Frank L. Smith, who had been refused his seat in the U.S. Senate for taking campaign contributions from Insull, the utility magnate, while still head of the State Public Utility Commission, were also defeated.

When the mayor got back from the National Republican convention in June, where no one seemed to want him to be president, he was faced with a court order from a suit brought by the Tribune to pay back to the city, personally, $2,455,604 for illegal payments made to so-called real-estate experts. Thompson's heyday was over. He was roundly defeated for mayor in 1931, tried to organize a far-right political party in 1936 with Huey Long and Father Coughlin, and rather pitifully ran for mayor again in 1939, but he was through. On the day after his defeat in April, 1931, the Tribune wrote his political epitaph:

> "For Chicago, Thompson has meant filth, corruption, obscenity, idiocy and bankruptcy. He has given the city an international reputation for moronic buffoonery, barbaric crime, triumphant hoodlumism, unchecked graft and a dejected citizenship. He made Chicago a byword of the collapse of American civilization."

The third aftermath, was the direct impact of the Thompson patronage system on the Chicago schools. Perhaps Thompson himself was through by April 1928; but the full force of what happened in the school system as a result of his invasion lasted twenty years—perhaps longer. When McAndrew was suspended by the Board in August, 1927, his assistant superintendent, William J. Bogan, was made acting superintendent and in June, 1928, was formally elected to the office. To the very best of his ability, Bogan defended the educational department against the onslaughts of the Thompson Board. There *were* onslaughts. President Coath called in some 200 elementary principals and scolded them for making speeches (of all things!) to Kiwanis Clubs—a clear warning against criticism of the regime—ending with the inspiring remark, "Some of you are unbearable. You must remember that you are no more than a small cog in a great educational machine."[24] Evidently the educational machine was also the political one. Superintendent Bogan was ordered by the mayor to have teachers distribute handbills to all children advertising his ill-starred city lottery scheme. (It never got off the ground because the Association of Commerce and the State Street stores would not participate.) The superintendent flatly refused. Thompson denounced him as heartless and impractical and assigned policemen to distribute the handbills outside the schools.

The Board did spend $6,000 on booklets containing patriotic songs and the "contributions of racial strains." The superintendent and parents found they could do little about the speakeasies that sprang up around the high schools. Parents reported five near Senn, six near Hyde Park, and six near Englewood to the police, but got no help.[25] In the 1931 mayoralty campaign the Board of Education authorized sending 20,000 special-delivery letters to Board employees on Board stationery the night before the election. The new president of the Board, Lewis Myers, refused to authorize the cost of the special-delivery stamps, since the Board had already had to skip one payday. A copy of a "School

Report," indirect Thompson campaign propaganda paid for from school funds, was, however, given to each child.

Racketeers Take Over Some School Jobs

Bogan's staunch defense of the educational department had no effect on the exploitation of the non-teaching force. Already a good sized army of approximately 3,000, it was annexed complete to the Thompson patronage machine, and became not only politically controlled but in some areas "underworld" controlled. Thompson's bootlegging friends demanded their share of the school loot in areas other than protected high-school speakeasies. When Joseph Savage, who had open Capone support, was defeated for the county judgeship, Thompson appointed him to the Board of Education.[26] It was generally believed that the Capone interests had contributed a quarter of a million dollars to the 1927 campaign. And certainly no Chicago policeman ever arrested Scarface Al himself. Daniel Serritella, Capone's lieutenant and a state senator, was appointed City Sealer—and arrested in 1931 for forcibly collecting money from "protected" short-changing store keepers.

One Jack Zuta, whose careful records of contributions (and loans to judges and the mayor of Evanston) were found in his pocket when he was finally shot, recorded a $50,000 contribution to Thompson's 1927 campaign. Among his papers was a complete analysis of the weekly take of the Moran gang of $400,000; Zuta's own department was collecting protection from houses of prostitution. A deputy sheriff's courtesy card along with the other records was in his pocket. He had been one of the 500 loyal Thompsonites who had accompanied Thompson on the presidential junket and had entertained as host all 500 junketeers at a regal banquet.[27] Zuta was a mysterious character who shifted his allegiance from Capone to Moran and back as easily as State's Attorney Crowe became pro- or anti-Thompson. He was one of the people accused of the murder of Capone's good friend, Tribune reporter Jake Lingle. When Zuta was shot, the executor of his will, to whom he left some money, was a friend named Nate de Lue. De Lue had been paid as a Thompson real-estate expert. His occupation was given as secretary of a distillery (during prohibition!).[28]

As soon as Thompson was elected in April, 1927, Nate De Lue was employed as an "inspector" in the business manager's office, on a sixty-day "temporary" appointment which was renewed as long as Thompson was mayor. On January 1, 1928, a loyal Thompson Board of Education member moved that he be promoted to assistant business manager and his salary raised to $5,200, and this was done.[29] The janitors and school clerks were already "civil service"; the director of the Playground Division had been dismissed and replaced by a more pliable administrator who urged that the playground directors also be put under "civil service." Todd, the Board attorney unacceptable to Thompson, was replaced (after an argument as to when his term began) by an ardent admirer of the mayor, Thomas V. Sullivan. Sullivan was the organizer of the ten-dollar membership drive for his national America First organization. At least he remained faithful to Thompson and was a candidate for attorney general of Illinois for the far right party in 1936. When Thompson was defeated by Cermak in 1931, the new mayor demanded the dismissal of De Lue, Sullivan, and Withal, who had gone to jail in the 1922 Thompson Board scandal—but was still on the payroll.

There were ninety-six different classes of "civil service" employees of the Board of Education by September, 1927. Twenty-five percent of them were not needed for the services of the schools, according to the business manager, and no janitors were in the schools on any election day. On March 2, 1929, the Tribune carried the story that the "Labor Bureau" of which De Lue was the head had forty employees and cost $150,000 a year, and that its abolition would save a million dollars of desperately needed school funds. By this time there were 2,500 sixty-day temporary political appointees in the ninety-six categories.[29] Their reappointment depended not on their services to the schools, but to the Thompson political organization. Civil Service examinations were seldom given, and when they were, the results were unchanged. One teacher clerk who took the clerks' examination said girls were passed on the stenography examination who didn't know one "hook" from another. Alderman Jackson of the Third Ward in an interview stated blandly to a University of Chicago student interviewer just how many janitresses from his ward would be passed on the next examination. President of the Board Caldwell sent a letter to the 1928 June graduates of the Normal Colleges telling them if they wished to be school clerks, to get a letter from their precinct captain and bring it to his office.[30]

The Board Proceedings were padded with recurring pages in fine print of the names of hundreds of employees appointed and dismissed. On August 11, 1927, 1,200 temporary appointees were employed and 800 separated. On May 9, 1928, about the same number of janitors, school clerks, truant officers, etc., were hired and let out. On June 20, 1929, not so many were hired, as there was no election in the offing. Every meeting of the Board had action on such a list until September, 1929. Every alderman had the list of those in his ward. Lewis Myers, who became president of the Board in 1930, denounced the Civil Service Commission (but not until *after* Thompson's defeat in 1931) to the effect that "They loaded us up with ward heelers and petty politicians, whose only value lay in their ability to get votes."

Racketeer Control

The situation became more vicious than ordinary patronage politics, however. There was an interlocking racket built in, to which many principals considered De Lue the key. The politically appointed janitors had been organized into a union in 1922. At first the initiation fee was $13, but it was soon raised to $50. A janitor was on probation for six months if he passed the Civil Service examination. If his "service" was not satisfactory, he lost his job—and his $50. What a temporary appointee paid for his job was a private matter; but the large numbers of probationers dropped was on record. Some janitors admitted they had dues collected from them twice at gun point.

The use of school funds and school payrolls to build a strong local political organization was, of course, no new thing in Chicago, or in other large cities the country over. But its sudden startling expansion and intrusion of known criminal elements into the gigantic apparatus was definitely contrary to the trend in other cities. The forces which had been successful in sending venal members of the Board of Education to jail in 1922, and in dislodging Thompson from the mayoralty in 1923, were equally vigorous in their opposition to Thompson's exploitation of the school in this current regime.

But the onset of the depression set a premium on the new school patronage system. All the local governments suddenly had less money to provide the jobs for precinct captains which were the lifeblood of any political organization whatever the party. Public employees who were not willing to contribute time and money to the party organization could expect less consideration in the allocation of the shrinking public funds. By the time Thompson left the City Hall in 1931, the huge patronage payroll in the schools was much more important to the Democrats than it had ever been to Thompson. The Democrats made no effort to reduce it—only to replace the Republicans with Democrats. The "reform" opposition which had been successful ten years before could get no support in either party now.

Chapter 10

THE SCHOOLS RUN OUT OF MONEY

The existence of the swollen patronage payrolls would not have been so serious a threat to the conduct of the schools had not the finances of the Chicago school system been gradually sliding into an untenable position even before the Thompson take-over and before the depression. When a well-meant effort to straighten out the tangled property tax system of Cook County collapsed and all tax collections were held up for three years until one-fifth of the working people of the city were unemployed, the schools were in dire distress. They had always been particularly vulnerable financially among the some 400 local taxing bodies in the county because of their dependence on the property tax. They had never been able to get enough funds either from the legislature or the city to provide seats for all the children they served, or for an average class size reasonable in comparison with those of other large cities. When the pie of available revenue was cut, either in the council or in the legislature, the Board members appointed by a mayor were usually loath to offend him by asking for a bigger share for schools than he found politically convenient to sponsor.

   In 1928 the Chicago Bureau of Public Efficiency, a private organization with roots in the Municipal Voters' League of the 90's, made a carefully documented study of the school system and of the growth of the procedures which had already brought the school finances into serious jeopardy by that year—meeting the growing cost of education by spending eleven years' taxes in ten years. They began with the reasons why the schools were costing more.

Costs Rise and Income Falls

   Enrolment in the Chicago schools shot up between 1915 and 1925. Such increase was inevitable. The city's population grew 21 percent. The economic life of the times required more skilled workers. A rising standard of living raised both expectations and opportunity. In 1914 30 percent of the children of

European immigrants, who then made up the largest sector of the city's population, had obtained work certificates at age fourteen,[1] but now more were in school. While the city's population grew 21 percent between 1915 and 1925, the elementary school enrolment increased 29.8 percent and the high-school enrolment 130 percent. The high-school enrolment in 1925 was five times that of 1906. Commercial and technical courses requiring added space and expensive equipment were in demand in the high schools. Manual training and household arts were available to all elementary pupils. Physical education at all levels was expanding, and classes for several kinds of handicapped children increased yearly. Kindergartens were taken for granted and were no longer rare exceptions. Eleven thousand additional children were expected annually.[2]

The child labor law of the state had raised the school leaving age to sixteen years, unless sixth grade had been completed, and continuation school attendance was expected in Chicago of children under seventeen who did leave school. Some 100 "truant officers" now pursued absent children to compel attendance, frequently with little understanding of the social problems involved, as the officers were not required to meet any standards except passage of a simple City Civil Service examination. A Bureau of Vocational Guidance since 1916 had directed a group of vocational advisers and sixteen visiting teachers, and had worked with the Children's Scholarship League, which, under private sponsorship, provided the means for keeping some children in school. The Montefiore and Mosely Schools were providing physical and psychological care for some socially maladjusted boys.

Text books were now furnished free, after forty years of argument. As early as 1885 the Illinois State Federation of Labor had sought free books. By 1896 free texts were compulsory in ten states and permissive in nineteen, and seventeen of the twenty-eight largest cities provided books for all children. Though supported by the Civic Federation, a 1901 bill in the legislature had been defeated by strongly organized German Catholic societies, and the Chicago Chronicle had opposed free books as straight socialism. Parents had to sign a statement saying they were too poor to buy books, to obtain for their children the "Fund Books" bought with money from private gifts to the school system. In 1919 the Illinois legislature passed a law permitting the use of public funds for free texts, after a local referendum. A petition circulated by the Chicago Federation of Labor, the teachers' organizations, and a number of civic agencies put the free textbook referendum on the ballot in 1921. The Chicago Board of Education and Mayor Thompson opposed the referendum, but it passed with a hairline majority of 7,000.[3]

There were other new expensive services. A flourishing Junior College in the Crane High School building enrolled more than 1,200 students. The Normal College had become a three-year course, grown from an enrolment of 866 in 1915 to 1,851 by 1925. Fifty-six playgrounds adjacent to school buildings had been taken over from the city by the Board of Education. Bus transportation for handicapped children, extension of "penny lunches" and bathrooms in schools in low-income areas all took more money. The 1922 teachers' pension law required that the Board of Education appropriate funds if the property tax rate set for pensions by the legislature did not bring in a given amount, and a quarter of a million dollars of educational funds were now going for pensions every year. Community centers and evening schools were drawing increasing numbers of adults. The inflation during World War I had increased all prices in 1917, and salaries after 1922. The addition of the non-teaching employees to the army of city political employees brought an increase in a decade of 324 percent in maintenance and operation as against an increase of 176.6 percent in instructional costs. The shift from cash to credit operation of the schools had increased debt charges to almost a million dollars a year. The $16,846,801 budget of 1915, had become $56,089,348 in 1925,[4] and $83,800,000 by 1929.

There had been no new school buildings during World War I. The tremendous increase in high-school enrolment after the war, and the creation of a system of junior high schools by Superintendent McAndrew, which required new, separate buildings, had added to an already existing seating shortage. The Report of the Educational Department to the Board of Education for 1926-27 showed a shortage of 428 high-school rooms and 842 elementary school rooms, although rapid shifts in population had left 341 elementary classrooms unused. Six hundred two portable school buildings were in use to provide space needed both in overcrowded neighborhoods and in the thinly populated newer areas at the edges of the city. The 1926 report stated that there were 3,000 pupils in portables in the outlying areas alone, that 37,500 other children lacked adequate building facilities and there was a need for adding 11,000 seats every year. In 1927 new buildings to accommodate 14,300 pupils were opened. But to acquire sites and to construct enough buildings to meet the actual seat shortage would have required expenditures of 31 million dollars. Approximately 9.5 million dollars worth of new construction each year would be necessary just to keep up with the annual increase in enrolment. The Building Fund tax rate as applied to the current assessed valuation in Chicago brought in $7,147,000 in 1926; but of this amount only 4.4 millions could be used to replace Civil War era buildings and to catch up with the seating shortage as the remainder was used annually for repairs and upkeep of existing structures.

All of these factors were at work in every large city school system, of course. But the Chicago schools had a special problem. For ten years they had been spending more than had been taken in each year. This miracle was possible because, up to 1915, the Board of Education had not spent tax money until after it was collected. The tax levied for 1914 was collected by the end of 1914 and was spent in 1915 as cash in hand. No money was borrowed for current expenses. But by state law, a municipality might spend the 1914 tax in 1914 if it wished, by the device of selling tax warrants up to 75 percent of the year's tax levy, before the taxes were completely collected. Between 1915 and 1926, the Board of Education shifted from cash in hand to credit by sale of tax warrants, and in doing so had used up almost eleven years of tax income in ten years time. In 1925 it based its current budget on 1925 taxes and counted anything left over from 1924 as surplus. In 1926 it spent 9 millions of this so-called "surplus." By 1927 the miracle was over. There was nothing to spend but the 1927 taxes not yet collected. The Board had reached the end of the line on fancy bookkeeping and was faced with the cold fact that there must be a sharp increase in its tax rate, more money contributed by the state, or higher assessed valuation of the property which was taxed.[5]

Every four years the Board of Cook County Assessors was obliged to revalue every piece of property in the county. Nineteen twenty seven was the year for this quadrennial assessment. The 1927 session of the legislature did increase the tax rate for Chicago schools by a small amount, and if the assessed value of the property in the city were increased by 230 million dollars, the schools could continue to operate on the 1926 scale with no improvements. In Superintendent McAndrew's Annual Report for 1926, after pointing out the progress the schools had made under his direction, he declared that the school's financial system was near the breaking point, now paying $921,148.28 in unproductive interest each year. He added

> "On the basis of present revenues, the schools can not complete the year 1927 without exceeding legal borrowing power, and unless additional revenues are provided at once, the schools can not go through the year 1927, without omitting some of the regular sessions, or cutting teachers' salaries, or eliminating present activities."[6]

It was clear that there must be more income from somewhere Aid from the state was rising, but very slowly in proportion to the Chicago budget. The original 1855 two-mill property tax had been changed to a flat million appropriation in 1871, and continued at that amount for 36 years until 1907, when a state educationl commission pointed out how much more the 2-mill tax would now be producing at current property values. The legislature added a million each biennium till 1925, when it set aside the sum of $16,114,000, without any relation to the old state property tax for schools. But Chicago's share of the 1925 state fund was only 6.1 percent of the city's expenditure for schools, as against 5.5 percent in 1915.[7] Fully 90.9 percent of the school income came from the local property tax. The remaining 3 percent came from rent and income from the school lands. The legislature had allowed a 140 percent increase in tax rate for the Chicago Board of Education since 1915, but the assessed valuation of the growing city was only 20.43 percent more than in 1915. Per capita costs per pupil throughout the state had increased from $37.54 to $95.01 between 1913 and 1925, but in Chicago only from $55.05 to $108.88, a considerable smaller rate of increase. Measured in 1913 dollars, not even the state figure had doubled.

The 1927 school budget raised the total estimated expenditures 2 million dollars over 1926. Each year $1,600,000 more was needed for the educational fund for new pupils alone. Each of the five separate funds set up by the legislature with separate tax rates (educational, building, playground, pension, and text book funds) had to have more money each year. Class sizes were already being increased. There were 45.5 pupils on the average per teacher in elementary schools, in 1926. Any reduction in class size, by just one pupil, would cost $350,000 in high schools and $400,000 in elementary. Proposals to raise salaries as recommended by McAndrew would eventually have cost 7 millions more. There was no prospect of replacing obsolete buildings or reducing the 37,500-seat shortage without more income. Five more playgrounds had been authorized for 1927, but the money to operate them would have to come from increased valuations. An increase in valuation might reduce the contribution to the pension fund from the educational fund, since the pension tax rate would then increase the pension fund income, and decrease the deficiency contribution from the general fund—but it might not, as the number of teachers retiring was increasing each year.[8]

New Property Tax Assessment

The quadrennial assessment could solve these problems. Building permits in the three years 1921 to 1924 showed $879,568,000 worth of new construction; but only $100,000,000 of these buildings had been added to the assessment rolls. Between 1915 and 1925 the population had grown 27.7 percent, and the Building Department had issued two billion dollars' worth of permits for new buildings. The assessed valuation of Chicago had been $1,562,683,000 in 1915, and it was only $1,882,067,000 in 1925. Between 1915 and 1926 the yearly increase in assessed valuation had averaged only 29 million a year, while the building permits averaged 200 million. While the assessed valuation barely changed, the real-estate tax collected per capita had risen from $1.77 in 1915 to $3.58 in 1925, doubling since 1915 and almost tripling since 1913. Moreover, the state legislature had ordered that the 1927 reassessment should be at 100 percent of full value, as required in the state constitution, not an arbitrary fraction set by local elected assessors.[9]

Of course, it was general knowledge that the assessing system was a haphazard, politically manipulated affair; people who might have had power to change it were apparently interested in keeping it that way, whether they were party leaders or large taxpayers, because few protests were heard. The Illinois Tax Reform Association had for years protested the increasing failure to tax personal property, and to tax corporations. "Everybody knew" the precinct captain could get taxes reduced. But financial problems were looming before all the local governments in Chicago. The City and the Sanitary District were also beginning to feel the pinch of inadequate income. To be sure, each of these branches was accused of having large numbers of employees who were really paid to work for the political organization instead of the government, and were either temporary appointees, supposedly under civil service, or straight political appointees. The Sanitary District had no civil service law at all until 1935, and had increased its payroll from 3 million dollars to 10 million in seven years with no increase in service.[10]

The school system and the city government under Mayor Dever had made some recovery from the blatant waste of the first Thompson regime. The city also had been able to increase its sources of income from areas other than the property tax. But sufficient concern about the future among the local governments prompted the city government, the Board of Education, and the teachers' organizations to cooperate in getting an appraisal of loop properties in 1926. The Board of Review of Cook County, however, refused to increase the loop valuations. Mandamus proceedings before the State Supreme Court to compel the Board of Review to do so were refused on the grounds that it was well known that property throughout the state was underassessed—in other words, since no one obeyed the tax laws, no one should be compelled to.

To the uninitiated it would have seemed that the way to get more money was to enforce the tax laws rather than ignore them; but no state or local official since 1872 had ever really considered such a thing. Of course the state constitution said beyond any shadow of doubt that all kinds of property must be taxed at full value and all at the same rate. In the pioneer society of 1848, when this constitutional provision had originated, property meant agricultural land, farm animals, and farm tools. Even in 1950 the personal property tax form, issued to the rare Chicago taxpayer who asked for it, required listing of the number of swine he owned, long since forbidden by law within the city limits. The greatest wealth of city people was no longer even the houses they lived in or could rent, but their possession of "intangible" personal property, of no value in itself except as it could produce income—stocks, bonds, mortgages, or franchises which allowed public utilities to operate. These the taxing authorities throughout the state calmly ignored, since collecting a tax on property useful only to produce income at the same rate as on real estate would confiscate the income. The tax assessors likewise made little effort to collect a tax on household furnishings, clothing, jewels, or other personal possessions except as an instrument of political retaliation. The railroads, however, did pay some 15 millions a year on their rolling stock by order of the Interstate Commerce Commission. Real estate in Cook County was estimated to be about one-third of the property in the county, but it paid approximately 85 percent of the property tax. It was this source of revenue on which the schools were dependent. Since this free and easy way of assessing property for taxation was almost at the whim of the elected tax assessors, the system was viewed with cynical suspicion by most citizens. So serious had the situation become in Cook County that a group of responsible bankers and business men took the initiative in trying to bring some order into the assessment process.

Investigation of Tax Graft

After considerable discussion, in January, 1927, the Cook County Board of Commissioners was induced to appoint a "Joint Committee on Real Estate Valuation," which included representatives of this group and county tax officials. However, the latter, five assessors and three members of the Board of Review, were all elected, and not under the jurisdiction of the County Board; they simply ignored the citizens' committee, and went about the 1927 assessment in their usual fashion. George Fairweather, business manager of the University of Chicago, which owned large loop properties, was chosen chairman, and John O. Rees, an expert from the Cleveland Bureau of Municipal Research at the time that city had revised its assessment system was employed as director. The committee set about collecting facts, a process complicated by the fact that the Board of Review flatly refused access to all records of previous assessments.

The negative attitude of elected officeholders toward the committee's efforts was encouraged when Thompson was reelected mayor in the spring of 1927. The mayor immediately assured all officeholders that this was no era of reform. One candidate on his ticket in 1928, Edward Litsinger, campaigned for reelection to the Board of Tax Review openly defending the method of giving favors to friends and promising to continue doing so. He was reelected.[11]

The quadrennial assessment had been made by the county assessors without regard to the Joint Committee's efforts. But the Committee published a preliminary report in June, 1927, immediately on completion of the new assessment, alleging that it was less uniform than that of the previous four years, and urging reconsideration on many points. The Committee's recommendations were supported by vigorous editorials in the metropolitan press and by civic organizations generally. Public meetings were held in many parts of the city by community organizations. The channels of communication offered by the Chicago Bar Association, the League of Women Voters, the Federation of Womens Clubs, the Federation of Civic Agencies, churches, forums, and the teachers' organizations were all used to spread concrete information on the seriousness of the tax situation and the failure of the reassessment to correct it in way. The assessors, among other items, had completely ignored the specific new state law requiring that all property be assessed at full or 100 percent value according to the constitution. Of course, most of the other assessors in the state ignored it, too. It was clear that the total valuation had not been increased to any extent, and this was a blow to the school people, teachers and administrators, alike.

The leaders of the teachers' organizations had known the discouraging school finance situation, whether others did or not. Ever since 1899 the teachers' organizations had taken the initiative in getting more money for the expanding school system, not the Boards of Education. In this emergency, they were already at work, planning to use the method by which Margaret Haley had been successful in 1899, high-school organizations taking the lead this time. They instituted court suits against corporations which failed to pay taxes on their capital stock as the law required. In 1916 Miss Haley and these high-school groups, then just beginning, had considered such legal action, but the Loeb rule fight and World War I had interfered. In 1925 Miss Haley had planned another suit, sending a letter to the Board of Education in 1925 offering to cooperate with it in "ferreting out tax dodgers." The Board showed no interest, perhaps partly because the President of the Board, Charles Moderwell, was an official of the Peoples Gas Company, an inevitable object of such a search of public utility franchise taxes. In 1924 the high-school unions set up an organized speakers' bureau and began collecting the thousands of dollars necessary to pay for suits, pointing out that platoon schools were not necessary if taxes were paid according to the law. In 1925 the Firefighters' Union of Chicago firemen won such a suit and thereby added $800,000 to the revenue of the local governments in the county. Plenty of other corporations could be attacked on the same basis. By 1926 the high-school unions were ready to enter two suits; but by this time Miss Haley had had what seemed her a better idea, and would not go along.

New Tax Laws and Reassessment

Miss Haley had been working since January, 1927, with the Joint Committee on Real Estate Valuation. In August, 1927, Mr. Rees had conferred with her on cooperation in getting the State Tax Commission to hold hearings on a request for a proposed second reassessment and perhaps to intervene in the "appalling condition of assessment in Chicago." In September, 1927, the Joint Commission formally asked for such a hearing, and on October 5 Miss Haley joined in the request.

It was at this point that the high-school unions and the Federation with Miss Haley as spokesman had their first serious confrontation. In November, 1927, the meeting of the Chicago Division of the Illinois State Teachers Association was the scene of sharp public disagreement. The high-school unions urged support of the suits, and rather gingerly supported the second reassessment, pointing out the grave danger of delay in getting paid. Miss Haley said the suits were too slow, and in an impassioned two-hour speech promised the teachers of Chicago fourteen millions more for schools from the proposed second reassessment, assuring them the city council would take care of credit in case of delay. She won four to one (the same proportion as elementary teachers to high), but the high-school teachers decided to push the suit anyway by themselves.

The hearing for a new assessment was held November 10. One of the grave points at issue was the failure of the Board of Assessors to publish the names of taxpayers with the amounts at which their properties were assessed. Such publication was required by law; but the law had never been complied within Chicago in twenty years. The Board of County Commissioners asked Cook

County State's Attorney Robert E. Crowe to enforce the law. He refused to admit that the law required publication; but Attorney General of Illinois Carlstrom ruled that the law did require publication of assessment rolls. On January 24, 1928, the chairman of the State Tax Commission, William J. Malone, ordered that the 1927 list of assessments be published. The Cook County Board of Assessors said that the State Tax Commission had no authority over them, and that there was no money to publish the list. Besides, they claimed, if they did publish it, they would not give names, only legal descriptions of property. After hearings in which the State Tax Commission was given clear evidence of flagrant inequalities in assessment, the Commission ordered that the 1927 assessment be held invalid and ordered a complete new quadrennial assessment.[12]

The Board of Assessors and Board of Review replied that the 1927 assessment could not be declared invalid because it was not finished. The Board of Review had a mountain of complaints to which it had given no hearings as yet, and there was no 1927 reassessment really until the Board of Review was completely through. On May 29, 1928, Attorney General Carlstrom held the objections of the Cook County tax officials valid, and ruled that no reassessment could be ordered as long as there were complaints to be heard. Such deadlocks could stop any action indefinitely. In the meantime, tax bills for 1928 should have been going out. The school system was already spending its 1928 income without knowing its extent, by selling tax warrants to be paid out of 1928 property taxes.

The deadlock was broken by legislative action. The 1927 session of the legislature had authorized the appointment by Governor Small of a "Legislative Joint Revenue Commission." The governor finally appointed the commission in May, 1928. It met immediately with the Joint Committee on Real Estate Valuation (which after all had been officially appointed by the County Board), with Miss Haley, and with representatives of other civic groups, and decided that new legislation was required. In June the governor called a special session which approved the legislation recommended by the new commission. It authorized the State Tax Commission to order a reassessment whenever it saw fit, and required that a quadrennial assessment must be published with name and address of each property owner.

The publication began. It produced immediate and startling explosions. The newspapers carried pictures of identical properties, with assessments varying by thousands of dollars—with as much as a ten-to-one difference. The State Tax Commission, now sure of its authority, on July 19, 1928, issued a second order for a repetition of the 1927 reassessment. A request for an injunction to stop it was presented to County Judge Jarecki's court. County Treasurer George Harding said he would honor no bills for it. Finally an expert, Harry S. Cutmore, was employed by the Board of Assessors to make the revaluation as ordered. The State Tax Commission ordered that a record card should be kept for each separate piece of property, with unit foot values of land, cubic costs of buildings, and the actual size of lot and building. This had never been done before by the Cook County Assessors. A manual for these measurements was prepared and a permanent record card printed. Instead of revisions being made by an oral request to any member of the Board of Review, a written complaint was required. Copies of this request were to be placed on file. The reasons for the complaint were to be entered on the permanent record card and a copy of any change made went to the State Tax Commission.

The State Tax Commission made a public statement as to the reasons it had ordered the reassessment. The average rate of assessment was 31 percent, instead of the vague "about sixty" which the assessors had previously claimed was their proportion of assessed to actual value or the 100 percent required by the Constitution and by recent specific state law. One quarter million pieces of property in Chicago were assessed at less than 20 percent of their value, and 90,000 pieces from 50 to 100 percent. Calumet Township was assessed at 10 percent, Rogers Park at 33.5 percent. Small homes were assessed at 33.5 percent, but large homes at 28. The rate of assessment in Chicago was higher than in most of the rest of Cook County.

The assessors and members of the Board of Review threw every obstacle they could devise in the way of the second assessment and actually were able to delay its completion for a whole year. Instead of being ready in 1929, it was not completed until April, 1930, after the primary election and long after the beginning of the October, 1929 depression. Since the work of the staff was only a reappraisal, there was no legal reassessment until the Board of Assessors declared it was made, and the Board of Review turned over its books for the entry of changes. Apparently they had had some hope that the new lists would be thrown out if there was enough delay. The first assessment had cost $812,000; the second $1,478,000. But these were not the only costs.

The second reassessment, when published, blasted all the hopes of increased income for the Board of Education and the other local governments. In January, 1929, the Board of Education estimated the income it would eventually receive from the tax levy of that year as $62,400,000; and in July, 1929, had increased its budget by $21,400,000 to $83,800,000, expecting the increase to come from property tax. With the tax rate allowed by the legislature, a valuation of $5,710,000,000 of all the property in the city would have been required to get this amount in taxes. But the original 1927 reassessment had set only $4,250,000,000 as the assessed value of city property and the second reassessment brought it down to $3,825,000,000. Clearly the tax rate applied to 3 billion dollars would not get the tax money expected from 5 billion. Not more than $52,500,000 could be collected to redeem tax warrants issued against 75 percent of the property tax in the $83,899,999 budget. Moreover, the 1930 budget estimates of the Board were already too high, because the legislature had reduced the 1929 educational tax rate of $1.47 to $1.35 in 1930 and no more than $48,500,000 could come in in 1930.

The reason the second valuation was so much lower for property in the city than the first was the attempt to equalize valuations between the city and the rest of Cook County, and between Cook County and the rest of the state. The total valuation for the County was lowered $440,000,000 below the original 1927 valuation, so that the average would be 35 percent, the average for the state in 1927, in spite of the specific legislation requiring 100 percent. Because the average for suburban Cook County was lower than that for the city, the city assessments were lowered from the 35.9 to 27.8 percent. The arithmetic was fair, but the results were disastrous. The only way the local governments could get money to operate was to sell tax anticipation warrants to the banks—who were far from eager to buy them. The Board of Education furthermore had already sold more warrants than the legal 75 percent of the levy. By the end of 1929 the city and the Board of Education owed $101,525,000 to banks, $49,115,000 to other sources, and were obligating themselves to interest payments of $4,000,000 a year.

Neither the high-school teacher unions nor Miss Haley had been right in their prophecies. The high-school suits were entered, lost, appealed and lost; the unions had spent more than $7,000 on their suits, collected from teachers. Miss Haley's promised fourteen millions of additional annual income if the assessment were redone had proved to be a mirage; instead, future income would be millions less. There were not only no pots of gold at the end of the rainbow; by October, 1929, there were no rainbows in sight in any direction.

The Depression Reduces Tax Collection

Now the grim presence of the depression became the overriding factor in the life of the city. The downward spiral of employment, the closing of banks in every area as unemployed workers could no longer pay on mortgages and loans, the unwillingness of banks, in fear of closing, to tie up their remaining cash assets in tax warrants which might be worthless—and in any case had no sure date of redemption—all pressed harder upon the schools than on any other local government. The sale of tax warrants in advance of property tax collections was practically the only source of income of the Board. Tax bills for 1928 and 1929, issued to fully employed people in those years, were clearly not now going to bring in full tax payments from people without jobs. It was hard enough to eat; taxes could wait.

The teachers' pay checks for November, 1929, were late. The pay checks for December, 1929, were late. The pay for January, 1930, came in March, four weeks' pay in ten weeks. There was serious discussion that no money at all would be available after October, 1930, and the schools might have to close Perhaps William McAndrew was lucky to be gone! Whatever mistakes he had made, this financial mess had been coming for many years and was not of his making.

Banks began to tighten up on their loans as people defaulted on mortgages and businesses wanted to trade gilt-edged securities, like Mid West Utilities, for loans to tide them over what most people still thought was a temporary financial setback. The Clearinghouse Association, supported by the banks, had offered $250,000 to hasten the reassessment and thereby reduce the issuance of tax warrants. The city council nervously asked the Joint Committee on Real Estate evaluation to suggest ways of relief. The Joint Committee organized a group of fifty-eight citizens to raise 74 millions in emergency loans to tide the local governments over until tax collections could catch up. Silas Strawn, former president of the American Bar Association, served as chairman. The staffs of various civic agencies were loaned to the committee to help speed its work. The 74 million dollars raised by getting taxpayers with large amounts of accrued taxes to buy otherwise unsalable tax warrants dated 1928, 1929, and 1930, and hold them until they could be turned in as payment for taxes with accrued interest.[13] Then the committee asked the governor to call a special session of the legislature to enact legislation they thought would help. They wanted the outstanding tax warrants, issued beyond the amounts permitted by the reduced assessments, to be made legal, and tax payments for 1929 and 1930 scheduled in five installments, to be paid every ten months until 1935. They urged that the city, the county, and the Board of Education be allowed to issue bonds to set up a working cash fund from which they could borrow at least part of their own tax anticipation warrants and eventually save much interest. They recommended that limits be set on the amount a government might guess its tax income would be, preventing mistakes of the kind the Board of Education made in 1929.[14]

Meanwhile the Governor's Legislative Revenue Commission had been meeting and had prepared a recommendation for a constitutional amendment, abolishing the uniformity provision and giving the legislature broad general power over taxation.

The special session was called and convened. The underlying conflict between Chicago and the rest of the state erupted as usual. Downstate members supported the general tax amendment which would allow the legislature to pass an income tax if it wished to. Chicago members opposed it, because the city would pay the major amount of an income tax, and the downstaters, who for thirty years had refused to reapportion the legislative districts every ten years as required in the state constitution (and who would not do so for twenty more years), would decide how the money was spent. In the wrangling, two changes in the original tax amendment were made. The proceeds of any income tax would be divided 85 percent to the county in which it was collected and 15 percent to the state. By eliminating a clause on exemptions, the amendment did not make possible exemption of intangible personal property such as stocks, bonds, and mortgages, from the property tax, even if there were an income tax. The amendment was distorted and poorly drawn, doomed to the failure it met at the polls in 1930. But some of the Strawn bills passed with little argument and immediately raised the level of credit of the local governments somewhat.[15]

The Board of Education had been harder hit than any of the other local governments when the 1928 valuation was $600,000,000 below the 1926 figure instead of the hoped for $500,000,000 above. The Building Fund lost $2,712,000 in revenue, in spite of the current seat shortage of 54,638 and twenty high schools operating 55 percent over capacity. The Teachers Pension Fund lost $81,000, which meant that much more must be taken from the already depleted Educational Fund. The Playground Fund lost $109,000 and eight of the sixty-five playgrounds had to be closed. And the auditor made the grim statement that "there are insufficient revenues in sight to meet teacher payrolls after October, 1920."[16]

No other great city in the United States was in such financial straits, and nationwide attention was focused on Chicago. The Literary Digest for January 25, 1930, carried an article, "Chicago—A Pauper City," showing a cartoon of squealing pigs at a trough labeled Chicago's Wasteful Politics, and alleging that crime was booming because 473 policemen had been fired. The Outlook for February 12, 1930 proclaimed "Chicago Broke": "The second American city can't pay its street cleaners, to say nothing of teachers, policemen and firemen," alleging civic corruption as one major cause. Douglas Sutherland, director of the Civic Federation, told "How Chicago Got That Way" in World's Work for May, 1930. "Corruption and inefficiency on a vast scale have plunged our second largest city so deep into bankruptcy that it is on the verge of closing its schools and losing police and fire protection." Paul Douglas, in the New Republic for February 13, 1930, said that "School janitors who were ward heelers got increases of 50 percent in two years, while instruction costs went up 9 percent in spite of rising enrolments. Any precinct captain can get taxes reduced."

Mayor Thompson meanwhile was blaming "the reformers" for all the city's troubles. He threatened to (but did not) lay off policemen and firemen, but did not even talk of dismissing any of the army of political appointees whose jobs were now more valuable than ever. In 1931 Thompson was ignominiously defeated by Anton J. Cermak, a Democrat. Cermak had the backing not only of the "wets," his original base of support, he had the solid backing of the business elite, of the Tribune, and also of some of the civic organizations. Although he had not reached the eminence of the presidency of the County Board without making some questionable connections of his own, Cermak had never openly defied the "respectable" element, as had Thompson.[17] Just what he would have done about the schools is difficult to say, as he was in office less than two years before he was shot while riding with Franklin D. Roosevelt in Miami. He did open his doors to the representatives of the teacher organizations and to the civic organizations concerned with the deterioration of instruction in the public schools. However, his major effort on schools in his two years in office was to criticize the Thompson appointees still on the Board for being unwilling to make the cuts business men recommended to restore credit. But he took no steps to reduce the excessive number of patronage jobs.

Since the Board of Education is not an elected body, it can not legally order a tax levy; it must have its annual levy approved by the elected city council. When the 1931 school levy came to the council for approval, action on the ordinance was delayed to bring pressure to reduce the total from 100 to 70 millions, but to no avail. The courts had held that the council can not legally change the school board levy.[18]

No Cash, Little Credit, Salaries Unpaid

Up to April, 1931, the school employees had been paid in cash, when the money finally came. From December, 1929, to March 1930, it was one to two months late. May, 1930, was on time, June, a month late. From September, 1930, to March, 1931, there were cash paydays on time, partly because of the efforts of the Strawn Committee. Then in April, 1931, the till began to run dry. Six weeks after it was due the April salary came in cash in May. In July and August teachers were offered scrip or tax warrants for services rendered in May and June. Scrip was paper stamped, over its printed value, "Not Sufficient Funds," issued to teachers in 1841 and 1878. Warrants could be used at face value to pay taxes in a year, but did not bring face value when teachers tried to sell them or offer them in payment for debt. Many teachers refused the scrip as illegal and worthless; the Federation challenged its legality in the courts. From March, 1930, to September, 1934, there were eight paydays on time for school employees and seven in the four years were in paper, not cash.[19]

Not only was there no money for salaries, there was no money to pay the banks interest on outstanding tax warrants, or to pay maturing bonds. The banks refused to buy more warrants. The tax assessing machinery was as thoroughly in disrepute as it had ever been, and the reduced income and financial uncertainty of the average taxpayer sharpened his resentment at his now well-publicized exploitation. An organized taxpayers' strike encouraged him not to pay any taxes even if he could. The realization that the depression was not a temporary matter deepened. The quadrennial reassessment, which should have been legally completed by the end of 1931—four years after 1927—had not even been begun by August 30 of that year. Tax bills for 1930 had not been sent out as ordered by the legislature. The tax machinery had again ground to a dead stop.

Part III

STRUGGLE TO DEFEND

INSTRUCTIONAL SERVICES

FROM POLITICAL

EXPLOITATION

Chapter 11

A GRADUATED INCOME TAX AND
A PLAN TO PROTECT INSTRUCTION

In June, 1931, Governor Emmerson appointed a Tax Conference to meet in July. Opening the conference, Governor Emmerson said "Bankruptcy and default stare us in the face in Cook County and some downstate counties. The people of Illinois and particularly of Cook County confront a revenue situation unparalleled in this or in any other state. We must solve this problem and solve it as soon as possible. . . . We must find some way of revising the tax system." The Tax Conference held thirty-three sessions. Leaders of industry and economic experts of the state agreed to serve, some fifty of them. The presidents of the three largest Chicago banks, Melvin Traylor, James R. Leavell, and Philip Clarke were among them. Fred Sargent, president of the Northwestern Railroad, Samuel Insull of the "gilt-edged" Midwest Utilities, Silas Strawn, Earl Smith of the Illinois Agricultural Association, C.V. Gregory of the State Street Council, George Nixon of the Real Estate Board, Douglas Sutherland of the Civic Federation, Victor Olander, Secretary of the Illinois Federation of Labor, Col. McCormick of the Tribune, Col. Frank Knox, owner of the Daily News, as well as the owners of the American and the Times, Mayor Cermak, and President Whealan of the Board of County Commissioners were all members. Samuel Insull was on the executive committee. The stated purpose of the conference was "To undertake a comprehensive study of the entire question [of taxes] in its relationship to both local and state governments, and to seek to find some feasible plan both for the immediate emergency for ultimate tax reform."

New Property and Income Tax Laws

On October 31, 1931, the Conference adopted a series of recommendations for legislative action. The most important were as follows:

193

1. Reorganization of the tax system in Cook County by the elimination of the present eight-member Boards of Assessors and Review, and the appointment by the Board of County Commissioners of a single board of three, one of whom shall be the assessor and the other two to act as reviewers with the assessor.
2. Issuance of bonds to retire tax warrants outstanding because of delayed tax collections, and to provide cash for purposes for which the levies were made.
3. Relief of real-estate tax payers by provision of new revenues from a graduated income tax and a tax on tobacco. "Every consideration points to the conclusion that the time has come for the enactment of a state income tax." The tax proposed had exemptions of $1,000 for single persons, $2,000 for couples, and $200 for dependents. Rates on taxable income were to be 1 percent on $1,000, 2 percent on $1,000-$4,000, 3 percent on $4,000-$9,000, 4 percent on $9,000-$16,000, 5 percent on $16,000 to $25,000 and 6 percent on all above $25,000. One hundred dollars of property tax was to be deductible. The revenue estimated was $30,000,000 a year. The new revenue was to replace the state property tax of 50 cents on $100 of property, to be divided between Cook County and the rest of the state for distribution to elementary school districts. The tax on tobacco was estimated to bring in $18,000,000 a year.
4. Creation of a state Department of Finance to administer income and tobacco taxes.
5. Collection of personal property tax on automobiles before granting a state license.
6. Payment of 1930 taxes in Cook County in six installments.
7. Equalization of property assessment by the use of a multiplier.[1]

In discussing the need for reduction in public expenditures by the local governments in Cook County, the report pointed out that in some instances there had been no effort to make reductions in keeping with falling costs. But it added "We are not unmindful of the fact that there are many essential expenses of government in which no reductions appear feasible. For example careful study of the salary scale of Chicago's school teachers is beyond the limits of our duties and opportunities. But it has not appeared to us that the salary scale is unreasonable." The report urged that reductions must be considered seriously, because it was certain that the 1931 quadrennial assessment when completed would reflect a fall in property values. "Unless municipalities pare their 1932 budgets to anticipate these tax reductions, there will be hopeless deficits and further impaired credit. If the local governments permit new deficits to occur in 1932, they will have only themselves to blame if the taxpaying and investing public refuses to come to their rescue." The report stated plainly that the measures proposed were not meant to be politically expedient. "Political expediency is almost wholly responsible for the situation in which we find ourselves. . . . The results of political expediency in public office are at the base of the taxpayers' distrust of the method in which public funds have been spent in Cook County. . . . No program shaped to conform to political expediency can pull us out of the morass."

When it adopted the report October 31, 1931, the Conference asked the governor to call a special session to enact its proposals, and he did so in November. The teachers' organizations opposed the proposal to grant the right to issue an unlimited amount of bonds for refunding or any other purpose, but supported the rest of the program with enthusiasm. But the city council voted on November 16 to oppose the change in the assessment machinery, although Mayor Cermak was on record as supporting it. It was clear that party leaders in either party in Cook County would not willingly give up one of their greatest sources of power. On November 18, Douglas Sutherland of the Chicago Civic Federation and Earl Smith of the Illinois Agricultural Association spoke to the legislature in support of the graduated income tax proposal, also opposed by Chicago members. On December 1, 1931, Melvin A. Traylor, president of the First National Bank, made a stirring address to the joint session of the legislature in behalf of the Governor's Tax Conference, urging the necessity of adoption of a graduated income tax.[2]

Traylor outlined the gravity of the situation in Chicago. Six hundred three and a half million dollars worth of tax warrants and bonds were now outstanding for the city, the county, and Sanitary District, the Board of Education, the three large Park Boards, and the Forest Preserve District. For 1932 a grand total of $186,494,000 was required just to pay current salaries, interest, and sinking funds for bonds. Only 82 percent of the taxes for 1928 had been collected by December 1931 and only 70 percent for 1929. The tax bills for 1930 had not yet been sent out. If only 70 percent of the 1930 taxes was paid promptly, it would not even amount to the 186 million dollars needed to pay basic current obligations. Already 150 millions of 1930 tax warrants had been sold—and they were the first claim on the 1930 taxes. The local governments could not pay 53 millions in interest due in 1932, nor certainly sell any more warrants on such hopeless credit. "This is Chicago now. Next year, it will be the state."

He said that there were valid reasons why people were not paying their property taxes. The first reason was that the revenue section of the 1870 state constitution was "utterly inflexible and impossible of legal enforcement." The people of Chicago had lost faith in the assessing system. A tax strike carried on by an organization of 30,000 members, who paid $10 apiece, was "murdering the credit of Cook County and Illinois." The Conference was attempting to lift from real estate the entire burden of supporting primary education in Illinois (which amounted to approximately 90 million dollars) and to substitute in lieu thereof a graduated income tax and certain sales taxes.

Said the president of the First National Bank to the Illinois General Assembly,

"I have always believed that everyone should pay some tax in proportion to their income. I think an income tax is the most equitable form of taxation in the world, if it is honestly drawn, and honestly applied. . . . The way to reach those who will not pay property tax is through an income tax, which I personally favor as against a sales tax. A sales tax penalizes the man or woman of small income to the advantage of the rich man. I have never favored a general sales tax as against a general income tax.

"What are the weaknesses in human nature that are paralyzing any attempt today to do anything constructive in Illinois? Selfishness, desire for special privilege, to escape a duty, to beat the game any way we can, apparently.

"There is an organized fight against the income tax. You say it is not constitutional, a thing about which I have serious doubts. If it is, we can change the constitution.

"We are obviously opposed to an income tax in Cook County because we would pay the larger share of the tax, and this legislature, dominated by downstate, will have the right to distribute it wherever they wish. Well, where in the name of Heaven are we going to get money to run the government except from those who have it?

"The time is gone for personalities; the time has come for adjournment of human selfishness in Illinois. The time has come when we can no longer play party politics. We can not trade the hungry, the unfed, the feeble voice of the sick, the empty bread basket of the unemployed against the maintenance of party preference or individual advantage."

Traylor's plea fell on deaf ears. While Cermak supported the Conference bills, the entire Chicago delegation in both Houses opposed them. Michael Igoe, Democratic leader in the House, had righteously denounced the corruption and misuse of the assessment system in 1930, and had sharply criticized the Strawn Committee for not presenting legislation to make drastic changes in it. But that was when he was minority leader and the Republicans controlled the tax machinery. Now that he was majority leader and the Democrats controlled the same machinery, it looked different to him, and he opposed any change whatever. Ex-governor Len Small and a group of his Republican followers also opposed any change. The Senate passed both income tax and appointed assessor bills in January, 1932, but the House stalled.

Teachers Get Million Signatures to Petition

In this crisis the teachers had not been idle. A corps of competent lawyers was employed by the major teacher organizations and they obtained 927,339 signatures to the following petition:

"TO THE 57TH GENERAL ASSEMBLY IN SPECIAL SESSION
The public schools of the City of Chicago have been supported since April 1931, by unpaid teachers and other school employees. Today the Board of Education owes over 18,000 teachers and employees more than twenty million dollars. These teachers and employees have used their savings, have borrowed money (often at 42 percent a year), have accumulated debts for food, clothing, rents and all other necessary expenses—to keep the schools open. They must have immediate relief. The General Assembly alone has the power to save our public schools by passing laws to restore public credit so that public obligations can be met and the school teachers and other employees be paid back salaries. It is the duty of the General Assembly as representatives of the people to pass whatever laws are necessary to provide relief for the Chicago schools. We call upon you, as our representatives, in this time of grave emergency, for Immediate Action to Keep our Schools Open."

The teachers' organizations rented the Stadium with the help of the Daily News, and held a huge mass meeting on January 4, 1932. An impressive roster of speakers urged legislative action to an overflow crowd of more then 27,000. Among them were Col. Frank Knox, later Roosevelt's Secretary of the Navy, Superintendent Bogan, James Mullenbach, member of the Dever Board of Education, Mayor Cermak, Mrs. Holland Flagler, president of the Illinois Congress of Parents and Teachers, Victor Olander, and Irwin A. Wilson, president of the Principals Club. Superintendent Bogan and Mrs. Hefferan urged the public to attend. On January 7, 1932, representatives of the teachers presented truckloads of the petitions to the legislature.

While the argument went on in the House of Representatives, further complications arose. On December 31, 1931, County Judge Jarecki held the entire 1928 and 1929 assessment rolls invalid, and thereby encouraged non-payment for those years. The State Supreme Court reversed this decision on April 9, but its effect had been serious. The Chicago Post of January 5, 1932, carried an announcement by County Superintendent of Schools Noble Puffer that thirty-five elementary schools in Cook County and the high schools in the Barrington area would have to close March 1, and that Oak Park schools would close April 1. The Cook County Real Estate Board came out against the income tax, although it had been represented in the Governor's Tax Conference. The Chicago Tribune, on January 9, 1932, ran an editorial, "The Blight of a New

Tax," complaining that so controversial a subject as income tax should not have been introduced at a session called to get money for schools. The Republican candidate for governor, William Malone, chairman of the State Tax Commission when the second reassessment was ordered, supported the whole program of the Governor's Tax Conference and declared that "Spoils politicians were more destructive than gangsters."

Income Tax Unconstitutional, Budget Cut

Both the bill on the income tax and on the change in the assessing machinery finally passed—after a month of wrangling, but not without amendments which made major alterations. The assessor and members of the Board of Review of Cook County were not to be experts appointed by the President of the County Board and approved by its members; they were to be elected on party tickets—and still are. The exemption on the income tax bill was raised to $2,500, which cut the amount expected for schools. On April 17, in the case of Bachrach versus Nelson, the State Supreme Court declared the income tax law unconstitutional on the grounds that it imposed a property tax in violation of the uniformity clause of Article IX of the State Constitution.[3]

The inheritance tax law, passed in 1895, had never had its graduated rates questioned, and in some other states, too, income had already been considered a privilege, not property, and not covered by the uniformity limitation on property taxes. All hopes of important new sources of revenue for 1932 vanished.

While the legislature was debating in January, 1932, the Chicago Board of Education was considering its 1932 budget. Since it was already evident that the value of real estate was down, and that the 1931 quadrennial reassessment when it was published would reflect this decline from 1927 valuations, the Board had announced on December 18, 1931, that it would cut 1932 expenditures 14 percent below 1931. The budget was presented on January 29. Omission of ten days of holiday pay made an 11.54 percent salary cut. One million thirty-five thousand dollars was saved by increasing the teaching load. School bathrooms in crowded areas were reduced by half, all sick leave pay was stopped, and there were sharp reductions in expenditures for the Normal and Crane Junior Colleges, for clerks, and for truant officers. Board member Savage suggested closing the Normal College and President Meyers said it could easily be closed for a year, as no new teachers were being hired. Board Member Brandenberg said it was Crane Junior College which should be closed. No one suggested reducing the maintenance patronage jobs.[4]

There were others who felt the Board must make further reductions somewhere. On February 23, George O. Fairweather, chairman of the Joint Committee on Real Estate Valuation, presented a statement to the Board to this effect. He pointed out that the Board was considering its 1932 budget while the tax bills for 1930 were just being sent out. The Board had sold 1929 tax warrants far in excess of the 75 percent legal limit of the actual tax income for 1929. Since the 1931 quadrennial assessment had not yet been made there could be no accurate estimate as to what the valuation for 1932 should be. He estimated that assessed valuation for Chicago would be at least a half billion dollars below that of 1930, and that even a 20 percent cut in valuation left mortgage holders uncertain as to whether it was worthwhile holding the property. He urged that all eight major local governments in Chicago cooperate in joint retrenchment amounting to 70 millions in their 1932 budgets. He indicated that the Board of Education had cut 2 millions in 1932 while the total of the budgets of all eight major local governments was actually 27 millions higher than in 1931. He urged "selective retrenchment," but carefully did not suggest what to select.[5]

Other sterner voices had already been heard. B. F. Kelly of the State Street Council on February 11 had demanded that the school budget be cut 25 millions for 1932. The Union League Club issued a statement demanding that further reductions be made before the adoption of the school budget. On March 1, 1932, the teachers were paid in tax warrants for work done in December, 1931. On March 3, the Board of Education adopted its budget without any further reductions. On March 11, Mayor Cermak announced that no more school tax warrants could or would be sold to the banks unless the "Thompson Board"—still dominated by six Thompson appointees—made more cuts. On March 14, the city council refused to approve the tax levy presented for approval by the Board of Education.[6] On March 14, Edward Rossiter, president of the Chicago Association of Commerce, did object to actual increases in the 1932 expenditures proposed for the business manager. On March 15, the legislature enacted a law which authorized the Board to issue "Not Sufficient Funds" checks on scrip for payment of salaries. Whereupon the investment experts, Chapman and Cutler, advised against any further purchase of school tax anticipation warrants, as the scrip lessened their value. On that day also, the Tribune stated that a group of business men who had served on the Joint Commission on Real Estate Valuation, on the Strawn Committee and on the Governor's Tax Conference would organize a new Committee on Public Expenditures of which Fred Sargent, president of the Northwestern Railroad, became the chairman.

Instruction Cut, Not Patronage

Continued pressure on the Thompson-appointed Board members did bring action, but no reductions in the business manager's department. On March 25, Walter Dill Scott, president of Northwestern University, opposed further cuts in educational services and pointed out that the high maintenance costs were due to extra patronage jobs. But on March 28, the evening schools were closed and twenty-five thousand adults shut out. On April 5, 8, and 21, teachers received two-week pay checks in cash, to bring pay to date through the first half of February. This money came from the state distributive fund. On April 19, Mrs. Holland Flagler, president of the Illinois Congress of Parents and Teachers, protested against any further cuts in the educational fund. On May 3, the State Senate defeated a bond issue which would have provided funds to pay salaries. The Civic Federation had pointed out that if warrants would not sell, neither would bonds. The interest on temporary school loans for the year was now $5,330,000 and for interest on and reduction of bonds $6,498,888, a total of almost 12 million dollars. Finally on May 24, the Mayor himself said 8 millions should be cut from the maintenance costs by dropping jobs controlled by Republicans, but pressed the matter no further.[7] Ninety percent of the teachers in high schools were carrying teaching loads beyond the maximum allowed by the North Central Association.[8] Salaries in elementary schools were below the depression level of twenty-six large cities. Superintendent Bogan urged that nine days be cut from the school term, and holiday pay dropped for the present, but that no other educational changes be made. And on May 28, the Association of Real Estate Taxpayers started another tax strike.

Rumblings about the amount of money spent for schools on "unnecessary" services began to increase in intensity. In September, 1931, the Tribune had expressed its indignation against Superintendent Bogan's suggestion that teachers should be trained for working with pre-kindergarten children, for whom he had four rooms open already. In December an editorial in the same paper justified cutting the teachers' pay, as only a fourth of them were college graduates, anyway, and 1,200 of them should be dropped entirely. It reiterated its old protest against the unnecessary "fads and frills" on which money was being spent. President Hutchins of the University of Chicago answered that the money needed *must* be found, so that youth would not be crippled. On May 12, 1932, the Board was reportedly considering closing all colleges and high schools. Sharpest opposition was to Crane Junior College, although the legislature had given specific authorization for its inclusion in the Chicago public school system, a piece of legislation criticized by the Tribune editorials. The opposition was of long standing. In 1923 the Committee on Education of the Chicago Association of Commerce had stated in a report, "There is a point where further taxation cripples community life more than further educational opportunity helps it. Higher education must be restricted to those who have brains and the inclination to cultivate them."[9] The inference was clear in the report that students who could not pay high tuition could have neither brains nor inclination. When the Strayer survey was published on June 2, 1932, recommending economies in business administration and giving high praise to junior high schools and other newer features of the school system, a June 6 Tribune editorial said it was not worth the $100,000 it had cost.

In October, 1931, the Board of Education had employed George D. Strayer, Director of the Division of Field Studies of Columbia University to make a survey of the Chicago schools.[10] The agreement setting up the survey had five sections: (1) a study of the efficiency of administration and supervision and recommendations for improvement, (2) a study of the business administration of the schools, (3) a survey of school buildings, (4) an analysis of present school costs, (5) a study of the progress of children in all departments of the school system. The report was published on June 2, 1932.

In the rush of other events, it had delayed impact on public opinion, but the most significant recommendations were recognized at once. First of all, the report recommended that the superintendent of schools be given responsibility for the entire system, including the business management. It included a list of suggested economies, amounting to more than 14 million dollars less than the 1930 expenditures, and still providing for the annual increase of 11,000 more pupils. Dr. Strayer urged that the schools be closed if additional reductions were to be made. His cuts centered on the business management. Five hundred two janitors should be dismissed as not needed at all, and the wages of the remainder be reduced and all maintenance costs be sharply reduced by using the wage level of other cities and postponing repairs which could wait. He pointed out that since 1928 a half million dollars a year had been saved by paying no part of the summer school expenses, that the continuation schools had been reduced by $200,000 in 1932 and that community centers had also been closed in 1932. In contrast, business administration of Chicago schools cost $2.54 per pupil, double that of New York City, while educational administration had only $1.75 per pupil to spend. He reminded the Board that children "have but one opportunity to get an education, and should not have to pay for the economic stupidity of their elders."[11]

Bank Failures, Tax Strikes, Payless Paydays

For the moment, however, the attention of teachers and the press was focused on Washington. The Reconstruction Finance Corporation legislation was before Congress, and there was a possibility of selling school board warrants, for which there were no local takers, to the new federal organization. A committee of teachers, headed by Charles Stillman, chairman of the Joint Conference of Teachers and Principals, representatives of the Board of Education, and other local Chicago governments descended upon Congress on June 5, 1932. The bill passed on June 19. Mayor Cermak went to Washington and urged the R.F.C. to take tax warrants for local governments in Chicago. He had been desperate enough to discuss selling Chicago's water system to a private New York City firm to get cash. On June 21, Fred Sargent, now chairman of a new Committee on Public Expenditures, and President Lewis Meyers of the Board of Education, joined him in Washington in an appeal to the R.F.C. Sargent pled that no city ever needed help so much. The Mayor said he would have to have money or troops.[12] But the Senate denied aid to Chicago and Cermak's subsequent personal appeal to President Hoover was without effect. The Board of Education still sat with tax warrants no one wanted to buy.

The downward spiral of the depression swirled more rapidly. By this time, the expectation of quick economic recovery had evaporated, and in face of grim reality the Board began to talk in earnest of more cuts. On July 11, 1932, it openly discussed closing the colleges. Board Member Buehler informed his fellow members that the banks would not lift a finger unless 15 millions were cut out of the 1932 budget. The next night, representatives of the three major banks and Mr. Sargent appeared before a special meeting of the Board with the starkly solemn message that no bank would buy any warrants from then on unless the 15 million dollar reduction was effected. They did not offer suggestions as to where the cuts should be made. Sargent gloomily added that they were not promising to buy warrants even if there were cuts.[13] The solemnity of the bankers was in part due to their foreknowledge that the Insull empire had collapsed, leaving them with enormous piles of the "best securities in Chicago, Mid West Utilities," now worth nothing, and that every bank in Chicago was in danger of bankruptcy. (This the public did not yet know.) But the bankers were not about to use their pitifully small reserves of cash to take up warrants which could not possibly be redeemed for two years—if then. Although Mayor Cermak in February, 1932, had promised that teachers would be paid whenever city employees were, City Comptroller Scymzak, in a letter to the attorney of one of the teacher organizations, announced that the city would no longer try to sell school warrants held in the traction fund, even at 6 percent interest. The Board acceded to the pressure and cut two weeks off the school term.

On June 5, 1932, Superintendent Bogan issued a strong statement defending the changes in public education which were taking place throughout the United States to make the schools more useful to children and to society at large, and pointed out the national significance of public education. On June 22, commenting on the trip of Board of Education members to Washington seeking an R.F.C. loan, a Tribune editorial opposed any request for federal help, but urged that salaries and services be cut to fit income. It did not mention maintenance costs. On June 22 the Herald Examiner complained that the Board had not made enough effort to get money. On July 22 an editorial in the Tribune attacked both Board and teachers. "With the school system a wreck about it, the school board has stubbornly adhered to the program of sacrificing city interests to their advantage. Another factor has been a radical element in school leadership which believes that the citizens are shirking their duties to the school system. The city as a whole has supplied money without stint." On September 9 a Tribune editorial claimed that Home Economics was not needed in grade schools, that 90 percent of the physical training in the schools was futile and superficial, and that the state law requiring it should never have been passed. On November 15 Professor Henry C. Morrison, emeritus Professor of Education at the University of Chicago, who had written a report for the National Association of Manufacturers urging reduction in school programs, was quoted as urging a simple curriculum to save school costs.[14] On December 12, 1932, the Tribune predicted that the "frills" like golf would be snipped off, and that it would probably be necessary to drop 1,200 teachers.

On July 13, 1932, the tax strike was declared illegal, the names of the "strikers" published and court action instituted against them. The teachers began a boycott of stores, hotels, and other businesses which had participated in the strike. But 47 percent of the 1930 taxes were still unpaid. On July 27, the State Supreme Court ordered the Chicago Board of Education to reduce the value of tax warrants it would issue against the levy for its educational fund to fit a total budget of 60 millions, not 75 millions. The Board took no definite action, but meditated aloud on charging college students $100 tuition. The teachers got two-weeks' pay in cash from state funds on August 6 (for work done in March). On August 11 Mid West Utilities publicly collapsed into dust, leaving $1,620,000,000 of securities of no value but to paper the walls of the Union League Club's "worthless security room." Samuel Insull began his journey around the Mediterranean in a rented yacht, touching only at points where no extradition treaties were in effect.[15]

The banks were now in a desperate state from which they did not recover until the R.F.C. a few months later took over 51 percent of their control. Some of them had already turned in Insull securities to the R.F.C. Ex-Vice President Dawes' bank had obtained a loan of 11 millions in June of 1932 on Insull paper. The reaction of the Board of Education seemed absurdly irrelevant. On August 17 President Meyers announced that all teachers must now live inside Chicago, and that new teachers would not be hired unless they reside in Chicago for a year previous to employment. The idea was of course not irrelevant to the notion that teachers should be grateful to their political superiors for having any jobs and should be willing to show their gratitude properly.[16] On August 20 it was announced that only 42 new students would be admitted to the Normal College in September. On September 7 President Myers declared there were 2,250 more teachers than were now needed, and the Normal College should be closed. On September 2 Superintendent Bogan mourned the 61,977 children without seats and schools without adequate toilets and other facilities. On September 27, 1932, shower rooms were closed in fourteen schools in the crowded areas of the city.

Teachers had not been able to sell the warrants given them in lieu of pay. The rate for Board of Education warrants on the open market was 72 cents on the dollar; however, for the year they were dated they were worth full value plus accrued interest to pay tax bills. With the help of P.T.A.'s and a few other groups, teachers began locating people to sell them at full value. On September 9, 1932, the teacher organizations jointly set up a Tax Warrant Pool office to facilitate this process, and gradually collected large amounts of warrants which were more easily salable to large taxpayers. They employed a young man named George Mahin to organize the sale. Department stores occasionally offered to take a few warrants in payment of bills, but most of the teachers' warrants were surrendered in emergency payments with a discount of 20 or more percent. One minor court decision helped a little. On October 11, as a result of a suit brought by the Teachers' Federation in September, 1931, Judge Finnegan's court ruled that the Board could issue no more scrip. This removed one minor obstacle the banks had said was in the way of buying warrants.

Another special session of the legislature opened September 1, 1932, and had begun consideration of a sales tax as a substitute for the income tax which had been declared unconstitutional in April. The teachers got two-weeks' cash in October, 1932 (for April work), and endeavored earnestly to sell their 1931 warrants. One case of tax objectors, involving thousands of names, was dragging along in the County Court. Judge Jarecki said they were all small taxpayers and there was no need for haste. The Federation of Women High School Teachers presented the judge with a list of 80 objectors in this Cisar case (obtained from the city council finance staff), whose uncollected taxes alone totalled $1,004,255, and insisted on action. The judge then issued an order to sell 100,000 pieces of property involved in the case as being withheld on unsufficient objection, and in a short time three millions in taxes were collected from the objectors.[17]

The Strayer Report Plan

By September many people had read the Strayer survey, not only the headline items, but the small print, and its significance began to be apparent. (Some of its excellent suggestions have not yet been put into effect, thirty-seven years later.) It took fifteen years more for the most important single recommendation to be adopted, that a superintendent be placed in charge of the entire system. The meticulous accuracy of the comparisons of expenditures with those of other cities, and the painstaking analysis of the present indebtedness and lack of resources, laid a basis for factual discussion quite different from the emotional name-calling by and at "Thompson Republican" board members, Democratic aldermen and officials, "taxcutters" and "tax eaters," about "fads and frills," "progressive education" and the "3 R's."

The report clearly demonstrated that the schools were being exploited for political profit. The teaching load in junior high schools averaged 224 students per day (on paper, counting non-teaching administrators) and in the senior high schools 177, both far above the maxima allowed by the North Central Association of Schools and Colleges. There were now not enough school clerks, and educational supplies were far too low. But the range of expenditures by the business department far exceeded those in comparable city school systems. The cost of new buildings was a third higher than in New York City, and electrical work just twice as high. Thirty-two new schools had been built so poorly and with such defective materials that before use they had to be repaired at a cost of $758,000. The architectural department had no connection with the superintendent of schools, and was still costing $554,000 annually, even though school building had ceased from lack of funds.

The president of the Board of Education actually had charge of purchasing—he personally signed requisitions—with four employees and expenses of $11,000 a year for his office, although there was no provision in the law for him to have any such authority. The acquisition and control of property and of school lands lay in the hands of three Board members, the president, the chairman of the Finance Committee and the chairman of the Committee on Buildings and Grounds, who did not need to consult the other Board members. In fact, any of the separate committees of the Board could still authorize expenditures the other Board members never heard about. Contracts were let casually without careful bidding, accounting was hazy and incomplete. and there was no concern about research to improve business methods. Per capita costs of maintenance and operation were more than twice as high as in New York. There was no responsible purchasing department and text book purchases were badly managed.[18] The survey recommended that the methods of approving expenditures be completely overhauled, and that the superintendent and not the business manager prepare the budget. "The business of the schools is to render instructional service, and the business activities exist only to facilitate instruction." This had obviously not been the motto of the Chicago Board of Education.

Strayer summed up the current financial dilemma of the Chicago school system:

> "The series of difficulties which followed the rejection of the 1927 reassessment by the State Tax Commission, aggravated by the economic depression which began in 1929, have resulted in the accumulation of audited vouchers and accounts, tax warrants, and other unpaid liabilities against the Chicago schools, which at the close of 1931 totaled $134,111,194.41. Portions of the 1928, 1929 and 1930 levies are not collected and 1931 has not yet been asked for.

> "Chicago has a school system basically sound. School organization has been maintained at a reasonable level of efficiency by a loyal personnel in the face of difficulties which are perhaps greater than any large system has had to contend with in recent times."[19]

The survey staff recommended no cuts other than the list it proposed, and commented that the present failure to pay teachers and creditors could not go on indefinitely, and that closing schools when funds ran out was better than allowing the system to deteriorate. The survey quoted the Report of the Governor's Tax Conference in 1931 on the essential expenses which should not be reduced and on the reasonable status of the present salary scale of teachers.

But Strayer saw no solution to the financial problems of the schools on the basis of the existing tax system.

"It can be stated with certainty that under the existing tax system of Chicago and Illinois, the Board of Education will always encounter difficulty in securing adequate funds for school support, whether times be good or bad. Approximately 94 percent of the local and state income of the schools comes from the property tax. The local property tax is universally condemned by competent tax authorities."

Approval was given to the plan for issuing 25 million dollars worth of bonds for a working cash fund, so that the Board itself might buy at least some of its tax anticipation warrants. But

"the tax problems of Chicago and the State of Illinois can not be solved on the basis of making minor modifications in the existing revenue system and of attempting to secure a more efficient administration of it. The improvement of the tax system should be accompanied by a modernization of the state's relationship to the support of public schools. A tax on personal income, for example, which will doubtless be necessary if any real effort is made to bring the revenue system of Illinois up to date, can not be locally administered. Revenues realized from these taxes by the state can in turn be apportioned to local communities according to a method of distribution which guarantees an equalization of the burden of school costs. Many states have traveled far on this road to better methods of supporting schools." [20]

There was no hurry about passing the 1933 budget. No one was going to buy the 1933 warrants anyway, since the banks were refusing those of 1931 and 1932. Because of over-issuance of tax warrants in the past, and because outstanding warrants for one year were a claim on succeeding budgets, it would be necessary to "find" four millions more somewhere to meet the budget as presented to the Board. Some encouragement was given by J. L. Jacobs, the new assessor, to the effect that the guess made by the Board as to what the 1933 valuation of property might be was a reasonable one. A new Citizens Committee, like the Strawn Committee, headed this time by Congressman Charles S. Dewey, was at work trying to sell warrants. The City Treasurer said the Dewey Committee was the only hope of a school payday. The Teachers Warrant Pool was having some success in selling—at full price—large batches of warrants it collected from teachers. The new Skarda Act provided that receivers assigned to properties in tax default would pay delinquent taxes from rents collected. An amendment to the R.F.C. law to permit loans to school districts was introduced in January, but died with the last "lame duck" Congress on March 4. A mass meeting had been held by teachers on February 16 which urged the Conference of Mayors then meeting in Washington to support the legislation.

Superintendent Bogan and City Corporation Counsel William H. Sexton had spoken at the meeting.

On February 15, 1933, a startling event changed the course of history in Chicago. While riding with President-Elect Franklin D. Roosevelt in Miami, Mayor Cermak was shot, and died on March 6. While Cermak had not fulfilled his original promise to see that school employees were paid when city employees were, he had been willing to meet often with representatives of the teachers and had seemed to be willing to accept some responsibility for the financial problems of the schools. The City Council immediately elected an unknown alderman, Frank J. Corr, to serve as temporary mayor, apparently because he had no possibility of competing with eventual contestants for the office. The General Assembly, then in session, enacted legislation to authorize the council to elect a permanent successor to Cermak. The party choice fell on Edward J. Kelly, chief engineer of the Sanitary District and a protege of Col. Robert McCormick, who had known him as a boy during a term as president of the Sanitary District. When the Republican members of the Sanitary District board had been indicted for flagrant misuse of public funds, Kelly, who could not possibly have been unaware of what was going on, had also been indicted. But the indictment against Kelly was quashed, although the others were sentenced to prison terms. It was alleged that Col. McCormick had used his influence on Kelly's behalf.[21]

As far as his attitude toward schools went, Kelly was an unknown quantity. But his complete loyalty to his political organization, thereafter known as Kelly-Nash, was unquestioned. Under his administration the payroll of the Sanitary District had grown from 3 million to 10 million—all political appointees—and he had a solid reputation for "taking care of the faithful." Whether the course of events would have been different had Cermak lived, there is no way of knowing. But Kelly lost no time in exercising his prerogatives in regard to the schools, and appointed seven members of the eleven-man board between May 10 and the first week of July, 1933. The Board members were also unknown quantities; but they were certain not to oppose the mayor's ideas in regard to schools.

The only pay for school employees between December, 1932, and September, 1933, had been four weeks of tax warrants in February and two weeks of cash in April. To express their frustration at the pay situation, the Federation of Women High School Teachers issued a bulletin in March 1932, entitled (a la Swift) "A Modest Proposal." It suggested that since both relief and school funds were exhausted by the same amount, the simplest way out was to feed the extra children to the reliefers. In a further attempt to dramatize the dilemma of teachers, they staged an operetta at the Goodman Theatre every night for a week in June, 1933, while the N.E.A. was meeting on Michigan Avenue, entitled "The Strangest Interlude in the Century of Progress."[22] The heroine, Miss Frill, looking vainly for her beloved Mr. Payday, discovered that Mr. Banker had abducted him, and found herself surrounded by insistent bills. Little "Scrips" sang "We have no mother, we have no father," and bedraggled

Warrants mourned they were abused and refused and not up to par. The Board members wondered indignantly, "How can they be so unloyal, when we've treated them so royal?" Anyway, "Though their money is all gone, they will labor on and on, on— and —on, on—— and ——on!" Other signs of frustration were the huge parades of the Teachers' Volunteer Emergency Committee down Michigan Avenue and to the banks. Radio Station WCFL and other stations gave free time generously for a long list of distinguished citizens to urge better treatment for school employees.

But rumors of impending change by the unknown school Board continued to swell. A recent publication of the United States Chamber of Commerce had been widely distributed in the city. It claimed that school expenses should be cut by simplifying services and curriculum. Specific suggestions offered were "transfer of supervisors to class rooms, shortening of school day, increase in size of classes, reduction of teachers' salaries up to 10 percent, discontinuance of evening schools and kindergartens, offering only three years of high school and charging tuition for high schools."[23] Superintendent Bogan sought every possible opportunity to explain why the educational services must be reduced no further and why any additional cuts would do irreparable harm. One by one he defended kindergartens, visiting teachers, vocational counsellors, and many other services. Dr. Nelson Henry of the University of Chicago and State Superintendent of Public Instruction Francis G. Blair went on radio to make vigorous pleas that no further cuts be made. But in the first week of July a Tribune headline declared that the Board of Education was millions of dollars in debt. There was no indication that the other local governments were also millions in debt for the same reasons. On July 10, 1933, the Federation of Women High School Teachers sent a letter to James B. McCahey, newly elected president of the Board, and pointed out that the current revenue for 1933 was sufficient to cover 1933 expenditures. If it was necessary to provide also for payment of 4 millions in debt for previous years, it should be met by shortening the school term. There was no answer to the letter.

Chapter 12

THE AXE FALLS ON INSTRUCTION—NOT ON PATRONAGE

A regular meeting of the Board of Education was scheduled for July 12, 1933, for 2 p.m. A crowded room full of spectators waited until 5:45 before ten of the eleven members filed in. Mrs. Helen Hefferan, the eleventh member, waited too, as she had not been invited to meet with the others.

Junior High Schools, College, Services Wiped Out

Quickly, Irwin Walker, a new Board member, read a long motion which was immediately passed by ten votes. The motion made the following changes in the school system.

Crane Junior College discontinued
Junior High School system abolished
Kindergarten reduced 50 percent
Parental School discontinued
Swimming instruction stopped
Number of high-school physical education teachers reduced 50 percent
All elementary school physical education teachers dropped
Athletic teams and coaching stopped
Visiting teacher service discontinued
Bands and orchestras discontinued
Bathing services in elementary schools reduced by 75 percent
Assistant superintendents reduced from five to three
District superintendents reduced from ten to five
All high-school teachers to have minimum of seven classes a day
Each elementary principal to supervise two schools

Continuation schools discontinued except for apprenticeships at
    Washburne

Bureau of Special Education discontinued

Text book purchases stopped until inventory

Manual arts and home economics classes stopped

Child Study department reduced to five psychologists

Bureau of Curriculum discontinued

Supervisor of social studies dropped

Printing classes stopped

Compulsory education staff reduced 50 percent

Lunch rooms to be supervised not by teachers, but by new civil
    service employees

Fourteen hundred teachers (10 percent of total) to be dismissed.[1]

Mrs. Hefferan voted against the entire program. One member voted against closing the junior college, and one against doing away with junior high schools. But there were eight votes for the entire program, enough to overrule the superintendent, had he objected. Superintendent Bogan had not been consulted in any way on this tearing up of the entire instructional system, planned by coal dealers and other small businessmen with little education themselves, and only a few days of service on the Board of Education. Quite apparently they were smugly sure that they were doing a necessary service to the city in spite of the selfish stupidity of the superintendent and the teachers, and of Mrs. Hefferan, their colleague. Superintendent Bogan sat with his grey head in his hands and said nothing. He had done everything he could to prevent such a disaster. He was convinced these were not temporary measures, but the permanent destruction of all the pitifully small gains attained painfully over so long a period of time to help the children of the city.

City Wide Public Protest

The stunned silence of the spectators at the Board meeting was succeeded by energetic action. By 7:30 that evening a "Save Our Schools Committee," made up of teachers and members of the P.T.A., the Womans City Club and the League of Women Voters, who had been present at 6 o'clock, was well under way. The next morning voter lists from every precinct were obtained from the Election Commissioners' office in the City Hall, and organized distribution of material begun, protesting the action of the Board. More than 5,000 teachers, seven months behind in pay, contributed an average of five dollars each, within three days. An office was set up in an unused floor of an office building on Wabash Avenue, managed by the member of the Board of Education who had voted to keep the junior college. Within the two weeks before the next Board meeting, more than 350,000 signatures to a petition were obtained:

"We the undersigned citizens of the City of Chicago, respectfully petition you to rescind immediately your hasty action of July 12, 1933, by which educational opportunities of our children were ordered eliminated or curtailed without consulting or advising with the Superintendent of Schools, without public notice to the parents of the school children or a public hearing to parents and other citizens."

The attorney of the Herald Examiner on July 28 demanded an injunction against closing the Parental School as the 1899 law made its conduct mandatory. The Board retreated and agreed to keep it open. Nine parents asked for an injunction to stop the entire program. This suit was dismissed by Judge Brothers on the ground that there was no evidence of fraud on the part of the Board.[2] The Board claimed first that the cuts would save 10 millions, and then 5 millions. The Citizens group issued a careful study made by C. C. Willard, principal of Phillips High School, who had been Director of Finance for McAndrew. There could be no more than $172,000 savings, he said, because the money saved by firing teachers must be spent to refit junior high buildings for other uses and to buy more elementary school seats and expensive high-school equipment. The dismissed teachers were ordered to attend the Normal College (of course without pay), where they would be taught by the junior college teachers who were *not* teaching 1,200 junior college students. Expensive junior high-school equipment in home economics and manual training shops disappeared and was never accounted for.[3] Ten percent of the high-school teachers were already meeting more than 200 students a day. No other city in the country had closed a junior college during the depression. Police and firemen were warned not to object to the school cuts—although many had children in school—because they would have no pay unless these reductions were made.[4]

The teachers presented the Board with an offer, signed by the president of every major organization, to work without pay long enough to make up any deficit rather than undergo the Board's drastic deletions, on the condition that the Board allow, at the teachers' expense, a recognized impartial auditing firm to make an audit of its books. There had been no such audit since 1930, and the Board seemed to use any figures which were convenient for its purposes, whether consistent with previous statements or not. The Board ignored the offer.

On July 21 the Citizens Save Our Schools Committee, the teachers' organizations, and the Illinois Congress of Parents and Teachers sponsored a mass meeting at the Stadium, which was attended by an overflow crowd of more than 30,000.

Professor Judd of the University of Chicago, John Fitzpatrick of the Chicago Federation of Labor, and Mrs. Holland Flagler of the P.T.A. were the principal speakers. No one from the business world could be induced to speak, although Charles E. Merriam tried to get participation. Superintendent Bogan asked to speak and urged that no changes be made in school services, since teachers' pay cuts had left enough money to continue all the services, and any further reductions should be made temporarily in shortening the school year.[5]

Opponents of the Board's action stated plainly that the cuts were not made to save money or to provide seats, but to cause "unfair reductions of taxes for big taxpayers and political control of school jobs as Thompson had controlled them." While the Board dropped 1,400 teaching employees, the city at the same time was adding 700 political appointees paid from the same tax source. School engineers for many years had received more salary than the principals in some schools, since engineers received full pay for hours the building was rented; but no school engineer was given two schools to manage. There was no reduction of 502 unnecessary politically appointed janitors as recommended by Strayer. Instead, aldermen were informed ahead of time just how many school janitor jobs their wards would get from the next "civil service" examination. The president of the Board of Education, who headed a coal company, had said soothingly that everyone had to take cuts in the depression, forgetting that the group of coal companies which divided the Board's million dollar annual coal order among them had received a 10 percent bonus when they had to wait for their money.[6]

The Board ignored the petition of a third of a million names presented in huge piles at the Board meeting July 26. They gave no sign of recognition to the protestations of the more than 30,000 persons who attended the mass meeting on July 21.

In September, 1933, all high schools and elementary schools opened in confusion. Hundreds of police patrolled the high schools, more than 100 at Phillips High School alone. Seventh- and eighth-grade children descended upon already crowded elementary schools. Ten new high schools in former junior high school buildings opened to children with no programs, no equipment, and no indication of what kind of subjects to provide teachers for. The original high schools had to find seats, programs, and teachers to fit a flood of ninth graders. In the meeting of the Board, Mrs. Hefferan attacked the Sargent Committee for demanding cuts only in the schools and then making no protest at the keeping of patronage employees. In October the Board reversed itself without formal action on several of the July deletions. Swimming pools *were* kept open. Printing shops did not close and high-school newspapers managed to publish. Bands and orchestras were kept; their instructors were called "music teachers." Only half, not three-fourths, of the bathrooms were closed.[7]

In November the Board published at considerable expense a sixteen-page pamphlet, "Our Public Schools Must Not Close," which defended the July cuts against "certain interests," who had wilfully misrepresented the facts.

> "Even now, for reasons which are known to many, and suspected by more, agitation continues. . . . When the present Board assumed office in the spring of 1933, it was confronted with an exhausted treasury, no credit, and an enormous and constantly increasing deficit. . . . Only the city government would come to the aid of the

schools. . . . High school teachers were teaching only 3 or 4 periods a day; the average was five. . . . The most costly branch was Crane Junior College maintained with questionable legal authority, where only 10 percent of those eligible were admitted. . . . Investigation disclosed that the Public School System . . . had accumulated many 'fads and frills' or 'extra curricula' [sic] activities and embellishments. . . . Vocational guidance teachers are not needed in a period of unemployment. . . . The Board sought the advice of authorities and experts versed in municipal finances and education. . . . Educators advised that the economies could keep the Board within its income [and the] Board's survey confirmed [this view. (The "educators" were not named nor was the "survey" published.)] The adoption of this program will save 10 millions a year. . . . All teachers are now required to do a full day's work. . . . Taxes will now be reduced."

The Daily News asked, in an editorial on August 25, why this expensive pamphlet had not been submitted to competent, impartial educators familiar with the evolution of and the scientific trends in education, pointing out that only the disinterested guidance of competent educators insures the proper kind of economy.

The Citizens Save Our Schools Committee continued to press for definite answers to their own analysis of the financial results of the alleged savings, but received none. The Board maintained sphinx-like silence toward all questions or objections. It was clear it felt completely secure.

On the other hand, those who made protests were sure that they were justified in their condemnation. None questioned the need for some adjustment in school expenditures. The change in the value of the dollar and in real estate valuation, combined with the Board's rash financial practices for previous years, the delay in tax collections, the tax strike, and the almost complete dependence of the school system on the vulnerable property tax, clearly reduced the amount of money the schools could spend. In every city changes had been made in school budgets to adjust to shrinking income, but in most cases under the direction of a capable superintendent with as little loss to educational services as possible. The Strayer Report in 1932 had recommended just such changes,[8] and so had Superintendent Bogan. But the new members on the Board of Education had completely ignored this expert advice, had not even notified the superintendent of their intentions, and had, on their own, cut deeper into the services to children than had any other urban Board of Education in the country. Moreover they had reduced no patronage jobs or unnecessary non-teaching services, like the large architectural department which was building no buildings, and were continuing to spend millions of dollars useful only to the local political organization.

Taxpayers' organizations in other cities had also demanded tax reductions. Some did ask for permanent reductions in educational opportunities, such as requiring tuition for high schools as recommended by the United States Chamber of Commerce. But in most cities the local business and industrial leadership had shown some respect for those in charge of schools. School terms were shortened, and salaries reduced in other large cities, but only in Chicago was one-tenth of the teaching force dismissed without warning. Only in Chicago were teachers paid in scrip and warrants, or delayed three-fourths of a school year for pay of any kind. Even in Chicago, the police and firemen had been paid in cash—on time and with less reduction in pay.

It is worth comparing the treatment of the public schools in Chicago with those in New York City, where reductions were not negligible, either. But the total saving in salary for New York was approximately the same as in Chicago, which had half as many teachers, and no pay was delayed or paid in any cash substitute. There were no classes for the handicapped in New York during 1934. Vacancies were filled by substitutes rather than by regular appointees. Vacation schools and athletic competitions were canceled for a brief time, and some health services cut temporarily. Repairs were trimmed by two million dollars and text book purchases reduced. Payrolls were sustained in New York by loans at 6 percent interest. The average number of pupils to a principal in New York was 550. In Chicago in 1933-34, it reached as high as 4,000.[9]

But in New York the state government increased its own support of schools during the emergency, until in 1934 one-third of the state budget was spent for education. When one state business organization tried to reduce the increased state school appropriation, the New York Citizens' Budget Committee, corresponding to the Sargent Committee in Chicago, effectively opposed the reduction.[10]

Moreover, there was no powerful voice in the Chicago press speaking so clearly in defense of public education as did the New York Times. That paper even went out of its way to comment on the contribution of several thousand dollars by unpaid Chicago teachers to help feed their students after state relief funds failed in March, 1932—an effort unnoticed by any Chicago paper. On July 24, 1933, the Times commented on the action taken by the Chicago Board twelve days before. "Shortening the school year, reducing teachers' salaries, failure to pay them what has long been due, denying the children the sort of training urgently recommended by high educational authorities—these are not fit acts of a community that was not daunted by the depression in building a Worlds' Fair," From the beginning of the depression the Times had felt that this was the time to lengthen children's schooling, not to cut it. It had urged that no pupil's education could be postponed without peril to the state, that the needs of the hour should not "make you forget to sow for the future," and that "we must not let false economy reduce educational opportunity." The Times urged that more money, not less, be spent on medical and dental services, and that vocational counseling and visiting teacher service should be increased during the depression, not decreased.

The most influential newspaper in Chicago, the Chicago Tribune, with double the circulation of the New York Times or of any other Chicago paper, held a completely opposite view. In the two-and-one-half years before July 12, 1933, it had published an average of three editorials a month demanding blanket reductions in school expenditures, the elimination of "frills" and no extension of school services, claiming editorially "There Can Be Too Much Schooling." After July 12, 1933, only three editorials commented on schools in five months, including complete support for the Chicago Board's deletions. Little lineage appeared in Tribune news columns on protests against those changes. The New York Times ran editorials during this period advising children to "Stay in School," stressing schools as "Democracy's Defense," and urging consideration for "The Children First."[10] The Chicago Herald Examiner, Tribune competitor with one fifth of its circulation, increased its circulation at the expense of the Tribune because it gave wide coverage of protest activities on which the Tribune was silent.

There was no question that the damage done to the educational structure of Chicago in 1933 was greater than that in any other large city in the United States, and the permanent effect more devastating. One national study, made in 1937, stated flatly that "The drive [against school services] has not been in any other city investigated, so demoralizing as it has been in Chicago."[11] Commenting on the Chicago situation, U.S. Commissioner of Education Zook said he was amazed at what seemed to be a return to the dark ages of education. President Robert Maynard Hutchins of the University of Chicago, in a signed Herald Examiner editorial on July 16, 1933, declared that the action of the Board was based "either on a complete misunderstanding of the purpose of public education, a selfish determination that its purpose shall not be fulfilled, or an ignorant belief that a system which has been wrecked can still function. The economic and social condition of Chicago will be worse for twenty five years because of what the Board of Education has done."

The 1934 Budget

By December, 1933, the 1934 budget was a source of bitter contention. Mrs. Hefferan denounced the 1933 curtailment without parallel in the cities of the United States and as a reactionary campaign against public education itself, and demanded reconsideration. Superintendent of Public Instruction Francis G. Blair urged that the state pay the 12 millions due the schools from obligations to the state distributive fund which had been voted but not paid in 1931 and 1932, and that the state purchase 50 percent of the outstanding warrants and "teachers' orders," (scrip) now being issued all over the state. Such a proposal would have rendered any reduction unnecessary for 1934, or for 1933 either. The amount spent for teachers' salaries in 1931 had been $38,971,664. The official report of expenditures for 1933 showed a decreased salary expense—for teaching at least 20,000 *more* children than in 1932. The Board claimed there were 15 millions less to spend in 1934 than in 1933. But the Board's own report showed that the actual income in its proposed 1934 budget was only $193,673 less than in 1933. The Board, however, pointed to another deficit in the educational fund for 1934, of $3,613,824. The reason given for the deficit was a valuation drop in the 1931 reassessment, published in 1933. Lessees of school lands owed $2,227,821, claiming the rent was based on old high valuations.

The total income of the Board for 1934 would not exceed $44,444,000, according to the business manager's report, and of this amount $23,693,304 was eaten up by deficit, interest, and retirement of bonds and warrants. This left only $20,750,696 to spend for the whole system in 1934—and teachers' salaries, with reduced staff and a 23.5 percent cut would still be $28,400,000, and other employees $7,078,000 more. Where would a 15 million dollar cut come from now? Without increased funds for 1934, the schools must close. The governor had signed a bill on July 11, 1933, authorizing a 40 million dollar bond issue to pay teachers to date, but the Board never mentioned this possible source, nor made any effort to market the bonds.

Junior College Back, New State Aid, A Federal Loan

Other school districts in Illinois were also in distress. A special session of the 58th General Assembly was called on February 13, 1934, to deal with schools. The governor had already issued two other calls, and three special sessions were meeting concurrently: the "relief" session, the "beer" session and the school session. The Senate said only one prayer a day; but in the House a prayer was said each time a different subject came up, for five dollars a prayer. Some observers wondered if more expensive prayers would help, as they listened to the quality of the debates on the floor. The leadership of business groups so articulate between 1927 and 1932 was now either silent, or in open opposition to proposed tax and school legislation.

A carefully prepared legislative program, supported by all the teacher organizations, the Citizens Save Our Schools Committee, the Illinois Congress of Parents and Teachers, and the League of Women Voters was presented to the legislature. It urged that state distributive fund allocations, authorized in 1931 and 1932 from the sales tax which was declared unconstitutional, now be paid to school districts (it never has been paid) and that the state distributive fund be increased from 6.5 millions to 35 millions, as the retailers' occupational tax income was increasing. They pointed out the familiar story that "Illinois ranks second in population, third in farm property, third in manufacturing products, second in income and forty-seventh in per capita expenditures on education in proportion to that income. Thirty-one states pay twice as large a share of school costs as does Illinois." The program urged a 4 percent net income tax on corporations and a 2 percent flat income tax with exemptions on personal income, the two to produce 62 millions in new income. State funds should give

$2,800,000 to high schools throughout the state. The Cook County government should share with other local governments the penalties on huge amounts of delinquent taxes which were gradually being paid.

The demand for help for schools all over the state was so general that it was clear something would be done, and the two political parties jockeyed for the credit of doing it. The Republicans got a bill through, earmarking income from the liquor tax for schools, but the Democratic governor vetoed that. The Democrats sponsored legislation to grant one-third of the income from the motor fuel tax to schools, taking one-third from each of the state, county, and city allocations. Half of the total of $6,654,257 would go to Chicago, by increasing the flat grant temporarily from $8 to $16 for each elementary pupil, and for the first time giving $7 for each high-school pupil. Since the flat grant went to schools in the state which did not need help as well as to those which did, the share of the total allocated to needy districts was reduced. But it would be cash on hand; people bought gasoline whether they paid their property taxes or not and the governor signed the motor fuel bill. An allocation from the new Retailers Occupational Tax was made to elementary schools.[12]

The amounts allotted to Chicago did not fill the gap the Board claimed existed. But three constructive measures affecting Chicago did go through. The first was the "pegged levy" bill of 1935. This law set an amount of 43 million dollars which the Chicago Board of Education could spend in the educational fund, and then legalized whatever tax rate would raise that amount from whatever the assessed valuation of the year turned out to be. 1935 was another quadrennial reassessment year. The total valuation from which the Board must derive its income would not be known until 1936, but the budget for 1935 must legally be passed by April 1, 1935. For the first time, Chicago school finance rested on a sound floor, below which the bottom could not fall out after the money was spent. By the time the pegged levy device was no longer needed, the schools were levying a tax rate far above the original legal limit. The necessity for this measure was emphasized on March 31, 1934, when County Judge Jarecki ruled that assessments on all small residences in the 1931 taxes be cut 15 percent. Protests asking for similar reductions in 1932 tax bills immediately poured in.

The second constructive measure was the validation of the Chicago Junior College. Under the persistent urging of Colonel Jacob Arvey, who was after all a National Democratic Committeeman, the legislature approved the existence of a junior college in Chicago divided into three branches—one on each of the three sides of the city. When the Board passed the 1934 budget on March 27, it quietly provided for the opening of these college branches in September and also for the return of elementary principals to each school. It did not answer its own flamboyant arguments for doing away with these services, and promptly claimed credit for having opened a junior college which had in fact been in existence since 1915.[13]

The third measure opened the way for federal help. Early in the session a federal bill was passed authorizing the Board of Education of any city, having a population exceeding 500,000, to mortgage certain of its school lands as additional security for bonds (not to exceed 40 million dollars worth) to be sold to any agency, corporation, or bureau of the United States, with the approval of three-fourths of the Board. The bill was signed in February, 1934. Representative Adolph Sabath had introduced this federal legislation to permit such purchase on January 18, 1934. The federal aid approach had been tried twice before with no results; but the teachers began to press for aid from Washington again.

The Board itself introduced legislation to decrease the building fund tax rate by 20 cents and add that amount to the educational fund. Since the only cash which could be used for construction might come from the federal Public Works Administration, this in no way reduced the actual amount of building which could be done. Several schools were standing unfinished in 1934.[14]

Nothing had been heard from the Sargent Committee on Public Expenditures for some time. At one time it had been willing to discuss the possible effect of educational cuts. But no word of protest had come from this powerful group on the actions taken on July 12, 1933 or thereafter. Now it began to oppose measures to restore salary and other cuts. On February 2, 1934, John Rees, who had worked so closely with teachers in 1926 and 1927, now Director of the Sargent Committee, stated his opposition to pegging the educational fund levy even at 37 million. The committee opposed any state distributive fund of more than 20 million dollars. They demanded a 3.8 million dollar reduction in the 1934 Educational Fund, knowing that it would come from employees' salaries if made. The teachers were furious. Of the 14.5 millions cut from the Educational Fund since 1931, 10.5 million dollars was in teacher salaries, 1.5 million in other salaries, and 1.5 million in interest on warrants used to pay teachers. Only a half million had been saved in any other way, in spite of the recommendations of the tax conference, of Superintendent Bogan, and of the Strayer Report.

It was clear that the size of salary cuts and reductions in services of the local governments were dictated in inverse ratio to the usefulness of employees and services in catering to partisan political interest. It was clear too that business interests had no intention of interfering with this arrangement. The government with the fewest cuts was the Sanitary District, with *only* political appointees and no civil service at all. Its employees had lost 10 percent for a short while, were always paid in cash, and by 1934 were up to date in wage payments. The South Park District employees, also without civil service, for a while had a slightly larger cut (now restored), payments in cash were now fully paid. Cook County employees, who could not fall under civil service in the sixteen-county "fee" offices because of a constitutional provision written before the adoption of the first civil service law in the United States, were two-and-one-half months behind. The city employees, under an almost meaningless civil service law evaded by employing large numbers of temporary appointees (particularly about election time), were only three months in arrears, and had always been paid in cash. In February, 1934, those self-righteous and superior teachers, who refused to bend the knee to Baal, still suffered a 23.5 percent salary cut, were six and one half months behind, and had been paid in scrip and warrants for six and one half months. Only the small number of Public Library employees had taken a greater reduction, 27 percent, but for a shorter time. By July 1, 1934, the city was only a month behind in wage payments, the county two-and-one-half, and school employees eight months—with no pay of any kind for services performed since October, 1933. Their resentment had been sharpened in March by the announcement by City Comptroller Upham that he was selling school tax warrants in the City Traction Fund, now salable, to pay city employees. City employees had never received anything but cash. Each time the school salaries and school budget had been reduced, it was claimed that the cut would restore credit and result in prompt paychecks. But there was no pay, and now cuts were still being demanded. When in July the Board ordered that all teachers sign a loyalty oath, their articulate indignation knew no bounds. [15]

A comparison of tax rates published by the County Treasurer on tax bills on February 17, 1934, showed increases in 1932 rates over 1931, for every local government except the Board of Education.

	Property Tax Rates for 1931	Property Tax Rates for 1932	Property Tax Rates for 1969
State	.39	.50	None
Cook County	.52	.58	.42
City	2.52	2.82	2.60
Board of Education	2.46	2.03	2.53 ⎫
Junior College Board	–	–	.18 ⎭ 2.71
Forest Preserve	.11	.14	.06
Sanitary District	.56	.87	.31
S. Park	.79	.99	.46*
	7.35	7.93	6.56

*All parks.

Patronage Costs Rise, Instruction Costs Fall

Not only was it clear that purely political decisions were influencing the division of tax income and credit among the local governments; more immediate discriminations were visible within the system. Annually $370,000 more was being spent on supervising, heating, and cleaning of school buildings than on directing the education of children. On July 22 the Board announced that so many school yard scales were broken that it would be too expensive to repair them, and therefore loads of coal delivered to schools would no longer be weighed.[16] Two members of the Board sold coal in the coal dealers' syndicate filling school orders. Coal was the only budget item not reduced at all during the depression. A boy in one of the forty portables (one-room shacks with stove) at Phillips High School watched a janitor dump two buckets of coal in the furnace on a May day when the temperature was 80° and wondered out loud how to get someone on the Board who sold chalk and erasers, of which there were none.

The attitude of the public toward the Illinois legislature, and toward the honesty of Illinois government in general, was not improved by the Chicago American's exposé on March 12, 1934, of Moe Rosenberg's income tax confession. Rosenberg was a junk dealer to whom Insull's Midwest Utilities had given enormous amounts of discarded copper waste. Some of Rosenberg's untaxed profit on sales of this copper waste paid for legislation Insull wanted. The newspapers carried a list of the amounts of stock rights in Mid West Utilities accepted by members of the legislature, from the speaker—who got $50,000, down to lesser lights who received $25,000. A Tribune school reporter who got $25,000 said to his teacher acquaintances, "We were poor fish to take it, because they were only rights to stock, and we had to put in some of our own money to take them up. Of course Insull got our money, and we lost it all."[17] A member of the legislature commented to one of the teacher representatives, "Ain't it awful it got into the papers?" The penniless Board of Education offered "Tug" Wilson, athletic director of Northwestern University a $4,000 salary to act as their "athletic adviser." Wilson accepted the money although on July 21, 1933, he had been quoted in the Herald as saying, "The work of years is being wiped out in one stroke. Heaven help the schools."[18]

The federal bill was moving along. It came out of committee in the House on May 12, 1934, and the President expressed himself as in favor of it. By June 5 it was in conference committee and on June 16 it had passed. The banks then claimed that the Board did not have separate bonding power from the city and that the two together had no bonding power left. The Board of Education on June 20 applied to the State Supreme Court for a ruling on its separate bonding power. On July 31, 1934, the Court ruled that the Board of Education had a separate 5 percent bonding power, the right to mortgage school lands and to issue 26 millions in bonds for the loan. In the arrangements made with the banks for the loan, one peculiar section appeared, sharply criticized by Arnold Baar, later president of the Citizens Schools Committee and subsequently Judge of the Federal Tax Court in Washington. The First National Bank was to collect the rents from lessees of school lands, as part payment for the federal government. If the lessees failed to pay, the land might become forfeit. Since the First National Bank was itself one of the lessees, it could, if it failed to pay its own rent, legally foreclose on the land it rented.[19] But nothing amiss developed from this arrangement.

On August 27, 1934, school employees lined up in front of windows at 130 N. Wells Street and waited hours to receive their seven-and-one-half months back pay in cash. From that time on, paydays were not delayed (except once in

1937), although at the end of each year it was frequently "touch and go." In 52 months they had enjoyed eight paydays on time and almost four months of paper in lieu of pay.

Schools opened on September 17 in 1934. The three Junior College branches had a new enrolment of 4,600. The elementary principals returned to their 1933 assignments. But the North Central Association in 1933 had refused to recognize the ten new high schools in the junior high-school buildings, and had warned the remaining twenty-four that their services were below standard. The high schools were disorganized, short handed, lacking in books and equipment. The Association report issued in April, 1934, stated that "Many recent changes were not based on sound educational advice, and that they have unquestionably impaired the efficiency and lowered the general intellectual and moral tone of the high schools." In May the Federation of Women High School Teachers published a sixteen-page statement on "High School Education in Chicago," which was reprinted in School and Society, October, 1934. Actual data from the high schools showed the average class load of 89 percent of the teachers was from six to ten above any acceptable standard of the North Central Association. More than 200 teachers were teaching seven classes a day instead of the normal five. The expenditures used for instruction were 5 percent below the average for the United States, and the percentage for operation and maintenance 4.5 percent above. Chicago was 21st in the list of 59 cities over 100,000, in all per capita costs for education. Five thousand copies of this high-school report were circulated.

One of the most extravagant wastes of funds in the high schools was the result of the order that no teacher might have less than six or seven classes. On May 23, 1934, in his annual report to the Board, President McCahey stated "All high school teachers are now required to do a full day's work, with the result that despite a large increase in high school attendance during the past year it was not necessary to employ additional teachers." [20]

In order to schedule at least six classes for each teacher, the schools had to remain open as much as three or four periods longer than a normal high-school day, burning more coal and using much more electricity. Some were suspicious enough to say that these extra expenditures were the purpose of the order, not the mere ignorance that teaching load was measured in number of children, not in number of classes. Since there was no saving in money whatsoever in having a teacher cover six classes of 40 instead of five classes of 48—and actual measurable increased cost instead—there was a concerted effort in September, 1934, to return to the ordinary 5-class day. A committee of teachers explained this waste to Fred Sargent, pointing out that neither Superintendent Bogan nor Benjamin F. Buck, assistant superintendent in charge of high schools, had recommended the plan. On July 19, 1933, however, McCahey had stated publicly that he would not be guided by the superintendents on such issues. Mr. Sargent wrote to McCahey asking for the change, and received a letter from the president of the Board dated August 29, 1934, stating that "it was necessary to follow the advice of the superintendents. It was difficult for the Board to act on its own judgment on matters of education." Mr. Sargent sent a copy of the letter to Mr. Buck and did no more.

One project that irked teachers was the demand made upon them to sell tickets to the Mayor's Christmas Charity football game, whose proceeds were used, according to public statement, to provide Christmas baskets distributed by Democratic precinct captains. In answer to a letter from the Citizens Save Our Schools Committee on this matter, protesting against the listing of teachers who refused to buy and the unprecedented use of the schools for openly political purposes, the Mayor answered in a letter dated December 14, 1934,

"We are definitely adverse to politics of any kind in the educational system of this city. I trust that the members of your committee realize that the Board of Education is a separate municipality and is entirely independent of the mayor or city administration. The mayor simply appoints the members for a five year term, after which they are on their own. Further, the mayor does not have the opportunity to go into the internal problems of the school board."

Four days later at a meeting of the city council on December 22, 1934, the members of the Chicago Board of Education presented Mayor Kelly with a huge gold-lettered, gold-tasseled, framed resolution—reputedly costing $500, which listed as *his* contributions to the schools "economies which have kept the schools from closing, and restoring the credit of the Board, saving the teachers by securing the money from Washington, and securing the help of industrialists in purchasing equipment for Lane High School."[21] In the school year 1934-35, 500 temporary certificates were granted to applicants with political sponsors, and 340 assigned to teaching positions for which there were 842 regularly certificated teachers waiting and eligible.

The outlook for the 1935 budget was still gloomy. The December, 1934 payroll had come through, but it was not certain there would be enough money for it until the day it went out. The proposed 1935 budget totaled $71,299,318, but $20,121,407 was required for debt service, interest on warrants, interest on and redemption of bonds due, and repayments to the working cash fund. The debt service was more than 28 percent of the entire amount budgeted. Forty-three millions was the levy for the educational fund "pegged" by the legislature to allow a tax rate sufficient to raise that amount, and another 6.5 millions would come from the state. The pegged levy laid a floor, to be sure, but there was not enough above the bottom. The total liability of the Board was $131,607,754, which was 6.5 millions more than the taxes now receivable—but not paid—from all the years between 1928 and 1934. Cuts made by assessors and by the courts (long after the Board had budgeted and spent larger amounts), along with the length of time for collections, the fluctuations in assessed valuation—all the vagaries of the property tax system greatly increased the financial burdens of the Chicago School Board. The promises of greater security after cuts were not kept. The deficit for 1935 was 5 millions higher than for 1934. Counting the money owed the Working Cash Fund, the liabilities of the Educational Fund were 284 percent above the 1935 appropriation for that fund. The federal loan offered no permanent solution; it must be paid back. The pegged levy was now 43 millions, but as the banks refused to buy the legal 75 percent of that amount, taking only 57 percent, they did not provide enough to meet payrolls for even the present nine-month term. Four millions more in cash must be made available if there was to be no pay stoppage.[22] The State still owed its school appropriations for 1931 and 1932, but showed no signs of paying. Five hundred of the 1,400 teachers dismissed in July, 1933, were still unassigned, and thirty-five elementary schools were on double shift—almost all in the Negro area on the South Side—with classes of 50 and 60.[23]

In spite of protestations by the mayor, it was clear that public employees who were not politically malleable, and particularly employees who were articulately and persistently critical were not to be favored as the financial situation of the local governments slowly improved. While the teachers' organizations and civic groups urged a 30 million dollar state distributive fund and distribution of those penalties on delinquent taxes when the 1935 session of the legislation opened, the Board of Education had different ideas as to what was needed. They re-introduced legislation to compel all teachers to live inside Chicago, and to require that teachers be required to take a loyalty oath—an inference of evil intentions not cast on any other local government employees, or on any other groups of citizens. Neither bill passed.

In June, without previous action or discussion of any kind, the attorneys of the Board introduced drastic changes in the pension law. Board members descended on Springfield to push through changes without committee hearings—or in fact reference to any committee. Mayor Kelly, the city corporation counsel, and leading aldermen also appeared in Springfield to support them and the entire Chicago delegation in the General Assembly voted for them as one man. When passed, the teachers' pension bills were included in the list of measures presented by the city administration.

There had been two separate pension systems for Chicago teachers since 1927. To one the teachers contributed, and from this they might receive $800 a year after twenty-five years of service and $1000 after thirty-five years. The other, the Miller law annuity, had been set up by state law in 1926 in McAndrew's administration, when there had been no compulsory age limit, to induce older teachers to retire. It provided that teachers who chose to work till age seventy would be retired at $2500 a year, and any who left at sixty-five, at $1000. Nine hundred two teachers were receiving this pension; 252 teachers already sixty-five had been assigned to continue teaching in September. Between the $1000 contributory pension and the $2500 maximum Miller law payment, a total of $3500 was more than any active classroom teacher at any salary level was receiving in 1935, and there clearly should have been some reduction. But the law set sixty-five years as the age for compulsory retirement, thereby dismissing 252 teachers without warning, and cut the Miller payment to $500, reducing the income of many of the 902 receiving it by $2000, also without warning. Incidentally it opened opportunity to assign not only low-paid substitutes but substitutes appointed through political sponsors.

Governor Horner expressed discomfort about the pension changes and refused to sign the bills, but he allowed them to become law without his signature. Finally, he supported legislation to raise the maximum possible on the contributory pension after thirty-five years of service to $1,200 instead of $1,000. The teachers were all the more angry because city civil service employees, who paid no contributions whatsoever to their pension system were getting $1,800 after thirty years of service. The Board announced it had saved the taxpayers $600,000 by the pension modifications.

The teachers' sense of insecurity was increased by the appointment of William H. Johnson as Assistant Superintendent of Schools in charge of high schools to succeed Benjamin F. Buck. Buck retired on July 24, 1935, and promptly offered his services to the Citizens Schools Committee. Superintendent Bogan stated that he had not recommended Johnson's appointment.[24] Mr. Johnson held a Ph.D. from the University of Chicago and Board members frankly boasted that he was the "educational expert" who had approved their July 1933 program.

William H. Johnson had a varied career, never staying long at any job. He had received a master's degree in chemistry at Northwestern University in 1918, served in the Chemical Warfare Division in Washington, been a chemistry instructor at Rockford College for a brief time, then Dean of a small junior college at Fort Knox, Kansas, and finally a teacher at Lane High School. While at Lane he worked on a doctor's degree (obtained in 1923) in Educational Administration at the University of Chicago. After teaching a short while at the Chicago Normal School, he passed a principal's examination and served as principal in three small elementary schools, the last one the Volta on the far northwest side.

Two evaluations of his professional methods are significant. One was that of Superintendent Bogan, his principal at Lane, who refused to recommend him for the assistant superintendency, and considered him an opportunist without much concern for the children he taught. The other was a report of the research assistant assigned by Superintendent Bogan's Advisory Council subcommittee on Civil Education, who visited him at the Volta School in 1931 because of an article he had written for an educational journal, describing in glowing terms his successful experiment in self-government in a six-grade elementary school. Johnson, eager for recognition, called a meeting of his council of students to demonstrate its success. Twelve little children sat on the school stage, staring vacantly at each other. Behind the two from each grade stood one teacher who told each child what to say, and made corrections if he failed to repeat the teacher's words accurately. He kept the council on the stage and those in the assembly hall seats for twenty minutes of their lunch hour in his effort to make a good impression. The researcher reported that Johnson was so ambitious for prestige he would write or say anything he thought might bring him recognition, but that he either did not recognize children's reactions to such a farce, or he did not care.[25] From the point of view of the Board, he was useful because he had never participated in any protests against actions of the Board of Education, and he had a doctor's degree from a recognized university.

The 1935 legislature, without encouragement by the Board, on its own initiative took some steps useful for Chicago schools. The state distributive fund was increased from 10.5 million to 13.5 million dollars for the biennium. Chicago schools would receive $700,000 a year more from this source, and an even larger sum, $875,000, was available annually to Chicago for deaf, crippled, and delinquent children. One extremely helpful item was the release of the Board from paying off old warrants from previous years with current income. In other words, 1932 warrants held in the working cash fund would have to wait until 1932 taxes came in to pay them off, instead of using 1936 income to do so. This provision alone released 9 million dollars for appropriation for 1936. The pegged levy for 1936 was set at 49 million dollars, and the state 1936 payment of $6,433,500 would again include 2 millions from the gasoline tax. A special session, called in October 1935, allowed monthly rather than quarterly state distributions of the state fund from the Retailers' Occupational Tax, and assured payment of the December payrolls.

It looked as if there might be a chance in 1936 of a longer school term and some pay restoration. The debt service was down. The pegged levy was up. Enrolment in elementary schools was down 30,000 from the peak of 330,704 in 1928, although high-school enrolment was still rising—126,455, up 40,000 since 1928. In ten of the fourteen largest cities, all cuts in time and pay had been restored. But the Board made no restorations of any kind in 1936. The North Central Report for 1936 charged that 50 percent of all high-school teachers were heavily overloaded, but no action was taken on the wasteful six-class day.

The Chicago Real Estate Board, however, entered objections to the 1934 tax levy when it came out early in 1936, and claimed that its objections should be extended to any taxpayer who protested, not merely to those who brought suit. County Judge Jarecki stated he was quite willing to make a general ten percent cut. The pegged levy legislation protected the schools from the disaster this would once have caused. The Board had finally sued for its share of the penalties on delinquent taxes; but the State Supreme Court had delayed decision on the plan.

A Compliant Superintendent

Superintendent Bogan died in March, 1936. One of the greatest tragedies of the decade between 1926 and 1936 was the complete frustration of one of the most creative and potentially useful leaders the Chicago school system had ever seen in its hundred years of existence. Like Ella Flagg Young, William J. Bogan began as teacher and principal in a deprived West Side neighborhood. Then, as principal of Lane High School beginning with 81 boys, he developed an institution whose enrolment reached 9,000, and whose reputation for high standards in vocational and general education was—and still is—nation-wide. After twenty-four years as principal and four as assistant superintendent in charge of high schools, he was made superintendent at the end of the McAndrew regime. The pressures of partisan patronage and of money shortages were already heavy and threatened to increase.

No isolated professional, Superintendent Bogan had been president of the Illinois State Teachers Association and of the Chicago Conference of Community Centers, and had been one of the leading spirits in the City Club for more than twenty years. He was chairman of the City Club committee which brought out its broad-based 1912 report on the kinds of vocational education the city needed (in opposition to the narrower Cooley plan), and had shared in all its efforts for more honest and efficient government. His national professional reputation had been recognized by frequent invitations to address and write for the National Education Association, and the American Federation of Teachers, and by his presidency of the Midwest Vocational Education Association.

The advisory council he created drew into the service of the schools some seventy specialists whose expertise in health, welfare, psychology, and social problems could bring new life and greater usefulness to the schools. In a day before the establishment of great foundations, he was able to get at least two small grants for the council. One went to the Committee on Juvenile Delinquency for a study of the best methods of helping truant and delinquent boys, which resulted in the Montefiore and Mosely Schools. A Union League Club grant was used to study ways to improve education for citizenship. Its recommendations were never even considered by the Kelly Board. The recreation subcommittee urged the wider use of school buildings for community purposes. A Committee on the School Budget pointed out how the budget could be simplified and clarified so that the public could understand it. (The budget instead became more mysterious as the Board altered yearly categories of expenditures so that changes could not be traced.) A Committee on Progressive Education studied the results of the application of John Dewey's ideas in urban schools.

The superintendent and the council divided the city into forty-one areas, and set about developing local community-school advisory committees in each area. Classes for pre-kindergarten children were set up on an experimental basis. The work of visiting teachers was encouraged. Studies of excessive class sizes were publicized. The Teachers Section included all organizations but the Federation, which refused to cooperate. The individuals and organizations cooperating in the council helped raise funds for an executive secretary, since tax funds were already scarce. Tax funds did pay for a small but useful periodical called "School

Facts," for two years between 1929 and 1931. At no time in the history of the system had the administration, the teachers, and civic leaders worked together so constructively to make the schools more effective.[26] After 1932 the Advisory Committee was lost in the financial turmoil. It was no wonder that most of its members helped the Citizens Save Our Schools Committee in 1933, which was trying to retrieve the gains which had been lost.

Moreover, William J. Bogan understood school finance, and knew beyond a shadow of a doubt how the figures presented by the Kelly Board were being rigged. Since 1920 he had worked to get more money from the state, and he was convinced that the claims presented for savings in the 1933 program were not honest, and that the amounts allegedly necessary to be saved in fact only reduced the children's chances for a better life. He was sure the businessmen who refused to distinguish between expenditures for education and for patronage were quite consciously willing to reduce their own taxes at the expense of youth. For three years Bogan was not consulted on the school budget. When Assistant Superintendent Buck retired, he was forced to accept as assistant a person he not only considered incompetent, but whom he did not respect or trust—a man clearly picked as his successor. Under other circumstances he could have carried the school system years ahead in its educational progress; instead he had to sit and watch it fall years behind.

Like William Wells and Ella Flagg Young, the teachers of Chicago considered William Bogan their friend. He was a welcome speaker in the Principals Club and the union groups, and had the cooperation of all organized groups (except the Federation, which was not really hostile). His quick warm smile and easy twinkle dispelled misunderstanding and invited confidence. The teachers did not blame Superintendent Bogan for their troubles. At his death the teachers' organizations and the Citizens Schools Committee raised a scholarship fund in his memory.

Although urged by the Citizens Schools Committee and other organizations to seek an experienced and creative successor to Superintendent Bogan, the Board lost no time in appointing William H. Johnson his successor, as had been expected.[27] To mollify the opposition, the mayor did reappoint Mrs. Hefferan to the Board.

In March, also, President McCahey announced that enough 1934 taxes had been collected so that 90 percent of outstanding 1934 tax anticipation warrants had been paid off. The first installment of 1934 taxes had been put in collection in November, 1935, and the second in March, 1936. Instead of being more than two years in arrears in tax collection, the local governments were now less than a year and a half behind. By the end of 1937 all 1936 taxes had been put in collection, and the system was practically back to normal. The enormous interest charges on tax anticipation warrants, which in 1935 consumed one-fourth of the entire school income, began to decrease.

There were sinister overtones of underworld connections with the Board of Education. In June, 1936, three of the largest and most reputable text book companies, Allyn and Bacon, Ginn and Company, and Harcourt, Brace, announced they would no longer do business with the Chicago Board of Education. It was alleged in the Chicago Daily News on June 5, 1936, that two of these companies had made their own investigation of the "Board's mysterious ways of doing business, with emphasis centered on evidence tending to show why a few text book publishing houses are paid for books sold the board, while others wait years without getting what is due them or any part of it." Publishers revealed that the Board still owed 2 millions on text books for bills incurred before January 1, 1934. There were charges that the Kelly-Nash machine instructed McCahey what to do, and that payments were based on political pull. Four days later, on June 9, the Daily News carried a front-page charge that "Billy" Skidmore, a syndicate gambler and Capone's current successor, had been making collections on text book sales, including a complete and sudden changeover in shorthand texts. No proof of these allegations was ever offered in a court. But there is no question of the withdrawal of these reputable book companies from business with the Board for a considerable time.

A New Cooley Plan, but Slow Restorations

By 1937 it was clear that the Board was deliberately dragging its feet on restoring services. A study made by Dr. William C. Reavis of the University of Chicago in December, 1936, contrasted administrative costs of Chicago schools with those of other cities as follows:

	Chicago	New York	Philadelphia
Business Administration	82.9%	34.5%	29.7%
Educational Administration	17.1%	65.5%	70.3%

An Office of Education study published a month before showed Chicago in 1935-36 to be the lowest in instructional costs per capita of the ten largest cities and the highest in non-instructional costs.[28]

Taxes were coming in regularly with the highest rate of prompt collection since 1926. Interest rates on tax warrants had been reduced from 6 percent to 3. A million dollars had been transferred by the legislature from the city gas tax to the schools. Of the fifteen largest cities, eleven had all pay and services restored; the Cleveland cut was still 4 percent, St. Louis 6 percent, Los Angeles 10 percent, and Chicago 23.5 percent. Only Boston and Chicago still had a short nine-month term. The average per capita cost of instruction in the seventy largest cities was $83.13. In Chicago it was $62.63.

The contrast in comparative expenditures with other Chicago governments was equally disconcerting. By January, 1937, all cuts had been restored to the Sanitary District employees, the county employees still had 7.5 percent off, the city from 7.5 to 10 percent, the Public Library 20 percent; school employees—

the only group which had no restoration at all—were still 23.5 percent off schedule. Moreover, five groups of these employees had been repaid in full for cuts they had suffered, to a total of four million dollars paid back to Sanitary District Trustees, county employees, Municipal Court employees, South Park employees, and to city employees—on the night before election, April, 1936. It is significant to note that except for nominally civil service city employees, all of these were straight political appointees whose work for the party was paid out of public funds. The cost of living had risen 13.1 percent from June, 1933, to March, 1937.

Dr. Nelson Henry of the University of Chicago estimated that each teacher had lost, on the average, $3,300 during this period. In 1937 the newly organized Chicago Teachers Union pointed out that the heads of other local government had been busy in Springfield on plans for employee salary restorations, but that the only mass invasion of the legislature by the Board of Education was in 1935 to get the pensions cut. The Chicago Democrats in the legislature voted en masse (with only two exceptions) against the proposal to increase the state school fund, and the Board of Education made no effort to get the increase.

Finally in July, 1937, the Board voted to add four days to the school term in September by opening the day after Labor Day, for which holiday the teachers were not to be paid. Restoring four of the twenty days discarded in 1933 increased salaries by 1.7 percent, leaving a total cut of 21.8 percent. Now none of the fifteen largest cities had less than a 38-week term, and only four had less than 40. Chicago had 36.8 weeks.[29] But the pressures on teachers, other than from loss of pay, remained. The rule dividing a high-school teacher's load into six classes rather than five still stood; and, in addition, Superintendent Johnson had just ruled that high-school students could take only three subjects instead of four, which was the universal standard, to the consternation of parents whose children would not be able to meet college requirements.[30]

Then in November, 1937, the superintendent outlined a plan by which only 20 percent of the high-school students in the city would take "general courses," the remaining 80 percent required to take vocational courses. This preliminary statement was given resounding praise by Mayor Kelly and President of the Board McCahey. The proposal was purportedly the result of a junket to California—at Board expense—taken by the presidents of two steel companies, the president of the South Side Chamber of Commerce, and Frank Righeimer, attorney for the Board since the 1922 Thompson Board days and prosecutor in the McAndrew trial. This proposal was much more restrictive than the old Cooley plan for a dual school system, since it seemed to allow only one-fifth of the high-school population any opportunity for higher education.

Professor William C. Reavis of the University of Chicago, president of the Citizens Schools Committee, immediately produced data showing that only 20 percent, not 80 percent of the students, in cities with much greater opportunities for choice than in Chicago, *chose* vocational education.

The Citizens Schools Committee opposed the scheme flatly, and set up an active committee to work on it, including some representatives of industry. Their activity culminated in a conference held in 1939, the results of which were published in a 70-page book which was widely circulated. Dr. John Lapp, chairman of the Committee, had been one of the authors of the Smith-Hughes law, the landmark vocational act passed by Congress twenty years before. Paul Douglas, Professor of Economics at the University of Chicago, Henry Heald, president of the Illinois Institute of Technology, and union leaders and industrialists joined in the protest against the vague, sweeping change proposed.[31] Finally, Superintendent Johnson announced he had never really proposed such a plan and it was never carried out. To the teachers the proposal had been a threat both to the whole purpose of public education and to the tenure of the whole teaching force. Moreover, it seemed to be a reopening of the old Cooley plan dispute, where business interests had been accused of depriving children of a real education in order to get cheap labor for themselves.

The 1938 budget totaled $73,312,389, 3 million above 1937. The school year was extended to 38 weeks by adding six more days, and leaving a 14.5 percent cut in salary. The five-class day was restored to the high schools. The three-subject rule in the high schools had been changed after violent protests from the P.T.A., allowing "the upper fourth" of the ninth graders to take four subjects. The North Central Association had expressed strong disapproval of this original notion and it was abandoned completely in September, 1938. The Citizens Schools Committee protested against the flood of politically sponsored temporary appointees given full-time classroom jobs for which fully qualified teachers were available. Paul Douglas, elected alderman from the Fifth Ward in 1939, stated that he had been offered as much as $300 to get someone a temporary teaching job. The Citizens Schools Committee also urged the Board to prepare the budget in such a fashion that the categories remained the same from year to year, so there would be some way of being sure how the money was being spent.

By January, 1938, all other local government employees had had full restoration of salary and in some cases refunds for past cuts, and 16,000 city employees got raises over their pre-depression wage. City Comptroller Upham said this was necessary because the cost of living had gone up 24 percent. The school employees still had a 7.5 percent cut in December, 1938.

The 1939 budget provided for a 39-week term. Tax collections were improving. Professor Herbert Simpson noted that a small group of large property owners were now responsible for half the present tax delinquency. Because of the fall of the birth rate during the depression, elementary school enrolment was dropping fast—another 10,000 below 1938—but the high schools were still growing.

By January, 1940, the numbers in the ninth grade began to decrease, and 21,000 fewer children entered first grade than at the peak of enrolment of 1934. The Board restored the 40th week of the school term, but did not return to the original 1922 salary schedule until 1943 when war prices were already mounting.

In 1944 the high-school union teachers approved of asking that only elementary teachers be given a raise in salary from the million dollars then available as a step toward a single salary schedule, and elementary teachers received $125 a year more, making their schedule $1,675 to $2,675. The high-school range remained $2,000 to $3,800. In that same year all police and firemen who received less than $3,000 a year were given a $200 increase to compensate for rising costs. Since all elementary teachers and approximately half of the high-school teachers received less than $3,000, the discrepancy in treatment was evident. Not until 1946 was any sick-leave pay restored, and that by a state law, not by action of the Board.

The Mayor's School Advisory Committee

Nineteen thirty-nine had been a mayoralty election year. The mayor, who on some occasions said he had nothing to do with the Board of Education except making appointments—after which members were on their own, gave the improved outlook for the schools as one of the chief reasons for reelecting him. In the February, 1939, issue of the Cook County Young Democrat—the cover of which was portrait labeled "Mayor Kelly with a Heart as Big as All Out Doors"—a long list of reasons is given why young voters should support him. Besides providing N.Y.A. and C.C.C. opportunities (both federal, not local programs), he had given Christmas baskets from the all Chicago football game (for which teachers were compelled to sell tickets), and he had paid the teachers (the only employees still not fully recompensed). He had brought Chicago schools back to normal, built new schools (with federal money) and abolished the portable one room buildings.

Mayor Kelly tried an old political trick before his 1939 reelection. He appointed a committee of distinguished citizens to tell him what to do about the schools.[32] The committee accomplished nothing. Professor James Weber Linn of the University of Chicago, who had suggested the idea, died. Three members, Charlotte Carr, who had succeeded Jane Addams at Hull House, Professor Frank Freeman of the University of Chicago, and Lester Selig, a businessman, resigned when it became clear the mayor had no intention of using their advice on school Board appointments—or on anything else. When the remaining four members of the Commission recommended three supporters of the mayor to replace Mrs. Hefferan who was retiring from the Board at seventy-five, the Citizens Schools Committee asked them to resign. Yet the mere appointment of such a committee won the mayor votes in 1939. It was one form of recognition of the steady and massive opposition to "Kelly School Board" policies.

Chapter 13

A CITIZENS COMMITTEE AND A TEACHERS
UNION OPPOSE THE BOARD

Although there was little other recognition by the mayor or the Board of Education of the continuing energetic opposition to the Board's program other than occasional attacks on the motives and personalities of its leaders, the appointment by the mayor of an advisory committee on schools, and the continuing lavish expenditure of public funds in defense of the Board's policies, were a tribute to the respect won by the Citizens Schools Committee, and to the impact of its steady hammering away after 1933 at distorted economies in instruction and continuing misuse of public funds for partisan ends.

Early Citizen Activity on Schools

When the Board refused to consider the petition signed by a third of a million voters on July 26, 1933, and ignored the mass meeting of more than thirty thousand on July 21, the Citizens Save Our Schools Committee settled down to a campaign of educating the public not only on the gross mistakes of the current Chicago Board of Education, but the financial and educational problems facing all public education. In the beginning most of the money and physical energy had been contributed by the teachers, and much of the distribution of material done by them, although many local P.T.A. groups had been as active. But from then on an active core of recognized leaders of the city's civic activities accepted responsibility for Chicago school strategy.

Under one name or another, these civic leaders represented the groups which had supported Ella Flagg Young, opposed the Cooley bill, protested the dismissal of Federation members, and created the Public Education Association in 1916 to support the Otis Law.[1] They had demanded the grand jury investigation of the Thompson Board in 1922, with the support of the Teachers Federation, and had continued to work in an informal group called the Joint

Committee on Public School Affairs in which the City Club, the Union League Club, the Chicago Woman's Club, the Womens City Club, the Chicago Womans Aid, the new League of Women Voters, the Y.M.C.A., the Y.W.C.A., and Settlement House Board were represented. When this group then supported Superintendent McAndrew it angered the Federation.

After McAndrew's dismissal, the Union League Club invited the Association of Commerce, the Chicago Real Estate Board, the Commonweal Club, the Western Society of Engineers, and some members of the 1922 Joint Committee to join in acting on school issues. This brief coalition disappeared into the sequence of businessmen's committees which crystallized into the Sargent Committee.

The member organizations of the 1922 Joint Committee on Public School Affairs furnished the leadership of Superintendent Bogan's Advisory Committee, but continued to meet separately. By 1931 it included some thirty-one participating organizations including the Urban League, the Association of Colored Womens Clubs, the Church Federation, the Chicago Dental Society, the Conference of Jewish Womens Organizations, the Chicago Federation of Settlements, and the Womens Trade Union League. Since the Citizens Save Our Schools Committee was an ad hoc organization intended originally only for the purpose of reversing the 1933 Board action, the Joint Committee continued to meet until the leadership in the permanent Citizens Schools Committee and the Joint Committee became practically identical, and until the Citizens School Committee Organization conferences of more than 100 groups became effective and far reaching. The Citizens Schools Committee received the support of many individuals whose continuing interest in schools had been evident through several of these past efforts. For instance, Henry Porter Chandler, president of the Union League Club, continued to support the Citizens Schools Committee though his organization seldom sent representatives. The Union League Club did defend the continuation of the Montefiore School against several attacks and had furnished money for the study of civic education made for Superintendent Bogan's Advisory Committee.

The Citizens Schools Committee

The experience of these participants during the years of public effort to help improve the schools, and their sophistication in the complicated political and economic problems of the city were placed at the service of the Citizens Schools Committee. The contribution of several individuals was of particular importance.

Two members of the 1923 Dever Board of Education, who had frequently disagreed with the majority of that Board in 1925, and who agreed still less with the actions of the Board in 1933, were particularly useful. The first of these, Mrs. William S. Hefferan, still a member of the Board of Education, was a lone voice in that body, speaking firmly against its entire program. On July 12, 1933, she had not even been informed of the plans of the majority of the Board.

A gracious woman of striking, poised presence, Helen Hefferan had not only an unusual background in public education, she was quite invulnerable to personal political attacks. A student of Col. Parker at the Normal School, a disciple of Ella Flagg Young, she had been the first president and the effective organizer of the Illinois Congress of Parents and Teachers. She had been chairman of the meeting at the Chicago Womens Club in 1922 when the new Joint Committee on Public School Affairs had demanded a grand jury investigation of the Thompson Board. The Catholic members of the Board whom she censored as using their religious and ethnic connections for personal ends could not approach her status in the Church. She had been president of the Illinois Catholic Womens' Association and her husband was the personal attorney of the Cardinal. She herself was a "public school Catholic" and had sent her children to public schools. Moreover she had been active in Democratic politics and had been president of the Illinois Democratic Womens' Club.

Other members of the Board could ignore her informed and parliamentarily skillful questions (she was the only experienced member of the Board), but they could not—and did not—treat her with disrespect, particularly after one taste of her rapier-like quick wit. In 1935 the mayor did not refuse to reappoint her, in spite of her complete opposition to almost every act of the Board. Her information and advice were at the service of the Citizens Schools Committee daily.

The second Dever Board member, James Mullenbach, was in Washington after 1933 heading one of the industrial commissions set up to facilitate economic recovery. In his brief intervals at home during the entire depression period he never failed to offer suggestions on strategy. He was one of those who made (unsuccessful) efforts to get President Roosevelt to bring pressure on Kelly to change his school policy.

A third adviser was Charles E. Merriam, chairman of the Department of Political Science at the University of Chicago. No academician in a grey stone tower, Merriam had served as alderman of the Fifth Ward for six years, been Republican reform candidate for mayor twice, and was the initiator of the Chicago Crime Commission and the city zoning plan. He had discussed school problems in the council, and protected the teachers' pension fund from a council raid, defended the teachers' right to organize, and engineered the council committee which recommended a tenure law. Now his intimate knowledge of the workings of the city government were at the disposal of the Citizens Schools Committee. Deeply disappointed when he was unable to convince any of his strong reform supporters to speak at the July 21, 1933, mass meeting, Merriam commented that this would not have happened in New York, where the political organization did not now exercise such ruthless power. He cautioned the opponents of the Board against undue hope for a rapid solution, although he urged that the strong pressure for change must continue, no matter how long it might take. He and Secretary of Interior Harold Ickes also tried to get President Roosevelt to interfere in the Chicago school situation. But the necessity for undivided national support for his recovery program was the president's overriding consideration.

Others with more direct connections to the formal organization of the Citizens Schools Committee also made major contributions to its efforts. William C. Reavis, chairman of the Department of Education at the University of Chicago, with the assistance of two of his staff, Nelson Henry and Newton Edwards, headed the committee between 1933 and 1937. Northwestern University was also represented on the advisory board by Ernest O. Melby, dean of the School of Education. The studies of the effect of the depression in other cities, made by Dr. Reavis, were particularly useful. He was succeeded by Arnold R. Baar, an attorney whose status in his profession and in the life of the city were evident in his later service as president of the City Club and the Civic Federation, and his eventual appointment as judge of the Federal Tax Court in Washington. John A. Lapp, who became president in 1943, had been professor of sociology at Marquette University, president of the National Catholic Welfare Council and of the National Conference on Social Work, and a member of several national commissions, including the one which drafted the Smith-Hughes Vocational Act. A recognized authority on vocational education, he was concerned with the current ineptness and paucity of vocational instruction in Chicago schools. He devoted ten years to the work of the Committee.

The Citizens Schools Committee had a small budget and staff, but was blessed with expert volunteers. Mrs. John M. Hancock, daughter of William Campbell (who had been the first examiner) and wife of Dr. John Leonard Hancock, dean of Crane Junior College up to 1933, had been chairman of the Educational Committee of the Chicago Woman's Club, and secretary of the Joint Committee on Public School Affairs. Under her informed leadership the monthly organization conferences of the Citizens Schools Committee drew representatives of more than one hundred agencies from all over the city to learn not only what was going on in the Chicago schools, but what progress was being made in other school systems. Her accurate analysis of the Board's budget was used by dozens of other organizations in their statements at annual public hearings, which were required by law and which were the only opportunity given to talk directly with a Board. She became editor of Chicago Schools and for a time served as executive secretary. [2]

The divided teacher organizations united in 1933 long enough to cooperate with the Save Our Schools Committee on the petition and mass meeting. But then the Federation and the groups it controlled withdrew. The other organizations, in a loose alliance called the Steering Committee of Teacher Organizations, helped raise funds for the S.O.S. and supported its program.

By the first of August, 1933, the Citizens Save Our Schools Committee had competent people, regardless of organization or teaching status, working on all kinds of projects—releases for foreign-language newspapers, investigation of the business activities of Board members, analyses of the fallacies in the Board's statements on savings and in its statements derogatory to the S.O.S. In July, 1934, it changed its name and was chartered as the Citizens Schools Committee. For several years it held general meetings downtown once each month and was able to develop active working groups in twenty-four of the fifty wards. It collected signatures on the petition to return Mrs. Hefferan to the Board and to add Mrs. Heineman. Its publication, Chicago Schools, reached every significant civic agency in the city with concise, accurate information on the actual state of school affairs, on the actions of the legislature and courts, and on the reports of state commissions. It summarized the warnings and comments of the North Central Association, which clearly was not satisfied with the progress of Chicago high schools. Its executive secretary, Mrs. Mabel Simpson, met indefatigably with community groups, Parent Teacher Associations and individuals, as they came to her office with protests, requests for help, and information on abuses of power. When she was killed in an accident in 1941 the Citizens Schools Committee suffered a serious loss.

The Citizens Schools Committee's special reports gave details on the appointment of unqualified temporary substitutes, on the comparative status of teachers' salaries, and on the delay in restoration of the salary schedule. The Church Federation was enrolled as one of the city-wide agencies to circulate all these materials. The Citizens School Committee's Conference on Vocational Education, held on October 29, 1938, attracted national attention, and the sales from its printed report paid for its costs.

Each of the pamphlets printed by the Board was analyzed and answered by the Citizens Schools Committee factually, and the cost of such publications noted. Twice a careful study was made of the overcrowding and other handicaps to education in the segregated schools on the South Side, pointing to the concentration of double-shift schools in the area.[3] The Committee urged that all qualified teachers anywhere be encouraged to apply for employment in Chicago, and that the source of elementary teachers not be restricted to graduates of the Normal College, who were guaranteed employment without an examination. It urged the wider use of school buildings at night for formal education and for general community use. It noted in its publications the population shifts taking place in the city, and urged recognition of the needs of new migrants by the schools. It sent the mayor names of distinguished citizens for his consideration for appointment to the Board of Education, and strongly opposed not only the original appointment of William H. Johnson as superintendent in 1936, but his reappointment in 1940 and 1944.

The circumstances surrounding the demotion and punishment of teachers and principals who publicly differed with the Board, and promotions to the principalship on clear grounds of partisan sponsorship, and the court cases arising from these actions, were reported accurately and fully in Committee publications. An example was Superintendent Johnson's use of school personnel, relieved of other duties (but paid by the Board of Education), to prepare a series of texts which he signed as author. By law he could not collect royalties on books used in Chicago, but since all his books used in Chicago were without competition from similar texts, the publishers used his reputation for sales in other school systems—from which the Superintendent could make considerable profit.[4]

The public meetings of the Citizens Committee, whether city-wide or in local communities, presented a wide range of informed and responsible speakers. Among them were Col. Frank Knox, Secretary of the Navy, federal Judge William Holly, Graham Taylor and his daughter Lea of Chicago Commons, Alderman Paul Douglas, Adlai Stevenson, Henry Heald, president of Armour Institute (later Illinois Institute of Technology), Jesse Newlon, president of the N.E.A., and Lyle Spencer. Each month representatives of more than one-hundred organizations met to discuss some important school issue.

In his article in the Survey Graphic for October, 1934, Charles Merriam commented on the energy and enthusiasm of the Citizens Schools Committee "The attack upon the Chicago school system . . . aroused the people of the city as they have not been for years. Men and women of all classes united in a common protest in behalf of their children and they will not rest until the educational system is restored to a satisfactory basis." In 1944 the Committee urged the National Education Association to make a study of the Chicago school situation, supported its recommendations, and financed the publication of the subsequent report.

The Chicago Teachers Union

The Citizens Schools Committee was not the only organized force to emerge from the conflict and confusion within the schools after the McAndrew era. In this period the focus of power among teachers shifted permanently from the Federation to the growing teacher union groups. Margaret Haley's reputation for infallibility was irreparably damaged by the results of the reassessment, and her influence inside and outside the schools suffered by her support of Thompson's outrageous campaign for mayor in 1927, in order to get rid of McAndrew. The growing number of junior high-school teachers resented her rejection of the middle school idea, and many of the junior and senior high-school teachers joined the union locals. Miss Haley's personal unwillingness to cooperate in any activity she could not control, and her continual reference to past triumphs, antagonized younger teachers.

The men and women's high-school groups which had cooperated since 1916, had by 1929 organized four more union locals—for elementary teachers, playground teachers, truant officers, and school clerks. These six groups had a Joint Board organization, a constitution, a common office, several clerical workers, and competent attorneys. In 1931 and 1932 they published a magazine with articles by distinguished local and nationally known contributors. They held public meetings, such as the dinner for Governor Emmerson, who discussed school finance in 1929, and in 1930 for Robert Maynard Hutchins, new President of the University of Chicago, who discussed the needs of public education and the record of organized labor in support of public education.[5] Many non-union teachers came to these affairs.

The union groups had free time on the Chicago Federation of Labor radio station, WCFL, and during the early '30's had eight hours a week "prime time." The members of the Federation of Women High School Teachers wrote and staged a "comic" opera, "The Strangest Interlude in the Century of Progress" in July, 1933, selling out the Goodman Theater for a week, with the cooperation of the other unions. When the R.F.C. amendment allowing the Board to sell warrants to it directly was under consideration in Washington, the union locals got the help of teacher unions in Atlanta and other cities in getting votes for the measure.

But in the minds of most of the payless teachers, such activity was not enough. They not only wanted results, the great mass, organized and unorganized, wanted to *do* something, not just sit and suffer while a few representatives interviewed and protested to Board members, legislators, newspaper editors, bankers, city council members, and citizens' committees. They simply insisted upon ways to express their personal indignation at the treatment accorded them. Teachers never before active in any organization, and some who had been, began to form more or less spontaneous groups to set up active projects. From 1930 to 1936 a half-dozen or so of such efforts of considerable size materialized.[6] Some died quickly. A few of their leaders got promotions and lost their reforming zeal.

By far the most dramatic and effective of these spontaneous activities was the Volunteer Emergency Committee. This group announced that it did not want to become a permanent organization and from the beginning of its activities urged teachers to join the established agencies; it was to operate only until pay was forthcoming. It was the brain child of four high-school teachers, only one of whom, John Fewkes, continued as active leader in teacher organizations after the group disbanded. In March, 1933, the Volunteer Emergency Committee called for a huge parade of all Chicago teachers, neighborhood mass meetings of parents and pupils with teachers, the elimination of organizational jealousy and conflict, and the unification of everybody in the Chicago schools behind an immediate action program. It kept contact with every school.

On March 21 several hundred teachers descended on the mayor's office to announce that they would return every Tuesday until they were paid. On April 15 some 8,000 teachers marched down Michigan Boulevard from Congress Street to visit ex-vice president Charles Gates Dawes, whose bank had just received a 90-million-dollar loan from the R.F.C.—and they wanted to know why teachers could not get cash on the Board of Education warrants. On May 1, 1933, a committee on the Volunteer Emergency Committee met with representatives of the five large banks and were promised that warrants enough would be purchased to pay the teachers up to January 1, 1933 within a week. But no money appeared within the week, and on May 13 a demonstration of at least 20,000 people—teachers, parents, and children—marched down Michigan Boulevard. A parade scheduled for the Saturday opening of the World's Fair was postponed, out of deference to President Roosevelt, and held the next Monday.

The Volunteer Emergency Committee posted a list of stores, hotels, and other businesses which were tax delinquent, and suggested doing no business with them. Then sent an automobile cavalcade to Springfield and a delegation to Washington on the R.F.C. amendment. A section of the parade to Dawes' bank had detoured to the Board of Education offices when it heard that James Meade, president of the Men Teachers Union, had been called down to the office of the president of the Board of Education because of his outspoken attack on the Board over WCFL.

Whatever else it did, the Volunteer Emergency Committee served a useful purpose in giving thousands of teachers a safety valve of action to express their pent-up anger, and it gave thousands, unconnected with any organization, a sense of the power that came from working with others. There is no question that the Volunteer Emergency Committee strengthened the conviction of many teachers that some way must be found to unify teachers so that their maximum potential influence could become effective. The Committee held a dinner on July 11, 1934, and formally disbanded, giving members an eight-page historical statement of what it had accomplished, and urging even greater unity among Chicago teachers.[7]

The Volunteer Emergency Council leaders had been right in observing that any efforts to get all the teachers to work together on the same projects simultaneously had never been successful for very long. As early as 1922 a Chicago Schools Committee included fourteen organizations which collected a half day's pay, successfully lobbying to get the school tax rates exempted from the Juul law, which set a maximum overall property tax rate for all local governments. The Joint Conference of Principals and Teachers succeeded this ad hoc joint effort and elected as chairman Charles S. Stillman, a principal, president of the Men Teachers Union and the first president of the American Federation of Teachers. In 1931 all the teacher organizations but the Federation worked together in the Teachers Section of Superintendent Bogan's Advisory Committee. After the Federation and its allies withdrew from the Save Our Schools activities at the end of 1933, for three years the rest of the teachers organizations worked with it through a loose alliance called a Steering Committee, made up of the Principals Club, the Teachers League, the Federation of Women High School Teachers, the Elementary Teachers Union, the Volunteer Emergency Committee (until 1934), and the Joint Conference of Principals and Teachers, which included several curricular groups. The Men Teachers Union withdrew when a splinter organization, the Subscribers, joined, but returned in 1936. The bulletins of the joint group went to every school, of which 225 sent representatives to its monthly Saturday morning meetings.

The Citizens Schools Committee and the Steering Committee coordinated their programs of action. In 1934 they concentrated on returning a principal to every elementary school and the reopening of the junior college. In 1935 they attacked the seven-class rule for high schools. In May, 1935, they jointly sponsored a Goodman Theater discussion by Professor A. W. Clevenger, who represented the University of Illinois in the North Central Association, to compare the conditions in Chicago high schools with those in other Illinois high schools and throughout the United States. That same month more than 2,000 teachers and others attended a dinner sponsored by the Steering Committee at the Stevens Hotel (now the Hilton) at which Dean Thomas Benner of the School of Education of the University of Illinois, Prof. Charles E. Merriam, chairman of the Political Science Department of the University of Chicago, and Harold L. Ickes, Secretary of the Interior, were the speakers.

In May, 1936, the Men Teachers Union elected as president John Fewkes, of the Volunteer Emergency Committee, on a platform calling for immediate amalgamation of the teacher unions. Letters inviting all teachers to discuss possible unity were then sent out to every teacher organization. The Principals Club and the Teachers League accepted; the Federation ignored the invitation. The High School Association refused, saying they did not believe in labor affiliation—and anyway that "Organized labor in Chicago helps us whether we are affiliated or not." (It changed its name to Association of Chicago Teachers.)[8]

In January the Joint Board of the Teachers Union, whose six constituent groups were now growing rapidly, resumed the publication of its substantial magazine, the Chicago Union Teacher, begun in 1931 but forced to stop for lack of funds in the payless period. Copies were sent to all teachers. The January, 1937, issue included plans on amalgamation, an analysis of the inequities of the pension system, a letter from John Fitzpatrick to the mayor on the injustice of the delay in restoring the pay cuts of teachers, and a speech by Prof Harold Groves of the University of Wisconsin on the value of union affiliation. In the February issue, Prof. Eugene Lawler of Northwestern, like Prof. Groves a union member, outlined the need for federal aid, and included a protest against Superintendent Johnson's current order allowing high-school students to take only three subjects instead of the usual four, and a chart of current teacher salary schedules in twenty-one large cities. The issue also included a tribute to Edward Nockels, vice-president of the Chicago Federation of Labor and creator of station WCFL, which had been so generous in the free time given teacher organizations to present school issues. The June, 1937, issue gave the speeches made at the May mass meeting which filled the Auditorium Theater and an article by Prof. Paul Douglas, long a member of the teachers' union, declaring that the spirit—if not the letter—of the 1935 Wagner Act opened up "the field of increasing unionization in the teaching profession."

The union Joint Board held a series of open meetings beginning in January, 1937, on the amalgamation. By April the four teacher union groups had elected a council, with one representative for each hundred members, which chose as temporary officers John Fewkes, now president of the Men Teachers Union, Helen Taggart, president of the Federation of Women High School Teachers, Charlotte Russell, for many years a president of the Teachers League, and Kathleen Crain, a member of the Elementary Teachers Union. Offices were opened at 185 North Wabash and five-dollar dues payments began to pour in.

On May 19, 1937, the new council held a meeting which again filled the Auditorium Theater. Four major speakers urged that all teachers join the new organization. John Fitzpatrick, president of the Chicago Federation of Labor was the first. The other three were the heads of the departments of education of the state's three major universities: Thomas E. Benner, University of Illinois, Ernest Melby, Northwestern University, and Charles H. Judd, University of Chicago.

Dr. Judd said that building a strong new union organization was the only way to "clean the Augean stables." He summed up the disasters inflicted upon the Chicago school system under the McCahey regime:

> "For years the public has been misinformed, misled, and maliciously hoodwinked by a potent organ of publicity. The teachers of this city have been scoffed at and misrepresented. I take it that what this great assembly wants is advice as to the ways in which it can bring truth to the people of this city. . . . What an individual hesitates to do, a group can do. . . . Your representatives told me, when they came to invite me to take part in this program, that you are self-selected members of the Chicago school system who are bent on the cultivation of a profession and are determined to insure to the people of Chicago a high grade, honestly and efficiently conducted school system. Tell the people of the city this. Chicago will rise as it has risen again and again, and will drive into oblivion those who trample on its children."

Dean Melby stated his belief that the only salvation for Chicago schools was through the organization and solidarity of the teaching profession itself. He assured the audience,

> "If the teachers of Chicago were organized in a body free from internal conflicts, bickering and inactivity, they would throw the fear of the Lord into the hearts of politicans interested in the schools only for selfish purposes. Had the teachers been solidly organized in 1933, no Board of Education could then have perpetrated the atrocities which then befell the school system. I believe your presence this evening is an evidence of the fact that you believe the time has come when all personal jealousies and differences among organizations must be laid aside. Whether your solidarity should be achieved through affiliation with the American Federation of Labor or otherwise is a secondary consideration. Years hence, the historian will be able to record whether or not the Chicago teachers were big enough to place the welfare of the children above their own personal differences; he will be able to record the degree to which these teachers possessed the courage of their convictions and devotion to their educational philosophy."[9]

The Teachers League in May voted to disband so that its members might join the new organization, after thirty years of separate existence. The four teacher union groups by the end of May had all voted to return their separate charters and to ask for one charter. The union council set up committees to enroll new members, write a constitution, and hire employees for the new organization. By October, 1933, there were 6,500 paid-up members, more than half the teaching force.

On October 28, 1937, the new organization was formally launched before an audience that filled the new Civic Opera House. The four unions surrendered their charters to the secretary treasurer of the American Federation of Teachers, and John Fewkes, as president, received a charter for the new organization. It was numbered Local One, the old number of the Chicago Teachers Federation, unused since 1917. The president of the Teachers League spoke on "One Union—A Dream Realized." John Fitzpatrick and Lillian Herstein rehearsed the long history of the concern for Chicago schools by the Chicago and Illinois Federations of Labor. Charles Stillman, first president of the American Federation of Teachers and for years chairman of the Joint Conference of Principals and Teachers related the turbulent history of the Chicago school system. The thousands present went home sure that they had witnessed a turning point in the grim school situation.

By November, 1937, there were 7,300 members. In December an election on voting machines chose as permanent officers the temporary list (working since April), and an executive board representing elementary, secondary, college, playground teachers, and principals. Each school elected a school delegate and representatives, one for each fifty members. The union grew steadily and by April, 1938, totalled 8,200 teachers—more than two-thirds of the entire force.

Encouragement poured in from many sources, some unexpected. On the program of the charter ceremony, Leonard D. White, professor of Public Administration of the University of Chicago and former member of the United States Civil Service Commission, urged the formation of unions among public employees as among the "strongest practical supporters of a sound merit system." Arnold R. Baar, president of the Citizens Schools Committee, past president of the City Club and of the Civic Federation, and soon to be a federal judge, stated his faith that

> "The new Chicago Teachers Union will be an effective agency for the public good, dedicated to a fine professional devotion to the schools and to the school children. After working with many leaders of the new union and its predecessors, I have yet to find an instance of disregard of the public welfare on their part or anything but a self-sacrificing citizenship and patriotism, which other groups and citizens might well emulate."

Victor Olander, Mrs. Hefferan, sole opponent of Kelly Board program on the Board of Education, and Eugene Lawler, professor of Education at Northwestern, were also quoted on the program. The next weekly bulletin of the union, dated November 10, listed a dozen more messages of encouragement from such people as Henry Heald, president of Illinois Institute of Technology, John A. Lapp of the National Catholic Welfare Council, Paul Douglas of the University of Chicago, Mrs. Holland Flagler, former president of the Illinois Congress of Parents and Teachers and the first president of the Citizens Schools Committee, and federal Judge William Holly. Notably absent were any such statements from leaders of industry or business, although efforts had been made to obtain them.

The metropolitan press gave considerable publicity to the start of the new organization. The Herald on October 29, in a sizable article listed the four objectives of the new union as the restoration of the basic salary schedule already in effect for other local employees, proper working conditions for both pupils and teachers, employment of qualified teachers only, and a thorough merit program for the entire public school system.

Clearly, the "one big organization" of teachers in Chicago had arrived. It had taken a long, long time. But at that, Chicago was the first of the large cities to have achieved such coordination in the action of its teachers. New York still had some 160 groups of one kind or another, and until 1960 in no other large city did any teacher organization have a majority of those eligible for membership.

Miss Haley, now seventy-six years old, ill, and retired to California, had left one tradition of great importance to the new union. Although her teachers had followed her in and out of the labor movement, without becoming deeply involved in it as individuals, the reasons Miss Haley had given them for affiliation in 1902 were equally valid in 1937. Whatever her disagreements with the other Chicago teacher organizations, they were not based on opposition to labor affiliation. John Fitzpatrick and Victor Olander had given unwavering support to the teachers and to the increase of educational opportunity for children, before the Board of Education, in the legislature, and in the press.[10] The business interests of the city, which had tried to get a dual system of vocational education in the first decades of the century, seemed to be consistently hostile toward paying the taxes needed to make a good general school system possible. They had not raised a hand in protest against the destruction of educational values in 1933 or against the open discrimination against teachers. It seemed clear to teachers where they might expect help.

The most unusual factor in the relation of Chicago teachers to the labor movement lay in the distinct difference between the attitude of the Illinois State Teachers Association and the Teachers Associations of other states, which were solidly hostile to union affiliation. The state association had always worked closely with the Illinois State Federation of Labor. In 1915 Robert C. Moore became the executive secretary of the Illinois State Teachers Association in an era when only seven such state groups had paid employees. The understanding and cooperation between Moore and Victor Olander, secretary of the State Federation of Labor, was a bond lasting until Moore's retirement in 1938.

Robert C. Moore was a regular attendant at the annual conventions of the State Federation of Labor with badge and button. The union teachers from Chicago, represented in the education committees of the labor convention, presented the State Association legislative program and frequently got it adopted completely without change. Olander and Moore worked together in the legislature for compulsory education laws, free text books, increased state funds, pension legislation, for tenure and specifically for the Otis law. They also fought together against the Cooley legislation for a dual vocational system. Olander was a speaker at the annual state teachers' convention in 1925 and at other times.

Not only had Robert Moore worked with the labor people, he had openly attacked the Illinois Manufacturers Association for attempting to separate the schools from the Federation because the Federation "was controlled by union labor." In the 1915 State Federation of Labor convention, wearing his delegate's badge, Moore warned:

> "There is a fight in the State of Illinois at the present time with regard to how far teachers shall affiliate themselves with the labor movement or cooperate with it to promote their common interests. I say frankly to you that a very large number of the teachers of the state are thoroughly in harmony with the thoughts I have expressed. . . . But we know also that a large number of them have the idea they should not affiliate or cooperate with any other organization—just drift along with the silent and powerful forces which some of us believe seek to control us in a way we consider harmful to the schools." [11]

Until 1938 when Robert Moore retired, the Illinois State Teachers Association followed this general policy. When he died in 1950 the Chicago Teachers Union paid him tribute. These long years of cooperation between teachers and labor on the state and local levels, and the absence of conflict on labor affiliation with the Chicago Division of the State Teachers Association, helped to create a climate in Chicago which had conditioned Chicago teachers not to consider labor affiliation as unusual or dangerous.

As long as Fitzpatrick and Olander were the spokesmen for organized labor in Chicago and in the state, there was an obvious practical reason for labor affiliation by Chicago teachers, whether accepted on an ideological basis or not. The refusal of the High School Association to join the new union, because organized labor would help whether teachers were affiliated or not, granted the reality of the labor support.

On the other hand, the new union was not really a union, any more than the Federation had been. Instead, it was the "one big organization" which teachers had been saying for years they would join. To many of them, as to many principals and to Dr. Judd, the labor affiliation was not a primary issue. The need for mobilizing all the forces available to rescue the Chicago school system was the paramount issue. It was on this basis the Chicago Teachers Union began. The "one big organization" had finally arrived, and it proceeded to tackle the grave problems which faced it with energy.

Plenty of long-standing headaches confronted the union, and new ones kept appearing. Only the state government could solve some of them. The failure of the state legislature to appropriate funds for public education anywhere near the national average of state support for schools, or to take any action to adjust the tax system of primitive pioneer days to a vast industrial complex, were plainly recognized by the union, which urged 50 percent support by the state and a graduated income tax. But there were more immediate concerns even in the legislature. The Board had introduced legislation in several sessions to dismiss married teachers, to dismiss teachers who lived in the suburbs, and to require teachers, alone among all public employees, to take a loyalty oath. None of these bills passed at this time, although the oath bill was adopted later. At home, the school administration was openly hostile to the union. The superintendent at first refused to recognize its existence and forbade circulation of union material (claiming it was not a teachers' organization), but relented after a year.[12]

The number of unqualified temporary appointess grew apace, while 800 qualified, certified teachers, both in elementary and high schools, waited for appointment or reappointment. A plan of Superintendent Bogan, approved by the Board, to set up an apprentice or interne system at the Normal College was ignored by Superintendent Johnson, and the Board promise of employment made to the apprentices was disregarded.[13] A chain of regulations on appointment of teachers became rigid. The Board controlled entrance to the Normal College as it had in the 1870's (and graduation also), and excluded all but Normal graduates from assignments to the elementary schools. For some years no Negro applicants were accepted at the Normal College. Only present elementary teachers were eligible to take high-school examinations. The conviction that the Board intended to have a teaching force fed and controlled by political influence—a mere adjunct to a powerful political machine—was a significant factor for the rapid growth and solid strength of the new union. The treatment of critics of the Board strengthened this conviction.

Several principals who spoke against Board policy were demoted. The first was William McCoy of Bowen High School, who was sent to a small elementary school. Another was Butler Laughlin, president of the Chicago Normal College, who was demoted to Lindblom High School and then to a smaller high school, Harper, to make way for a relative of the President of the Board at Lindblom. When the new Phillips High School (now Du Sable), was opened in 1935 only the intervention of Negro aldermen, who respected him, kept Chauncey C. Willard, the principal, from demotion. McAndrew's budget director, he had furnished the figures used in the suit to enjoin the Board om making the cuts of 1933. McCoy had also been long a leader in the Men Teachers Union, and the Chicago Teachers Union took his case to court. But the court held that there was no special certificate for high school principals, and that the Board could move him anywhere it chose. The Board gave as the reason for his demotion the failure to have repairs made in the school building. His records showed he had asked for these repairs every year for several years, but the Board had granted no funds to make them. The repairs were completed as soon as he was demoted.[14]

The 1936 Principals' Examination

The most flagrant example of open interference on the basis of partisan politics was the list of persons announced in 1937 as having qualified for the principalship. A few days after Superintendent Johnson's appointment, he had announced an examination to replenish the eligible list of principals. Eight hundred thirty applicants took the examination and 155 received certificates.

When Johnson had been appointed assistant superintendent in 1935 he announced he was a candidate for the superintendency, in which office he would head the Board of Examiners. He went so far as to state that his classes in administration, which continued after his securing the superintendency, would be preparation for a coming principals' examination. Just before the examination, though he was superintendent and head of the Board of Examiners, he accepted money to tutor a special group to pass it. There is no record of Johnson's tutoring price, but rumors were that it was high, and the existence of the class was never denied. Twelve of the first fifteen principals assigned, including Board President McCahey's sister (who had failed previous examinations), had been students in the special tutoring class.

Eighty-one percent of the 155 who were awarded certificates had failed the written examination but were declared passed on an "oral examination," in which Johnson provided the list of those he approved. One hundred twenty of the 155 had been Johnson's students. Of the 54 applicants who did pass the written examination, 25 failed the "oral" when the superintendent ordered they be given such low marks that they could not pass in the total average. He changed the rules (after the examination was given) to say that an applicant must make 75 on the oral, no matter what his other grades were. This oral examination was given by a group of district and assistant superintendents, one of whom, J. J. Zmrhal, was so disgusted that on March 19, 1938, he signed an affidavit, accepted by the court as evidence, stating the facts given above. The names and connections of almost all of the 155 successful applicants were traced without difficulty to some immediate relative or sponsor with a "clout."

One other factor about the examination was disturbing. The Otis law of 1918 had set up a three-man Board of Examiners to prevent political influence. The superintendent was one of the three and its chairman. It was his responsibility to nominate to the Board for their approval, the other two examiners for a two year term. Neither of the two examiners in 1936 had been approved by the Board, although they continued to serve from day to day at the pleasure of the superintendent—who could appoint someone else at any time he chose. One of the two (whose son-in-law was among the 155 who passed), was over sixty-five and faced a small pension if he displeased Johnson and had to retire from the very lucrative assignment. The superintendent was the only examiner present at the "orals"; he decided who should pass and who should fail, and by himself wrote the numerical grades in the oral, without consulting either the "oral board" or the other two examiners.[15]

The Chicago Teachers Union, backed by the Citizens Schools Committee, supported three suits on this examination for principals. The first case attacked the validity of the examination procedure and asked for an injunction to void the whole list. The judge—in spite of the fact that he needed the support of the Mayor for renomination—granted the injunction, and stated flatly that there was evidence of fraud of a serious nature. The Board of Education appealed this decision and engaged a Tribune attorney to help fight the case. Righeimer, the regular attorney for the Board, made no effort to refute the factual charges in the Appellate Court, but held that the plaintiff, the highly respected retired principal of Hyde Park High School, Hiram Loomis, had suffered no personal monetary loss as a result of the facts alleged. On this basis the Appellate Court set aside the injunction.

The second case, brought by Raymond Cook, a teacher at the Normal College, attacked the procedure of the superintendent in changing, without public notification, the grades required for passing *after* the examination had been given. The court agreed with the plaintiff and ordered that a certificate be granted Raymond Cook, whose written average was more than 90. Again, the Appellate Court overruled the lower court. This time it held that the Otis law gave unlimited power to the Board of Examiners, and that no one could challenge it on any grounds.

The third case, brought by Lemuel Minnis, who had passed the written examination, was based on District Superintendent Zmrhal's statement that the oral board had given Minnis a passing grade, and that the superintendent, by himself, had changed it to 60 in order to fail him. The lower court merely quoted the previous ruling of the Appellate Court that the Board of Examiners was infallible whether legally constituted or not. The actions of the Board and the superintendent in the conduct of the 1936-37 principals' examination cemented the union teachers into open opposition to such crass corruption. It seemed obvious that neither ability nor hard work—nor anything but money or "clout"—would win any teacher or principal advancement as long as Johnson was superintendent.[16]

Effort to Change Board of Examiners Law

If the courts held the Board of Examiners legally infallible, no matter what it did, the system clearly should be changed. The Chicago Teachers Union and the Chicago Division of the Illinois Education Association, with the support of the

Citizens Schools Committee, introduced legislation in 1941 and 1947 to create a new kind of Board of Examiners independent of the Superintendent, chosen for training and experience in personnel work, and definitely limited in authority. The original Board of Examiners had been a hasty, makeshift device to limit the Thompson Board's authority over appointment and tenure in 1918. Other school systems had devised better procedures by 1941, and standards in personnel work were rising in industry as well as in civil service. But both these efforts were defeated by the opposition of Chicago members of the General Assembly. The 1918 law still stands.[17]

Punitive Demotions

The opposition of the union to abuses of power by the Board and the superintendent won for it the respect of many thoughtful people outside the school system. But it did not aid in solving the problem closest to the teachers, themselves—the restoration of pay cuts. By the time the union was chartered in 1937 eleven of the fifteen largest cities in the United States had restored full salaries to their teachers, and Chicago was the only one with less than a nine-and-a-half-month school year. The per capita cost for instruction in Chicago was $20 per child less than the average in the seventy largest American cities. While other local employees were being repaid their previous cuts from the general tax funds, no consideration was given to such action for teachers. In 1939 the mayor publicly promised union leaders he would support a "pegged levy" of sufficient amount to provide for considerable pay restoration. But when the votes were counted in the House of Representatives, only 14 of the 35 votes in the mayor's bloc were cast for it, in spite of his explicit promise.

In 1939 the Board provided for a thirty-nine-week year and reopened kindergarten for all five-year-olds. Although the fall in the birthrate during the depression years had lowered the enrolment in elementary schools to 296,632 that year, the high-school enrolment had now reached its all-time high of 145,050, and the total costs of the schools did not go down.[18] By 1943 the 1922 schedule was again in effect, but in a period of such rapid inflation it was worth only two-thirds of its 1922 value. For thirteen of the twenty-one years in which the 1922 schedule had been the legal schedule, it had not been paid in full.

The use of demotions to throttle dissidents continued. The most dramatic were those of Raymond Cook and Lyle Wolf. In 1937 Raymond Cook, supervisor of student teaching at the Normal College, appealed to the court when he failed the oral principals' examination, although his written grades were almost at the top of the list. Cook was active in the union, which supported his case. He was transferred immediately to classroom teaching at Hyde Park High School, along with Lyle Wolf, who had been active in the Steering Committee as executive secretary of the Principals Club. Cook had seniority in three areas in the Normal College, the quality of his services had never been questioned, and even the Board-oriented new president of the College had not recommended his demotion. In 1938 the Chicago Normal College began offering a four-year degree, changed its name to Chicago Teachers College, and applied for membership in the American Association of Teachers Colleges. The Chicago Teachers Union protested the admission of the Chicago Teachers College to the Association, using the demotions of Cook and Wolf as a reason. After a series of editorials in the Daily News, and persistent action of the Citizens Schools Committee, the two men were finally returned to the college staff on the reluctant recommendation of the superintendent.

Then Raymond Cook compounded his sins. At the 1941 convention of the N.E.A., the principals from the 1937 list, who had now taken over control of the Principals Club, staged a campaign to get William H. Johnson elected to the presidency of the N.E.A. The Chicago Teachers Union, belonging to the N.E.A. as an organization, sent Raymond Cook to the convention as its official delegate with the expressed purpose of preventing Johnson's nomination as president elect. He was completely successful and Johnson's stock in N.E.A. circles began to fall from that time on.

As a result of the draft and other war-time situations, the 1942 enrolment of the Chicago Teachers College fell from 2,000 to 800, and forty-two teachers were dropped. All those with tenure were transferred to the junior college or to high schools, except Raymond Cook. On the ground that he had a junior high-school, not a senior high-school certificate, he was demoted to a third-grade room in a small elementary school in the inner South Side and to an elementary teacher's salary—by action of the same Board which had assigned him to Hyde Park High School, five years before.[19] In order to support his family he worked in a war plant during 1944-45, and the schools lost his services for that year.

Another demotion with clear patronage overtones was that of Mrs. Olive Bruner, principal of the Spalding School for Crippled Children. In 1942 she was directed by telegram to report to another school and was replaced by a newly appointed principal from the 1937 list with no background in special education; she was, however, the sister of the Democratic floor leader of the lower house of the legislature. No reasons were given for Mrs. Bruner's removal. The Chicago Teachers Union got the Chicago Federation of Labor to protest Mrs. Bruner's transfer, despite the opposition of the unions which had now been won over by the City Hall. The Citizens Schools Committee marshalled a long list of organizations into a public protest.

In 1944 Thomas J. Crofts, also a union member, was demoted as principal from Manley High School, when the Board allowed the Navy to take over the building. He was transferred to a small elementary school at a time when there were several openings in other high schools. His protest that Manley, which was serving a deteriorating West Side community well, should be continued and that the Herzl Junior College Building, where the draft had lowered enrolment, should be offered to the Navy, was the only obvious reason for his treatment. Again that year, the Board ordered curriculum changes in the Teachers College. John De Boer, director of student teaching, was summarily transferred to a junior college when he objected to the changes. More than 600 teachers were transferred without their request or consent. Whether these demotions and changes were punitive, or convenient to make way for promotions of Board friends and relatives, other political figures, in no case was a hearing granted the teachers transferred.[20]

Board Saps Opposition

Not only did the Board and the administrators who supported it punish individuals, they tried to gain control of the teachers organizations, beginning with the Chicago Division of the Illinois Education Association, which Miss Haley had controlled for forty years. But Miss Haley was now gone and the Federation torn within itself. The nominating committee slated new officers who were clearly Board supporters. The union presented an opposing slate. More than 4,000 people attended the annual meeting, November 12, 1938, which included a considerable number of new members who were not teachers, but patronage appointees from the downtown offices. The Federation supported the Board slate, but the union candidates were elected. Until 1948 candidates supported by the union were elected to leadership in the Chicago Division. Edward E. Keener, who had been active in the principals' group in the union, was elected president in 1940.

As late as 1949 a Ph.D. thesis at the University of Chicago on the Chicago Teachers Union stated there had never been a serious rupture between the union and the I.E.A. and that officers of each organization had been active in both.[21] The union and the Chicago Division cooperated on all major issues between 1938 and 1947. The union urged its members to belong to the non-union state organization, and as a body held membership in the N.E.A., as well as in the American Federation of Teachers, of which it was the largest local. Representatives of the union were active in the 1941, 1943, and 1944 N.E.A. conventions. Members of the Chicago Union were invited to speak at meetings of downstate divisions of the Illinois Education Association. The I.E.A. and the N.E.A. both supported the right to tenure of Mary Wheeler and Ralph Marshall, teachers of Proviso High School who were refused contracts because they had organized a teachers' union. The executive secretary of the I.E.A. who had succeeded Robert Moore in 1938, Irving Pearson, contributed to the union bulletin and magazine. In 1947 the Chicago Division backed the union's single salary proposal. Both groups cooperated in drafting bills in 1941 and 1947 to change the Board of Examiners and to give the superintendent of schools full authority over the entire system.

This close cooperation still continued for a while after a sharp change in

N.E.A. policy on the scope of state teachers organizations. In 1947 the N.E.A. announced that state organizations should turn their local branches into general welfare organizations instead of limiting them to matters of state legislation. The N.E.A. membership in large cities was small and union groups in large and middle-sized cities were now increasing.[22] Even in some forty smaller Illinois towns there were teachers' unions by 1947. Protests against forced collection of I.E.A. dues, in order to receive pay for a day spent at compulsory County Institutes, threatened the 100 percent membership of which local superintendents had boasted. Rockford and other cities in Illinois where there were A.F.T. locals set up their own institutes and refused to pay I.E.A. dues. The Chicago Division began its competition with the union by setting up a small credit union, competing with the union group in existence since 1931, and a separate insurance plan. Gradually union members withdrew until the Chicago Division membership fell from 10,000 to 3,000, some of whom were anti-union and some of whom thought the union not militant enough, and it became a rival, not an ally of the union.

The Chicago Teachers Federation was an easy prey. Margaret Haley had been so completely its dominating force that conflict over filling her place was inevitable. A number of long-time Federation leaders like Susan Scully had already become active in the union. The group which won the internal struggle in the Federation recognized the union as a greater threat to its shrinking organization than the Board of Education. In 1939 the Federation challenged as illegal the reelection of Lyle Wolf, the union candidate, as president of the Chicago Division. It attacked the union as an enemy of the single salary schedule for elementary teachers, although a single salary scale was one of the policies adopted at the very first meeting of the Union House of Representatives. In December, 1941, the Federation told its members to withdraw from the Chicago Division. In a sharp debate within the Federation on trends in the pension in 1940, seven of its most experienced and able members had resigned from the board. When the union, the Chicago Division, the Citizens Schools Committee, and other civic groups introduced legislation to modernize the system of examining teachers in Chicago, the Federation joined the Board in opposition, claiming that it was a vicious attack on tenure and on the Otis law. In 1945 a further division in the Federation gave rise to a smaller new organization, the Council of Elementary Teachers. In 1946 this second group sent a letter to Mayor Kelly urging him not to ask for the resignation of McCahey, as his "service has merited the commendation and gratitude of the citizens of Chicago."[23]

The collapse of the Chicago Teachers Federation as a force for justice and professional integrity among Chicago teachers was a tragic end to Margaret Haley's remarkable and courageous efforts. But even more serious in its current effect on school policies was the complete reversal of the position of the Chicago Principals Club. As the 155 principals certificated in 1937 were appointed and joined the Club, the balance in favor of Johnson and McCahey was tipped. In

1939 the executive secretary who had succeeded Lyle Wolf was dismissed, and the club became a most useful sounding board for the administration. After the members voted down a resolution to support the choice of principals by merit, introduced by Edward Keener, some 200 of the older principals became active members in the Chicago Teachers Union—knowing that by doing so they lost all chance of promotion as long as Johnson was superintendent.[24]

The Illinois Congress of Parents and Teachers had also retreated from the militant opposition to the Board's policies displayed by Mrs. Holland Flagler, its president, in 1933. Action on Chicago issues could be taken only at the State P.T.A. convention. The local P.T.A.'s in Chicago which opposed the Board found it difficult to get downstate members to give time or attention to city problems. Moreover, the political pressures which could be (and were) applied on business favors and tax bills of the husbands of P.T.A. leaders discouraged crusading in the state and local organizations. Until May, 1946, when an active group of Chicago P.T.A. leaders obtained from the state convention the right to have a Chicago regional organization, the P.T.A. had become a negligible factor in school policies, although some individual local associations continued to be vocal in their protests.[25]

The opposition of another powerful force to the Kelly control of schools had also weakened. In spite of Fitzpatricks's forthright personal support, it became increasingly difficult to get the Chicago Federation of Labor to oppose actions of the Chicago Board of Education. Some of the union leaders felt that labor support of the Roosevelt-Democratic national policies was more important than action on local issues. This had been the position of Roosevelt himself when approached by some of his strong Chicago supporters who opposed the Board.[26]

But at least two other influential groups in the Federation of Labor were now completely in Kelly's camp, and neither Fitzpatrick's directness nor Lillian Herstein's oratory had any effect on them. The building trades, the largest single group in the Federation, always generally conservative and unsympathetic with labor as a social movement, gradually lost its older leadership, which in the painters' and carpenters' locals particularly had given strong support to Fitzpatrick on the school issue. The new leadership was able to make contracts with local governments which guaranteed building trades workers the permanence of civil service—and at the same time a high hourly scale for construction work based on intermittent private employment.[27] The second large group was the flat janitors local of the Building Service union. Now headed by the president of the Thompson-controlled school janitors' union of 1928, the union gave complete support to Kelly and staged a huge mass meeting of the membership at the Stadium to support his relection in 1939. Flat janitors were ordered to distribute Kelly's campaign publicity throughout the city.[28] The members of the Building Service union who were employed by the schools were sometimes successful in blocking recommendations brought by the Chicago Teachers Union to the Education Committee of the Chicago Federation of

Labor. The last important direct protest against a school Board action by the Federation of Labor was the vote to condemn the replacement of Mrs. Bruner at the Spalding School by Celestine Igoe in 1942. Fitzpatrick died in 1946, and Lillian Herstein, the most eloquent spokesman for the union teachers, was not reelected to the executive committee of the Chicago Federation of Labor on which she had served for twenty years. The Chicago Teachers Union was not ignored; but it was not able to muster the full strength of the Federation behind it on controversial issues. While the C.I.O. unions, mainly steel and automobile, sometimes supported school issues, in Chicago they have not constituted more than a third of the total organized labor force.

Program and Problems of the Union

The war seriously hampered the work of the union. Gasoline was strictly rationed and public transportation difficult. All of the growing social activities of the union, a chorus, a drama group, a bowling league and other enterprises, came to a dead stop. Such activities were beginning to knit warm personal relationships among teachers of the various levels, long separate and cool toward each other. Moreover, all over the nation, teachers were asked to assume arduous and time-consuming new duties to help the war effort. In 1940 Chicago teachers spent a twelve-hour day registering young men for the draft. They gave out cards for sugar and other commodities rationed in the school neighborhoods. They collected keys for scrap and paper for reuse.

The union itself organized classes in civilian defense procedures to prepare teachers for instructing the government-prepared courses on what to do with magnesium incendiary bombs or several kinds of gases. Hundreds of teachers participated in training classes under Professor Albert Lepawsky of the University of Chicago, director of civilian defense for Chicago. When the project succeeded completely, Prof. Lepawsky's lectures and outlines were reprinted under William H. Johnson's name, and the entire project claimed as the work of the Board of Education, without reference either to the union or to Prof. Lepawsky.[29] A union teacher organized the blood bank set up by the Chicago Federation of Labor. The union housed a large and active Red Cross unit and raised funds for the U.S.O. During and toward the end of the war the union distributed O.P.A. price control and rationing pamphlets, thousands of copies of the Atlantic Pact, and early material on the United Nations, particularly UNESCO. In 1944 the annual Educational Conference dealt with Democracy at War, and the union magazine carried several articles on the war's impact on child labor and juvenile delinquency. In 1946 Laird Bell was the featured speaker at the educational conference, discussing the international economic problems of peace.

More serious than the interruption of union development by the war, however, was the conflict within the union itself over retention of its executive secretary, Kermit Eby. An earnest social activist, a pacifist and a firm believer in the possibilities of the teachers' union as a redeeming force for the city, Eby worked tirelessly and wrote well, but he tended to assume a superior attitude to those who were not his intellectual equals, and tended also to assume the center of the stage in an organization where he was an employed and not an elected officer. In general, he failed to recognize the sincerity of union members who did not accept his analysis of the scope of the union. Conflict arose when he demanded that the current president of the union somehow force the members of the executive council of the American Federation of Teachers to keep on its staff an editor of whom he approved, although the president of the A.F.T., Professor George Counts, recommended removal. Eby went so far as to threaten to release attacks in the press on the past and current leadership of the union if this were not done. Charges brought against him by the executive Board,[30] and heated support by those who appreciated his devotion and ability and agreed with his wide ranging goals for the union, resulted in a disruptive dispute in the union, resolved by a close vote for his dismissal. A definite drop in membership, especially in the high schools and colleges, followed. Perhaps the heightened emotions of the war period played a part in the decision of Eby and his supporters to fight for his position. The sense of rapid change on great issues, and the need to go the limit for ultimate values were real factors in 1942.

Disputes in voluntary organizations are not uncommon, particularly when a crisis-produced group has not yet determined its permanent direction. But in the case of the Chicago Teachers Union, the timing of any such conflict was unfortunate. It broke wide open the slowly knitting ties between high-school teachers and the large group of elementary teachers with only two years of normal training, between those who believed deeply in the importance of the labor movement in American society and those who had little knowlege of or concern for it, between teachers who felt the union should be a major force in solving political and social problems of the city and others who saw only need of a good, orderly school system where they could do their day's work with dignity. Moreover, in the heat of argument accusations had been made which diminished respect for union leaders on both sides. Discussions on issues involving social problems became polarized around personalities, and objective decisions on them more difficult. Political division within the union (in itself not unhealthy), sometimes became bitterly personal rather than constructive in advocating new policies. In 1943, despite a well-organized drive to elect as president Susan Scully, an ex-Federation elementary teacher, failed by a small number of votes.

The damaging results of the dispute were not what Kermit Eby had wanted or intended. In fact, the conflict over his dismissal tended to delay the maturity of the union and kept the governing apparatus largely in the control of the older elementary teachers, conscientious in their work for the union, but cautious in adopting changes in policy or leadership and in employing the skilled staff needed to make the union attain maximum usefulness in any area.

Two other sharp differences opened old seams among the leaders in this period. One arose from debate on the union position on aid for instruction in parochial schools. After the union legislative committee presented a report detailing the arguments pro and con, the union House of Representatives voted against federal support for church schools in the form of instruction and transportation, but for all other aid—such as food and health services—to children without discrimination. This also became the position of the American Federation of Teachers in 1947. But the extended arguments became heatedly emotional and some of the old antagonisms between the Teachers League and the Chicago Teachers Federation became visible.

The second rift was opened by a number of men teachers at Lane High School. Impatient with the slow pace of salary increase in the face of war-time inflation, they organized a Men Teachers Club to seek more money for men teachers than for women, presenting their requests to the Board of Education for several years. Some of them remained in the union and some did not.

But in spite of its internal dissension, the Chicago Teachers Union did grow in breadth of understanding of its professional responsibilities, though not as far or as fast as some of its members wished. The content of discussion at annual educational conferences and the articles in its thirty-page monthly magazine indicate such growth. The responsibility of the union for enlarging the opportunities of minority group children and of those generally underprivileged was a continuing thread in the educational conferences. Two workshops on minority groups heard Ethel Alpenfels and Margaret Mead. Articles on the injustice of the poll tax and on the myths of prejudice appeared in the magazine with the encouragement of an able volunteer editor, Ethel Parker, who had before the amalgamation written the bulletin for the Federation of Women High School Teachers. Robert Weaver contributed an article on the F.E.P.C. There were articles on the new "intercultural education," on the forms of racist discrimination, on the increasing in-migration to the city, and one by a displaced Japanese on the tragic Nisei internment camps. Accounts of the activities of the Urban League and of the new City Commission on Race Relations, appointed by Mayor Kelly in 1943, appeared.[31] The Union was represented on the Advisory Committee of this city agency and a union member served as its secretary for its two first years.

Discussions in the magazine and in the conferences by Jessie Binford, Lea Taylor and Lester Schloerb described what the war was doing to children. Child labor and dropouts were explored by national figures such as Floyd Reeves, who was on the board of the Citizens Schools Committee. D. E. Mackelman, beginning his career as a housing expert, analyzed the mounting housing problem of Chicago. In February, 1942, the union magazine pointed out the need for increasing the scanty health services available to Chicago children. Improvements in elementary school libraries, in teaching reading, and in the too narrow opportunities for gifted children were urged. Radio programs produced by teachers and by recognized authorities supplemented the written articles on these subjects.

Income from the annual card party given by the union was combined with the bequest of Ella Flagg Young to the largest teachers' organization in the Chicago schools, to provide eye-glasses for needy children. Union members contributed generously to pay the salaries of Mary Wheeler and Ralph Marshall, dismissed for organizing a teachers' union in Proviso High School in Maywood, and the union in 1941 finally helped to get a tenure law (of a kind) for all downstate teachers.

After the war, the union participated in local and national conferences on UNESCO, distributed to teachers material on UNESCO and the new United Nations, and put on an exchange exhibit of artwork of children from European countries, under the earnest direction of an interested union member. There was clearly a wealth of genuine goodwill for mankind and an honest interest in solving human problems outside the narrow perimeter of the Chicago school system; but it seldom focussed into organized action. The union did, however, in 1943 urge Harold Ickes to run for mayor of Chicago.

The final step in the ousting of the Kelly Board of Education was initiated by the Chicago Division of the Illinois Education Association in 1943 by Edward E. Keener. The union supported the request to the N.E.A.[32] and made available all of its records to the N.E.A. Committee under Donald Du Shane, paid $1,000 to have the N.E.A. report printed, and urged its distribution by members. Chicago teachers were understandably annoyed when the superintendent of schools of Kansas City, Kansas, at the moment president of the N.E.A., instructed his teachers not to join the newly chartered Kansas City local of the American Federation of Teachers because the Chicago Teachers Union had done nothing, obliging the N.E.A. to come in and "save" the schools—since this was the first notice the N.E.A. had taken of the tragic situation of Chicago schools in twelve long, hard years. The union representative at the city council hearing on the N.E.A. Report recounted the union's fight against the 1937 principals' list. When Mayor Kelly appointed another advisory committee at the end of March, 1946, a committee of union officers, headed by Arthur Walz, its president, presented a detailed statement listing the abuses of the school system during the Kelly regime.

The union clearly had a long way to go to reach its maximum usefulness, but it had made a start and included two-thirds of all the city's teachers.

Chapter 14

A BOARD REMAINS FOR THIRTEEN YEARS

Why did the new inexperienced members of the Chicago Board make such radical changes in the entire school system without public discussion before or after its action? Why were they so adamant in ignoring all criticisms? Why was the opposition to the Thompson Board's activities in 1922 almost immediately successful in sending Board members and employees to jail and in preventing the re-election of Thompson as mayor in 1933, when the same forces of the city's life—greatly augmented by many more organizations and by thousands of previously unconcerned indignant voters who were the parents of the children in the schools—could not budge the Kelly Board of Education for more than a decade? The answer to these questions lies not within the Board of Education itself, or within the school system, but in the interrelation of the political and economic forces within the city during the depression.

Kelly-Nash Strength in Chicago

The major reason for the security of the Board of Education's stance was the simple fact that for the first time in its turbulent history, not only one party, but just one faction within that party controlled almost every significant segment of the complicated maze of some 1,700 local governments in Cook County. Moreover, this faction profited enormously politically from the popularity of the national administration, which it did little to help, with the all-important exception of delivering a huge supporting vote in national elections. In 1922 the Republicans were divided into the Thompson and Deneen-West factions, and the entire city press opposed Thompson and his Board of Education. No division was possible within the Kelly-Nash organization and the support of the ultra-respectable Republican Tribune was a plus of considerable value. [1]

The second important reason was that the business interests of the city were more concerned with saving their own financial skins during the depression than with what happened to any government services (except perhaps the police). They were certainly unconcerned with what happened to the schools, which had never been of much consequence to them at any time in the city's history. Sargent got a loan of 8 million dollars for his railroad, but made no effort to get a federal loan for the school system. Their precious skins could not be saved except with the cooperation of the all-powerful leaders of the faction in power—who had no intention of reducing the sources of that power—too complete in their control of all government functions to be opposed or even criticized by any who wanted favors. Sargent visited Kelly his first day in office as mayor. [2]

The third reason lay in the obvious fact that voting strength in Chicago had always been in the wards dominated by large ethnic groups, sometimes with venal leadership. Only eight of the fifty wards could easily be influenced by middle-class reform groups. The flight to the suburbs, already increasing in population three times as fast as the city, reduced both this upper-middle class element and its potential leadership. That most of the ethnic groups were strongly Catholic and that almost one-third of the children in the city attended parochial schools lessened the general concern among voters and party leadership for what happened to public schools. [3]

The depression introduced a new element. The unemployed on federal relief and made-work stipends were encouraged to believe that the local Democratic party, whose agencies administered these funds, could cut them off at will, and that support of Chicago Democrats was necessary if aid were to continue.

The huge patronage payroll of federal, county, and local governments was at the disposal of the Kelly-Nash group. At least three-fourths of the Democratic precinct captains in the county in 1936 held some public job.[4] Failure to deliver a precinct might deliver the job holder immediately into the limbo of unemployment, as a captain would earnestly explain to his good friends and neighbors. The school janitors alone covered half the precincts in the city, and there were none in any school building on any election day.

All of the punitive, regulatory, and permissive powers of government were under party control. Judges were no longer nominated by the squabbling factions of two parties. Any sitting judge recognized the imminence of the possibility that his own ward committeeman might fail to nominate him for reelection if his decisions offended City Hall. The tax assessing and reviewing machinery, the county treasurer's office with its millions to deposit in the local banks (which always "went along"), the council power over licenses and code violations, and the entire election machinery were now in the hands of one tightly controlled faction.

Organized labor, with membership reduced by continued unemployment, supported the national Democratic administration so wholeheartedly that it was hard to arouse opposition to the sins of the party locally, lest it be weakened nationally.[5] The teachers were divided within themselves, ineffective in 1933 in comparison with their power in 1902 and 1916.

The press was now also divided in its attitude toward the city administration. The Tribune supported it and the business interests in their demand for reduction in the cost of public education. For fifty years the Tribune had consistently fought new services in the schools, calling them "fads and frills," and several times had stated that any education beyond elementary school levels should not be given at public expense. The Herald for four years made a major issue of opposition to actions of the Kelly Board. Then its two excellent school reporters went on to greener fields and its coverage suffered. The Daily News was not vitriolic in its opposition, as the Herald had been in 1933, but it did oppose the economy program as an unnecessary attempt to reduce the opportunity of the city's children and particularly publicized the illegal aspects of the 1936 principal's examination. The American gave little space to school issues but did not support the Board. The Times in 1933 was shocked with the attack on athletics. The Sun, which began in 1941 as a morning counterweight to the Tribune, was from its inception forthright in demands for improvement of the battered school system.

One other element in control of the city's government under Edward J. Kelly cannot be omitted. Under all the surface manifestations of power lay an illicit connection with organized crime, as actual if not as blatant as in Thompson's day. The Kelly-Nash machine received campaign funds and its managers accepted personal payoffs from the purveyors of gambling and prostitution—contributions blinked at by the respectable leaders of organized business because they did not involve tax income, and because they would have lost their own favors had they protested.[6] Many of them had been very self-righteous in their criticisms of Thompson, who made less personal profit from illicit sources than did Kelly.

For the first time in Chicago a political organization, as all-inclusive and powerful as Boss Tweed's Tammany at its zenith, controlled every phase of local government. This was happening in Chicago at a time when LaGuardia, elected in New York as a reform mayor, was sending letters to a hundred thousand public employees telling them that their jobs did not depend upon their voting for him, and at a time when Philadelphia was also shedding some of its ancient political shackles. Thompson had left a pattern in Chicago which had been seized upon by shrewd successors and ruthlessly extended. All elements in the rest of the city's power structure now had to dance to the tune of city hall. Public utilities, real estate operators, bankers, contractors, hotels, liquor dealers, and organized illicit enterprises had to come to terms with it or suffer immediate and serious punishment. Contributions to campaign funds were a must; opposition could not even be considered. Removal of public deposits could wreck a bank during the depression. Increase in taxes or adverse decisions of the Board of Tax Review were too serious to fool with. Withholding of licenses or of police protection was easy.

If city hall could dictate so easily to legitimate business, it was obviously even simpler to collect from illegitimate activities which could be stopped at any time by ordinary enforcement of the law. Those in control of gambling and prostitution not only contributed to campaign funds, they produced thousands of voters for Kelly (as they had for Thompson), including an army of "floaters" who went from one precinct to another and accounted for a considerable part of Kelly's huge majority in 1935.[7]

In 1930 the Cermak faction in the Democratic party, whose strongest base lay in the United Societies composed of ethnic groups opposed to prohibition, had taken over control of the Board of County Commissioners, the County Treasurer's office, the Assessor's office, and the Board of the Sanitary District, each with an army of already existing patronage jobs. In 1931 Cermak, then president of the County Board and chairman of the Cook County Democratic Central Committee, was elected mayor of the city. A year later the Cermak faction elected the states' attorney, the Board of Tax Review, and in the national Democratic sweep, the governor and a United States senator, adding some state and federal patronage perquisites. By April, 1933, when Kelly took over the Thompson and Cermak structure, the Kelly-Nash faction gained complete control over all major sources of political power within Cook County. The Republicans had access neither to campaign funds nor to patronage jobs. The Kelly-Nash reign was so complete that in 1933 there was only one candidate for alderman in 21 of the city's 50 wards, and in 15 of the 19 state legislative districts within the city there was no contest at all. In 1935 the Republican County Committee put up no fight for mayor and gave no real support to Emil Wetten, who had really been nominated as token opposition by the Democrats.[8]

The relation of the Kelly-Nash machine to the Democratic national administration was never spelled out, any more than in Hague's Jersey City or Pendergast's Kansas City. After Kelly received almost 800,000 votes for mayor in 1935, as against Wetten's 167,000, he was so important to Farley's organization that no questions were asked on local issues or how Kelly got his votes, and no remonstrances by Secretary of the Interior Harold Ickes, or others high in New Deal councils, had any effect. In a city where the country's strongest press criticism of the Roosevelt administration was being spewed out daily by the Chicago Tribune, that kind of unchallenged vote was a blessing not to be questioned. When Eleanor Roosevelt, speaking in Chicago on October 31, 1933, was quoted in a Daily News editorial as urging an enlarged educational program during the depression because the first duty of this generation was to its youth and because it was no economy to produce delinquents and to pay for jails, the President of the Board of Education, James B. McCahey, felt quite at ease in snorting "Poppycock" at her statement. In areas where strong opposition to the Board of Education program existed, precinct captains circulated petitions asking for signatures to "support the president and the mayor."

Business and Chicago Politics

The business leadership, for which the Sargent Committee assumed the right to be spokesmen, had never shown any great concern for public education. Its most significant effort had been aimed at establishing a dual system of expensive vocational education to produce skilled workers during the beginning years of the century when the demand for skilled labor was strong. In 1933 there was an excess of all workers, skilled and unskilled, and no direct advantage to business and industry in spending money for schools.

The Sargent Committee itself was a somewhat amorphous body. It was sometimes listed as having 32 members, sometimes 165, sometimes 250, but the letterhead carried only the eight names of its moving spirits. All of the lists, however, contained names whose prestige was sufficient to carry weight with lesser lights. Only three of those on the list of 165 had ever sent children to the public schools, and then only for a short time, and two-thirds of them listed suburban residences.[9]

Members of the committee were probably quite convinced that they were doing a service to the city as well as to themselves by forcing tax reductions. They also understood clearly that the political organization which alone could compel reductions would not tolerate cuts in areas which would weaken its own position. Since educational employees and educational services were no longer of patronage value to the political powers—almost the only group of employees of which this could be said—it was inevitable that this would be the area in which reductions could most easily be made. The Sargent Committee simply accepted this as a matter of fact and at no time made any effort to change it.

In a Saturday Evening Post article for January 14, 1933, the chairman of the committee, Fred Sargent, president of the Northwestern Railroad, stated its purpose and modus operandi.

"The Committee on Public Expenditures is made up of one hundred men whose only right to interfere is their love of their city and their desperation as taxpayers. We find ourselves dealing with city officials who want our aid and are going a long way to get it. . . . Our Committee members are not crusaders condemning the past."

Sargent listed the essential government services which must be protected as police, fire and health (with no mention of education), and stated that the committee intended to stand pat and see that the banks bought no tax warrants from any government without its recommendation. He went on, however, to comment on the schools, then costing a million dollars a week, to the effect that, "Boards of Education and Superintendents are not the only intelligences to decide what shall be paid for schools. . . . It would be fine when every child in America can be guaranteed not only a high school education, but four years of college." But the question "as to how much is essential and how much merely desirable, must be determined by the people who pay the bills. The business men of Chicago have learned their lesson. We have not decided how we shall work out the method of future control."

Although reform political movements in other large cities were now being initiated by business leaders, the traditionally self-made businessmen of Chicago had no intention of being "crusaders," or of veering from their long accepted pattern of using political agencies to get what they wanted and not otherwise interfering in any of the political operations, no matter how disgraceful or illegal. The director of the Sargent Committee in a recent interview stated that the "Committee on Public Expenditures was never particularly interested in the educational system, whether they had junior high schools or this or that and the other. All that they were interested in was getting them to slow up the rate at which they were piling up obligations."[10] When it was ascertained that the cost of erecting school buildings in Chicago was from 50 to 100 percent higher in Chicago than in the suburbs, the Sargent Committee made no protest against the obvious loss of public funds in political kickbacks; they merely ordered all school construction stopped. They offered no apologies for their actions. They assumed without question that they were the people who knew what was good for the city, just as in later years a national official was surprised at objections to his statement that what was good for General Motors was good for the country. Neither did the small businessmen sitting on the Board of Education question the omniscience of their betters; they were equally sure they were performing a proper and necessary service—and were being quite unjustly persecuted.

At the same time they were ruthlessly enforcing heavy reductions in educational expenditures, these same businessmen were urging public expenditure for an extravagantly expensive World's Fair (from which they hoped to profit), planned from the beginning with Kelly, who had been head of the South Park Board. The Fair opened with a flourish, totally ignoring the army of unemployed, the unpaid teachers, and the corrupt city government. One critic suggested that as usual, Chicago had "accomplished the impossible and ignored the essential."[11]

The place of Samuel Insull in the constellation of business leadership in Chicago gives a measure of the level of its public mores. Donald Richberg accused Insull of being "more responsible than any one man in Chicago's history for the degradation of munincipal government to its lowest level of corruption and incompetence." Insull regularly made huge campaign contributions to both parties, and sometimes to all factions of both parties. His contribution to the campaign fund of Frank L. Smith for U.S. Senator, while the latter was still chairman of the State Public Utilities Commission, cost Smith his Senate seat.

The publication of Moe Rosenberg's income tax confession indicated Insull's method of buying votes in the state legislature. The confession listed the name of almost every member of the legislature as a recipient of Mid-West Utility stock rights, supposedly worth thousands of dollars. The Speaker of the House, later a federal judge, got $50,000 worth. This particular deal, however, carried its own penalty, as the stock was already worthless and the payments made by recipients to validate the rights were swept away in Insull's fall. The Federal Trade Commission investigation of the attempts of the National Electric Light Association to color school curricula with propaganda against control of public utilities showed Samuel Insull a major force in this effort. But Insull was a respected and accepted member of the powerful inner circle of businessmen in Chicago who forced school cuts—that is, until his own inflated empire was punctured by his rivals in the East. All the men who associated with him in the long succession of businessmen's committees on government problems, before and after 1926, knew his record and did not find it beneath their standards.[12]

When Charles Merriam grieved that no businessmen in Chicago had the courage to speak at the mass meeting on July 21, 1933, and compared it with the higher level of political morality among the same group in New York City, he had recognized a fact which had been one of the great handicaps in the development of a sane and reasonable form of government in Chicago and Illinois.

When the long list of cases challenging the authority of the Board of Education and the Board of Examiners was brought in courts in Chicago, any judge who heard them knew he risked his renomination if his decision were unwelcome at city hall. Park District employees similarly refused community organizations the right to hold discussions on school problems in park buildings, or tried at least to limit the scope of the meetings. A huge personal property tax bill was sent to the husband of the president of the Citizens Save Our Schools Committee, in 1934—he had never received one before. The Civic Council on Vote Frauds produced, from the records of the Election Commissioner's office, an eighty-page publication listing voting irregularities—on which no action was ever taken. In May, 1935, an audit of the books of the County Treasurer showed a shortage of $400,000, also never accounted for and never repaid.[13]

Crime and the Kelly-Nash Machine

Even more disturbing was the plentiful evidence of the connection between Chicago Tammany and organized crime. Capone's headquarters in Cicero remained undisturbed by County law enforcement agencies during Cermak's administration of the County Board. When he became mayor, the city policeman assigned as his bodyguard was arrested for shooting one Frank Nitti, a known gangster enemy of the Moran gang which succeeded Capone in power. Nitti refused to testify, and the policeman was dropped from the force. The Better Government Association in 1931 had refused to support Cermak as no better than Thompson.[14]

Both Kelly and Nash made settlements out of court on income tax not paid on their personal income between 1926 and 1932, the heyday of wild Sanitary District expenditures which had increased from three to ten millions in seven years. One example of the ease with which incumbent officials made money was giving away of cinders from the huge District pumping plants to a favored customer who promptly sold them back to the District at a high price to pave the bridle path along McCormick Boulevard. Soldier Field Stadium cost eight millions; a similar stadium in Los Angeles, $1,700,000. Nash as a sewer contractor had won some 8 million dollars' worth of contracts from the District. Edward J. Kelly's salary as chief engineer of the Sanitary District was $6,000. He was, according to the press, called to account for not paying income *tax* of $450,000.[15] As chief engineer he could not have failed to know how the tripled budget of the District was being spent, but when the Republican Sanitary District trustees were sentenced to prison for spending it, the indictment against him was quashed.

On October 30, 1934, the Chicago Daily News accused Kelly of accepting a million dollars a year from the enterprises run by Skidmore, who had now inherited the illegal domains of Capone and Moran. The Daily News and John Flynn in the July 6, 1940, issue of Collier's Magazine stated flatly that Skidmore was collecting kickbacks on textbooks for Chicago schools. So matter-of-fact was the acceptance of gambling protection that when a group of Fifth Ward citizens in 1935 protested to their Democratic ward committeeman about an open gambling house at 63rd Street and Cottage Grove, he responded indignantly that he had nothing to do with it; all the money from 63rd Street went down town to Skidmore.[16] Mayor Kelly, after $6,000 a year as salary from the Sanitary District, received $15,000 as mayor. When he died he left a fortune including a home worth a half million. When the mayor criticised Governor Horner in 1936 as an inept politician, the governor retorted, "If to amass a fortune on a modest salary is to be a politician, I am not a politician."[17]

Kelly's opposition to Horner was based in part on the governor's veto of bills relaxing somewhat the laws against gambling and on his support of the League of Women Voters' permanent registration bill. Vote frauds were so common that support from the Capone gangsters Thompson had used, in some West Side precincts in 1927, was not even necessary. State Senator T. V. Smith, professor of philosophy at the University of Chicago, speaking in behalf of the permanent registration legislation said "Our party is truly the party of democracy; we believe not only in the right of a vote for each of the living, but even for the dead!" The army of floaters, who carried slips with the names of those not yet voted from one precinct to another, was estimated to have cast as many as one-third of the votes in the 1935 mayoralty election.

All this was the monolithic "establishment" which confronted those who tried to reverse the action of the Board of Education in July 1933, and to obtain a more equitable division of public funds. At no time in Chicago's history had a city administration been so impregnable. The complete support of the most powerful newspaper in the city was only a bonus; it would have been secure without it, but perhaps for not so long. The corruption of the Thompson administration, at which the Tribune had aimed its righteous thunderbolts, was no worse than that of the Kelly administration which it ignored. That there were thousands of dissenters in 1933, instead of the hundreds in 1922, was not enough to budge city hall.

The individual members of the Board of Education were quite insignificant figures in the total city picture, "small fry" in comparison to the industrial leaders and bankers in the Sargent Committee. Many of them were still preoccupied with contracts for their friends who would then return favors over the years—coal dealers, an oil dealer, small bankers, real estate managers, union officials (not recommended by the Chicago Federation of Labor), and lawyers. One member lived in Barrington, one in Winnetka. Aside from Mrs. Hefferan, whose personal status exceeded that of any of her colleagues on the Board, representation carefully followed the old ethnic pattern of Irish, Polish, Czech, German, Scandanavian, and Jewish. After 1944 there was always one Negro. In 1938 the mayor appointed Mrs. Walter Heineman, after two years' urging by the Citizens Schools Committee and the Chicago Woman's Club, so that, as Mrs. Hefferan remarked, she might get a second to her motions.

As a group the Kelly Board members were quite sure, in conducting the affairs of the schools, they were doing nothing different from what had been done by previous Boards of Education. In this assumption they were unfortunately very nearly right. They were flattered by their importance in the eyes of such leaders as the Sargent Committee and the mayor, and sincerely indignant at the reception of their efforts by the teachers. When the teachers' offer to work without pay, if the Board allowed an audit of its books, was read in the 1933 Board meeting, one member roared that such an offer was exasperating to a person who was trying to do something for children. When the roomful of teachers laughed, he stormed that he would get their names and prefer charges against them. His colleague Joseph Savage, a Thompson appointee, now a loyal Kelly man, said the Board should dismiss any employee who did not see that "Our program is for the benefit of the children."[18] The Kelly appointees on the Board had only to stand pat, with the power of the wide-based city political organization behind them, and they did just that.

Appointments of substitutes to the increased number of unfilled vacancies in the schools were on political status, according to statements from independent Alderman Paul Douglas, who was approached for jobs. The evidence presented in the principals' examination court cases, on the open political sponsorship of almost all who were passed, was never questioned as to fact. One woman, a temporary clerk in the Board of Education offices, was tried in Municipal Court for stealing $1,000 from a church to get a promotion to be a music supervisor. She pleaded guilty, gave her reason for the theft, and no question was raised in court as to who promised her the promotion or who received the money.[19] Union members who spoke for the Board slate in the hotly contested Chicago Division election in 1938 got immediate promotions. No opponents of the superintendent or the Board, whatever their qualifications, received promotions of any kind—and punitive demotions have been noted in previous chapters. The Dean of the School of Education of the University of Illinois, Thomas E. Benner, who had been sharp in his public criticisms of the Chicago Board was scheduled to address a meeting of the American Association of University Professors in Chicago on March 12, 1938, to discuss the "Situation in the Chicago Schools" The president of the Chicago Board called the president of the University of Illinois on the telephone, and threatened drastic cuts in the university budget, then under consideration by the legislature, if Benner spoke. The Daily News of March 12, 1938, carries this story. Benner called a member of the board of the Citizens School Committee to ask her to take his place and to explain why he could not come.[20]

Not only did the Board of Education punish its opponents, it treated the whole education department with scorn, even its own choice as superintendent. After the new Chicago Teachers Union had tried for a year to meet with Superintendent Johnson, it managed with the active help and actual presence of John Fitzpatrick, to get an interview with the president of the Board, James B. McCahey. When the union president protested against Johnson's treatment of the union, McCahey said "Don't pay any attention to him; if you want something, you've got to come to me." Johnson sat in the corner and said nothing.

School Taxes for Political Propaganda

One of the problems of those who opposed the Kelly Board of Education had been the large sums of tax money spent by the Board of Education and the city government in their own defense. Even in 1933 the Board had spent a very considerable part of its depleted funds, not on paying employees, or giving school services, but on printing more than a half million pamphlets defending its actions. In December, 1933, a copy of a sixteen-page illustrated pamphlet, "Our Public Schools Must Not Close," was given to every school child and distributed widely throughout the city. The pamphlet (described in Chapter 11) restated the claims made by the Board to justify its actions on July 12, that no opportunity for children had been reduced, that enormous savings had been made, and that taxes would now be reduced. The first page gives the Board's explanation of the opposition to its program.

> "Considerable agitation against this program of economy and efficiency was stirred up by certain interests, and the facts have often been wilfully or ignorantly misrepresented. Even now, for reasons which are known to many, and suspected by more, agitation continues, though on a constantly diminishing scale."

Innuendoes such as these were the frequent answer to questions, or to allegations of fact. The Citizens Schools Committee answered these publications factually, point by point, with clear exposition of the misstatements of facts; but its mimeographed answer could reach only a tiny fraction of the hundreds of thousands who had received the expensive pamphlet.

A second broadside from the Board at public expense was issued in 1937 as the Chicago Teachers Union was being organized. This was a 44-page book with 67 illustrations entitled *Our Public Schools*, again distributed by precinct captains and given to every pupil. This publication claimed credit for the junior college which the Board had destroyed and which had been restored by legislation the Board did not support, only by the personal intervention of Col. Jacob Arvey, National Democratic Committeeman, without support from the Board. It pointed out how remarkable were the junior college lectures of which it had made fun in 1933. It lauded the bands, the music and art classes, and the instruction in physical education and swimming, all of which it had voted to eliminate four years before. It claimed credit for building twenty-eight new schools, all of which had been paid for out of federal P.W.A. funds. The last page was a eulogy of Superintendent Johnson, stating that Superintendent Bogan had recommended his appointment as assistant superintendent, although thousands of people in the city knew beyond a shadow of doubt that this was not true.

Just before the 1939 mayoralty election, the Board published another sixteen-page pamphlet entitled "Half a Million Prepare for Life's Battle" and distributed it not only to the half million who were being prepared, but through all the regular political channels of the County Democratic Committee. This praise of what Chicago schools were doing in vocational educational followed Johnson's backing down on his vague plan to make the school system 80 percent vocational which had aroused criticism from organized labor and teachers' organizations, and prompted the Citizens Schools Committee to organize a conference on vocational education using business leaders from the city and nationally known figures in the field of vocational education.

In 1942 the Board published James B. McCahey's speech of acceptance upon election to his tenth term as the Board's president—in another sixteen-page illustrated pamphlet. This publication again claimed credit for the "great development" of the popular junior college since 1933, without mentioning its destruction as a worthless extravagance. It boasted that the Board's finances were now in order and that expenditures were below the 1931 budget, without acknowledging that this was possible only because teachers' salaries were still $4,754,000 below the 1931 level, long after all other public employees had begun getting increases to compensate for war-time inflation. All credit for instruction in war work, fully financed by the federal government, was assumed by the local Board. One paragraph reiterated the "dangers of unjust and uninformed criticism" from a "mistaken minority group" who "for self-promotion would besmirch the schools."

In 1943, the mayoralty election year, another pamphlet went out to the more than half million children and the precinct captains. It compared the stupid waste of resources and the lack of educational accomplishments in the Chicago schools before 1933 with the quite marvelous deeds now being accomplished in 1943 by "capable teachers using modern methods"; even the "capable teachers" were quite surprised having after all had few additions to their ranks since being castigated in 1933. Few of the activities praised were new in the ten-year period and some, like the "adjustment service plan" and elementary home economics, had been deleted in 1933 as fads and frills. Again the account of additions to school housing failed to mention that the "unfinished structures before 1933" had actually been completed by the Public Works Administration.

The 1944 "Message to the Schools" capped the list. It named the schools in the Negro area on the South Side, giving the cost of 12,534 new seats, and of Du Sable High School, one of the "unfinished structures," which had waited three years for the P.W.A. to complete. It claimed that the Board had spent 6 million dollars on South Side schools, although almost every cent came from Washington. Then it listed the number of migrant children from each southern state, Mississippi heading the list with 34 percent. Pictures of ramshackle one-room Negro schools in Mississippi were placed opposite pictures of Chicago schools, without mentioning that the Chicago buildings shown were jammed with children on double shifts, while in white areas only a very few schools in outlying areas were so crowded. Du Sable and Phillips High Schools between them had 3,000 children more than their seating capacity that year.

In 1945 a large publication entitled *One Hundred Years of Educational Progress,* 1845-1945, showed pictures of the first schools in the pioneer settlement, and then went on to make enlarged claims for the current Board of Education. On page 2 it stated that the Board had saved 20 million dollars in 1933—and had paid "all back salaries" out of the savings! It had never claimed savings of more than five or ten millions before, and certainly had paid no "back salaries." As a war-time contribution, Superintendent Johnson's "Americanism bulletins were developing a deep and understanding patriotism in children."

Mayor Kelly had profited politically from the more than three million expensive publications for which the city administration and the Board of Education had used tax funds to attack critics and defend their actions. In a 1943 campaign folder labeled "Mayor Kelly talks on a subject vital to every taxpayer," half of the eight pages dealt with bitter attacks on his opponents, accused of "venomous bile," "personal self-seeking and intrigue," and "deliberate fakery." The unfair opposition press (apparently the Sun and the News) and the "twisters of truth" and "hate breeders" who "undermine our school system," were accused of breaking down the morale of the teachers. The Mayor asked rhetorical questions, such as "What of the 28 New Schools?" (built with P.W.A. money); "What of Chicago's Own Christmas Benefit that has collected over a million dollars to clothe needy children?" The Christmas benefit was the football game for which the Board tried to force teachers to buy and sell tickets so that precinct captains could distribute food and clothing to those who "went along." (In 1937 the School Children's Aid had furnished the names of families, but the machine still got the credit.) The pamphlet urged "Keep out the self-appointed brigadiers of destruction! Be proud to call Chicago—Your Home Town!" Thompson had never tooted his horn any louder.

The N.E.A. Investigation

The final step in the ousting of the Kelly Board from its strangle-hold on school progress was initiated by the Chicago Division of the Illinois State Teachers Association in 1943, under the leadership of Edward E. Keener, its president. Keener had been active not only in the Principals Club and the Chicago Teachers Union but also in the N.E.A. Association of Elementary Principals. He urged the National Education Association to institute an investigation of the activities of the Chicago Board of Education and of Superintendent William H. Johnson. In this request, he was supported by the Citizens Schools Committee, the Chicago Teachers Union, and by other organizations.

The N.E.A. had held its 1933 convention in Chicago a few days before the crushing program of July 12 was adopted; but it had never taken official cognizance of that official action or of any other Chicago school difficulties for ten years thereafter.

In fact, had it not been for the alert opposition of the union and the skill of Raymond Cook in 1941, Superintendent Johnson had had a good chance to put himself in line for the N.E.A. presidency in that year's convention. In 1943 the Johnson favorite (whom the union had defeated for president of the Chicago Division in 1938) was in line for chairmanship of the N.E.A. committee on tenure, and was kept from getting that office by the 1943 union representative at the N.E.A. meeting. But both Willard Givens, secretary of the N.E.A., and Donald Du Shane, while president, had contributed to the union magazine, and Du Shane in particular had clearly shown his personal concern about the grave situation of public education in Chicago. Donald Du Shane was head of the N.E.A. Commission for the Defense of Democracy through Education, and he welcomed the Chicago Division's invitation. The Citizens Schools Committee enlisted a large number of organizations to support the request. The Chicago Teachers Union offered Du Shane the briefs of all the court cases on which it had spent some $20,000, and any other records he wanted, and he gladly accepted them. The union contributed $1,000 and the Citizens Schools Committee $1,500 to cover the total cost of printing thousands of copies of the report for distribution.

The investigation was thorough. It summarized all the major issues raised against the Chicago Board of Education and its superintendent in 1933 and thereafter in concise, factual form. It stated in detail the unprofessional acts of Superintendent Johnson—his coaching of candidates for the 1936 principals' examination for pay while superintendent and one of the examiners, and the evidence of grade "fixing" on the subsequent oral examinations in favor of those he had coached and those who had known political sponsors. It described the demotions of Raymond Cook and others, and summarized the evidence that the demotions were purely punitive. It gave the decisions of the courts in the challenges to the principals' examination and in the demotions. It noted the clear discrimination against teachers in salary restoration, as compared with other local government employees.

Having reviewed these data, the investigation committee set forth direct recommendations. The Superintendent of Schools of Chicago should have control over all employees and activities in the entire school system, not merely over instruction. The Board of Examiners as constituted should not be continued; instead there should be a group of persons trained in educational personnel problems, who should have tenure. The superintendent should not regard the examining system as his personal province, with the right to disregard the examiners he appointed and controlled if he so chose. Before any teacher or principal was demoted, he should be given a hearing and a statement of the reasons for the action. Teaching positions should be open to any qualified instructor, not merely to graduates of the Chicago Normal College or to elementary teachers from the Normal College who were already in the system. The superintendent's control over and leadership of his teachers should be established by his "fairness, knowledge, integrity and a deep interest in the welfare of the city." The superintendent should provide channels of communication so that "the ideas of teachers could be given his careful consideration." The report, seventy pages long, was issued in May, 1945. In January, 1946, the N.E.A. voted to expel William H. Johnson for unprofessional conduct, an almost unheard of procedure.[21]

The Chicago Board of Education had ignored the investigation completely. It had refused Donald Du Shane access to its records—the only instance of such refusal in the experience of the N.E.A.[22] The Board likewise ignored the report when issued—but the newspapers did not. Summaries of its main points and its recommendations appeared in the Daily News, and Marshall Field's new newspaper, the Sun, carried long accounts. One chain of neighborhood newspapers, whose owner, Leo Lerner, had been at one time president of the Citizens Schools Committee, carried the entire report in serial form. The Citizens Schools Committee urged Republican Governor Green, who had promised in his platform to rid the schools of exploitation for personal or political profit, to hold hearings on the report; it was also supported by the State Superintendent of Public Instruction, but the governor was reluctant to act on this as on his other promises.

The city council was urged to hold a public hearing on the charges made in the report, a request echoed by dozens of organizations and many local P.T.A.'s. The council finally voted to hold such a hearing and appointed a committee of five aldermen, all of whom were staunch supporters of Mayor Kelly, to listen. For two days the city council chamber was packed while a stream of speakers from the Citizens Schools Committee, the Chicago Teachers Union, the Chicago

Division, The Independent Voters of Illinois, Women's Clubs, the City Club, P.T.A.'s, settlement houses, and dozens of other organizations gave the committee their reasons why the council should support the recommendations in the report. The representative of the Chicago Teachers Union summarized the story of the 1937 principals' examination.

For two days the aldermen listened stolidly, and then issued a mimeographed statement, some four pages long, in which they stated that they had heard no evidence to support the charges, and they therefore concluded that the charges were unfounded, a mere rehash of old rumors—and besides, the North Central Association had always accredited the schools and therefore nothing could be wrong with them. This "white-wash" report was adopted by the city council and then distributed through the schools by the Chicago Teachers Federation, now an ally of the Board. President McCahey in a speech to an engineers' group (reprinted at public expense), related the savings and progress made by the Board of Education since 1933. But the newspapers had given wide coverage to the statements made at the city council hearing by obviously responsible persons, and there was no question that the Kelly regime had suffered serious political damage. The school issue would clearly loom large in the 1947 mayoralty campaign.

The North Central Association Warning

Just one week after the hearings in the council chamber and one day after the publication of the council committee's report, on March 30, 1946, the annual report of the North Central Association of Schools and Colleges on Chicago high schools was released. Usually this report was sent only to the superintendent. But this time it was released to the press, as well. It contained a peremptory warning to the superintendent and Board of Education that any further accreditation of Chicago high schools would be dependent upon the centering of responsibilities in the office of the superintendent of schools and upon the provision for a politically independent Board of Education. Every paper gave headlines to this bombshell, particularly since the council report had based its defense on the approval of Chicago schools by the North Central Association.[23]

The warning by the North Central Association, which set standards of accreditation in thirty states, was the climax to a series of warnings since 1933. The accrediting committee of the Association in any state is composed of representatives of the State Department of Public Instruction, the School of Education of the State University, administrators from the local district, and others from public or private schools not amenable to pressure because of elective or appointive office or of funding by the legislature. The tone of the annual reports on Chicago had varied as pressures had been applied, but there had never been open denunciation. In 1934 the Association refused to accredit the ten new high schools, paying a tribute to Superintendent Bogan who it found "forced to carry out orders not based on sound educational advice." In 1935 three older high schools were warned. In 1936 the report had stated "there is evidence that the Board of Education or certain members of the Board are attempting to perform certain duties which should be performed only by a trained school administrator. The six class rule is one." Non-educational items, the report went on, eat into educational funds, and teachers look at the Board as the administrative head of the schools, and some seek help from local politicians. In 1938 all the high schools were warned on overcrowding, and the chartering of the Chicago Teachers Union noted as increasing the morale of the teachers. By 1946 the weakening of Kelly control on the public agencies involved in the North Central so lessened the pressures upon it that at last its representatives felt free to speak their minds.

The Mayor's New Advisory Committee

On April 1, just four days after the city council by solemn vote had decreed that there was nothing at all wrong in the school system, Mayor Kelly appointed another school advisory committee, as he had in 1939. This time it was to consist of the presidents of the University of Chicago, the University of Illinois, the Illinois Institute of Technology, Northwestern University, DePaul University, Loyola University, and a representative of the North Central Association. The advisory committee must tell the mayor what to do to avoid the interdiction of the North Central Association. The president of the University of Chicago, mindful of the mayor's ignoring the recommendations of the 1939 committee (on which two of the university's faculty had served), refused the invitation, not wanting to be used to save the mayor's face. But the others came, electing Henry T. Heald, president of the Illinois Institute of Technology, as chairman. President Heald had no intention of being used to save anyone's face.[24] He presided over hearings at which most of the same groups appeared as had come to the council hearing. While the committee was by no means unanimous—the president of at least one university was an outspoken supporter of the Board of Education—it proclaimed, as a whole, a series of recommendations on June 18, 1946, which could not but be unpalatable to the mayor. It flatly stated that the superintendent and the entire Board of Education should resign and a completely new Board selected on the advice of civic agencies. Superintendent Johnson and one Board member did resign immediately. The superintendent was not dismissed, but demoted to head the colleges at a high salary.[25] By September three more Board members resigned, leaving six vacancies on the eleven-man Board.

This time Mayor Kelly had gone too far to turn back or to ignore the recommendations which, sight unseen, he had pledged to support. He invited the five universities to help him choose new Board members, and, on the advice of the Heald Committee, invited eight more city-wide organizations to send representatives to the commission to participate in screening Board nominees. The Heald committee had said that these organizations should be representative of business, education, home, labor, the professions, and welfare, "city wide, nonpartisan, non-racial, non-ethnic and non-religious." On the basis of this recommendation, the mayor invited the following organizations to send representatives:

Chicago Association of Commerce
Chicago Bar Association
Congress of Industrial Organization
Chicago Federation of Labor
Chicago Medical Society
Chicago Technical Societies Council
Civic Federation
Illinois Congress of Parents and Teachers

To the universities and North Central Association, he added three other organizations, the American Legion, the Illinois Club for Catholic Women, and after some urging, the Welfare Council. The Citizens Schools Committee was not included. This time both the University of Chicago and Northwestern refused to serve, the latter giving as its reason (as did the North Central Association), that the whole Board of Education had not resigned.

From the nominations submitted to him by the screening committee, the mayor chose six names to replace the four Board members who had resigned and the two whose terms had expired. McCahey announced that he would retire in May, 1947, when his term as president expired. The six new members, who now constituted a majority, took their places on September 25, 1946; they included Mrs. Clifton Utley, recommended by the League of Women Voters; Mrs. Harry Mulberry, president of the Chicago Region of the P.T.A., a representative of the Steel Workers Union, an Italian doctor, two businessmen of high standing, and in the next year, the vice president of Swift and Company, William Traynor, who was elected president.

Though four other members never resigned and remained in office against the express recommendation of the Heald Committee, the majority of the board after September, 1946, seemed clearly committed to "cleaning the Augean stables" as Charles H. Judd had urged in 1937, and to pulling the schools out of the morass in which they had so long foundered. Even so, one of the new appointees nevertheless voted quite consistently with the remainder of the old Board.

The mayor was in difficulty in many other areas than schools. The first major blow at Kelly's complete control came in 1936, when Governor Horner was reelected by downstate votes, though he carried only eight of Chicago's 50 wards. Those who had always opposed Kelly, along with disappointed patronage and privilege seekers, rallied to Horner's faction within the city. A small block of alderman opposed to Kelly gradually increased. Kelly had no choice but reluctantly to support Paul Douglas for alderman from the Fifth Ward in 1939 since his major opponent was an out-and-out Horner man. Alderman John Boyle aided Douglas in his efforts to change the school situation and ran against Kelly in the 1943 Democratic primary for the mayoralty nomination. The demands from this growing group of aldermen increased after the new Sun in 1941 began a campaign against the mayor's administration. By 1945 demands of aldermen for accounting for the names on the patronage payrolls, for the actual expenditures of the $78,000 spent in Kelly's own office, and for a huge budget item for killing rats—when there was no evidence of any decline in the rat population—made good newspaper copy in the Sun and the News.[26]

The New Deal and war days were over. There were no Roosevelt coat tails to slide on. The polls, national and local, indicated that President Harry S. Truman would not be reelected in 1948. Since 1940 there had been Republican governors in Springfield, though they had done little to bother the mayor in spite of campaign promises. The big campaign contributions from Republican businessmen were falling off, as war-time prosperity made them less dependent on the machine. Reform elements were taking heart and organizing again. The Fifth Ward, ever since the days of Alderman Charles E. Merriam forty years before, had been able to nominate and elect independent aldermen like Merriam and Douglas, even though they had not always done so. Now similar groups had coalesced into a growing city-wide organization calling itself the Independent Voters of Illinois, which not only supported aldermen but members of Congress like Emily Taft Douglas, Paul Douglas' wife, who was elected congresswoman-at-large after Alderman Douglas enlisted in the Marines.

In the fall of 1946, Marshall Field III, who had invested the millions of three Field generations to create a morning opposition to the Tribune while supporting the New Deal, the League of Nations, and municipal reform, had now absorbed the Evening Times. With Leo Lerner, president of the Independent Voters of Illinois, Field told Kelly that their combined forces would oppose him if he ran for mayor in 1947. They pointed out that the liberal Democratic vote would be absolutely necessary if the Democrats were to win in 1947 and 1948, and suggested that he support Major Paul Douglas, now home from the war, for governor, and Adlai Stevenson, with experience in the new United Nations as a State Department aide, for United States Senator. The mayor replied he did not want Douglas in Springfield, but he would back him for the United States Senate and they could send the "striped pants guy" to Springfield. Several possible candidates were suggested for mayor. Kelly did not run in 1947, and the "organization" did support the candidates suggested for mayor, senator, and governor.

Not only was the forthright opposition of the Field newspapers a serious threat, with that of the News a close second, but now even the Chicago Tribune had finally deserted Kelly. It had given him staunch support during the flurry over the N.E.A. report and the North Central Association edict, when the Sun had given 2,200 column inches of space, and the Times and News 1,000 each on attacks on the Kelly Board. At that time, it had accused Du Shane of

Communist connections and told the N.C.A. to mind its own business. But by June 19, 1946, it was criticizing Kelly for not defending McCahey, and by December 10, 1946, a Tribune editorial stated that "McCahey had been the School Board for a decade and the others only stooges," that McCahey had now "outlived his usefulness, which once had been considerable"and that "Johnson's pliant subservience," the consistent success of relatives or pets of politicians in winning promotions, had "harmed the reputation of the schools which was never very good." The editorial added that there was no point in the mayor's "hollering that it was a dirty Republican plot." In four months the Sun carried 34 biting editorials on the school issue with 18 front-page streamer headlines, and the Daily News 18 editorials and several acidly effective cartoons.

Kelly's successor was Martin Kennelly. With no real experience in Chicago politics, Kennelly had been active in civic affairs, notably the Red Cross, and was earnest about the school situation, public housing, and public transportation improvement. He promised the Citizens Schools Committee that he would continue using the screening commission in appointing the school Board and added the Citizens Schools Committee, the University of Chicago, and Northwestern to its membership. He attended the public affairs of the Citizens Schools Committee and of the Chicago Teachers Union, and frequently used the slogan that a great city must have a great school system. But as might be expected, he had enormous difficulty in managing the closely knit web of privilege and patronage left by his predecessors and in withstanding the pressures put upon him. When the nominating committee refused to recommend Bernard Majewski—who had been on the Board since 1936, served as a vice president under McCahey, and had refused to resign in 1946—Mayor Kennelly, responding to the cries of the importance of the Polish vote and to the size of Majewski's campaign contributions to party coffers, reappointed him in 1951 anyway, in spite of his promises.

Law Gives Superintendent Control of Entire System

The first and foremost task of the Board of Education was, and still is, the selection of an able and trustworthy superintendent of schools. But no such superintendent was willing to take on the Chicago schools when the Board of Education still retained its direct management of a large part of the school system, not only over contracts, but in personnel and budget making, excluding him from any control whatsoever in these areas. Following the series of recommendations made by every serious student of public education in Chicago from William Rainey Harper in 1898, the Strayer survey in 1931, and the Heald committee in 1946, the Chicago Teachers Union and the Chicago Division of the Illinois Department of Education jointly had drafted a bill to create the office of General Superintendent of Schools. The Citizens Schools Committee organized strong support for this legislation. The new Chicago Region organization of the

P.T.A., authorized in 1946 to speak for Chicago members, approached downstate as well as Chicago legislators in its behalf. But after its Education Committee had approved the bill, without any notice to the Chicago Teachers Union, pressured by the engineers, janitors and other non-teaching Board unions, and their national head, William McFetridge, the Chicago Federation of Labor came out against it. John Fitzpatrick had died in 1946. Since the Illinois Federation of Labor could not oppose the Chicago Federation on local matters, Victor Olander, executive secretary of the Illinois Federation of Labor, was unable to support the measure.

Olander, however, had urged this very step of giving the superintendent complete control when the Otis law had been passed, and his influence in the legislature was needed to obtain passage. Many of the local Chicago legislators would certainly vote against the bill, fearing they would lose their precinct captains, janitors on the school payroll. At a meeting in Mayor Kennelly's office, on the urging of the Chicago Teachers Union, Olander got agreement from the dissident non-teaching union groups in the schools for him to support the superintendent's bill if the attorney were not under the direction of the superintendent. With Olander's help, the bill passed. When Olander died in 1949 the public schools of Chicago lost a consistent and intelligent friend.[27] In actual fact, the status of the Board attorney was not significant. In many large school systems there is no legal service for the schools separate from that of the city government. The 1947 effort to change the Board of Examiners, supported by the union, the I.E.A. and the Citizens Schools Committee, however, failed as it had in 1941.

By June, 1947, the governor had signed the legislation creating the office of General Superintendent of Schools of Chicago. Herold C. Hunt, superintendent in Kansas City, was chosen by the new Board to replace William H. Johnson. When the bill was safely signed, Hunt agreed to accept the appointment and entered on his new duties in August 1947.

The scars left on the Chicago school system by the years in which school resources were diverted from instruction to other uses were deep and permanent. Years in which the school system of a great city should slowly have been struggling toward more skilled and understanding service to children had been distorted into a battle to keep at least what had been left after the collapse of the tax system, multiplied by the effects of the depression. In many services, such as those of school social workers, the Chicago schools still lag far behind those of other cities which really had no more resources than did Chicago. The new superintendent entered a system where the administrative staff he inherited had acceded to political pressures and corruption for a dozen years and where the entire non-teaching personnel was hostile. Hunt faced no easy task, and he knew it.

Chapter 15

A SUPERINTENDENT CLEANS THE AUGEAN STABLES

No superintendent of schools had ever been welcomed to Chicago with such warm offers of cooperation as was Herold C. Hunt when he arrived in August, 1947. The September issue of the Citizens Schools Committee publication, Chicago Schools, carried praises of his past accomplishments from its former president, William C. Reavis, under whom the new superintendent had once studied. The current president, Dr. John A. Lapp, wrote,

> "You have been summoned to heavy duty. It is probable that no educator in America ever faced problems more intricate. All who know the difficulty of your task will give sympathetic understanding to your efforts. The Citizens Schools Committee and associated groups will stand guard over the gains which have been made and will be in readiness to support progressive advances. We have been by necessity severe critics in the past. We believe confidently that your record of educational leadership promises us the opportunity to play a happier role. We pledge our cordial support in redeeming Chicago's schools and placing them in the forefront."

On October 18, 1947, the Citizens Schools Committee held a civic assembly to give the new superintendent an opportunity to meet hundreds of concerned citizens and talk to them directly. Representatives of more than one hundred organizations were present. Every member of the Board of Education was present or sent regrets. Ten aldermen came. Mayor Kennelly stressed the necessity of a great school system as the foundation of the city's life.

The September issue of the eight-page Chicago Teachers Union newspaper carried a picture of the new superintendent on its first page, and a greeting from him to the membership praised not only the strength of the union, but "its marked degree of professionalism, desire for high standards and eagerness for the best possible education for Chicago's girls and boys. I hope to merit your confidence and support." On October 3, the new superintendent and the new president of the Board of Education spoke to a meeting of union teachers which crowded Orchestra Hall. Mrs. Hefferan, whose lonely fight against exploitation and corruption had won her the respect and love of teachers and other citizens alike and who had served on the Board for almost twenty years, was a guest of honor, as was Victor Olander, whose wise counsel had helped find a way out of many tight corners, from the days of the Otis law to the recent passage of the bill creating the general superintendent's office. John Fitzpatrick was now dead. His successor was present, as was Major Paul Douglas, recently home from military service, Mrs. Holland Flagler, president of the Illinois Congress of Parents and Teachers who had so forthrightly opposed the economy program in 1933, and Dr. John Lapp, now president of the Citizens Schools Committee.

In announcing the meeting, the union paper had said,

> "The dramatic changes in the Chicago schools which culminated in the appointment of Superintendent Hunt have opened wide new avenues for cooperative action to improve the working conditions of employees and to widen and deepen the opportunities for children. On October 3, the Chicago Teachers Union will look back over ten years of accomplishment and conflict, and toward a brightening future. . . . Every ounce of the energy spent unselfishly by thousands of teachers in the building of the union can now achieve results ten-fold. The program of the union, forged with painful care is ready."

The Chicago Division of the Illinois Education Association gave a reception for Dr. Hunt on September 30, and that of the new Chicago Region of the Parent Teachers Association followed on November 22.

These were the organizations which had opposed the old regime. Significantly, however, they were not the only groups to welcome him. On September 23, the Union League Club also invited its members to meet him. In October, the Negro Chamber of Commerce gave a dinner in his honor. The metropolitan press was also uniformly friendly. The Tribune, which so recently had attacked the N.E.A. and its report, and which had castigated Mayor Kelly for failing to support his school Board, in a long article in its September 21 Sunday Magazine on the many accomplishments of "Chicago's Hearty Headmaster," referred to him as president of the American Association of School Administrators (a part of the N.E.A.)—and with no invidious inferences.

Many Changes

The new superintendent wasted no time getting down to business. It became clear quickly that such "business" was not to include vindictive punishment for past sins, but a constructive effort to improve school services with what material was available. Two of William H. Johnson's staff were kept as assistant superintendents, but new faces were promptly added. Edward E. Keener, president of the Chicago Division of the Illinois Education Association, and past vice president of the Teachers Union—more responsible than any other single person in breaking the log jam with the N.E.A. report—was appointed Director of a new Department of Personnel. This department included not only the entire instructional force, but the army of non-teaching "civil service" employees who ever since 1927 had been patronage employees.[1] In one year half of those positions were filled by persons certified by a new City Civil Service Commission, and in two years, more than 90 percent. Butler Laughlin, demoted twice by the Kelly Board, became assistant superintendent for high schools. Raymond Cook, treated so outrageously by the old Board, was appointed president of the Chicago Teachers College, for which office he held a certificate. One of the rebels against the Principals Clubs' pro-Johnson policy became Director of Finance, and another, the ex-business manager of the union magazine, became head of the Department of Extension Education. A new Department of Instruction and Guidance was created. The business manager was incorporated into the general staff. The choice of the staff had been based not on any past posture; two who had been for one reason or another on the 1937 principals' list now became assistant superintendents. When George Cassell was retired from his position as assistant to the superintendent, Hunt appointed James F. Redmond, who had been on his staff in Kansas City, in his place.

Early in 1947, at the request of the new superintendent, the Board authorized a survey of administrative practices and salary scales to be made by an established management consultant firm—a practice consistently followed thereafter by Superintendent Hunt in search of sound bases for new policies.[2] But some changes required no long study. An examination to fill the long list of vacancies in principalships was announced in November, 1947, with the statement that all papers would be marked by a professional, completely non-partisan agency, the American Council of Education, and records kept of all oral examinations. This and all succeeding examinations for all positions would be open to all qualified citizens of the United States. Graduates of the Teachers College would be certified by such examinations and no longer guaranteed employment on graduation. The purchasing department was reorganized although troubles in that area persisted; finally Redmond was placed in charge of it.[3] Text books were now chosen by committees of principals and teachers competent in each area, and no book company was to approach any committee member individually. The rules of the Board of Education were revised and published in 1951 for use of both staff and the general public. There was clearly a general relaxation of the tensions and fears among school employees which had for so long been a real deterrent to good service.

The new superintendent stated his plans for involvement of teachers and the public in planning improvements—and he carried them out. He wanted an advisory council of teachers and administrators and in 1948 set up a tentative body to plan for a permanent organization, such as had been suggested in the N.E.A. Report. He wanted another advisory group of representatives from high-school student councils. He wanted workshops for teachers, regular conferences of principals and administrators, and encouragement of voluntary efforts to increase the skills and interests of the staff. He invited representatives of major civic organizations to join the staff for a general review of the curriculum and for advisory aid in revisions of separate subject fields. This council approved a statement of philosophy for the Chicago Public Schools, and agreed on a list of some nine "functions of living" around which the curriculum should be built.[4] In order that the public might have adequate information on what was happening in the schools, a four-page publication called "Educational Progress" was issued and an annual summary of basic facts on enrolment and finances began publication in 1950. An effort was made to make budgets more intelligible. The new superintendent established a reputation for answering every letter sent him promptly and courteously.

The curriculum could not be completely redone all at once, but some changes were made quickly. Elementary "home mechanics" became a part of the regular curriculum. An industrial arts program in elementary schools, driver education and aviation courses in high schools (where equipment was available) were new additions. An annual Science Fair stimulated creative interest in science at both elementary and secondary levels. Plans for sex education were presented, but discouraged by the Board.[5] A course leading to a practical nursing certificate, and another in diesel engines, were offered to adults. Increased emphasis on "developmental reading" in all curricular areas began some improvement in reading levels. The offer of the Chicago Symphony Orchestra to provide free concerts at schools was eagerly accepted. One major curricular change was the development of a "civics" course in American Problems which was required for the last semester of the twelfth grade.

Public Informed on Needs of Schools

The dearth of auxiliary services for pupils in comparison with those available in other large cities was still an obvious and serious lack in Chicago. The corps of visiting and vocational guidance teachers had been broken up in 1933 and the "adjustment teachers" added under the Kelly Board were too few and too limited in their training to replace the former services. Other cities were developing a staff of school social workers to bridge the gap between childrens' homes and their schools. There were too few psychologists in the Bureau of

Child Study. No more training was required of truant officers (now called attendance personnel), than had been the case fifty years before. No educational qualifications were set for them—only the passage of a simple City Civil Service examination. In terms of modern school services, their work, even if done well, touched only one phase of the schools' problems.

Health services formerly provided by the Health Department in the schools had almost disappeared. A study by the United States Bureau of Public Health in 1947 pointed out how far Chicago lagged behind other systems in the care of the health of its children. For instance, the New York City schools were spending $2.11 per pupil on health care; Chicago schools were spending only fifty cents.[6] Some schools still had no playground space and few buildings were used after school hours for community purposes.

The money to provide all these kinds of services well was not available; but a beginning was made. In 1949, $50,000 was set aside for screening the vision and hearing of elementary pupils. In 1950 a physician was appointed as Director of Health, and a year later ten school health nurses were employed. The School Health Committee of the Citizens Schools Committee and city-wide School Health Council of the Welfare Council urged and applauded these additions and asked for more. A Citizens Committee on the Wider Use of Schools, joining together the City Recreation Commission, headed by Lea Taylor, the Chicago Region of the P.T.A., and the Citizens Schools Committee, pressed for an extended "lighted school house" program to use school buildings after normal hours. This committee obtained authorization from the legislature for a referendum (for the addition of a 1¼ cent increase in the property tax) for an after-school community program, and was successful in getting approval in 1952.[7] The school administration worked out plans with the Chicago Park District for use of swimming pools and libraries by the Park and Library Boards after school hours in new buildings.

In his public statements at the annual civic assemblies of the Citizens Schools Committee, the Educational Conferences of the Chicago Teachers Union, P.T.A. meetings, and City Club Forums and organizations of businessmen, the superintendent continued to demonstrate the need for school social workers, more psychologists, reduction in class size, and the great possibilities to the community in the wider utilization of buildings. He urged higher salaries for teachers, in which training was recognized as a factor.

Through all the channels available to him and through new ones he himself created, Superintendent Hunt tried to make the general public aware of the changes taking place in the life of the city, their impact on the lives of the children in the schools, and the responsibilities such changes entailed upon the school system. As opportunities for unskilled labor disappeared and the schools increasingly neglected to train large numbers of students in the skills needed for employment in a technological society—and frequently failed even to prepare them for success in the upper years of high school—"dropouts" began to loom as a major problem. For a hundred years no one had really worried about the "school leavers." Fifth grade had been as far as most children went in the '90's, and the age standard of sixteen years was comparatively recent. But those who left school at sixteen in 1950, unready either for an available occupation or for responsible citizenship in an increasingly complicated society, were now clearly in distress. Some were actually "push-outs," not dropouts, as some school administrators often informed school failures they had had their chance and must leave. A staff committee headed by Miss Helen Campbell, an early vocational guidance pioneer, worked diligently to reduce the number of dropouts in the Chicago system.[8]

Another social problem with immediate impact on school success was the increasing transiency of residence within the city, particularly in low-income areas, and the swelling wave of post-war in-migration from southeastern United States. The Citizens Schools Committee study of one West Side school district in October, 1952, showed that in the first four months of that year there had been 2,338 transfers in and out of schools in that district, a fourth of them from outside the city, more than a fourth from one school to another within the district, and more than a third from other districts in the city. Of the forty school buildings in the district, 65 percent were fifty to ninety-five years old, without many facilities found in newer buildings. Sixty percent of the teacher vacancies in these old schools had been caused by the transfer of discouraged teachers. The administrative staff and the West Side Council of the P.T.A. were alarmed at the situation, only one of many such, which had been accumulating in depth for years.

Emphasis on Human Relations

A major effort of the superintendent was directed at what was then labeled "Intercultural Relations." He was deeply concerned with the role of the school in fostering group understanding, religious, ethnic—and increasingly in Chicago—racial. A few weeks after his arrival, he asked the cooperation of a Committee on Education, Training and Research in Race Relations of the University of Chicago, directed by Prof. Louis Wirth, in organizing a Technical Committee to advise him to this end. The Technical Committee enlisted the help of specialists in the institutions of higher learning in the Chicago area. A second committee was organized of key citizens, interested and knowledgeable in the field of race relations. Eventually there was to be a staff director for this area of work, but the goals, resources, and procedures for the program needed to be determined first. The Technical Committee set about making studies on school boundaries, assignment, promotion, and transfer policies, materials for curriculum, extra-curricular activities, relations with community groups, teacher attitudes, discrimination in higher education, and the adjustment of emergency situations as they arose. In November, 1949, the superintendent estimated that the Technical Committee had already contributed at least $25,000 of free time to the school system.[9] In-service training for teachers began with a workshop at the University of Chicago in the summer of 1948, with the expressed purpose of instilling "in all school employees a thorough going sense of the need for seeing that all pupils obtain equal advantages and services in their school living and learning." The Technical Committee also helped plan classes for parent organizations and for the police department. Cooperation with minority group organizations and direct contact with public officials concerned with problems of minority groups was taken for granted. Eventually a director would serve as a link with the Curriculum Council.

These plans did not all work out. No agreement was reached with the Board on the appointment of a director.[10] Instead, in 1950, a committee of administrators and teachers, headed by Dr. Hunt himself, took on the responsibility of directing the program. The Technical staff realigned the boundaries of the rapidly increasing elementary schools, eliminating some overcrowding, and quietly achieving some integration. Plans were made for boundary changes in high schools; but the enrolments there were now falling because of the low depression birth rate, and the actual changes were postponed until the post-war elementary increase reached the high schools. (This high-school plan was presented later to Superintendent Willis, but was never used).

The superintendent consistently stressed the basic American philosophy of equality of educational opportunity in his public statements. In 1952, speaking for the sixth time to the civic assembly of the Citizens Schools Committee, he pointed out that 10 percent of the entire population of the city is actually within the walls of public schools daily, and that the school system has the opportunity to "build a greater city where men and women may live together harmoniously and in a spirit of cooperation and understanding." In 1951, at the civic assembly of that year, Paul H. Douglas had reminded the audience of the kinship between Ella Flagg Young and Superintendent Hunt in the wideness of their vision of the place of public education in a democratic society.

The Citizens Schools Committee gave enthusiastic support to this phase of the superintendent's program. The efforts of the committee in the same direction were recognized by awards given to two of its presidents for this period by the Chicago Commission on Human Relations. The Chicago Teachers Union also took an active interest. The union had furnished active leadership in the Advisory Committee on Education of the City Commission since its inception in 1943, and had encouraged its members to cooperate in the new activities within the system. A group of new teachers, working in the school districts where poverty and transient residence were common factors, made a study (for the union) of the actual inequality in education offered by 85 such schools with specific recommendations to reduce the inequality.[11] In its annual Educational Conferences, the union elaborated these problems in detail. Active committees of the Chicago Region of the P.T.A. were also concerned. Under the skilled leadership of Mrs. Stella Counselbaum, the Chicago branch of the

Anti-Defamation League held a conference on Discrimination in Higher Education in 1949, where it was pointed out that only 3 percent of the students in institutions of higher education were Negro, and that 85 percent of that number attended segregated Negro colleges. These organizations, with others, sponsored an annual November 11 conference of hundreds of students from Chicago and suburban high schools to discuss specific problems of human relations.

Enrolment and Class Size Rise

Recognition by the school leadership of the responsibility of the schools for some share in solving the increasing social problems of the city did not, however, minimize the significance of the long-standing dilemmas of overcrowding and underfinancing; in fact, it could not help but emphasize them. As "war babies" began to enter school the enrolment rose from 289,000 to 330,000 in the six years of Superintendent Hunt's service. The high-school enrolment receded from 103,000 to 92,000 in the same period, but there was still a net increase of 40,000. Students in the Teachers College increased from 900 to 2,000, while the Junior College total fell from 9,500 to 8,500 because of the Korean War draft. By 1953 the total number of teachers was 14,000 and of all school employees, 21,000.[12]

In spite of great effort, no way was found to decrease the average elementary class of 39.60 in 1947 below 35 in 1953. Since these figures were averages, not maxima, many classes were much larger. In the high schools, where enrolment was shrinking, an average reduction from 31.03 to 29 was easier to achieve. In 1953 Superintendent Hunt pointed out that Chicago had the dubious distinction of larger class loads than any other large American city.

Income Increases More Slowly than Enrolment

The total budgets increased from $103,461,000 to $146,452,000 in the six-year period; but any gains were minimized by continuing inflation and increase in enrolment. There was however a substantial increase in state aid, sponsored vigorously by Governor Adlai Stevenson. The approval by the public of a bond issue on June 4, 1951, added the new funds.

The bond issue of 50 million dollars was for new school buildings. The schools had never been able to keep up with the rapidity of growth of the city, and even now, when the total population was no longer increasing, the school system was continuing to expand. The legislature authorized a referendum to be voted on in 1951 and it had been approved by a vote of more than three to one, with a majority for it in every ward. The need for new construction was now generally recognized throughout the city. The crowded schools were not only the old buildings in the center of the city with mostly Negro children; many were now in newly built-up outlying areas, where few people had lived before the war but where blocks of new houses now stretched. Fifty-one schools averaged 41 per class; ten of these were on double shift. What empty seats there were (and these were published in periodic inventories) were far away from the crowded schools, either in the center or the periphery. In 1947, 5,200 children had been on half-day schedules, and there were still 8,269 in 1953, even with the schools erected with part of the new bond issue. It was estimated that 206 new rooms were needed in 1953, 130 of them for outlying areas, and—with the children already born and preparing to enter school—1,250 rooms by 1956. Even though the general high-school population was falling, a new building was greatly needed for the Dunbar Trade School on the South Side, and the Jones Commercial School, planned forty years before, was still housed in one of the oldest school structures in the city.

The Strayer report had lamented the use of obsolete and dangerous buildings in 1932. Most of those so designated were still in use more than fifteen years later. Almost all were in the inner city, where they compounded educational problems by their lack of modern facilities and their discouraging appearance. Twelve buildings dated to the 1870's or earlier, and 141 of them to the 1880's and 1890's. Seventy-five percent of these old buildings had inadequate toilet space and poor lighting. Ten percent lacked playgrounds.[13] The survey of facilities made in 1953 indicated the necessity of successive bond issues if the goal of a seat for every child—even in classes too large—were ever to be reached.

Improvement in State Aid

The increase in state aid was encouraging, however. Illinois had always been far below the state average in share of school support provided by the state government. Despite a high level of personal income, Illinois for decades had never been listed above fortieth among the states in its total provision for schools in proportion to its wealth. In 1948 Mayor Kennelly pointed out that it was forty-third. By 1950, according to the Council of State Governments, it had slipped to forty-eighth, in spite of Governor Stevenson's efforts and some long overdue changes in the state school system. The most basic of these was the cutting off of state aid to very small one-room districts—of which Illinois had had the largest number for many years. The total number of school districts in the state in 1945 was 11,555, 3,000 more than in any other state. More than half of these districts had less than eighteen children, but they were receiving far more money per capita than were effectively organized districts, particularly those few, which (like Chicago) included both elementary and secondary schools in the same district.

Since 1927 the state school fund had been distributed in two ways. A "flat grant" was given for every elementary pupil in a district according to "average daily attendance." This amount rose from $9 in 1927 to $47 by 1955. Every school district received the same amount per child, whether it was wealthy and did not need the money, or whether it was desperately poor and taxing itself at a much higher rate than the rich districts in order to exist at all. A flat grant of $2 was given to high schools in 1943, and raised to $7 in 1947. The second basis of distribution was intended to equalize the great differences among districts. The legislature fixed a minimum tax rate which each district must levy on the property in each area. The tax funds derived from this levy were divided by the number of children in the district. If this per capita tax product, plus the flat grant per child did not reach a sum fixed by the legislature—called the equalization level, the difference per pupil was paid by the state to the district. It was this equalization level which Governor Stevenson had pressed to have raised from $90 to $160 per child.

This system penalized Chicago in several ways. The provision of large sums for one-room schools of six to eighteen children was one. These small schools had received flat grants for thirty children, and received a teacher's salary of $850 besides, paid from state funds. But the state law also subtracted all the expenses for salary and operations for the 102 elected county superintendents before any money was spent on children. In Chicago a local tax rate and teacher contributions paid for teachers' pensions; outside Chicago there was no local tax for teachers' pensions, and all tax contributions for pensions were charged to the state school fund. Finally, a small share of the Chicago Pension Fund tax contribution was being paid from the state fund. The method of distribution, however, failed to recognize the effort of a school district like Chicago, which was almost always taxing itself not at the minimum rate set by the state, but at the maximum, beyond which state action or local referendum was required. Real estate valuations in parts of the city and in some of its suburbs in Cook County were high; but so was the number of city children. The low figure for real estate valuation per school child in the city put rich Cook County with its extremely wealthy suburbs in the lowest two-fifths of Illinois' 102 counties.[14] Most Illinois high schools—all in Cook County outside Chicago—were in districts separate from those for elementary schools. The districts where all age levels occurred in one district were called "unit districts" and were penalized by not being allowed to tax at as high rates as a similar area with two kinds of districts. Most of the total number of children in unit districts in the state were in the one district of Chicago.

In one area of state help for schools, however, Chicago had always received more than the proportion of its children. This was in special allocations for the excess costs of educating children handicapped physically or mentally or needing special "social adjustment." The city provided more care for large numbers of such children than smaller districts could give for a small group. It also received a larger share of federal funds for vocational education, distributed through a state agency, because it had more schools which met the federal standards.

One of the factors contributing to the continuation of this obsolete system of state school finance lay in the Jacksonian philosophy embodied in the 1870 constitution, whereby a State Superintendent of Public Instruction was elected on a party ticket. He then directed one of the largest departments of the state government, staffed by patronage and without the benefit of a state school board. Illinois was one of two states in the union without such a board. A long series of educational commissions, appointed by governors since 1907, had uniformly recommended modernization of the state school system, but to no effect.[15] In 1951, to fill this gap in part, Governor Stevenson created a School Problems Commission with five members from each house of the legislature and five citizens. One of the first citizens appointed was a member of the Chicago Board of Education, Mrs. Clifton Utley, who made a constructive contribution not only to the solution of some of Chicago's problems, but also to those of the schools of the rest of the state.

Clearly the state government was not accepting a fair share of responsibility for its constitutional charge of providing a thorough and efficient education for all the children of the state. The Citizens Schools Committee urged the Chicago Board of Education and the State School Problems Commission to ask state aid, not only for elementary and high schools, but for summer schools, evening and trade schools, and for the junior college. They also pointed out the failure of the State Department of Public Instruction to enforce six laws on the statute books forbidding segregation of school children by race. Fifteen counties in southern Illinois did so segregate, and the printed state reports listed the Negro and white schools separately. The Superintendent of Public Instruction, in response to a protest from the Illinois Commission on Human Relations in 1947, had ruled that any action on such laws must come from the elected state's attorneys in those counties!

Although little progress was made in the financing of the public schools in Chicago, there were some other gains. Dr. Hunt used every possible opportunity of winning public support for improvements in the schools. Each year he used the public platform given him by the Citizens Schools Committee in its annual civic assembly. The Committee rendered solid and organized support for the bond issue referendum and for tax rate increases. Too, dozens of organizations each year profited from Mrs. John L. Hancock's analyses of the budget, and the annual public hearings on the school budget, required by law, became a means of public education through the press. Each month the Citizens Schools Committee presented, to a large group of organizations, staff and outside experts in discussions of the services given and needed in the schools. At the meetings of the Chicago Region of the P.T.A., Superintendent Hunt was a regular attendant and was elected vice president of the state organization. He missed no opportunity of urging P.T.A. membership and in 1951 noted in his annual report his pleasure at its growing membership, now 151,887. The City Club paid him honor in 1950, along with Charles E. Merriam of the University of Chicago, Mayor Kennelly, and the Citizens Schools Committee. At the 1950 Civic Assembly of the Citizens Schools Committee, Governor Stevenson, Senator Paul

Douglas, and Mayor Kennelly united in praise of what Hunt had done for Chicago schools.

The polarization of business and labor, so evident in school affairs for more than forty years had begun at last to disappear. In October, 1951, the president of Time, Inc., speaking at the Citizens Schools Committee assembly, pointed out that while the money price of good education is substantial, it is not a one-thousandth part of the loss caused by ignorance. The presidents of the Association of Commerce and of the Illinois Manufacturers' Association were guests. In 1952, at the next assembly, President Guy Reed of the Chicago Association of Commerce spoke on "Business' Stake in Public Education," Stanley Johnson, secretary of the Illinois Federation of Labor, on "Labor's Stake in Public Education," and Superintendent Hunt on "The Public's Stake in Public Education." Reed stressed the increasing importance to business and industry of the development of the dormant unused talent of the uneducated, and "that support of improved educational opportunity was an economic necessity."

Victor Olander had died in 1949. The quality of Olander's public service could be measured by the tribute paid him on February 6, 1949, by the Chicago Tribune (which so seldom agreed with him):

> "He had everyone's respect—earned by fair dealing in a long and useful career. His death deprived the community of one of its most stalwart and useful citizens."

The Superintendent and the Union

The relation of Superintendent Hunt with the Teachers Union was probably warmer than with any other group. He spoke at every annual educational conference of the union during his term in office; he was invited to return in 1956, and similarly welcomed again by the Citizens Schools Committee in 1958. For the cover of the December, 1950, issue of the union newspaper President of the Board of Education William Traynor with comparable cordiality wrote a Christmas message. But a more convincing example of cooperation among superintendent, Board, and union occurred long before.

In 1948 the city council had refused to approve a considerable increase in the levy for schools, although the raise was within the limits set by the legislature. Charles J. Whipple, President of the Board of Education, Herold C. Hunt, General Superintendent of Schools, and John M. Fewkes, President of the Chicago Teachers Union, stood side by side before the city council to point out that the city council had no legal control over the tax levy voted by the Board of Education, except, as an elected agency, to declare it valid.[16] The council knew that the union had voted to strike, not against the Board, but against the council itself, if it failed to approve the levy. Never before in the history of

Chicago schools had there been such evidence of close cooperation and good will among these three essential elements of the school system. The union supported the program of the superintendent for six years—except for two of his plans. These, however, were important, both to the superintendent and to the union.

The first concerned the relationship between superintendent and teacher organizations. The second concerned salaries.

Ever since its first meeting in 1937, the union had asked for the right of collective bargaining as the organization to which a majority of Chicago teachers belonged.[17] Since public employees were not included in the National Labor Relations Act which compelled a private employer to recognize one organization to which a majority of its employees belonged, there was no legal way to force recognition—and certainly no possibility of voluntary recognition by the Kelly School Board, which the union had so consistently and openly opposed. In 1949 the union had introduced state legislation making recognition of teachers' organizations by Boards of Education specifically permissible, to counter the argument of Board attorneys that the Board could not make binding contracts with employees. But it had not been passed. To the Chicago Teachers Union, therefore, a return to the theory of teachers' councils of the '90's or the '20's was unthinkable.

Superintendent Hunt Revives the Teachers Council Idea

But in his first public speech Superintendent Hunt announced his intention of doing just that. In 1948 district superintendents made suggestions for an interim council, appointed in May, 1949. The union printed the interim council's minutes. In 1950 the interim council announced its plans for the election by all teachers of a permanent council. The next issue of the union newspaper, in May, carried on its cover the words of the Declaration of Independence, "Governments are instituted among men, deriving their just powers from the consent of the governed," and devoted most of the paper to the arguments given for and against the council.

The permanent council was duly elected, although most of its members were active members of the union, including the union vice president. The council served no real purpose not already met by the union, but it gave the superintendent a neutral stance among teacher organizations, both locally and nationally. The union audit for 1950, sent to the superintendent, members of the Board of Education, and of the legislature, showed 8,209 union members, and estimates of other teacher organizations (which were not contradicted): 2,809 for the Chicago Division of the Illinois Education Association, 400 for the Principals Club, 300 for the Chicago Teachers Federation, 300 for the Association of Chicago Teachers, 200 for the Men Teachers Club, and 25 for the Council of Elementary Teachers. In 1953 no election was held for the council and it disappeared. There was little reason for the union to be exercised about the council's doings—except for hurt pride. The teacher council movement gradually disappeared everywhere, because it inevitably became either an echo of the administration, or, as in Miss Haley's day, a sounding board for the most powerful organization at the moment.

The second disagreement was on a salary schedule. Had more money been available, there might have been no dispute at all. The increased tax levy, which stuck in the throat of the city council members in 1948, had been needed for Chicago's first single salary schedule, sponsored by the union. Because elementary teachers had a five-hour day, and (since 1914) the high schools had had a six-hour day, the elementary salary was set at five-sixths of the high-school salary on each step. There was no increment for training. The Griffenhagen report, authorized by the Board in 1947, had shown Chicago was seventh in elementary teachers salaries and sixth in high school—and first only in salary paid the president of the Junior College, William H. Johnson, erstwhile superintendent up to 1946. The "poverty level of $3,000" was above the salaries of all public beginning teachers, who were therefore eligible to apply for public housing.

After the 1948 increase, the scale for elementary teachers ran from $2,240 to $4,400 in ten years, and for high schools from $2,640 to $4,800. Wartime inflation and payment of federal income tax since 1939 brought the actual buying power of these salaries below those so frequently delayed in 1931. In 1949 the union asked for $3,200 to $5,000 as an elementary scale, and $3,840 to $6,000 for high schools with a $300 increment for a masters' degree, which new high school teachers were now supposed to have.

In 1952 the union reiterated its 1949 request, which had not yet been reached. Instead, Superintendent Hunt proposed a fourteen-year, not a ten-year schedule, with a six-hour day for elementary teachers. The basic schedule was $3,000 to $5,400 for all, with $300 more for high-school teachers because of the new requirement for a higher degree. The proposal "blanketed in" all elementary teachers without A.B. degrees and all high-school teachers without M.A.'s. The union objected that the maximum increases came from stretching the schedule and that no teacher would actually get more income over a long period of years. The Board then voted an 8 percent increase on the old five-sixths scale, with maxima of $4,910 and $5,890. Since the 1952 dollar was worth .53 on pre-war prices, the 1952 high-school maximum had to be $7,834 to deliver the same buying power as the 1922 high-school maximum during the depression years.[19] When the union asked for an $8,000 maximum in 1953 and got nothing, a letter to Superintendent Hunt was authorized, thanking him for his effort to increase the schedule by at least $100.

The union had its say on these two issues and did not seem to hold a grudge against Dr. Hunt. When the Board of Education gave him a second term in 1951, an editorial in the union newspaper was headed, "We're Glad You're Going to Stay," and went on, "The union has not always agreed with Dr. Hunt on all his policies; but it respects his integrity, his skill and the sincerity of his desire to give Chicago's children a better chance than they have had for many years." Distributed to all teachers, the union newspaper carried the superintendent's picture twenty times in his six years in office.

Opposition from Holdovers and Far Right

The superintendent's way of dealing with all groups was frank, open, and always courteous. To the casual observer it would have seemed that he was sailing along through calm sea, blue sky, and friendly winds. Moreover, no one would have known from his serene countenance and easy poise that there were violent storms raging around him.

In the first place, some members of the Board of Education had not been as enthusiastic about Dr. Hunt or his activities as were the Kelly Board critics. Not all the members of that Board had resigned. Four remained, and Bernard Majewski, vice president of the previous Board, was a vocal member of the new one, and one new appointee frequently sided with him. Only six votes were required to reject almost all recommendations made by the superintendent according to the new 1947 school law. When the vote was taken to invite Herold Hunt to be superintendent, Majewski and one other had voted for him—only after stating they would have preferred George Cassell, who had been William H. Johnson's first assistant.

The new device of a screening committee to suggest candidates to the mayor for school board posts by no means worked perfectly. The original recommendation of the Heald Committee had been for a nominating commission of

> "... representatives of a workable number of those Chicago organizations which as accurately as possible reflect the social interest of the entire community. These representatives should be selected or appointed annually by the organizations themselves. Organizations having membership on the commission should be representatives of business, education, the home, labor, the professions and welfare. They should be city-wide in scope, non partisan, non racial, non-ethnic and non-religious in character. The commission must be small enough to be workable; its members should not exceed 15 in number."

The committee went on to suggest the following eight organizations as its recommendation for the makeup of the nominating commission:

Chicago Association of Commerce
Chicago Bar Association
Congress of Industrial Organizations
Chicago Federation of Labor
Chicago Medical Society

Chicago Technical Societies Council

Civic Federation

Illinois Congress of Parents and Teachers

On his own initiative Mayor Kelly included DePaul and Loyola Universities, the Illinois Institute of Technology, and the University of Illinois. (He was accused of adding organizations which would follow his wishes.) Northwestern University and the University of Chicago were invited but did not accept until 1948. The mayor also added the Illinois Club for Catholic Women, the American Legion, and after some urging, the Welfare Council. In 1948 Mayor Kennelly added the Citizens Schools Committee and in 1949 the Chicago Region of the P.T.A. replaced the state-wide organization. The mayor chose the organizations, and new invitations were sent out each year; he might drop organizations if he chose. In 1950, when Bernard Majewski's term expired, the commission voted three to one against recommending his appointment and other names were sent to Mayor Kennelly for his consideration. To their surprise, Kennelly, the "reform mayor," reappointed Majewski, even though his name was not on the list. Majewski was a heavy contributor to party coffers and influential with the large block of Polish votes.

When Edward E. Keener had been nominated to direct the Department of Personnel, now governing non-teaching employees, there had been two votes against him and Majewski had passed his vote. After 1950 the superintendent found increasing difficulty in getting his appointments approved, though there was never open conflict between him and any members of the Board of Education. The Citizens Schools Committee, in April 1950, commented on Majewski's reappointment, finding him playing from the beginning "the part of a petty obstructionist with no apparent constructive intent to measures of the present school administration."[20]

Another source of opposition to the superintendent arose out of the post-war hysteria about the danger of Communism within the United States, reaching its climax in the McCarthy hearings. Chicago staged a series of dramatic episodes of its own, centering around the school system, in which, openly or by association, the superintendent of schools was the object of attack. His opponents on the Board found frequent pretexts to embarrass him. The Chicago Tribune was now as violent a critic of the United Nations as it had for years been of Roosevelt and the "New Dealers" as active Communist plotters. The Hearst papers also were looking for Communists, and on July 25, 1947, the Herald, a Hearst paper, published a long article on the "Twenty-Five Year Effort by Reds to Indoctrinate Teachers with Communism," attacking among others Dean Ernest Melby of the Northwestern University School of Education. This article did not mention Dr. Hunt, but repeated the charge of a "Security Committee of 85" that the N.E.A. was publishing "Communist leaning pamphlets." During the discussion of the N.E.A. Report in 1946, the Tribune had stated that Donald Du Shane, chairman of the committee investigating Chicago schools, and other N.E.A. leaders were "under investigation by the authorities."[21] Dr. Hunt was then president of the American Association of Administrators, a division of the N.E.A. He had also been invited by Dr. Milton Eisenhower to serve on the United States Commission for UNESCO.

Within two months of his arrival, through no fault of his own, Dr. Hunt was caught in the middle of a newspaper war between the Tribune and the Chicago Sun, Marshall Field's morning paper, new in 1941. The Sun had attacked the Kelly regime in the schools, had supported the demand for public hearings on the charges in the N.E.A. report and had welcomed the new superintendent. Now the Sun was wholeheartedly in favor of the United Nations, and particularly excited about the possibilities of UNESCO. The Sun donated enough money for an ambitious project to send a student from every public and parochial high school in the Chicago area to New York to visit the United Nations in the month of October, 1947. For eighteen days the Sun carried interviews with enthusiastic high-school students. Commendations of the plan from the president of the Illinois Congress of the P.T.A., from the director of parochial schools, from President Stoddard of the University of Illinois, and from Mayor Kennelly appeared in the Sun. Dr. Hunt made no statements about the trip, but merely excused students from school so that they might go. Not only did the Sun advertise its trip, it carried two editorials directly reproaching the Tribune for its opposition to the United Nations.

This was more than the Tribune could stand. The schools were being used "to propagandize children" with ideas which were clearly evil. Frank Hughes, Col. McCormick's personal aide on the latter's special projects, produced a series of long and conspicuously placed articles in answer. These articles openly attacked the United Nations, UNESCO, and Columbia University as Communist controlled and quite specifically mentioned Superintendent Hunt's connection with each. He had received his Ph.D. degree from Columbia. On October 7, an article accused the N.E.A. of selling "pro-British, New Deal, anti-monopoly pamphlets" for school use. On October 9, an attack by the American Legion on textbooks written by Harold Rugg of Columbia furnished the meat of another article. It complained that one objection to Rugg's books was that they did not teach children why the white race was the best on earth. On October 10 an article accused Henry Luce of approving N.E.A. New Deal pamphlets written by Moscow authors and published by Harcourt, Brace and Ginn and Co., two of the book companies which had refused to deal with the Kelly Board. The October 13 installment expressed horror at the N.E.A. claim that UNESCO was "one of its proudest achievements." On October 24 the series ended with an all-inclusive broadside at the N.E.A., the American Historical Association, the Carnegie Foundation, and Mrs. Franklin Delano Roosevelt, climaxed by a reminder that Superintendent Hunt was a member of the UNESCO Commission.

Superintendent Hunt suavely stated that he would send all the material furnished him to Secretary Givens of the N.E.A., and that all Chicago books were safe. There had certainly been no evil N.E.A. pamphlets purchased unless by individual teachers, since the old administration would not have bought them and the new one had no money. The Tribune assured him that he should do more than inform the N.E.A., he must "clean it up." The other papers, including the Herald, took no part in this blast at the superintendent. But thousands who knew nothing about the schools read the articles.

The war on the U.N. trip was accompanied by efforts to alienate the Chicago Teachers Union from the superintendent. A letter to the Tribune "Voice of the People" accused Dr. Hunt of forcing Chicago teachers to join the evil N.E.A. The superintendent asked that the union print in its paper, which went to all teachers, a statement "advising his associates in the public schools that affiliation or non-affiliation with any organization is a matter of personal choice and individual responsibility" and that if pressure were put upon any teacher to join any organization, he would be grateful to have it reported to him. The attack on the U.N. certainly had no effect on the union. It had printed the UNESCO constitution as a great document, sent representatives to UNESCO conferences, and contributed $5,000 to the United Nations Appeal for Children.

The Chicago American fired the next broadside. In June, 1948, it published three articles accusing a social science teacher at Senn High School of teaching Communism. The only basis for the attack lay in inaccurately quoted remarks of students. Investigation by the superintendent's office revealed no basis of any kind for the charge and a vote by the Board completely cleared the teacher.[22]

In 1950 a significant curriculum revision of the twelfth grade social science course was completed. It included studies of urban housing, race relations, and international relations. The Tribune and some organized far-right groups immediately attacked the new course. At a meeting on February 14, to which teachers and the public had been invited, Frank Hughes denounced the revision because it recognized that changes were taking place—and change was necessarily Communism. Then on October 10, the Tribune picked out one reference, on a long bibliography for the use of teachers, entitled "I Want to Be Like Stalin," a translation by Dr. George S. Counts of the untruths told about America in Russian textbooks. It was clearly a bitter attack against Communist twisting of the truth. The Tribune announced that Superintendent Hunt had ordered every child in the high schools to read the book, giving nothing but the title. The Communists themselves could not have twisted the truth more consciously.

Such attacks on schools were being made by far-right groups all over the country. A pamphlet called "The Little Red Schoolhouse," alleging that the schools were full of Communist teachers, was widely distributed in Chicago. The Los Angeles Board of Education forbade mentioning UNESCO in the schools. In Houston, a mediocre, commonly used civics text was attacked as preaching "creeping socialism," because, for one reason, it stated that the Post Office was a government-owned business. Superintendents of schools in Scarsdale, Indianapolis, and Pasadena were under attack by far-right groups. A group of members of the Chicago Region of the P.T.A. were determined to stop any teaching about UNESCO and caused long, hot arguments within the P.T.A. In the Illinois General Assembly a series of laws to limit freedom of teaching, to require legislative inspection of materials used in teaching, and to exact loyalty oaths of all teachers was passed in 1951, but vetoed by Governor Stevenson.

The anti-Hunt members on the Chicago Board of Education approved of this "Broyles" legislation. When the oath bill was vetoed by Governor Stevenson, Board member Majewski introduced one for Chicago at a Board meeting. At a hearing on the proposed oath bill for Chicago, Dr. John Lapp, president of the Citizens Schools Committee, and also of the City Club, appeared in opposition. Dr. Lapp was well known as a trusted adviser and staunch supporter of Superintendent Hunt. At the hearing the American Legion representative attacked Dr. Lapp as a Communist sympathizer, stating that he had belonged to unnamed organizations listed as "unAmerican" by the Dies Committee, and alleged that there was an international scheme among Communists to conduct "school affairs to their liking"—clearly inferring that Dr. Lapp's interest in public education was a part of such a plot. He urged that the Board adopt the oath, "to keep faith with the boys in Korea." The Tribune carried the story on its first page, with the heading, "Foe of Anti Red Oath Branded Aid to Commies." The Sun and Tribune both carried Majewski's comment that

> "This board has been castigated and assailed by an organized clique—the same fellows that have been doing it for years. Maybe some of the rest of the Board members have to sit here and take this, but I am under no obligation to a clique. I am glad to find out who are the people so opposed to Americanism in the schools."[23]

The teacher organizations varied in their response to the oath proposal. The Chicago Teachers Federation asked for time to study it. The Principals Club approved it. The Chicago Teachers Union opposed it, as it had opposed the Broyles bills in Springfield, pointing out that there was no reason for singling out teachers only for suspicion, and adding that oaths in themselves were no assurance of anything. Every member of the General Assembly of Illinois took an oath to put into effect everything in the state constitution, but for fifty years the majority of these oath takers had consistently voted against redistricting the state every ten years—so clearly required in the constitution they had sworn to uphold.

The attack against Dr. Lapp continued in the legislature. On March 28, 1951, a member of the legislature introduced a resolution calling for an investigation of the activities of Dr. John A. Lapp, "a most influential member of Mayor Kennelly's board to choose school board members." The resolution declared,

> "As president of the Citizens Schools Committee, John A. Lapp went on record as opposing the loyalty oath of the Board of Education. He was a member of the advisory committee on Social Studies which proposed a history and civics course which extols collectivism and the principles of Communism, thereby leading to an

attack by the local press and civic organizations, and this committee recommended the book 'I Want to Be Like Stalin' to be placed as reference for high school students in civics.

"John A. Lapp was instrumental in bringing Herold C. Hunt to the $25,000 a year job as superintendent of schools, and has substituted for the General Superintendent Herold C. Hunt as the main speaker at educational conferences, which function should not be the prerogative of outsiders."

A committee of Senate and House members was to inquire of Mayor Kennelly why Dr. Lapp was so recognized in view of his influence on 375,000 children.[24]

The resolution did not pass. But in the minds of any who accepted any part of these wild statements, Dr. Hunt was clearly tarred with the same brush. No such general publicity was given to the dinner held in honor of Dr. Lapp on June 18, even though its hundred or more sponsors included some of the city's most distinguished citizens. Governor Stevenson, Dr. Hunt, state and federal judges, aldermen, members of the legislature including State Senator Richard J. Daley, the Republican candidate for mayor in 1943, two congressmen, U.S. Senator Paul Douglas, leaders of the three major religious faiths and labor leaders including Arthur Goldberg were on the sponsoring committee. Mrs. Utley and Sidney Brown from the Board of Education made a point of attending. But irreparable damage had been done to Superintendent Hunt's status in some quarters.

Post-War anti-Communist hysteria was not the only source of attack, however. Some of those within the system who owed their promotions to the old regime steadily undercut Dr. Hunt's efforts by half-hearted implementation of changes or by open discouragement of their teachers. The union newspaper commented in 1951, "That some of the forces which have opposed good public education in Chicago in the past have expressed opposition to Dr. Hunt is to his credit, not to his dishonor." Worse than this, a long series of anonymous letters accusing Dr. Hunt of professional fault and personal offenses to decency were circulated in quantity within and without the school system at obvious considerable expense and effort. President Traynor, who gave Hunt complete support, asked and obtained from the Board of Education a unanimous vote of confidence against these malicious and unfounded attacks.[25] No more carefully planned attacks had been made in Pasadena or in other cities where superintendents had been persecuted than were aimed at Superintendent Hunt.

In the spring of 1953 Superintendent Hunt announced that he was accepting the post of Eliot Professor in the Harvard Graduate School of Education. At the annual meeting of the Citizens Schools Committee in April, he voiced his appreciation of the support he had received and noted particularly the help of Dr. Lapp (who was now retiring from the presidency of the Committee), and described his past six years as a challenging and stimulating experience—but a mission completed. The announcement was received with apprehension in many quarters. The April issue of Chicago Schools pointed out that ambitions, friendships, resentments, and factions that had existed in the pre-Hunt era still remained and that much of his work "has not had time to jell. To be frank, some of it has not even started, and we are not sure it ever will, after he takes his pectin elsewhere." The Board of Directors of the Citizens Schools Committee sent a telegram to the Board of Education urging that no one now in the system be chosen to replace him, unless Dr. James F. Redmond could be released from his commitment to become superintendent of the New Orleans schools, and that if necessary, a canvass of the entire country be made for his successor.

No farewell to Superintendent Hunt was more explicit or more warm than that of the Chicago Teachers Union. The cover of the June, 1953, newspaper read as follows:

REPORT CARD
FOR A GRADUATING SUPERINTENDENT

IN 1946, the school system of Chicago was in a demoralized state. After thirteen years of protest from teachers and other citizens, the North Central Association of Schools and Colleges threatened to remove all Chicago high schools from the accredited list, because of the clearly recognized political control of appointments and contracts. A committee of presidents of the universities in the Chicago area, appointed by the Mayor to investigate, recommended that the Superintendent of Schools resign his office and that a new school board be appointed. The political control of Chicago's public schools was a major issue in the 1947 mayoralty campaign.

IN 1953, even the non-teaching employees, for three generations almost entirely spoils jobs, now hold secure civil service positions, for which employees are chosen for competence. The examinations for teachers, now open to all, are not influenced by political considerations. A major building program to replace over-age buildings and to meet the increased demands is under way, by means of a bond issue voted by the public. Redistricting of elementary schools on the basis of the needs of children is only one of the steps which have been taken to provide equal opportunity for all. The militant drive of the Chicago Teachers Union for more adequate salaries has received firm administrative support. Promotions have in the main been based on competence without relevance to past or present group allegiances. Significant steps have been taken in curriculum revision.

The General Superintendent has made a vigorous and enthusiastic effort to increase the interest in and understanding of the problems of public education in Chicago and has worked in hearty cooperation with the Citizens Schools Committee and the P.T.A. Toward the teaching staff, he has shown a warm and friendly courtesy which has raised teacher morale and encouraged teachers to contribute their best.

The Chicago Teachers Union has by no means always agreed with DR. HUNT. In fact, it has had a considerable number of deep differences of opinion with him. But it has always been able to discuss these differences frankly and with considerable give and take; and in most cases a meeting of minds has been arrived at. The Union took strong objection, and still does, to the establishment of a Superintendent's Advisory Council, when a democratic procedure for sounding the opinion of the majority teaching force already exists. We are glad to note that no election for such a Council was held in 1953 and that the Council has been allowed to die.

THE CHICAGO TEACHERS UNION TAKES THIS OCCASION TO MAKE PUBLIC RECOGNITION OF THE GAINS IN OUR PUBLIC SCHOOL SINCE 1946, THE

INCREASING HARD WORK OF DR. HUNT IN HIS EFFORTS, THROUGHOUT HIS ADMINISTRATION, TO IMPROVE OUR PUBLIC SCHOOLS, AND TO BETTER THE RELATIONS BETWEEN THE SUPERINTENDENT AND THE UNION. WE HOPE HE CAN TRAIN OTHER SUPERINTENDENTS TO BE EQUALLY EFFICIENT, FORWARD LOOKING AND FAIR.

JUNE, 1953

HEROLD C. HUNT

A FOR EFFORT
A FOR ACCOMPLISHMENT
A FOR SINCERITY AND FAIR PLAY

Part IV

URBAN SCHOOLS

FACE NEW

PROBLEMS

Chapter 16

THE CITY CHANGES FASTER THAN THE SCHOOLS

The Chicago of 1953 was not the Chicago of 1933, or 1893, or 1853. Nor was the urban technological complex, in which the city's children would live, the kind of a society which had existed before World War II. The years required in school for earning a livelihood, and the necessity for understanding the economic and international problems upon which voters must voice decisions, put new responsibilities upon schools few had appreciated before. Some were not willing to recognize them now. The flight to the suburbs was reducing the economic level of urban dwellers. The city was growing old. City planning and urban renewal were changing its physical aspects. A great surge of people from the rural areas to the South, where unskilled labor was no longer in demand, flooded the great cities—which could use unskilled workers even less. Many of them came not only in expectation of work, but in the hope of better education and opportunities for their children. Some of these were white, some Puerto Rican; but most were now rural Negroes. They brought the product of three centuries of repression and mistreatment to the doorsteps of Northern school systems which were no better adapted to solve their problems than they had been to solve those of their European predecessors seventy-five years before; but now these problems could no longer merely be ignored.

Changes in Population and the Economy

In 1860, 52 percent of the people living in Chicago had been born outside the United States, most of them in Europe. In 1930, 65 percent of the people of Chicago had been either foreign-born or children of foreign born. By 1960 only 12 percent were foreign-born and 23 percent, second generation. But there were still forty foreign-language newspapers—in eighteen languages—which found it profitable to publish in Chicago. As the nation had prospered, so had the early immigrants. By the third generation, many, but not all, considered themselves far removed from their European backgrounds. The more affluent joined the trek to the suburbs north and west of the city. The less affluent found homes in the close-in industrial suburbs or in new communities on the edges of the city, and joined the ranks of small home-owners, proud of their status and suspicious of any threat to it. Only a few ethnic groups, notably some of the Poles, tended to remain in their original location in the city. Into the buildings of the older central areas, worn out by decades of successive migrations, poured the new migrants from the South.

There had always been Negroes in Chicago. In fact, the first recorded resident was a Negro, Jean Baptiste Point Du Sable. The 1840 census counted 53 Negroes, 1.2 percent of the population. By 1900 there were 30,000, but still only 1.8 percent of the total. Between 1900 and 1950 the Negro population rose from 30,000 to 492,000, or to 13.6 percent of the city's people. Between 1950 and 1960 it almost doubled. The 1960 census figure was 812,637, 23.6 percent. By 1966 it had reached 27 percent and was still rising.[1]

As the earlier immigrant population had increased in number and income, it had gradually spread from the center of the city into outlying neighborhoods, sometimes in clusters, sometimes as single families. As the Negro population grew, it pushed against rigid barriers of race prejudice which dammed the rising numbers within fixed limits. Housing laws were disregarded as old buildings were divided into illegal living spaces, rented at prices higher than those charged for comparable quarters elsewhere. Until 1948 the Negro areas in Chicago were ringed with "restrictive housing covenants" wherein property owners agreed not to rent or sell to Negroes, and sometimes not to Jews or other ethnic groups as well. The declaration by the United States Supreme Court in 1948 that such contracts were unenforceable in any court of law by no means solved the problem. The pressure within the segregated area and the opposition to it from without resulted in inch-by-inch, block-by-block incursions, often met by violence. Housing within the segregated ghetto took on the pattern of the city itself, with pleasant middle-class homes on the edges of slums. After World War II, more of the newcomers rushed into the older and more deteriorated housing of the inner West Side than into the already crowded areas south of the Loop.

The schools on the South and West Sides were jammed with children. Most of the school buildings were already old, some pre-Civil War. They had once accommodated a population where a considerable number of pupils had attended ethnic, parochial schools. Now almost all the children of a much denser population were in the public schools. In North Lawndale, between 1950 and 1960, 76,300 white people had moved out and 100,700 Negroes had moved in. Not all the double-shift schools were now in Negro areas, however, as they had been in 1940. Large numbers of Jewish residents along South Parkway had moved to the South Shore, Hyde Park, and Rogers Park areas. In the outlying areas, miles of new homes were built after the war where there had formerly been neither houses nor schools. The children here, too, went to public schools which became more crowded.

The "flight to the suburbs" had begun in 1910 when the rate of increase in the city's growth began to slow down. Between 1910 and 1950 the suburban population tripled, and between 1950 and 1960 it doubled again, until it was three-fourths that of the city—and still growing rapidly. The central city lost in total population. The effects of this change on the school system were measurable. As the property in the inner city deteriorated with age, and the proportion of children in the public schools to adult population increased, the assessed value of the city real estate per public school child went down by some $3,000 per child,[2] while in most of the suburbs it increased. There was measurable reduction too in the proportion of city children attending parochial schools. The demolition of buildings for the construction of wide roads to facilitate automobile transportation to the suburbs reduced the taxable area. This reduction in taxable property was increased by the replacement of slums by acres of public housing which did not pay full taxes.

Opportunity for employment in the city changed radically. The acceleration of scientific discovery—a result of the tremendous outpouring of money for defense—began to alter civilian industry at a pace faster than such changes had ever taken place during the ages when men slowly learned to replace muscle by machine. Nuclear energy, computers, and new electronic devices opened rapidly widening vistas in the production of goods and services. These fields had little need of unskilled labor. In 1910, 36 percent of the people at work in Chicago had been unskilled. By 1950 it was only 19 percent, and by 1960, 9.5 Cotton-picking machines and huge coal cutters were replacing hand labor in the South, driving the uneducated and unskilled workers from the fields and mines into the cities, where they were even less ready to do the work for which labor was needed.

In 1960, 5 percent of the male workers of the city were unemployed. While 35 percent of the Negro population were middle-class in income, 53 percent were unskilled laborers, and 11 percent—not 5—were unemployed, double the city ratio. In 1960 the median family income of the city was $6,738, but for the Negro family it was only $3,763, near the "poverty level." By 1950 thirty-one of every 1,000 persons in the city were receiving public assistance. Of the 272,860 persons receiving public assistance in 1962, 90.5 percent were Negro. The welfare system and the inability of men to earn enough to support a family discouraged normal family life. Chicago had the highest degree of residential segregation of any city in the United States. Seventy percent of the Negroes on public assistance lived in six communities each almost 100 percent Negro.[3]

Children from the homes of migrants from the rural South—where education for Negroes had been so substandard as to be almost without meaning—came into schools with cultural handicaps, aggravated by lack of health care, overcrowding of housing, and, frequently, vicious community influences. The schools were not ready to overcome these handicaps or to give children the kind of educational experiences which the steadily rising standards of education— both in excellence and duration, demanded for their success. The children of the poor *never* had an equal opportunity for education, as Hannah Clark and William Rainey Harper had made very clear in the 90's.

But a strong back and a willing hand had made it possible, once, for the fifth grade "school leaver," with little reading skill, to make a happy and useful life for himself and his family. No longer was this true. Even a high-school diploma was now no guarantee of a job—only the possible "ticket" for a chance to be shown how to do one. By 1950 a low reading level meant continued failure in school, subsequent dropping out at sixteen, or getting an almost worthless diploma at eighteen. Such an education offered little chance even at a dead-end job, assuming one could be found by a Negro. The schools of the Northern cities had neither the financial or professional resources to give children the counseling and extra help needed. Many of the teachers in the overcrowded schools were dismayed at the results of their efforts to make the standard curriculum useful to children to whom it made little sense. The really astonishing thing was the number of Negro children who managed to get a sound and useful education and find places for themselves in an unhelpful world.

Many school systems were developing methods to meet not only the problems of children from the poor homes, but the problems of all children in coping with the stress of life today on their physical, mental, and emotional growth. But the Chicago schools never had money enough to do more than scratch the surface with such services. There was really no school staff to help parents understand and cooperate with the school during the one-seventh of a child's life spent there.

Some children did not even spend one-seventh of their time in school, because they did not attend for a full day. The perennial problem of lack of space was intensified partly by building restrictions during two wars and by the tremendous increase in the birth rate at the end of World War II, which brought the number of students in Chicago elementary schools from 279,267 in 1953 to 418,251 in 1965. While the high-school enrolment had fallen to a low of 86,954 in 1953 (because of the birth-rate decrease during the depression), the wave of increased elementary enrolment began to reach the high schools by the end of the decade, and by 1966 saw 127,544 in high school. The prospect of providing schools for a city full of new children, when there never had at any time been enough seats for their predecessors, was enough to appall any school administrator. The school population rose 180,000 between 1953 and 1966, while the population of the city fell 70,000.[4]

This was the Chicago and this was the school system which faced Superintendent Benjamin Coppage Willis when he arrived from Buffalo to succeed Dr. Herold C. Hunt in September, 1953. Much had been done since 1947 to correct some of the gross wastes of the past. A real beginning had been made on the building situation by the passage of a bond issue for 50 million dollars in 1951. The morale of the teaching staff had definitely risen. Civic agencies were encouraged at the prospects and willing to help in further improvements. The waste of funds in politically dictated contracts, and in unnecessary political jobs in the non-teaching services, had been practically stopped. There was now a chance to get ahead with new and constructive ways of making the schools useful to the city and its people.

The new superintendent was greeted as warmly as his predecessor. The Citizens Schools Committee gave him a rousing welcome at a Civic Assembly, where hundreds of people came to meet him directly and where he could present his own program for their support. With this audience he discussed the great need for sufficient buildings well adapted to their purpose, for a reasonable standard of living for teachers with a salary schedule recognizing their level of training, and for emphasis on the main purpose of the schools, the education of children.

On the cover of the Chicago Teachers Union newspaper for September, 1953, a Chicago American cartoon of June 9, 1953, showed a smiling Willis flying in from Buffalo, with applause from the tall buildings below him, and a caption, "Happy Landing." The new superintendent was invited to speak to the union members at the Sherman Hotel on October 6. To them, he stressed the importance of the human element in teaching, the need for good personnel policies as well as for buildings and sound administrative procedures, and urged that channels be opened between parents and teachers. An editorial in the union paper described him as a "modest, friendly, capable and intelligent school administrator." The newspapers noted his coming as an asset to the city and continued for almost eight years to give him and his administration solid support.

Improvement in Salaries, Services, and Seats

In his first year Dr. Willis and the union worked out a new salary schedule which provided a six-hour day for all teachers, a $500 increment for a Master's degree, and $500 more for thirty-six hours of graduate work beyond the Master's. The 29 percent of elementary teachers who did not have A.B. degrees were "blanketed in" as if they had. The A.B. salary began at $3,400, now at least above the accepted poverty level, with a maximum $6,650 after ten years of service. Year by year the salaries rose, so that when Superintendent Willis left in 1966 the minimum was $5,500 and the maximum $10,250 after thirty-five years of teaching.[5] There had of course been great pressure from the teachers to reach these levels. But Dr. Willis had evidently meant it when he stressed the need for higher salaries, whether he acceded to every request or not. Chicago teachers' wages were not the highest in the country, however, and other cities were competing for the scarce supply of teachers. In 1966 more than 6,642 were still not fully certified, in a total educational staff of 24,000.

Now that war-time restrictions were lifted, the new superintendent could attack these problems. By increasing the number of seats and the number of teachers he was able to reduce the average elementary class size from 39 in 1953 to 32 in 1963. Since these figures were averages (not maxima), counting staff other than class-room teachers, there were still many rooms of 40, some of 50 and a few of 25. In 1957 the curriculum for high schools was overhauled and made more flexible. Curriculum guides were prepared at all levels. The Curriculum Council with its advisory members from civic agencies was continued. Opportunities for vocational education were offered in nine schools, and work-study plans in distributive education developed in the general high schools. Rooms for trainable mentally handicapped children, previously not provided for, helped parents appreciably. New buildings were provided for two schools for the socially maladjusted and new experiments to help these children begun. In 1959 the Chicago Teachers College increased the proportion of general to special education in its curriculum. Gifted children were recognized as a group to be given special attention.

Special help also for children in low income areas was provided through some after-school speech and reading clinics, and through after-school remedial reading classes for some students. An "Urban Youth" program to help dropouts offered guidance, training, and employment to dozens. With Ford Foundation help, a program was set up on the inner South Side for boys and girls fifteen or over still in elementary school. Beginning in 1960 experimental summer schools, with class size limited to 25, set a successful pattern; all the system's auxiliary aids were available, and with parental cooperation a basic factor of the plan, 60,000 children in one summer eventually profited. General summer-school enrolment was encouraged by eliminating all tuition in 1955, and it increased six-fold to 124,000 in 1966. The use of non-graded classes emphasized the necessity of recognition of individual needs and abilities. Extra funds were budgeted for supplies and books for schools in high transiency areas. The number of teacher nurses reached 139 by 1963, compared to 21 ten years before, and referrals for hearing and vision treatment in the lower grades were made for more than 100,000 children. The "Lighted School House" program for adults and children was extended from 51 schools to 132 by 1963. Only one school social worker was at work in 1963, although one for each district was provided for in the budget. The number of psychologists was almost doubled, to 113.

Efforts were made to try out new educational methods through the use of television and teaching machines, and language laboratory equipment in the high schools and colleges. Courses in adult education provided training which led to a practical nursing certificate. The school lunch program served 24 million meals in 1963. The junior college enrolment approached 40,000. Allocations for school libraries, both elementary and secondary, were increased and these facilities became centers for audio-visual materials as well as for books. The time spent on administrative records by teachers was reduced by the adoption of the annual admissions plan in 1961. All schools in an area were placed under one district superintendent, instead of having high schools separated from elementary, and the number of districts enlarged to twenty-four. Each district superintendent was to appoint an advisory committee from the community in his area. Federal funds amounting to 1.3 million dollars, most of it from the National Defense Education Act, were used after 1953 for improvement of instruction in foreign language, mathematics, and science. Programs broadcast from the Board of Education radio were increased, and children participated in producing them. Television instruction for credit was offered by the City Junior College, and twenty-seven schools participated in an experiment with air-borne television. Each of these innovations in the vast system required meticulous planning and many conferences. [6]

In the eternal problem of finding roofs and seats for the endlessly increasing number of children Superintendent Willis made his major contribution to the Chicago school system. The 1951 bond issue had provided a start. Successive bond issues for 50 million dollars apiece in 1955, 1957, and 1959, all approved by public vote, brought the total available, beyond the comparatively small amount from each year's budget, to 200 million dollars. A fifth bond issue for twenty-five millions was authorized by the legislature in 1961, but it was not voted upon by the public until November, 1966, after Dr. Willis had left. These large sums of money were spent with great care and hard work in planning, much of it done by the superintendent himself. That not one rumor of scandal ever rose as to its spending was in itself a remarkable achievement. Eminent architects and builders submitted competitive bids and thus replaced the old Bureau of Architecture, of which the Strayer Report had so heartily disapproved. The actual cost of construction was reduced in a period of sharply rising materials and labor costs, so that more buildings were erected with the money available then would have been otherwise possible. Critics complained that the superintendent spent so much time on the details of the building program that he neglected his public leadership responsibility. Thirty-five percent of the new buildings were in the low income areas. By 1963, 40 percent of the children in the system were housed in new or modernized buildings. Two-hundred eight elementary schools were either erected or enlarged. Thirteen high schools, one junior college, and a second, beautiful, modern Teachers College on the North Side, went up. Modern design devices to increase functional usefulness changed the inner and outer appearance of the attractive new buildings, at lowered costs. By January, 1963, for the first time in Chicago public-school history there was a seat for every child in the city's elementary schools. [7]

By 1964 the building funds had run dry. Now there was no money to continue providing seats for elementary children, since the annual increase in the elementary schools was greater than could be provided for from the current building tax rate. The enrolment in the high schools had risen by 1964 to 123,974, and 40,000 high-school students were now without seats except on a shortened pupil day and longer hours for the schools. [8]

Not only had $288,663,294 been spent on buildings in the first ten years of Dr. Willis' service as superintendent, the total budgets had increased from $158,448,000 in 1953 to $387,990,000 in 1966. By that year, 12.2 percent was coming from new federal sources, and 24 percent from the state, with only 65 percent now from the local real estate tax. But to get money for the greater number of children, the local property tax rate for schools had been raised from $1.85 to $2.27 per $100 of assessed valuation. The school's share of the total local property tax for the six local governments—county, city, Sanitary District, Park District, Forest Preserve District, and the Chicago Board of Education—had risen from 39 to 42 percent. The biennial appropriation for the state school distributive fund had gone up from $139,838,000 in 1952-53 to $559,251,000 in 1965-66, and Chicago's share had risen accordingly, from 11.3 percent of the Chicago school budget in 1953 to 19.3 percent of the much larger budget of 1966. The special state aid to Chicago for the handicapped, the gifted, driver education, and vocational and adult education had also risen from 1.8 percent of the budget of 1953 to 5.2 percent in 1966. Reimbursement for the Chicago Teachers College and for some junior college aid was reduced in 1965 when the Board of Education turned the Teachers Colleges over to the state system of higher education. Continuation of the *Facts and Figures* booklets made all this information available to any citizen.[9]

The record made by Superintendent Willis was recognized outside Chicago. In 1955 he was appointed to an eleven-man advisory commission of the Foreign Operations Administration. In 1961 when the superintendent of the New York City schools resigned and Dr. Willis was suggested as his successor, the Chicago newspapers were unanimous in protesting that he could not be spared.[10]. In 1963 he was invited by the State Board of Education of Massachusetts to direct a survey of the schools of that state. In 1964 he was cited by the National Vocational Association for his work as chairman of a committee to advise Congress on new federal legislation for vocational education. A month later the Maryland State Board of Education stated that it wished it could offer him enough money to serve as state superintendent of schools, but it could not compete with his Chicago salary. The Chicago Board of Education was paying him $48,500, the third highest salary for any public official at any level of government in the United States.

Superintendent Becomes Focus of Controversy

Why, then, were Dr. Willis' last three years so full of tension—conflict with the Board of Education, with the teachers, with the civic agencies which had once given him such strong support, and above all, why was the more articulate black community increasingly critical? Only one of the major newspapers, the Tribune, continued to support him and his actions were reported in the press with front-page headlines and unfriendly cartoons.

Three main reasons account for the change of attitude of a considerable number of people. One was Dr. Willis' own definition of the responsibilities of a school system in the solution of social problems, and his fixed assumption that decisions on such matters were the prerogative of professionals, not laymen on the Board of Education or anywhere else.[11] The second reason lay in his own inability to accept criticism from any source, and his resentment against critics for their lack of appreciation of the real progress made in a school system with a long record of conflict, political mismanagement, and open corruption, and retarded educational development. Since some members of the Board of Education accepted neither his definition of the social responsibilities of the schools nor his assumption that only he determined such policies, there was increasing criticism from the Board, and increasing stubborn refusal by him to accede to changes suggested by individual Board members or by the Board as a whole—which assumed it was empowered by law to make such decisions.[12]

The third base of conflict, less dramatic in the public eye, was the determination of the Chicago Teachers Union (to which a majority of the teachers had belonged for almost thirty years), to achieve a collective bargaining agreement, which they insisted grew more necessary as they saw the superintendent growing less responsive to them.

The year after Superintendent Willis came to Chicago the United States Supreme Court had declared unconstitutional the legal segregation of Negro children in public schools, ordering the Southern states, which had such laws, to desegregate their schools. By 1960 Negro leaders in every Northern city were pointing out that the reasons given by the Supreme Court against segregation in schools imposed by law were just as valid against "de facto" segregation caused by residential segregation. The effects on the "hearts and minds" of the children were the same, it was claimed. In every large city most Negro children went to school only with other Negro children.

In Chicago, segregation was particularly disturbing, because it was now accepted that the city had a higher degree of residential Negro segregation than any other large Northern city. The expert research department of the Chicago Urban League analyzed the expenditures of individual schools and established beyond question that the segregated Negro schools were actually getting less in school funds per child than those in more prosperous white areas. There were, to be sure, some extra allocations for supplies to these schools; but the percentage of highly paid experienced teachers was low, and the proportion of low-paid substitutes was high, so that the total expenditure for teaching was demonstrably less. Moreover, the allocation for maintenance and operation per child in the segregated schools was less. All but one of the largest elementary schools, those over 1,600, were in the Negro areas. The cost per child for maintenance in a large crowded building was less than in a small uncrowded one.[13]

Efforts to find out the number and location of unused class rooms which could be utilized to reduce the overcrowding met with frustrating postpone-ments and unclear figures. When this information was finally given to the Board members who asked for it, some unused rooms in white schools were still not listed, as they were assigned to extra services (such as nurses) for which the Negro schools had no comparable space. One report was based on what rooms would be unused if there were 30 children in a class—when the current average was 32 and many in the Negro schools were above 40. This last fact was recognized when a transfer plan was announced in 1961 to relieve overcrowding. No Negro child could ask for a transfer unless his school averaged more than 40 to a class room, and no white school was listed for accepting transfers unless it had an average of less than 30 to a room.[14] Busing children at public expense, a practice in use in several large Northern cities, was ruled out by a majority of the Board as too expensive. The superintendent did not encourage busing, considering it an improper use of educational funds. He felt that the established pattern of neighborhood schools should not and could not be changed.

Dr. Willis' unyielding attitude on the subject of school responsibility for creating an integrated city aroused the bitter opposition not only of Negro parents but of many community leaders. They felt that all agencies, public and private, must make some contribution to keep the city from splitting into two hostile worlds, and that the future of the city depended in a very large measure on what the schools did in race relations. Negro parents alleged the large number of new schools in Negro areas had been put there to perpetuate segregation. Their location seemed to be based on continued containment within the ghetto, particularly when the system took no action to promote integration. When there was no more money for new construction and well-built, air-conditioned portable buildings with seats for only 30 children were used to accommodate the steady pupil increase, their use in Negro areas was bitterly resented and they were dubbed "Willis wagons."[15] Sit-ins at the Board of Education, picketing and disturbances at sites where the portables were being installed, marches to picket the Board of Education Building, the City Hall, the homes of Board members, the superintendent, and the mayor followed. As early as 1961, the N.A.A.C.P. and other Negro organizations and newspapers were demanding that Dr. Willis be dismissed.

Law suits were filed against the Board of Education on the grounds of discrimination in educational opportunity. A group of Negro and integrated civil rights organizations, called the Coordinating Council of Community Organizations, complained to the United States Civil Rights Commission that the Chicago schools were receiving federal funds without complying with the Commission's regulations. The investigators sent by the Commission met reluctance on the part of the superintendent and the Board to discuss the problems referred to in the complaint, and found that records of the racial composition of individual schools, or of the system as a whole, did not exist. Widely different guesses as to unused space had not been met with an official statement since 1957. The Daily News pointed out in an editorial on January 18, 1962, that such class room inventories had been published regularly by Dr. Hunt as a matter of course.

Protests against the purchase and use of expensive portables, instead of the utilization of space already available, were not accepted as valid by the school administration. The transfer plan initiated in 1961 had been criticized by the Chicago Urban League because of the difference in class sizes set for white and Negro schools. The use of the Washburne Trade School for training apprentices by unions which did not admit Negroes was especially noted by the Commission investigators.

One of the suits, the Webb case, filed in September, 1961, by a group of Negro parents, had been dismissed on the grounds that other possible steps to a solution had not yet been taken. But the federal district judge in dismissing the suit said, "Chicago can not deny the existence of 'de facto' segregation or excuse it on the pretext of benign indifference. . . . Separation can not be defended on the ground that it is the result of a high concentration of Negroes in a school district." In January, 1962, another group of parents of children at the Burnside School had brought suit against the Board, alleging manipulation of boundaries and transfers to keep an underpopulated school all white, while nearby Negro schools were on double shift. Parents demonstrating within the Burnside School were arrested, but the cases were dismissed.[16]

The federal investigators stated that the allegations of the Chicago Urban League that less was being spent per child in Negro schools than in white were reasonably substantiated. They also found that data collected by the Chicago Teachers Union on the wide variation in class sizes among districts were similarly reliable. The number of double-shift schools had been decreased, but the actual number of half-day children had actually increased, since the double-shift schools again were almost entirely in Negro areas with the largest enrolments. Most of the double-shift schools over a thirty-year period had been in segregated schools. The report stated that no official information was available on achievement levels in any particular school. But one-third of the high school graduates who entered the South Side Junior College branch were ready to do only remedial, below college level work. They had had a median reading level of eighth grade.[17]

The report commended the decision of the Board of Education to make an independent survey of the system as had been urged by the P.T.A., the Citizens Schools Committee, and other groups. It further recommended clarification of transfer plans proposed, and concluded,

"In a city where it has been impossible to obtain an open occupancy ordinance, and where the city administration and council have passed up numerous opportunities to promote residential integration, is it reasonable to expect the school administration to undertake by itself a positive program of integration? . . . A program of carefully planned zoning in fringe areas, coupled with a sound transfer policy might not only provide the first steps toward integration in the schools, but could encourage the other organs of the city government to undertake with new spirit the herculean task of housing desegregation." [18]

School Policy on Integration

This report from the Civil Rights Commission in 1962 emphasized the reluctance of both superintendent and Board to accept any positive responsibility for doing anything about integration. The committee of teachers and administrators which Dr. Hunt had created, and his technical and lay advisory committees had all ceased to function—the latter two as soon as Dr. Hunt left. Mrs. Annabelle Prescott, with a Ph.D. degree in the field of human relations from Columbia University had been assigned to work with the staff committee before its dissolution, and in 1958 was appointed Director for Bureau of Human Relations without any staff. She offered a series of in-service training courses for which Teachers College graduate credit was given, taken by several hundred teachers after school hours. Positions provided in the budget for the Bureau of Human Relations were left unfilled, however, and on her retirement her position was vacant until the dean of Wright Junior College took a leave to extend the work of the Bureau. However he received little encouragement and did not stay. His successor, highly trained in the field, planned television instruction and gave in-service training courses in individual schools; but his work was severely limited by his lack of staff and by isolation from the general administrative activity. The Bureau was clearly not considered important, in spite of repeated requests at public hearings for its extension, and for an unequivocal statement of policy on integration by the Board of Education.

In response to mounting requests, the Board appointed a committee of its members to prepare a statement of its integration position. Many organizations throughout the city presented detailed suggestions to the committee for its consideration, and found its final action disappointing. The official statement of policy did not even mention integration or any other positive goal. Adopted by the Board on January 14, 1959, it began,

> "Better human understanding among all peoples, based upon deeper mutual understanding, is a primary objective of the entire educational program in Chicago's public schools. All activities under the jurisdiction of the Chicago Board of Education shall be so organized and all persons so directed as to bring this desirable objective to closer fulfillment, promptly and prudently." [19]

The organizations which had asked for a positive statement on integration considered these generalities meaningless, a mere evasion of clearly obvious issues, where prudence was clearly employed at the expense of promptness. Superintendent Willis took occasion to deny publicly that there was any segregation in Chicago schools, as all children went to the schools in their own neighborhoods. [20]

The Chicago Teachers Union by action of its House of Representatives, in 1961 had pledged itself to work for integration within the system so as to equalize educational opportunity, and the following year presented specific proposals with the statement that the neighborhood school policy should not be used as an excuse for segregating children. The Citizens Schools Committee continued to press for advisory committees, an independent survey of the system, a policy of continuous redistricting and special aid for all economically underprivileged children through reduction of class size, extra materials, and auxiliary services, and for the assumption of integration as a positive and explicit goal. The Chicago Region of the P.T.A. took similar positions. The Urban League issued a series of studies, and held a Schools Seminar in March, 1962, at which Dr. Dan Dodson of New York University and President Davis of the Cleveland Board of Education discussed practical steps toward integration. The latter pointed out that 3,000 children in Cleveland were already being bused at a cost of no more than $18 per child a year. The League stated that while only one-tenth of the children in Chicago schools had been culturally deprived in 1950, one-third were in 1960. The South East Community Organization, largely white, asked for a regional exchange for South East Side high schools to promote integration and to stabilize the already integrated schools.

The superintendent answered all these proposals with a four-point program for "Problem Area Pupils." Two-hundred truant officers were to visit homes before school opened. Fifty elementary high schools would open early in order to place transient pupils properly. General high schools would open three days early to orient freshmen, and sixty elementary schools would provide help two days a week after school for "floundering children." [21] The groups which wanted the school system to accept its share of responsibility in doing something about the major social problem of the city which affected so deeply the life and learning of so large a portion of the city's children, felt that there was no communication between them and the superintendent on this issue. This conclusion on their part was intensified when district public hearings were discontinued.

The Board of Education was not all of one mind on the issue. As early as 1956, Dr. Joseph Pois had spoken to the Citizens Schools Committee on the importance of the schools in the necessary effort to make the city an integrated community. Since 1962 and 1963, Warren Bacon and Dr. Bernard Friedman had clearly, courteously, and consistently urged action to integrate the schools. Other Board members had made clear their impatience with the superintendent's and the Board's unwillingness even to recognize the issue. While president of the Board between 1962 and 1964, Clair Roddewig met with representatives of several Negro groups, and was the guest of honor at the annual dinner given by a group of teachers who had attended Human Relations Workshops sponsored by the National Conference of Christians and Jews. The speaker at the dinner was

Prof. John Coons of Northwestern University Law School, who had written the 1962 report on Chicago for the U.S. Civil Rights Commission. At least three other Board members urged definite action on some steps toward integration. Information requested by Board members to help formulate such steps came from the school administration very slowly. But other members of the Board generally supported the superintendent's position and some went even farther in disclaiming any responsibility for the public schools except in professional instruction on subject matter.

The Board was, however, compelled by court action to do something. The suit brought by the Burnside parents was settled out of court by agreement of the Board on August 28, 1963, to select a panel of five experts

> ". . . to analyze and study the school system, in particular in regard to schools attended entirely or predominantly by Negroes, define any problems that result therefrom, and formulate or report to this Board as soon as it may be conveniently possible a plan by which any educational, psychological and emotional problems or inequities in the school system that prevail, may best be eliminated."

It was finally decided that the committee would report in March, 1964.[22]

In August, 1963, also, Superintendent Willis presented to the Board a new permissive transfer plan; the Board approved the scheme for allowing honor students in crowded high schools to transfer into twenty-four less-crowded high schools. Subsequently, without notification or discussion by the Board, the superintendent reduced the number of receiving schools from twenty-four to nine. At the Board meeting on September 25, President Roddewig suggested reinstating two of the receiving schools to make a total of eleven. The superintendent was present and raised no objection.[23] Twenty-four students, mainly Negro, had already applied for transfers to these two schools. The superintendent delayed in issuing the transfers. The parents of the twenty-four children sued in Superior Court for an order to the superintendent to carry out the Board's directive. Thomas Murray, vice president of the Board, who had voted for the directive, appeared in court to oppose granting the order. On October 3, the court did direct the superintendent to order the transfers, clearly authorized by the Board of Education. The students were then transferred.

Willis Resigns

Superintendent Willis thereupon sent his resignation to the Board and called a press conference on October 4 to explain his reasons for doing so. He stated that the order of the court placed him in a position of carrying out an order which he considered discriminatory, and which violated his "principles and sense of professional integrity." He added that he had been dissuaded from resigning after the meeting on the 25th, although for a year the Board had been encroaching on his administrative activities. The latest incident of such "administrative activity" on the part of the Board came September 25, when,

> ". . . without requesting a report on the status of the permissive plan, or prior notice to me, the president of the Board suggested an administrative action and directed its adoption. I can no longer continue to discharge my responsibilities under such circumstances since the present practice is counter to all the fundamentals of good Board-staff relations here and elsewhere." [24]

This reaction of the superintendent toward the Board occurred amid increasing turmoil in the city over de facto segregation in the schools, evidenced in demonstrations, efforts to stop the installation of portables, court suits, and open threats that future referenda against bond issues for buildings would be defeated.

Superintendent Willis then disappeared. Deputy Superintendent James H. Smith stated to the parents who had brought the suit that he would do his best to see that the twenty-four transferred children remained in their new schools. Other than the Tribune, the metropolitan press took issue against the superintendent, and the largest Negro newspaper attacked him forcefully:

> "[Dr. Willis] . . . is not irreplacable. . . . We do not think that the Board should be turned from its own concept of progress by the petulance of its administrator." [Editorial, Chicago Daily News, October 9, 1963]

> "The resignation of Dr. Benjamin C. Willis has been inevitable for some months. . . . Whatever the reasons may have been, Dr. Willis lost contact both with his board and his public. . . . It is the obligation of the superintendent to carry out the policy of the board, once decreed, or, if he disagrees, as Dr. Willis did, to resign." [Editorial, Chicago Sun Times, October 6, 1963]

> "We wish the superintendent well; there are many positions, we're sure, that will benefit from a hard-driving executive who wants his word to be law. But in this tense and touchy year of 1963, the directorship of the Chicago school system is not one of them." [Editorial, Chicago's American, October 7, 1963]

> "[Dr. Willis is] still not without his own power. He's the Madame Nhu of racial progress in Chicago—the Charles DeGaulle of American education—the Gov. Wallace of Chicago standing in the doorway of an equal education for all Negro kids in this city—a one-man educational John Birch Society, incarnate and inviolate." [Editorial, Chicago Defender, October 12, 1963]

Others, however, rushed to his support. Without waiting to secure information from both sides, the chairman of the Illinois State Committee of the North Central Association intervened, threatening loss of accreditation for the city's high schools, saying (according to the Sun Times of October 7), "From the information I have at this time, it seems that the president and some members of the Board of Education have been in violation of North Central criteria." A significant group of business leaders sent a telegram to the Board urging that the superintendent be continued in office, in recognition of his economical expenditure of tax dollars and modern methods of conducting the largest single business enterprise in the city.[25] A barrage of letters from within the system flooded members of the Board; it was rumored that the campaign had been organized by some members of the administrative staff.

On October 7, the Board of Education went into executive session to consider the resignation. Vice President Murray moved to refuse the resignation, and to send a committee of the Board to call upon Dr. Willis to discuss "improving relations between Board and superintendent." Two members voted against the motion and six for it. Board member Fairfax Cone had announced his resignation when the superintendent resigned, giving as his reason his new position as chairman of the Board of Trustees of the University of Chicago; he therefore passed his vote. On October 9, the Board again met and reconsidered its action in replacing the two schools on the list. The final vote on this proposal was four to support the superintendent, one to oppose cancellation of the September 25 action, with three members passing their votes.[26] The court then dismissed the case brought by the parents, since there was no longer a Board action which had been disobeyed. On October 16 the superintendent appeared at the Board meeting and made a public statement that he would abide by the Board's decision to reject his resignation, and that he and the Board had agreed to outline principles of operation and "to delineate areas for action."

The three newspapers criticized the Board's "caving-in." One showed a cartoon of the Board crawling on hands and knees toward a throne on which Dr. Willis sat. But the Board was in a difficult position. At least two members considered the resignation a blessing. Some members always had accepted the superintendent's view; others who did not condone his present actions were appalled at their taking responsibility for a school system without a capable head—particularly a system in which all administrative power had been concentrated so tightly in the hands of one person. The superintendent's unwillingness to delegate authority was brought into sharp relief in the crisis. It would be impossible to find a successor immediately (Deputy Superintendent Smith had, some time before, asked for a leave of absence for illness); any person capable of administering so vast and complicated an organization was not idle in October of any year and would not be available on short notice. It was as if the superintendent had engaged in a one-man strike in an essential industry where his services were irreplaceable, and where his demands must then be met.

Willis not only lost the support of most of the press; the organizations outside the schools which had welcomed him so warmly ten years before were now sharply critical both of his attitude toward the Board and to the "community," particularly the Negro community. The Citizens Schools Committee issued a release on October 8, stating that the superintendent had not provided the Board with pertinent information on school population changes and on the use of class room space, had not cooperated in seeking an independent survey of the system (until, under threat of resignation, he had been made part of the survey staff), had shown no interest in the work of the five-man panel to study the impact of segregation on quality of education, and had "failed to establish harmonious community-school relations, thereby leaving a vacuum that had to be met by the Board." The release went on:

> "The issue is whether the Board will determine policy or whether the General Superintendent will be the sole arbiter of the public policy of the Chicago schools. The Citizens Schools Committee strongly urges the Board to arrive with the superintendent at a definite understanding as to the responsibilities and authority of each before Dr. Willis resumes his office, and to obtain from him an assurance that he will carry out the policy directives of the Board of Education. The Citizens Schools Committee also feels it is impera-tive that Dr. Willis offer active cooperation to the two committees set up by the Board to survey the Chicago school system."

Dr. Willis attended no more of the Civic Assemblies which had been created by the Citizens Schools Committee to provide a platform from which a superintendent of schools might speak to the people of the city. The Chicago Teachers Union newspaper printed the release of the Citizens Schools Com-mittee in full in its October, 1963, issue, and added that the definition of a superintendent's duties, as set up in the 1947 law, were not being accepted by the present incumbent.

The Coordinating Council of Community Organizations had rejoiced at the resignation. When it was withdrawn, the organization printed the newspaper comments, listed community and religious organizations of all three major faiths which had recommended acceptance of the resignation; it announced a boycott of the schools for October 22 in protest against the reinstatement and demanded a new superintendent.[27] At the boycott approximately half the children in the school system remained away from school, a considerable number of them white. Tension tautened when the mayor in May, 1964, reappointed Mrs. Wendell Green, a Negro board member who supported Willis, against the vigorous expressed opposition of every considerable Negro organization in the city.

New Board Policy on Integration

The conflict between Superintendent Willis and the Board was never satisfactorily resolved. Dr. Willis invited the Board members to lunch to discuss the problems involved, or "anything they wished to discuss." Two Board members refused the invitation, holding that the 1957 state law required open discussion on all but a few matters specifically exempted in the law.[28] Under President Roddewig's leadership, the Board adopted a policy statement on integration on October 13, 1964, as follows:

> "The members of the Chicago Board of Education believe that this city and this country would be healthier economically, educationally, and morally if Chicago, Illinois, and all sections of the country, reflected the kind of racial and ethnic diversity characteristic of the nation as a whole.

> "We have already made clear our opposition to segregation or discrimination in planning attendance areas and educational programs. We believe the children of Chicago would be better prepared for today's world if their classrooms and school staffs reflect a racial and ethnic diversity.

> "We are now seeking guidance in meeting any educational problems which may be inherent in the school which is all, or practically all, Negro. We hope later to seek similar guidance in relation to the school which is all, or practically all, white. However, we see no single over-all step or action by which such diversity can be brought immediately to all our schools by the Board of Education alone.

> "We shall continue to seek, and promptly take, any practical steps by which, in conformity with sound educational procedures, racial and ethnic diversity in schools and classrooms can be promoted. We shall continue to be guided by, and comply with, state and federal laws and the spirit of the 1954 Supreme Court decision on desegregation.

> "Therefore, we reaffirm and publicly declare a policy of racial integration. We shall endeavor to effect the development of a continuous program to achieve this goal."

When President Roddewig announced in February, 1963, that he did not wish to continue on the Board, every newspaper in the city paid tribute to him. The Tribune on February 19 inferred that he was leaving because Negroes picketed his home while his wife was ill. The News said he had done well "in the hottest seat in the municipal hierarchy." The Sun Times claimed he had inherited Chicago's long refusal to face up to the facts of school integration, a "problem made no easier by Willis staging a sit-down of his own in the middle of controversy." The comment made by the superintendent was that "The major issues in today's urban schools are clouded by civil rights, or whatever people may mean by civil rights."[29]

Uncertain Relation of Superintendent with Board

On April 23, 1964, the Board adopted a "Statement of Principles and Procedures," which was not completely satisfactory to all Board members as a definition of the division of authority between Board and superintendent. Two objectionable clauses required that (1) Board members be limited only to the superintendent in their contacts with school personnel and that (2) all communications received by Board members concerning the administration of the schools be sent directly to the superintendent, "for his investigation and report."[30]

On October 27, 1964, the Board discussed a policy statement on stabilization, and adopted it on November 12. The statement read as follows:

"While the Board continues to search for ways to increase the interracial association of students, it has also a responsibility to help preserve, as far as possible, such associations in areas where they now exist.

"Therefore as one of our important objectives in the field of integration, the Board of Education hereby asserts that it is its policy to seek and to take any possible steps which may help to preserve and stabilize the integration of schools in neighborhoods which already have an interracial composition."

But the issuance of statements without subsequent positive implementation resolved no difficulties. Since implementation of changes within the system required initiation by the superintendent—who did not approve of such changes—the Board was at a stalemate.

Chapter 17

BOARD, UNION, AND BLACK COMMUNITY
OPPOSE A SUPERINTENDENT

Two surveys authorized by the Board were ready in 1964. The first, describing the impact of segregation on the quality of education in Chicago schools, was presented on March 31. The five experts who prepared it were led by Dr. Philip Hauser, head of the sociology department of the University of Chicago. Dr. Sterling McMurrin, former U.S. Commissioner of Education, was vice chairman. The president of Howard University, the assistant program director of education for the Ford Foundation, and a professor of education from Stanford University were the other members of the panel. The eighty-five-page report stated the facts of residential segregation in Chicago and the results of the head count in the schools, finally taken in October, 1963. The count showed 54 percent of the elementary pupils in the public schools Negro, and 36 percent of those in high schools. Negro children however, constituted only 34 percent of the elementary age group in the city, and 27 percent of the secondary-school age group. There was no data on the race of teachers, as the Board attorney had ruled that it was illegal to collect it.

The Hauser Report on Effect of Segregation

The report summarized the court decisions as to the responsibility of the Board of Education on school segregation caused by residential segregation, and stated:

> "The neighborhood elementary school, which has served this nation
> well historically, operates now to retard the acculturation and

integration of the in-migrant Negro in Chicago and in metropolitan United States as a whole. Earlier in the century, the neighborhood elementary school actually helped to bring persons of diverse ethnicity and culture together, because foreign immigration was on a smaller and more gradual scale than in the recent in-migration of Negroes. . . . The public school must do its share in breaking down walls of segregation and paving the way for the exercise of free choice on the part of the Negro, as for all citizens, in respect to his life pursuits."

The extent of segregation in the Chicago schools was clearly stated. Of 148,000 Negro elementary students, 90 percent were in schools at least 90 percent Negro, and 10 percent in integrated or 90-percent white schools. Of 17,000 Negro students in upper grade centers, 97 percent were in Negro schools. Sixty-three percent of the 36,000 Negro general high-school students and 45 percent of the 7,000 Negro vocational students were in all-black schools.

Forty percent of the Negro schools had an average of more than 35 students per classroom as compared with 12 percent of white schools. The city-wide average was 32.5. Five of the 8 Negro high schools had enrolments 50 percent over capacity, but only four of the twenty-six white high schools. The median dropout rate for Negro high schools was 9 percent, for white 4.2 percent. But almost 82,000 Negro children were in buildings constructed since 1951, as compared with 28,000 in white schools, and 9,500 in integrated buildings. Seventy-three percent of the 215 mobile classrooms were in use in Negro schools. These facts were illustrated with maps and charts.[1]

The report made eleven recommendations, as follows:

1. Modified open enrolment in elementary schools, with enlarged attendance areas to include at least two contiguous schools; racial integration as a major consideration in locating upper-grade centers; open enrolment for all general high-school students living within enlarged high-school districts, each to include three or more general high schools; open enrolment in all vocational and special schools.
2. Free transportation from overcrowded to under-utilized schools for distances over a mile; no use of mobile units to perpetuate segregation.
3. Location of new schools and boundary lines to foster racial integration.
4. Integration of faculties in all schools.
5. Assignment of teachers to distribute experience and professional training fairly.
6. Encouragement of teacher training institutions to develop a more effective program for the education of teachers for

schools with high turnover, heavy retardation, and limited educational achievement.

7. In-service education of teachers and administrators in the history of minority groups in America, in the content and method of teaching children of different cultural heritages, and in human relations practices.

8. Substantially increased funds for the schools described in 6, above the city average.

9. Increased programs to raise linguistic and mathematics skills in such schools closer to grade expectancy.

10. Increase in guidance and counseling services.

11. A saturation project in one or more districts, using the best educational practices. [2]

Six days after the presentation of this report to the Board of Education, the administrative staff issued a critical "Study Guide" to the report, citing among other things what had been done by the school administration in the location of buildings according to the Armstrong law (in effect over the state since August, 1963). The law had stated that

"The Board shall, as soon as practicable, and from time to time thereafter, change or revise existing sub-districts or create new sub-districts in a manner which will take into consideration the prevention of segregation and the elimination of separation of children in public schools because of race, color or nationality. All records pertaining to the creation, alteration or revision of sub-districts shall be open to the public. In erecting, purchasing or otherwise acquiring buildings for school purposes, the board shall not do so in such a manner as to promote segregation and separation of children in public schools because of color, race or nationality."

To many of those in and out of the schools, the "Study Guide" seemed to be a defense of the present system and an effort to minimize the report's importance. Seventeen of 72 questions contained in the Study Guide suggested implications not mentioned in the report, or inferred problems not covered. One question reexamined the advantages and disadvantages of providing information on race. Another clearly asserted contradictions within the report. Certainly the Study Guide showed no enthusiasm for the report or its implementation. [3]

On April 8, the Board adopted the Hauser report "in principle," but took no further action except to appoint the advisory committee of "Friends of the Schools" suggested in the report. [4] In May Superintendent Willis and the new Board president, Frank Whiston, presented a substitute for the panel's suggestion of clustering schools into larger districts. The plan differed little from the previous voluntary transfer plans adopted in November, 1962, and December,

1963. No transportation was provided. The plan adopted in May was to be operative in September, 1964.[5]

The Board had been concerned in April and May with a proposal on the sharing of the facilities of a new public high school on the far West Side with a nearby parochial school, possessing less scientific and gymnasium equipment. After a public hearing at which considerable opposition was voiced on the basis of the need for separation of church and state, the Board voted tentative approval of a "shared time" plan as an experiment, the results of which were to be reported to it.

In June the superintendent declared in a television interview that Negro schools were not inferior to white schools, and stated that he was not responsible for the neighborhood school policy he had inherited.[6] But arguments on overcrowding and possible empty space continued. The superintendent held that there were only 12,809 empty seats, if an average of 30 to a room was the base. Dr. Hauser pointed out that 30 was *not* the base, and claimed that there were 26,000 empty seats which could be used immediately. School opened in September with no action taken on the proposed transfer plan. In New York City there was a massive boycott of the Negro schools. In Philadelphia, 1,500 Negro children were taken to less crowded schools by bus.[7]

The Havighurst Survey on Quality of Education

The second report was not presented to the Board of Education until November, but it had had a long history before that time. For six years the Citizens Schools Committee had been asking for such a general study of the Chicago school system. Only two such surveys had occurred in the 130 years of Chicago school history—the Harper report in 1898 and the Strayer survey of 1932. The Chicago Region of the P.T.A. and other groups had also asked repeatedly for such a study. In November, 1961, Board member Fairfax Cone had been appointed chairman of a committee to plan such a survey. The committee had first suggested that the superintendent's staff make a study with the help of Prof. Eldridge T. McSwain of Northwestern and two other advisers. Dr. McSwain said he saw no need of a survey. The committee then settled on Dr. Robert S. Havighurst of the University of Chicago, who had made a number of surveys both in this country and abroad. Dr. Willis frankly expressed his disapproval of this choice, saying that it indicated a definite change in Board policy toward neighborhood schools and indicated to Board members that he might resign if Havighurst was employed. Finally in May, 1963, the Board voted to put the direction of the proposed survey in the hands of three people—Dr. Havighurst, Dr. Alonzo Grace, Dean of the School of Education of the University of Illinois, and Dr. Willis himself.[8] Far-right groups raised objection to the employment of Dr. Havighurst, citing his activities for peace and civil liberties,[9] but the planning went ahead and a design for the survey was approved by the Board in December, 1963.

For six months the superintendent did not meet with the committee, although in August he publicly opposed the recommendation of the other two members that the state take over responsibility for the operation of the Teachers and Junior Colleges, and accused the Board again of "usurping his power." In September Dr. Grace threatened to resign from the survey unless the superintendent shared the work as he had agreed to do.[10] The News cartooned Dr. Willis "moonlighting" in Boston –doing a survey there while far below him the little Chicago survey circled lonesomely in space. The Sun Times in an editorial criticized him for working on the survey for which he got a large extra fee, but not on the one at home. When Dr. Havighurst formally presented the Chicago survey, with its recommendations, to the Board of Education on November 4, 1964, the superintendent ignored his presence and made no comments, either to the Board or to the press. There was wide demand for copies of the report, and Rand McNally offered to reprint them for sale at a low price, but the offer was refused by the Board.

The survey was a full-scale 500-page study of a vast and complicated urban school system. Some of the sections evaluated highly technical phases of modern education. But the entire study was set against the background of the city as it was, and of the children as they were. The chapter "Schools and the Development of the City" indicated two alternatives for the future of Chicago. One was to let present population trends continue, resulting in fewer and fewer white people in the city and increased segregation. The second alternative was to stabilize the proportion of white to Negro population, to retain a majority of white collar workers in the city, and to cause a slow and steady movement toward residential integration and an eventual decrease in Negro segregation. The second choice, said the report, was already supported by the Chicago Commission on Human Relations, by the Comprehensive Plan for Chicago, and by many civic and religious organizations.

The report alleged that the policy of the school system toward the relation of the races was a crucial factor in determining the future of the city. If the schools remained a passive element, efforts at community renewal would probably fail. A passive school attitude was in keeping with the "four walls" philosophy, concerned only with what happens to children inside a school building and rejects involvement in efforts to renew the physical and social environment in which they live. On the other hand, if the school system were an active element, it would follow the developing philosophy of an urban community school, and cooperate actively in social and physical city renewal. Said the report, "They [community-involved planners] will develop programs and standards of instruction and attendance, aimed at keeping middle income people, white and Negro, in the city and encouraging them to live in integrated local communities." There was no doubt that two of the three members of the survey committee agreed with the second alternative.[11]

The superintendent immediately took public exception to three major recommendations. He did not want the Chicago Teachers Colleges to become a part of the state system of higher education, as recommended in the state master plan, since he felt that it would be easier to recruit elementary teachers for the city if the Teachers Colleges remained part of the local school system. The same master plan had recommended that the state junior colleges, of which the Chicago Junior College was by far the largest, come under a state-wide junior college board with a separate local board. Since Illinois had always been more generous in providing for higher education than in aiding local school districts, new buildings and equipment would be available to both kinds of colleges at state expense, which could not be expected from the always-too-limited local property tax resources of the Chicago Board of Education. Dr. Willis objected also to the division of the city schools into three districts and to the appointment of an assistant superintendent to develop integration.[12] The other major recommendations of the report are briefly summarized below.

1. Increased in-service training for teachers.
2. Additional specialists to help local schools adapt curriculum and materials to their children.
3. Strengthened status and longer service for principals, to give leadership to communities.
4. More auxiliary staff—social workers, psychologists, counselors, nurses, clerks, and school-community coordinators.
5. Pre-kindergarten classes for socially disadvantaged children and earlier admission to kindergarten.
6. Reduction of class size to 30, with provision for special help for maladjusted children.
7. Expansion of programs for marginal adolescents.
8. Reorganization of vocational education with a critical examination of present practices.
9. Expansion of adult education with a much larger staff and city-wide center.
10. Greater use of new technological devices, such as television, teaching machines, and language laboratories.
11. Use of volunteers and non-professional aides, with a full-time coordinator.
12. Administrative encouragement of experienced teachers to work in "difficult" schools.
13. Permanent technically competent research staff to evaluate educational experiments.
14. Continuation of the advisory committee recommended by the Hauser report, for a year, to work on programs for the socially disadvantaged.[13]

The effect of the two surveys on the actual conduct of the schools was negligible. In August, 1964, the Urban League placed a full-page advertisement in each of the metropolitan newspapers, signed by distinguished citizens whose names filled the page in fine print, urging immediate action on the Hauser report. On leaving the Board in May, 1964, President Roddewig was quoted (by the Tribune) as saying, "The largest educational problem is to prepare thousands of Negro youngsters so that they can qualify for various jobs. This will require greater emphasis on the Negro than on the white pupil." He urged the "saturation" experiment as the most significant part of the Hauser study. In December, 1964, the Bryn Mawr P.T.A. brought in a carefully worked out plan to stabilize the school and general population in that part of the South Shore area. Dr. Willis presented a substitute plan. In August, 1964, the committee of Board members which had been appointed to make recommendations to the Board on the Hauser suggestions, favored the cluster idea of several high schools in a district for the Bowen High School area, and also the employment of an assistant superintendent for integration, in agreement with the Havighurst survey.[14] The advisory committee on the Hauser report was discouraged at the lack of progress and half of the members threatened to resign.

On one issue, however, the Board and superintendent were in accord. In January, 1965, a parent of a Wright Junior College student protested against the inclusion of *Another Country* by James Baldwin on a reading list. The city council set up a committee with the approval and encouragement of the mayor to investigate the use of such a book. Both Board and superintendent supported the college.[15]

In March, 1965, the president of the Principals Club was appointed to recruit and train volunteers. In August the superintendent nominated, and the Board approved, an assistant superintendent in charge of integration, but no program of integration was suggested or approved for her to implement, and no mention was made of the detailed proposals in the Havighurst survey. In October, 1965, a Sun Times editorial reminded the Board of Education that the Havighurst report had never even been formally considered in the eleven months since its submission and that no real recommendations of the Hauser survey had been put into effect after eighteen months. The editorial was entitled "Making Molehills out of Mountains." In February, 1965, however, the Board voted—over the outspoken objection of the superintendent—to turn the Teachers Colleges over to the state, and in November, 1965, to approve the separation of the City Junior College from the system.[16] (The only two municipal teachers' colleges left in the U.S. were in St. Louis and Washington, D.C.)

Friction Between Board and Superintendent

Conflict between the superintendent and the Board had not disappeared with the adoption of the guidelines. In January, 1965, the Board asked Dr. Willis to submit more than one nominee for promotion to a vacancy.[17] He answered that such a request was a return to the manipulation of schools by pre-1946 politically controlled Boards. In March, 1965, Assistant Superintendent Milton Cohler resigned—with a blast at the Board, which had no respect for profesionally expert administrators, "who are made [by the Board] to prove everything they say"; it should not, he claimed, have commissioned the two reports. The superintendent was quoted in all the newspapers as saying "I agree with everything Dr. Cohler has said [about the eleven-man Board] as laymen not properly respectful of professional experts." The Principals Club supported Dr. Cohler.[18] The News on March 31, 1965, commented that "Education, like war, was too important to be left to the generals."

In September, 1965, the superintendent proposed the division of the city into 42, not 24 districts and the appointment of 18 additional district superintendents. In October a Board member urged the superintendent to release the achievement scores of individual schools, as was done regularly in New York and other city systems as a matter of course. This was never done by Dr. Willis. In November a Board member accused the superintendent of "pocket-vetoing" the requests and decisions of the Board, complaining that they waited as long as eighteen months for important requested information. That month, also, Deputy Superintendent James H. Smith resigned from his $27,000 post to teach in a local university. The Board asked him to stay, and Chicago Teachers Union urged his retention as a "symbol of stability, integrity and educational excellence."[19] In December the superintendent reported that in nine months ten volunteers had been recruited and that a sex-education pilot program was planned for fifth grade. Mr. Murray, vice president of the Board, commented that sex education was the business of parents and that schools should stick to the 3R's.

In January, 1966, parents staged a revolt at the Jenner, a very large Negro school in a public housing project close to the Loop. They asserted that the principal was rude to Negro children and teachers. The conflict in and around the school, reported at length in the newspapers, continued for weeks. In February several Board members objected to a new salary schedule for top administrators, higher than that approved in the 1966 budget. On March 4, the Board voted to employ a management consulting firm to study its own operation and that of the non-teaching services.

On March 4, too, Board member James Clement resigned, giving as his reason the excessive amount of time required of members because of the obstruction, opposition, rudeness, and contempt shown to them by the superintendent. He stated that the superintendent had been defensive and defeatist in his opposition to any policies involving integration.[20] On March 6, the Sun Times commented on five competent Board members who recently had either resigned or announced they did not wish reappointment. Fairfax Cone, who had become president of the board trustees of the University of Chicago, Mrs. John B. Allen, who had left the city, Cyrus H. Adams III, Raymond Pasnick, and James

Clement all had differed with the superintendent on significant issues. In March, President Whiston informed Board members that the results of the head count of teachers by race, which they had commissioned, were secret, but might be seen if the members came to his office. On May 8, a newly appointed Board member complained that it took ninety minutes to pass a resolution asking the superintendent to make one telephone call to settle a dispute about over-crowding in the shared-time high school.

The Jenner School dispute continued. The Board appointed a committee to ascertain the facts. The principal demanded that fifteen teachers be transferred immediately. Twenty-one teachers who had not supported the parents in the boycott asked that the principal be transferred as not supporting the teachers with parents. The superintendent objected to the Board's action, refused to come to its committee hearing, and ordered the principal not to appear as well. On April 15, the parents were still picketing the school. A week later the principal was granted a leave of absence for illness; an experienced and competent administrator took her place, and there was peace. [21]

Collective Bargaining with the Union

The organized teachers had played little part in these months of frustrating and futile conflict, except for the Principals Club, which had openly supported the superintendent both at the time of Dr. Cohler's resignation and that of his own. The Chicago Teachers Union, which had included a majority of the teaching force since 1937, longer than in any other large city, had asked for collective bargaining agreements at various times in its long history. In January, 1963, the union newspaper had praised the procedures arrived at with Dr. Hunt, for settling grievances, but asserted now that the present administration was less cooperative.

With a request for a collective bargaining election, presented in January, 1963, the union sent to the Board of Education a petition signed by 65 percent of the teaching force asking for recognition as its bargaining agent. In April the Chicago Education Association, a part of the Illinois Education Association and the N.E.A., presented its request for an agreement on professional negotiations. In May, 1963, the superintendent urged the Board to reject both proposals and said he wanted a council of teacher and civil service employee organizations. The Board set October 23, 1963, as the date on which they would discuss these proposals, but Dr. Willis' temporary resignation upset the timetable. Finally on May 3, 1964, the Board approved a memorandum of agreement with the union, and a week later gave the same agreement to the C.E.A., refusing to authorize an election to determine a bargaining agent. The N.E.A. was now withdrawing its opposition to collective bargaining agreements and several of its affiliates had obtained them at such elections.

In January, 1964, Board vice president Murray had held up passage of the annual budget until increases were granted for non-teaching employees, but not for the teaching force. The union members marched in protest and considered striking. The union voted to strike in September, 1965, unless action were taken on their salary requests and on a collective bargaining election. Having secured the backing of Mayor Daley and supported by the president of the Chicago Federation of Labor, the union appeared at a Board meeting to ask again for a collective bargaining election. This time the Board voted to hold such an election—Board members rumored to be influenced by the mayor casting the deciding votes.[22] Suits brought by the C.E.A. to stop the election were settled and in June of 1966 the election was held, with the following results: for the Chicago Teachers Union 10,936; for the C.E.A., 364 [it had asked its members not to participate] ; for the Chicago Teachers Federation, 16. It had taken the union thirty years to reach this goal. The superintendent's open disapproval of the whole procedure widened the rift between teachers and administration.

Disagreements Over Federal Funds

Two other major sources of conflict emerged in the last three years of the superintendent's service. The first was over the use of federal funds and the second was the bitter fight over his re-election for a fourth term in 1965.

The report of the U.S. Civil Rights Commission in 1962 had already raised questions on the status of racial discrimination in the Chicago schools, and a federal judge in the same year had also questioned their procedures. Federal funds for education were rising fast. In 1963, $1,335,119 had been received on allocations under the National Defense Education Act. Large sums were appropriated in 1963 in the Elementary and Secondary Education Act, for uses in keeping with the Civil Rights law. Commissioner Francis Keppel of the Office of Education, on receipt of complaints from the Coordinating Council of Community Organizations in October, 1965, delayed payment of the money for which Chicago was eligible under the new legislation, pending investigation. The superintendent accused Commissioner Keppel of despotic and illegal action.[23] It was widely rumored in newspapers and news periodicals that the mayor used his influence in Washington to cause a reversal of the delaying order. In any case, the Board of Education stated on October 5 that it would comply completely with Title III of the Civil Rights Act in regard to the apprentice training program, open enrolment for vocational and trade schools and district boundaries.

On December 13, 1965, the Board sent a progress report on these items, as it had agreed to do. On December 29, John Gardner, Secretary of the Department of Health, Education and Welfare, answered that the apprenticeship progress was acceptable, but that no other changes had been made, that only 12.8 percent of Chicago school children were in integrated schools, and that present system policies were preserving segregation or failing to reduce it where possible.

Secretary Gardner asked the Board to direct the superintendent to cooperate with his staff members who would arrive in Chicago in January.[24] The Sun Times commented on January 1, 1966, that the action of the Board had been evasive and confusing, inept and uncooperative—and had literally "invited federal interference." The Board voted that Secretary Gardner's men should deal only with the superintendent, not with the Board.

On February 9, Dr. Willis ordered principals not to answer questionnaires sent out from the Census Bureau at the request of the Office of Education.[25] On March 9, the Illinois Superintendent of Public Instruction briefly held up 7 million dollars due for work performed in Chicago in January under the federal program. On April 29, the Board voted to ask approval of the State Superintendent to use a small amount of the federal money for milk and cookies for the children in the underprivileged areas who were staying after school for remedial help under the federal program, as the superintendent had ruled the funds could not be used for this purpose. On May 15, 1966, it was announced that $7,280,000 in federal funds had been lost for Chicago schools, because the applications for their use had not been sent before the deadlines set.[26] (The other four of the five largest cities in the United States were spending the full allocations for their schools.) On June 23, 1966, the superintendent told the Board that it had approved five projects costing 2 million dollars in January, although no member of the Board recalled doing so. On July 14, the superintendent presented requests for spending 27 million dollars in federal funds for the coming year.[27] The law required Board approval on all such applications but the Board—not wishing to lose them—approved them without having time to read or consider them. The use of the federal funds was a frustrating experience for both Board and superintendent.

Conflict on a Fourth Term

The second conflict, over the re-election of the superintendent for a fourth term, reached a boiling point in 1965. His third four-year term was concluded at the end of that school year. Three of the city's major newspapers opposed his retention beyond that date. The Negro organizations had opposed his continuation in office during his whole third term. The Citizens Schools Committee and other organizations sent the Board lists of qualifications for the selection of a useful superintendent and urged careful Board consideration in making its decision. Dr. Willis seemed to have been a political liability to the city leadership and many people did not expect his re-election.

Strong voices, however, were raised to keep him. As early as December 11, 1964, his twelve top aides sent a letter to the Board of Education asking that he be retained in May. In January, 1965, large posters with Dr. Willis' picture and the caption, "Willis for Mayor," were (according to the press) distributed by the Kilbourn Organization, an outlying neighborhood group violently opposed to any change in community school policy. A month later a dinner was given for

Dr. Willis at which the main speakers were a congressman of Polish descent and a Negro minister, both outspoken opponents of school integration. On March 6, 1965, the Board attorney ruled that the superintendent could not be chosen until May, after newly appointed members had taken their places.[27] Both Dr. Willis and Dr. Hunt had been selected before May in the years when they were first chosen. The attorney had previously stated that a superintendent of schools in Chicago must live in Illinois for a year before being elected, as the office was mentioned in state law and was therefore an office of the state government. A Board member (who was a lawyer) laughed at that ruling, as it had never been applied to Dr. Willis, to any of his predecessors, or even to any other superintendent of schools in the state.

In March, also, a group of Willis supporters appeared at the City Hall wearing togas, to warn of the Ides of March. Eight thousand signatures to petitions collected by organizations opposing integration, asking to keep Dr. Willis in office, were presented at the City Hall. Vice President Murray said that the superintendent must be kept and paid a higher salary. When the Urban League urged the Board not to reappoint him, the superintendent commented that leaders in Negro organizations obviously had to stir up trouble to keep their own jobs. The Principals Club endorsed another term for him. An organized campaign within the schools to send letters to the Board urging his retention was sharply criticized in News and Sun Times editorials. On April 3, groups of anti-integrationists, wearing caps and gowns, distributed pro-Willis literature on State Street.[28] Buttons bearing his name began to appear on audience lapels at meetings of the Board. Fifty-thousand copies of an anonymous folder listing Dr. Willis' accomplishments were widely distributed.

The mayor said that he did not intervene in school matters. Some local political analysts felt that he might wish the superintendent to stay, in order to please the segregationists, since he could count on many Negro votes without making any concessions to them. In May the Republican-dominated State Senate passed a resolution giving high praise to Superintendent Willis. Organizations from the edges of the city sought a permit for a "Tribute to Willis" motorcade.

The majority of the Board decided to ask Dr. Willis whether he wished to remain. He refused to answer until he had been offered the position. On May 14, by a vote of 7 to 4, as a committee of the whole, the Board voted not to give him a new contract, although it had taken no steps to find anyone else. On May 28, after a discussion with him on "mending his ways," three members changed their votes and the Board gave him a four-year contract—with the understanding that he would not remain beyond his sixty-fifth birthday, which would occur in December, 1966.[29] (Willis was not actually required by the 1926 Miller Law to retire at 65, as all other members of the teaching force were.) A second boycott by Negro children in June followed his re-election.

The Board then appointed a committee of its members to search for a successor. The president of the American Association of School Administrators protested against such an inquiry while the superintendent was still in office, but the Board appointed three advisors to help them in their search and went ahead.[30] In May, 1966, Dr. Willis announced that he would resign as of the end of August instead of December, and that he would teach in a branch of Purdue University and offer consulting services for school systems. When he did leave in August, his supporters on the Board gave him an ovation, which was not, however, unanimous.

The conflicts within the Chicago schools have frequently been more dramatic than those in other urban centers. Certainly the necessity of finding new ways of interpreting the relationship of the school administration to the community which pays for the schools and trusts its children to them was never more dramatically illustrated than in Superintendent Willis' last years in Chicago. Such strains have indeed been evident in other large cities, although without open personal conflict with a superintendent. It was clear also that the role of the Board of Education—and its relation to the people of the city and to the city's political leadership—also stood in need of review in the light of changes taking place in the city and in the schools.

As it had been decades before, the whole city was again sharply divided on a significant school issue. At the beginning of the century the argument involved separate schools for the affluent and for the poorer children. For twenty years between 1927 and 1947 the dispute raged around the ability of school professionals to determine educational policy independent of the ends of an established political regime. Now the issue was whether the schools should accept some responsibility for desirable social change, or indeed, whether Negro children in the schools should have any consideration at all for their special problems. Many of the descendants of the European immigrants were displaying toward the new settlers some of the attitudes their own grandfathers had resented.

The part played by business leaders in the retention and final departure of Superintendent Willis was probably important. Many of them were his personal friends in the Commercial Club, of which he was a member, and in the Association of Commerce, of which he was an ex-officio director. He was accepted as one of them: after all he was acknowledged the competent director of a half-billion dollar business with thirty thousand employees, paid the third highest public administration salary in the country. Some of the undisputed leaders in the city's business world had signed their names to a telegram sent the Board and the press on October 7, 1963, to the following effect:

"The Chicago schools need leadership from a great superintendent and an effective Board of Education. We urge you to meet with Dr. Willis and reconcile your differences, to guarantee stability and progress in our educational system."

However, on July 12, 1965, after the superintendent's term had been extended until December, 1966, some of the same business leaders and others endorsed the following letter to the Board and to the press, urging prompt action in choosing his successor:

> "As business citizens of Chicago, we are conscious of our responsibility to share in the solving of problems which are ever present in a dynamic, changing city such as this.
>
> "The health and growth of our business depend on the health and growth of the city. The welfare and happiness of our employees and their families depend on the prospering of the concerns which employ them. Their jobs and their purchasing power depend increasingly on a good education for all.
>
> "It is your responsibility to insure that all children of Chicago receive educational opportunities of the highest order and we of the business community endorse this objective completely.
>
> "You have committed yourselves to the selection of a new general superintendent of schools to take office when the present general superintendent retires at the end of 1966.
>
> "It is imperative that the choice of his successor be completed promptly.
>
> "We have no doubt that any persons selected by you will possess pre-eminent professional qualifications. But we urge you at once to determine and make known your educational goals which should include:
>   1. The highest possible educational standards;
>   2. Special programs to assure such standards in areas where the quality of education has been substandard, and
>   3. Equal access to our schools by all races, with a positive policy and program to eliminate segregation.
>
> "Any candidates for selection as general superintendent should be questioned and considered in the light of such clearly stated objectives, based on research studies already available to the Board or commissioned by them in the future."

All of the signers of this letter were members of the Business Advisory Committee of the Chicago Urban League.

A graduate student at the University of Chicago interviewed some twenty of the signers of these communications. Their comments indicated a definite change in attitude between 1963 and 1965, based not so much on whatever their individual approaches were to the social issues involved, as on a growing conviction that the superintendent's rigidity toward those who differed with him no longer made him useful in a period of serious, growing conflict which had reached an impasse not resolvable as long as he remained.[31]

The mayor made no public comment on the disputes centering around the superintendent—other than the cliche (of any mayor trying to keep out of controversy) that he merely appointed the Board which was thereafter on its own. Several of the businessmen interviewed, formerly supporters of the mayor for re-election, took for granted that he had exerted influence directly or indirectly on the Board members who were loyal to him. The mayor did express his open anger at the marches and demonstrations of the Coordinating Council of Community Organizations in protest against Willis' return to office and the extension of his contract. He went so far as to say, on June 19, 1965, that they were financed by "outside sources for political reasons," and on June 30 that they were caused by "Communist influence."[32]

The conflict was clearly complicated by the personal attitudes of the general superintendent. In no other city had the superintendent taken so rigid a position that any disagreement with the decisions of the professional staff were in the same category as the misdeeds of Boards of Education which in the past had looted the treasury and sold teaching jobs. Dr. Willis was clearly convinced that he was defending the educational profession from encroachment by outsiders. He was also convinced that the good education he wanted for children had little to do with forces outside the schools. In 1966 he gave as the Horace Mann lecture at the University of Pittsburgh, "Social Problems in Public School Administration." Here he maintained that "Quality education is best summed up in the word, 'Professionalism.' Career teachers who are ever seeking more knowledge for themselves and higher skills in student relationships provide the basic ingredient for quality education."[33] "Social problems confronting the schools," he continued, "are but a reflection of the profound social problems, with all their attendant issues, confronting America today." To the child on West Madison or South State Street, and to his teacher, the social problems of the schools were not a reflection; they were the real thing, and must be confronted directly within the school itself, as in the community outside.

Superintendent Willis left a school system where bureaucratic control had become tightened and where isolation of the schools from the actual lives of children and people of the city had worsened. While this was happening in Chicago the top leadership in other large systems was making efforts—to be sure, some fumbling and some successful—toward making greater sense of school experiences to children and their parents. In Chicago, instead, there was increasing increasing conviction on the part of minority groups, that the education given their children was inferior and futile and that they were powerless to change it. This conviction intensified their mounting resentment toward the economic and political power structure of the city which had done so little to meet their demands and expectations in other areas. One caustic critic of the Willis era said the superintendent had created a situation in which "guaranteed rioters are being produced."[34]

It was clear that any new superintendent had to find better answers to many troubling questions than his predecessor, if there was to be peace in the city—already torn by Puerto Rican and Negro riots—and in the schools, already failing to help adequately so many of their children. At the meeting of the Board of Education in May, 1966, when Dr. Willis announced his resignation, they voted to ask James F. Redmond to be his successor.

Chapter 18

THE SCHOOL SYSTEM BEGINS TO CHANGE DIRECTION

The Chicago of 1966 was not the Chicago of 1953. The number of migrants from the South had approximately doubled. The demands for training of workers had increased. There had been gains for the migrants in housing, income, and status, but most of the rising expectations were not being fulfilled and the Negro community was increasingly resentful of its inability to help itself. The parents who had hoped for greater opportunity for their children in the good schools of a rich Northern city were disillusioned as they saw their children growing up with no more chance to be successful, self-respecting, and respected contributing workers—accepted as first-class citizens and equal human beings—than they had themselves. Instead they saw raw, overt race prejudice become more articulate and organized. As the segregated areas spread block by block, as industry moved away from the city, as the unemployed youth, ill-prepared by the schools for useful work, organized into too-well-advertised gangs (for want of anything else to do), resentment pervaded all economic layers of the Negro communities, acerbated by the open allegations of inherent Negro inferiority from those who opposed open occupancy laws and school integration.

Only a few voices in the city government were raised to protest this powerlessness. Most of the powerful in city government were still the descendants of earlier immigrants. In the spreading Negro sections political control was still exercised by white people who frequently did not even live in the area, or exercised by black people under obligation to whites.[1] Widely publicized civil rights and anti-poverty laws had had little effect on most of the city's poor, plagued by the depressing atmosphere of segregation, continuing unemployment, and the increasing failure of the school system to help its children escape the lower caste status—the fate of their people for three centuries.

Civil Rights Movement Shifts Emphases

From the schools, now, the people in the black areas wanted more than just seats in an uncrowded school, or instruction up to grade level in the basic skills. Nor would it be enough to have integrated experiences with white children. The goal of the black community now included a demand that their children—and all children—in whatever school, be taught directly that they were not inferior human beings—that it was a proud thing to be "black." They wanted their children—and all children—taught the contributions of black people to the history of this country and to the world. Many of them discarded the word "Negro" as having slave connotations, calling themselves "Afro-Americans" and "blacks" as, indeed, other migrant groups had been recognized by names indicating ethnicity or history. Since many white teachers did not understand these demands, or lacked the background to meet them (as in fact did many Negro teachers), the lament that experienced white teachers did not remain in black schools was replaced by insistence on the employment of black teachers for black children, particularly young men. Some insisted they wanted only black principals and more Negroes to be appointed to general administrative positions, if their children were to be motivated to seek success.[2]

In order to bring these results about, groups of Negro parents in many Northern cities were demanding to have something to say about the schools which their children attended. They indicated plainly that going hat-in-hand to school principals, to the downtown administration office, and to the Board of Education got them no results. In New York these reactions were even stronger than in Chicago. The New York City Urban League suggested that Harlem be made a completely separate school district, to be run by its own people.[3] The Chicago Urban League continued to work with the Chicago school system, trying to change it from within. This drive to help children escape hopeless blind alleys was the strongest single force in the demand for decentralization of the school system which by 1966 was now rising one way or another in every large city.

Background of New Superintendent

A "new breed" of school superintendent was developing. It recognized these factors in planning curriculum, administration, and buildings, and it considered its main responsibility the winning of public support for a more socially useful kind of public education, rather than managing the countless details of a vast organization. James F. Redmond was one of this "new breed."

Redmond had been through two hard schools, each at least as important to him as his doctorate from Columbia University. As Superintendent Hunt's close associate in Chicago he had seen the gradual reclaiming of an administrative staff, the rescuing of a teaching force, and the severance of corrupt business affiliations in the school system of a great city. He had seen the ethnic patterns and conflicts of that city, watched its municipal government in action, and knew the traditions and legal status of its Board of Education. The second hard school had been in the office of the superintendency in New Orleans. The federal court order to integrate the New Orleans schools had brought violent reactions from segregationists in the city and in the Louisiana legislature. No devices could be tried by segregationists in Chicago which would be new to him. When he left New Orleans he had spent some time as educational consultant for the management relations firm which the Chicago Board of Education had already employed to study its problems, and in such service had witnessed changes in school systems across the nation. Perhaps one of his greatest assets for Chicago schools at this moment in history was a quiet dignity with which he habitually met differences of opinion, and a habit of emphasizing issues and goals rather than his own personal importance.

When he arrived in October 1966, Superintendent Redmond found many things waiting to be done for which he had no opportunity to set a time-table. He followed Dr. Hunt's example in keeping most of the administrative staff he inherited. There was considerable criticism, however, because changes still evolved so slowly, and more importantly, because he retained as spokesmen for the new administration those whose past attitudes had been considered hostile by the black community and other groups. The election which chose the Chicago Teachers Union as bargaining agent in June, 1966, required the immediate negotiation of a contract, about which nothing had been done before the arrival of the new superintendent except the appointment of three Board members as a negotiating committee. Dr. Redmond offered to work with the Board committee in the negotiations and spent many days doing so. Whether or not he approved of the union's demands for deficit financing (by including in the budget salary raises dependent upon future tax referenda or additional state appropriations), he abided by the agreements and worked to get the additional funds.

Superintendent Redmond set about deepening and widening channels of communication with business and industrial leaders, with the Board of Education, with the legislature, and with as many elements in the city at large as he could reach. He had the support of some agencies to begin with. The Citizens Schools Committee gave a reception in his honor the week after his arrival, to which 1,500 people came to meet him. The Chicago Region of the P.T.A. found him ready to cooperate; many of its people had known him when he had been on the staff in Chicago. More significantly, within his first month in the city he explained the urgency of the schools' financial situation to the fiscally cautious Civic Federation—and won its approval of a tax referendum for 25 million dollars for buildings, to be voted in upcoming November elections. The referendum had been authorized by the legislature in 1961, but there never seemed to be a propitious time to put it on the ballot. A fellow participant in the integration disputes in New Orleans—who had integrated that city's parochial school system—was now archbishop and later cardinal in Chicago. Archbishop Cody also urged support of the referendum for the bond issue.

The reactions of leaders in the black community were cautious. When Dr. Redmond accepted the superintendency in May, 1966, he had said he wanted his door open to those who wished to talk to him. At the June national conference on Civil Rights in Washington he had met the leaders of Chicago Negro organizations and had invited their help.[4] When he arrived in Chicago he received parents' groups urging higher achievement levels in segregated schools and listened to them. The Chicago Urban League continued its steady flow of careful studies and recommendations. Dr. Redmond attended the League's annual meetings and the conference held by its committee of school principals. Analyses of his own reports and proposed plans by any groups were recognized and accepted.

The Coordinating Council of Community Organizations and the Chicago chapter of C.O.R.E., however, showed continued suspicion of Dr. Redmond's motives and hostility toward his plans. The C.C.C.O. urged that the referendum for building bonds be voted down in November, as there was no assurance the money would be spent to increase opportunity for black children. When desegregation plans were published in August, 1967, the C.C.C.O. urged the Office of Education to stop all federal grants to Chicago, because the proposed solutions were inadequate.[5] During the same period, C.O.R.E. urged that Negro communities be given the money for their schools and be allowed to spend it themselves.

In the adjustments made as his program developed, Dr. Redmond did increase the number of black administrators. He appointed two assistants to himself as superintendent, one of whom was black. Another was made a member of the Board of Examiners, which had been accused of bias. Following the recommendation of the Havighurst report, he divided the city into three areas each under a separate assistant superintendent: the superintendent for the West Side was black. There were some other appointments to lesser administrative positions. The curriculum department prepared high-school courses in Afro-American history which began in two schools in February, 1968. A revised high-school transfer plan resulted, with applications from 1,050 students, in some integration in all but two high schools. The achievement levels asked for by some Board members were published by districts.

The Board of Education and the superintendent worked without visible strain on either side. Dr. Redmond presented his proposals far enough ahead of Board deadlines for decision, so there was time for discussion. One member of the Board was quoted in the August 27, 1967, Sun Times as saying of Redmond, "He rarely gave directions. He just asked leading questions. He never forces his views on people, but he manages to get a census through dialogue." He took pains to credit his predecessor for the marked reduction in new school construction costs, and on some issues won the support of at least one of Dr. Willis' supporters on the Board. A Tribune Sunday Magazine article called him

"Redmond the Conciliator" and acknowledged his capacity for leadership. A Daily News article called him "Gentleman Jim" and asserted that he was

> ". . . in his own cautious way emerging from a cocoon of polite, good natured conciliation to a position of patient but persistent leadership. Under his low key stewardship, the massive school system is confronting with uncustomary candor the issues that threaten to overwhelm every big city school system, the issues of money, race and bureaucratic centralization. Victory may be years away, but it doesn't seem so hopelessly elusive as it once was."

When the proposal for a tax increase referendum was first considered by the Board, its president (a past president of the Chicago Real Estate Board) voted against it—but eventually he supported it too. The superintendent frequently asked members of the administrative staff to answer Board members' questions, rather than preparing all responses himself. When the Board failed to approve a proposal, he did not hesitate to bring it up again, as he did when the Board refused to allow public listing of school telephone numbers.

Studies as Basis for New Plans

At the end of the superintendent's first year his general plans became clearer. He had asked and obtained from the Board authorization for a series of studies on which recommendations for a building program could be constructed to achieve social and educational goals necessary for the welfare of the city. In December, 1966, the first of these appeared, *Design for the Future: A Recommended Long Range Educational Plan for Chicago, 1967-1971*, relying largely on data collected before his coming. The cost of implementing the plan was estimated at 750 million dollars. This report received considerable criticism as being vague and based on past planning.

In May, 1967, the management firm previously employed by the Board presented its *Organization Survey: Board of Education of the City of Chicago*. The report began with the significant statement that "The organization of the Chicago school system has evolved largely in response to factors unrelated to educational and administrative requirements"; it then commented on the wide variations in its responsibility and effectiveness during the administration of different superintendents. The report recommended specific changes in Board procedure. The Board should no longer spend at least 80 percent of its time reviewing detailed administrative and houskeeping items for which its members had no special competence, and should be free to deliberate on major issues of policy, to evaluate alternate courses of action, and to be responsive to the educational needs of the city. It stated that these were the reasons for the Board's existence and the areas in which it could be effective. For Board members the report urged staff assistance in analyzing reports and doing independent research. Committees of Board members should prepare reports ahead of time to facilitate Board discussion.

On the other hand, the management experts stated that the general superintendent should have enough additional assistance in the tremendous task of coordinating divisions of the huge school organization so that he could have time to work on major problems with the members of the Board. Developing plans for integration and for increasing the financial resources of the schools requires the full cooperation of the Board of Education and can not merely be a side issue for the superintendent, left over from his other duties. More areas of decision-making and administrative responsibility should be delegated to area and district superintendents, not merely to reduce the drain on the general superintendent's time, but more significantly, to tailor a school's services to the needs of a particular group of students at the local level, and to work with parents and community leaders in doing so. Services such as curriculum planning should be distributed among the districts. But a human relations department should be included at the top administrative level, as well as at lower levels. The top administrative staff should be able to operate as a team so that the general superintendent, again, might be relieved to work closer with the Board and to handle educational matters outside the school system. In February, 1968, the Board of Education voted to accept these recommendations and to use them as a basis for streamlining its activities.[6]

On August 23, 1967, the superintendent presented his next report, entitled *Increasing Desegregation of Facilities, Students and Vocational Education Programs,* generally spoken of as the "Redmond Report." It restated the Board's 1964 policies on integration and stabilization. Experts from ten universities, from the school staffs of three other large cities, from several national and local organizations, including the Chicago Urban League, representaties of Chicago teacher organizations, and of the Chicago school administrative staff, and also teachers below the administrative level served as consultants in drawing up its recommendations. The report made clear that it was an answer to the questions raised by the Office of Education in January, 1967, and that its preparation had been financed by a planning grant from the Office of Education. The introduction stated the basic assumption on which the report's recommendations were based:

> "Particularly are we concerned about racial and economic depriva-
> tion in our midst. . . . When a condition so pervasive in our city bears
> in upon the schools, the schools can not hope to solve the problem
> except in commitment and action shared by the community—a
> genuine shared commitment with all groups who can make common
> cause with the Board of Education for quality education for
> all. . . . We see an obligation to undertake a comprehensive educa-
> tional program aimed at reversing a pervasive social condition that

has become deeply rooted in our society... and seek educational pathways to a better society."[7]

The specific recommendations were in four areas: faculty assignment patterns, boundaries and student assignment patterns, vocational education, and "public understanding," summarized below.

Principals should have experience in lower socio-economic areas before assignment and should have continued in-service training after assignment. The rapid turnover of principals should be reconsidered. Teachers should be assigned so that the proportion of experienced teachers in any school was no less than the proportion of regularly certified teachers in the whole system (72 percent). The collective bargaining agreement signed by the Chicago Teachers Union has pledged that the union and the Board will "work cooperatively to develop and implement policies with respect to the assignment of teachers in such a manner as to lead to the achievement of representative social composition of school faculties and of a more equitable distribution of regularly assigned teachers." The current rule on transfers was that a teacher might ask to transfer to any school with not over 90 percent certified teachers (not 72 percent).

On the assignment of children to schools, the report recommended that groups of students should be assigned, with free transportation, from over-crowded fringe areas to schools less threatened by racial change, and that any student might be allowed to transfer from a ghetto school. Since large-scale integration can be attained only on a metropolitan basis, a Metropolitan Educational Council should be established to work toward solutions. Magnet schools offering special opportunities should be placed in non-residential areas, in integrated areas, in white peripheral areas and along the lake. There should be no further building in Negro areas except when no space is available in integrated areas.

The report asserted that, to achieve these results, the "anachronistic" system of school finance in Illinois must be revised, because its chief source, real estate, is no longer an accurate barometer of wealth. It pointed out that Illinois is the forty-third state in its collection of per capita state and local taxes, and almost at the bottom of the fifty states in its per capita support of public education in proportion to its income. The federal government, which collects two-thirds of all taxes, must also increase its share of the cost of education, now less than 10 percent.

The summary on vocational education was not encouraging. On the lack of admission of black students to apprentice programs using public school facilities—so sharply criticized by the U.S. Civil Rights Commission—there had been a little improvement. In the training courses the number of students had risen from 1 to 2 percent in one year, and of those entering for the first time, 7 percent were now black. Theoretically the vocational schools had open enrolment; but there had been no change in the actual fact that only two of the ten vocational schools were really integrated, and that more than two-thirds of the students in these schools were black, most of them in segregated schools.[8]

The authors recognized the difficulties involved in carrying out the report's recommendations. "Meaningful mitigation of segregation in a city as racially polarized as Chicago will require wholesale changes in public attitudes, changes which are not readily legislated." Giving this as a reason for improved communication facilities it goes on to say about Chicago, "No urban school district is confronted with greater challenges—integration of students and faculties, adequate financing, community attitudes, decentralized administrative services, employee morale, instructional improvement—and has been employing such primitive information services in pursuit of its objectives."[9] The report closes with a long list of questions, raised in each of the four areas, for further research.

Four months later, in December, 1967, the Real Estate Research Corporation presented the Board with a demographic study of city, school, and racial populations, on which projections for future school enrolment could be based. One significant factor in considering enrolment changes was the possibility of adjustments in the parochial school system which had for decades provided education for almost one-third of Chicago's children. The majority of these children were from homes whose forebears had come from Europe. Only a few of the new in-migrants were Catholic in faith. Parochial school enrolment had fallen as second and third generations moved to the suburbs. It was now only 27.9 percent of the total number of children in public and private schools; it was expected to fall still further by 1980, but to no more than 23.6 percent. There were 13,000 fewer parochial students in 1966 than in 1961. Forty-three percent of the white children in the city were now attending parochial schools, but only 7 percent of the black children.[10]

The parochial systems in all large cities had been under considerable stress. They were able to operate financially because the cost of teachers from religious orders was very much less than the cost of lay teachers. Because of the great increase in the total number of children enrolled and a decrease in the number of religious teachers available, however, the parochial schools were now employing large numbers of lay teachers who asked salaries comparable to those of their public school colleagues. Class sizes reluctantly had been raised. Any reduction in class size in the parochial schools, the deletion of some grades from the system (already effected in some cities), or a considerable extension of facilities "shared" with the public schools, would further decrease the proportion of city children in parochial schools, and add to those for whom the public schools must make some provision. Some lay leaders within the church were recommending that the whole parochial school system be discontinued entirely. These considerations were of particular importance to the Chicago public school system, as the Chicago archdiocese, which covers most of the metropolitan area, was the largest in the United States.

The study gave detailed information on the rapid changes taking place in the Austin, South Shore, and Harper High School areas, and stated flatly that any alterations aimed at stabilizing the racial balance in those areas must be made almost immediately if they were to have any effect.[11]

Proposals to Build New Kinds of Schools

In January, 1968, Dr. Donald Leu, one of the consultants on the long-range building plan, presented the first of a series of new reports, entitled, *A Feasibility Study of the "Cultural-Educational Park" for Chicago.* Dr. Leu outlined a thirty-year plan for replacing obsolescent school buildings and for developing a new concept of educational parks for the city intended to improve instruction and increase integration. An educational park was defined as

> "A clustering on one site of large groups of wide age differences and varying socio-ethnic and religous backgrounds. Student groups are decentralized within the total site, with shared use of specialized staffs, programs, support services and facilities. [Such centers could provide] cultural, recreational and social services to public, private and parochial school students and coordinate these programs with other public service institutions (parks, libraries, museums, housing, higher education, social services, health, highways, etc.)"

The report pointed out the advantages of the neighborhood school concept and the disadvantages of the educational parks as well as their advantages, but, noting a considerable number of other cities now planning such groups of schools, recommended the construction of the parks. As the basis for its approval of the new idea, the report continued:

> "The transition of our society from a simple, rural, family centered structure to an urban, impersonalized, highly complex configuration has resulted in expanding the schools' role from one of an agency responsible for the impartation of factual knowledge to that of an all-encompassing multi-purpose, multi-faceted agency. The evolution of the school as the agency to serve from the cradle to the grave and to participate in resolving the social issues of the present and the future strongly indicates a change in the concept of the school."

The report further made explicit the importance of resolving the issue of minority group status within the schools and within the city.

> "If we believe that our system of democracy can not succeed unless means are found to provide successfully integrating experiences for all; if we believe that segregation is deteriorating and dangerous to the fabric of our democratic society, then we must do everything within our means to break down existing barriers to desegregation and to encourage participation by all segments of our society. The consultants believe that the cultural educational park is one of the

many educational tools that may be employed to help reverse the existing trend toward segregation within our metropolitan school systems."[12]

In May, 1968, a second section of the Real Estate Research Report supplemented Dr. Leu's second report, and urged that the highest priority be given to immediate improvements in ghetto schools—whose shortcomings were the result of environmental deficiencies for which the long-range solution is integration. For current action, it was recommended that schools be non-graded so that pupils could progress at their own rate, that they be equipped with "schomes" (a model-city nursery school concept combining features of school and home) to accept children at the age of three, that there be special teacher training to deal with inner-city culture, that the curriculum be geared to increase the communication skills of inner-city children, and that the ghetto community be involved in curriculum changes and administration for its schools. The estimated cost of putting such plans into effect in twenty years was 1 billion dollars.[13] This estimate was presented by Dr. Redmond to the subcommittee on urban education of the State School Problems Commission on June 15, 1968, with a detailed list of the needs that must be met.

All of these reports were duly noted in the public press. Only one, *Increasing Desegregation of Faculties,* attracted wide and open opposition, although the same assumptions underlay all of them. On August 23, 1967, the Board of Education approved the "Redmond Report" in principle.[14] The press gave it wide coverage for some weeks. For fifty days the Daily News each day summarized one important recommendation made in the report, and urged editorially that the plan be tried. On August 25, its editorial said it was time to end the wavering which had characterized the school system in the recent past, and now applauded the superintendent and Board for their courageous action:

> "The implementation of the plan [said the News] will require courage on the part of everyone concerned, white and Negro community leaders, teachers, parents, the children themselves. But the point to remember is that when change is inevitable, it is essential to face it and to try to shape it to constructive ends, rather than allow unplanned change to destroy a city."

The Sun Times carried editorials praising the plan, defending it against its detractors, and calling attention to the current, peaceful, successful integration of all the elementary schools in adjacent Evanston. It declared the Redmond plan modest in comparison with similar efforts in other large cities, and urged that Chicago take the lead in such innovations, even if it cost twice the money now being spent on schools. On August 25, the Sun Times called the new plan an educational Burnham plan for Chicago in keeping with the demands of modern living, and included the completion of the Redmond plan as an essential part of the paper's platform for Chicago. The American gave less space but in the main showed approval. Only the Tribune's news coverage and editorials indicated open disapproval. On August 24, a Tribune editorial headed "Racial Mixing in the Schools," denounced the plan as "official Washington doctrine," and added, "Many things ought to be done to improve Chicago schools. We fear, however, that nothing will be done as long as all the authorities are obsessed by the notion that improvement in the schools requires racial mixing." The Tribune gave more space than the other papers to news on the activities of opponents of the plan.

Opposition to Integration Proposals

Objections to the Redmond Report came from two sharply different groups. On September 9, the spokesman for the Coordinating Council of Community Organizations attacked the plan as racist and inadequate, and sent a request to Washington that further federal funds be withheld from Chicago schools. Several organizations which had belonged to the C.C.C.O. took issue with the C.C.C.O. and stated publicly their support of the plan. Dr. Robert J. Havighurst made the front pages with a statement that the C.C.C.O. attack was completely unjustified.[15] The Chicago Defender said there was now no retreat; Dr. Redmond would integrate the schools.

The mayor called the plan bold and imaginative. but did not commit himself in support of it.[16]

But the groups which had so earnestly wished the retention of Dr. Willis, and which had so heartily supported his approval of the neighborhood school, wasted no time to make their displeasure known. On August 27, the Tribune gave considerable space to a protest motorcade displaying signs which read, "Redmond and Cody Must Go." Cardinal Cody had urged integration in the parochial school system, taking in suburban as well as city areas, and Bishop McManus, head of the 220,000-student parochial school system and the Catholic Interracial Council had also praised the Redmond plan. Many of the protesting groups from the outlying areas of the city were members of the Roman Catholic church, as their ancestors had been.

On September 20, three of the dissident organizations, in an effort to block implementation of the plan, filed a suit which was dismissed. Members of the state legislature from these areas threatened to get legislation passed to stop any steps toward integration in the schools, and, if the Board of Education continued its present course, to abolish the Board and require the election of a new one. These neighborhood and taxpayer groups claimed they could and would defeat any referenda on bond issues for new school buildings or on tax rate increases.[17] (One tax rate increase for 15 cents had been approved by a referendum in February, 1967, and another was being considered.)

Work on the plans proceeded, however. On December 6, the fiscal committee of the Board approved the long-range building program and debated whether to ask for a referendum vote on the 120-million-dollar bond issue already authorized by the legislature, or on the 15-cent tax increase. On December 12, the Chicago Urban League proposed a system of thirty-two educational parks for a long-range building program. On December 20, the federal government agreed to sell the lake-front site of an obsolete hospital for the building of a magnet school. On December 27, the superintendent presented to the Board two relatively small plans to implement recommendations for integration in two of the rapidly changing areas, Austin and South Shore. Some 500 Negro children in the Austin area would be bused from presently integrated, but overcrowded, schools to those with empty seats in outlying—stable—white areas. On the South Shore a comparable number of white and Negro children would be transported by bus to equalize racial percentages. These were areas where the Real Estate Research study had said action must be taken immediately if it were to have any influence on stabilizing integrated communities and on stemming the flight to the suburbs. The Board voted to approve these transfer plans, President Whiston and Vice President Murray dissenting.[18] The Board also voted to approve an application for federal money to fund "Operation Wingspread," a proposal for an eventual city-suburban interchange of more than 3,000 students, and another federal request for an experimental program in segregated schools in Woodlawn, worked out jointly by the University of Chicago and T.W.O., the Woodlawn Organization. The Daily News commented that at last the school system had reached the action stage and deserved support in so doing.

Dissidents Invade Board Meeting

By January 8, the opposition had begun to gather steam. A Northwest-side organization called a meeting to protest the transfers, attended by some thousand persons, including a congressman and seven members of the legislature —all of whom spoke against bringing the Negro children into their area. One alderman offered to pay $1,500 for buses to carry objectors to the Board of Education meeting during the discussions.[19] Edward Vrdyolak, a South East Side attorney, and Alderman Aiello of Austin filed a suit to stop the transfers on the ground that the integration plans had been formulated at secret, illegal meetings to which the public was denied admission. The attorney (who became a candidate for ward committeeman), implied the mayor was waiting for some sign of protest.

On January 10, fifteen-hundred people appeared at the Board rooms, some of them seven hours before the scheduled meeting, literally screaming "allegiance to the neighborhood school." The confrontation that day was the most crowded and emotional session ever witnessed at a Board of Education meeting in Chicago. The Board, six to four, voted to defer action until February 28 rather than to postpone it indefinitely, as suggested by President Whiston.

Superintendent Redmond recommended deferral until public hearings took place. After the meeting fifteen elected officials met with the Board and reiterated the threats of four months before to defeat the referenda and to make the Board elective; they restated their opposition to increased state aid for schools unless the busing plans were shelved immediately.[20]

At the public hearings set by the Board, a wide variety of ideas were expressed for some areas, but only blind opposition in others. In the South Shore area, those who approved of busing to stabilize the community felt the plan too small to serve its purpose, and urged revamping. At a hearing of city-wide organizations held at the new Jones High School, there were statements of support from the Citizens Schools Committee, the Chicago League of Women Voters, the Anti-Defamation League, the Church Federation of Greater Chicago, the Independent Voters of Illinois, and from the Chicago Region of the P.T.A. The latter organization, to which all local P.T.A.'s belong, in January had voted down two-to-one a motion to oppose the busing plan, but representatives of seventeen local P.T.A.'s appeared at this hearing to oppose it.

The meeting in Austin approved of the plan for its area, except that objections were made to one-way compulsory transfers for Negro children only. A representative from one of the crowded schools, from which transfers were to be made, said he could not see why public hearings allowed the North West Side people to determine what was good for all the children of the city.

At the large meetings on the North West Side, speakers violently railed against the plan; the few individuals who raised lone voices in its defense were booed down. Petitions claiming 60,000 signatures were presented at the February 19 meeting of the Board. One state representative begged that integration not begin with "innocent children." The president of the Polish Home Owners' Council said busing would cause "population pollution." The chairman of the Greater Northwest Civic Association, at a Sunday rally of his organization, urged citizens to withhold the payment of taxes, to plan secession of the North West Side to the suburbs, to get the superintendent fired, and to demand that all school plans be submitted for the approval of citizens.[21]

On February 24, the Illinois Advisory Committee to the U.S. Commission on Civil Rights urged the Chicago Board of Education to put the busing plan into effect immediately. A few days later the Chicago Urban League and the Chicago Teachers Union issued statements in support of the busing plans. Also making their support public were the Leadership Council for Metropolitan Open Communities, the Chicago Conference on Religion and Race, and the United Auto Workers. Cardinal Cody sent a pastoral letter to be read in churches on the urgent necessity of such busing programs for both public and parochial schools. Four executives of the Presbytery of Chicago issued a release in support of the busing program.

The Board met on February 28. By a five-to-five vote they failed to approve the Austin transfer plan and by a vote of nine-to-one they asked the Superintendent to revise the South Shore plan. The director of the Urban

THE CHICAGO SCHOOLS

League lamented that the Board's rejection of such small plans makes Negroes lose hope that anything could be done about the schools. The Sun Times accused the Board of lacking backbone and suggested a dose of vitamins. Dr. Philip Hauser said that "The hysteria of first and second generation immigrants is not to be confused with a majority of opinion in Chicago. . . . Individual neighborhoods do not have the right to abrogate the Constitution of the United States." The head of "Operation Crescent," a segregationist organization, an independent candidate for governor, claimed the Board's action was due to Democratic fears of losing the 1968 elections. The superintendent was quoted in the press as saying quietly, "I do not feel that the Board has stopped me from using any or every way to relieve overcrowding and implement our desegregation report." On March 1, the *Report of the National Commission on Civil Disorders*, commonly known as the Kerner Report, became public. It recommended school integration and specifically reproved Chicago whites of European descent for saying "If my father made it, why can't they?" when their fathers would not have "made it" in today's world, either.[22]

On March 2, the president of the Board called a special meeting for March 4. At this meeting the Austin plan was changed by allowing Negro parents the choice as to whether their children should be transferred, instead of marking off areas from which children would be transferred automatically. The revised plan was approved by a vote of eight to one. Vice President Murray stated that he was still firmly opposed to busing, and was voting "reluctantly" for a "minor plan."[23] Superintendent Redmond quoted the Kerner Report to the effect that the issue was "assimilation of black and white in an America which belongs to both, by no merit of either."

The North West Side organizations thereupon staged a boycott which kept 75 percent of the children in the receiving schools at home for two days. Meeting in Slowik Hall on North Milwaukee Avenue, they laid plans to get parochial school children in the area to transfer to public schools to fill up the empty seats. Leaflets were distributed, attacking the policies of the Church since the second Vatican Council, and urging readers to "Save the last bastion of the Republic, what is left, the neighborhood school." There were no noticeable transfers from the parochial schools, however, and the 1,700 seats remained empty.[24]

Some of the parents of Negro children in the two overcrowded schools were understandably loath to send their children into neighborhoods where according to newspapers, there was talk of overturning buses and keeping children out by violent means. But 296 signed up for immediate busing. Voluntary transfers increased gradually until they approximated the number originally set. The boycott ceased. For a little while hostile parents jeered the Negro children as they alighted from buses, but that ceased also. The handful of children who had transferred to the far South West Side Mt. Greenwood School under a previous transfer plan continued to attend in spite of organized picketing by hostile persons, some of whom did not even live in the neighborhood.[25]

There remained, however, the threats made by the legislators of reprisal by state law. When the recessed session of the 1967 legislature reconvened in January, 1968, bills were introduced into both houses to forbid busing. The House promptly voted down the resolution presented to it, and the Senate Education Committee buried its bills on the subject in a subcommittee, although 250 opponents of busing appeared in Springfield. Their case was weakened in May, 1968, when the Illinois Supreme Court reversed itself and declared the Armstrong law constitutional. In doing so, the Court admitted that the Illinois Constitution did permit state action to reduce and eventually to eliminate "de facto" segregation in the schools.[26] When the recessed session convened again in June, no proponents appeared at the anti-busing legislation hearing, while President Whiston of the Board of Education and the president of the Chicago Teachers Union spoke against it, as did representatives of the League of Women Voters and the two state-wide teachers' organizations. Its sponsor, Senator Krasowski, asked for postponement and managed to get it referred to the subcommittee, threatening to hold hearings every week during the summer. A critic of the senator suggested that the hearings would be a part of the senator's campaign for Congress and would stop after November. The House of Representatives briskly—by a two-to-one vote—defeated three anti-busing bills and the bill to elect the Board of Education of Chicago. The legislators clearly had been powerless to carry out their threats.[27]

On June 13 the Board voted to allow Negro students at Austin High School to transfer to other less crowded schools with their bus fare paid. On June 18 in his presentation to the subcommittee on urban problems of the State School Problems Commission, Dr. Redmond stated that he hoped to transfer children from some thirty integrated, overcrowded schools to the remaining empty seats on the periphery of the city, busing a total of some 10,000 children—about two percent of the total enrolment—in order to stabilize changing communities and to integrate others. On July 10, the Board approved a revised plan for the South Shore area in which some 300 children would attend two new small "magnet schools," with smaller classes than other schools and special services and opportunities. The superintendent announced that plans were being drawn for a much larger magnet school in the area. (On June 11 the referendum, which the segregationist groups had threatened to defeat, passed with a 52 percent majority vote; the full support given it in black areas negated the efforts to defeat it in the outlying neighborhoods.)

Business Aid on School Finance

One reason for the success of the referendum was the effort of the Better Schools Committee, made up of businessmen, bankers, and other city leaders, who had been asked by the Board in January to find additional sources of revenue for the schools. A subcommittee of this group, headed by former Board of Education President Roddewig, had recommended in March that the Board

ask the Chicago Public Buildings Commission for a grant of 140 million dollars
for school buildings, instead of asking for a referendum vote to approve the 120
million dollar bond issue authorized by the legislature. The Public Building
Commission was authorized to sell bonds to pay for the construction of public
buildings for local governments in Chicago. The Commission would finance the
construction of buildings and the user would pay rent until the bonds were paid
off. The mayor is chairman of the Commission. On March 27, the Board of
Education accepted this plan for financing buildings and postponed action
indefinitely on the referendum for a separate school bond issue. The city council
approved the use of the Commission's funds for school buildings on April 18.
The Board thereupon decided to ask for a referendum for another 15 cent tax
increase at the June 11 election. The Better Schools Committee took over the
publicity to win support for this tax increase; among the methods used was an
urgent reminder in the June bill received by all city telephone subscribers of
reasons to vote for the 15-cent tax increase. Powerful leaders in the economic
life of the city were now assuming some positive responsibility for the city's
schools.

Method of Choosing Board Members an Issue Again

When the Booz, Allen and Hamilton management survey of Board procedures
commented that the Chicago school system had evolved largely in response to
factors unrelated to educational or administrative requirements, they might well
have included one significant phase they omitted—the selection of the members
of the Board of Education.

As cities had grown from small towns, where neighbors planned their little
schools, little change took place in the pious words used to describe such
services, and except in the very large cities little change resulted in the New
England township method of electing those who performed them. But in the
great cities the power over vast expenditures for contracts, and over thousands
of jobs useful in perpetuating partisan control, brought on a long era of open
exploitation of school resources for purposes not even remotely concerned with
the education of children. Whether to facilitate such exploitation or to avoid
huge campaign expenses for an unpaid office, all but two of the large cities had
for decades chosen Board of Education members by appointment. In a city with a
million voters, any candidate for election as a member of the Board of
Education must either be wealthy enough to pay for a campaign to convince the
large electorate of his qualifications, or he must put himself under obligation
either to an organized political party or to some other partisan agency for its
financial support. Clearly neither method would guarantee that Board members
would be thoughtful, independent citizens, really representative of the interests
of all the children and all the people of the entire city. If a city Board of
Education is to be appointed, on the other hand, the mayor is in the best

position, since he is the only individual elected by the whole city, although large cities in Pennsylvania had their Boards appointed by state judges for many years.

But it had been the mayors who had appointed the Chicago Boards which so grossly had exploited children in the nineteenth century and the early years of the twentieth. Since this era of crass and open exploitation lasted longer in Chicago than in any other large city in the United States, those who changed it in 1946 wanted to provide safeguards against its recurrence. The use of a citizen advisory committee to recommend possible choices for Board members to the mayor was considered this kind of insurance. To be sure they were not merely a hand-picked "mouthpiece" for a mayor, the members of the advisory committee on school Board nominations were not to be chosen as individuals by the mayor himself. Instead, responsible organizations were invited to choose their own representatives to share in its deliberations. In 1961 New York City had adopted this plan for recommending school Board nominations for the mayor's consideration, according to a method fixed by state law. In 1965 Philadelphia, using its new Home Rule powers, had set up a similar law by city ordinance.

The committee of college presidents headed by Henry Heald in 1946 had outlined the general plan for the advisory commission. It prepared a list of responsible organizations to be invited to send representatives, already noted in Chpater 14, with a further suggestion as to the kinds of interests with which such organizations should be concerned. Mayor Kelly's immediate inclusion of one public and five private universities, and of the Illinois Catholic Woman's Club, did not really follow the original recommendation.

Theoretically each representative was to speak from the experience and research of the organization he represented. But from the beginning some members did not accept this interpretation of their role, and assumed they were invited as individuals—and expected reappointment year after year. The chairman was supposed to be chosen by the group each year, but for many years one representative, also an appointed public official, assumed re-election. The commission was not a continuing body. Each year's group might recommend procedures to the next group, which was under no obligation to follow such recommendations. However, there were actually few changes in the personnel of the commission from year to year. It became established tradition that no priest, minister, or rabbi should be recommended to the mayor. The old ethnic categories of Board members, whereby there was always at least one Italian, one German, one Irishman, one Czech, one Pole, one Jew, and one Scandinavian on the Board did not entirely disappear, but they were partly replaced, tacitly, by categories of business, labor, and women, including a P.T.A. parent. But the old ethnic categories were not completely gone. If a Negro or a Jew or a Pole left the Board he was very likely to be replaced by another. A sitting Board member was usually renominated if he wished to be.

Mayor Kennelly added three agencies to the list of organizations. Mayor Daley included Roosevelt University, and the Cook County Physicians Association and the Cook County Bar Association (both segregated Negro groups), when he was urged to include the Chicago Urban League, which came under the original list. Finally the Urban League was asked to send a representative in 1967. If the mayor did not wish an organization which had served one year to serve the next, he simply did not invite it. The Illinois Catholic Woman's Club and the Welfare Council thus disappeared; and in 1968, the Cook County Physicians' Association and two of the original list, the Chicago Medical Society and the Chicago Technical Societies Council, were not invited.

Gradually the procedure became a little more efficient. At the urging of the Citizens Schools Committee representative, forms were prepared on which were entered the qualifications of persons whose names were suggested for consideration. The commission in the last four years had interviewed those persons whom they considered most likely to be acceptable. At times the mayor had not published the names of those recommended to him; at other times he gave them to the press.

Since Mayor Kennelly was the "reform candidate," it was expected that he would abide by recommendations of the commission which was so important a part of the reform. When Mayor Daley had first been a candidate for mayor, speaking at the annual meeting of the Citizens Schools Committee in 1955, he promised: "I have stated repeatedly that I will maintain the present screening committee for selection of members of the Board of Education and I pledge that I will observe their recommendations, regardless of any political or personal consideration." At a similar meeting in 1959 a representative of the mayor read the identical speech on schools he had made in 1955, containing the same pledge. He was not asked to put it in writing again in 1963 and 1967.

The system really never quite worked as planned. When the term of the pre-1946 vice president of the Board expired, the advisory commission voted not to recommend his reappointment. He had been a party to all of the sins of the Kelly Board and had refused to resign as he had been asked to do. But he was a large contributor to party coffers and had great influence in a politically powerful ethnic bloc whose support was essential to party success. The "reform mayor" reappointed him. Once when the C.I.O. notified Mayor Daley of its choice for a representative, the mayor himself chose another C.I.O. representative. Twice after the list recommended to the mayor's consideration had been sent to him, other names were added at his suggestion, according to a member of the commission interviewed by the Citizens Schools Committee.[28]

The year 1968 was crucial both for the mayor and the general superintendent of schools. Since there had been two resignations, there were five positions to be filled, and their appointment could destroy or greatly advance the superintendent's program. The mayor, on the other hand, was now finding this same program a threat to the control of the city's unity by his political organization—control which he could justify as necessary to continue and advance his program of economic progress in a declining city. Since 1931 all mayors of Chicago have been Democrats. With one exception, no Republican candidate since Thompson has tried to get the black vote. As candidates of the Democratic party have been sure of the large black vote, they have tended to try to please other ethnic groups with promises not always acceptable to black neighborhoods.

On the issue of busing, opposition candidates for Congress and the state legislature were now openly making converts. The outlying communities claimed they had no voice on the Board of Education. For months the city had been in an uproar on busing. It was quite clear that the school position on integration was likewise a major political issue for municipal and state government representatives as well, and simply could not and would not be ignored as a matter of practical politics.

In March, 1968, the mayor invited the six universities and eleven organizations to send representatives to the advisory commission. The majority of the 1968 commission were clearly of the mind that Superintendent Redmond should not be hamstrung by a Board which would not give a fair trial to his program. They did not feel that sitting members should be reappointed if they had not supported that program. Moreover they thought there should be new and vigorous leadership on the Board, and recommended to the next year's commission that no one over seventy years of age should be considered. Then they acted on their own advice, and a majority of the commission voted not to recommend for reappointment the president and vice president of the Board, one of whom was 73 and the other 76. Both had been strong supporters of Dr. Willis, had "reluctantly" (according to the press) supported some of Dr. Redmond's proposals, and had "caved in" when opposition arose. Both had said they wished to continue on the Board. The commission sent the names of eleven other persons to the mayor from which he was to choose five.

The mayor was in a serious quandary—and he had plenty of other problems without this one. The riot which broke out after the assassination of Martin Luther King had burned down buildings for almost a mile along West Madison Street. The chairman of the nominating commission, generally assumed to be the spokesman for the mayor, had publicly ridiculed the members of the commission—to their justified indignation. He had previously criticized the "leadership of the Board" in the press, although he had then voted to retain the president and vice president on the Board. It seemed possible that the mayor had wanted them there as a not too dangerous sop to the opponents of Dr. Redmond's plans. Moreover the mayor had a particular problem in the case of the vice president, who was an official of the Chicago Federation of Labor (one of the strongest bases of support for the mayor), and who was also head of the Building Trades Council and a long-time official of the International Brotherhood of Electrical Workers. Several members of his family had held political offices. These aspects were the "personal and political considerations" he had once promised to ignore.

Mayor Daley chose to recommend to the council only two persons on the long list sent to him. One was Warren Bacon, an able and contributing Negro Board member who had been a frank and outspoken opponent of Dr. Willis and was keenly interested in developing new approaches. The other had a good civic record and a name indicating East European ancestry. Then—breaking his long-time pledge—he appointed three members to the Board who had not been recommended by the advisory commission. One did not represent a serious infraction of his pledge: she was secretary of the Urban League. and had been proposed by the commission in 1967. (She was not considered in 1968 because the mayor had appointed her to the new Junior College Board in June, 1967; Daley had been urged either to ask the present advisory commission for suggestions for that Board, or to organize a new commission for those appointments. He had done neither, appointing the members of the Board directly.) The other two appointees were the president and vice president of the Board who had been refused approval by the commission. The council approved the five names sent by the mayor, over the strong opposition of a few aldermen—particularly the black aldermen from middle class areas. The two Board officers were then reelected by the Board to their former positions. Shortly thereafter, the Board president appeared at the State School Problems Commission, of which he had been made a member by the governor—from which he had been conspicuously absent for some time—and spoke in opposition to anti-busing bills at the legislative hearing previously mentioned.

From the point of view of the mayor, these appointments were a wise compromise. There were now at least five on the Board who could be counted upon to support Dr. Redmond's programs. The appointment of those who had been in agreement with Dr. Willis was a concession to the opponents of integration. But there were now two Board members serving five-year terms who were more than 75 years of age and one other more than 70. One of these had voted consistently against every proposal aimed at integration and another was still convinced that the neighborhood school was the best policy and should never be changed. Moreover, the whole institution of the advisory nominating commission was in a shambles. Unless there were some resolution of its status before March of 1969, there would be great difficulty in getting responsible organizations to participate in it. The carefully prepared recommendations made by the Citizens Schools Committee and the City Club in 1964 for its reconstitution had been presented to the mayor but had never been given consideration. But the mayor could no longer retreat behind the cliché that he just took the advice of the nominations commission and had nothing to do with the Board thereafter. Whatever stormy issues developed in the Board of Education—and it was inevitable that there be some—he was now publicly and clearly directly responsible. It was quite clear that the schools of Chicago still did not operate in a sterile antiseptic vacuum where professionals, undisturbed by the turmoil outside, make decisions which are not to be questioned.

Obstacles to Change

By the end of his second year in office, Superintendent Redmond had laid before the people of Chicago a comprehensive program which not only offered to the children of the city steadily increasing opportunity, but to the city itself a major tool in solving some of the problems of its people. He was faced, however, with a Board of Education whose leadership could not be counted upon to implement this program, and of whom only a minority gave it solid support. One major financial problem had been solved, at least for a time, by the grant of 140 millions from the Public Buildings Commission to construct the kind of school buildings essential to the plans; but funds were simply not available to reduce class size, to continue increasing salaries in competition with other cities, to humanize the unwieldy school administration by breaking it into smaller units, and to put enthusiastic life into the whole fixed educational process. The local property tax and Illinois' niggardly state aid for schools—only half the average contribution of the fifty states—simply did not provide enough. Meanwhile, the teachers and the black communities were growing increasingly restive because "Nothing was happening" in spite of plans on paper.

Certainly there was no answer to the question asked by the superintendent in his 1968 Report, "How do you stir a city, Board members, citizens, students" to the "solution of problems which the cynic says are insoluble?"

Chapter 19

LACK OF MONEY AND OF FULL
BOARD SUPPORT HINDERS PROGRESS

School plans were not just on paper. Blueprints were growing for twenty new buildings to implement the ideas in the piles of long reports. Some plans were reaching the brick and mortar stage. Five hundred children were participating in an integrated, two-way exchange with seven suburban schools. In 1968 the highly successful special summer schools had enrolled more than 60,000. Two hundred and fifty thousand children shared in some summer-school activity. Experiments in Afro-American history in four high schools in early 1968 were followed by 114 classes in 36 high schools in September, in all high schools predominantly black and in some that were 20 percent or less black. Six teachers were helping Spanish-speaking high-school students with English. There were more teacher aides to free teachers to help children. Camp programs, both in winter and summer, were provided from federal funds. Two thousand teachers participated in summer in-service training. Gifted pupils in some inter-city areas were given special opportunities. There was a summer program for children with language difficulties. Summer head start programs enrolled 21,300 pre-schoolers. Fifty-two classes for teachers, dealing with many aspects of human relations, opened in September, 1968. Two small integrated "magnet schools" drew children from several areas. Five hundred elementary children in Englewood were aided in reaching their potential by a special federal grant. Three hundred members of the Chicago Teachers Corps Consortium, supported by federal funds, were at work in classrooms learning how best to help city children.[1]

But there were almost 600,000 children all together. To parents and other citizens impatient with present conditions and results, any such efforts seemed only a drop in a very large bucket. There was no further money from any source, either for new projects or simply to relieve the daily frustrations of all the

361

teachers, students, and parents who were sure the schools could do better. Class size in some suddenly overcrowded small buildings still reached 50, and many rooms contained far over the average of 34. At least 18,000 seriously emotionally disturbed children needed special care, both for their own sakes and for the welfare of other children. Such care at a minimum costs twice as much as instruction in regular classrooms, and there was money to help only a few hundred. Almost all the high schools had more students than seats, but the inner-city segregated high schools were the most crowded; the shifts of population within the city, furthermore, were making rapid changes in the ethnic and economic levels of their students. To most people in and out of the school system there were few visible, dramatic signs of constructive change in spite of all the plans and projections.

The racial count reported on November 11, 1968, showed 87.4 percent of all children in Chicago to be attending schools still 90 percent black or white. The needs of the Spanish-speaking 4 percent were certainly not being met. Only 8.8 percent of elementary school children were in integrated schools in spite of the busing program, and only 31.7 percent of the high-school students in spite of opportunities for transfers. There had been no measurable increase in integration since the publication of the Hauser and Havighurst reports in 1964. There were fewer vacant rooms of any kind, and higher class sizes in the inner-city schools than in most of the outlying areas, in spite of efforts to reduce the discrepancies. Extra-curricular activities in each high school received an allocation of no more than $8,000 for a year, although some suburban high schools spent as much as three times that amount on athletics alone. Average reading levels of first-year high-school students in many segregated high schools were too low for standard high-school work. Dropouts were increasing rather than decreasing. The unemployment rate of non-white teenagers was 32 percent. The programs open to dropouts through the school system and other agencies were limited. Street gangs flourished, whether parents approved of them or not.

Student Demands on Civil Rights

Many of the students in the segregated high schools and their parents saw no indication of any immediate change in the drift toward a frustrating dead end. For a decade the demand from the black communities had been for open housing and integrated education. When the dust of battle over efforts to put the "Redmond Plan" into effect settled, it was clear to everyone concerned that massive integration was simply not going to take place for some time. Moreover, the tone, temper, and direction of the whole civil rights movement was shifting. A rising spirit of black pride, black independence, and black self reliance tended to regard integration as certainly nothing to beg for—perhaps something that was not wanted at all. Black student demands in most of the nation's great universities for curricula of greater relevancy to their experience, to their needs, and to their day and age was being reinforced by even larger numbers of white students who wanted some share in planning *their* own higher education. The violent deaths of Martin Luther King and Robert Kennedy, who represented to many young people leadership against injustice and oppression, discouraged reliance on slow, conventional methods of social change. The announcement of the plan to elect local school boards in New York City received nation-wide attention. Some supporters of the plan justified it on the assumption that discrimination against schools in black communities was based on a deliberate plan to keep black people down, and prevent them from becoming first-class citizens. This was an expression of a general attitude appearing also in Chicago ghettos.[2]

All these factors of social change were not lost on high-school students in Chicago and elsewhere. The ghetto continued to spread, not so much because of increasing migration from the south, but because of displacement of low-income populations by urban renewal and highways. Black children were becoming the majority in some recently all-white high schools. In some of these schools the principals and teachers were not always sensitive either to the children's needs or to the shift in attitudes of the black parents. Particularly in the rapidly changing high schools with few black teachers, a tinder box of unresolved grievances and resentment was accumulating. Insistence upon "consent of the governed," and demand for some share in determining the kind of people and methods of instruction to which students were expected to conform—so forcefully expressed by rebellious minorities on college campuses—was heightened within the ghetto by a sense of the powerlessness of the whole black community to make any real decisions as to its own fate on any issue. A few sparks fanned by militants ignited an emotional conflagration in the high schools in October 1968.

On October 2, 55 percent of the students enrolled at Harrison High School walked out of the building in protest against a long list of grievances. Harrison had once been solidly Czech, and was now more than half black. The students demanded a new principal, more black teachers and counsellors, a black R.O.T.C. commander—in general, black control of the school. They wanted school holidays on the birthdays of black heroes like Martin Luther King and Malcolm X. They wanted food *they* liked in the school cafeteria, and insurance for their athletes. They wanted effective vocational education and "more homework." In an assembly, with the principal sitting on the stage, the leaders of the boycott told the students to withhold their applause for the principal's going-away party. Not all the black students agreed with these activities. More than 200 black students at Harrison signed a statement that they wanted good teachers of any kind, not necessarily black ones. Most of the teachers supported the principal.[3]

On October 8, conflict erupted at Austin High School, close to the western edge of the city. Austin had been all white in 1963, and was 49 percent black in 1968. At an assembly black students demanded a black principal and black teachers. Two hundred white students walked out of the auditorium. The next day a thousand black students stayed out of three high schools as an expression of support.

On Monday, October 15, 28,000 students boycotted 32 high schools. The Chicago Defender claimed that 35,000 of the 60,000 black high-school students in Chicago schools were absent. "Operation Breadbasket," the arm of the Southern Christian Leadership in Chicago, supported this general resistance movement, and 300 teachers who worked with that group also stayed away from school. The leaders of the boycott, students and others, announced that such boycotts would occur every Monday until their demands were met. On Monday, October 22, there were 20,000 out. Of fourteen segregated high schools, four reported more than 70 percent absent, and in thirteen integrated high schools, two reported more than 60 percent out. Students in the Vincennes Upper Grade Center, housed in an old building once an orphan asylum and then a venereal disease hospital, walked out. One hundred twenty five Spanish-speaking students marched in front of Lake View High School on the North Side, asking language help and courses relevant to their background and culture.[4]

At the meeting of the Board of Education on October 23, the superintendent presented an answer to the demands of the students. He explained that 34.1 percent of the teaching force was black, as was 21.9 percent of the administrative force, but made it clear that by law only ability and qualification could be considered the bases for assignment. Other demands were carefully examined:

> "While we appreciate the idea of providing a positive image for black and other children, we do not think that any of us wish to accept the position that only a black teacher can relate to black pupils, or only a white teacher to white pupils. We believe that an educator who has sensitivity and personal security and a real concern for people, as well as a basic respect for the individual person at every level and of every background is the type of person we are seeking for all positions of responsibility in this school system. . . .

> "We will continue our efforts to achieve a racial integration of staff throughout the system. Our most recent effort in this direction is the opening of 17 new divisions for the assignment of additional assistant principals to improve the integration of administrative staff at certain high schools.

> "Efforts are continuing to locate Spanish speaking and other minority people qualified as administrators, teachers or teacher aides.

> "For the past two years, school community representatives in eligible schools (federally financed) have been hired from the community which the individual school serves. These people represent the ethnic background of the school area.

"A 20 week course in Afro American history is being offered in 114 classes being taught in 30 high schools at the twelfth grade level throughout the city. At this time a year ago there were none. . . .

"Additional text book funds have been made available to enable the purchase of new and relevant instruction materials in the social studies area. $300,000 had been allocated for Afro American and Latin American history course material, and $600,000 to provide students from seventh to twelfth grades with materials which place greater emphasis on the contribution of minority groups.

"During the last two years more than 28.5 millions of dollars have been spent to repair old and run-down school plants. Years of inadequate financing have caused buildings in all parts of the city to continue to deteriorate.

"In the 1969 budget it will be possible to add 5 million dollars additional money for repair and rehabilitation because of our new arrangement for financing school construction [through the Chicago Public Building Commission].

"Holidays to observe the birthdays of national heroes are traditionally established by legislative action. . . . Most community leaders and educators believe that more significant observation of such events can be made while schools are in operation.

"The Illinois School Code provides that only moneys derived from athletic activities may be used to pay the cost of insurance for athletes. We shall recommend that a greater athletic allotment be made in the 1969 budget to all high schools, so that gate receipts may be used for insurance coverage in interscholastic athletics.

"Knowing how great is the feeling for Afro American history and culture, we have found one television station . . . which will use the services of able black teachers for programs if a foundation grant of $250,000 is available. A request is being made for such a grant. The Board of Education radio station WBEZ was carrying programs on Afro American history.

"Accept our commitment to improve the schools and consider your needs and consider your mission of dramatizing our needs accomplished.

"I have listened to what you are saying to me, and I have answered your questions. You say to me that you are searching for dignity, respect and a meaningful education. As you give thought and attention to Afro American history and culture, you will find that each of the great men you seek to emulate found dignity and respect as every other human being found it, within himself as a person and as a member of the human race. You can not—neither can I—have dignity and respect unless we share it with every man, regardless of his race, nationality or religion. I can not compromise with this belief. Dr. Martin Luther King lived for every man and this is the legacy he left for us.

"During the past few weeks, students have assaulted the dignity of teachers and principals. This can not be permitted if education is to be meaningful. . . . Together the teaching staff and the student body must build pride through school spirit. I ask both to work toward this end.

"The events of the past two weeks indicate that we can no longer live in a complex society and have power and authority emanate from only one man. As we examined the records of attendance on Monday night, we realized how difficult it is to pass judgment on the motives of every student and teacher who was absent." [5]

Dr. Redmond then urged principals to work with parents on chronic truancy and asked the boycotting students to return to school where problems can be worked out, and parents and community leaders to work with school personnel in bringing them back to classes.

This statement of the superintendent was released to the press.

After the superintendent had spoken, on a motion by Mr. Bacon the members of the Board voted six to five to hear the student movement leaders and those of the teacher groups supporting the boycott the next week on October 30. The superintendent expressed some doubt as to the value of a hearing, pointing out there was no objective way of even recognizing who were the student leaders. When students were named by principals to participate in the hearing, some refused to come. On October 28, a group from several high schools staged a "funeral" for the Board of Education. But on the third Monday, October 29, only 9,000 boycotting students were out beyond the usual absences.

On October 30, nine members of the Board of Education and the superintendent listened to three teachers and fifteen students from ten high schools, four each from the West and South Sides, and two from the North Side. Four of these schools were completely black, four were both black and white and two were white with a considerable number of Spanish-speaking and Appalachian students. Twenty-nine students who had been invited either did not come or did not speak when their names were read.

The responses from the students varied in tone and content. Some emphasized the need for help for Spanish-speaking students in learning English, in studying "their own roots," and for school personnel who could converse with them and their parents. Some asked for repairs of school equipment and buildings. One asked for four years of black studies, not one semester. A North

Side white student wanted democracy applied in high schools so that students, black or white, would not be "pre-processed machines all set with preconceived, unchanging attitudes." Some of them had a take-it-or-leave-it attitude, and one accused the Board of "playing dumb" as if it did not know the needs of the black people in the ghettos. Another announced he was too busy to be bothered with such triviality as the meeting and left. Mr. Bacon asked for suggestions as to definite ways in which students could be involved in sharing decisions within the school, and was referred by one student to their advisor, Mr. Harvey.

The three teachers also spoke from different points of view. The first, from the Black Teachers Caucus, indicted the Board for criminal miseducation of black children and demanded that black people control and direct their own schools. To him, integration was quite irrelevant, believing the racist society of the United States must be changed or destroyed. The second teacher said his group, working with Operation Breadbasket, supported the boycotts to help dramatize the conditions to which the courageous children were calling attention and urged a change in the white-oriented, middle-class policy of the Board of Education; he stressed the need of varying degrees of local control as one of the significant ways in which the Board could improve the education of black children. The third teacher represented black teachers in his now all-black school. He accused the "power base of the Chicago Public School system" of not wanting black children to achieve at an equal level with white children and suggested a list of changes to achieve equality—among them black success images in the schools, creative, relevant instruction, adequate physical facilities, and involvement of the black community in educational policy.

When the teachers finished, Mr. Bacon asked his question on ways in which students could be involved in school decisions, of James Harvey, advisor of the boycotting students. Mr. Harvey did not answer, but announced that other forms of protest to grip the entire school system were being prepared unless the demands were met. In response to an admonition by the president of the Board, he retorted, "Baby, this is our meeting, and not the Board's." The president adjourned the meeting abruptly.[6]

The disturbances receded, but did not entirely cease, and similar outbursts took place in a number of nearby school districts outside the city. In December the principal of Calumet invited parents to discuss the sporadic disorders taking place in that school for almost a year. The suggestions of the parents who attended were over-ruled by some seventy-five students who disagreed with their elders. In February the vice president of the Board of Education stated that sex education, which he opposed, was the cause of the boycotts. In March the Chicago Vocational School was closed briefly after fights in its halls. In April, 200 students walked out of Lindblom High School for a day, fighting on the streets erupted near Tilden, and parents insisting on a new building for the Vincennes Upper Grade Center kept their children out of classes for a week. In May students at Englewood, protesting the transfer of a substitute teacher, caused the resignation of the white principal. Fenger High School was closed briefly because of fighting.[7]

The impatience and unrest of the black communities was not confined to the high schools. Parents at two elementary schools, one on the West and one on the South Side, demanded Negro principals. At one old school on the far South Side, a 90 percent boycott was encouraged by parents to emphasize the need for better lighting and for mobiles to relieve overcrowding. In March the Organization for the South West Community called a boycott in twelve schools. The school administration invited parents to come in and discuss the school's problems and the plans being made to solve them. One thousand parents appeared.

In November and December, 1968, the number of black administrators was increased by the appointment of seventeen high-school assistant principals and seven elementary, and by the appointment of a black administrator as deputy superintendent, next in authority to the superintendent himself. The number of Negro top administrators and principals in Chicago far exceeded the number in New York City schools (a much larger system), and in other large cities as well, but was not in the same proportion as black to white students.[8]

Opposition in the areas which had objected to the Redmond plan was not lessened by the outbursts in the high schools. Parents on the far southwest part of the city threatened a march on the Board if black children from an overcrowded school were assigned to elementary schools in their area. In October a few pickets marched in front of the eight northwest area schools to which black children were being bused. They were organized by supporters of "the neighborhood school" in the Polish Home Owners Association, the Kilbourn Organization, and the Greater Northwest Civic Association.[9] By January, however, the busing was proceeding peacefully without interference. Perhaps more important in the total school situation than the conflict over busing was the statement of the Civic Federation at the December public hearing on the 1969 budget that class size and spending per pupil had little influence on education—as family background was more important. The Federation did not attempt to suggest what the schools could do to change family background in order to improve educational results.[10]

The segregationist organizations were not idle, however. Thomas Sutton, who had been active in opposition to the Redmond plan, was organizing a Legion of Justice, and openly recruiting students at the Circle Campus of the University of Illinois to deal with "scum." On May 28 a group of some 600 Gage Park parents and some of their children wearing Neighborhood School badges picketed the meeting of the Board of Education. Those who were admitted to the meeting applauded vociferiously at the re-election of President Whiston and Vice President Murray—and were not rebuked by the chairman for doing so. On June 11 another group demanded that schools west of Ashland Avenue not be integrated, and six protesters were removed by police. There was little doubt that the disorders in the high schools had intensified opposition to integration, and added strength to the demand for public aid for parochial schools, only 11 percent of whose children were black.

Integration of Teachers

At its June 11 meeting the Board discussed data on the discrepancy in per pupil expenditures between schools in low-income areas and those in more privileged neighborhoods (currently revealed in the Sun Times[11] and established by Urban League studies years before). The difference lay in the higher salaries paid more experienced teachers, most of whom were in middle income white areas, as against the lower salaries of new and substitute teachers who made up most of the school faculties in low-income areas, rather than in any difference in allocation of other funds.

The reasonable proposal that the same amount be spent on salaries in each school, ran up against the perennial lack of funds. Without more money, there were only two ways to equalize salary expenditures among schools—either compulsory transfer of experienced teachers to inner-city schools and of substitutes, largely black, to the white schools, or increase in the class size in more favored schools by transferring experienced teachers to reduce class size in inner-city schools. Such procedures had been requested at one time by black spokesmen, but now the demand of many of them was instead for black teachers who understood black children. Some black teachers were now less interested in token integration than in helping black children. Older white teachers, drafted against their will and unfamiliar with the black communities, might now be unwelcome and unsuccessful, even if the collective bargaining agreement with the union permitted such involuntary transfer. With more money available, on the other hand more teachers could be added and class size reduced in the schools now suffering discrimination in total salary expenditure. This solution was proposed by the union, which had included in the 1969 agreement (approved by the Board on May 28) 725 new teachers to reduce class size, to be assigned first in inner-city schools.[12]

A Six-month Budget for Lack of Funds

The members of the Chicago Teachers Union, like many students and parents in the black communities, had also been critical of the slow pace of change. In the 1967 and 1968 collective bargaining contracts signed by the Board of Education, the Board had agreed to give services and salaries from funds not yet received from the state or provided by a referendum to increase the property tax. In September, 1968, the money available from all sources was insufficient to fulfill the contract. The reduction of class size, the extension of new services such as teacher aides and the salary increases promised would cost eight and one half millions more than was on hand. Teachers were given a $60 a month increase, considerably below the agreement. When in November the Mayor agreed to raise salaries of police and firemen so that they would reach $10,000 in three and one-half years, the teachers pointed out that it took nine years for a teacher to reach that salary. To help pay for the increase given teachers in September, the number of day-to-day substitutes was cut in half, and no new teachers added. Class sizes therefore rose rather than fell. For its 1969 contract the union asked for a minimum salary of $8,500, a raise of $1,500 a year, and for a long list of other changes—almost all requiring additional money—in previous contracts, such as reduction in class size. Many of the proposals were directly for improvement in instruction. [13]

Without additional money from the 1969 session of the legislature, there was not enough to keep school services and salaries at the 1968 level, to say nothing of providing the services and salaries asked for by the union. The Board of Education refused to vote a deficit budget a third time without any real indication as to what increases, if any, the legislature would make in state aid for schools. The superintendent was unwilling merely to divide the money then in sight by the total months of the school year, with the resultant reduction of all expenditures and services in January, while it was still possible that the legislature would supply additional funds. At his request the Board of Education approved the 1969 expenditures only for the first six months of the year, such expenditures to be based on the 1968 level. Then the superintendent outlined what would have to happen in September, 1969, if the legislature failed to act. Average class size would have to go up from 34 to 45. Seven thousand teachers would have to be dismissed. No new services could be added, and no extensions made of those now in use. [14] In January, 1969, the union was divided on its course of action. At a membership meeting, a majority of some 3,000 in attendance voted to strike—a decision reversed after a vote in the schools of 9,022 to 5,206 to accept the extension of the 1968 contract for the present.

While the underlying plea of the high-school students for teachers with understanding of their problems and faith in their potentialities, was not merely a matter of money, it was obvious that more money would have to be found to make it possible even for the best teachers to help all the students who needed special aid. Smaller classes, special individual instruction, sufficient numbers of counsellors, plentiful up-to-date materials, new kinds of auxiliary staff services to diagnose and solve individual problems—all these cost money. Moreover, at no time in history had children in the Chicago public schools ever had enough buildings, seats, and equipment. The Public Building Commission could help catch some of the long-standing deficiencies, but there was still no assurance of enough money to renovate all the older buildings (one-third were over sixty years old), equip new vocational schools, and provide space for the annual increase in enrolment. The continual shifts of population within the city, which sometimes increased enrolment unexpectedly in a given school, required funds for seats and equipment, and frequently, mobile classrooms. If dropouts could be held in school, there must be room for them. If classes were to be smaller, there must be more rooms for more classes. There just were insufficient funds available to provide the kind of school system which would meet the most obvious needs of the city's children.

Students and parents, and some teachers, blamed the Board of Education for the lack of resources. Some Board members themselves showed deep concern over the lack of present resources and future prospects for more. Others tended to accept the traditional attitude of those in charge of public education that it was not their responsibility to find money, only to decide how to use what there was. By April, 1969, however, the Board had voted to urge the raising of the level of state aid to $800 and a change in the formula by which state aid was divided among local districts; some members had appeared in the legislature in active support of these issues.

Pressure for More State Aid

The 1969 session of the Illinois General Assembly was faced with the simple fact that it could no longer run the state government on a sales tax. The revenue system of Illinois, dating back to 1848, was an anachronism, no longer a viable method of financing the government of an industrial state of ten million people, only 20 percent of whom now lived in rural areas. It could no longer continue to finance the services already provided for its people, to say nothing of others furnished in many other states—for which clamor was being insistently raised in Illinois. It was at the bottom of the fifty states in state tax-produced revenue in proportion to the personal income of its citizens. It was forty-seventh in its support of public elementary and secondary education, far down in its provision for mental health facilities and for physical health care of children. Local governments depended mainly on a uniform property tax which had never, since the tax strike of 1872, been actually applied as the 1870 State Constitution required. It was second only to West Virginia in the extent of its reliance on regressive sales taxes for support of state government.[15]

After decades of dodging the inevitable, both political parties in the state finally recognized the sheer necessity of some kind of income tax. Also after decades of refusal to admit that a single-rate income tax was not in contradiction to the State Constitution, they went even farther and proposed a flat-rate income tax which would allow exemptions. The Republicans supported a tax at the same rate on personal incomes and on corporation incomes. The Democrats insisted that the rate on corporation income be higher. In April, the governor proposed a 4 percent tax on personal and corporation income, with an exemption of $1,000 for each member of a family. A bill was introduced by Democrats for a 2 percent tax on personal and 5 percent tax on corporation income, and there were other variations considered.

In his budget message the governor stated that he gave public education priority in expenditures. He called on the legislature to raise the level of state aid for schools from $400 per pupil to $500. He added that there should be additional money for crowded urban areas, and specifically for inner-city schools. This increase would still leave Illinois far below the average state support of elementary and secondary education, which was 40 percent. Five hundred dollars was actually far less than the average cost of education of the children.

In any case, the complicated distribution formula did not mean that the state really gave $400 or $500 for the education of each child—far from it. The formula required that approximately half of the money appropriated for state aid to schools first be distributed to every school district in the state at the rate of $47 for each child. This money went to the districts with the highest property values per child in the state as well as to those with the lowest. Then, each district was required to levy a property tax at not less than a certain rate. If the "qualifying tax rate" plus the $47 per child did not produce enough money to reach the level for each child set by the state, e.g., $400, the state made up the difference. In 1968 the actual state aid for Chicago had not been $400 per pupil but only some $172. In order to keep the schools going, the citizens of Chicago had been paying almost twice the rate of property tax which the state set as a minimum requirement for state aid—in fact as much as state law would allow the school district to tax, even with a special referendum of the voters. The maximum tax rate assessable in unit districts like Chicago, where elementary and secondary schools were in the same district, was lower than in dual districts, where high schools were under separate school governments. [16]

The money which Chicago schools would receive from the state if the level of aid were set at $500 would not even keep the Chicago schools operating on the 1968 basis. The superintendent of the Chicago schools informed the State School Problems Commission that at least $600 would be necessary to meet the 68 million dollars required for the rest of 1969 and urged a level of $800 as a realistic approach to provide education needed for all the city's children.

The voice of the Chicago superintendent was not the only one raised in protest against the governor's proposal. State and local teachers organizations, the Illinois Congress of Parents and Teachers, the Illinois School Board Association, and the Illinois Association of School Administrators were equally vehement. The Citizens Schools Committee of Chicago and other civic organizations stated the reasons for more adequate state support for public schools. The State Superintendent of Education asked that the level be $550. The School Problems Commission, ten of whose members sat in the legislature, in March had also recommended a $550 level. The Education Committee of the House of Representatives unanimously recommended $550. An amendment on the floor of the House to raise it to $600 lost by only 13 votes. In May, raising his figure a little, the governor finally said it could be $520.

Critics of the governor's proposal pointed out that the Task Force on Education, appointed by his predecessor, had recommended a level of $600 in December, 1966, and that the cost of living had risen steadily since. They compared the budget allocation for highways of $1,114,000,000 with that for the education of all the children of the state at $1,111,000,000. They reminded the governor that the State Constitution put the responsibility for elementary and secondary education squarely on the shoulders of the state government. Even the federal courts provided them an argument. In a case brought by Lawndale parents, the court held that there was obvious inequity in the apportionment of state funds for education, but that the remedy lay in the hands of the legislature, not the courts. The three-judge court accepted as fact that a school district with real estate valued at $3,000 per child could not offer the quality of education to its children which could be given by an Illinois district whose real estate was valued at $114,000 per child.[17]

There were opponents to any increase, or to any considerable increase in state aid. The Illinois Chamber of Commerce claimed that $500 was too high. Others said there just was not money for more than $500. One Chicago member of the legislature attacked the Chicago schools as offering luxuries. In any case, unless there was some kind of income tax, there would be no increase in school funds.

Ever since his arrival in Chicago in October, 1966, Superintendent Redmond had been waging a steady, constant campaign to get more money for the Chicago system. His first public statement on arrival, made to the Civic Federation, stated his conviction that much more money must be found if the schools were to carry out their responsibility to children. He attended committee hearings of the 1967 legislative session, supporting the Task Force findings. In November, 1967, he stated that there must be an increase of at least 54 millions from some source, if the city system was not to lose ground and that 728 million dollars should be spent in Chicago in 1968, not just the 426 million being budgeted. He urged the Illinois Associations of School Boards and School Administrators to organize a state-wide campaign to get more funds and explained that money must be found if Chicago schools were to be able to implement integration, to explore adequately the values of shared time projects, and to provide leeway for collective bargaining. In July, 1968, speaking to the School Problems Commission subcommittee on Urban Problems, he voiced a positive hope for results in the 1969 session, pointing to signs of greater understanding of public education needs.

In November, 1968, the 1969 Chicago school budget was in preparation. The superintendent had made it very clear to the Board, to the union, and to the public that there was not enough money to continue the present program through the next school year, and no funds for new or added services or for additional salaries. In January, 1969, the superintendent and the president of the union had appeared before the School Problems Commission and urged an $800 level of state aid, for changes in the distribution formula to reduce discrimination against unit districts like Chicago, and to allocate aid not on attendance, but on the number of children enrolled, since that was the basis of assigning teachers and space.

In February, 1969, accompanied by the president of the Chicago Board of Education, the president of the Illinois Association of School Boards, and the secretary of the Better Schools Committee, the superintendent had two conferences with the governor and leaders of the majority party in each House, urging a substantial increase in state aid based on what the schools needed, not on what was politically convenient. Also in February, he appeared before Congressional committees urging larger and more flexible grants for big city schools. In March he told the Chicago Association of Commerce that "What we really want is a Marshall Plan for our underdeveloped American common school system."[18] In April, with the president of the Chicago Board, he returned to the School Problems Commission to explain in detail why the $550 recommended by that body was not enough for Chicago. When the governor's budget message of April 2 ultimately contained a recommendation for only $500 for state aid, the superintendent reluctantly cut the 1969 Chicago summer school program in half.

The superintendent made clear in all these statements that more money was needed not merely to keep the present system running, but because its present state was far from what it must be. The "underdeveloped" school system was a failure in vital respects. In speaking to the representatives of Illinois school boards and administrators in March, he stated flatly,

> "There is not one administrator or Board member who can escape the indictment of unequal education for some of the children in his school system. Integration is a national challenge which must be faced and resolved by those of us concerned with public education. Unless we are a vital force in the social order, assuming some responsibility for directing it and forming it, education will become just another problem to add to pollution, transportation, sewage and blight."[19]

At last, administrators were hearing Jacob Riis' lone voice of the 1890's which had cried that the battle of the slums must be won in the schools.

Not only did Superintendent Redmond and some members of the Chicago Board of Education speak vigorously and directly for a new view of school legislation in Illinois, now there was also support from some of the business community. The Better Schools Committee, which had obtained the grant for buildings from the Public Building Commission, urged that the legislature set at least a $550 level for state aid, that a state income tax be adopted and that aid be divided among districts on the basis of membership, not attendance. Its chairman, the president of the Illinois Bell Telephone Company, had employed expert help in preparing a series of full-page ads run in all the metropolitan press several times. They used such titles as "Pick the Kids Who Don't Deserve a Good Education" under a group picture of eager children.[20] Thousands of pamphlets on the need for more money for schools were circulated. A year before, the telephone company had included in its June bill a reminder to customers to vote for an increase in the Chicago school tax rate. The Better Schools Committee invited the members of the Chicago legislature to visit the Chicago schools and appraise their needs for themselves. These were new and heartening attitudes in the business leadership of the city, which had for so many decades ignored the education of the city's children.

The metropolitan press varied in the degree of its support for more state aid. The Sun Times was the most vehement. Its editorials alleged that for decades the Illinois legislature had shirked its responsibility for public education, so explicitly stated in the state constitution. On March 26 it declared that "The legislature must change its long standing view that its sole responsibility is to figure out a formula for distributing to the schools what money is available," and went on to say that the present demand for action "comes after a long period during which Illinois has short-changed its children and its teachers." It pointed out that the $550 would give Illinois only 32 percent of the cost per child, a long way from the 40 percent average of the fifty states. The Sun Times also ran a series of news stories on the financial troubles of school districts in many parts of the state, and on the enormous inequities in the financial resources of elementary school districts in Cook County. The News firmly urged more state aid than the $550 level, pointing out that present level and traditional attitudes toward public education were remnants of a pioneer rural society and that it was unthinkable that education in Chicago should stand still—to say nothing of slipping backward. All the metropolitan newspapers supported some kind of income tax. On April 2 a Tribune editorial headed "For an Income Tax, But—" accepted an increase of state aid to $500, but warned that the convention meeting in December to frame a new state constitution must set limits on any income tax.

Mayor Promises Money to Settle Union Strike

By April, 1969, no contract for 1969 had been signed either by the union or the Board. As the session wore on with no commitments from the governor or majority party leaders to a level of state aid necessary to provide money for the 1969 contract proposed by the union in December, the union took dramatic action to force the issue. On April 22, 6,000 teachers paraded through downtown streets in a cold rain, asking for better schools for children and a cost of living salary increase. On April 29, during the spring vacation, 2,000 teachers appeared in the Capitol at Springfield, to interview their legislators and the governor. On May 14 the union House of Representatives voted to hold a referendum of the members as to whether there should be a strike on May 22. By a vote of 10,944 to 5,435, the union members voted the strike. Their intention was to obtain a 1969 contract from the Board of Education containing an agreement that there would be no lay-offs or cutbacks, and that those items in the 1968 contract which had not been fulfilled because of lack of funds in September, 1968, would now be implemented. Class sizes would be reduced to the level agreed upon in 1968, but not just to an average figure. There would be a maximum which was not to be exceeded. There was to be a new program to improve the inner-city schools and a salary increase of $150 a month.

One further request was included which had been argued long and hard among the teachers. Those full-time teachers who fulfilled state requirements, but who did not have Chicago certificates, were to be given Chicago certificates after two years of satisfactory service, entitling them to qualify for service-based increments in the salary schedule. The majority of these Full Time Substitutes, (F.T.B.'s) were black, and many of them claimed they had been discriminated against for that reason. They had demanded full certification after one year when they organized a strike the year before. A competent black principal had been appointed one of three examiners to allay fears of discrimination at that time. The black teachers in the union were divided on the strike. Some refused to honor the picket line and entered the schools to teach, proclaiming their first responsibility was to their black children.

Seventy-six percent of all the teachers in the city participated in the strike on May 22. The superintendent ordered the schools closed, and only a few, where the black teachers refused to strike, were open. He had urged the teachers not to strike. The Board of Education admitted it had no more money to meet the requests of the union than it had had in December, 1968. Then Mayor Daley offered his services as mediator, and talked to the governor. By the evening of the second day of the strike the union and the Board had come to an agreement based on conferences between the mayor and the governor. On Sunday afternoon, May 25, union members voted on acceptance of the agreement for the remainder of 1969. It was affirmed by a vote of some 9,000 to 585, and the schools reopened on Monday, May 26. On May 28 the 1969 collective bargaining agreement between the Board and the union was approved by the Board by a vote of 6 to 4. The Board members voting against it stated that again the Board was promising to spend money it did not have—and might not get. The new contract provided for a $100 salary increase and certification without examination after three years of satisfactory service for F.T.B.'s, rather than two.[21] The House of Representatives in Springfield approved of the $550 level with allocation on membership rather than attendance and a higher allocation for high-school aid, which had not been given high schools in unit districts in 1967, when all other high schools did receive it. It looked as if there might be money to fulfill the contract.

While the Board of Education was discussing its agreement with the teachers' union on May 28, Vice President Murray raised the issue of increase in the wage rates of electrical workers asked for by their union, of which he was an officer. Some weeks before, Board Member Dr. Bernard Friedman had questioned (1) the size of raises sought (38 percent) over a ten-month period, and (2) the policy of paying rates set for private, intermittent contracts to school electrical workers who were guaranteed permanent, steady employment under civil service. He pointed out that the wage requested (over $13,000 a year) was almost $4,000 more than was paid for identical work at federal installations.[22] This arrangement had been in effect in the schools and in the city for more than thirty years, going back to the days of the Kelly regime. The Board had voted to ask the superintendent to employ experts in this field of work to recommend a policy to them. Vice President Murray moved to pay the higher rate asked for until the experts reported their findings. This was approved, but not unanimously.

There were other issues directly affecting Chicago schools before the 1969 session of the legislature. The first was supported by those who objected to the U.S. Supreme Court ruling forbidding prayers in public schools. It provided that there be a minute at the beginning of each day's school session for undirected silent prayer or "meditation on the activities of the day." Just what a ten-year-old boy would think about as "meditation on the activities of the day" was not made clear. This law was passed and signed by the governor.

The second was an effort to curb the limit of the bonding power of the Chicago Public Buildings Commission so there could be no further use of it to solve the financial school building problem. The Civic Federation had backed this proposal, which would have required referenda on all bond issues to build schools in Chicago. One June 10 this bill was defeated, but a bill to allow a 350 million dollar bond issue without referendum to complete the long-term plans of the Sanitary District was passed with little opposition. [23]

The governor's proposal to give 32 millions to parochial schools passed the House and was defeated in the Senate. The chief argument used to support it was that it was cheaper to subsidize parochial schools than to add their enrolment to already overcrowded and underfinanced public schools. One claim used by both proponents and opponents was that aid to parochial schools would most certainly increase the proportion of black children to white in Chicago public schools.

Changes in Choosing Board Members

Two bills, introduced by senators from "backlash" districts, proposed election, not appointment, to the Chicago Board of Education. One, a return to a Board of 21, elected from state senatorial districts within the city, was defeated by one vote in the Senate. The other, for a Board of 13–seven elected, three appointed by the mayor, and three by the governor–passed the Senate, but never got to a vote in the House. Senator Lanigan, who introduced it, however, was successful in getting approval for a commission of senators to investigate the Chicago Board of Education on deficit financing and on racial policy–a procedure used only once before in the history of Chicago schools, in 1915. [24]

These bills, if passed, would not have gone into effect until July 1, 1969, without an unlikely two-thirds vote. However, the terms of two members of the Chicago Board of Education expired May 1. By March, the mayor had not committed himself to the continuation of the screening committee for nominating Board members. On March 4 the Citizens Schools Committee presented him with a revision of its 1964 plan for reorganizing the screening committee, and the mayor agreed to try it for 1969. The commission was to be limited to thirteen members. Five were to be chosen by specific organizations, namely the Association of Commerce, the Federation of Labor, the Citizens Schools Committee, the Chicago Region of the P.T.A., and the Urban League. Five were to be chosen by organizations selected by panels of city-wide groups with like interests, such as the universities in the city, civic organizations, professional groups, human relations organizations and welfare agencies. Three members were to be selected by the mayor at will. The organizations involved were summoned by the mayor to a meeting and duly selected their representatives. The mayor added a Puerto Rican and two persons from fringe areas which had protested their lack of representation. The head of the Department of Education of the University of Chicago was chosen chairman by the commission and the president of the Citizens Schools Committee, vice chairman. On June 12, six names were presented to the mayor. On July 15 he sent to the council for confirmation the names of a Puerto Rican woman social worker and a black business man with a record of civic leadership.[25]

Financial Dilemma Remains

On June 28 money for schools still had not been provided by the legislature because the income tax conflict had reached a stalemate. On that day—the last on which legislation could be initiated in time to go into effect on July 1, 1969—a compromise was reached to levy a 2.5 percent personal income tax, and a 4 percent corporation income tax. The governor said the compromise reduced the estimated revenue from the income tax by 48 millions, and refused to allow state aid higher than the $520 level, or to change the formula by allocating aid by number of children enrolled, not the number who came each day. To answer the protests of Chicago legislators that this arrangement did not give enough operating money for the Chicago schools, the bill was amended to allow the city government to give its 23 millions in new income tax revenue to the schools, if it wanted to. The revenue from a one fourth cent jump in city sales tax was promised for salaries for city employees and other city purposes.

When the smoke of legislative battle cleared away, the Chicago school system still faced grave financial dilemma. The new formula for state aid for schools would provide no more than 33 million dollars for Chicago. Superintendent Redmond's current estimate of the additional funds needed for the remaining months of 1969 was 73 million. There were 11 million dollars in the school treasury, but there was still a deficit of 29 millions. The Board of Education, relying on the mayor's and governor's promises, had signed a firm contract with the Chicago Teachers Union to spend the 29 million they did not have. The teachers' governing body had voted to strike in September if the contract were not kept. The promised pay raise was only 11 of the 29 million dollars, and if the teachers wanted to give it up they still could not provide the remaining 18 million needed to keep the schools operating at the level of the first six months in numbers of staff and amount of supplies.

The governor said the mayor could use his 23 millions of new income tax money to help the Chicago schools. The mayor pointed out that while collection of the income tax was to begin August 1, he would not receive the state allocation until 1970. The city financial experts claimed it was not legal to issue tax anticipation warrants on expected revenue from the income tax. [26]

Justice Department Orders Teacher Desegregation

While the Board of Education was debating its way on finances on July 10, it received a peremptory order from the United States Department of Justice to desegregate its teaching force, and to offer a plan within two weeks to accomplish such desegregation, or be sued by the federal government. One Board member asked why the order applied only to desegregating teachers and not to children. The segregation of teachers was so obvious in the 1964 surveys, and in the current reports of the school administration, that there was no argument about the fact. Some Board members blamed the union. The Union refused to accept involuntary teacher transfers—both white and black members in agreement in their opposition—and pointed out its long series of unanswered requests for smaller classes, additional instructional aids, and other improvements in inner-city schools, which would have equalized the difficulty of teaching. It also pointed out that new teachers were not assigned by the administration in ways which would increase integration. Black teachers refused to transfer to white areas for token integration, since they claimed they were needed to help black children, and white teachers who had remained for years in all-black schools pointed out that they were no longer welcome in some schools. Furthermore, white teachers forced to transfer into black communities, with whose problems they were not familiar, would be even more unwelcome. The mayor said to pay the teachers in the inner city more. The Board replied that it lacked even the 29 million dollars the mayor had promised them, and where would they get more to pay such extra salary? The superintendent said he would have some plan ready by the end of the two weeks. [27]

This unhappy state of the Chicago school system varies only in detail, amount, and particular causes from that of its thirteen previous decades. But the pressure gauge within and without the system has risen. The resentment of the black communities at the quality of education many of its children are receiving grows more bitter daily. The strongly organized teachers in Chicago and elsewhere now see no reason why they should continue to make up the difference between what the public demands of the schools and what the public pays to support them. The public now expects an excellence in instruction and an extension of years in school which students have never before enjoyed—but for which it is not yet willing to pay. A superintendent with vision for improvement is confined by the inherited structure and leadership of a vast system, by timid support from the Board of Education, and by a city administration sensitive to its own insecurity in the face of change.

The present situation gives the mayor of Chicago open control of the policies of the Board of Education. For two years, at least, the mayor and the city council have veto power over funds necessary to carry out the improvements projected by the superintendent. It is easier for the members of the Better Schools Committee, many of whom live in the suburbs, to use their influence to help reach higher standards in buildings and instruction in the city schools, than it is for aldermen from "backlash" wards to face their constituents after voting money for busing black children into their neighborhoods.

The outlook looks bleak. But the bleakness is due to failure to move fast enough, not to failure to move at all. The schools with all their glaring faults and failures are improving the opportunities of more and more children. But every year the number of ways in which such opportunities can be increased grows greater, and even more significantly, the gap between what children are now getting in school and what all of them must have to survive in an exploding, scientific society widens daily. There is never enough of anything to catch up with. In fact, there are only two things of which the Chicago schools have always had more than enough—children and crises!

Chapter 20

IT CAN BE DONE!

The story of how the Chicago school system took its present shape is a strange saga, long, confused—and still confusing. The breath taking, cliff-hanging suspense of waiting for a decision by the 1969 session of the legislature on the fate of Chicago schools for the next two years is only one of many such crises. No single thread of dominant purpose has bound its history into a logical sequence, or given it permanent direction. Most enterprises of such scope and cost have been built around some generally agreed upon objectives which take precedence over other considerations in decisions as to their creation and conduct. There has been no such real agreement as to the central purpose of public education in Chicago, or elsewhere, throughout its decades of existence.

Why Public Education?

The history of the public schools of Chicago reflects a conflict of forces seeking widely divergent and frequently contradictory goals. The simplest and commonest of these was that every other place had a school where children could learn to read and write and add, and therefore there should be one in Chicago. Some people just wanted to keep children off the streets until they were old enough to work. Other groups wanted the schools to train children to be useful in some particular segment of society, such as employers in a given industry, or an ethnic group wishing to perpetuate its own culture. As the money spent on schools increased, and the number of employees rose, the right to divert money and jobs to their own ends, asserted by those in power, became a controlling factor in what schools could and would do. There has been a general assumption that the public schools were to train children to conform to the beliefs and customs acceptable to their elders in the community; but when sharp differences arose within the city as to what were acceptable beliefs and customs, and when the beliefs and customs of a local area ran counter to those of city, state, or nation, conflict has been inevitable even on the assumption that schools were to train children to accept the status quo. In recent years, there has been increasing emphasis on the need for actual proficiency in the tools of learning, such as reading, computing, and scientific skills, to provide vast numbers of competent workers needed in a technological society.

But there have been a few people through the years who have insisted that the purpose of public education was to give every child the opportunity, full and equal for all, to develop his abilities and his special talents, whatever they might be, in order to become, to the extent these allowed, a self-directed, creative human being, able not only to make a constructive contribution to society, but also to live his own life with satisfaction. This last goal has been frequently mentioned in respectful oratory on formal occasions; but it has never been seriously considered as a base for the operation of a school system by any considerable number of legislators, mayors, city councilmen, or Board of Education members. Parents may say they want such a goal for their own children, but too few have been concerned with what happens to other people's children. Those among the teaching staffs who have sought to make the schools a path to such a goal have found little support in the past from those in power.

It is this confused conflict of narrow, limited purposes which has precipitated the Chicago public schools into successive financial crises. There never has been any sustained, conscious effort to find the funds to finance any one of the conflicting goals, except, perhaps, just to maintain the existence of a school system. Other major enterprises in the city—and the nation—have not been forced to drift so helplessly. When it was decided to turn the Chicago River backward in order to stop typhoid fever, engineers estimated the cost, and the money was found. When the cost was more than the original estimate, for whatever reasons, more money was found. When wars have been declared, or fought without a declaration, there has seemed to be no limit to the billions paid for them out of current taxation and debts passed on to future generations. When Congress determined that it was in the national interest to send men to the moon, billions were spent on experiments to find the most effective way to achieve this scientific feat, and more billions to carry out the operation. This huge expense was justified as advancing mankind's basic knowledge of the origin of earth and moon and the physical make-up of the universe—and before the Russians did it.

No responsible agency has ever taken careful thought as to how present knowledge of the physical and social sciences could be employed to help children develop bodies, minds, and personal and social values with which to continue the search for truth for themselves and for the shrunken world of which our nation is a decreasingly important part. Nor has any estimate ever been set on how much such exploration might cost, to say nothing of estimates of putting such findings into effect. Is money spent for such ends, or the use of human knowledge for such purposes, of any less value to the human race than finding out the exact content of the moon's dust or strengthening one theory or another of how our lifeless globe came to be, eons ago—or beating the Russians in a game? The affluent United States could feed its hungry, educate its children well, and send a man to Mars if its people wanted these things; it is the *only* nation in the troubled history of the world which could. The affluent state of Illinois, third among the fifty in its personal wealth per capita, most certainly could contribute as large a share of that wealth to its schools as Mississippi and Arkansas contribute to theirs, from their lesser resources. And the city of Chicago could at least provide a seat for every child in its public schools—never done since the first school opened—and could give all its children a real opportunity to learn at least the basic tool subjects of learning, which it has never given all of them and it is not giving all of them today.

Gains Made by Emerging Labor Movement and by Blacks Today

The discrepancy between a vague ideal and an incongruous reality exists, of course, in other areas besides education. It is this inconsistency between noble platitudes and obvious cold fact against which protests are being made by growing numbers of youth today, some through anti-social and some through traditional channels. It is perhaps a tribute to the blundering success of our educational system, as well as to instantaneous, vivid, and world-wide education by television, that so many of them see the inconsistencies so clearly. As this generation becomes the major sector of the population in the next decade, such outspoken criticism of the gap between what we say as a nation and what we do—which Myrdal called the "American dilemma"—may become a stronger force for social change.

There have been two eras of history, in the nation and in the city, when strong voices have been raised expressing demands for change in public education. Both have been eras of open social conflict. Neither group raising the outcry was considered really respectable by the established social order of its day. Yet both succeeded in making permanent changes in the direction taken by public education.

The first group was the explosive—and frequently violent—emerging labor movement of the last half of the nineteenth century and beginning of the twentieth, which insisted that the slogan of the Declaration of Independence, that governments were insituted and allowed to exist by the "consent of the governed," applied to economic control as well as to political. They demanded and obtained child-labor and compulsory education laws, and a general education for all children which included useful vocational training and free text books. They insisted that human rights took precedence over property rights and that school standards for children of common people should be as high as those for children of the wealthy. In scope and intent their demands far exceeded mere justice for their own children. The labor movement in Chicago was more successful than in some other areas because of the exceptional quality of its leadership. Its efforts brought the city's public schools several long steps closer toward equal opportunity for all children.

The second era began in 1954 with the Supreme Court decision declaring school segregation by state law contrary to the federal Constitution. The civil rights movement of the second half of the twentieth century, like the earlier labor movement, has overtones of anger and threatened or actual violence. It also directly challenges the failure of the public schools to provide equality of educational opportunity. The high expectations of a better life for their children, one of the motives which impelled millions of black people to leave the South for Northern cities, have met with cruel disillusionment. Faith that they could "overcome," by non-violent reminders that they too were a part of an American dream, is fading into frustration at continuing powerlessness to escape crowded housing in anti-social environments, to find employment, and to give their children a chance in this generation. Many are now convinced that the schools of the city are not teaching their children to read, nor to compete in a hostile world; they feel that the city as a whole does not care what happens to them or their children. They want their children to be taught subject matter that makes sense to them, to have teachers who believe in them and respect them, and to become self-respecting, confident, and competent adults.

Resistance to Change in Schools and in Society

The migrants from the South had mistakenly assumed that equality of opportunity, so firmly stated in Supreme Court decisions, was the actual basis on which city school systems operated, and many of them are convinced their group is the only one to which such equality has not been granted. That they are in error in this belief is not really important today. The gap between the quality and quantity of education necessary for economic and social security today is so much greater than it was when William Rainey Harper pointed it out in 1898, that black parents today have the right to judge the schools only by present results. But while the new migration from the South believed in the noble promises of educational equality, the legislators and city political powers, used to pleasing dozens of opposing forces—just enough to hold their votes for the next election, have shown little indication of changing their long-held view of education as only one of those competing forces to be placated as little as possible. Few of them have shown the remotest intention of departing from the record of the past one hundred years to make an effort to provide equal opportunity for all children. The desperate, explosive reaction to this blank indifference, not merely by "militants," but by the mass of black people in the city, is taking many forms, such as decreasing concern for efforts at integration, insistence on black history, black teachers, and administrators, and on some actual control by themselves over what the schools are doing with their children. This pressure will inevitably increase until the black communities find answers to their demands which convince them that real changes are taking place which will really help their children.

Public Education Must Serve All Children and Adults

It is not merely the black population which is openly demanding change; Mexicans and Puerto Ricans are also vehement in their expressed dissatisfaction with what is happening to their children. Without any such outcry, the children of the mountain whites, ex-coal-miners, and ex-sharecroppers and of scattered American Indians on the city streets, need much more help than any of them are now getting to grow into human beings who can with self respect and confidence share in a pluralistic society. But it is not merely the economically handicapped who need new kinds of education. The stresses of city life, the sudden disappearance of values once held immutable, even the very affluence of our society, are creating problems which many homes at all economic levels are not solving and which the schools perforce must consider. Neither the schools, the churches, or the homes of many middle-class children are really helping to make sense to them of the world they see around them. Many parents merely want their children to attend schools like the ones they remember, and are apprehensive of new ways of any kind. Youth who use drugs are found in the wealthiest suburbs, not merely in the slums. A whole new approach to education is needed.

Another service to our urban society, which no school system is really providing on a scale commensurate with the need, is education for adults without presently useful skills, to help lift themselves to a new level of competence and self respect. The "community school" experiments in New Haven and in some other cities foreshadow what could be done in this direction. The changes now being seriously discussed to reorganize the socially and financially wasteful welfare system point toward the necessity of a great expansion of such service from urban educational institutions. Such work has begun in several ways in the Chicago schools, but it is hopelessly handicapped at present by lack of space, equipment, and staff to work with industry.

Positive Forces for Change

Clearly the demands upon urban public education are multiplying, and there is no indication that their number, cost, or complexity will diminish, even though improved service from physical and mental health agencies ought to relieve the schools to some degree. If there were no hope of more public support—both in resources and understanding—the outlook would be dark, indeed. But there are encouraging signs both within and without the schools.

One such encouraging sign is in the political maturing of the black communities, which are beginning to translate resentments into use of the political power their numbers and concentration can give. Such revolt against exploitation according to the ancient ethnic pattern in the city not only makes possible change by slow, traditional methods, but offers immediate bargaining strength in a city where the black vote holds the balance of power. Recent elections indicate that this change is taking place. A realization of the dammed-up resentment in the ghettos is deepening throughout the rest of the city. No smug minimizing of the 2 percent involved in riots or the small number actually in street gangs can diminish the growing manifestation of black peoples' anger at the failure of the city to give the children of the ghetto their chance. There have been—and still are—thousands of black products of the Chicago public schools who have achieved success in every area of the city's life. But the black communities know that there should have been hundreds of thousands more.

The "fire next time," prophesied by James Baldwin in 1963, has already begun to burn. Perhaps fire is better for the nation than the slow freezing of dreams of equal opportunity which have been deadening in the schools for years. As James Redmond said in 1967, unless our schools actually provide real opportunity to all our children, they become just another evidence of urban blight, like air pollution and choked transportation. Moreover, they guarantee that the caste system which began with slavery will be extended indefinitely, perhaps permanently, and that our claims in a world of new rising nations to be the leader of the "free world" will become ridiculous.

A second hopeful sign is the very real improvement within the school system itself. Only in the last twenty-five years has exploitation by local political power in the crude control of promotions and contracts disappeared from Chicago schools. The rising standards of training for teachers now require at least a degree from some institution of higher education. With all the faults and narrow traditions of many such institutions, they have on the whole produced teachers with a greater understanding of urban and national social problems, and the relation of public education to these problems, than was true of their predecessors. Many institutions in the Chicago area are making valuable contributions to the training of teachers for urban schools. Federal funding of the small numbers in the Teachers Corps is a recognition of a real need. The Chicago system has given some thought to aid for new teachers and new experiences for older ones, but much more is needed.

This attainment of professional status by teachers is partly the cause and partly the result of the organization of teachers to support their demands not merely for fair salaries and reasonable working conditions, but also for a share in planning their own creative activity as teachers. Salary scales in Chicago have risen since 1943—the year they finally reached the maximum set in 1922. The rise has been due partly to the law of supply and demand, partly to pressure from the teachers themselves, and partly to a slowly increasing general recognition that they are still too low for the kind of service needed in urban schools. Pointing out that the 1969 contract of the Chicago Teachers Union, not yet funded, still requires eight years of service before a beginning teacher reaches the salary level attained by policemen and firemen in three and one half, does not minimize the importance of other city services, but indicates the slow pace of change within the schools.

Those who criticize a teacher's expectation of salary comparable to those of his colleagues in other professions as being paid "at the expense of the children" are still accepting the old notion that there should be only so much money for schools, and that if it is insufficient, the teachers should make up the difference, not the taxpayers. Teachers must now be considered professionals and treated as such, and other kinds of professionals beside classroom teachers must be added to their ranks in greater numbers than at present, if children are to get the help they need. One of the major gains in the growing strength of teacher organizations is the intercommunication of ideas and enthusiasms within the teaching force itself. Emerging among teachers is leadership for the development of schools which are not alien institutions in a community, set down by some distant "foreign" power, but are an integral part of the life of that community. Without such developing awareness among the teaching force, there can be no such schools. Such understanding can not be imposed by orders from above.

School administrators are changing, too, not only in their relations with teachers, but in their willingness to share the concerns of people outside the schools and in the image of their own role in society. A school superintendent of today must be really a social engineer dealing with all the elements, explosive and reactionary, in the city he serves. If he refuses all change, one element explodes. If he seeks change, another attacks him. Such a posture on the cutting edge of social interactions requires courage and patience, and perhaps willingness to risk a career. In any large city the superintendent of schools is not merely the chief administrator of one of the largest businesses in that city. He must steer his efforts for educational change through reefs of teacher contracts, Board of Education reluctance, and violent opposition from some element in the city—and then he still has, somehow, to get the money to execute his plans. He can no longer merely be an educational technician. School principals in less degree face the same array of problems, which some of them already find overwhelming.

One of the grave problems in school administration today is the lack of definition of the complementary roles of superintendent and Board of Education. This is complicated by the fact that each Board member defines his own responsibility on the basis of his own background and his past and present commitments. One problem has been that state law requires that the time of the Chicago Board of Education be frittered away on many minor matters, most of which are not in its field of competence—whatever that might be.

No great city has really solved the problem of selecting persons of competence and social understanding necessary for the awesome, and time consuming, if unpaid, task of making legal decisions as to the direction of education for hundreds of thousands of children. Some of the largest cities elect their Boards; but the results of that process have not been encouraging. Three have chosen the method used in Chicago (since 1947) of a screening committee to nominate candidates for the mayor's appointment. Such a committee was set up by state law for New York City schools in 1961, and by city ordinance for Philadelphia in 1965. New York City, in its effort to reduce the impersonality of its vast school system of a million children, plans to increase the involvement of local communities. Among the many recent convulsions has been the sudden replacement of the 1961 law, in 1969, by one requiring election of part and appointment of part of the central Board and the election of some thirty district boards. One result of the conflicts in New York over local school boards seems to be indication that all concerned elements must have some responsible involvement in planning the major outlines of any decentralization scheme, if it is to work.

The origin and history of the screening commission for school board nominations in Chicago has been related in detail in preceding chapters. The mayors of Chicago can ignore its recommendations—and have done so several times. It is clear that at least some appointments to the Board have been made with a weather eye on the political security of the mayor and his party, rather than on the necessity for obtaining the highest quality of farseeing, constructive leadership for a vast school system. Mere geographic, economic, or ethnic representation does not guarantee such quality either. Howver, in the present state of mind of the black people who send 53 percent of the children to Chicago public schools, the present representation of their racial group by only 27 percent of the Board of Education seems unreasonable. Whether the changes made in 1969 in the operation of the screening committee will result in the selection of more members of the dedicated quality of some now serving—who can and do offer the leadership so desperately needed—time will tell.

One of the most hopeful omens for the future of public education in Chicago is the appearance of a new generation of business leaders, some of whom are demonstrating in word and deed an enlightened self interest far different from the callous disregard of almost all their predecessors from 1835 to 1935. The younger businessmen of today have been brought up on the need for an expanding Gross National Product, an increasingly productive working force, and the necessity of increasing profit not only by higher productivity but by raising the buying power of the mass of the people—notions few of their fathers (and none of their grandfathers) gave thought to. Most of them are well aware of the economic validity of the current advertisement slogan of a nationally known corporation, inscribed beneath a picture of many kinds of children: "If they don't make it, we won't." One striking illustration of this changing point of view is the difference among the generations of the Marshall Fields. The first Marshall Field saw little in life beyond his creation from scratch of a great business and a large personal fortune, and had little but scorn for those who had not been as successful as he. He could never have understood his grandson's book entitled *Freedom is More Than a Word,* or the policies of the newspaper founded with grandfather's wealth. The members of the Better Schools Committee, who have devoted time and influence to extend the resources of the Chicago schools, and of the Business Advisory Committee of the Chicago Urban League, are only two examples of this change. The skill and expertise of such leaders should be included in the membership of the Board of Education, as well as the concern of those who can speak clearly for the needs of the children of the "inner city."

Most of these hopeful signs are common to all large cities, not merely to Chicago alone. But there are some situations peculiar to Chicago and Illinois which also seem a little closer to improvement. The century-old state constitution with its unworkable tax system and its rural control over a metropolitan area in which live 60 percent of the ten million people of the state, is now in process of revision. It can scarcely get worse. There is some real possibility that Chicago and its schools may at least win some modicum of home rule so that they need not wait helplessly for months to find out what rural downstate legislators, hostile to what they have always considered alien and inferior city populations, will allow done. One important step has been taken; in 1969 an income tax stopped being an unmentionable curse, and was seriously considered as a solution to the financial difficulties of the state, among which its responsibility for its schools and universities were given some priority. The expensive and inefficient system of county and state superintendents of schools elected on a partisan ballot and saddled with hundreds of patronage jobs is likely to be modified in the constitutional convention. The unenviable distinction of Illinois as one of two of the fifty states with no citizen state board for elementary and secondary education may be erased.

It cannot be hoped that all of the inequities in the relations of one large city to the rest of the state will disappear, because the state—like Gaul—is now divided into three sections, not merely two. The central city is losing population and revenue, but it still contains a third of all the people in Illinois. The other section of the metropolitan area, made up of suburbs with a total population now almost as large as that of the city (and still growing), is widely divergent in wealth and in opportunity for its children. In the remaining third, urban populations like that of East St. Louis suffer even more from rural domination than does the one large city. But changes in some of the ancient handicaps are sure to be made if a new constitution is adopted.

A reversal of policy on federal aid to education by the national Congress is also significant cause for new hope for city schools. Since public education was only a gleam in the eye of a few dreamers like Thomas Jefferson in 1787, it was not even mentioned in the federal Constitution, and the states, as they developed, did little or much with it as they chose. The disastrous discrepancies in what the states did do with education have caused many of the present troubles of urban schools. The subsidies for vocational education, result of a drive in the World War I period, spearheaded by organized labor, the G.I. Bill after World War II, the National Defense Education Act after Sputnik were funded by Congress as a result of specific pressures—not because of acceptance by the federal government of any general responsibility for public education.

The 1954 decision of the Supreme Court, however, decreed that the federal government had responsibility for equalizing educational opportunity in states where laws required separate schools for black and white children. The Civil Rights Act of 1963 extended that interpretation to segregation in schools in general, and the Elementary and Secondary Act of 1964 initiated the assumption of some financial responsibility for equalizing education opportunity for the children of low-income families. The present allocations, which look large in total, are only a trickle for any one large school system. But the trickle is not likely to stop and almost certainly will increase, particularly whenever military costs are reduced. To begin tapping the vast resources of the national government is a long step forward in the recognition of the necessity for effective public education for all the children as a national—not merely a local—responsibility.

Today we have no choice but to assume that these converging factors of change will eventually produce school systems which can reach a goal of real opportunity for all children. To assume otherwise is a numbing, defeatist acceptance of the hopeless failure of democratic government here or anywhere else. There is no point singing such a Jeremiad of final disaster until the last possible effort has failed—and we are a long way still from that day. The kind of public education our urban society needs is becoming clear. Those who see it must work unceasingly to reach it.

But the grim fact that must never be forgotten is that each child goes this way but once, and every day one child is cramped and hampered and fails to grow, takes its toll not only on him but on the future of the city and the nation. We can only echo the cry of Ella Flagg Young—

"How long, O Lord, how long?"

APPENDIXES

Appendix A

FEDERAL LAND GRANTS FOR EDUCATION

There are 1,905,000,000 acres of land within the limits of mainland United States. Of this area, 463,000,000,000 acres lay within the boundaries of the thirteen original states. Between 1781 and 1853, 1,442,000,000 additional acres came under the direct control of the federal government. Of this vast area, one-fifth or 226,000,000 acres were donated to states for several purposes, the largest amounts being given for education. Some 132,000,000 acres, or 9.7 percent of the land of the United States east of the Alleghenies, were given to states for schools, and Texas set aside 23,000,000 of its own land on the same basis. Railroad grants totaled 90,000,000 acres, 6.2 percent of the total. Two and two-tenths percent of the land was reserved for the Indian tribes.

Addition of territory beyond the mainland increased the total area by one-fifth and the public domain by 98 percent of the expanse of Alaska; but the federal government has aided education in these states and possessions in other ways than by the granting of land.

Several such land grants were made at different times. Two were the most important. The Ordinance of 1785 provided for laying out the whole new Northwest Territory into six-square-mile townships, one mile of which in each township was to be set aside for a school. This mile was originally in the same place in each township, the 16th section in the middle tier. When Ohio was admitted as the first state from the territory, the grant of the 16th section was officially reaffirmed. Except for Texas, Oklahoma, and West Virginia, the gift of land for schools was made to every succeeding new state and in 1848 was increased by the addition of a second square mile, the 36th section. Kentucky, Tennessee, and Vermont had not been included. Texas set aside its own land in 1866. The Indian Territory was given other aid as so much of its area had been allotted to Indian tribes. West Virginia, a part of old Virginia, was not granted land. In most of these states from two to seven six-mile-square townships were also granted for seminaries and university at the time that Section 16 was given for "common schools."

The second general gift came under the Morrill Act of 1862, intended to promote higher education in "agriculture and the mechanical arts." Each state was allowed to apply for 30,000 acres of the public domain according to the number of representatives and senators it had sent to Congress. Every state did so apply. The thirteen original states received "scrip" for land outside their territory. There have been a few other separate gifts to schools of mines, for example, and to Howard University.

The new states of the Northwest Territory also received 5 percent of the proceeds of the general sales of public land in their states; in 1841, for that year, nine states received 10 percent of all land sales. Some states used these and other grants made by the federal government for schools, whether Congress had so earmarked them or not. In 1841 one-half million acres were ceded to eight new states for internal improvements. Wisconsin and Illinois used the proceeds from the sale of their share to increase their state school funds. In 1850 fifteen states were given 80,000,000 acres of swamp land, which had not been sold by the central government. Ohio, Wisconsin, and Illinois assigned income derived from the sale of this land to their state school funds. One grant—of money, not of land—in 1836 came from the division, among the existing states, of $27,306,943 of "surplus funds" after the closing of the United States Bank. Indiana and Illinois added two-thirds of their share to their state school funds.

Theoretically, all these lands were to be held as an endowment, rather than sold. No formal authorization for their sale was made by Congress until 1843, when decision as to their management was turned over completely to each state. But most states, including Illinois, allowed the land to be sold without such authorization—and at very low rates. One-third of all the Sections 16 in Illinois had been sold by 1831, more than 300,000 acres. Pressure to sell came from two sources—from those who wanted to buy land cheap, and from those who wanted schools and saw no other source of income for them. Until 1850, and in some cases long after, the existence of schools depended on whatever income could be derived from the sale or rent of the school lands and whatever small amounts could be obtained from state school funds. If these were not sufficient to pay teachers their tiny stipends, or if parents wanted more than five or six months of school, rate bills of some two and a half cents a day might be levied on parents and guardians. Some states used lotteries, so respectable a method of obtaining money for schools that Congress passed fourteen laws between 1814 and 1835 authorizing such lotteries to provide schools in the District of Columbia. Other supplementary sources of income sometimes used were liquor and gambling licenses and fines imposed by the courts.

Township, county, or state governments might control the school land, according to the law of a given state. In the beginning the results were equally disastrous whichever governmental agency was in charge. Later, the states which had assumed control salvaged more land and income than those where unsupervised township and county officials sold the land and disposed of the funds. Every state suffered from at least two problems, squatters who never paid for their land, and those who took the timber, and then abandoned their claim.

Most of the school land was practically given away. In Illinois the buyer need make no down payment, if he paid his 10 percent interest in advance, and remitted the original price within three years. When the collected money was invested, local individuals in charge decided whether any security was required for loans. In states where some security was required for credit on the original purchase, groups of buyers would agree not to "bid up" the price and to pledge security for each other. Speculators in school lands could and did make fortunes in two years' time.

Prices per acre began as low as fifty cents, although the Ordinance of 1785 had stated that none should be sold at less than a dollar. Many Ohio lands sold for less than a dollar an acre, and records show that land with current value admittedly $50 an acre was sold for $6. Kansas sold most of its lands at 20 to 40 percent of current value and at considerably less than adjacent property being sold at the same time by the Santa Fe Railroad.

When school lands were sold the money sometimes disappeared completely. California records show 2,000,000 acres as sold by local authorities for which no accounting of any kind was ever made. The Indiana commissioners who sold that state's swampland for $850,000 never turned the money in to the state school fund. An 1870 report of the State Superintendent of Public Instruction in Missouri listed the reasons given by officials of 49 counties for the disappearance of their school funds:

(1)   The court house burned.
(2)   The township treasurer defaulted with the money.
(3)   Borrowers were insolvent and had given no security.
(4)   Notes of borrowers were worthless.
(5)   The school funds had been stolen.
(6)   No records had been kept of any transactions over school lands.

No state in the union received federal land grants for schools without repetition of this grim story, over and over. When state governments were responsible, the records are clearer, but with results little different. Not only did the local Sections 16 disappear, the state school funds sometimes vanished into thin air. Oregon, South Dakota, Utah, and Wyoming kept what state school funds they had intact. All the other states invested part or all of these funds in "internal improvements," sometimes corruptly, and sometimes just unwisely, and although ostensibly only borrowing them, never paid them back. Ohio called its lost school fund an "irreducible debt." Mississippi invested much of its school land in the Planters' State Bank which failed. Indiana still pays interest each year on a nonexistent state school fund of $10,641,226; Michigan on an imaginary

$5,201,852; Wisconsin 7 percent on $2,251,000; and Illinois pays $57,000 on its long-gone $7,033,753. The interest comes, of course, from current taxation, and completely defeats the purpose for which the original gift had been made—of adding each year to current resources for education from the endowment from the land.

One might hope that the more recently admitted states have learned from the past how to conserve their school lands. But Arizona, admitted as a state in 1912, has not done much better. In 1861 the territory was promised four sections of land in each township for schools when it became a state, the largest allocation made to any state. In 1871 the governor asked if some school land might be sold to supplement the income from gambling licenses, then the only source of school income for the 1,621 children of the state (only 149 of whom were in school), but the request was refused. As the sections of land for common schools were gradually located, some were found to be already occupied, some were on Mexican grants, Indian reservations, or forest reserves, and many in hopelessly arid spots. In 1898 the state was permitted to rent the lands, but until 1905 no more than $5,800 a year had been realized in rents from the few sections located in the scarce farming areas. When the lands began to be sold after 1912, the sections first snapped up at low rates were those which have since become the most valuable. A 1925 report from the State Department of Education divulges that income from all the school lands in Arizona even in 1920 was only 3 percent of state school costs.

Texas saved a considerable state fund from the proceeds of the 23,000,000 acres of its own land reserved for schools in its 1866 constitution. But more than one-tenth of it was sold at fifty cents an acre, and up to 1900 $700,000 had been lost by default on payments. Only one-tenth of the price was paid in Texas at the time of purchase and the remaining nine-tenths need not be paid for ten years. However, in 1905, Texas did have an actual school fund of $52,660,489, the income from which was sufficient to pay 27 percent of all state school costs that year.

Minnesota's conservation policy saved some of that state's most valuable school land. In 1849 the territory had been promised 2,955,902 acres for schools. When it was admitted into the union in 1858, the state took control of these lands from the townships. In 1861 the governor pointed out that Iowa and Wisconsin had received virtually nothing from land now worth two million dollars, and urged that Minnesota take greater care. The warning apparently had some effect, as in 1911 the state had $21,500,000 in its state school fund and a million acres still unsold. More than 20,000 acres of the unsold land were in the iron producing area, and protected by state mineral laws. Lessees of such land paid taxes and a 25-cent-a-ton royalty on all ore removed. It has been stated that one such section has already earned more for educational purposes than the millions of acres of school lands in Michigan, Wisconsin, and Iowa now will ever pay.

In 1906 eight states derived more than 10 percent of all school revenue from the income on land grants. But all of these were western states with sparse populations. Only in Minnesota has any such state school fund actually increased. Per capita costs for education have jumped from twenty or thirty dollars to several hundred, as high schools grew and compulsory education laws were enforced, and the relative importance of these fixed original funds shrinks every year. In 1837 the income from the school lands of Chicago was 100 percent of the income of the schools. In 1969, although rents from the few remaining scraps—like the loop block and Midway Airport—bring in more than a million dollars yearly, they constitute less than one-fifth of 1 percent of the total annual school budget.

Although the tenth of the public domain set aside for schools does not now provide for the opportunities that millions of today's children desperately need, it did serve one purpose. It made possible some kind of public education, no matter how meager, in the period when bitter opposition to any free public instruction made general taxation for schools impossible. It was not until 1850 that even scanty taxes were generally levied—and not until 1855 in Illinois. However, the question as to whether it would have been better to hold the land is purely academic now. The irresistible thirst of the pioneers for land, no matter how obtained, was as violent and emotional as the gold rush to California or the Klondike—and much more rewarding for most participants. Officials who wanted to continue in office made little effort to stem this tide, justifying their failure to enforce existing regulations by the need to encourage population growth and put empty land to profitable use. John Quincy Adams lamented that his dream of the use of the national domain to produce "an inexhaustible fund for progressive and increasing internal development" had never materialized.

It is now impossible to estimate the present value of the original 132,000,000 acres of school land, and not worth the effort to try. But it is discouraging to realize that no single section of it lost so much for so many as did the square mile at the center of Chicago, sold in 1833 for a pittance.

Today, it is probably more significant to question whether this generation is not wasting as carelessly an even more important national resource. The acres that were lost are now paying either land or income taxes to the most affluent nation in history. But we are failing to use that affluence and the scientific knowledge of our day to provide equal opportunity in our schools to develop millions of children to their most socially useful and personally satisfying potential. The failure to use this resource to the full may be more finally decisive of the fate of the nation and the dream it has represented to the rest of the world, than the loss of all the long-gone lands which might now be helping to prevent that failure.

Appendix B

LEGAL RIGHTS TO EDUCATION
OF BLACK CHILDREN IN ILLINOIS

The first settlers in Illinois were Southerners who crossed the Ohio. Although the Ordinance of 1787 had declared the Northwest Territory "forever free," the territorial government legalized slavery by merely calling it "voluntary indenture," supposedly reviewed every year, and giving control over the children of the "indentured" for their continuing "indenture" also. Congress accepted this provision in admitting the state in 1818. By state law, slave owners entering the state could not set their slaves free until 1825. A "free" Negro could not enter the state without a "certificate of freedom," and was to deposit $1,000 as security with the bond. He could be kidnapped and sold into another state with impunity. Without the bond, his services were sold by a sheriff at public auction as late as 1858. There were 746 registered slaves in Illinois in 1830, and they were freely bought and sold as late as 1854. By state law, white persons aiding the Underground Railway were liable to a fine of $500.[1]

In all the early laws, only the white population was counted, whether as voters, children in school, or in any other category. There is no record of slaves being owned in Chicago—which was as far north as Boston—and it was for years one of the most important stations in the Underground Railroad system which helped slaves escape to Canada. Public opinion was vocal against the efforts of slaveholders to capture slaves in Chicago under the Fugitive Slave Law. Chicago had sent a company of volunteers to Kansas, and there had been outspoken opposition to the Kansas-Nebraska Act, despite its being the brainchild of Stephen A. Douglas, a Chicagoan of whom his fellow citizens had been proud.

When the original Black Code for Illinois had been amended in 1853 to keep free Negroes from entering the state, representatives in the legislature from Chicago voted against the amendment. However, they also voted to exclude from any court the testimony of a Negro against a white person. In southern Illinois the pattern of segregation was as complete as in any southern state. The first school law for Chicago, in 1835, had said that "all white children" might attend. The state law of 1855 specified that "persons of color" were to receive state school funds in proportion to the taxes they paid, clearly inferring they were not to go to school with white children, and if they paid no taxes, had no claim to public provision for education whatsoever.

In Chicago, Negro children did attend the public schools, even though no state aid was received for them. But the plight of black children in other parts of the state was described in the Biennial Report of the State Superintendent of Public Instruction for 1867-68, as follows:

> "The larger portion of the aggregate number of colored people in the state are dispersed through the different counties and school districts in small groups of one, two, or three families, not enough to maintain separate schools for themselves, even with the help of the pittance paid for school taxes by such of them as are property holders. This whole dispersed class of our colored population are without the means of a common school education for their children; the law does not contemplate their co-attendance with white children and they are without recourse of any kind. I think it safe to say that at least one-half of the six thousand colored children between the ages of 6 and 21, are in this helpless condition in respect to schools."[2]

The Negroes in Chicago had not been helpless in 1863. In 1889 the General Assembly amended the state school law to make Boards of Education liable to a fine of from $5 to $100 for excluding a child from a public school in Illinois on account of his color. However, in the fifteen southern Illinois counties, and in many other areas as far north as Springfield and Quincy, this law was completely disregarded.

Until 1947, there was no real challenge to the complete public segregation in schools for all Negro children in the fifteen southern counties in Illinois. The State School Directory for that year listed Negro and white schools separately. Some towns, like Edwardsville, had four-year white high schools and three-year Negro. At that time the Illinois Commission on Human Relations pointed out the six state laws forbidding these practices, and urged the State Superintendent of Public Instruction to withhold state aid from districts which refused to obey the law. He replied that he had no authority to make such investigations unless the elected state's attorneys in those counties initiated suit against the elected school boards.[3] In Cairo, Illinois, actually farther south than Richmond, Virginia, no elected state's attorney had any intention of initiating suits to compel integration.

More recent laws, such as the Armstrong Act forbidding gerrymandering of school districts to avoid integration, and the U.S. Civil Rights and 1965 Elementary and Secondary Education Acts have brought perfunctory compliance in this southern tip of the state; but general residential segregation and generally low real estate values in the area have tended to negate the effect of the legislation.

The energetic and successful resistance of the black citizens of Chicago to the 1853 Black Law segregating their children was no new attitude on their part. In 1850 when the harsh Fugitive Slave Law was passed, they organized a Liberty Association which most of the five hundred black residents joined. At a public meeting, well and favorably reported in the press, they organized a police system of their own with six persons on patrol every night in each of seven areas. At this mass meeting they agreed to defend each other at any risk, but to use violence only as a last resort. The papers reported their claim that no colored man in the United States could be free as long as the statement of a person who tried to capture him was considered evidence without proof. They proceeded to take action against the first man who showed up to capture a fugitive. His name was Uriah Hinch, and he came from Missouri with a "trusty slave" to help identify those he sought. A committee of "respectable citizens" called upon him and warned him that his enterprise was risky business in Chicago. The "trusty slave" was delighted to find himself on a boat, bound for Canada. Hearing rumors of possible tar and feathering, Hinch consulted a judge and a lawyer, both of whom told him he had best leave, whereupon he did.

That this organized resistance of black citizens had general support in the city is borne out by the action of the city council on October 21, 1850. By a vote of 9 to 2, it denounced the Fugitive Slave Act and ordered city police to abstain from its enforcement. At a public mass meeting in the City Hall on the same night, a resolution was passed calling northern members of Congress who voted for the law, Judas Iscariots, pointing out that the law applied to white persons also, and stating that "resistance to tyrants is obedience to God." This was too much for Senator Stephen A. Douglas, who had been one of the sponsors of the Act.

Douglas called a mass meeting at the City Hall on October 25; he defended himself for three and a half hours and then introduced a resolution urging citizens to stand fast with the Constitution and all its compromises, calling the council action nullification. This resolution passed the meeting, but the newspapers did not support him. The council finally passed a substitute resolution, which did not tone down its opposition to the law, but stated that since the Supreme Court had held that state officers are under no obligation to fulfil duties imposed upon them by act of Congress, it is not necessary to counsel the city officers to abstain from aiding in the search for refugees. They added, "We do not believe our harbor appropriations will be withheld, our railroads injured, our commerce destroyed or that treason has been committee against the government"[4]—all obviously reasons given for accepting the law.

This kind of group activity among black citizens in Chicago forced the withdrawal of the black school law.

CHICAGO PUBLIC SCHOOL STATISTICS, 1840-1970

Table 1. Enrolment in Chicago Public Schools

Year	City Population	Elementary	High School	College		Total
1840	4,470	317				317
1850	29,963	1,919				1,919
1860	112,172	6,539	312			6,851
1870	298,977	27,342	602			38,939
1880	503,185	58,519	1,043			59,562
1890	1,099,850	131,341	2,825			135,541[a]
1900	1,698,755	215,660	10,201	N	497	255,718[a]
1910	2,185,283	257,620	17,781	N	700	301,172[a]
1920	2,701,705	291,678	36,433	N[d] J[e]	513 491	393,918[a]
1930	3,376,438	326,000[b]	103,851[b]	N J	1,281 3,374	444,816[a]
1940	3,396,809	318,443	144,671	N J	2,074 6,193	399,438[a]
1950	3,620,962	293,142	96,786	N J	1,688 11,126	410,025[a]
1960	3,550,404	410,206	102,886	N J	2,558 23,116	513,092
1969	3,550,404	434,367	145,925		c	580,292
1970	3,332,855	433,319	142,834			576,253

a. These totals include evening, summer and special students, not included in regular day schools, and also administrators.

b. Junior high school; seventh and eighth grades included in elementary, ninth grade in high school.

c. Colleges no longer under jurisdiction of the Chicago Board of Education.

d. Normal School.

e. Junior College.

Table 3. Training and Salary of

Year	Minimum Training Elementary	Salary Scale Elementary	Salary Scale High School
1840		Women $200-$400 Men $400-$800	
1860	2 years of high school	Women $200-$500 Men $500-$1,000	
1880	4 years of high school	Women $400-$775 Men $500-$1,000	Women $850-$1,245 Men $2,000
1900	2 years of Normal School	$650-$1,225 in 10 years	$1,245-$2,000
1920	2 years of Normal School	$1,200-$2,000 in 10 years	$1,600-$3,400
1940	4 years of Normal School	$1,387.50-$2,312.50 in 10 years	$2,035-$3,515
1960	A.B. Degree Certified by Examination	A.B., $5,000 to $7,300 in 10 years; $8,500 in 35; M.A., $5,250 to $7,750 in 10 years; $8,750 in 35; M.A. + a year, $5,500 to $8,000 in 10 years; $9,000 in 35.	
1970	A.B. Degree Certified by Examination or 3 years as substitute	A.B., $8,400.00 to $13,387,50 in 15 years M.A., $8,977.50 to $14,382.50 in 15 years M.A., $9,345.00 to $15,067.50 in 15 years	

Chicago Public School Teachers

*Minimum Training
High School*   *Pension*

Most had A.B. degrees

A.B. Degree Certified by Examination	$400–After 20 years, Women; After 25 years, Men
A.B. Degree Certified by Examination. 2 yrs. experience outside Chicago	$800 after 25 years $1,000 after 35 years
A.B. Degree from Normal College. Examination. Experience in a Chicago Elementary School	$1,000 after 25 years. $1,200 after 35 years +$500 if remaining till age 65
(1950 M.A. Degree) A.B. Degree Certified by Examination	Approximately 41% of salary up to $15,000 after 25 yrs. of service; 51% after 35 yrs at age 60
A.B. Degree Certified by Examination or 3 years as substitute	Same as 1960

Table 2. Number of Teachers in Chicago Public Schools

Year	Total Enrolment	Elementary Teachers	High School Teachers	College Teachers	Total Teachers
1840	317	4			4
1850	1,919	21			21
1860	6,851	126	9		135
1870	38,939	515	22		537
1880	59,562	901	33		958[a]
1890	135,541	2,591	120		2,711
1900	255,718	5,104	306	20	5,806[a]
1910	301,172	5,800	640	33	6,390[a]
1920	393,918	7,398	1,342	38	8,778
1930	444,816	10,171[b]	3,208[b]	209	13,688
1940	399,438	8,613	4,866	370	13,902[a]
1950	410,025	8,601	3,943	411	13,423[a]
1960	513,092	14,939	4,955	636	20,912
1969	580,292	16,223	6,767		26,701[c]
1970	576,253	16,541	6,090		26,884[d]

a. This number includes teachers in special kinds of work, not in regular classrooms.

b. Junior high school teachers included with elementary.

c. There are 3,761 educational employees not listed as regular elementary or secondary teachers. This figure includes administrators and specialists in central and district offices and 2,612 assigned to federally funded projects. (Facts and Figures, 1969, p. 63.)

d. There are 4,253 teachers not listed as regular elementary or high.

Table 4. Expenditures of Chicago Public Schools

Year	Population of City	Expenditures of Schools	Enrolment
1840	4,470	$3,307	317
1860	112,172	$83,834	6,851
1880	503,185	$1,000,003	59,562
1900	1,698,755	$9,970,813	255,718
1920	2,701,705	$31,101,147	393,918
1940	3,396,962	$71,443,560	399,438
1960	3,550,404	$294,376,333	513,092
1970	3,322,855	$561,511,498	576,253

NOTES AND REFERENCES

NOTES AND REFERENCES

1. THE SCHOOLS OF FRONTIER CHICAGO

There are scant records left of the early history of the Chicago schools. Many were destroyed in the fire in 1871. Few of the people who wrote of the city's beginnings thought the schools important enough to mention. Although the first volume of Bessie L. Pierce's *A History of Chicago** lists 32 pages of bibliography, there are few references to schools in these sources. Only one of the published reminiscences of pioneers gives any description of schools.

The archives of the Chicago Historical Society contain newspapers, letters, speeches, and copies of early reports on the beginnings of the Chicago schools which can not be found anywhere else. The textbooks used in Chicago before the Civil War are in the Center for Research Libraries in Chicago.

The following are the most useful sources of information for the period:

Clark, Hannah B., *The Public Schools of Chicago: A Sociological Study.* Chicago: University of Chicago Press, 1897.

Johnston, Shepherd, *Historical Sketches of the Public School System of Chicago: The 25th Annual Report of the Chicago Board of Education of the Year Ending December 31, 1879.* Chicago: Clark and Edwards, 1880.

Morgan, William P., "The School Fund Land of Chicago, with Its History Prior to 1880." Master's Thesis, University of Chicago, 1905.

Pierce, Bessie L., *A History of Chicago; Vol. I, The Beginnings of a City, 1673-1848.* New York: Alfred A. Knopf, 1937.

Wells, William Harvey, "Annual Report of the Superintendent of Schools of Chicago, 1857-1858."

1. Henry E. Hamilton, *Biographical Sketches* [of Richard Hamilton by his son], 1888. Henry R. Hamilton, *The Epic of Chicago.* Hamilton's grandson includes his data in the 1932 published work.

2. Pierce, Vol. I, pp. 318, 333-34.

3. Chicago Democrat, Nov. 26, 1833.

4. School Law of Illinois, 1869, pp. 33-39; Morgan, pp. 7-13.

5. See Appendix A.

6. The Illinois School Code, 1963, p. 160, still includes the following provision: "Whoever without being authorized cuts, fells, boxes, bores or destroys or carries away any tree, sapling or log standing or being on school lands shall forfeit and pay for every tree, sapling or log the sum of $8.00."

*Complete citations for all works referred to may be found in the Bibliography.

7. Chicago Democrat, Feb. 4, 1834. Tuition of $2.00 a quarter was asked but not required of parents.

8. Letter of Frances L. Willard, January 17, 1838.

9. Johnston, pp. 6-7; City Charter of 1837, Sec. 83-92.

10. City Charter of 1837, p. 179; the 1841 report of the Committee on Schools of the Common Council.

11. Pierce, Vol. I, pp. 67-74.

12. Ibid., pp. 179, 418.

13. *United States Sixth Census, 1840,* pp. 359, 377, 449.

14. Fletcher H. Swift, *A History of Public Permanent Common School Funds in the United States, 1795-1905,* p. 63.

15. Johnston, p. 17.

16. Mary H. Porter, *Eliza Chappell Porter, a Memoir.* Eliza Chappell married Jeremiah Porter, the first Presbyterian minister in Chicago.

17. Edwin O. Gale, *Reminiscences of Early Chicago and Vicinity,* p. 211.

18. Johnston, p. 17.

19. Gale, p. 211.

20. Johnston, p. 14.

21. Clark, p. 14; Summary of the Report of the Committee, 1838.

22. Johnston, pp. 24-25; Annual Report of the School Inspectors, 1849.

23. Illinois School Finance and Tax Commission, State Support of Public Education, Springfield; 1947, pp. 34-35.

24. Edith Abbott and Sophonisba P. Breckinridge, *Truancy and Non-Attendance in the Chicago Schools.* p. 27.

2. FRONTIER SCHOOLS BECOME A TOWN SYSTEM

The Report of the Superintendent of the Schools of the City of Chicago in 1855 was the first of the continuously printed records of the school system. Since that time there have been annual reports of superintendents for almost every year, and after 1857, of the Board of Education. In 1846 the inspectors had ordered that the proceedings of their meetings be published in any newspaper which would do so free. Beginning in 1867, the Board published its own Proceedings. Issues of these Proceedings after 1874 are available in every major library in the Chicago area.

Complete sets of the early reports from 1855 to 1873 are in the Chicago Public Library and in the collection of the Chicago State College, formerly the Chicago Normal School. There are scattered copies in other libraries. Proceedings between 1867 and 1873 may be found in the Chicago Public Library. Copies of *The Graded School,* the graded curriculum introduced by Superintendent Wells in 1861, are in the files of the Chicago Historical Society, the Chicago State College, Northwestern University, the University of Chicago, and the Chicago Public Library.

Clark, Johnston, and Morgan remain major sources of information for the period between 1853 and the fire in 1871. The following can be added:

McManis, John T., *Ella Flagg Young and a Half Century of Chicago Schools.* Chicago: A. C. McClurg, 1916.

Pierce, Bessie L., *A History of Chicago; Vol. II, From Town to City, 1848-1871.*
New York: Alfred A. Knopf, 1940.

Wells, William Harvey, *The Graded School. A Graded Course of Instruction for the Chicago Public Schools, with Copious, Practical Directions to Teachers and Observations on Primary Schools, School Records.* . . . Chicago: A.S. Barnes, 1962. 2nd, 3rd editions–Chicago: Dean And Ottoway, 1866, 1867.

William Harvey Wells, 1812-1885. In Memoriam. Sketches of his life and character, memorial addresses and resolutions of public bodies on the occasion of his death. Chicago: Fergus Printing Co., 1887.

1. Report of the Superintendent of Schools, 1855, p. 12.

2. Johnston, p. 33.

3. *William Harvey Wells. In Memoriam,* p. 80.

4. Johnston, pp. 48-53.

5. The author's grandfather, who taught in an Ohio academy, died in 1867. He left a copy among his books.

6. Report of the Superintendent of Schools, 1859, p. 19.

7. Johnston, p. 47. A table of the population of Chicago under 21, and of the enrolment, average membership, and expenditures of Chicago schools from 1837 to 1879.

8. Ibid., pp. 39, 44. In 1865 the legislature changed the number of members of the Board of Education from the fifteen set in 1857 to sixteen, and required that the common council elect one from each ward. (In 1872 the legislature reenacted the 1857 law.)

9. *William Harvey Wells. In Memoriam,* pp. 42-44.

10. Ibid., p. 86.

11. Johnston, p. 34.

12. Morgan, p. 52; Pierce, Vol. II, p. 268.

13. Pierce, Vol. I, p. 512.

14. See Appendix B.

15. McManis, pp. 51, 134.

16. Ibid., p. 53.

17. Chester C. Dodge, *Reminiscences of a School Master,* p. 122.

18. Pierce, Vol. I, p. 382.

19. Johnston, p. 47.

3. THE TOWN BECOMES AN INDUSTRIAL CITY

Besides the reports and proceedings of the Board of Education, three other easily available sources of information on this period are useful:

Abbott, Edith and Sophonisba P. Breckinridge, *Truancy and Non-Attendance in the Chicago Schools.* Chicago: University of Chicago Press, 1917.

Pierce, Bessie L., *A History of Chicago; Vol. III, The Rise of a Modern City, 1871-1898.* New York: Alfred A. Knopf, 1957.

Staley, Eugene, *The History of the Illinois State Federation of Labor.* Chicago: University of Chicago Press, 1930.

1. Clark, p. 22.

2. Johnston, p. 42.

3. Eleventh Annual Report of the Board of Education of Chicago, 1864-65, p. 20.

4. John D. Philbrick, *City School Systems in the United States*. Bureau of Education Circular of Information, No. 1, 1886, pp. 14-15.

5. Johnston, p. 38.

6. See Appendix B.

7. Pierce, Vol. III, p. 383.

8. Clark, p. 44.

9. Clark, pp. 53-54, 62; Morgan, pp. 46, 50.

10. Proceedings, 1879, pp. 126, 149, 163. School was closed a half day, June 12, 1879, so that teachers might get the scrip being paid them for services given in February, March and April. Warrants were given teachers in 1881. Pierce, Vol. III, p. 324; McManis, p. 62.

11. Johnston, p. 43, quoting the law.

12. Dodge, p. 40.

13. Ibid., pp. 38, 119.

14. *A Statement of the Theory of Education in the United States of America, as Approved by Many Leading Educators*. Washington: Government Printing Office, 1874.

15. Citizens Association of Chicago, "Report of the Committee on Education," p. 22.

16. Pierce, Vol. III, p. 389.

17. Philbrick, pp. 14-15.

18. Clark, p. 41.

19. Philbrick, p. 155.

20. Pierce, Vol. III, p. 387.

21. *Eleventh Census of the United States, 1890*, "Population," Part II, p. 117.

22. Proceedings, 1874-75, pp. 21, 31.

23. Pierce, Vol. III, pp. 24, 385-86.

24. Abbott and Breckinridge, p. 55.

25. Robert A. Nottenberg, "The Relationship of Organized Labor to Public School Legislation in Illinois, 1880-1948." Ph.D. Dissertation.

26. Proceedings, 1888-89, p. 75.

27. Abbott and Breckinridge, pp. 58-60.

28. Ibid., pp. 60-62.

29. Ibid., pp. 77-78; Thirty-Ninth Annual Report of the Chicago Board of Education, 1893, p. 5.

30. Abbott and Breckinridge, pp. 78-81; Fortieth Annual Report of the Chicago Board of Education, 1894, pp. 155-59.

31. Staley, pp. 8, 37, 156, 354.

32. Ibid., pp. 19, 33, 150-74; Pierce, Vol. III, pp. 269-71.

33. Pierce, Vol. III, 257, 271-74, 281, 289-91.

34. Ibid., Vol. III, pp. 272-81; Staley, pp. 65-69.

35. Pierce, Vol. III, p. 374.

4. FRONTIER VILLAGE TO WORLD METROPOLIS IN SIXTY YEARS

These are the special sources for this period:

Harper, William R., Chairman, "Report of the Educational Commission of the City of Chicago, Appointed by the Mayor, Hon. Carter H. Harrison." Chicago: R. R. Donnelley and Sons, 1898.

Young, Ella Flagg, *Isolation in the Schools.* Chicago: University of Chicago Press, 1900.

1. Clark, p. 30; Pierce, Vol. III, pp. 331-33.
2. Illinois Public Laws, 1891, pp. 144-45; Clark, p. 101.
3. Illinois Revised Statutes, Chap. 122, Secs. 144, 145; Harper Report, pp. 225-26.
4. Chicago School Extension Committee, Reports, 1898-1912; Harper Report, p. 221.
5. Proceedings, 1893-94, pp. 443-44; Clark, p. 77.
6. John M. Beck, "Chicago Newspapers and the Public Schools, 1890-1920." Ph.D. Dissertation, pp. 117, 206, 209, 234.
7. Proceedings, 1895-96, June 17, 1895.
8. Jack Campbell, *Colonel Francis W. Parker, The Children's Crusader,* pp. 129-46.
9. Clark, p. 54.
10. Ibid. p. 56; Report of the Chicago Board of Education, 1859, p. 63. On April 27, 1969, Chicago newspapers stated that four blocks including the former school land had been sold by the railroads, then holding deeds to the land, for ten million dollars.
11. Clark, pp. 54, 57; Morgan, p. 47.
12. Clark, p. 61. Table of value of lot at State and Madison Streets ranging from $20 in 1833 to $1,250,000 in 1894.
13. Pierce, Vol. III, pp. 324-25; Clark, pp. 57, 58.
14. Clark, p. 60; Pierce, Vol. III, p. 325.
15. Journal of the State Senate of Illinois, 1895, pp. 252-54.
16. Report of the Chicago Board of Education, 1885, pp. 20-22.
17. Pierce, Vol. III, p. 389.
18. Hoyt King, *Citizen Cole of Chicago,* pp. 16, 22-23, 75-77.
19. Dodge, p. 123.
20. Proceedings, 1874-75, pp. 75-76, 130.
21. Dodge, p. 72.
22. Harper Report, p. 35.
23. Henry E. Dewey, "The Development of Public School Administration in Chicago." Ph.D. Dissertation.
24. Theodore R. Sizer, *Secondary Schools at the Turn of the Century,* pp. 66, 131-32.
25. Lawrence A. Cremin, *The Transformation of the School,* p. 85.
26. Harper Report, p. 19.
27. Ibid., pp. 65-66.
28. Ibid., p. 64.
29. Ibid., p. 172.
30. Ibid., pp. 167-68.
31. Ibid., pp. 139-43.
32. Clark, pp. 109, 115.
33. Young, pp. 139, 12, 17.

5. TEACHERS TAKE ARMS AGAINST A SEA OF TROUBLES

There are no detailed published accounts of the beginnings of the organization of teachers in Chicago schools. The Bulletins of the Chicago Teachers Federation from 1901 to 1907 and the Reporter of the Chicago Principals Club, beginning in 1911, are useful. Two unpublished dissertations are pertinent:

Anderson, Olive O., "The Chicago Teachers Federation." Master's Thesis, University of Chicago, 1908.

Reid, Robert, "The Professionalization of Public School Teachers; The Chicago Experience, 1895-1920." Ph.D. Dissertation, Northwestern University, 1968.

1. Anderson, p. 1.

2. Clark, p. 98. The Chicago Record, June 24, 1985, stated that seven years was the average.

3. Harper Report, p. 86

4. Ibid., pp. 167-68.

5. Young, p. 55.

6. Elmer J. Ortman, *Teacher Councils,* p. 1.

7. Chicago Record Herald, Feb. 2, 1902.

8. Anderson, pp. 1-33.

9. Charles E. Merriam, *Chicago: A More Intimate View of Urban Politics,* p. 125.

10. Anderson, p. 34.

11. Stephen G. Wood, "The Retirement System for Public School Teachers in Chicago." Master's Thesis, pp. 8-24.

12. Anderson, p. 5.

13. George S. Counts, *School and Society in Chicago,* pp. 95-96; Chicago Teachers Federation Bulletin, Dec. 20, 1901; Chicago Record, Oct. 17, 18, 1900; Anderson, pp. 8-16.

14. Anderson, pp. 14-16; Chicago Teachers Federation Bulletin, Sept. 5, 1902; Chicago Record Herald, July 10, 1902; Reid, p. 74. The city used its new money to raise salaries of policemen and firemen.

15. Proceedings. 1906-07, p. 1033; Chicago Tribune, Jan. 17, 1907.

16. James W. Linn, *Jane Addams: A Biography,* p. 223.

17. Chicago Teachers Federation Bulletin, Dec. 18, 1903.

18. Proceedings, 1906-07, pp. 569, 601.

19. Anderson, p. 4.

20. Proceedings of the N.E.A., 1904, pp. 145-52.

21. Proceedings, 1905-06, pp. 760-62.

22. Linn, p. 230.

23. Counts, pp. 248-50.

24. Jean E. Fair, "The History of Public Education in Chicago, 1894-1914." Master's Thesis, p. 54.

25. Chicago Record Herald, March 7, 1914.

6. THE BOARD ATTACK ON THE FEDERATION

The following are the most useful sources for the first sixteen years of the twentieth century:

Beck, John M., "Chicago Newspapers and the Public Schools, 1890-1920." Ph.D. Dissertation, University of Chicago, 1953.

Margaret Haley's Scrapbook. (In the files of the Chicago Teachers Union.)

Margaret Haley's Bulletin, 1902-07, 1915-16.

1. Abbott and Breckinridge, p. 88.

2. Proceedings, 1904-05, p. 520, 1905-06, p. 627.

3. Chicago Daily News, Feb. 11, 1969. Superintendent Cooley is quoted in the "Sixty Years Ago" column: "For nine years it has been fight, fight, fight. There can be no assurance it will not continue to be so. I am tired and sore."

4. Young, *Isolation in the Schools*, pp. 3, 22, 47.

5. Sixty-first Annual Report of the Chicago Board of Education, 1915, p. 185.

6. Proceedings, 1913-14, p. 596, 1914-15, pp. 2, 368, 601; Chicago Record Herald, Dec. 2, 1913.

7. Harper Report, p. 206.

8. Proceedings, 1908-09, p. 547.

9. Counts, p. 139; Staley, pp. 527-28.

10. Counts, pp. 145-51, 168-69.

11. Proceedings, 1913-14, pp. 572-73; Chicago Record Herald, Sept. 6, 1913.

12. Chicago Tribune, July 17, 1915.

13. Beck, p. 84; Report of Chicago Federation of Teachers, April 15, 1913.

14. Proceedings, 1915-16, p. 734.

15. Merriam, p. 128.

16. Margaret Haley's Scrapbook, p. 20.

17. Chicago Herald, Sept. 16, 1915.

18. Reid, pp. 166, 185.

19. Proceedings, 1915-16, p. 963.

20. Margaret Haley's Bulletin, Oct. 21, 1915, p. 6.

21. United Federation of Teachers of New York City, The United Teacher, Dec. 14, 1966, p. 9.

22. Proceedings, 1915-16, pp. 3080-91.

23. Proceedings, 1916-17, pp. 1730-31.

7. A TENURE LAW LEAVES MANY PROBLEMS UNSOLVED

Essential reference material for this period:

Committee on Schools, Fire, Police and Civil Service of the City Council of Chicago, "Recommendations for the Reorganization of the Public School System of the City of Chicago, 1916."

Counts, George S., *School and Society in Chicago*. New York: Harcourt, Brace and Co., 1928.

Reports of the Elementary Teachers Council, 1921-25.

Public Education Association, Bulletins 1-4, 1917.

1. City Council Committee, p. 1.

2. Ibid., pp. 4-8.

3. Public Education Association, Bulletin 2, pp. 3-5.

4. Lloyd Wendt and Herman Kogan, *Big Bill of Chicago,* p. 175.

5. Margaret Haley's Bulletin, Dec. 31, 1927.

6. Reid, pp. 149, 258.

7. Proceedings of the N.E.A., 1904, pp. 145-52.

8. Ibid., 1912, p. 72; Ibid., 1914, p. 914.

9. Mildred S. Fenner, *N.E.A. History,* p. 155.

10. Staley, pp. 364-65.

11. Counts, pp. 251-53; Proceedings, 1918-19, pp. 24-26; Ibid., 1919-20, pp. 1-3, 853.

12. Wendt and Kogan, p. 175.

13. Counts, pp. 68-70, 253-57.

14. Proceedings, 1918-19, Vol. 2, p. 243.

15. Constitution of High School Council, June, 1922.

16. Reports of Elementary Teachers Council, 1921-25, pp. 28-29.

17. Bulletin of the Women's City Club, 1923, p. 274; Counts, 223-25.

18. Counts, pp. 259-63; Wendt and Kogan, pp. 209-11.

19. Reports of Elementary Teachers Council, p. 157.

20. Report of the Superintendent of Schools of Chicago, 1926, pp. 15-16; Proceedings, 1925-26, pp. 1162, 1337, 1442.

8. MODERNIZATION OF SCHOOLS ORDERED BY SUPERINTENDENT

The most important source of information for the McAndrew era is George S. Counts, *School and Society in Chicago.*

1. Report of the Superintendent, 1918, p. 9.

2. Counts, pp. 105, 198-99.

3. Proceedings, 1924-25, pp. 1342, 1649.

4. Joint Bulletin of High School Teachers Federations, April 1925, p. 5.

5. School Facts, Feb. 11, 1931. This Bulletin was issued from the Office of the Superintendent between 1929 and 1931.

6. Federation News (Vol. 12) Dec. 23, 1924, p. 11; Counts, pp. 179-84.

7. Proceedings, 1924-25, p. 59.

8. Reports of the Elementary Teachers Councils, pp. 157-63.

9. Proceedings, 1924-25, pp. 964-47; quotation from Proceedings 1906-07, pp. 760-61.

10. Report of the Superintendent, 1924, p. 10; Ibid., 1926, pp. 31-36.

11. Young, p. 106.

12. Report of the Superintendent, 1926, p. 55.

13. Proceedings, 1924-25, p. 955.

14. Ibid., 1927-28, p. 973.

15. Counts, pp. 194, 200.

16. Proceedings, 1924-25, pp. 102-104.

17. Annual Report of the Chicago Association of Commerce, 1926, pp. 16, 21.

18. Counts, pp. 158-59.

19. Proceedings, 1924-25, pp. 72-74.

20. Ibid., p. 1496.

9. THE NON-TEACHER PAYROLLS BECOME THOMPSON PATRONAGE LISTS

Books worth consulting for impact of the second Thompson era are:

Lewis, Lloyd and Henry Justin Smith, *Chicago: The History of Its Reputation.* New York: Harcourt, Brace and Co., 1929, re. ed. 1938.

Merriam, Charles E., *Chicago: A More Intimate View of Urban Politics.* New York: The Macmillan Co., 1929.
Wendt, Lloyd and Herman Kogan, *Big Bill of Chicago.* New York: Bobbs Merrill, 1953.

1. Proceedings, 1924-25, p. 973.
2. Ibid., 1925-26, pp. 264, 456, 561.
3. Ibid., 1926-27, pp. 9, 104, 337, 1263.
4. Mary J. Herrick, "Negro Employees of the Chicago Board of Education." Master's Thesis, 1931.
5. Proceedings, 1926-27, p. 1670, 1927-28, p. 1384.
6. Ibid., 1927-28, pp. 217-20.
7. Wendt and Kogan, pp. 250-77.
8. Proceedings, 1927-28, p. 972.
9. John Landesco, *Organized Crime in Chicago,* 1929.
10. Proceedings, 1926-27, p. 1500.
11. Wendt and Kogan, p. 277.
12. Olander and Fitzpatrick did not support Thompson.
13. Proceedings, 1925-26, pp. 1779, 1802.
14. Ibid., 1926-27, pp. 1511-13.
15. Ibid., 1927-28, pp. 214, 220.
16. Wendt and Kogan, 185, 204. He is still in the employ of the Board in 1970.
17. Ibid., p. 302.
18. Proceedings 1927-28, pp. 337-38, 343, 956, 1037-50; Counts, pp. 276-84.
19. Wendt and Kogan, p. 296.
20. Proceedings, 1927-28, pp. 955-66.
21. Wendt and Kogan, p. 300.
22. Merriam, p. 112.
23. Lewis and Smith, p. 478.
24. Wendt and Kogan, pp. 284-85.
25. Proceedings, 1927-28, p. 360.
26. Carroll Wooddy, *The Pineapple Primary,* p. 209.
27. Wendt and Kogan, p. 278.
28. Herrick, pp. 59, 66.
29. Proceedings, 1928-29, p. 8.
30. Herrick, pp. 49-52.

10. THE SCHOOLS RUN OUT OF MONEY

Sources of information on the financial collapse of the Chicago school system are:

Chicago Bureau of Public Efficiency, "Chicago School Finances, 1915-1925, with Addenda for 1926." Chicago: 1927.
Simpson, Herbert D. *Tax Racket and Tax Reform in Chicago.* Menasha, Wis.: Collegiate Press, 1930.
——, *The Tax Situation in Illinois.* Evanston: Institute for Research in Land Economics and Public Utilities, Northwestern University, 1929.

1. Sixty-first Annual Report of the Chicago Board of Education, p. 185.
2. Chicago School Finances, 1915-1925, pp. 27-29, 35, 41-49.
3. Staley, pp. 526-27; Chicago School Finances, 1915-1925, p. 35.
4. Chicago School Finances, 1915-1925, pp. 142-43.
5. Ibid., pp. 99-111, 219.
6. Annual Report of the Superintendent of Schools, 1926, p. 75.
7. Chicago School Finances, 1915-1925, pp. 37-38, 170-73, 225.
8. Ibid., pp. 101-103.
9. Simpson, *Tax Racket and Tax Reform in Chicago*, p. 224.
10. Merriam, p. 30.
11. Simpson, *Tax Racket and Tax Reform in Chicago*, p. 155.
12. Ibid., p. 130.
13. Ibid., pp. 185-86.
14. Ibid., pp. 186-88.
15. Ibid., pp. 190-93.
16. School Facts, June 18, 1930, p. 3.
17. Alex Gottfried, *Boss Cermak of Chicago: A Study of Political Leadership*.
18. Nelson B. Henry and Jerome G. Kerwin, *Schools and City Government*, p. 53.
19. Federation of Women High School Teachers, Bulletin, June 26, 1934.

11. A GRADUATED INCOME TAX AND A PLAN TO PROTECT INSTRUCTION

The five volumes of the *Report of the Survey of the Schools of Chicago*, made by the Division of Field Studies of Teachers College, Columbia University, under the direction of George D. Strayer, analyze not only the desperate financial situation of the school system, but the complete control of finances and of non-teaching personnel by the Board of Education as well as the helplessness of the superintendent.

The Survey Graphic "Chicago Issue," October 1934, has a series of articles dealing with this period, and Fortune for August 1936 gives Kelly's record in the Sanitary District in an article, "The Kelly-Nash Machine."

A Ph.D. dissertation (University of Chicago, 1968) by Stephen D. London, "Business and the Chicago Public School System, 1890-1966," analyzes the makeup and motives of the Sargent Committee, with interviews of surviving members.

1. Governor's Tax Conference, "Report of the Executive Committee." Springfield: 1931, pp. 2-7.
2. Traylor, Melvin A., "On the Need for a Graduated Income Tax for Illinois." Address to the First Special Session of the 57th General Assembly, Dec. 1, 1931, pp. 12-14.
3. The decision is quoted verbatim in "Report, [Illinois] Commission on Revenue," Springfield, 1963, pp. 362-66.
4. Proceedings, 1931-32, pp. 717-18. Francis X. Busch, President of the Union League Club, asked for cuts in nonteaching employees and services comparable to those being made in the educational department.

5. Joint Committee on Real Estate Valuation, "Property Assessments, Public Revenue and Retrenchments for 1932: A Statement Presented to the Chicago Board of Education."

6. Chicago Daily News, March 3, 1931; Chicago Herald Examiner, March 28, 1932.

7. Chicago Herald Examiner, March 24, 1932.

8. Federation of Women High School Teachers, Bulletin, May 1932.

9. Chicago Commerce, July 14, 1923, p. 9, quoting this remark from President Hadley of Yale.

10. Proceedings, 1931-32, p. 340.

11. Strayer et al., Vol. I, pp. 173, 232-37, 199-201.

12. Washington Herald, June 22, 1932; Chicago Herald Examiner, June 12, June 21, 1932.

13. Chicago Daily News, July 13, 1932. The Proceedings do not record this public hearing.

14. William Wattenberg, On the Educational Frontier, p. 39; Chicago Tribune, Nov. 15, 1932.

15. The dramatic collapse of the Insull empire is recorded in Forrest McDonald, Insull, and in contemporary periodicals. See Survey Graphic for a series of articles: e.g. V. O. Key, p. 474, gives the Insull story in detail. Donald Richberg, "Gold-Plated Anarchy," in Nation, April 5, 1933, deals with Insull's influence in the city. Harold Gosnell, Machine Politics, Chicago Model, p. 5, says of him, "In Chicago, both the Democratic and Republican leaders had aided and abetted Insull in his savage struggle for economic power. Both accepted huge campaign funds." Richberg adds, "Insull was more responsible than any other man in Chicago's history for the degradation of municipal government to its lowest level of corruption."

16. Chicago Daily News, August 17, 1932.

17. Federation of Women High School Teachers, Bulletin, Dec. 7, 1932. The list was given them by a staff member of the Finance Committee of the City Council who could not act himself.

18. Strayer et al. Vol. I, pp. 11-16, 27, 30-35, 97, 150, 184; Vol. IV, pp. 7-8, 35-41, 135, 170-74.

19. Ibid., Vol. I, pp. 168, 221.

20. Ibid., Vol. I, pp. 238-42.

21. Fortune, pp. 117, 126.

22. New Republic, July 5, 1933.

23. Wattenberg, p. 20; The American Teacher, April 1933.

12. THE AXE FALLS ON INSTRUCTION–NOT ON PATRONAGE

Indispensable for understanding the cuts made in school services and their effects are the following:

Citizens Schools Committee, "Chicago Schools," June 1934-present.

——, News Releases, 1933-34.

Federation of Women High School Teachers, "Financial Outlook for Chicago Schools," Feb. 1934.

——"High School Education in Chicago," May 1934.

——" 'A Thorough and Efficient System' of Schools for all the Children of the State has not been provided by the Illinois General Property Tax," 1935.

The Federation's monthly Bulletins and radio speeches are also pertinent.

Wattenberg, William, *On the Educational Frontier: The Reactions of Teacher Associations in New York and Chicago.* New York: Columbia University Press, 1936.

1. Proceedings, 1933-34, pp. 24-27; Chicago Tribune, July 13, 1933.
2. Federation of Women High School Teachers, Bulletin, July 18, 1933.
3. Chicago Herald Examiner, August 4, 1933.
4. Save Our Schools Committee Flier, August 5, 1933.
5. Chicago Herald Examiner, July 26, 1933.
6. Ibid., July 22, 1933; Chicago Tribune, July 22, 1933.
7. WCFL, 10 p.m. broadcast, Feb. 20, 1933.
8. Strayer et al., Vol. I, pp. 202-12, 232-37.
9. Wattenberg, p. 29.
10. Burton Duffie, "Educational Policies of Two Leading Newspapers." Master's Thesis.
11. Henry and Kerwin, pp. 29-30.
12. Federation of Women High School Teachers, "Financial Outlook for Chicago Schools," and Bulletin, April 1934.
13. Chicago Schools, Oct. 1934.
14. In 1932 DuSable High School consisted of three stories of steel framework with a cement stage and swimming pool. In 1935, the walls were built.
15. "Financial Outlook for Chicago Schools," pp. 5-6.
16. Chicago Herald Examiner, Oct. 1, 1933, July 22, 1934.
17. Oscar Hewitt, Chicago Tribune School Reporter. He was dismissed by the Tribune and appointed Director of Public Works for the City.
18. Chicago Herald Examiner, July 21, 1933.
19. Chicago Schools, Jan. 1935.
20. Proceedings, 1934-35, p. 338.
21. Chicago Schools, Jan. 1935.
22. " 'A Thorough and Efficient System' of Schools has not been Provided," p. 3.
23. Chicago Schools, Jan. 1935; N.E.A., "Report of an Investigation: Certain Personnel Practices in the Chicago Schools," p. 44.
24. Federation of Women High School Teachers, Bulletin, August 1935; N.E.A., "Report of an Investigation," p. 57. Superintendent Bogan made this statement to a committee of the Citizens Schools Committee.
25. Report to Sub-committee on Civic Education, of Superintendent Bogan's Advisory Council, Feb. 1931.
26. School Facts, Jan. 1931.
27. Proceedings, 1935-36, pp. 1178-79.
28. Chicago Schools, Nov. 1936.
29. Chicago Teachers Union, "Why No Pay Restoration?" July 1937.
30. Chicago Schools, June 1937, June 1938.
31. Citizens Schools Committee, "Charting the Course for Vocational Education," 1939.
32. Chicago Tribune, April 22, 1938; Chicago Schools, March 1939, May 1940, April 1941.

13. A CITIZENS COMMITTEE AND A TEACHERS UNION OPPOSE THE BOARD

1. Chicago Tribune, Nov. 21, 1916; Chicago Herald, May 7, 1916, May 29, 1917; Chicago Schools, May 1936.

2. Chicago Schools, Jan. 1950.

3. Ibid., Oct. 1939, Feb. 1941, April 1941, Nov. 1943, August 1945, Nov. 1947.

4. Chicago Schools, March 1944; N.E.A., "Report of an Investigation," pp. 45-47.

5. American Teacher, June 1930.

6. Levitt, "Activities of Local Teacher Organizations Since 1929." Master's Thesis, University of Chicago, 1936. A description of the Volunteer Emergency Committee, the parades, and other transient organizations is included.

7. Wattenberg, pp. 82, 94; Bessie Slutsky, "The Chicago Teachers Union and Its Background." Master's Thesis.

8. High School Teachers Association, "Teacher News and Views," May 1, 1937.

9. Chicago Teachers Union Magazine, June 1937, pp. 3-9.

10. Illinois Federation of Labor, Weekly News Letter, Dec. 23, 1932; Counts, p. 167; Staley, pp. 501, 536; Merriam, pp. 128-29, 210.

11. Illinois Federation of Labor, Proceedings, Oct. 18, 1915, p. 1; Illinois State Teachers Association, Illinois Teacher, Oct. 15, 1915; Staley, p. 536.

12. Chicago Teachers Union Bulletin, Feb. 26, 1938, Sept. 16, 1939.

13. Chicago Daily News, June 22, 1936.

14. Chicago Schools, Nov. 1937; Chicago Daily News, June 24, 1937; N.E.A., "Report of an Investigation," pp. 32-34; Chicago Teachers Union Bulletin, June 1937.

15. Chicago Unitarian Council, "Appeal for Civic Action, The Record of William H. Johnson," Chicago: 1938; Chicago Schools, June 1937, June 1938; Chicago Teachers Union Bulletin, March 30, 1938, April 16, 1938, Nov. 22, 1938; N.E.A., "Report of an Investigation," pp. 37-40, 58. The ZMHRAL affidavit is included here.

16. Ex. Rel. Cook V. Board of Education, 295 Ill. App. 41 (1938) Chicago Teachers Union Bulletin, Feb. 26, 1938, Oct. 29, 1938, Dec. 3, 1938; Chicago Schools, Jan. 1938; N.E.A., "Report of an Investigation," p. 39.

17. Chicago Teachers Union Bulletin, Sept. 13, 1946, Dec. 3, 1947; Chicago Teachers Union Magazine, April, 1941; Chicago Schools, March 1939; N.E.A., "Report of an Investigation," pp. 35-37.

18. Chicago Schools, April 1939. Sixty-two thousand children were on half day schedule.

19. Chicago Daily News, Editorial, Oct. 23, 1937, "Are Only Dumb Teachers Wanted?" Chicago Daily News, March 3, 1938, April 25, 1938, Feb. 11, 1939; Chicago Tribune, April 25, 1938, N.E.A., "Report of an Investigation," pp. 20-28.

20. Chicago Schools, April 1942; N.E.A., "Report of an Investigation," pp. 27-32.

21. Robert F. Pearse, "Studies in White Collar Unionism. The Development of a Teachers Union." Ph.D. Dissertation, University of Chicago, 1950, pp. 244, 261.

22. Ibid., pp. 162, 261.

23. Chicago Teachers Federation Bulletin, Dec. 16, 1941, Jan. 1947; "Letter to Mayor Kelly," June 18, 1946.

24. Chicago Teachers Union Bulletin, Oct. 7, 1939; Chicago Schools, Nov. 1939, April 1940.

25. Chicago Schools, June 1946.

26. Gosnell, Fortune, p. 19. Roosevelt in 1935 wired congratulations to Kelly on his overwhelming victory of 800,000 to 167,000.

27. Pearse, pp. 57, 198, 205; J. David Greenstone, Labor in American Politics, pp. 86, 93, 95, 125, 127. Greenstone points out that the Democratic party in Chicago has preferred

to deal with individual unions, and has discouraged union political organizations, such as COPE, in sharp contrast to union action in Detroit.

28. Sun Times, March 16, 1969; Pearse, p. 63.
29. Chicago Schools, June 1942.
30. Chicago Teachers Union Bulletin, Feb. 15, 1943; Pearse, pp. 152-53; Slutsky, pp. 172, 180.
31. Chicago Teachers Union Magazine, June 1937-June 1947.
32. Chicago Teachers Union Bulletin, Nov. 5, 1944; Chicago Schools, Nov. 1944.

14. A BOARD REMAINS FOR THIRTEEN YEARS

Three periodicals describe the reasons for the invulnerability of the Kelly-Nash organization, its connection with organized crime, its use of Roosevelt's popularity for its own end, and the reasons for its treatment of the public schools:

Flynn, John T., "These Our Rulers," Colliers (Vol. 106) June 29, July 6, July 13, July 20, 1940.
"The Kelly-Nash Machine," Fortune (Vol. 14) August 1936.
Survey Graphic, "Chicago Issue," (Vol. 23) Oct. 1934. This issue contains articles by V. O. Key, Milton Mayer, Charles Merriam, Donald Slesinger, and Louis Wirth.

Twelve years of conflict over the management of the schools are summed up in the report made by the National Commission of the Defense of Democracy of the N.E.A.

National Education Association, "Report of an Investigation: Certain Personnel Practices in the Chicago Public Schools." Washington: 1945.

1. Fortune, August 1936, p. 114; Colliers, June 29, 1940, p. 43.
2. Fred W. Sargent, "The Tax Payer Takes Charge." Saturday Evening Post. (Vol. 205) p. 24; London, "Business and the Chicago Public Schools," Doctor's Dissertation, pp. 103-105, 114-24; V. O. Key, "The Unholy Alliance," Survey Graphic, pp. 473-75. London points out that although 65 of the 165 listed on the Sargent Committee did not live in the city, it included all the major real estate firms, the State Street Council members, and others interested in reduction of real estate taxes. Sargent's railroad, for instance, owned much land within the city.
3. Gosnell, p. 17; Fortune, p. 114; Louis Wirth, "The Land and its People," Survey Graphic, p. 469.
4. Gosnell, p. 54; Donald Slesinger, "The Second Century." Survey Graphic, p. 462.
5. Interview with Joseph Keenan, Secretary of the Chicago Federation of Labor, 1949.
6. Fortune, pp. 114-18; Chicago Daily News, Oct. 30, 1934.
7. Fortune, pp. 118, 123-24.
8. Stuart, The Twenty Incredible Years, p. 547.

9. Chicago Tribune, July 13, Dec. 9, 1932; Chicago Principals Club Reporter, Dec. 7, Dec. 19, 1932; London, pp. 92-93; Hazlitt, "Crisis in School Government," Doctor's Dissertation, pp. 32-33.

10. London, p. 10.

11. Donald Slesinger, Survey Graphic, p. 512.

12. Donald Richberg, "Gold Plated Anarchy," Nation (Vol. 146) April 1935, p. 368; London, pp. 78-79; Gosnell, p. 6, Fortune, p. 126; Colliers, July 6, 1940, pp. 22, 24, 56, Survey Graphic, pp. 473-74, 479.

13. Colliers, July 6, 1940, p. 22; Gosnell, p. 19.

14. Colliers, June 29, 1940, p. 40; Milton Mayer, "Corrupt and Contented," Survey Graphic, p. 478.

15. Merriam, p. 30; Fortune, pp. 114-17, 126; Gosnell, p. 15; Colliers, June 29, pp. 14-15, 42-45, July 6, 1940, p. 56; Chicago Sun Times, June 24, 1951.

16. Fortune, p. 126. Prof. Harold Gosnell was Chairman of the committee which interviewed Committeeman Lindheimer.

17. Colliers, July 6, p. 60, July 13, 1940, p. 48; London, pp. 106-107, 124; Chicago Tribune, May 10, 1933; Gosnell, p. 15.

18. Atlantic Monthly, "Spasmodic Diary of a Chicago Teacher." (Vol. 152) Nov. 1933, p. 513. An anonymous article—the author was never discovered by the Board.

19. Chicago Schools, Jan. 1936.

20. Chicago Schools, Nov. 1904; Chicago Teachers Union Bulletin, Nov. 4, 1944; N.E.A., "Report of an Investigation," p. 6.

21. Chicago Sun, Jan. 18, 1946. In the Chicago Tribune, Jan. 19, 1946, Johnson is quoted as saying the N.E.A. was "only a hiking club."

22. N.E.A., "Report of an Investigation," p. 6; Chicago Tribune, Jan. 18, March 3, March 21, 1946.

23. Chicago Tribune, Chicago Sun, March 31, 1946.

24. Chicago Sun, June 18, 1946.

25. Proceedings, 1946-47, p. 1245.

26. Chicago Sun, Sept. 20, 1946.

27. Merriam, p. 210; Chicago Teachers Union Bulletin, March 3, April 21, June 17, 1947.

15. A SUPERINTENDENT CLEANS THE AUGEAN STABLES

The Annual Reports of the General Superintendent of Schools, the issues of Educational Progress and Facts and Figures furnish complete and reliable data on the activities of the school system. The Chicago Teachers Union began a monthly 8-12 page newspaper in September 1947.

1. Proceedings, 1947-48, pp. 47-48, 1010-16. The Chicago Tribune, Jan. 25, 1949, accused the Superintendent of "making a pay-off" to the N.E.A. in appointing Keener.

2. Proceedings, 1947-48, pp. 221, 375.

3. Ibid., 1951-52, pp. 318, 531-45. The purchasing agent ordered 400 automobiles for someone, at the Board of Education discount. He said at first that they had been ordered at the request of a Board member, but later denied this. The Board members refused to approve of his dismissal.

4. Annual Report of the General Superintendent, 1949-50; Educational Progress, June 1949, pp. 3-4, May 1952, p. 12.

5. The Superintendent was quoted in the Herald American, Dec. 10, Dec. 23, 1947, as planning sex education classes. No action was taken on these plans.

6. The summary of the extensive survey of health in Chicago and Cook County, made by the U.S. Public Health Service in 1947, headed its comment on Chicago schools, "School Health Services—Lacking," and stated that systematized and effective medical and nursing service were almost completely absent in both public and private schools in Chicago. ("A Blue Print for a Healthy Community," pp. 25-27).

7. Francis McKeag in Chicago Schools Journal, Sept.-Oct. 1955, p. 2, details the development of the Social Center Program, sponsored by the citizen groups.

8. Chicago Schools, March 1949, Sept. 1951, Oct. 1951.

9. Educational Progress, Oct. 1949; Chicago Schools Journal, Nov.-Dec., 1949.

10. Proceedings, 1949-50, pp. 1310, 1439. The nominee of the General Superintendent had been an active opponent of the previous administration. Five Board members passed their votes, and the President of the Board was absent. This was the first nomination made by Hunt not approved by the Board.

11. Chicago Union Teacher, Jan. 1948, p. 5.

12. Facts and Figures, 1953, p. 10.

13. Report of the General Superintendent, 1949-1950, p. 67.

14. School Finance and Tax Commission, "State Support of Public Education in Illinois." Springfield; 1947, pp. 106-107.

15. Reports of the Educational Commissions of 1909, 1925, and 1935.

16. Chicago Union Teacher, Jan., Feb. 1948. All the metropolitan press had Jan. 26, 1948, headlines on this confrontation.

17. Chicago Union Teacher Magazine, June 1943, Feb. 1947. Workshops and methods of collective bargaining were set up in 1946 and 1947 by the Union.

18. Chicago Union Teacher, Dec. 1949, Dec. 1950, Dec. 1951.

19. Proceedings, 1946-47, pp. 1245-46.

20. Citizens Schools Committee, "Report of the Committee to Study the School Board Nominating Process in Chicago," Sept. 1, 1964, p. 2.

21. Chicago Tribune, March 21, 1946. It followed up the attack on Dushane with an editorial entitled, "There is No Such Thing as Red-Baiting," on April 5, 1946.

22. Proceedings, 1947-48, pp. 1443-45; Chicago Union Teacher, June, Oct. 1948.

23. Chicago Union Teacher, April 5, 1951; Chicago Tribune, March 16, 1951, carried a first-page story with the heading, "Foe of Anti-Red Oath Branded Aid to Commies."

24. Chicago Tribune, April 28, 1952, carried the full resolution.

25. Proceedings, 1949-50, pp. 528-30; Chicago Sun Times, Feb. 1950.

16. THE CITY CHANGES FASTER THAN THE SCHOOLS

Sources of information for the 1953-1964 years:

"We Build: Ten Years of Growing, 1953-1963." Annual Report of the General Superintendent of Schools, 1963.

Facts and Figures, 1954-1964.

News of the Chicago Public Schools, 1963-1964.

U.S. Commission on Civil Rights, "Civil Rights, U.S.A. The Public Schools: Cities in the North and West," 1962, pp. 175-248.

Chicago Urban League, "Schools Seminar," 1962.

Pois, Joseph, The School Board Crisis: A Chicago Case Study. Chicago: Educational Methods, Inc., 1964.

Prof. Pois was a member of the Chicago Board of Education from 1956 to 1961. He has a Doctor's degree in Political Science from the University of Chicago, a law degree; he is a C.P.A., and was Illinois Director of Finance in Gov. Stevenson's cabinet. He is now on the faculty of the University of Pittsburgh.

1. Drake and Cayton, pp. 8-13; Duncan and Duncan, p. 37; *Statistical Abstract of the United States,* 1969, p. 19; Bogue and Dandekar, p. 7; Pois, p. 17.

2. Facts and Figures, 1966, p. 93.

3. "Local Community Fact Book, Chicago Metropolitan Area, 1960." Chicago: Chicago Community Inventory, University of Chicago, 1963, pp. 2-5, 67-73, 83-89; Chicago Sun Times, Nov. 23, 1964.

4. Annual Report of the General Superintendent, 1963, pp. 3-6, 52.

5. Ibid., p. 36.

6. Ibid., pp. 10-22, 39-43, 52; Report on Special Summer Schools, 1963.

7. Ibid., pp. 22-33.

8. Proceedings, 1964-65, pp. 2834-44; Facts and Figures, 1965, pp. 28, 36, 39.

9. Facts and Figures, 1966, p. 82.

10. Chicago Daily News, August 19, 1961, Editorial, "A Compliment for Chicago Schools"; Chicago Sun Times, August 19, 1961, "A Memo to New Yorkers."

11. Benjamin C. Willis, "The Need for Professionalism in Education Today." Chicago Schools Journal, March, 1954, pp. 273-80. Questions posed in this article are "Shall we be errand boys or leaders? Are we only to respond to trends and pressures? . . . I know of no patient who, upon entering a hospital, dictates to his physician concerning the program of medication. His family does not do so either." "Much of what is wrong with education today, can be attributed to the fact that educators . . . have abdicated from positions of educational leadership, and have permitted themselves and their schools to be swayed by the winds of uninformed public opinion." "I speak of the position of the teacher in society . . . as the custodian of a technique." "Should the schools employ social workers and teach driver education? . . . How far does the school responsibility extend in relation to the home and community?"

12. Pois, pp. 85-98, 118-25, 207-12.

13. Chicago Urban League, "An Equal Chance For Education." Chicago: Research Department, 1962, p. 10. The Crisis, "De Facto Segregation by the Chicago Public Schools." (Vol. 65, No. 2) Feb. 1958, pp. 87-93.

14. Proceedings, 1961-62, pp. 924, 925, 1025; "Civil Rights, U.S.A.," pp. 191-94, 200, 233; Chicago Daily News, Oct. 5, 1963.

15. "Civil Rights, U.S.A.," pp. 196-97, 232.

16. Ibid., pp. 209-15. The Webb Case (Civ. No. 61C1569DC.N.D.Il.) and the Burroughs Case (Civ. No. 62C206,D.C.N.D.Ill.) protested the overcrowding of the Burnside segregated school, immediately adjacent to a white school whose unused rooms housed blind and deaf students from many areas.

17. Ibid., p. 226, quoting Dean Charles Monroe of Wilson Junior College.

18. Ibid., p. 23.

19. Proceedings, 1958-59, p. 830.

20. New York Times, Sept. 16, 1961.

21. Chicago Daily News, May 7, 1962.

22. Proceedings, 1963-1964, pp. 274-76.

23. Ibid., p. 446.

24. Pois, pp. 109-12; Chicago Daily News, Oct, 4, 1967.

25. London, "Business and the Chicago Public School System, 1890-1966." Doctor's Dissertation, p. 134. The telegram stated: "The Chicago schools need leadership from a

great superintendent and an effective Board of Education. We urge you to meet with Dr. Willis and reconcile your differences to guarantee stability and progress in our educational system."

26. Proceedings, 1963-64, p. 452; Pois, pp. 112-14.

27. The Superintendent was quoted in the Chicago Sun Times, Nov. 23, 1963, as stating that 244,770 out of the total of 466,738 were absent.

28. Chicago Sun Times, Editorial, Nov. 2, 1963; Pois, pp. 134-39.

29. Chicago Tribune, Feb. 20, 1964.

30. Proceedings, 1963-64, pp. 2212-14. Pois compares an alternative set of guidelines presented by one Board member and supported by others, pp. 288-309.

17. BOARD, UNION, AND BLACK COMMUNITY OPPOSE A SUPERINTENDENT

To understand the bases of conflicts of the years 1964-1966, refer to the studies published in 1964 and one current Ph.D. Dissertation:

Advisory Panel on Integration of the Public Schools, *Report to the Board of Education of the City of Chicago: Integration of the Public Schools— Chicago.* Chicago Board of Education, March 31, 1964.

The panel consisted of Philip M. Hauser, Chairman, Sterling M. McMurrin, Vice Chairman, James M. Nabrit, Jr., Lester M. Nelson, and William R. O'Dell. (Usually called "Hauser Report.")

Havighurst, Robert J., *The Public Schools of Chicago: A Survey for the Board of Education.* Board of Education of the City of Chicago, 1964.
London, Stephen D., "Business and the Chicago Public School System, 1890-1966." Ph.D. Dissertation, University of Chicago, 1968.

1. Hauser Report, pp. 11, 52-71.

2. Ibid., pp. 25-39.

3. Pois, pp. 94-95, reproduced in full, pp. 225-37.

4. Proceedings, 1963-64, pp. 2157, 2215.

5. Ibid., p. 2713.

6. Chicago Daily News, June 15, 1963, quoting WBBM TV news broadcast.

7. Ibid., Nov. 11, 1964; Chicago Sun Times, Nov. 8, 1965.

8. Proceedings, 1962-63, pp. 2233, 2300.

9. Chicago Daily News, Nov. 30, 1964. Members of the Birch Society distributed leaflets attacking Dr. Havighurst.

10. In August, 1964, the survey task force under Dr. Grace's direction issued the section of the survey on colleges, which the Board had specifically directed them, on May 27, to report upon. It is entitled "Report on Chicago Teachers College and Chicago City Junior College." The Chicago Tribune, August 27, 1964, carried Superintendent Willis' denunciation of the survey recommendation that the state take over the colleges. Dr. Grace then said he would resign unless the Superintendent met with the other two members of the

Committee. President of the Board Roddewig heartily approved the idea of state control. See Chicago Sun Times, May 14, 1964.

11. Havighurst Survey, pp. 369-74.

12. Chicago Daily News, Nov. 20, 1964.

13. Havighurst Survey, pp. 402-406.

14. Proceedings, 1964-65, p. 2713; Chicago Sun Times, August 12, 1964.

15. Proceedings, 1964-65, pp. 2064-71. Vice President Murray and Judge Scheffler did not vote to keep the book as recommended by the college faculty. Chicago Sun Times, Jan. 28, 1965.

16. Proceedings, 1964-65, pp. 2179-82. The Superintendent objected to the action.

17. Ibid., pp. 2120-21. The Superintendent commented that the discussion on January 27 asking for more than one nominee had "badly shaken the faith of the staff in the intent and integrity of this Board. What is being envisioned by the staff is a return to the practice prevalent in Chicago many years ago, under which staff appointments were made on a political basis." Chicago Daily News, Feb. 11, 1965.

18. Chicago Sun Times, April 3, 1965, carried the Superintendent's comment.

19. Chicago Sun Times, Nov. 24, 1965; Chicago Union Teacher, Dec. 1964, Feb. 1965.

20. Chicago Sun Times, March 4, 1965.

21. Proceedings, 1964-65, pp. 2254-59. On Jan. 27, 1965, the Chicago Sun Times carried a statement from the Superintendent that the Jenner dispute was a power dispute between him and the Board. The Board set up a hearing for the community representatives and asked the Superintendent to have the principal attend. He told her not to do so.

22. Chicago Union Teacher, March 1963, Nov. 1963; Proceedings 1963-64, p. 2116. The Mayor's influence in obtaining the collective bargaining agreement for the Chicago Teachers Union is related in Greenstone, p. 95. The Chicago Sun Times, Sept. 26, 1965, says that the Mayor called the President of the Board, who called a special meeting to avert the threatened strike.

23. Chicago Sun Times, Oct. 7, 1965; Chicago Daily News, Oct. 27, 28, 1965; Chicago Urban League, "Title VI of the U.S. Civil Rights Act of 1964, and the Federal Aid Controversy in Chicago," Nov. 6, 1965.

24. Chicago Daily News. Dec. 30, 1965; Chicago Sun Times, Jan. 6, 1966.

25. Chicago Sun Times, Feb. 9, 1966. The Superintendent told his press conference that he had ordered principals not to participate in the Office of Education survey set up under the Civil Rights Law.

26. Chicago Sun Times, March 14, 1966.

27. Proceedings, 1965-66, pp. 36-37, 58-68.

28. Chicago Sun Times, March 5, April 3, 1965.

29. Proceedings, 1964-65, pp. 2582, 2592-2600. The long debate in the Board meeting occurred because of an effort to get the Superintendent to be explicit in the public meeting on his agreement to retire in December 1966 if he were given a four-year contract in 1965. He insisted on saying it was "presently his intention" to retire in 1966.

30. Proceedings 1964-65, June 24, p. 2788.

31. London, pp. 134, 139, 147-49. All the business leaders who signed both the 1963 and 1965 statements were interviewed. Their comments centered on inflexibility of personality, not on recognized ability. "The racial thing came to an impasse: His attitude and that of the Civil Rights Groups hardened." "I thought him an extremely able fellow, but he stuck his foot in his mouth. He was too arrogant." "I think at one time he had 90 percent or more of the business community with him; by the time he left, he had only about half."

It is interesting to note that the labor leadership of the city had become so much a part of the local Democratic party apparatus (Greenstone, p. 94-97) that they played no part in this discussion as an organization. However, Thomas Murray, Chairman of the Building Trades Council, Vice President of the Chicago Federation of Labor, and Vice President of the Board of Education, was one of Willis' strongest supporters.

32. Ibid., pp. 136-52; Chicago Sun Times, June 30, 1965.

33. Willis, p. 144.

34. Charles and Bonnie Remsberg, "Chicago, Legacy of an Ice Age." Saturday Review, (Vol. 50) May 20, 1967, pp. 73-75, 91-94.

18. THE SCHOOL SYSTEM BEGINS TO CHANGE DIRECTION

Detailed studies of the problems of Chicago school organization and planning were authorized by the Board of Education and published in 1967 and 1968. To meet the needs of the city and the current school population, now more than half black, the studies contain recommendations on reorganization of the system and of the Board itself.

Booz, Allen and Hamilton, Inc. "Organization Survey: Board of Education of the City of Chicago," Chicago Board of Education, May 1967.

Chicago Board of Education, "Increasing Desegregation of Faculties, Students and Vocational Educational Programs," August 1967. (Usually called "Redmond Report.")

Real Estate Research Corporation, "Preliminary Findings and Projections of Population and School Enrollments For Chicago, Illinois, 1970-1980," Chicago Board of Education, Dec. 1967.

Leu, Donald J. and Carl Candoli, "A Feasibility Study of the 'Cultural-Educational Park' for Chicago." East Lansing: Michigan State University, College of Education, Jan. 1968.

——, "Design for the Future. A Recommended Long Range Educational Plan for Chicago," Vol. 1. East Lansing: Michigan State University, College of Education, Oct. 1968.

——, "Design for the Future. Educational Facilities Data," Vol. 2. East Lansing: Michigan State University, College of Education.

Chicago Urban League, "Plan for a System of Educational Parks in Chicago." Chicago: Dec. 1967.

U.S. Commission on Civil Rights, "Racial Isolation in the Public Schools." Washington: 1967.

1. Chicago Urban League, "Negroes in Policy-Making Positions: A Study in Black Powerlessness." Chicago: 1968.

2. Young, Beyond Racism, pp. 33-34, 156-62; Carmichael and Hamilton, pp. 9-10, 158, 169.

3. New York Times, Nov. 2, 1967, p. 50.

4. Chicago Sun Times, June 1, 1966.

5. Ibid., Nov. 12, 1966; Chicago Daily News, Nov. 11, 1966.

6. Booz Report, pp. 23-26, 27-33.

7. Redmond Report, Introduction, p. 1.

8. Ibid., A 22-33, B 26-30, C 3-27.

9. Ibid., B 15, D 7.

10. Real Estate Research Report, Addenda, Tables A4, A5, A6.

11. Ibid., p. 14, 68-75.

12. Leu, "Feasibility Study of the 'Cultural Educational Park.' " A 1, C 19, B 1.

13. Leu Report, Vol. 1, F 8.

14. Proceedings, 1967-68, 100-page insert between pp. 534 and 535; Chicago Daily News, August 28, 1967.

15. Chicago Sun Times, Sept. 11, 1967; Chicago Defender, Sept. 13, 1967; Chicago Daily News, Sept. 12, 1967, Editorial, "Give the School Plan a Try."

16. Chicago Sun Times, August 26, 1967; Chicago Tribune, Sept. 6, 1967.

17. Chicago Daily News, August 24, Sept. 20, 1967.

18. Proceedings, 1967-68, pp. 951-55; Chicago Daily News, Dec. 13, 1967.

19. Chicago Daily News, August 24, Sept. 20, 21, 1967; Chicago Sun Times, Sept. 21, 1967; Chicago Tribune, August 27, 1967.

20. Chicago Daily News, Jan. 11, 1968; Chicago Sun Times, Jan. 11, 15, 1968.

21. Chicago Sun Times, Feb 20, 1968. On Nov. 2, 1968, the Sun Times quoted State Senator Krasowski as a supporter of Wallace. He denounced "Fair Housing" as a Communist plot to destroy democracy, said welfare recipients must be forced to work, and attacked Cardinal Cody because of "his crazy stupid programs like Civil Rights." The Cardinal had arranged busing of inner city parochial students to the suburbs and had publicly supported the Redmond Plan. Chicago Sun Times, March 26, July 3, 1968.

22. Kerner Report, p. 281.

23. Proceedings, 1967-68, pp. 2430-36, 2436-37.

24. Chicago Sun Times, March 6, April 4, 1968; Chicago Daily News, March 12, 1968; Chicago Tribune, March 27, 1968.

25. Chicago Sun Times, Jan. 31, Feb. 1, 2, 1968; Daily News, Feb. 3, 1969.

26. Redmond Report, B. 19.

27. Chicago Sun Times, Jan. 17, June 15, 1968; Daily News, Feb. 16, 1968.

28. Citizens Schools Committee, "Report of the Committee to Study the School Board Nominating Process in Chicago," Sept. 1964.

19. LACK OF MONEY AND FULL BOARD SUPPORT HINDERS PROGRESS

Activities within the system are described in Annual Reports of the Superintendent and in the monthly periodical, News of the Chicago Public Schools. The 1966 report of the Task Force on Education appointed by the Governor, "Education for the Future of Illinois," describes the financial problems of public education in Illinois, with considerable attention to Chicago.

1. News of the Public Schools, Issues of Oct. 1967-Dec. 1968; Annual Report of th General Superintendent, 1968, pp. 9, 10, 13, 23, 25, 31; Proceedings, 1968-69, pr 2501-502.

2. Young, Beyond Racism, 135-43; Carmichael and Hamilton, pp. 42-43.

3. Chicago Tribune, Oct. 18, 1969.

4. Ibid., Oct. 22, Oct. 25, 1969.

5. Proceedings, 1968-69, pp. 700-704.

6. Stenographic Report of the Hearing, Oct. 30.

7. Chicago Sun Times, Sept. 26, Dec. 21, 1968; Chicago Tribune, Dec. 22, 1968; Chicago Sun Times, March 28, April 10, 24, 25, 26, 1969.

8. Chicago Sun Times, March 7, 13, 14, 1969. There were 31 black principals in Chicago, 6 in New York, a system of 60,000, not 24,000 teachers. The New York Times, Sept. 9, 1968, Sec. 4, p. 1, stated that only 10 percent of teaching staff in New York were black, that there were only 200 blacks above the classroom level, and that the first black high school principal was appointed in 1968. In Chicago, 33.9 percent of the teachers are black, and 25 percent of the assistant principals alone were black, almost as many in that one group of administrators as the total of the black administrators in New York.

9. Ibid., Nov. 14, 1968.

10. Ibid., Dec. 13, 1968.

11. Ibid., June 1, 2, 3, 4, 8, 12, 1968, July 8, 1969.

12. Proceedings, 1968-69, pp. 3007-13.

13. Chicago Union Teacher, Dec. 1968.

14. Proceedings, 1968-69, pp. 832-34.

15. Statistical Abstract of the United States, 1968, pp. 417, 420; Chicago Sun Times, May 5, 1968.

16. Education for the Future of Illinois. Report of a study by the Task Force appointed by the Governor, Dec. 1966, p. 104; Facts and Figures 1968, pp. 98, 112.

17. Report of Task Force, p. 115; Chicago Sun Times, Nov. 19, 21, 1968, March 25, 1969.

18. Proceedings, 1968-69, p. 2759.

19. Chicago Sun Times, Nov. 21, 1967.

20. Chicago Daily News, April 22, May 14, 22, 26; Chicago Sun Times, March 11, 18, April 17, May 2, June 4, 1969.

21. Chicago Sun Times, May 10, 19, 20, 21, 23, 24, 25, 26, 1969; Chicago Daily News, May 17; Chicago Tribune, May 22; New York Times, May 23, 1969.

22. Chicago Daily News, April 8, 10, 11, 1969.

23. Chicago Sun Times, May 21, 29, June 29, 1969.

24. Chicago Tribune, June 25, 1969. Included also as items to be investigated were sex education and methods of choosing members of the Board of Education.

25. Chicago Sun Times, April 2, 9, 26, July 16, 1969; Chicago Daily News, March 17, April 23, 1969; Chicago Tribune, April 4, July 30, 1969; Chicago American, April 8, 1969.

26. Chicago Daily News, June 30, July 12, 1969; Chicago Today (new name for Chicago American), July 10, 1969; Chicago Sun Times, July 11, 1969.

27. Chicago Daily News, July 11, July 16, 1969; Chicago Sun Times, July 11, 1969.

APPENDIX A. FEDERAL GRANTS FOR EDUCATION

REFERENCES

Arizona State Board of Education, "A Survey of the Arizona Public School System." Phoenix: 1925.

Cubberley, Ellwood P., School Funds and Their Apportionment. New York: Columbia University Press, 1905.

Iverson, Samuel G., "Public Lands and School Funds of Minnesota." Minneapolis: Minnesota Historical Society Collection (Vol. XV) 1911, pp. 287-314.

Martzoff, Clement L., "Land Grants for Education in the Ohio Valley States." Columbus: Ohio Archaeological and Historical Society, 1915-16, pp. 24-25.

McCrea, Samuel P., "The Establishment of the Arizona School System." Thesis in History, Leland Stanford, Jr., University, 1902.

Reazin, Bruce D., "The Permanent School Fund in Arizona." Master's Thesis, University of Southern California, 1933.

Swift, Fletcher H., *A History of Public Permanent Common School Funds in the United States, 1795-1905*. New York: Henry Holt and Co., 1911.

Taylor, George R., *The Turner Thesis*. New York: D. C. Heath and Co., 1954.

Texas State Teachers Association, "The Permanent School Funds of Texas." Fort Worth: 1934.

Turner, Jonathan B., "Influence of Government Land Grants for Educational Purposes upon the Educational System of the State." Illinois State Historical Society, Vol. VI.

U.S. Department of Commerce, Bureau of the Census, *Historical Statistics of the United States, 1960; Statistical Abstract of the United States, 1967*.

APPENDIX B. LEGAL RIGHTS TO EDUCATION OF BLACK CHILDREN IN ILLINOIS

1. Harris; Ph.D. Dissertation, pp. 11-15, 23, 51-59, 62.

2. Abbott and Breckenridge, pp. 375-377; Mason, "The Policy of Segregation of the Negro in the Public Schools of Ohio, Indiana and Illinois." Master's Thesis, 1917.

3. The author was a member of the committee of the commission which interviewed Superintendent Vernon Nickell, Feb. 12, 1947.

4. Mann, "The Chicago Common Council and the Fugitive Slave Law of 1850."

APPENDIX C. CHICAGO PUBLIC SCHOOL STATISTICS, 1840-1970

Data for Tables 1, 2, 3, and 4 are taken from the following sources: Johnston, *Historical Sketches of the Public Schools of Chicago* (1880); Clark, *The Public Schools of Chicago* (1897); School Facts, June 18, 1930; Annual Reports of the Board of Education and of Superintendents of Chicago Schools; Facts and Figures (1953-69); 1970 Budget of the Chicago Board of Education.

BIBLIOGRAPHY

BIBLIOGRAPHY

BOOKS

Abbott, Edith and Sophonisba P. Breckinridge, *Truancy and Non-Attendance in the Chicago Schools.* Chicago: University of Chicago Press, 1917.

Addams, Jane, *Twenty Years at Hull House.* New York: The Macmillan Co., 1910.

——, *The Public Schools and the Immigrant Child.* Proceedings of the National Education Association, Washington: 1908.

American Federation of Teachers, Commission on Educational Reconstruction, *Organizing the Teaching Profession: The Story of the American Federation of Teachers,* New York: Free Press of Glencoe, 1955.

Benson, George C. S., Sumner Benson, Harold McClelland, and Proctor Thompson, *The American Property Tax: Its History, Administration and Economic Impact.* Claremont, Cal.: College Press, 1965.

Bogue, D. J. and D. P. Dandekar, *Population Trends and Prospects for the Chicago-Northwestern Indiana Consolidated Metropolitan Area, 1960 to 1990.* Chicago: Population Research and Training Center, University of Chicago, 1962.

Britton, Gertrude Howe, *An Intensive Study of the Causes of Truancy.* Chicago: Hollister Press, 1906.

Campbell, Jack, *Colonel Francis W. Parker, The Children's Crusader.* New York: Teachers College Press, 1967.

Carmichael, Stokely and Charles V. Hamilton, *Black Power.* New York: Random House, 1967.

Clark, Hannah Belle, *The Public Schools of Chicago: A Sociological Study.* Chicago: University of Chicago Press, 1897.

Conant, James Bryant, *Slums and Suburbs.* New York: McGraw-Hill Book Co., 1961.

Counts, George S., *School and Society in Chicago.* New York: Harcourt, Brace and Co., 1928.

Cremin, Lawrence A., *Public Schools in Our Democracy.* New York: The Macmillan Co., 1956.

——, *The Transformation of the School.* New York: Alfred A. Knopf, 1961.

Cubberley, Ellwood P., *School Funds and Their Apportionment.* New York: Columbia University Press, 1905.

Dodge, Chester C., *Reminiscences of a School Master.* Chicago: Ralph Seymour, 1941.

Donovan, Frances R., *The Schoolma'am.* New York: Frederick A. Stokes Co., 1938.

Drake, St. Clair and Horace R. Cayton, *Black Metropolis.* New York: Harper and Row, 1945, revised 1962.

Duncan, Otis Dudley and Beverly Duncan, *The Negro Population of Chicago. A Study in Residential Succession.* Chicago: University of Chicago Press, 1957.

Fenner, Mildred Sandison, *N.E.A. History.* Washington: National Education Association, 1945.

Field, Marshall, *Freedom is More Than a Word.* Chicago: University of Chicago Press, 1945.

Gale, Edwin O., *Reminiscences of Early Chicago and Vicinity.* Chicago: Fleming H. Revell, 1902.

Gosnell, Harold Foote, *Machine Politics, Chicago Model.* Chicago: University of Chicago Press, 1937.

——, *Negro Politicians. The Rise of Negro Politics in Chicago.* Chicago: University of Chicago Press, 1935, 2nd ed. 1967.

Gottfried, Alex, *Boss Cermak of Chicago: A Study of Political Leadership.* Seattle: University of Washington Press, 1962.

Greenstone, J. David, *Labor in American Politics.* New York, Alfred A. Knopf, 1969.

Haig, Robert Murray, *A History of the General Property Tax in Illinois.* Urbana: University of Illinois Studies in the Social Sciences, Vol. III, No. 5, 1914.

Hamilton, Henry E., *Biographical Sketches* [of Richard Hamilton by his son] Manuscript, 1888.

Hamilton, Henry Raymond, *The Epic of Chicago.* Chicago: Willett, Clark and Co., 1932.

Harris, Norman Dwight, *The History of Negro Servitude in Illinois, and of the Slavery Agitation in that State, 1719-1864.* Chicago: A. C. McClurg, 1904.

Harrison, Carter H., *Stormy Years, The Autobiography of Carter H. Harrison, Five Times Mayor of Chicago.* New York: Bobbs Merrill Co., 1935.

Henry, Nelson B. and Jerome G. Kerwin, *Schools and City Government.* Chicago: University of Chicago Press, 1938.

Hosman, Everett M., *State Teacher Organizations.* University Place, Nebr.: National Association of Secretaries of State Teachers Associations, 1926.

Howatt, John, *Notes on the First One Hundred Years of Chicago School History.* 1940.

Howland, George, *Practical Hints for Teachers in the Public Schools.* New York: Appleton and Co., 1898.

——, *Moral Training in our Public Schools.* Chicago: Jamieson and Morse, 1882.

Hoyt, Homer, *One Hundred Years of Land Values in Chicago.* Chicago: University of Chicago Press, 1933.

Illinois State Historical Association, *Influence of Government Land Grants for Educational Purposes Upon the Educational System of the State,* Publication 706. Springfield: 1901.

Iverson, Samuel Gilbert, *Public Lands and School Funds of Minnesota.* Minneapolis: Minnesota Historical Society Collection (Vol. XV) 1911, pp. 287-314.

James, Edward Janes, *Charters of Chicago.* Chicago: University of Chicago Press, 1898.

Johnston, Shepherd, *Historical Sketches of the Public Schools of Chicago.* Reprint from the 25th Annual Report of the Chicago Board of Education. Chicago: 1880.

Judd, Charles H., *Measuring the Work of the Public Schools.* Cleveland: Cleveland Foundation Survey, 1916.

King, Hoyt, *Citizen Cole of Chicago.* Chicago: Munroe and Southworth, 1931.

Kitigawa, Evelyn M. and Karl E. Taeuber, *Local Community Fact Book, Chicago Metropolitan Area.* Chicago Community Inventory, University of Chicago. Chicago: 1950 ed. 1953, 1960 ed. 1963.

Landesco, John, *Organized Crime in Chicago.* Chicago: Illinois Association for Criminal Justice, 1929.

Lewis, Lloyd and Henry J. Smith, *Chicago: The History of Its Reputation.* New York: Harcourt, Brace and Co., 1929, rev. ed. 1938.

Linn, James W., *Jane Addams: A Biography.* New York: Appleton, Century Co., 1935.

McAndrew, William, *The Public and Its Schools. A Statement of the Means of Finding What the Intelligent Public Expects of Children and How a School System Can be Managed to Deliver the Goods.* Yonkers, N.Y.: World Book Co., 1917.

McDonald, Forrest, *Insull.* Chicago: University of Chicago Press, 1962.

McManis, John T., *Ella Flagg Young and a Half Century of Chicago Schools.* Chicago: A. C. McClurg, 1916.

Mann, Charles W., "The Chicago Common Council and the Fugitive Slave Law of 1850." An Address read before the Chicago Historical Society, Jan. 29, 1903.

Martin, James W., *Revenue Potentials of the States.* Washington: N.E.A., 1964.

Martzoff, Clement L., *Land Grants for Education in the Ohio Valley States.* Columbus: Ohio Archaeological and Historical Society (Vol. 25) 1916, pp. 59-70.

Merriam, Charles E., *Chicago: A More Intimate View of Urban Politics.* New York: The Macmillan Co., 1929.

National Industrial Conference Board, *The Fiscal Problem in Illinois.* New York: Harper and Bros., 1927.

National League of Teachers Association, *Yearbooks,* 1923-1931.

Ortman, Elmer J., *Teacher Councils.* Montpelier, Vt.: Capital City Press, 1923.

Pasley, Fred D., *Al Capone: The Biography of a Self Made Man.* Garden City, N.Y.: Garden City Publishing Co., 1931.

Pierce, Bessie L., *A History of Chicago. Vol. I. The Beginnings of a City, 1673-1848* (published 1937); *Vol. II. From Town to City, 1848-1871*

(1940); *Vol. III. The Rise of a Modern City, 1871-1898* (1957). New York: Alfred A. Knopf.

Pois, Joseph, *The School Board Crisis: A Chicago Case Study.* Chicago: Educational Methods, Inc., 1964.

Porter, Mary H., *Eliza Chappell Porter, a Memoir.* Chicago: Fleming H. Revell, 1892. Published for the benefit of the Oberlin Missionary Home Association.

Propeck, George and Irving Pearson, *The History of the Illinois Education Association.* Springfield: Illinois Educational Association, 1961.

Rice, J. M., *Public School Systems of the United States.* New York: The Century Co., 1893.

Simpson, Herbert D., *Tax Racket and Tax Reform in Chicago.* Menasha, Wis.: Collegiate Press, 1930.

——, *The Tax Situation in Illinois.* Evanston: Institute for Research in Land Economics and Public Utilities, Northwestern University, 1929.

Sizer, Theodore R., *Secondary Schools at the Turn of the Century.* New Haven: Yale University Press, 1964.

Staley, Eugene, *The History of the Illinois State Federation of Labor.* Chicago: University of Chicago Press, 1930.

Stead, William T., *If Christ Came to Chicago.* London: British Review of Reviews, 1894.

Stuart, William Harvey, *The Twenty Incredible Years.* New York: Donahue and Co., 1935.

Studensky, Paul, *Teacher Pension Systems in the United States.* New York: D. Appleton and Co., 1920.

Strayer, George D., Fred Engelhart, John K. Norton, Lester Dix, and Newton H. Hegel, *Report of the Survey of the Schools of Chicago. Vol. I. Administration, Business Management, Financing, Educational Personnel, Social Services; Vol. II. Fitting the School to the Pupil, Secondary and Higher Education; Vol. III. Teaching and Supervision in Elementary Schools, Health and Physical Education, Vocational Education; Vol. IV. Housing the Schools, Operation of School Plant; Vol. V. Findings and Recommendations.* New York: Columbia University, Bureau of Publications, 1932.

Sullivan, Edward Dean, *Chicago Surrenders.* New York: Van Guard Press, 1930.

Swift, Fletcher Harper, *A History of Public Permanent Common School Funds in the United States, 1795-1905.* New York: Henry Holt and Co., 1911.

Swift, Fletcher Harper, Frances K. Del Plaine, and Oliver Leonard Troxel, *Studies in Public School Finance: The Middle West.* Minneapolis: University of Minnesota, 1925.

Taylor, George Rogers, *The Turner Thesis.* New York: D. C. Heath and Co., 1954.

Taylor, Graham, *Pioneering on Social Frontiers.* Chicago: University of Chicago Press, 1931.

Taylor, Howard Cromwell, *The Educational Significance of the Early Federal Land Ordinances.* New York: Columbia University, 1922.

Vieg, John Albert, *The Government of Education in Metropolitan Chicago.* Chicago: University of Chicago Press, 1939.

Wattenberg, William, *On the Educational Frontier: The Reactions of Teacher Associations in New York and Chicago.* New York: Columbia University Press, 1936.

Wells, William Harvey, *The Graded School. A Graded Course of Instruction for the Chicago Public Schools, with Copious, Practical Directions to Teachers and Observations on Primary Schools, School Records, ...* Chicago: A.S. Barnes, 1862; 2nd, 3rd editions, Dean and Ottoway, 1866, 1867.

Wells, William Harvey, 1812-1885. In Memoriam. Sketches of his life and character, memorial addresses and resolutions of public bodies on the occasion of his death. Chicago: Fergus Printing Co., 1887.

Wendt, Lloyd and Herman Kogan, *Big Bill of Chicago.* New York: Bobbs Merrill Co., 1953.

Wesley, Edgar B., *N.E.A., The First Hundred Years.* New York: Harper, 1957.

Willis, Benjamin C., *Social Problems in Public School Administration.* Pittsburgh: University of Pittsburgh Press, 1967.

Wooddy, Carroll, *The Pineapple Primary.* Chicago: University of Chicago Press, 1928.

Young, Ella Flagg, "Ethics in the School." Contribution to Education, No. IV. Chicago: University of Chicago Press, 1902.

——, *Isolation in the Schools.* Chicago: University of Chicago Press, 1900.

——, *Scientific Method in Education.* Chicago: University of Chicago Press, 1903.

Young, Whitney M., Jr., *Beyond Racism. Building an Open Society.* New York: McGraw-Hill Book Co., 1969.

REPORTS AND DOCUMENTS OF GOVERNMENT AGENCIES

CHICAGO BOARD OF EDUCATION

Annual Reports of Board and Superintendent, 1854 to 1969.

Proceedings of Chicago Board of Education, 1867-1969.

Facts and Figures, 1950-1968.

School Facts, 1929-1931.

Statistical Bulletin, 1929-1932.

Elementary Teachers Councils, Reports, 1921-1925.

High School Teachers Council Constitution, 1922.

Manual for Teachers, 1878.

Rules of the Board of Education, 1859-present.

School Census, 1885-present

"Address by James B. McCahey on his 10th Re-election as President of the Board," 1942.

"Address by James B. McCahey before Western Society of Engineers," April 23, 1946.

"Forward with Youth," April 7, 1943.

"Half a Million Prepare for Life's Battle," 1939.

"A 1944 Message about Chicago Schools."

"One Hundred Years of Educational Progress," 1845-1945.

"Our Public Schools," 1937.

"Our Public Schools Must Not Close," December 1933.

Advisory Panel on Integration of the Public Schools, "Report to the Board of Education of the City of Chicago, March 31, 1964." (Usually called "Hauser Report.")

"Fiftieth Anniversary of the Chicago City Junior College 1911-1961."

Havighurst, Robert J., "The Public Schools of Chicago: A Survey for the Board of Education." Board of Education of the City of Chicago, 1964.

"Quality Education: Improved Educational Opportunities." A Report to the Board of Education by the General Superintendent, Benjamin C. Willis, Nov. 25, 1964.

"Report on the Special Summer Schools," 1964.

Booz, Allen and Hamilton, Inc., "Organization Survey: Board of Education of the City of Chicago." Chicago Board of Education, May 1967.

"Elementary and Secondary Education Act Status Reports, Titles I, II, and III." From the General Superintendent of Schools, July 12, 1967.

"Increasing Desegregation of Faculties, Students and Vocational Educational Programs, August 1967." (Usually called "Redmond Report.")

Leu, Donald J. and Carl Candoli, "Design for the Future. A Recommended Long Range Educational Plan for Chicago, Vol. 1. Educational Facilities Planning Study No. 2." East Lansing: Michigan State University, October 1968.

——, "A Feasibility Study of the 'Cultural-Educational Park' for Chicago. A Preliminary Report. Educational Facilities Planning Study No. 1." East Lansing: Michigan State University, January 1968.

——, "Design for the Future. Educational Facilities Data, Vol. 2." East Lansing: Michigan State University, College of Education.

Real Estate Research Corp., "Preliminary Findings and Projections of Population and School Enrollments, for Chicago, Illinois, 1970-1980." Chicago Board of Education, December 1967.

CITY OF CHICAGO

"Report on Common Schools," 1838.

"Basic Policies for a Comprehensi,e Plan for Chicago," 1964.

Civil Service Commission, "Report on the Budget of the Board of Education," 1914.

——, "Report on the Investigation of Engineer and Janitor Service, Board of Education," 1913.

Committee on Schools, Fire, Police and Civil Service of the City Council of Chicago, "Recommendations for the Reorganization of the Public School System of the City of Chicago," Dec. 9, 1917.

——, "Report to the City Council of Chicago on Investigation of N.E.A. Report on Chicago Schools of May, 1945." 1946.

Harper, William R., Chairman, "Report of the Educational Commission of the City of Chicago, Appointed by the Mayor, Hon. Carter H. Harrison." Chicago: R. R. Donnelley and Sons, 1898. (Usually called "Harper Report.")

STATE OF ILLINOIS

Board of Higher Education, "A Master Plan for Higher Education in Illinois, Phase I and II, December 1966."

Commission on Human Relations, Reports, 1947, 1948.

Commission on Revenue, Report. Springfield: Frye Printing Co., 1963.

Commission on Taxation and Expenditures, "Report and Recommendations," Jan. 4, 1933.

Department of Public Instruction, "Reports of Superintendent, 1915-1930."

——, "Sesquicentennial, 150 Years of Education in Illinois," 1968.

"Education for the Future of Illinois." Report of a study by the Task Force appointed by the Governor, December 1966.

Educational Commission, "Report to the 46th General Assembly," 1909.

——, "Report to the Governor and the 54th General Assembly," 1925.

——, "Report of the Advisory Staff," 1935.

Governor's Tax Conference, "Report of Executive Committee," Oct. 31, 1931.

Legislative Council, "Some Aspects of School Administration in Illinois," August 1938.

Legislative Reference Bureau, "The Constitution of Illinois: Problems Arising under the Constitution of 1870," 1934.

School Finance and Tax Commission, "State Support of Public Education in Illinois," 1949.

School Problems Commission, Reports, 1951-1969.

State Tax Commission, "Illinois Revenue System, 1818-1936," 1936.

UNITED STATES

Bureau of Education, "City School Systems in the U.S.," No. 1, 1885.

——, "State School Taxes and School Funds," Bulletin 29, 1928.

——, "Tangible Rewards of Teaching," Bulletin 16, 1914.

Commission on Civil Rights, "Civil Rights, U.S.A. The Public Schools: Cities in the North and West," 1962.

——, "Racial Isolation in the Public Schools," 1967.

National Advisory Committee on Civil Disorders, Report, March 1968.

Office of Education, "Deepening Crisis in Education," No. 14, 1933.
——, "Education an Answer to Poverty," 1965.
——, "Equality of Educational Opportunity," 1966.
——, "Public School Finance Programs of the 48 States," Circular No. 274, 1953.
——, "Race and Place: A Legal History of the Neighborhood School," 1967.
——, "Revenue Programs for the Public Schools in the United States," Misc. No. 38, 1959-60.
——, "State Programs for Public School Support," 1965.

OTHER REPORTS

Chicago Association of Commerce, Annual Reports, 1924, 1925.
——, "Industrial and Commercial Education in Relation to Conditions in the City of Chicago," 1909.
——, "Report on the Administrative Organization and Business Procedures of the Board of Education of the City of Chicago," 1943.
Chicago Bar Association, "Report of the Special Committee on the Revenue System of Illinois," 1879.
Chicago Bureau of Public Efficiency, "Chicago School Finances 1915-1925," with Addenda for 1926, December 1927.
Chicago High School Teachers Club, "Obstacles to Effective Teaching in the Chicago High Schools," Report of the Education Committee, 1923.
Chicago School of Civics and Philanthropy, "Finding Employment for Children who Leave Grade School to go to Work." Chicago: Hollister Press, 1911.
Chicago Teachers Federation, "Report Showing Results of Fifteen Years of Organization," Dec. 1, 1908.
Chicago Teachers Union, "Modernize Illinois Taxes Now," June 1960.
——, "Pay Restoration, 1936-1937."
——, "Statement at City Council Hearing on N.E.A. Report," 1946.
——, "Steps Toward a Long Range Tax Program for the State of Illinois," February 1957.
Chicago Unitarian Council, "Appeal for Civic Action: The Record of William H. Johnson," 1938.
Chicago Urban League, "An Approach to a New Era in Race Relations," Jan. 31, 1969.
——, "Black Powerlessness in Chicago." Reprint from Trans-action, Nov. 29, 1968, pp. 27-33.
——, "Plan for a System of Educational Parks in Chicago," 1967.
——, "Racial Aspects of Urban Planning: An Urban League Critique of the Chicago Comprehensive Plan," 1968.
——, Schools Seminar, 1962.
Chicago-Cook County Health Survey, "Blueprint for a Healthy Chicago," Report of the Advisory Committee on the Survey conducted by the U.S. Public Health Service, 1947.

Citizens Association of Chicago, "Report of the Committee on Education."
    Chicago: George K. Hazlitt, 1881.
——, "School Fund Lease Crisis," 1933.
Citizens Schools Committee, "Charting the Course for Vocational Education." A
    Broad expression of public opinion by Industrial, Labor, Civic, Business
    and Educational Leaders, April 28, 1939.
——, "Report of the Committee on Compensatory Education," 1964.
——, "Report of the Committee to Study the School Board Nominating Process
    in Chicago," Sept. 1, 1964.
——, "Scrap Book." Releases and Bulletins, 1933-1934.
City Club of Chicago, "Report on Vocational Training in Chicago and Other
    Cities," 1912.
——, "Teacher Personnel Practices," March 1, 1943.
Commercial Club of Chicago, "Vocational Schools for Illinois," 1912.
Committee on Public Expenditures, "Analysis of Financial Status of Chicago
    School System as of June 30, 193," August 17, 1933.
Coordinating Council of Community Organizations, "Action for Quality and
    Equality for all Public School Children in Chicago," Oct. 18, 1966.
Federation of Women High School Teachers, "Financial Outlook for Chicago
    Schools," February 1934.
——, "Handbook on Chicago High Schools," 1923.
——, "High School Education in Chicago," May 1934.
——, " 'A Thorough and Efficient System' of Schools for all the Children of the
    State Has Not Been Provided by the Illinois General Property Tax," 1935.
Illinois Chamber of Commerce, "Five Steps in the Right Direction: Tax
    Modernization," 1942.
Illinois Education Association, "School Finance: Tax Problems," 1960.
Joint Committee on Real Estate Valuation, "Property Assessments, Public
    Revenue and Retrenchments for 1932: A Statement Presented to the
    Chicago Board of Education." Chicago: February 1932.
——, "A Study of the Present Financial Difficulties of Local Governments and
    Their Causes," 1929.
National Association of Manufacturers, "Industrial Education," 1913.
National Committee for Support of the Public Schools, "The Struggle for Power
    in the Public Schools." Washington: 1968.
National Education Association, "Report of an Investigation: Certain Personnel
    Practices in the Chicago Public Schools." Washington: 1945.
National Federation of Settlements, "Rise of Community Schools in Urban
    Education." New York: 232 Madison Ave., 1968.
Public Education Association, "Student Grievances in the New York City High
    Schools." New York: 20 W. 40th St., May 1969.
Texas State Teachers Association, "The Permanent School Funds of Texas."
    Fort Worth: 1934.

Traylor, Melvin A., "On the Need for a Graduated Income Tax for Illinois." Address to the First Special Session of the 57th General Assembly, Dec. 1, 1931.

PERIODICALS

GENERAL ARTICLES

American Teacher, "Chicago Number." (Vol. XI, No. 8) April 1927.

Atlantic Monthly, "Spasmodic Diary of a Chicago School Teacher." (Vol. 152) November 1933, pp. 513-26.

Bogan, William S., "The Danger to Free Public Education." American Teacher (Vol. XVIII) pp. 1-8.

Cooke, Flora J., "Col. Francis W. Parker: His Influence on Education." Chicago Schools Journal (Vol. 19) March 1938.

The Crisis, "DeFacto Segregation in the Chicago Public Schools." (Vol. 65, No. 2) February 1958, pp. 87-93.

Douglas, Paul H., "Chicago's Financial Muddle." New Republic (Vol. 61) Feb. 13, 1930, pp. 324-26.

Elementary School Journal, "Tragedy of Chicago Schools." (Vol. XXXIV) September 1933, pp. 1-9.

Flynn, John Thomas, "These Our Rulers." Colliers (Vol. 106) June 29, 1940, pp. 14-15; July 6, pp. 22-23; July 13, pp. 18-19; July 20, pp. 39-40.

Fortune, "The Kelly-Nash Machine." (Vol. 14) August 1936, p. 51.

——, "The Chicago Tribune," (Vol. IX) May 1934, pp. 14-25, 101-103.

Goggin, Catherine, "Inaugural Address." Chicago Teacher and School Board Journal, June 1899, pp. 309-11.

Hard, William, "Chicago's Five Maiden Aunts." American Magazine (Vol. 62) September 1906, pp. 484-89.

Hunt, Herold C., "After Two Years." Chicago Union Teacher (Vol. XV) October 1949, pp. 5-6.

Hutton, Harry K. and Charles Galcoci, "The McAndrew Case: Britain at the Chicago Bar." School and Society (Vol. 98, No. 2323) February 1970.

Literary Digest, "Chicago a Pauper City." (Vol. 104) Jan. 25, 1930, p. 12.

New Republic, "Chicago Interlude in a Century of Progress." (Vol. 75) July 5, 1933, pp. 203-205.

Outlook, "Chicago Broke." (Vol. 154) Feb. 5, 1930, pp. 213-14.

Remsberg, Charles and Bonnie, "Chicago, Legacy of an Ice Age." Saturday Review (Vol. 50) May 20, 1967, pp. 13-17, 73-75, 91-94.

Richberg, Donald, "Gold-Plated Anarchy." Nation (Vol. CXXXXVI) April 5, 1933, pp. 368-69.

Sargent, Fred W., "The Taxpayer Takes Charge." Saturday Evening Post (Vol. CCV) Jan. 14, 1933, pp. 21, 24-28, 80-82.

School Review, "Disemboweling Chicago Schools." (Vol. 41) October 1934, pp. 483-91.

——, "High School Education in Chicago." (Vol. 42) October 1934, pp. 565-68.

Stillman, Charles B., "Chicago, a Key Situation." American Teacher (Vol. XVII) October 1932, pp. 19-21.

——, "Protest Against Citizens Committee 48 Million Budget Limitation." Chicago Principals Club Reporter (Vol. XXVIII) Dec. 19, 1932.

Survey Graphic, "Chicago Issue." (Vol. 23) October 1934: Carroll Binder, "Hot Spot of American Labor," pp. 484-87, 513-16; V. O. Key, "The Unholy Alliance," pp. 473-77; Milton Mayer, "Corrupt and Discontented," pp. 478-81, 521-28; Charles E. Merriam, "Snapshots of Chicago Leaders," pp. 504-505, 525-26; Donald Slesinger, "The Second Century," p. 462; Louis Wirth, "Chicago, the Land and the People," pp. 468-71, 520-25.

Sutherland, Douglas, "How Chicago Got that Way." World's Work (Vol. 59) May 1930, pp. 53-55.

CHICAGO SCHOOLS

Bulletins of the Chicago Federation of Men Teachers and the Federation of Women High School Teachers, 1919-1928.

Chicago Board of Education, Bulletin, Nos. 1-36, 1902-08.

——, Chicago Schools Journal, 1918-64 (thereafter Illinois Schools Journal).

——, Chicago Teacher, 1873-75.

——, Chicago Teacher and School Board Journal, 1899-1901.

——, Digest, Department of Human Relations, 1969-present.

——, Educational Bimonthly, 1906-18.

——, Educational Progress, 1947-60.

——, News of the Chicago Public Schools, 1964-present.

Chicago Principals Club Reporter, 1911-40.

Chicago Teachers Union, [Weekly] Bulletin, September 1937-September 1947.

——, Chicago Union Teacher Magazine, January 1937-June 1947.

——, Chicago Union Teacher Newspaper, September 1947-June 1968.

Citizens Schools Committee, Chicago Schools, July 1934-June 1963.

——, Report, October 1963-present.

Federation of Women High School Teachers, Bulletins, 1919-37.

——, Weekly Radio Speeches, 1927-37.

Margaret Haley's Bulletin, 1902-07, 1915-16, 1926-31.

Men Teachers Union, Bulletins, 1919-37.

Public Education Association of Chicago Bulletins 1-4, 1917.

UNPUBLISHED THESES

Amerman, Helen, "Impact of Inter-group Relations on Nonsegregated Urban Public Education." Ph.D. Dissertation, University of Chicago, 1954.

——, "Survey of Human Relations Problems and Projects in the Chicago Public Schools." Project of the Technical Advisory Committee of the Chicago Public Schools. Chicago: Committee on Educational Training and Research in Race Relations, University of Chicago, 1952.

Anderson, Olive Orton, "The Chicago Teachers Federation." Master's Thesis, University of Chicago, 1908.

Beck, John M., "Chicago Newspapers and the Public Schools, 1890-1920." Ph.D. Dissertation, University of Chicago, 1958.

Bell, John Wesley, "The Development of the Public High School in Chicago." Ph.D. Dissertation, University of Chicago, 1929.

Bigham, Truman Cicero, "The Chicago Federation of Labor." Master's Thesis, University of Chicago, 1924.

Dewey, Henry Evert, "The Development of Public School Administration in Chicago." Ph.D. Dissertation, University of Chicago, 1937.

Dolnick, David, "The Role of Labor in Chicago Politics Since 1919," Master's Thesis, University of Chicago, 1939.

Duffie, Burton, "Educational Policies of Two Leading Newspapers." Master's Thesis, University of Chicago, 1934.

Fair, Jean Everhard, "The History of Public Education in Chicago, 1894-1914." Master's Thesis, University of Chicago, 1939.

Farley, Nancy Lee, "Educational Publicity in the Newspapers of Chicago. A Study of Six Dailies." Master's Thesis, University of Chicago, 1927.

Gibney, Esther F., "The Public School Teacher in a Metropolis." Ph.D. Dissertation, Northwestern University, 1947.

Graham, Polly Jo, "An Investigation of the Chicago School Redistricting Program." Master's Thesis, Univeristy of Chicago, 1952.

Hazlitt, James Stephen, "Crisis in School Government: An Administrative History of the Chicago Public Schools, 1933-1947." Ph.D. Dissertation, University of Chicago, 1968.

Herrick, Mary J., "Negro Employees of the Chicago Board of Education." Master's Thesis, University of Chicago, 1931.

Jerrems, Raymond L., "A Sociological-Educational Study of a Public School in a Negro-Lower Class Area of a Big City." Ph.D. Dissertation, University of Chicago, 1965.

Johns, Elizabeth, "Chicago Newspapers and the News." Ph.D. Dissertation, University of Chicago, 1942.

Kawalek, Thaddeus P., "The Educational Implications of Property Assessment Practices in Illinois." Ph.D. Dissertation, University of Chicago, 1959.

Levit, Martin, "The Chicago Citizens Schools Committee, A Pressure Group." Master's Thesis, University of Chicago, 1947.

Levitt, Emma, "Activities of Local Teacher Organizations Since 1929." Master's Thesis, University of Chicago, 1936.

London, Stephen D., "Business and the Chicago Public School System, 1890-1966." Ph.D. Dissertation, University of Chicago, 1968.

Mason, Mame Charlotte, "The Policy of Segregation of the Negro in the Public Schools of Ohio, Indiana and Illinois." Master's Thesis, University of Chicago, 1917.

McCrea, Samuel Pressley, "The Establishment of the Arizona School System." Thesis in History, Leland Stanford, Jr., University, 1902.

Miller, William Allen, "A History of the Illinois State Teachers Association Since 1912." Master's Thesis, University of Chicago, 1930.

Morgan, Walter Piety, "The School Fund Land of Chicago, with Its History Prior to 1880." Master's Thesis, University of Chicago, 1905.

Munson, Oscar Francis, "Salary Schedules for Teachers in One Hundred American Cities." Master's Thesis, University of Chicago, 1915.

Nottenberg, Robert Arthur, "The Relationship of Organized Labor to Public School Legislation in Illinois, 1880-1948." Ph.D. Dissertation, University of Chicago, 1950.

Patrick, George Walter, "History of the Illinois State Teachers Association, 1854-1912." Master's Thesis, University of Chicago, 1928.

Pearse, Robert F., "Studies in White Collar Unionism. The Development of a Teachers Union." Ph.D. Dissertation, University of Chicago, 1950.

Powers, Dorothy E., "The Chicago Womans Club." Master's Thesis, University of Chicago, 1939.

Reazin, Bruce D., "The Permanent School Fund in Arizona." Master's Thesis, University of Southern California, 1933.

Reid, Robert, "The Professionalization of Public School Teachers; The Chicago Experience, 1895-1920." Ph.D. Dissertation, Northwestern University, 1968.

Romberg, Hildegarde, "The Origin and Development of Public Elementary Schools in Chicago." Master's Thesis, University of Chicago, 1938.

Sanders, James W., "Education of Chicago Catholics: A Social History." Ph.D. Dissertation, University of Chicago, 1970.

Slutsky, Bessie, "The Chicago Teachers Union and Its Background." Master's Thesis, Northwestern University, 1945.

Spackman, Barbara S., "The Women's City Club of Chicago. A Civic Pressure Group." Master's Thesis, University of Chicago, 1930.

Staerkel, William Max, "A Case Study in Public School Leadership [The career of Herold C. Hunt]." Ph.D. Dissertation, Leland Stanford, Jr., University, 1955.

Staunton, George Edgar, "Activities of the Illinois Congress of Parents and Teachers." Master's Thesis, University of Chicago, 1934.

Stephens, Kenton E., "Collective Relationships Between Teachers Organizations and Boards of Education." Ph.D. Dissertation, University of Chicago, 1964.

Stevenson, Fred Gay, "Teachers Contracts in City School Systems." Master's Thesis, University of Chicago, 1929.

Winget, John Arthur, "Teacher Inter-School Mobility, 1947-1948." Ph.D. Dissertation, University of Chicago, 1952.

Wood, Stephen Gaskell, "The Retirement System for Public School Teachers in Chicago." Master's Thesis, University of Chicago, 1935.

INDEX